P9-EAJ-625

Helping in Child Protective Services

Helping in
Child Protective Services

A Competency-Based Casework Handbook

SECOND EDITION

Edited by

Charmaine Brittain and
Deborah Esquibel Hunt

OXFORD
UNIVERSITY PRESS

2004

OXFORD

UNIVERSITY PRESS

Oxford   New York

Auckland   Bangkok   Buenos Aires   Cape Town   Chennai
Dar es Salaam   Delhi   Hong Kong   Istanbul   Karachi   Kolkata
Kuala Lumpur   Madrid   Melbourne   Mexico City   Mumbai   Nairobi
São Paulo   Shanghai   Taipei   Tokyo   Toronto

First edition published in 1980 by the American Humane Association
First Oxford University Press edition, 2004

Published by Oxford University Press, Inc.
198 Madison Avenue, New York, New York 10016

www.oup.com

Library of Congress Cataloging-in-Publication Data
Helping in child protective services : a competency-based casework
handbook / edited by Charmaine Brittain and Deborah Esquibel Hunt.
—2nd ed.
p. cm.
Includes bibliographical references and index.
ISBN 0-19-516189-0; 0-19-516190-4 (pbk.)
1. Child welfare—United States.   2. Maternal and infant
welfare—United States.   3. Child welfare workers—United States.
4. Social work with children—United States.   5. Family social work
—United States. I. Brittain, Charmaine. II. Hunt, Deborah Esquibel.
HV741 .H45 2003
362.71—dc21   2003004586

9 8 7 6 5 4 3 2 1

Printed in the United States of America
on acid-free paper

For all the children whose lives we touch.

If you find it in your heart to care for somebody else,

you will have succeeded.

—Maya Angelou

Preface

Change is inevitable and Child Protective Services (CPS) practice continues to evolve in response to our dynamic economic and political environment. Similarly, the landscapes of the families involved in the child protective services system are ever changing. The topography of both has become increasingly more complex and difficult to navigate effectively and efficiently. Therein lies the impetus for the latest version of *Helping in Child Protective Services: A Competency-Based Casework Handbook*, or, as it has come to be called, the *Helping Handbook*. When originally published in 1992, the *Helping Handbook* contained the latest information, policy direction, and practice guidance in CPS. In ten years' time, however, the CPS practice environment has changed significantly, and the book required revision. You will find that much about the revised *Helping Handbook* is familiar—the structure, the practice philosophy, and the emphasis on information that workers need to do their job. Much of it, however, is new and reflects the evolution of CPS practice and changing families.

About American Humane

Mission and Vision

American Humane envisions a nation in which no child or animal will ever be a victim of abuse or neglect.

The Mission of the American Humane Association, as a national network of individuals and organizations, is to prevent cruelty to and abuse, neglect, and exploitation of children and animals and to assure that their respective interest and well-being are fully, effectively and humanely guaranteed by an aware and caring society.

American Humane has a long history of protecting children from abuse and neglect. In 1877, a group of humane societies from across the United States—including the New York Society for the Prevention of Cruelty to Children and the American Society for the Prevention of Cruelty to Animals (ASPCA)—joined forces to establish the national American Humane Association (AHA). In 1886, AHA formally amended its constitution to encompass the protection of children as well as animals. Emphasizing the important role that family plays in children's welfare, AHA encouraged its member organizations to protect families and to remove children from their parents only when absolutely necessary.

Today, American Humane (AH) supports the development and implementation of effective community, state, tribal, and national systems to protect children and strengthen families. American Humane provides consultation to courts, public and private child welfare agencies, and community organizations; trains workers and supervisors on best practice; conducts research and publishes findings; analyzes child protection systems and offers recommendations to improve practice; advocates for new legislation; and disseminates information about innovative practice models and procedures to not only child welfare and other professionals but also a wide audience of concerned citizens. American Humane works to ensure that services are in place throughout the country to protect children from abuse, neglect, and exploitation and to increase families' ability to nurture and protect their children. American Humane recognizes that, to succeed in this work and truly help children, it will need to involve professional partners, community advocates, and concerned citizens to develop a broad array of effective supportive services. In addition, we must recognize the strong, protective elements of culture and seek to assure that child protective services are truly culturally responsive to the increasing diversity within families.

■ Developing and Writing the *Helping Handbook*

Developing the revised *Helping Handbook* was a lengthy process of considerable breadth and depth. It was broad in the scope of diverse opinions sought and deep in the accumulation of information on important practice elements. Initially, American Humane identified Child Protective Services (CPS) subject experts and invited them to serve on an Advisory Committee and to use a highly structured, comprehensive tool to review the 1992 edition of the book for such areas as relevancy to today's practice, currency of research findings, and use of examples. Anonymous reviewers at Oxford University Press also offered excellent feedback. In addition, American Humane solicited feedback via a survey on the American Humane website. The editor provided chapter authors aggregated information from these sources to guide their revision efforts.

Chapter authors were chosen for their knowledge of the field and, most importantly, for their practical, direct service experience in CPS. Each of them conducted an extensive literature review and drew upon practice experience to write the chapters. The editors worked closely with chapter authors to ensure that specific themes were covered. Key themes included culturally responsive practice, strengths-based practice, permanency, safety, well-being, community-based practice, partnering with the community, shared decision-making, and an outcomes orientation. Most importantly, American Humane strove to make all content relevant to workers in the field who need practical guidance to help children and families.

Families involved in the CPS system are complex. They have many untapped strengths, struggle with an array of difficult issues, and come from diverse cultural backgrounds. A criticism frequently leveled at CPS is the lack of emphasis on culturally responsive practice. Sensitive to this concern, American Humane editors and staff reviewed the text carefully (and repeatedly) to ensure that the *Helping Handbook* is culturally responsive. To that end, co-editor Dr. Deborah Hunt reviewed the book in its entirety through a cultural lens. The final product benefited enormously from her keen eye and quiet wisdom in considering if there were cultural implications or if examples would enhance content. She wrote many examples illustrating diverse cultures and situations. Deborah also helped the staff at American Humane gain an understanding of the intended and unintended effects of public policy on populations of color through history and how that might influence these populations' ongoing interaction with CPS systems.

For the final review process, key American Humane staff and other CPS experts used a structured evaluation tool and their own expertise to assess the adequacy of each chapter. Through this intensive, multilayered effort, chapters were revised numerous times to ensure that they reflect both a cogent structure and provide the key information that workers need most to do their jobs.

■ Using the *Helping Handbook*

The *Helping Handbook* offers users multiple purposes. Workers and supervisors should use it as a desk reference to help guide practice. For example, a new worker in a rural county is just about ready to go out and conduct an investigation for possible sexual abuse of an eight-year-old child. The new worker is apprehensive, and, because her supervisor is in the next county attending training, there is no one to turn to for help. Seeing the *Helping Handbook* on her desk, the new worker turns to the chapter on interviewing and reads the section on protocols for sexual abuse interviews and takes notes on how she will use this information during her own investigation. She continues to thumb through the book and finds some key information on the medical evaluation of sexual abuse. Now, she feels more confident and ready to conduct the investigation.

In another situation, a supervisor could use the book as a tool to support on-the-job training. The supervisor could assign the chapter on assessment as a reading for a new worker and then ask her to use it as a guide as she uses agency forms to assess a family. In yet another situation, a college professor might use the *Helping Handbook* as the text for a course on Child Protective Services. For a field assignment, she could ask students to use the chapter on child development to assess the developmental level of several children. Other readers may find it useful it as a guide to understanding the Child Protective Services system.

Whatever its specific application, American Humane hopes that it helps guide practitioners through the complex and changing field of CPS so that they are able to provide appropriate services that result in better outcomes for children and families.

Acknowledgments

Many people contributed to the monumental task of revising the *Helping Handbook*. Their contributions are acknowledged in no particular order of effort toward or importance to the final product.

The *Helping Handbook* was initially funded by the Children's Program at the Edna McConnell Clark Foundation. I appreciated the continual support and assistance provided by the new Center for Community Partnerships in Child Welfare of the Center for the Study of Social Policy in Washington, D.C. The *Helping Handbook* would not have been possible without its financial support in the beginning phase of the project.

This latest revision of the *Helping Handbook* continues American Humane's long tradition of promoting excellence in CPS practice. The first version was published in 1980 by the American Humane Association with the Texas Department of Human Services and Worden School of Social Services at Our Lady of the Lake University of San Antonio, Texas, was adapted, revised, and published as *Helping in Child Protective Services: A Competency-Based Casework Handbook* in 1992. Authors of the 1992 *Helping Handbook* were:

Rebecca L. Benton	Nancy B. Mann
Jane Berdie	Nancy McDaniel
Karen J. Farestad	Joyce K. Moore
Judee Filip	Anne Parks
John Fluke	Desmond K. Runyan
Sol Gothard	Patricia Schene
Norma Harris	Jean C. Smith
Ray Kirk	

Thank you all for setting the bar so high.

Jane Berdie treated me to boundless wisdom over the years and was the initial champion of this latest version of the *Helping Handbook*. Throughout the writing process, she was an invaluable problem-solver and idea catcher, as well as an inspiration for ensuring the integrity of the process and the product. Many thanks to Jesse Rainey for her steadfastly positive attitude, infinite patience, and tireless assistance. Knowing I could count on her made this sometimes daunting task possible. Much appreciation to Deborah Hunt for opening my eyes and guiding my thoughts on culturally responsive practice. Ga Du Gi! ("Working together" in

Cherokee language) will be a treasured memory. Thank you, Sharon O'Hara, for believing in the potential of the *Helping Handbook* and for your unwavering, optimistic encouragement throughout the process. Nita Lescher, oh, you wordsmith extraordinaire, thank you for your contribution to tightening selected passages and chapters. The book benefited enormously from your command of the language. Anna Gonce nudged the *Helping Handbook* boulder up the publishing hill, helping to make this latest edition a reality. Thanks, also, to all the staff at American Humane who are so passionately committed to protecting children and animals.

As the project began, the Advisory Committee offered diverse opinions and astute impressions of the book to start molding what it eventually became. Thank you one and all:

Shirley Alexander	Susan Klein-Rothchild
Lucille Echohawk	Moria Krueger
Norma Harris	Lloyd Malone
Cathryn Potter	Pat Schene

Many thanks to Joan Bossert, American Humane's editor at Oxford University Press, who believed so enthusiastically in the book's potential and offered her positive encouragement throughout the process and took at least that pressure off the worried editors.

Several staff at American Humane offered to critique "final" versions of chapters, and their contributions improved the work enormously. Many thanks to Carol Harper, Kim Murphy, Leslie Wilmot, Myles Edwards, Greg Tooman, Lisa Merkel-Holgúin, and Robin Leake for your candid and astute reviews.

Outside CPS experts also provided key perspectives. Thank you to Shirley Alexander for your gentle wisdom and sharp sense of CPS practice. Thank you, also, to Janine Tondrowski and the Hon. Judge Moria Krueger for your keen and helpful insights.

I also acknowledge the support of my family—Jeff, Devyn, and Colton Frasier—who endured the early mornings, late nights, and crowded weekends that were necessary to get the manuscript finished. Deborah Hunt sends the same heartfelt message to Antonio Esquibel. You sweeten our lives and make it all worthwhile.

Of course, last but certainly not least, a special thanks to all the authors whose contributions and willingness to work with the editors made the effort such a positive and worthwhile experience—because of the process and the product we developed together. In alphabetical order, these talented and perceptive individuals are:

Shirley Alexander	Linda Metsger
Anne Comstock	Kimberlee Murphy
Deborah Esquibel Hunt	Edward Nowak
Susan Klein-Rothschild	Ingo Schamber
Nita Lescher	Andrew Sirotnak
Nancy McDaniel	Janine Tondrowski

Kathryn M. Wells Leslie Wilmot

Carol A. Wahlgren Amy Winterfeld

In the course of developing the book, many individuals supplied input and guidance. They are so numerous, in fact, that I may have overlooked their contributions. I take full responsibility for any inadvertent omissions from this acknowledgment section and offer a blanket thank you to all individuals and organizations who contributed in any way to the 2004 edition of *Helping in Child Protective Services: A Competency-Based Casework Handbook.* May you all know the joy that touching the life of a child can bring.

—Charmaine R. Brittain, M.S.W., Ph.D.

Contents

Contributors

Book Editors

Charmaine Brittain, MSW, PhD
Manager, Education & Professional Development
Children's Services
American Humane
Englewood, Colorado

Deborah Esquibel Hunt, LCSW, PhD
Denver, Colorado

Chapter Authors

Shirley Alexander, MSW
Child Welfare Project Manager
Bureau of Child and Family Services
Boise, Idaho

Charmaine Brittain, MSW, PhD
Manager, Education & Professional Development
Children's Services
American Humane
Englewood, Colorado

Anne Comstock, MS
Consultant and Trainer
Denver, Colorado

Deborah Esquibel Hunt, LCSW, PhD
Denver, Colorado

Susan Klein-Rothschild, MSW
Director
Clark County Department of Family Services
Las Vegas, Nevada

Nita C. Lescher, MSW, LICSW
Director, Program Planning, Eastern Region
Children's Services
American Humane
Silver Spring, Maryland

Nancy McDaniel, MPA
Director, Program Planning and Operations
Children's Services
American Humane
Englewood, Colorado

Linda Metsger, MA
Training Supervisor and Curriculum Specialist
Institute for Families
University of Denver
School of Social Work
Denver, Colorado

Kimberlee C. Murphy, PhD
Research Analyst
Kansas Action for Children
Topeka, Kansas

Edward Nowak, MSS
Director, Philadelphia Department of Human Services
Philadelphia, Pennsylvania

Ingo Schamber, MSS, LSW
Social Work Administrator
Philadelphia Department of Human Services
Philadelphia, Pennsylvania

Andrew Sirotnak, MD
Associate Professor of Pediatrics
University of Colorado School of Medicine
Director, Kempe Child Protection Team
The Children's Hospital
Denver, Colorado

Janine Tondrowski, MEd
Curriculum Development Specialist
Virginia Institute for Social Services
Training Activities
School of Social Work
Virginia Commonwealth University
Richmond, Virginia

Carol A. Wahlgren, MSW, LCSW
Child Protection Treatment Program Supervisor
Child Welfare Services
Colorado Department of Human Services
Denver, Colorado

Kathryn M. Wells, MD, FAAP
Instructor in Pediatrics
University of Colorado Health Sciences Center
Denver, Colorado

Leslie Wilmot, MSSW
Senior Program & Policy Analyst
Children's Services
American Humane
Englewood, Colorado

Amy Winterfeld, JD
Children's Advocate
Centennial, Colorado

Glossary compiled by
Jesse Rainey
Research Assistant
Children's Services
American Humane
Englewood, Colorado

Helping in Child Protective Services

1

Charmaine Brittain
Kimberlee C. Murphy
Leslie Wilmot

The CPS Experience
Working with a Family from Beginning to End

- The Report

- The Investigation

- The Safety Assessment

- Gathering Informatiom for the Investigation

- The Temporary Coustody Hearing

- Referral and Preparation for Family Group Conference

- The Family Group Conference

- The Risk Assessment

- Case Transfer to Ongoing Services Unit

- The Dispositional Hearing

- The Initial Service Plan

- The Follow-up to the Initial Family Group Conference

- The Change of Placement Hearing: The Return Home

- The One-Year Review

- The Risk Reasssessment

- Closing the Case

This handbook covers the various practices and procedures used in child protective services (CPS) work. If you are new to CPS work, you may find it somewhat difficult to understand how all aspects of the work fit together for the life of a case. This case diary, written from the perspective of the workers assigned to the case, will show you how a family moves through the CPS system and how the various players in the CPS system handle their portions of the case. For educational purposes, these notes reflect some of the workers' thought processes, and they include more detail than would notes for an actual case. The names and scenario are fictitious; any resemblance to actual people or situations is purely coincidental.

	Name	Role
Immediate family	Monica Herrera	Rosa's mother
	Frankie Mandel	Rosa's father
	Rosa Maria Herrera	Female infant—subject of CPS report
	Ramone Herrera	Rosa's brother
	Victor Jaramillo	Live-in boyfriend of Rosa's mother
Extended family	Horace and Muriel Herrera	Rosa's maternal grandparents
	Gina and Alfred Perez	Rosa's maternal aunt & uncle by marriage
	Crystal Mandel	Rosa's paternal aunt
	Lynette Owens	Rosa's paternal great aunt
	Emelda and Enrique Martinez	Rosa's maternal great aunt & uncle
	Carmen McNay	Cousin of Rosa's mother
Professional support	Rennie Vrain	CPS investigation worker
	Pat Wolfe	CPS ongoing services worker
	Trent Aberdeen	Next Step counselor for Rosa's mother
	Lia Fau	Visiting nurse, Home Visitation Program
	Father Juan Gomez	Priest at Our Lady of Lourdes Church
	Kendall Washington	Family group conference coordinator

■ The Report

On January 21 at 11:20 a.m. a call came into the state child abuse and neglect hotline on a possible child neglect situation. The following case notes were made by the hotline employee.

January 21, 11:20 a.m. T/C [telephone call]: I received a call about the possible risk for child neglect of a 5-day-old infant. As a professional mandated by state law to report suspected child abuse or neglect, a hospital social worker called about her concern that the infant was born addicted to cocaine and that the mother may not be able to care for her once she is discharged from the hospital in about a week. On the basis of the information I collected to complete our hotline screening tool,[1] the report fits the criteria for possible child neglect and requires further investigation. After checking our automated system for prior reports, I emailed a summary of the report to the Haverson County Department of Children and Families for further investigation and indicated a needed 24-hour response time.[2] The following is the summary.

See Chapter 12: Accountability in Child Protective Services.

See Chapter 6: Intake and Investigation: Initial Stages of the CPS Process.

Summary of Report

Baby (5 days old) may be at risk for neglect upon release from County General Hospital on January 25 or 26. Full-term baby was born low birth weight (4 lb, 12 oz), tested positive for cocaine, is not taking a bottle well, and has ongoing respiratory problems. The mother shows little interest in feeding, changing diapers, and looking after baby's oxygen equipment. Reporter and hospital staff suspect possible developmental disability and substance abuse problems with mother, and are concerned that she will not be able to look after baby's needs upon release from hospital.

Child: Rosa Maria Herrera

Child location: County General Hospital, Haverson County

Child age: 5 days old

Allegation(s): Neglect

Reporter: Sue Murray—social worker, County General Hospital Haverson County, 555-5555

Mother: Monica Herrera

Father: Unknown

Alleged perpetrator: Monica Herrera

Relation to child: Mother

Response Classification: Level 2 (24 hours)

---

1. A *hotline screening tool*, called different names in different locations, is used by staff who take reports of possible child maltreatment. The tool often consists of a checklist of criteria for the conditions or actions that constitute child abuse or neglect. Based on the types and number of conditions/actions checked, the staff determine whether the report matches the state's criteria for child abuse or neglect, the severity of the potential maltreatment, and within what time CPS investigators must respond to the call.

2. Reports received by hotline staff are categorized by the severity of the potential maltreatment. Some reports require immediate response (within 3 hours), others a 24-hour response, and still others a response within 3 or more days. Response times vary based on the state (if in a state-run system) or agency (if in a county-administered system).

■ The Investigation

See Chapter 6: Intake and Investigation: Initial Stages of the CPS Process.

The referral for investigation of the Herrera case arrived at the Haverson County Department of Children and Families on January 21 at 2:58 p.m. Agency staff processed the referral and gave it to the CPS supervisor responsible for assigning CPS investigators. The Herrera case was assigned to CPS investigator Rennie Vrain. The following are her case notes.

January 21. Received the Herrera case for investigation today. T/C to the County General Hospital social worker (the reporter) and am meeting with her tomorrow at 8:30 a.m. for greater detail about her concerns. Checked our local records to see if there were any other reports or information on the family and found nothing. Will visit the baby (Rosa Maria Herrera) at that time. T/C to mother (Monica Herrera) to set up an initial meeting with her. Will meet her tomorrow to review the concerns in the report and obtain further information. Need to bring Jose with me as an interpreter—Monica speaks some English, but says she is more comfortable conversing in Spanish.

Note: Will need to bring an interpreter with me whenever I talk with Monica.

January 22. F/F [face to face]: Met with the County General Hospital social worker and two nurses. They said that on January 16, Monica Herrera (23-year-old mother) gave birth to Rosa Maria. The hospital released Monica within 24 hours but kept Rosa because of health problems. Rosa was full term (38 weeks gestation) but weighed only 4 pounds, 12 ounces. Because she displayed shaking and Monica asked the nurse if occasional cocaine use before birth would hurt a baby, Rosa was tested for cocaine—she tested positive. Three days ago, she became sick with a high fever and a respiratory infection. She requires around-the-clock supervision and oxygen equipment to assist her breathing and will require the equipment once discharged.

Nurses say Monica visits Rosa daily, but they are concerned about her ability to care for Rosa after discharge from the hospital. They report that Monica, who is developmentally delayed, does not respond to Rosa and shows no interest in learning how to operate the oxygen machine, feeding the baby, or holding her. She has refused to change Rosa's diaper and has said "That's what nurses are supposed to do." Monica denies using drugs, but the nurses have often seen her sit impassively "with her eyes glued to the TV" while the baby cries for her bottle. When Rosa became sick at 3 days of age, Monica seemed unable to cope with Rosa's discomfort. Instead of trying to console the baby, she handed her to a nurse and said that she was afraid she would make her sicker. Monica also seems to have difficulty picking up on Rosa's cues (e.g., for hunger). Given these issues, they worry that Monica may not be able to meet Rosa's basic needs or medical needs.

No information on Rosa's father. The hospital staff have not seen a male figure, other than Monica's father—Rosa's grandfather.

F/F: Saw Rosa in the Newborn Intensive Care Unit and she is small, but seems alert. The nurses said she should be ready to discharge in another few days.

January 22. F/F: Met with Monica today to discuss the child neglect report received and to do an initial assessment of her situation. We met at the hospital before her visit with Rosa. Jose was our interpreter.

See Chapter 5: Interviewing Children and Families.

Monica's Background

- Monica has two children. Rosa (6 days old) and Ramone (9 years old).
- Rosa's father is Frankie Mandel, Monica's ex-boyfriend. Frankie is in jail for physically assaulting his current girlfriend's child. Monica said that Frankie has not contacted her since their breakup and did not respond to her letters when she wrote him about the upcoming birth of the baby.
- Frankie's parents are not in the picture. Frankie's mother is deceased, and his father is estranged from Frankie and lives over 2,000 miles away. Frankie's sister (Crystal Mandel) is Monica's friend.
- Monica and Ramone live with her father and stepmother (Horace and Muriel Herrera). Monica sees her older sister (Gina Perez) regularly.
- Monica has a developmental disability and does not currently receive educational, occupational, or parent training. Monica did not recall getting occupational or parent training in the past.
- Monica is not currently employed but receives Social Security Disability Income because of her developmental disability.
- Neither Monica nor Frankie are members or potential members of an American Indian tribal group. Monica's family is originally from Mexico. By his sister's report, Frankie is Caucasian. Therefore, there is no apparent need to further pursue compliance with the Indian Child Welfare Act[3] for Rosa.

Concerns

Reviewed these concerns with Monica to get her perspective. Monica seemed relatively comfortable talking with me and readily admitted her own challenges.

- Rosa is an infant who has special needs requiring ongoing close monitoring. She is low-birth-weight and currently requires oxygen that will continue on discharge from the hospital.
- Monica has a developmental disability and appears to be uninterested in learning how to care for Rosa, according to nursing staff.
- Monica may have a substance abuse problem—Rosa tested positive for cocaine. Monica said substance abuse is not an ongoing issue. She said she just used drugs once or twice before Rosa was born. I told her I thought it would be good for us to assess her drug use and see if she needed treatment.

3. The Indian Child Welfare Act was established to help preserve an American Indian child's tribal heritage; tribes must be notified and involved if there is a tribal membership or the potential for it.

- Monica stated several of her own concerns. She said that there are a lot of things to remember for Rosa and she's not sure how to care for her—working with Rosa's oxygen equipment, changing her diapers, and knowing when to feed her. She also mentioned that she had no baby supplies. She knows there isn't much room for her at her father's house and her stepmother is really ill, making it unlikely she'll be able to get much help from them.

Monica's Strengths

The following strengths of Monica may help to reduce Rosa's immediate safety concern and may offer solutions for how to address the concerns outlined above.

- Monica visits Rosa in the hospital daily.
- Monica lives with her son and meets his needs, with help from her father and stepmother.
- Monica has a relatively good support network that can offer her help and/or possibly serve as placement options to assure permanency if Rosa cannot live with Monica:

    Monica's father and stepmother (Horace and Muriel)—Monica and her son (Ramone) live with them.

    Monica's older sister (Gina) lives close by and sees Monica regularly.

    Our Lady of Lourdes—Monica's church, although she does not attend regularly, the priest visits the family on a regular basis and has expressed concerns regarding what would happen when the new baby arrived.

- Monica states that she is interested in learning how to care for Rosa, although hospital staff did not observe her interest.

■ The Safety Assessment

As part of her initial work to determine whether Rosa was at immediate risk for child abuse or neglect, Rennie completed the safety assessment tool.[4] She referred to the questions in the tool as she interviewed Monica and the hospital staff and observed Monica with Rosa, so that she could be sure to get all the information she would need in order to determine Rosa's current level of safety.

> *See Chapter 7: Assessment.*

January 22. F/F: As I talked to the hospital staff and Monica today, I was able to complete much of the safety assessment. Given the concerns outlined, the factors associated with the concerns, and the strengths of the family now, Rosa's safety *will* be in immediate jeopardy once she is discharged from the hospital.

---

4. A *safety assessment tool* is an instrument that is often used by CPS investigators to determine whether children are in immediate danger of moderate to severe harm. Such tools vary by location but often include a checklist of potential dangers and factors that may be associated with the possible danger. Also included is information on family strengths and mitigating circumstances that may affect the possible danger.

January 22. Reviewed the Herrera case with my supervisor. She suggested I pursue Rosa's father's relatives for other possible supports. We agreed that Rosa's safety under Monica's care is likely to be in danger upon discharge from the hospital.

January 22. CT [court]: I filed a request for temporary custody with the court to request the state to take temporary custody of Rosa while I complete the investigation. Will look into possible placement options as I gather information so that I can suggest a placement option at the temporary custody hearing.[5] Will also ask the judge to make an order asking for cooperation with the visiting nurse for whoever cares for Rosa temporarily—to train the caregiver and Monica on the oxygen equipment and how to monitor Rosa until she is stronger.

■ Gathering Information for the Investigation

Because Rennie and her supervisor determined that Rosa would be at immediate risk for child neglect upon discharge from the hospital, she filed a request with the court to temporarily take custody of Rosa at least until Rennie could complete her investigation. With that done, she then began gathering information on Monica and the family so that she could complete an assessment to determine Rosa's risk of longer term neglect. To do this she used her skills as an interviewer, read available records on Monica and Rosa, and observed Monica's environment and interactions with her extended family and children.

January 23. H/V [home visit]: Met with Horace and Muriel Herrera (Monica's father and stepmother) at their home to gather more information.[6] Also wanted to find out if they were willing to support Monica by helping her care for Rosa. Although Jose came with me to interpret for us, the Herreras are comfortable conversing in English. They did not notice Monica drinking or using illegal drugs before Rosa was born, but said that they aren't around her 24 hours a day to know for sure. They mentioned that Monica was excited about the arrival of Rosa, but they worry that she is not prepared to care for her, particularly considering the fact that she required a great deal of help in caring for Ramone when he was a baby. Although Horace and Muriel want to help Monica, they are not able to help care for Rosa. Muriel has breast cancer, so is not well enough to help raise a baby; and Horace said that he does not know how to care for an infant with special needs—he had not been the primary caregiver for Monica when

---

5. The temporary custody hearing, typically occurring within 48–72 hours of a case being assigned for investigation, is held for the purpose of determining whether a child needs to be temporarily placed into the custody of the state (or county, if a county-administered system) to assure his or her safety. See chapter 6.

6. A professional systematic, informed approach to gathering and evaluating specific information about the family. Uses information gathered from initial screening, safety assessment, risk assessment, and various other sources of information that shed light on family connections and capacities. This assessment includes family interactions and relationships, strengths and supports, developmental issues, physical and mental health, educational history, social adjustment, substance use or abuse, domestic violence, the environment, culture, and the community, and any other factors that affect the family's ability to resolve concerns that led to involvement with CPS.

she was a child. Horace suggested that I talk to his older daughter, Gina Perez, who had helped to care for Monica when they were children.

January 23. T/C; H/V: Talked with Gina Perez by phone after this morning's meeting, then met with her later in the afternoon. I wanted to gather information and ask about her possible interest in taking Rosa temporarily. Gina lives six blocks from the Herreras' home and sees Monica regularly. She stated that with help from her and their parents, Monica has been able to care for Ramone's daily needs. When asked about Monica's substance use, Gina indicated that Monica had experimented with drugs in her teen years but didn't seem to be a regular user. However, she did notice that Monica seemed to be high on something a few days before she gave birth to Rosa.

Gina is 28 years old, married, and has 2 children (5 and 7 years of age) and does not work. She says that she would be willing to care for Rosa if the agency would give her supplies and financial assistance. I will get the police and social services check done on her and her husband (Alfred Perez) so that we can place Rosa in her home. She agreed to enroll in the next available foster parent certification class.

January 24. H/V: Rosa is still running a fever and not breathing well. Gina says the doctors are going to try a new medication. Horace, Muriel, and Gina provided me with some preliminary information on Monica's family history. Information includes the following:

Monica is one of three children. Gina Perez is her older sister and has a close relationship with her. Michael Herrera, Monica's older brother, has limited contact with her—he lives about 800 miles away.

Monica's parents both came from Mexico. Horace is one of five children and emigrated with his family from central Mexico to the U.S. when Horace was an adolescent. One of Horace's siblings is still living and lives about 500 miles away. Monica's mother (deceased) was the youngest of three children and came to the U.S. with her family from northern Mexico when she was a child. Monica's mother's other sister, who is developmentally delayed, lives in a nearby assisted living facility. Monica's father was a machinist in a local clothing factory, and her mother a seamstress in her home. Monica's parents were married for 30 years before the mother died in an automobile accident—Monica was 17 years old at the time. Horace remarried two years later to Muriel. Muriel has worked closely with Monica to help her raise Ramone.

Monica's maternal aunt and uncle (Emelda and Enrique Martinez) live in the area and have 6 children who are now grown. Aunt Emelda helps Monica from time to time with the care of Ramone—particularly since Muriel was diagnosed with cancer.

Monica's family is religious. Although Monica does not attend church regularly, she is a member of her church, Our Lady of Lourdes. Father Juan Gomez is close to the family and has visited the Herrera home often since Muriel was diagnosed with breast cancer and since Monica became pregnant with Rosa.

Monica was diagnosed with a developmental disability when she was a child. Monica was last assessed by a psychologist in junior high school, and Horace provided me with a copy of the evaluation report. She was found to have mild retardation with an IQ of 70. According to this report, her developmental delay was caused by a shortage of oxygen at birth. As the youngest of the three Herrera children, and because she was an adorable baby with special needs, Monica was coddled and doted on in her childhood. Emelda Martinez told Pat, "Someone was always rescuing her from one mishap or another." Reportedly, Monica was a sweet and compliant child who did not make waves. Sometimes she made poor choices about friends and, according to family members, "did a lot running around, hanging out, and generally getting into trouble." One of these "trouble incidents" led to her sexual assault by a stranger when she was in grade 9. Monica became pregnant with Ramone from that assault. She completed grade 8 (receiving special ed services) before dropping out of school towards the end of grade 9. Since then she has not received educational, occupational, or independent living training and has never held a job. She has lived with her family since birth. According to Emelda Martinez, Horace drank a little too much and was a very strict but loving father. It appears that Monica's own mother and other family members were Ramone's primary caretakers when he was an infant and small boy. The Herreras were a religious family, especially Monica's mother, Maria Rosa. She was killed when Monica was 17, and then Gina stepped in and helped with Ramone.

■ The Temporary Custody Hearing

See Chapter 11: The Legal Framework for Child Protective Services.

To determine whether Rosa would be placed into temporary custody to assure her safety while Rennie completed the investigation, Rennie, Monica, and her family went to court.

January 25. CT: Went before the judge today for the temporary custody hearing pertaining to Rosa. Monica attended with her father and stepmother. I met with Rosa's guardian ad litem (GAL)[7] before court to review the case. The GAL was just assigned to Rosa late yesterday afternoon so did not have a chance to visit her at the hospital before the hearing. However, she agreed with the placement recommendation. The judge heard my testimony on the case and asked Monica if she had any questions—she did not. I didn't know how much she understood, so I met with her and her family after court to try to explain what was said. The judge told Monica she would get an attorney who can legally represent her rights as she goes through the child welfare process.[8] The following are the court orders:

1. Rosa Herrera will be placed temporarily into the custody of the state[9] and will live with her maternal aunt and uncle, Gina and Alfred Perez, upon discharge from the hospital.

---

7. A guardian ad litem (GAL) is a person assigned by the court to represent the child's best interests in court.

8. Whether parents have their own attorney varies by location. Not all parents involved in the child welfare system have legal representation.

9. The custodian for a child in an out-of-home placement varies based on the location. Children may be in the custody of the state, the county, or the agency.

2. The Department of Children and Family Services will arrange for WIC services for Gina Perez.[10]

3. The Department will arrange for a visiting nurse from the Home Visitation Program for Gina and Monica. The nurse will check on Rosa in Gina's home as needed and will train Gina and Monica to monitor and care for Rosa's special needs.

4. Monica will visit Rosa no less than 3 times per week in Gina's home. Visits will be supervised by Gina.

5. The Department will refer Monica to Next Steps for a substance abuse assessment and possible treatment. Monica will participate in assessment and treatment as needed.

6. The jurisdictional hearing[11] is set for February 4 at 2:00 p.m.

See Chapter 10: Intervention with Families.

January 25. T/C: Referred Monica to Next Steps for a substance abuse assessment and possible treatment. One of their counselors, Trent Aberdeen, speaks Spanish, so I requested that he conduct Monica's assessment. It is scheduled for February 11. Also arranged for WIC for Gina (to cover costs of baby supplies) and for the visiting nurse from the Home Visitation Program to visit Rosa at Gina's home. Provided Gina with a voucher to a thrift store to buy other baby supplies.

January 29. H/V: Rosa was discharged from the hospital and placed into Gina's home today. Monica was present when I came to take Rosa to Gina's home. Although she knew Rosa would be placed with Gina and understands the need, she was quite upset when the time came for me to take Rosa. I did my best to reassure her that our permanency goal was to reunify her and Rosa and only if that was not possible would we pursue other options, like maybe having Gina adopt Rosa. Visits between Monica and Rosa (supervised by Gina) will begin this coming weekend. Ramone will also spend time with his little sister at Gina's house.

See Chapter 6: Intake and Investigation: Initial Stages of the CPS Process.

H/V: I talked with Monica about the possibility of conducting a family group conference (FGC) so that she and her family could come up with a plan to address Rosa's safety and permanency concerns. Monica liked the idea of involving the family as a part of the team that would develop a plan for Rosa's safety and agreed to meet with Kendall Washington, our FGC coordinator, to discuss the family group conference process in greater detail. I will make the referral.

See Chapter 4: Key Partners in Protecting Children and Supporting Families.

February 4. CT: Had the jurisdictional hearing this morning. Monica's attorney was there to represent her rights as she makes her way through the process. The judge reviewed my report outlining the current concerns and information obtained.

---

10. Women, Infants, and Children (WIC) is a program operated by the U.S. Department of Health for low-income mothers and their children 0 to 3 years of age. It provides financial assistance for baby supplies and food, as well as medical care.

11. The jurisdictional hearing is also called the plea hearing.

Monica did not deny any of the concerns described, and indicated that she is willing to cooperate with the court and agency to get Rosa back. Rosa's GAL agreed that her best interests are being served by her current placement with Gina. The dispositional hearing is set for March 22 at 11:00 a.m.

February 16. H/V: Visited with Gina, Monica, and Rosa today while Ramone was at school. Rosa seems to be doing well and is responding to her medicine. Monica seemed stiff as she held Rosa, didn't look at her, and did not pick up on her cues. Gina took the baby from Monica to give her a bottle. She says Rosa has no schedule yet and is up several times a night. I told Monica again that our first plan was for Rosa to eventually go home with her. Then I told about our need to make a concurrent plan and asked them about who might adopt Rosa. Gina said there was no way Rosa would leave her house except to go home with Monica and committed to talking about adoption just in case. Gina says Monica is trying to do her best as a mother and visits almost every day. Gina hosted a family dinner on Sunday, and Horace and Muriel came over to visit Rosa.

■ Referral and Preparation for Family Group Conference

As a way to address and remedy the safety concerns that prevented Rosa from going home, Monica decided to participate in a family group conference.[12] What follows are the notes of the FGC coordinator, Kendall Washington, as she coordinated the conference.

February 6. T/C: On January 30, I received a referral from Rennie Vrain on Monica Herrera and her then 2-week-old baby, Rosa Maria. Rennie gave me brief information on the family's issues as well as contact information for Monica and several of her family members. I called her today for a brief update on the status of the Herrera case. She gave me the names and contact information on the service providers currently working with Monica and Rosa so that they can be invited to the FGC.

February 11. H/V: Met with Monica to explain the purpose and procedures of the FGC. Jose interpreted for us. She seemed to understand the purpose/procedures, but questioned the need to include Rosa's father (Frankie Mandel) in the process, and how we could do it since he is in prison. I explained that his family can help support her and be involved in Rosa's life and that we could involve him perhaps by phone or letter. Monica consented to the conference. She identified her sister, father, step-mother, and cousin (Carmen McNay) as important FGC participants. She also mentioned that she'd like Frankie's sister (Crystal Mandel) to come—one of her best

---

12. Family group conferencing (FGC) is a decision-making process that encourages and broadens family inclusion and responsibility for the safety, permanency, and well-being of children. Families are engaged and empowered to make decisions and develop plans that protect and nurture their children from further maltreatment. Carried out in four stages (referral, preparation, actual FGC meeting, and follow-up), the conference involves bringing family member and friends together so that they can hear information on safety concerns and create a plan to assure child safety. It simultaneously fosters a partnership with the family and child welfare and other community agencies involved in supporting the family.

friends. I will invite the people Monica and Rennie suggested and possibly get additional participants once I start talking with these people about the conference.

February 22. T/C: Contacted the treatment coordinator at the county jail to discuss Frankie Mandel's ability to be involved in planning for Rosa's care and treatment. He arranged for a teleconference with Frankie. He is interested in the idea of an FGC and wants his sister, Crystal, and his aunt, Lynnette Owens, to attend in his absence. He said he was angry with Monica for getting pregnant but cares about Rosa and wants to be a part of her life. He is going to write a letter explaining his thoughts so that we can read it during the conference. The conference is set for March 5.

■ The Family Group Conference

The Herrera family group conference was convened in the basement of Our Lady of Lourdes, the family's church. All of the family and friends Monica and Frankie invited were present, and everyone brought their favorite dish to share for a pot-luck dinner. In addition, a number of support professionals were present to share information: the CPS worker (Rennie Vrain); the visiting nurse from the Home Visitation Program (Lia Fau); Monica's Next Step counselor (Trent Aberdeen); and Rosa's GAL (Paula Thompson).

March 6. F/F: FGC was a very positive experience for all who attended. It was conducted in Spanish, and an interpreter translated the meeting into English for the few participants who did not speak Spanish. After initial introductions, the family asked Father Gomez to open the conference with a prayer and blessing to guide them in their work. Rennie Vrain then presented information on the safety concerns that the family was being asked to address through the conference, and the other service providers provided a brief summary of the status of Monica and Rosa. Once the information was provided, Monica's family and friends were left alone for private family time to think through the information and then develop a plan that would support Rosa's continued safety and address her ongoing special healthcare needs. Since Frankie had sent a letter for the conference, Crystal read the letter as the family and friends started discussing the information presented. In it he said he would support whatever plans the family made but wanted a picture of Rosa and monthly letters updating him on Rosa's growth. Based on the planning portion of the conference, the family came up with the following plan for Rosa.

1. Rosa will continue living with Gina, and Monica will visit at least three times a week.

2. Gina will continue to help Monica learn to care for Rosa. Aunt Lynette (Rosa's paternal great-aunt) will meet with Monica on Tuesdays, cousin Carmen on Thursdays, and aunt Emelda (Rosa's maternal great-aunt) on Saturdays to help her improve her parenting skills and provide respite for Gina.

3. Aunts Lynette and Emelda will help Monica take Rosa shopping, to the park, and to other community places.

4. Monica will try to not use cocaine or any other illicit substances. She will attend group therapy at Next Step twice a week.

5. Monica will start attending Narcotics Anonymous (NA) meetings. Crystal (Monica's friend and Rosa's paternal aunt) will attend with her and provide transportation.

6. If Monica relapses, she will ensure Ramone's safety by leaving him with her father (Horace Herrera) or her sister (Gina Perez).

7. Monica and Gina will both go to Rosa's doctor appointments and meet with the visiting nurse once per week to learn how to handle Rosa's oxygen equipment and monitor her health.

8. Horace (Ramone's grandfather) will take Ramone to soccer practice at Our Lady of Lourdes while Monica attends her NA meetings.

9. Crystal will write monthly letters and send a picture of Rosa to Frankie.

10. Gina will monitor the family plan and, aside from Monica, will be the primary contact with the Department.

11. In six months or when Monica, her family, or her worker feel like Monica is ready for Rosa to return to her primary care, they will reconvene the FGC to review information and create a support plan to help make that possible.

Rennie Vrain fully supported the family's plan as one that is safe and addresses the issues that brought Rosa and Monica into contact with the Department. She will attach the plan to and incorporate it into her court report and recommendations. She will also inform all family members of the date of the dispositional hearing so that they can attend and present their family plan to the court with the Department's support.

■ The Risk Assessment

As Kendall was coordinating the family group conference, Rennie was continuing her investigation by interviewing Monica, her family, and the service providers involved with the family, observing Monica and her baby, and reading reports from others involved with the family. This information helped her complete the *risk assessment* that she used to determine the family's future risk for maltreatment.[13]

See Chapter 7: Assessment.

March 8. Completed the risk assessment to determine longer-term risk for child neglect to Rosa. Considering the risk factors related to child safety and the strengths of Monica and her family, Rosa is at high risk for future maltreatment. I continue to

13. A risk assessment is carried out for the purpose of assessing a child's future risk of child maltreatment. It is often guided by a tool that contains a checklist of potential dangers and factors that are associated with child maltreatment. Risk assessments are typically conducted during the investigation process, every 6 months, and when significant changes take place in placement or family situation.

support the family's decision to have Rosa remain with Gina until Monica can address and remedy some of the concerns currently putting Rosa's safety in jeopardy. See summary of risk factors and strengths that follows.

Concerns

- Rosa is an infant who is too young to care for herself or seek help should she need it.
- Rosa has special needs requiring ongoing close monitoring. She is low-birth-weight and currently requires oxygen and medication.
- Monica has a developmental disability and lacks parenting skills and knowledge.
- Monica is reluctant to carry out basic caregiving tasks for Rosa. The visiting nurse, Gina, cousin Carmen, and aunts Lynette and Emelda all report that Monica has refused to touch Rosa's oxygen equipment and only diapers Rosa when asked to do so repeatedly. When changing diapers, Monica will not wipe Rosa's bottom because it is "messy and smells."
- During visits with Rosa, Monica has to be repeatedly reminded to give Rosa her medicine, according to Gina.
- Monica has occasionally used illegal substances and does not recognize it as a problem.

Note: Trent Aberdeen completed Monica's substance use assessment. He has found her to be a binge user of cocaine (1–2 times per month at most). Monica reported experimenting with drugs in junior high, and sporadically since then. She used again just before her baby's birth and again the day that Rosa was discharged from the hospital and placed with Gina. Trent is going to work with Monica and enroll her in group therapy for a total of two contacts per week. He's also suggested random UAs.

Monica's Strengths

- Monica visits Rosa regularly at Gina's home.
- Monica is following the court orders and is cooperating with the various professionals involved in her case.
- Monica has a good support network: her father, stepmother, Gina, cousin Carmen, aunts Lynette and Emelda, and Crystal (friend and Rosa's paternal aunt).
- Monica is a member of Our Lady of Lourdes, and although she does not attend church regularly, she does have a supportive relationship with her priest.
- Monica is successfully parenting Ramone with family supports.

■ Case Transfer to Ongoing Services Unit

After the CPS investigator, Rennie, completed her investigation, finding that Rosa's safety was in immediate jeopardy (based on the safety assessment) and that the family was at high risk of future maltreatment (based on the risk assessment), she and her supervisor determined that the Herrera family would need ongoing support and services to remedy the safety concerns. The Herrera case was, therefore, referred to the ongoing services unit. Because Monica converses primarily in Spanish, Pat Wolfe (fluent in Spanish) was assigned to the case. Rennie met with Pat to provide details on the family, explain the key issues, and transfer the case. Pat Wolfe's case notes follow.

March 12. I met with Rennie Vrain, the investigator for the Herrera case, to get her file, information, and thoughts on the family's needs. I'll be meeting with Monica Herrera and Gina Perez on March 14 to get information on how the family is currently doing and gather information for the family assessment.[14] I also want to get their opinions of the status of the family, the family plan developed during the family group conference, and what may need to be changed (if anything) to help her accomplish the work toward getting Rosa back. In the meantime, I'll contact Monica's Next Step counselor (Trent Aberdeen) for substance abuse and the visiting nurse from the Home Visitation Program (Lia Fau) to get their information and thoughts.

March 14. H/V: Met Monica and Rosa at Gina's house. Baby is small but is smiling and seems to respond to Gina. Monica was visibly scared at meeting me and did not say much during our meeting. Did tell me that she's going to Next Step and it's helping. She let Gina take care of Rosa while I was there. Gina says she's stocked up on supplies and formula for now.

March 19. T/C: Trent Aberdeen has worked with Monica on her substance abuse issues twice per week for the last 2 weeks. Monica had her first UA. He says that Monica is showing up for appointments. Lia Fau (the visiting nurse) indicates that she has worked with Monica on how to read Rosa's cues (e.g., when she is hungry) and how to work with the oxygen equipment. Gina and cousin Carmen are teaching Monica basic parenting skills such as bathing, feeding, diapering, nurturing, and playing. Gina reported that although her sister visits Rosa every other day, she has little interest in changing diapers and only feeds her with a great deal of help. Monica will continue to work with Trent, the visiting nurse, and her family members. I'll make sure she has tokens for transportation to her substance abuse treatment and doctor appointments.

■ The Dispositional Hearing

March 22. CT: Had the first dispositional hearing for the Herreras today.[15] Monica came with her father, stepmother, sister, and attorney. Monica's attorney met with her 15 minutes before the court hearing to go over her thoughts and to prepare her for the hearing.

The judge heard testimony and reviewed the reports that Trent Aberdeen, Lia Fau, and I submitted on the Herreras' current situation, the status of services being provided, and

14. A family assessment is carried out as part of the investigation and is done for the purpose of gathering information on the family's functioning. Information on family history is gathered as part of this assessment to determine family patterns in strengths, in challenges they have encountered, and in how they have handled those challenges.

15. Dispositional hearings are carried out by the court for the purpose of developing court-sanctioned case plans for the safety and permanency of the child. They typically occur within 60 days of investigation and every 6 months after that (if the case remains open).

their recommendations. She concluded that Rosa is a dependent child in need of services. If Monica shows that she can look after Rosa's needs and has 3 consecutive months of UAs that come back negative for illegal substances, we will be able to go before the court for a change in placement hearing before the next scheduled dispositional hearing in September. The following are the court orders for the Herrera case.

1. Rosa will continue to live with Gina Perez until such time as Monica is ready to assume full-time caregiving responsibility.

2. Monica will visit Rosa at least three times per week during visits supervised by Gina Perez.

3. The Department of Children and Family Services will continue to provide for ongoing assistance for Gina (e.g., WIC).

4. Lia Fau from the Home Visitation Program will continue to visit Rosa weekly as needed.

5. Monica will continue getting help for parenting from the family.

6. Monica will continue in substance abuse treatment at Next Step as recommended by the program.

7. Monica will continue to submit weekly urine samples for random UAs.

8. The Department will continue to give Monica bus tokens for doctor visits, Next Step appointments, and agency visits.

9. The Court accepts and includes the family group conference plan developed on March 5 as part of this court order (see attached plan).

10. The next dispositional hearing and permanency plan review is set for September 23 at 2:30 p.m.

I'll get in touch with Trent Aberdeen and Lia Fau about their continued work with Monica and the family. I'll continue to meet with Monica and her family at least once per month to monitor the progress being made.

April 15. T/C: Trent Aberdeen, Gina, and aunts Lynette and Emelda all reported that Monica is doing well. Gina mentioned the need for Monica to continue working on her ability to pick up on Rosa's cues (e.g., feeding) and engaging her. She does seem to be getting better about diapering and seeing the importance of giving Rosa her meds as needed. Trent mentioned that Monica has only missed one appointment. She is attending NA meetings and has a backup plan to call her cousin Carmen in case she relapses and uses again. Carmen will make sure that Ramone and Rosa are safe.

■ The Initial Service Plan

April 20. H/V: Met with Monica, Gina, Crystal, and Lia Fau to review the family's status and develop a service plan. Trent Aberdeen wasn't able to make the meeting, but talked with me last week about Monica's progress and current needs. See April 15 notes. According to Gina and Lia, Monica is making progress regarding Rosa's care, but still struggles to engage Rosa through eye contact, singing, or playing baby games.

Gina said that since Carmen has become more involved, she has seen an improvement in Monica—evidently Monica admires Carmen and seems to imitate her when Carmen models good parenting skills with Rosa.

Monica has started attending her church more regularly and just attended an informal social event in the parish last weekend. Father Gomez is going to christen Rosa on April 24, and Emelda and Enrique Martinez (Rosa's great-aunt and great-uncle and Monica's own godparents) are organizing a family celebration after the ceremony. Monica says she is still working with Trent Aberdeen weekly on substance abuse issues. She says she has not used cocaine since Rosa was placed with Gina in late January.

Given the current status of the family, the family plan that was developed during the family group conference on March 6, Trent's recommendations for continued services, and the court orders from the March 22 dispositional hearing, we agreed on the following services for Monica and Rosa.

- Ongoing assistance for Gina (e.g., WIC).
- Visiting nurse from the Home Visitation Program weekly at Gina's home.
- Bus tokens to Monica for doctor visits, Next Step appointments, and agency visits.
- Substance abuse treatment at Next Step as recommended by Trent Aberdeen.
- Random weekly UAs.

May 14. T/C: Lia Fau called yesterday to tell me that Rosa's health is greatly improved and that Gina and Monica are comfortable monitoring Rosa's meds. Rosa was taken off of oxygen 3 weeks ago. She indicated that there is no longer a need for her weekly visits but is willing to resume visits should Rosa's condition worsen. Gina and Monica indicated (by phone this morning) that they feel comfortable meeting Rosa's medical needs and are fine without the nurse's visits.

May 18. H/V: At Gina's house with Monica and Rosa present. Rosa was sleeping at the time, so I didn't get a chance to see Monica interact with Rosa. Gina said that Monica is visiting five to six times per week and is much better about looking after Rosa's feeding, diapering, and medication needs without being repeatedly reminded. Because Monica is doing so well, Gina asked if the visits between Monica and Rosa could be unsupervised.

Monica is happy with how things are working. She reports having learned a lot about parenting from Gina, aunts Lynette and Emelda, and Carmen, and says they don't step in to help her as much as they used to. She says that Trent Aberdeen still works with her on substance abuse issues twice per week but that she has had negative UAs since the end of January, so wonders if she needs to see him so often. Monica was particularly excited about her new boyfriend, 31-year-old Victor Jaramillo. Victor is unemployed but receives Social Security Income because of a seizure disorder from a beating as a teenager.

Muriel Herrera (Monica's stepmother) isn't doing well. Her cancer is not responding to treatment, so she is sick much of the time. Despite Muriel's illness, Monica continues to care for Ramone (according to Horace Herrera) and is still making progress in what she is trying to accomplish regarding Rosa's return home. Monica and Gina wondered if they could have a follow-up family group conference, since things have significantly improved, to explore the possibility of Rosa living with Monica.

Gina thinks Rosa may be somewhat delayed—she's not as responsive and exploratory with objects as her own kids were at that age. She wonders if Rosa should be tested. I'll set up an appointment for assessment with the Child Development Team at Haverson Children's Hospital.[16]

See Chapter 8: Child Development and Its Importance to Child Protective Services.

May 21. T/C: Talked with Trent Aberdeen after an administrative review meeting we both attended today. He reported that Monica is doing well. I asked him about his thoughts on cutting back the frequency of contacts with Monica. He saw no problem with going down from twice to once per week. He'll talk with Monica about the idea when he sees her on Thursday.

May 24. Met with my supervisor today to review the Herrera case. We both agree that given the progress being made by Monica and the improved health of Rosa, it is time for a follow-up family group conference. I'll contact Kendall Washington again to get it scheduled.

■ The Follow-up to the Initial Family Group Conference

When using a family involvement model such as family group conference, the family continues to be involved in all key decisions. The family decided it was time to have another conference, earlier than expected, because the family reported that Monica was doing very well and they wanted to see if they could make a recommendation that Rosa live with her mother.

June 20. The Herreras had their follow-up family group conference at their family's church yesterday. Kendall Washington coordinated it. Everyone from the original conference was there (except for the visiting nurse and the CPS investigator, who are no longer on the case), along with Monica's new boyfriend, Victor Jaramillo. To date, Monica has remained clean and sober for just about 6 months, validated by random and ongoing UAs that all came back negative. She continues to see Trent Aberdeen weekly for substance abuse treatment and has not missed a meeting in the last 2 months. She also continues to attend NA meetings with Crystal (friend and Rosa's paternal aunt). Trent said that Monica has done well with her treatment. He believes she has made enough progress to reduce their meetings to every 2 weeks.

Victor has begun to help Monica care for Rosa, and her skills have improved, according to Gina, Carmen, and Aunt Lynette. They said that she seems more in tune with Rosa and no longer needs to be reminded or asked to feed, change, and put her to sleep. They also said that Monica not only attends to Rosa's physical needs but also

16. A developmental assessment typically consists of a combination of observations of the child and questions to the caregiver on the child's behaviors. The observations and questions often target how the child's behaviors and skills compare to the developmental milestones that are typical for the age of the child being assessed.

tries to engage her by holding her and singing lullabies. I did find out that Victor has no history of criminal history or drug or alcohol abuse. He used to take care of his sister's children while she worked, so he has some experience caring for young children. Victor enjoys visiting with Rosa and has been observed by Gina to be a good caregiver. I was happy to be able to report that Rosa had participated in a developmental assessment and that her development was within normal range.

Given the information provided, the family decided that Rosa should return home to Monica's care. Their reunification plan is as follows.

1. Rosa will move back into the Herrera home with Monica (dependent on court approval).

2. Monica will not use cocaine or any other illegal substances. She will continue to see Trent Aberdeen every 2 weeks and will attend NA meetings with Crystal.

3. Crystal, Carmen, and aunts Lynette and Emelda will take turns caring for Rosa and Ramone one evening each week and on occasional weekend overnights to give Monica a break.

4. Gina will help Monica shop for baby supplies for her home before Rosa's return.

5. Monica will be responsible for scheduling and attending Rosa's medical appointments. Gina will assist when necessary.

6. Horace will spend one afternoon a week doing something fun with Ramone.

7. Crystal will continue to write monthly letters about Rosa to Frankie.

8. Horace and Muriel, despite her very poor health, agreed to help in whatever way they could.

9. Gina will continue to monitor the family plan and, aside from Monica, will be the primary contact with Pat Wolfe.

The family decided that Horace and Gina will attend the change of placement hearing with Monica to support the court's acceptance of their new family plan. My agency just changed its policy and now all workers stay with a case no matter what the placement status is.

■ The Change of Placement Hearing: The Return Home

Pat fully supported the family's plan for reunification and agreed that it would help assure Rosa's safety and well-being. She then filed a request with the court for a change of placement hearing so that they could request that the judge approve Rosa returning home to Monica.

July 5. CT: We just had the hearing today. Monica and her family were in attendance, along with Monica's attorney, and Rosa's GAL. All agreed that Monica is ready to assume full-time caregiving responsibilities. The judge agreed that Rosa would return to Monica, with the State maintaining custody so that we can continue case monitoring as Monica and her family make the adjustment to Rosa's return home. Because the hearing was held today, the second dispositional hearing has been rescheduled to January 10 at 9:30 a.m.

July 9. H/V: Visited with Monica, Horace, and Muriel Herrera. All are making the transition to having Rosa home. Monica and Victor are currently looking for an apartment together. They plan to have Rosa and Ramone live with them. Given Muriel's poor health and Monica's progress, the family supports this move. Horace, Gina, Carmen, and Crystal all plan to visit Monica regularly, so that Monica gets multiple visits per week from family members.

July 29. H/V: Visited with Monica, Victor, Rosa, and Ramone at Horace's house. Rosa appears to be healthy and was smiling and cooing when I played with her. Monica reports that she's starting to take solid food and usually sleeps through the night. Monica says Muriel is really sick and it is really hard to live there right now because the doctors don't think she'll make it through the summer. Victor and Monica have found an apartment close to Gina's house but are having problems finding the money for the deposit. Since the family and I both believe that Victor and Monica have demonstrated the capacity to care and provide for the children independently, I'll see if I can help cover the deposit.

July 31. T/C: Talked to Monica and told her I made arrangements to cover the deposit for their new apartment. Monica was thrilled and says they can move in on Saturday.

August 8. H/V: Visited with Monica, Victor, Rosa, and Ramone in their new apartment. They aren't unpacked yet but seem really happy about their new place. Rosa was healthy and engaged during the visit.

August 11. T/C: Gina called. She said Ramone was over at her house yesterday and they were talking about CPS and how they help keep children safe, and he disclosed that Frankie Mandel (Rosa's father) had sexually molested him right around the time school started last year. Gina wants guidance on where to go. I told her that we would proceed and conduct an investigation. I called in the report to the hotline.

August 12. T/C: Talked to Monica today. She is very upset about Ramone, said she always thought Frankie was "bad." She pledged cooperation with the investigation. Says Ramone is scared but relieved to have told his secret. Told her that we will get help for Ramone. Ramone referred to the Kids First child advocacy center (CAC) for an assessment with law enforcement assisting.

See Chapter 5: Interviewing Children and Families.

August 12. T/C: Talked with Kids First counselor. Said the interview occurred this morning and was videotaped as per policy. Ramone disclosed that Frankie had sexually molested him on several occasions last fall, starting around when school started. The abuse ended when Frankie and Monica broke up around Halloween. Law enforcement will be interviewing Frankie sometime in the next couple of days. Counselor recommends ongoing therapy for Ramone. Made some phone calls to find a therapist specializing in child sexual abuse close to Monica's home and made the referral.

August 20: Based on the evidence, the report on Ramone was substantiated. Since I'm already working with the family, I'll keep the case and address Ramone's issues as well. The district attorney charged Frankie with sexual abuse.

August 25. T/C: Muriel lost her battle with cancer over the weekend. Although the family is all right, Monica seems pretty distraught because she said it's reminding her of her biological mother's death. The family is meeting with Father Gomez from their church tomorrow. I'll check with Monica and Victor to see how they and the children are doing.

August 28. T/C: Father Gomez and I talked this afternoon. He met this week with the Herrera family to pray and share memories of Muriel. They also discussed the challenges that might lie ahead without Muriel and how they would meet them. Horace agreed to spend more time with Ramone as a way to help them both deal with Muriel's death. Horace and Ramone decided that they would work on Muriel's neglected gardens. Horace will take on Ramone's religious education. Ramone will start catechism classes next month and, in the meantime, Horace will take his grandson to mass on Sunday mornings and be more involved as his first padrino. Horace will also read him bible stories from a child's bible storybook that Father Gomez gave them. Father Gomez said he will support the family as he can.

August 30. H/V: Visited with Monica and Victor at their apartment. Monica was visibly upset over Muriel's death. She says the funeral was really beautiful but very sad. Ramone is pretty upset about it right now too, especially because of all the other stuff happening with him. Called Ramone's therapist to let him know of events in Ramone's life. Counselor says he's met with Ramone once and has another meeting next week. Will send monthly reports to me.

September 12. T/C: Monica called to request more bus tokens. She says Rosa has been really fussy, running a fever, and throwing up and she needs to take her to the doctor. Also said that Ramone had spent the weekend with Horace and he and his grandfather set to work on Muriel's overgrown flower and vegetable gardens. She said they worked all weekend long, weeding to bring the gardens back to life and salvage the harvest. She said they had a good time together and ended the weekend fishing at a nearby lake.

September 23. H/V: Visited with Monica, Victor, and Rosa today. Ramone was at school. Monica said Rosa had some kind of virus and she's still not eating well. Monica related well with Rosa and responded to her cues. Observed Victor with Rosa and he seems to be quite fond of her and changed her diaper to give Monica and me a chance to talk. Said she still feels sad most of the time, can't stop thinking of how her mom died and now her stepmom. Says she's been spending a lot of time with Gina and going to mass like she never did before. Says it's helping. I talked to her about connecting to JOBS, Inc.—a local agency dedicated to helping persons with developmental delays to find, apply for, and keep jobs. This will help Monica to become more self-sufficient. She was reluctant but said she'd check it out, so I gave her their business card.

September 28. T/C: Talked with Trent Aberdeen today. He reported that Monica's UAs came back negative for illegal substances again, and that Monica has remained clean over the last 8 months. Despite the tremendous stress she has been under with Muriel's death, Ramone's disclosure, and moving to her own apartment, she has been doing well. He increased his meetings with her to once a week after hearing about Muriel's death, but Monica is now settling down and no longer needs the weekly contact. He will reduce his meeting with her to once per month, and says that as long as she continues to attend her NA meetings, she no longer will need her group therapy sessions.

September 30. T/C: Gina reports that she, Aunt Emelda, Horace, and Cousin Carmen all visit Monica at least twice a week, going at different times. Things seem to be going well. Crystal indicated that she has also seen Monica and Rosa twice and agrees that things are going well. Monica is glad for the assistance that WIC provides.

October 20. H/V: Visited with Monica, Ramone, and Rosa today. Rosa was asleep so did not get to observe Monica and Rosa together. Monica says Rosa continues to be fussy, thinks maybe she's teething. Says she made an appointment with JOBS, Inc. for October 29.

November 2. T/C: Monica missed her appointment with JOBS, Inc. the other day, according to a JOBS, Inc., rep, and chose not to reschedule the appointment. Monica then called me this morning to tell me that she and Victor had a terrible fight last week—probably affecting her decision to make the JOBS appointment. Evidently, they had some misunderstanding about a call Frankie made to the house asking about his daughter, Rosa. When Victor reviewed the phone bill and saw the charge for a collect call from the jail, he flew into a rage, called her names, grabbed her, and shoved her out the door. Monica stated that never before had Victor become physically abusive with her. Monica went to her father's house with Rosa and Ramone. She had no clothes or supplies. I suggested that she stay with her father until she and Victor can get some help with their problems and to borrow clothing and supplies from Gina and Carmen. Monica said Ramone was happy to be staying with Grandpa again.

November 8. T/C: Talked with Victor, who explained the reason for the blowup. He said that he was sorry he had blown up. He and Monica talked yesterday and want to work things out. Not knowing if such blowups are normal for Victor, and suspecting that Monica could use some help learning how to handle future situations if they arise, I suggested that they may benefit from a few couples counseling sessions—for Victor, to help him better handle his anger, for Monica, to teach her how to handle such situations. Victor thought that might help. Will call Father Gomez to find out what they offer at the church.

November 18. H/V: Visited with Monica today. Rosa was alert and quite happy during the visit, sitting on Monica's lap and playing with her hair. She said that Ramone and his grandfather went to a basketball game over the weekend. She's glad to see Horace spending special time with Ramone. The rest of the family is all right. Monica hopes that things will settle down in the next few weeks—she's been getting a lot of family and church visitors since Muriel's death. She and Victor are doing great again, says she has an appointment with one of the priests at the church for some couples counseling. Monica says she really doesn't want a job right now but will think about it after the first of the year.

December 4. T/C: I checked with Trent Aberdeen to see how Monica was doing with her substance abuse issues. Trent thinks Monica has maintained her abstinence from cocaine, alcohol, and other drugs.

December 10. H/V: Rosa had her regular checkup at the Family Clinic last week. According to Victor and Monica, the doctor expressed concern that the baby hadn't gained much weight since the last visit and was showing some developmental delays. Although Rosa was always on the lighter side, hovering in the 30th percentile of weight, this was the first checkup in which she substantially dropped below this and weighed in at the 20th percentile. The doctor also mentioned that Victor and Monica may want to try boosting their level of engagement with Rosa—particularly as it pertained to increasing her mobility and helping her eat.

December 17. T/C: Got a call from Gina. She said that she, Carmen, and Monica have come up with a plan to increase Rosa's mobility and have revised the feeding schedule. Victor thought the low weight was probably a result of the few weeks after Muriel's death when things were so crazy and Rosa was so sick. I'll recommend another developmental assessment if things don't improve with Rosa in the next few months.

December 20. T/C: Trent Aberdeen contacted me to let me know that he's going to move toward closing his case with Monica. She has continued her NA meetings and has remained clean for the last 11 months, even during the highly stressful period when Muriel died and Monica and Victor moved to their new apartment. He said that Monica was comfortable with their working relationship coming to an end. He will meet with her monthly for another two sessions and will then close the case. However, he said he'd be happy to work with Monica again, should she need it in the future.

December 23. H/V: Visited Monica and Rosa today at the apartment. Ramone continues to spend private time with Horace and is now playing soccer with boys from church. For a few weeks after Muriel's death, Ramone was aggressive and angry at school. However, after the school's social worker called Monica and learned about Ramone's recent loss and disruption (moving out of his grandparents' home), the school set up a meeting with Monica, Victor, and Horace to talk about how they might support Ramone during this difficult time. They came up with a plan for school and home on how Ramone can express his angry and sad feelings without throwing and hitting things. They also decided it would be fun for Ramone to join the church's soccer team, thinking that it might be a good outlet for his anger. Ramone was brought in for the last part of the meeting and helped make this plan. In the last 2 weeks, the teachers have told Monica that Ramone is getting back to his old self. Monica thinks that the visits with Horace have helped Ramone deal with his anger and sadness over his grandmother's death.

The family is still working with Monica to improve Rosa's mobility. Rosa is eating better these last couple of weeks, according to Monica.

January 10. H/V: Visited Monica, Victor, and Rosa at their apartment. Rosa was cheerful and sat on the floor on a blanket during our meeting. Seemed healthy but not interested in crawling or walking. I reapproached the subject of Monica getting a job. Both she and Victor seemed to have no problem with this idea, although Monica said she just wants a part-time job so that she can spend time with her kids. I'll call JOBS, Inc., about setting up an appointment for Monica. Assured her that they help people who have never held a job or even applied for one.

January 16. T/C: JOBS, Inc. counselor called and said she met with Monica this morning. Monica signed a release and she wants more information about her, and her capacities to help Monica find the best fit for a part-time job. She thinks she can find Monica a good situation but will need to make sure Monica has daycare to look after Rosa.

See Chapter 4: Key Partners in Protecting Children and Strengthening Families.

■ The One-Year Review

Because it had been a year since Rosa was placed, Pat held an administrative review to discuss the family's current situation, challenges, and progress.

January 20. F/F: We had the 1-year Administrative Review today. Monica and Victor attended, along with Horace and Gina, Monica's attorney, Rosa's GAL, and Father Gomez. In our review of the past year, the team seemed pleased with the progress made by the family. Monica and Victor continue to live in their apartment and participate in couples counseling through the church. Rosa has regained some weight and is now in the 25th percentile, but is suspected of being developmentally delayed. She will be assessed next week. Ramone is doing well in school, plays soccer with his church group, and has developed into a "spirited soccer player," according to Monica. He is doing better in school and no longer displays the aggression he had earlier in the year. He and Horace have continued their get-togethers and both report enjoying their time together. Horace continues to drive Ramone to catechism classes and then takes him to dinner afterward. They go fishing together a couple of times a month. Reviewed a report from Ramone's therapist. She was pleased with his progress and recommended monthly, rather than biweekly, counseling. Given how well everyone is doing, we talked about terminating Department involvement, if a reassessment of risk for future maltreatment shows low risk. The family, the GAL, and Monica's attorney all support the idea.

January 31. H/V: Visited with Monica, Victor, and the kids late today. Monica and Victor report that things are going well. Ramone's time with his grandfather has been good for both of them. They still attend church together and read stories from time to time. Horace thinks that after Muriel's death, if it hadn't been for his grandson's need for special attention, he might have fallen back into his old drinking habit. He recalled his close relationship with his own grandfather in Mexico. He stated that his grandfather had helped shape his own life and felt contentment, knowing that he had honored their cultural traditions in helping to raise his grandson. Rosa's weight is back within normal range but she is still not interested in exploring, either through crawling or walking.

February 5. T/C from Monica. She's going to start a part-time job next week and needs daycare. She said she took Rosa over to the daycare place I referred her to but wasn't comfortable and wouldn't leave her. She said Carmen suggested that she try the daycare program at their church. Monica is much more comfortable with this idea and will check it out.

February 19. T/C: Talked with Gina today. Says she sees Monica a couple of times a week. Carmen and Aunt Emelda also go over at least once a week. I am concerned about Rosa's development, and Gina says she noticed as well and that Rosa seems far behind her own kids at that age. Rosa still appears to be developmentally delayed—at almost 13 months of age, she is not crawling well or standing with support. Although Monica has made progress in engaging Rosa and providing her with opportunities for exploration and mobility, I suspect that Monica may still have some trouble engaging Rosa on a regular basis—when I asked Monica about Rosa's exploration and mobility, Monica said that she tries to get Rosa to do things but that the baby "would rather just sit and watch everyone else." I'll make an appointment with the child development team at the Haverson Children's Hospital.

February 26. H/V: Visited Monica and Victor at their apartment. Rosa seemed cranky today, Monica says it was just about time for her nap. Saw Ramone and he seems to be doing well. Was excited about an upcoming field trip to the zoo. Monica started her job and is working 15 hours per week at a special workshop for people with disabilities. She says it's okay, but it's hard with the kids. Rosa's been attending the church daycare for a couple of weeks and seems to be okay but she always throws a fit when Monica leaves her. Rosa's appointment for the developmental screening is March 1.

March 16. The report from the Haverson Children's Hospital came in on Rosa's developmental assessment. The psychologist indicated that although Rosa's motor skills are on the low end of the normal range, her cognitive and communication skills are within normal range. He recommended that Monica continue to encourage Rosa to crawl and stand with support, and suggested that Monica come in again for some training on helping Rosa with her mobility. They are glad to hear Rosa is attending a structured daycare setting and think that she needs it at least half time to be engaged in structured play and other stimulating activities with other children. I'll call Monica with the results.

March 28. H/V: Talked with Monica about the results of Rosa's developmental assessment. Monica says she got some good ideas from the hospital and is using them with Rosa. Talked to Monica about thinking about closing the case. I'll do a formal risk reassessment to determine whether Rosa's safety is still in jeopardy.

■ The Risk Reassessment

When workers start to recognize that the safety concerns that brought CPS involvement have been addressed, it is time to consider a formal reassessment of risk.

April 7. H/V: Conducted another risk assessment to determine whether Rosa's risk for future maltreatment is still significant. Talked with the family and other professionals still involved in the case and have summarized the case activity over the life of the case. Using the risk assessment tool once again, I've confirmed my own feelings that although some of the risk factors for maltreatment still exist (e.g., Rosa is still too young to care for herself, Monica still has a developmental disability), others have been alleviated (e.g., Monica no longer uses cocaine, her support network is stronger, her parenting skills and knowledge are significantly better). Monica's living situation is still not totally stable (e.g., still somewhat new to her part-time job, just finished couples counseling with Victor) and she has a tendency to minimize Rosa's developmental problems and her own need to provide developmental opportunities (although Rosa's attendance at Our Lady of Lourdes Church Daycare Center is likely to supplement her developmental opportunities). Overall, however, risk for future maltreatment is no longer high. A summary follows of the safety concerns addressed over the life of the case, the actions taken to address those concerns, and the outcomes of those actions.

Safety Concern	Actions to Address Concern	Outcome
Rosa was a medically fragile newborn, needing ongoing medication and oxygen.	Rosa was placed with her aunt and had a visiting nurse who checked on Rosa weekly and taught Gina and Monica to use the oxygen equipment.	Rosa no longer is considered medically fragile and does not need ongoing medication or oxygen.
Monica has a developmental disability and lacks parenting skills and knowledge. She did not respond to Rosa's medical and physical needs—did not diaper, feed, or give Rosa medication without repeated prompting.	Family members taught Monica parenting skills and knowledge and modeled parenting behavior.	Monica has learned to care for Rosa—she learned to provide medication and now looks after diapering, feeding, and providing opportunities for learning. Victor coparents Rosa.
Monica lacked infant care supplies and gear.	The Dept. set her up with WIC.	Monica acquired supplies and gear over time and learned where to go for help.
Monica's substance abuse posed a potential risk for caregiving—she binged on cocaine before Rosa's birth and once after Rosa was placed with Gina.	Trent Aberdeen from Next Step assessed Monica's drug use and worked with her. Crystal takes her to NA meetings.	Monica came up with a plan to assure Rosa's and Ramone's safety in case of relapse, but has remained clean for over one year.
Rosa was suspected of having developmental delays.	Rosa was assessed on two separate occasions.	Both assessments found her to be within normal range.
Monica and Victor had a fight that resulted in Monica and the kids having to move back to her father's home.	Monica and Victor participated in couples counseling for conflict resolution skills.	Monica's and Victor's relationship stabilized, and they continue to live together with the kids.
During the life of the case, the family experienced two serious crises: the grandmother's death and the report and substantiation of Ramone's sexual abuse.	Ramone received appropriate therapy, school, social, and religious support to help him deal with the sexual abuse and the loss of his grandmother.	The family coped successfully with the grief and loss by supporting each other and receiving help.
Monica's social support did not formally extend beyond her parents and sister. With Muriel's illness, her support was not able to meet her needs once Rosa was born.	The family had an initial and followup family group conference to plan on how to help Monica with Rosa.	Plan was implemented and resulted in Monica's family and other supports helping with Rosa and Ramone. Dept. assisted with supports for Monica and Victor.

■ Closing the Case

Pat and her supervisor both agreed that with the support of a team of professionals, community resources, and the family, Monica had successfully remedied the safety concerns that prompted CPS involvement. Pat, therefore, filed a request with the court for a final dispositional hearing. Pat's supervisor commended her on doing a good job of working with the family to assure Rosa's safety, documenting the work and progress made by the family, working with the other service providers and family as a team, and helping to provide Monica with what she needed to achieve her goals.

See Chapter 12: Accountability in Child Protective Services.

April 12. H/V: Monica and Victor are thrilled about the possibility of closing the case and hope that the judge will agree with us. I talked with them about their plans in the next few months, and we reviewed where they would go for support if they run into difficulty in the future. They just moved into a 2-bedroom apartment—now that Monica is working, they can afford a larger place. Monica and Victor told me that they wanted a dining-room table, so they could eat together as a family. I told them I could get a voucher for a thrift store and we'll go on Friday to pick one out and bring it back to their apartment in my car.

Ramone's First Communion and Reconciliation (confession) is happening next weekend. The family is going to celebrate the event with a big feast at Gina's house. Special traditional foods are being prepared, including Aunt Emelda's homemade tamales and Grandpa Horace's famous menudo (tripe stew), with Ramone's green chili that he tended in Grandma's garden. Ramone has chosen his Aunt Gina and Uncle Alfred to be his second set of padrinos (godparents). Horace, as the first padrino, was particularly proud of his grandson's achievement and pleased that he had played an important role in Ramone's religious education.

May 10. CT: Had the final dispositional hearing today. Monica and Victor were there, along with Horace and Gina. When the judge was asking Monica questions, she proudly told him that she, Victor, and the kids now live in a bigger apartment and that she has her first job. All parties agreed that Monica and her family are doing well and no longer need Department involvement. Monica told me afterward that she knew she had needed help in the past and was glad that her family and the Department were there to help her. She's confident that she and Victor are now ready to handle any situation that comes their way, but knows where to get support when needed. I wished them much happiness and future success.

2

Nancy McDaniel
Nita C. Lescher

The History of Child Protective Services

■ The Beginnings of Child Protection

In the United States, the child protection movement was tied to and gained momentum from other social justice reform movements that occurred throughout the country in the mid- to late 1800s. In addition to championing suffrage, the women's rights movement confronted and drew public attention to issues of family violence (Costin, Karger, & Stoesz, 1996). The animal welfare movement was particularly influential, as was the American Society for the Prevention of Cruelty to Animals (ASPCA) that supported and aided early efforts to legislate state authority to protect children. With the assistance of the ASPCA, in 1874 New York passed the Protective Services Act and the Cruelty to Children Act, thereby becoming the first state to enact legislation intended to safeguard the rights of children.

☐ The Story of Mary Ellen Wilson

By the end of the nineteenth century, child abuse and neglect had shifted from being largely a private matter to being one of public concern. In 1875, after the much-publicized case of Mary Ellen Wilson, a young child who was abused by her caregivers, New York City established the country's first Society for the Prevention of Cruelty to Children. The case involved a concerned citizen, Etta Angell Wheeler, who tried to get help for the child from various social service agencies in New York City. Frustrated by their lack of response, she sought support and ultimately obtained legal assistance from Henry Bergh, president of the ASPCA.

The Real Story of Mary Ellen Wilson

Over the years, in the retelling of Mary Ellen Wilson's story, myth has sometimes been confused with fact. Some of the inaccuracies may stem from colorful but erroneous journalism, others from simple misunderstanding of the facts, and still others from the complex history of the child protection movement in the United States and Great Britain and its link to the animal welfare movement. While it is true that Henry Bergh, president of the ASPCA, was instrumental in ensuring Mary Ellen's removal from an abusive home, it is not true that her attorney—who also worked for the ASPCA—argued that she deserved help because she was "a member of the animal kingdom."

The real story—which can be pieced together from court documents, newspaper articles, and personal accounts—is quite compelling, and it illustrates the impact that one caring and committed person can have on the life of a child.

Mary Ellen Wilson was born in 1864 to Frances and Thomas Wilson of New York City. Soon thereafter, Thomas died, and his widow took a job. No longer able to stay at home and care for her infant daughter, Frances boarded Mary Ellen (a common practice at the time) with a woman named Mary Score. As Frances's economic situation deteriorated, she slipped further into poverty, falling behind in payments for and missing visits with her daughter. As a result, Mary Score turned 2-year-old Mary Ellen over to the city's Department of Charities.

The department made a decision that would have grave consequences for little Mary Ellen; it placed her illegally, without proper documentation of the relationship and with inadequate oversight, in the home of Mary and Thomas McCormack, who claimed to be the child's biological father. In an eerie repetition of events, Thomas died shortly thereafter. His widow married Francis Connolly, and the new family moved to a tenement on West 41st Street.

Mary McCormack Connolly badly mistreated Mary Ellen, and neighbors in the apartment building were aware of the child's plight. The Connollys soon moved to another tenement, but in 1874, one of their original neighbors asked Etta Angell Wheeler, a caring Methodist mission worker who visited the impoverished residents of the tenements regularly, to check on the child. At the new address, Etta encountered a chronically ill and homebound tenant, Mary Smitt, who confirmed that she often heard the cries of a child across the hall. Under the pretext of asking for help for Mrs. Smitt, Etta Wheeler introduced herself to Mary Connolly. She saw Mary Ellen's condition for herself. The 10-year-old appeared dirty and thin, was dressed in threadbare clothing, and had bruises and scars along her bare arms and legs. Ms. Wheeler began to explore how to seek legal redress and protection for Mary Ellen.

At that time, some jurisdictions in the United States had laws that prohibited excessive physical discipline of children. New York, in fact, had a law that permitted the state to remove children who were neglected by their caregivers. Based on their interpretation of the laws and Mary Ellen's circumstances, however, New York City authorities were reluctant to intervene. Etta Wheeler continued her efforts to rescue Mary Ellen and, after much deliberation, turned to Henry Bergh, a leader of the animal humane movement in the United States and founder of the ASPCA. It was Etta Wheeler's niece who convinced her to contact Mr. Bergh by saying: "You are so troubled over that abused child, why not go to Mr. Bergh? She is a little animal surely" (Watkins, 1990, p. 3).

Mrs. Wheeler located several neighbors who were willing to testify to the mistreatment of the child and brought written documentation to Mr. Bergh. At a subsequent court hearing, Mr. Bergh said that his action was "that of a human citizen," clarifying that he was not acting in his official capacity as president of the NYSPCA. He

Henry Bergh

emphasized that he was "determined within the framework of the law to prevent the frequent cruelties practiced on children" (Watkins, 1990, p. 8). After reviewing the documentation collected by Etta Wheeler, Mr. Bergh sent an NYSPCA investigator (who posed as a census worker to gain entrance to Mary Ellen's home) to verify the allegations. Elbridge T. Gerry, an ASPCA attorney, prepared a petition to remove Mary Ellen from her home so she could testify to her mistreatment before a judge.

Mr. Bergh took action as a private citizen who was concerned about the humane treatment of a child. It was his role as president of the NYSPCA and his ties to the legal system and the press, however, that brought about Mary Ellen's rescue and the movement for a formalized child protection system.

Recognizing the value of public opinion and awareness in furthering the cause of the humane movement, Henry Bergh contacted *New York Times* reporters who took an interest in the case and attended the hearings. Thus, there were detailed newspaper accounts that described Mary Ellen's appalling physical condition. When she was taken before Judge Lawrence, she was dressed in ragged clothing, was bruised all over her body, and had a gash over her left eye and on her cheek where Mary Connelly had struck her with a pair of scissors. On April 10, 1874, Mary Ellen testified as follows.

> My father and mother are both dead. I don't know how old I am. I have no recollection of a time when I did not live with the Connollys. . . . Mamma has been in the habit of whipping and beating me almost every day. She used to whip me with a twisted whip—a raw hide. The whip always left a black and blue mark on my body. I have now the black and blue marks on my head which were made by Mamma, and also a cut on the left side of my forehead which was made by a pair of scissors. She struck me with the scissors and cut me; I have no recollec-

Mary Ellen at Discovery   Mary Ellen post-trial

tion of ever having been kissed by any one—have never been kissed by Mamma. I have never been taken on my mamma's lap and caressed or petted. I never dared to speak to anybody, because if I did I would get whipped. . . . I do not know for what I was whipped—Mamma never said anything to me when she whipped me. I do not want to go back to live with Mamma, because she beats me so. I have no recollection of ever being on the street in my life. (Watkins, 1990, p. 502)

In response, Judge Lawrence immediately issued a writ de homine replegiando, provided for by section 65 of the Habeas Corpus Act, to bring Mary Ellen under court control.

The newspapers also provided extensive coverage of the caregiver Mary Connolly's trial, raising public awareness and helping to inspire various agencies and organizations to advocate for the enforcement of laws that would rescue and protect abused children (Watkins, 1990). On April 21, 1874, Mary Connolly was found guilty of felonious assault and was sentenced to one year of hard labor in the penitentiary (Watkins, 1990).

Less well known but as compelling as the details of her rescue is the rest of Mary Ellen's story. Etta Wheeler continued to play an important role in the child's life. Family correspondence and other accounts reveal that the court placed Mary Ellen in an institutional shelter for adolescent girls. Believing this to be an inappropriate setting for the 10-year-old, Mrs. Wheeler intervened. Judge Lawrence gave her permission to place the child with Mrs. Wheeler's own mother, Sally Angell, in northern New York. When Sally Angell died, Etta Wheeler's youngest sister, Elizabeth, and her husband, Darius Spencer, raised Mary Ellen. By all accounts, her life with the Spencer family was stable and nurturing.

Mary Ellen as an adult, with her daughters

At the age of 24, Mary Ellen married a widower and had two daughters—Etta, named after Etta Wheeler, and Florence. Later she became a foster mother to a young girl named Eunice. Etta and Florence both became teachers; Eunice was a business-woman. Mary Ellen's children and grandchildren described her as gentle and not much of a disciplinarian. Reportedly, she lived in relative anonymity and rarely spoke with her family about her early years of abuse. In 1913, however, she agreed to attend the American Humane Association's national conference in Rochester, New York, with Etta Wheeler, her longtime advocate, who was a guest speaker at the conference. Her keynote address, "The Story of Mary Ellen Which Started the Child Saving Crusade throughout the World," was published by American Humane. Mary Ellen died in 1956 at the age of 92.

☐ Early History of Child Protective Services

The late 1800s. From late in the nineteenth century through most of the first half of the twentieth century, private nonprofit societies for the prevention of cruelty to children initiated and took responsibility for child protection efforts. In 1877, humane societies from across the country—including the New York Society for the Prevention of Cruelty to Children (NYSPCC) and the ASPCA—convened in Cleveland, Ohio, and founded the national American Humane Association (AHA). In 1886, American Humane (AH) amended its constitution to include the protection of both children and animals, a mission that it supports to this day (Douglas, 1998).

The early 1900s. In 1909, President Theodore Roosevelt convened the White House Conference on the Care of Dependent Children, but the federal government did not enter the child welfare arena officially until 1912, when it established the Children's Bureau. In the 1920s, there were more than 250 humane societies working to bring resources to families and to protect maltreated children through the courts. Gradually, however, public social services agencies took on more responsibility in this area. It was not until the era of the New Deal, however, that the federal government took the lead in child welfare, sponsoring the 1930 White House Conference on Child Health and Protection and introducing programs for maltreated children through various titles of the Social Security Act of 1935, most notably Aid to Families with Dependent Children (AFDC) (Costin, Karger, & Stoesz, 1996).

The mid-1900s. As early as 1946, pediatric radiologists began drawing attention to issues of child abuse and "battered" children (Caffey, 1946, as cited in Pecora, Whittaker, Maluccio, Barth, & Plotnick, 2000). The 1960s brought major changes in this country's response to child maltreatment. An article and accompanying editorial published in 1962 in the *Journal of the American Medical Association* (Kempe, Silverman, Steele, Droegemueller, & Silver, 1962, as cited in Pecora et al., 2000) received widespread media attention.

By 1966, due to the efforts of child welfare professionals and the medical community's recognition and publicizing of the "battered child syndrome," 49 states passed mandatory reporting laws obligating certain professionals working with children to report child abuse or neglect to public departments of social services (Pecora et al., 2000).

Federal recognition of this serious societal issue resulted in Congress passing Public Law 93-247, the Child Abuse Prevention and Treatment Act (CAPTA) in 1974.

■ Historical Perspective of the Intended and Unintended Consequences of Public Policy

The professionals who responded to child abuse and neglect for most of the twentieth century believed in helping rather than in criminalizing families involved in child maltreatment. To this day, the *intent* of child welfare policy is to ensure that families receive the supportive services they need to protect and parent their children in their own homes.

☐ The Experience of Families of Color

In this country, the child welfare system has always treated children and families of color[1] differently. It was, in fact, an openly segregated system until the mid-1940s. In the late 1800s, wealthy white do-gooders took on the task of saving impoverished children from cruelty and deprivation. They established orphanages for white children and relegated black children to inferior, overcrowded "colored orphan asylums" (Roberts, 2002, p. 7). Other minority populations experienced similar discrimination. As long ago as 1860, the U.S. government supported military-type boarding schools for American Indian children. In 1879, just 2 years after the humane societies' meeting in Cleveland, the first group of American Indian children was sent by train to just such an institution in Carlisle, Pennsylvania, where they were to be stripped of their customs and assimilated into white, middle-class culture (Roberts, 2002).

Remarking on what they term the history of racism and differential treatment of children and families of color in America's public child welfare system, Billingsley and Giovannoni (1972) describe a shift from total to partial exclusion. While new federal legislation opened the doors to blacks in the 1930s, discriminatory state-based policies and rules on home stability, substitute fathers, illegitimate children, and men in the house continued to ensure that they were denied equal services (Lawrence-Webb, 1997). In her 1983 study, Close says bluntly that the public child welfare system is "less committed, in practice, to the welfare of children of color and their families" (p. 19).

☐ Disproportionate Representation of Minorities in the CPS System

Relative to their numbers in the general population, children of African American and American Indian/Alaskan Native heritage are overrepresented in the child welfare system, and white or Asian/Pacific Islander children are underrepresented (Earle & Cross, 2001).

- Child protective services agencies receive and substantiate more maltreatment reports on children of color and provide fewer services to them.

Statistics show that these children spend a longer time in care, have a higher rate of reentry into care, have less stability in their out-of-home placements, and wait much longer to be adopted (Courtney, Barth, Berrick, Brooks, Needell, & Park, 1996).

- A 1980 Youth Referral Survey conducted by the U.S. Office of Civil Rights showed that prevalence rates for out-of-home placement per 1,000 children were highest for black and American Indian children.

- According to a 1986 nationwide survey, American Indian children entered the foster care system at a rate 3.6 times higher than any other group of children.

- Data from California, Illinois, Michigan, New York, and Texas indicated that in 1990 black children were more likely to be placed in out-of-home care (Courtney et al., 1996).

- A 1999 analysis of data in the Multi-State Data Archive found that black children stay in the foster care system longer than white children in 11 states (Alabama, California, Illinois, Iowa, Maryland, Michigan, Missouri, New Mexico, New York, Ohio, and Wisconsin) (Derezotes & Poertner, 2002).

- In 2000, the Administration for Children and Families of the U.S. Department of Health and Human Services reported that while blacks represented only 17% of the country's youth, 42% of the children in foster care were black (Roberts, 2002, p. 8).

☐ Differential Treatment

There is no shortage of research on and documentation of the differential treatment of minority populations in the child welfare system (Brissett-Chapman, 1997; Close, 1983; Courtney et al., 1996; Jorge, 1989; Stehno, 1982). The literature shows a "pattern of inequity, if not discrimination, based on race and ethnicity in the provision of child welfare services," with children of color—blacks in particular—achieving poorer outcomes (Courtney et al., 1996, p. 112).

Research suggests various (and sometimes contradictory) explanations for this situation, including institutional racism, poverty, substance abuse, and poorly trained child protection staff.

☐ The Negative Consequences of Laws and Policy

Despite the good intentions of this country's legislators and policy-makers, from Colonial times to the present, people of color—particularly blacks and American Indians—have experienced institutionalized discrimination and differential treatment on many fronts. Consequently, they often distrust and resent the public child welfare system, a powerful arm of the federal government. Examples follow of policy and legislation that have had unintended negative consequences for populations of color.

Slave Law (seventeenth century). The brainchild of white lawmakers, slavery gave plantation owners total authority over their labor force. The system was intended to help "uncivilized Africans" acquire "moral values" (Roberts, 2002). Instead, it destroyed families, deprived children and adults of rights, and thoroughly subrogated the race.

Freedmen's Bureau (eighteenth century). Free black children were given access to almshouses and were indentured, but they received harsher treatment than their white counterparts (Hogan & Siu, 1988).

Apprenticeship Laws (eighteenth century). After Emancipation, laws were passed to enable children of former slaves to learn a trade. The courts, however, abetted plantation owners' tendency to exploit the legislation. Judges had the authority to declare the children's parents unfit and return them to plantation owners' custody, thereby separating recently reunited families and reinstating the master/slave relationship (Hogan & Siu, 1988).

Orphanage System (nineteenth century). In the 1800s, social services were segregated, and children of color were excluded from the developing orphanage system. A separate substandard white-run system of care existed for black children, and their families were seldom consulted in planning for their future (Hogan & Siu, 1988).

Supreme Court Ruling of 1832: Worcester v. State of Georgia (nineteenth century). Historically, U.S. federal and state governments have manipulated and exploited the treaties they signed with tribal nations. The Supreme Court ruling of 1831 established sovereignty for tribal nations, giving them the authority to govern themselves and make treaties with the United States. In 1885, however, Congress passed the *Seven Major Crimes Act*, which firmly established the federal court on American Indian land and diminished the hard-won rights of the tribal courts. In 1887, the federal government struck another blow to American Indians with the *General Allotment Act*, which gave Congress authority to section tribal territory into 160-acre tracts and sell "surplus" land to non-Indian settlers. Within 25 years of the act's passage, American Indians lost an additional two-thirds (or almost 90 million acres) of their land (Johnson, 1982). With the loss of land came increased poverty.

Aid to Families with Dependent Children (AFDC) (twentieth century). Introduced in 1935, this New Deal welfare program was established to prevent child welfare authorities from removing children from their parents for financial reasons. It supported what were considered the worthy poor, or poor white widows. Prior to the civil rights movement, social services remained segregated, and few mothers of color benefited from AFDC.

War on Poverty (twentieth century). This national effort in the 1960s saw the expansion of welfare entitlements to help America's poor. As the percentage of black welfare recipients increased, however, states reduced cash benefits, cut back on services, imposed behavior modification rules and other punitive measures, and instituted work requirements, thereby perpetuating the notion of an unworthy poor (Roberts, 2002).

Indian Adoption and Termination Era (twentieth century). The overall policy of this era was aimed at ending the trust relationship extended from the federal government to Indian tribes that had been established by *Cherokee Nation v. Georgia* in 1831 and further clarified in *Worcester v. State of Georgia* in 1832.

During this era thousands of Indian families were stripped of their land and encouraged to "relocate" to urban areas with the promise of employment and an end to poverty. American Indian policy analysts consider the relocation program a fiasco due to lack of training and support and an increase in family breakup. The program was intended to assimilate Indians into mainstream society. The intent was similar to previous attempts to end an "inferior" culture by "civilizing" the Indians.

Similar thinking pervaded the Indian Adoption Project, which removed Indian children from their families and placed them with more affluent, white families. Poverty was the justification for children being removed from their families and familiar communities. According to George (1997), the project established a "clearinghouse for the interstate placement of Indian children with non-Indian families" and was based on the philosophy "that the 'forgotten child, left unloved and uncared for on the reservation, without a home or parents he can call his own' could be adopted 'where there was less prejudice against Indians'" (p. 169).

Child Abuse Prevention and Treatment Act (CAPTA) (1974) (twentieth century). By attaching federal funding to various aspects of child welfare, this legislation actually created incentives for states to remove children from their homes and place them in foster care. Public agencies expended less energy and money on keeping families intact and allocated their dollars to support out-of-home placement. Since most families involved in the child welfare system are poor and most of the poor in this country are black, American Indian, Hispanic, or another immigrant population, the lack of family preservation services affected people of color disproportionately.

Indian Child Welfare Act (1978) (twentieth century). American Indian tribes' role within the federal system as sovereign, domestic nations has been established by the Supreme Court and through treaties. There is *no direct relationship between states and tribes.* Tribes do not yet have direct funding for child welfare programs. Although the Social Security Act mandates states to administer social service and financial assistance to American Indians on reservations, it does not offer guidelines on how tribal governments are to be involved in the federal/state partnership for program delivery. Tensions over funding and jurisdictional disputes are ongoing, increasing the likelihood of inferior service delivery to reservations (Johnson, 1982). In addition, as is not the case with other federal child welfare legislation, there are no fiscal sanctions against states that do not comply with the practice requirements of the Indian Child Welfare Act. Furthermore, there are no guidelines about how tribes are to respond to the states' attempts to comply with the requirements of the act. While some states are making concerted efforts to improve compliance, no states have achieved full compliance. Child welfare systems continue to fail to identify Indian children, to properly notice tribes, and to apply the legal and practice best-interest standards that are defined for Indian children within the act.

Adoption Assistance and Child Welfare Act (1980) (twentieth century). This act was intended to reverse the effects of CAPTA by emphasizing preventive services and family preservation/reunification programs. It also, however, encouraged termination of parental rights (TPR) to expedite permanency. If children's families could not be rehabilitated in what judges deemed a reasonable period of time—and the depth of problems poor families of color experience (including domestic violence and substance abuse) can require extensive, long-term intervention—they ordered TPR. Consequently, family ties for large numbers of children of color were permanently severed (Roberts, 2002).

Adoption and Safe Families Act (ASFA) (1997) (twentieth century). Illustrating Congress's shift from supporting prevention and reunification programs to reducing the number of children in foster care, ASFA dramatically increased the number of children adopted into permanent homes. Unfortunately, most of the children waiting to be adopted are black. It was their families who did not receive preservation/reunification services and were unable to meet the shorter time frames for reunification. It was their families whose parental rights were terminated because they were in foster care too long, and before the multiple challenges of their parents could be resolved (Roberts, 2002).

☐ Working toward a More Equitable CPS System

As professional child welfare practitioners in the twenty-first century, then, our challenge is to guarantee that policy is carried out in practice and that practice is culturally responsive. Research reveals that as child welfare advocates and practitioners, we need to improve our cultural competence and responsiveness and ensure culturally sensitive and appropriate services to all children and families. We also must renew our commitment to writing equitable, equal, and adequate policy and carrying it out consistently. American child welfare policy will be equitable when children and families of color receive the same combination of services, exit at similar rates, and achieve permanency at the same rate as white children. It will be equal and adequate when populations of color entering the child welfare system get equal treatment, benefit equally from a full range of appropriately funded services, and are not overrepresented in the foster care population (Everett, Chipungu, & Leashore, 1991).

■ The Legal Base

Child protective services are guided by federal laws enacted in the late 1900s. (For more information related to the legal basis and policies, see chapter 11.) Brief descriptions follow of some of the most influential federal child welfare legislation.

The Child Abuse Prevention and Treatment Act of 1974 (CAPTA) (Public Law 93-247), revised and updated regularly since enactment, ties federal funding for states to systems of identification, reporting, and response to child abuse and neglect.

The Indian Child Welfare Act of 1978 (Public Law 95-608) emphasizes the role of Indian tribes in decision-making around the protective needs and placement of American Indian children. Through this act, Congress sought to address the systemic bias that appeared to be the foundation for out-of-home placement for up to 35% of all Indian children, with more than 90% of these children placed in non-Indian homes. The law includes mandates on state courts and procedural safeguards, such as tribal notification and active efforts to preserve the unity of families and the integrity of children's tribal and cultural affiliation.

The Adoption Assistance and Child Welfare Act of 1980 (Public Law 96-272) ties federal foster care funding and fiscal incentives to the implementation of policies related to family preservation and permanency planning. Workers and courts are obligated to demonstrate and certify that reasonable efforts were made to preserve families before children can be placed in foster care or made eligible for adoption. This legislation provides fiscal incentives to support the adoption of children determined to have special needs.

The Omnibus Budget Reconciliation Act of 1993 (Public Law 97-35) included the Family Preservation and Support Program (FPSP) to fund a range of services and activities designed to strengthen families (including adoptive and extended families) and prevent out-of-home placement (Costin et al., 1996).

The Multiethnic Placement Act of 1994 (MEPA) (Public Law 103-382) and the *Interethnic Adoptions Provisions Act of 1996* (IAP). MEPA legislation eliminated policies that favored same-race placements. Amendments to MEPA, found in the IAP legislation, established Congress's intent to prevent discrimination or delays in foster care or adoptive placement and specifically prohibited delays in or denial of foster care or adoptive placement on the basis of race, culture, or ethnicity. Due to the unique political status and separate coverage by ICWA, Indian children are specifically excluded. In other words, Indian children must be tribally or racially matched under ICWA.

The Adoption and Safe Families Act of 1997 (ASFA) (Public Law 105-89) provides both changes to and clarification of policies of its antecedent legislation, PL 96-272 (the Adoption Assistance and Child Welfare Act of 1980). The legislation is intended to improve the safety of children, promote adoptions and permanent homes for children, and support families. Significantly, ASFA:

- Stipulates that child safety is of paramount importance during reunification efforts and provides exceptions to reasonable efforts requirements.
- Mandates shorter timelines for reunification before actions to terminate parental rights may occur.
- Requires concurrent permanency planning.
- Provides financial incentives and technical assistance to states to promote adoption activities.
- Includes system accountability and reform provisions and outlines required performance measures for state child welfare programs (National Association of Public Child Welfare Administrators, 1999; Pecora et al., 2000).
- Promotes the study of kinship placement feasibility.

☐   State Response to Child Abuse and Neglect

All states have laws that support and complement federal legislation. In 1911, Ohio was the first state to develop and use a children's code—or catalogue of existing legislation that affected children's lives—to improve program planning and legislation. These state laws define child maltreatment, specify reporting responsibilities and procedures, and articulate the overall purpose, focus, and organization of the local child protective services systems. In addition, all states and some local departments of social services have manuals outlining regional policies and procedures for CPS workers who must intervene in cases of abuse and neglect.

Federal Definitions

- *Maltreatment.* An act (or failure to act) by a parent, caregiver, or other person as defined under state law that results in physical abuse, neglect, medical neglect, sexual abuse, or emotional abuse. Or an act (or failure to act) that presents an imminent risk of serious harm to a child.
- *Neglect or deprivation of necessities.* A type of maltreatment that refers to a caregiver's failure to provide needed, age-appropriate care despite being financially able to do so or being offered financial or other means to do so.
- *Physical abuse.* A type of maltreatment that refers to physical acts that cause or could cause physical injury to a child.
- *Psychological or emotional maltreatment.* A type of maltreatment that refers to acts or omissions—other than physical abuse or sexual abuse—that cause or could cause conduct, cognitive, affective, or other mental disorders. This includes emotional neglect, psychological abuse, and mental injury and frequently occurs as verbal abuse or excessive demands on a child's performance and may result in a negative self-image and disturbed behavior.
- *Sexual Abuse.* A type of maltreatment that refers to the involvement of a child in sexual activity to provide sexual gratification or financial benefit to the perpetrator, including contacts for sexual purposes, molestation, statutory rape, prostitution, pornography, exposure, incest, or other sexually exploitative activities.

Source: Administration on Children, Youth and Families, Children's Bureau (2000).

■   Current Practice and Policy

☐   Philosophy

When a parent or caregiver abuses, neglects, or is clearly unable or unwilling to protect his or her child, society responds to ensure the child's safety. Public child protective service (CPS) agencies—traditionally a specialized component of the broader child welfare system—are the legally mandated social agents responsible for meeting the needs of these unprotected children and their families. Although these agencies are mandated to respond to reports of child abuse and neglect, in recent years the broader community also has begun to share in the responsibility for ensuring children's safety and well-being.

As child welfare practitioners, we must be guided by a philosophy of family preservation. Rather than removing or rescuing children from abusive families, we build on families' strengths and enhance their capacity to nurture and protect their children. Restoring families and ensuring that they develop adequate parenting skills is our objective. For the vast majority of families involved with the child welfare system, this is a realistic goal.

Removing children from their homes should be the exception rather than the rule. Family preservation is not only a more desirable outcome, it also is a much more cost-effective alternative to long-term, out-of-home care.

There are times, however, when families cannot be restored or preserved. In some cases, children's safety can only be ensured by removing them from their homes and placing them in foster care.

Whenever possible, the extended family should be the first placement option, and children should be returned as soon as the immediate safety concerns are remedied.

☐ Emphasis on Achieving Permanency

Permanency, which can be defined as "a sense of belonging and legal, life-time family ties" (Pecora et al., 2000, p. 73), may be achieved with a kinship placement, a permanent guardian, an adoptive family, or a foster family committed to raising the child to adulthood.

Permanency planning involves identifying a permanent home and preparing the child and family, both the biological and foster or adoptive family, for the placement.

Concurrent planning is necessary to achieve permanency. This process begins immediately (or as soon as a case is opened) and involves simultaneous, careful planning efforts. While planning for and providing services to ensure the families' reunification/restoration, one also must explore and develop viable, permanent, out-of-home placement options.

☐ Community Response

As child welfare practitioners, we have come to understand that families reported for alleged child maltreatment require different levels and types of formal response or investigation. States have adopted various strategies to ensure that their public child protection systems are directing their resources appropriately. For example, some locales/states partner with communities to provide an alternative response to reports alleging harm to a child. In this way, they are able to provide a less intrusive and ideally more targeted service to vulnerable or at-risk families who, with adequate support, can ensure the safety of their children.

☐ Current Focus on Outcomes

In recent years, agencies have become much more focused on outcomes, or on the results of interventions and services for children and families served by the

CPS system. We have gained a great deal of experience in and knowledge about defining and developing measures to collect information on child safety, permanency, and well-being, the three outcomes that are monitored by ASFA legislation and the federal Child and Family Services Review process. Experts in the field continue to explore ways to ensure that we, as professional child welfare practitioners, fulfill our societal and legal responsibilities to ensure children's safety, permanency, and well-being.

■ The Principles of Child Protective Services

☐ Characteristics of CPS Work

Child protective services casework has the following unique characteristics that distinguish it from other publicly provided social services; CPS:

- Emphasizes reaching out to children and families involved in child maltreatment
- Gives critical safety and risk assessment responsibilities
- Gives authority to protect children
- Requires knowledge of the law and the skillful use of the court
- May necessitate an immediate response
- Requires a careful balancing of the rights of involved parents, children, and society at large

☐ CPS Goals

In summary, CPS includes a continuum of services and interventions that are directed toward accomplishing the following goals:

- Receiving and assessing allegations of abuse and neglect
- Assessing safety and risk to children and evaluating families' capacity to accept and use help
- Planning and coordinating the services and interventions available from all resources
- Initiating court involvement for both the removal of children and the provision of mandatory protective services to resistant parents or caregivers
- Assuring that children are receiving a minimum standard of care before closing a case
- Achieving outcomes related to safety, permanency, and well-being in a time-limited way
- Educating the public about the purview of the formal child protective services system
- Developing and coordinating community resources and services

■ Summary of Competencies

This handbook is designed to help you get a better understanding of the public system of child protective services; the criteria for decision making at every stage of the casework process; the dynamics of the family situations encountered; the methods of interviewing and helping children, parents, and caregivers; and the coordination of the casework role with other community services and institutions. This chapter covers the following knowledge areas:

1. Overview of the development of the child protection movement in the United States.

2. Framework of federal legislation and policy in child protective services.

3. The intended and unintended effects of public policy on populations of color.

4. Philosophical basis of CPS as a specialized set of services intended to ensure child safety while preserving families.

Note

1. Categories and terms used for race and ethnicity are consistent with those used in the annual *Reports from the States to the National Child Abuse and Neglect Data System*, prepared for the U.S. Department of Health and Human Services, Administration on Children, Youth and Families.

References

Administration on Children, Youth and Families, Children's Bureau. (2000, March). *National Child Abuse and Neglect Data System (NCANDS) Glossary (SDC and DCDC Combined)*. Retrieved September 2002 from: http://www.acf.dhhs.gov/programs/cb/dis/ncands98/glossary/glossary.

Billingsley, A., & Giovannoni, J. (1972). *Children of the storm: Black children and American child welfare*. New York: Harcourt Brace Jovanovich.

Brissett-Chapman, S. (1997). Child protection risk assessment and African American children: Cultural ramifications for families and communities. *Child Welfare, 76*, 45–63.

Close, M. (1983). Child welfare and people of color: Denial of equal access. *Social Work Research and Abstracts, 19*, 13–20.

Costin, L., Karger, H., & Stoesz, D. (1996). *The politics of child abuse in America*. New York: Oxford University Press.

Courtney, M., Barth, R., Berrick, J., Brooks, D., Needell, B., & Park, L. (1996). Race and child welfare services: Past research and future directions. *Child Welfare, 75*, 99–137.

Derezotes, D., & Poertner, J. (2002). *Factors contributing to the overrepresentation of African American children in the child welfare system: What we know and don't know*. Urbana-Champaign: Children and Family Research Center, School of Social Work, University of Illinois at Urbana-Champaign.

Douglas, A. (1998). *The American Humane Association: 1877–1945*. Unpublished manuscript.

Earle, K. A., & Cross, A. (2001). *Child abuse and neglect among American Indian/Alaska Native children: An analysis of existing data*. Seattle: Casey Family Programs.

Everett, J., Chipungu, S., & Leashore, B. (1991). *Child welfare: An Africentric perspective*. New Brunswick, NJ: Rutgers University Press.

George, L. J. (1997). Why the need for the Indian Child Welfare Act? *Journal of Multicultural Social Work, 5*(3/4), 165–175.

Gooden, M., & Hunt, D. E. (2000). *Resource guide for Indian child welfare practice: Ensuring safety and permanence for Indian children.* Salt Lake City: Graduate School of Social Work, University of Utah.

Hogan, P. T., & Siu, S-F (1988, November). Minority children and the child welfare system: An historical perspective. *Social Work, 33*(6), 493–498.

Hunt, D. E., Gooden, M., & Barkdull, C. (2001). Walking in Mocassins: Indian child welfare in the twenty-first century. In A. L. Sallee, H. A. Lawson, & K. Briar-Lawson (Eds.), *Innovative practices with vulnerable children and families.* Dubuque, IA: eddie bowers.

Johnson, B. (1982, January). American Indian jurisdiction as a policy issue. *Social Work, 27*, 31–36.

Jorge, I. (1989). *Cultural responsiveness and sensitivity in risk assessment.* Paper presented at 1989 CPS Risk Assessment Conference, Los Angeles, CA.

Lawrence-Webb, C. (1997). African American children in the modern child welfare system: A legacy of the Flemming Rule. *Child Welfare, 76*, 9–29.

National Association of Public Child Welfare Administrators. (1999). *Guidelines for a model system of protective services for abused and neglected children and their families.* Washington, DC: American Public Human Services Association.

Pecora, P. J., Whittaker, J. K., Maluccio, & Barth, R. P., with Plotnick, R. D. (2000). *The child welfare challenge: Policy, practice, and research.* Hawthorne, NY: De Gruyter.

Roberts, D. (2002). *Shattered bonds: The color of child welfare.* New York: Basic Civitas Books.

Stehno, S. (1982, January). Differential treatment of minority children in service systems. *Social Work, 27*, 39–45.

Watkins, S. A. (1990). The Mary Ellen myth: Correcting child welfare history. *Social Work, 35*(6), 500–503.

3

Anne Comstock
Nancy McDaniel

The Casework Process

The casework process is the approach to practice used in child protective services. It involves integrating the legal mandates for CPS, as well as the values of social work practice, in working together with families on resolving the issues that precipitated their involvement with CPS. In this chapter we first explore the philosophical foundation for CPS practice, and then we discuss the casework process, from the thinking behind it to the tasks within it. When conducting casework, you will have multiple roles, and you must be comfortable moving among all of them. You will also have to balance your use of authority with your engagement with and provision of help to the family. Your self-awareness can help to facilitate this balance. Finally, in this chapter we present the factors that make CPS a challenging experience and strategies for overcoming them to make the casework process a better experience for everyone involved.

■ The Philosophical Foundation of Child Protective Work

Definition of CPS. Child protective services are defined as specialized supports and interventions for neglected, abused, or exploited children and their families. In CPS, workers focus on rehabilitating the family and home through interventions and services that address the specific situations and conditions that lead to child maltreatment. The term *family* is used broadly, and persons within a family should make the designation of who to include in the family unit.

The Mission of CPS. The National Association of Public Child Welfare Administrators (1999) says that the mission of CPS agencies is

> to assess the safety of children, intervene to protect children from harm, strengthen the ability of families to protect their children, or provide an alternative safe family for the child. Child protective services are provided to children and families by CPS agencies in collaboration with communities in order to protect children from abuse or neglect within their families. (p. 12)

The public child welfare agency is mandated by federal and state laws to respond to reports alleging child maltreatment, to determine the safety of the identified child immediately, and to establish the course of the initial response.

The core beliefs of CPS are as follows:
- This country's laws, policies, and cultural mores reflect our belief that children deserve to be protected from abuse and neglect and to have their basic physical, emotional, and educational needs met.
- Parents, family, and kin are the best source of protection for children, and they—as primary caregivers—have an obligation to meet children's basic needs.
- Parents have the legal responsibility to ensure the health and welfare of their children and to act on their behalf in matters related to their health and well-being.

- However, when parents or caregivers are unwilling or unable to protect their children from neglect and abuse, or when they are the cause of the maltreatment, society has an ethical and legal obligation to step in on behalf of the children.
- With appropriate and adequate support, most parents or caregivers can and will change their behavior.
- The best way to protect children from maltreatment is to provide services that ensure that parents or caregivers are able to provide a basic standard of care.
- It is always best to allow children to continue to live with their parents. If, however, it becomes clear that their safety and healthy development cannot be assured—even with supportive intervention—you, the worker and agent of the formal child protective services system, must make other arrangements for temporary or permanent placement.
- When workers find it necessary to remove children from their homes, they must make every effort to place them with and maintain their connection to family members, kin, and community.

CPS Standards. National organizations and professionals who work in the field of child protective services have developed practice standards, policies, guidelines, standards for accreditation and standards of excellence for service delivery. They may have different philosophies and may take different approaches to practice, but they do tend to agree on many aspects of CPS work. Areas of commonality include the following:

- Child protective services should be child centered and family focused. The child's protective needs are at the center of decision-making, but the service is focused on building the family's capacity to care for and protect the child. When this is not possible, the formal CPS agency should move toward placing the child outside his or her home in a safe setting.
- Child protective services should be a specialized child welfare service and not the only entity available in communities to help vulnerable children and families. Community organizations and the broader network of community services, both formal and informal, need to be involved in responding to abused and neglected children and their families. CPS works with the community in the following ways:

    CPS receives reports from the community and must give feedback to reporters.

    Formal interagency agreements should exist between CPS agencies and other partners in the CPS system to coordinate intervention on cases and foster sound decisions to mobilize resources that protect children and strengthen families.

    CPS needs to be able to access or purchase social services support from a spectrum of individuals, agencies, and organizations in every community.

- There is a clear intent to reserve CPS for cases in which the child has been or is likely to be demonstrably harmed by the parent, caregiver, or other family member.
- All reports indicating child neglect or abuse should be assessed.
- A CPS case can be defined as one in which a child is being harmed or is at great risk of being harmed by the abuse and/or neglect of parents or caregivers who are unwilling or unable to ensure protection.
- Agencies and workers must be culturally responsive and able to intervene appropriately and work effectively with families with diverse ethnic, racial, religious, and socioeconomic backgrounds, as follows:

    Agencies' policies must delineate the importance of cultural responsiveness.

    Workers and supervisors must receive training to develop both knowledge and skills to relate to all cultural groups appropriately.

    Decision-making on cases must be culturally responsive and tailored to the particular circumstances of individual children and families.

- Workers cannot make assumptions about the nature of families' needs/problems or strengths without careful assessment.
- Careful assessment involves being open to resources that are available from the extended family, faith-based groups, neighborhood support systems, and other resources that may be more available in certain communities or cultural groups than in the general population.
- The types of maltreatment to be addressed by CPS include physical abuse, neglect, sexual abuse or exploitation, and emotional maltreatment. CPS is focused on intrafamilial situations of abuse and neglect in which the parents or caregivers are unwilling or unable to protect the child.

■ The CPS Casework Process

The CPS casework process is systematic and involves a series of steps directed toward helping people solve specific behavior-related problems. The process provides a structure to guide your work and increases your confidence and level of comfort in doing your job. It also enables you to assess your own performance and gauge the effectiveness of your interventions and your progress in working with the child and family. You should describe and explain it to families to increase their level of comfort and confidence and reduce their fear of the unknown. The family is your partner in the process, so you must engage them in it fully.

□ The Functions of CPS in the Casework Process

Because CPS is directed by the mission and values of the organization mandated to provide CPS and is guided by law and policy, child protective services staff must:

- Determine the immediate safety of a child and assess the potential risk of future harm.
- Determine if abuse or neglect has occurred.
- Assess the strengths and needs of the target child and family to identify the issues associated with risk of harm.
- Determine the need for services.
- Provide direct services to strengthen families and protect children.
- Coordinate community services.
- Seek family involvement in case decisions while drawing on the knowledge and expertise of a multidisciplinary team of professionals.
- Be culturally responsive when assessing and serving families of various backgrounds.

In addition, the CPS casework process:

- Incorporates a unified approach based on step-by-step procedures.
- Emphasizes the interconnectedness of the steps of the process. The process is progressive in that each step builds on previous steps, and the success of later steps depends on how well you accomplish earlier steps.
- Allows you to be flexible and to respond spontaneously to the family's needs.
- Requires that you be flexible enough to back up and reprioritize tasks or redefine families' strengths/needs; your relationship with a family is dynamic, so you must always be flexible and open to change.
- Requires that you convey a sense of confidence and control in managing crises.
- Requires that you take enough time to deal with and resolve the complexity of issues facing families. Progress often occurs incrementally, and while small changes may at times seem insignificant, over time they can lead to success.
- Uses an analytical model for problem solving that includes:

    Exploring all of the dimensions and dynamics of the problem situation.

    Assessing the immediate safety of the child and the strengths that exist in the family.

    Assessing the potential risk for harm to the child and the likelihood of successful intervention strategies.

    Choosing among alternative intervention strategies and community resources.

    Continuously evaluating the effectiveness of the selected strategies and services.

- Uses a family's strengths to resolve the issues that led to CPS involvement. This identification of and strengthening of the family's intrinsic assets characterizes the process from beginning to end. Each step in the process is intended to contribute to the successful outcome(s) of safety, permanency, and well-being.

- Involves careful decision-making around: children's safety and the risks they face; family strengths and resources; minimal standards of parenting behavior; and design and negotiation of desired outcomes or changes expected from the family as a result of the relationship.

☐ **Basic Steps**

When a referral is received by CPS, the following seven basic steps are followed.

1. *Intake.* It is the first step, and it includes:

Receiving the report or referral.

Making collateral contacts as needed and checking written and/or electronic records.

Exploring the appropriateness of the referral.

Determining the urgency of the report and the level of response

Assigning the report for agency and/or community follow up.

Documenting the information in an electronic and/or written record.

2. *Investigation.* It includes:

Making initial contact with the child and family.

Coordinating the immediate response of other service providers if warranted; for example, law enforcement, medical professionals, and so on.

Assessing the immediate safety and well-being of the child.

Making subsequent assessment visits.

Assessing the potential for continuing risk to the child.

Evaluating the family indicators of abuse or neglect.

Determining if abuse or neglect has occurred.

Identifying cultural heritage; specifically asking if a family has Indian tribal affiliation.

Determining the need to invoke the authority of the court.

Providing emergency services as needed.

Providing feedback to appropriate persons, including notifying Indian tribes (or the Bureau of Indian Affairs, if the tribe is unknown), if there is clear and convincing evidence that the child must be removed from the home.

Documenting the information in an electronic and/or written record.

Providing parents or custodians with their rights and remedies.

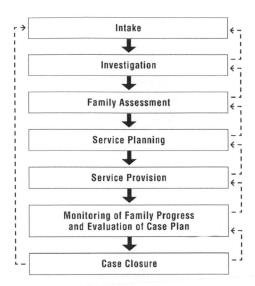

3. *Family assessment.* It includes:

Working with the family to identify the family problems in more depth from a causal perspective.

Assessing strengths and assets within the family and the extended network of social supports (cognizant of cultural and community norms and mores) that can minimize risks and identify areas for improvement in family functioning.

Understanding the family's history and current circumstances and their potential impact on risks and strengths.

4. *Service planning.* It includes:

Determining both the formal and informal services and resources available to and needed by the family, and making sure the services are seen by the family as culturally responsive.

Specifying the changes that need to occur to assure the child's continued safety, permanency, and well-being.

Deciding what services will be given: to whom, by whom, how often, and for how long.

Establishing dates for review.

Documenting the service plan.

5. *Service provision.* It includes:

Involving the family in formulation of the service plan and ensuring that it is understood.

Arranging for and coordinating services provided by other agencies, organizations, or individuals.

Eliminating obstacles to service provision.

Providing direct services.

Documenting the progress of all services.

6. *Monitoring family progress and evaluating the case plan.* It includes:

Contacting all service providers for a review of the case.

Working with the family and other providers to evaluate the family's progress.

Updating the assessment.

Making decisions with the family to continue the plan, revise the plan, or terminate the plan.

Documenting the record.

7. *Closing the case.* It includes:

Evaluating goal attainment with the family.

Analyzing the potential for the family to remain stable.

Examining the need for referral to other continuing services.

Advising and preparing the family for termination of services.

Advising other agencies or involved persons.

Documenting the record with the rationale for case closure.

■ Child Protective Services Roles

CPS work is difficult and complex. You are the individual most directly involved in safeguarding the rights and welfare of children. As a professional, you embody the principles, standards, theories, and techniques of social work as a method of interacting with people. In addition, as a CPS worker, you have specific roles and responsibilities you must perform. An understanding of these various roles and responsibilities will assist you in the complex work of protecting children and strengthening families. Your roles include the following.

☐ Evaluator

As evaluator, you *study and analyze* information about the family, the family's problems, strengths, available resources, services, and treatment strategies, and you *assess* the results of interventions. As an evaluator, you conduct an assessment.

- In response to allegations of child maltreatment, you are expected to conduct a comprehensive assessment that will allow you to make critical decisions regarding child safety, the risk of future maltreatment, the needs, and existing resources of the family.

- Many agencies have developed and implemented specific assessment instruments for workers to utilize during this phase of the case. These instruments identify content areas and factors to be considered in conducting your assessments.

- When interpreting assessments, you must determine whether cultural norms are sufficiently considered in your conclusions. Most assessment instruments have not been validated for different cultural groups. Check with your supervisor if you have concerns about the cultural fit of instruments. In the overall evaluation summary, you may want to comment on any items that you believe do not fit the cultural norms of the family.

- Assessments will also help to identify strengths within the family's informal and formal support network that could mitigate safety and risk concerns.

In addition, you make decisions. Your assessment should enable you make decisions regarding safety, risk, and needs.

- You will determine if the child can safely remain in his or her current environment with the parents or caregivers.

- You will determine the likelihood of future maltreatment of the children.

- You will also be working with the family to identify their needs and strengths, specifically related to their ability to care for and keep their children safe. Family needs cover a broad spectrum, from housing and employment, to drug treatment, to parenting support groups. Strengths can include extended family and non-kin support, cultural identity and values that inspire resilience, spiritual or religious connection, informal community supports, or a desire to change.

☐ Case Manager

As case manager you are expected to oversee the helping process. This could involve planning, referring, implementing, and evaluating services. As case manager, you facilitate follow-up activities related to your cases and coordinate the agency and community systems assisting families. You empower the family to use these formal and informal systems to encourage positive change. The aim of these services is, first, to protect the child from further maltreatment, and then to try to help the family members build on their strengths, capacities, and resources to be able to relate to each other in more responsible and productive ways.

You *work with the parents and other partners* to prioritize these needs, identify strengths, and develop a realistic service plan:

- You may negotiate specific goals with the family.

- You negotiate specific dates, times, and places for subsequent contacts.

- You identify the need for and arrange for referrals to other agencies or services. You should make referrals only if you are certain that they are in the best interest of the family, that is, they are part of your service plan.

- You follow up on referrals that you make.

You *remain actively involved* with the family and the implementation of the service plan by:

- Having regular contact and visits with all involved members of the family.
- Continuing to develop a deeper understanding of the family's feelings, relationships, environment, special problems, strengths, and challenges, and the interrelationships among these factors.
- Evaluating your assessments, that is, you determine the validity of the information you have and change your perceptions in the light of new information.
- Assessing community resources in order to determine their availability and appropriateness for serving the family.
- Encouraging and supporting changes that are moving the family toward successful completion of the plan.

In your professional capacity, *you meet certain legal roles and responsibilities.*

- Your legal role consists of knowing the laws and statutes that provide CPS authority for intervention, including when and how to invoke the authority of the court for specific actions, e.g., removal of a child or the filing of a court petition.
- You must fully document your efforts in the event that you become involved in the legal process.
- You must be prepared to provide required information to the court. You will do this via written reports, as well as court testimony.
- You must be prepared to have contact with and consult with others involved in the legal system, including attorneys, advocates, and potential witnesses.
- You must be prepared to testify. If you do testify, keep in mind that your role is to provide neutral and factual information to the court, not to advocate on behalf of any party: the parent, the prosecutor, or the child.

☐ Collaborator

As collaborator, you partner with family members and with community-based professionals who bring valuable knowledge and resources to protect the child and support the needs of the family. You involve extended family, tribe or community professionals, and service providers in the partnership of protecting children and strengthening families.

You formalize the involvement of all the partners (parents, caregivers, extended family, worker, providers, and the community) through their signing of the family services plan.

You have a responsibility to be a professional agency representative, as follows:

- You are the agency's spokesperson: the agency mission, federal and state laws, and community standards for child protection determine your actions; and your agency has policies and procedures that direct your practice.

- You interpret your agency's mission, policies, and procedures to the family, CPS partners, and the community.
- You are an integral part of the agency. Your input related to its organization, operation, and administration is important; and while you should not discuss the shortcomings of your agency with families or the community, you have a responsibility to let the appropriate people in your agency know of problems you perceive.

☐ **Therapeutic Treatment Provider**

In this role, you work directly with families to help them stop the maltreatment and learn new ways of relating to and being responsible for their children. You have a responsibility to serve as an *educator* for parents, as well as a role model through your professionalism.

- You should provide the parent(s) with an understanding of the law and its purpose.
- You should help the parent(s) understand your role and focus on family-centered, culturally relevant child protection.

☐ **Advocate**

In this role, you represent both the child and the parents or caregivers and speak for them in all agency matters.

☐ **Administrator**

In this role, you maintain accurate records and document your work.

- In addition to your direct work with families, you are also responsible for organized and accurate record keeping.
- You must document all of the information you gather about a family, as well as all of your activities related to the family.
- You must also complete all necessary documentation, following standard procedures.
- Sometimes CPS workers get frustrated and discouraged by all the paperwork they must complete, by hand, computer, or some sort of automated system. They often see paperwork as bothersome and time-consuming. If you do not recognize the importance of paperwork, it seems like a waste of time; however, because you represent the larger agency and the community, you are accountable.

    You must demonstrate your accountability by recording what you do. "Work not written is work not done!"

By recording what you learn about the family and the abuse or neglect incident, you can be assured that the information is there when you need it for making decisions. (This information is essential should you have to involve the court.) In addition, keeping records ensures that important information is not lost, in case you are not available and someone else must deal with a case, or if the case is transferred to another worker. By adhering to good documentation practices, you also participate in adding to the fund of knowledge in the child protective services field.

☐ Supervisee

In this role, you maintain close contact with your supervisor for assistance in decision-making and in dealing with complex issues and the potential conflicts that protective services work can cause.

As a CPS worker, you perform all of these roles at different times, and you are the sum of these roles at all times.

■ The Casework Method: Balancing Authority and Helping

☐ Integrating the Use of Authority with the Helper Role

One of the challenges of CPS work is building a trusting relationship with the family by integrating your use of authority with your ability to be a supporter and helper for the family. This is called the *casework method*, because the casework process allows this integration.

Use the casework method to develop a positive, trusting, collaborative relationship with the family. The helping relationship is based on several fundamental principles:

- An individual has the right to determine his or her own destiny, to make his or her own choices and decisions, and to deal with any resulting consequences of his or her action or inaction.
- An individual has the right to be treated with respect, regardless of weaknesses, faults, or conditions.
- An individual has the right to be accepted as a human being of worth, despite certain actions.
- An individual has the right to have personal information maintained in professional confidence.

☐ Use of Authority

As a CPS worker, you represent the public concern and commitment for the protective needs of children and support of families. The community gives you the difficult task of protecting children and strengthening families who have maltreated their children. Immediate response to referrals is often necessary, and often you must make difficult decisions on the basis of a limited amount of information.

Offer the family the choice of collaboration first, before using authority. Leverage change, if necessary, by using the prescribed power of the profession to gain entry to communicate the importance and seriousness of the situation while simultaneously striving to create a collaborative partnership.

Authority must be carefully exercised to effectively intervene and secure the child's safety. To use authority effectively:

- Be well informed to make critical decisions.
- Base your actions on your assessment of the best interest of the child.
- Use authority to help parents become more self-sufficient and responsible.
- Recognize that your intervention creates a crisis without which many parents would not be motivated to change their treatment of their child.
- Initiate the protective services process to provide the parents with help they need to become more effective parents.
- Recognize that in some cases your authoritative intervention alone may cause the parent(s) to become motivated to change.
- Understand the family history with authority, especially prior involvement and outcomes with child welfare systems.
- Recognize the resistance to or immediate overcompliance with authority as a reflection of the family's position in the broader power structure related to poverty, race, and possibly the gender of the worker.

Your own underlying attitude toward authority will determine, to a great extent, how effectively you use your power.

- The greater your awareness of your internal feelings about authority, the more capable you will be in appropriately exercising authority and control.
- A lack of awareness of your own personal dynamics and feelings about authority may make you vulnerable to inaccurate perceptions and irrational responses to families. Discuss this use of authority with your supervisor.

Be aware of feelings that cause you to lose objectivity, as well as personal experiences that affect your use of authority and infringe on the establishment of the helping relationship.

- Because of your own childhood experiences, you may become angry about a maltreatment situation. Seeing the child as the only victim of the situation may motivate you to use your authority to remove the child from the parent.
- You may be stern with a parent because of some event in your past that causes you to feel resentment about your own parents.

- You may have had negative experiences or been raised with deep-seated prejudices or stereotypes about a particular ethnic or religious group that make you want to change or control things about people based on your own beliefs.

Examine your attitudes toward authority by considering how you respond to the following questions.

- Do you view authority as a coercive means of controlling parents and obtaining their submission?
- Do you expect the parents to be motivated just because you approach them with authority?
- Do you use your authority to punish or "get back" at parents?
- Do you refrain from taking firm action because you want the acceptance or approval of the parents?
- Do you avoid using your authority because you fear the resulting rage of the parents?

You may experience conflict and difficulty in deciding generally how to exert your authority.

- Your agency expresses its authority by responding to reports and complaints of abuse and neglect. Some parents cannot or will not provide acceptable standards of care for their children. Out of pity or sympathy for the parents you may hesitate to take the action required. You may experience difficulty in making a decision.
- Some parents may want to be relieved of their parental responsibilities and may want you to assume the management and control of their children. You may experience difficulty in dealing with these demands.
- Because of the slow pace of the parents' responses, you may want to use your authority to take over the parental role.
- To deal with such difficulty, you should strive to maximize your effectiveness by increasing your knowledge and skill in dealing with families. The more you may be lacking in knowledge and skills, the more likely you will be to rely on your authority.
- In order to be certain your authority is being used in constructive ways, you should consult your supervisor.

You may experience particular difficulty in deciding to initiate court action, including the very serious consideration of removing a child from his or her home.

- You may be uncertain about the potential harm to the child.
- You may be uncertain about the resources available in the community to meet the needs of the child.
- You may have questions about the effect of the court action on the family relationships and your relationship with the family.
- You may have fears about becoming involved in the legal process.

- Nonetheless, if you determine, after a complete assessment, that the separation of the child from the parents is necessary, it is your responsibility to seek the legal authority required by your state law to take this action.

Although it is important for the family to understand the source of your authority, they do not necessarily need to have this information immediately.

- Many parents will offer no resistance to your intervention. You will be able to gain entry by a simple statement such as: "I am (name) from the Department of Human Services and I would like to talk with you about your child."

- If you do achieve immediate acceptance, you may feel it is not necessary to talk about the responsibility and obligations of your agency to protect and safeguard the welfare of children. However, at some point during the initial contact, you should clearly explain to the parents your role and function. The parents must understand the specific reasons for the intervention and your authority to act on behalf of the children. (See Chapter 6.)

You should use your authority in a warm, personal, supportive manner that shows an understanding of the parents' feelings about the problem.

- A family may feel less fearful of your authority if you demonstrate a nonthreatening and noncoercive attitude.

- Demonstrate your authority in a manner that indicates that you have no hidden agenda, that is, be honest.

- Clarify your protective service role and function. Do not retreat from your responsibility. Make the family aware of the expectations for change and the consequences of no change in their behavior. Make them aware that you will develop a plan with them for your work together, and that there are consequences if the changes in their behavior do not occur and their children are considered to be at risk for maltreatment.

- Make the family aware of your understanding that CPS intervention is likely to be traumatic and that you will do your best to minimize that trauma. Remember that the experience may be traumatic for both children and parents. In particular, it is not uncommon for parents who face losing their children to foster care to have been placed in foster care as children themselves. The parents' beliefs and capacity to hope for reunification with their children may be based on personal or family historical experience with the child welfare system.

■ The Key Values of the CPS Worker

The work of CPS is guided by the values and ethics of the profession of social work. According to the National Association of Social Worker's code of ethics, "This constellation of core values reflects what is unique to the social work profession. Core values, and the principles that flow from them, must be balanced within the context and complexity of the human experience" (National Association of Social Workers, 1999, Preamble section, para. 4).

☐ Ethical Principles

The following broad ethical principles are based on social work's core values of service, social justice, the dignity and worth of the person, the importance of human relationships, integrity, and competence. These principles set forth ideals to which all social workers should aspire.

Value: *Service*

Ethical principle: *Social workers' primary goal is to help people in need and to address social problems.*

Social workers elevate service to others above self-interest. Social workers draw on their knowledge, values, and skills to help people in need and to address social problems. Social workers are encouraged to volunteer some portion of their professional skills with no expectation of significant financial return (pro bono service).

Value: *Social justice*

Ethical principle: *Social workers challenge social injustice.*

Social workers pursue social change, particularly with and on behalf of vulnerable and oppressed individuals and groups of people. Social workers' social change efforts are focused primarily on issues of poverty, unemployment, discrimination, and other forms of social injustice. These activities seek to promote sensitivity to and knowledge about oppression and cultural and ethnic diversity. Social workers strive to ensure access to needed information, services, and resources; equality of opportunity; and meaningful participation in decision-making for all people.

Value: *Dignity and worth of the person*

Ethical principle: *Social workers respect the inherent dignity and worth of the person.*

Social workers treat each person in a caring and respectful fashion, mindful of individual differences and cultural and ethnic diversity. Social workers promote clients' socially responsible self-determination. Social workers seek to enhance clients' capacity and opportunity to change and to address their own needs. Social workers are cognizant of their dual responsibility to clients and to the broader society. They seek to resolve conflicts between clients' interests and the broader society's interests in a socially responsible manner that is consistent with the values, ethical principles, and ethical standards of the profession.

Value: *Importance of human relationships*

Ethical principle: *Social workers recognize the central importance of human relationships.*

Social workers understand that relationships between and among people are an important vehicle for change. Social workers engage people as partners in the helping process. Social workers seek to strengthen relationships among people in a purposeful effort to promote, restore, maintain, and enhance the well-being of individuals, families, social groups, organizations, and communities.

Value: *Integrity*

Ethical principle: *Social workers behave in a trustworthy manner.*

Social workers are continually aware of the profession's mission, values, ethical principles, and ethical standards and practice in a manner consistent with them. Social workers act honestly and responsibly and promote ethical practices on the part of the organizations with which they are affiliated.

Value: *Competence*

Ethical principle: *Social workers practice within their areas of competence and develop and enhance their professional expertise.*

Social workers continually strive to increase their professional knowledge and skills and to apply them in practice. Social workers should aspire to contribute to the knowledge base of the profession.

In addition to abiding by the code of ethics, other attitudes and values are essential. Child protective services work is a complex and challenging process. The first step in being an effective CPS worker is to know yourself. Awareness of your culture, values, beliefs, and styles of working with people and how they influence your interactions with children, families, and professionals is a critical element in the work that you do. This self-assessment and understanding is key to maximizing objectivity in casework intervention.

☐ Self-Awareness

Self-awareness is your ability to recognize how you react to people and situations, and how your attitudes, values, and behaviors might affect others. Self-awareness is an ongoing process of understanding yourself so that you can better understand others. When you know, understand, and respect yourself you are more likely to embrace and appreciate diverse cultures. Respect is a key value in working with families, regardless of similarities or differences. The essential elements of self-awareness are as follows.

Asking yourself who you are as a person.
- Your personality is the accumulation of your life experiences.
- You have your own unique background characteristics—culture, gender, religion, social status, economic status, education, and special interests.
- Your unique characteristics and life experiences combine to develop your sense of values.
- Your values determine how you behave—your perceptions, motives, and expectations.

- Your values are so deeply entrenched that

    you are apt to believe that *your* way is the *right* way;

    you may believe that your code of behavior applies to others, as well as yourself; and

    you may act and react automatically—so automatically, in fact, that you may not be able to see the effects of your values and behavior on others.

Consider the following example.

> *The 6-month-old child of Mr. and Mrs. Scott has been admitted to the hospital with a skull fracture and bruising to the buttocks. Mr. Scott has allegedly subjected the child to abusive treatment because the child continually cries. You meet the Scotts at their home to investigate the complaint.*

What thoughts go through your mind as you confront this couple for the first time?

- Do you wish that you could somehow inflict the same kind of punishment on them?
- Do you conclude that they must be mentally ill?
- Do you have the urge to bring the full force of your authority to bear on them?

If you have such thoughts but are not consciously aware of and do not control them, you will react in a hostile and discourteous manner.

- You may not listen to what these people say because you have already judged them.
- Your manner or nonverbal cues may indicate that you believe they are of little worth.
- You may refrain from asking pertinent questions because you have already formulated the answers in your mind.

The better you understand how your values and beliefs can impact your interactions with others, the more likely it is that you will be able to control and direct your behavior.

Looking at yourself critically. When doing so,

- You must be honest in your self-appraisal.
- When working in CPS, it is also imperative to be aware of your own feelings, reactions, and motives and to determine how appropriate they are, given a specific situation with a child or family.
- There are times when emotions such as anger, warmth, guilt, or irritation are entirely appropriate, and there are many more times when they are not. If you find that you are angry, frustrated, irritated, unusually positive, guilty, or overprotective with a person, it is helpful to ask yourself several key questions:

    Is the person doing something to activate these feelings?

    What am I feeling as I am communicating with this person?

> If I were to release my most impulsive responses, what would they be?
>
> Does the person resemble someone in my life?
>
> What role do I find myself playing with this person?
>
> For what reason did I make a certain response?
>
> Does this situation remind me of a trauma I have experienced?
>
> Is my objectivity clouded because of my own feelings?
>
> Am I looking to the person to meet my needs?

- It is not appropriate to expect families to meet your basic personal needs.
- You must be genuine and authentic, but that does not mean that you relate to the parent or caregiver as you would to any other person.
- In the worker-family relationship you must put aside many of your usual ways of relating to others.
- You may see your own life reflected in the life of a family. If you are experiencing a situation similar to that of the parent, you may overidentify with her or him.
- Instead of dealing with the family's difficulties, you may also use the relationship as a means of trying to meet some of your own unresolved personal needs and resolve some of your own problems.
- Just like others in your life, sometimes a person involved in a case is able to figure out how to "push your buttons." This can result in you doing or saying something either reactively or impulsively.
- You should recognize that families, like anyone else, will become aware of your real feelings, even if you make a conscious effort to hide them.
- If you understand yourself, you can capitalize on your personal assets and minimize your personal liabilities.

Understanding yourself. This requires practice. You can practice by doing the following.

- Identify how you behaved in a situation.
- Ask yourself about the consequences of that behavior.
- Ask yourself if those consequences were what you intended.
- If they were not, identify what it was that you did intend.
- Ask yourself what you should have done to get the intended result.

Practicing self-awareness as an ongoing process. Self-awareness is not a skill or a technique. It is the outcome of continually applying skills and techniques, such as questioning and reflection, to your own personality in order to understand it. Self-awareness is the result of honest self-appraisal; of observing yourself as you interact with others; and of understanding the relationship between "stimuli" (e.g., other people) and the "effect" (e.g., your behavior in relation to other people). Self-awareness is enhanced by asking others, such as your supervisor, for insight and objective feedback.

Changing behavior. Once you become aware of attitudes or behaviors that are not helpful or productive, it is then your responsibility to begin the sometimes challenging process of change. Changing behavior is extremely difficult and it may often be painful. Be patient and enlist the support of others, such as your peers and your supervisor, as you try to change behavior to improve your relationships and interactions with others.

Understanding your own culture and the culture of the children and families with whom you interact. It is often easier to understand someone who is more like oneself than different from oneself. In CPS work, you will be working with many people whose cultures and beliefs are different from your own. You will be expected to treat them with dignity and respect and to do your best to understand and honor their cultural beliefs and practices.

Cultural differences can create numerous challenges in the communication, in the relationship development, and, most critically, in the assessment and information-gathering stage of a case. Cultural differences can create communication problems and may lead to inaccurate conclusions being drawn.

You may look upon the other culture as deviating from the usual. The danger here is that you may view perspectives that are different from your own as "not normal" and therefore "wrong" or "bad." Consider this example.

> The local daycare center called to report possible child abuse. Staff reported that a 4-year-old Vietnamese child has reddish/purple, linear bruising on her chest and upper back. Daycare staff said the child had been out for the past 2 days with a cold. When asked about the marks, child said, "Mommy did it." The daycare center's reaction was one of disgust and disbelief that a parent could possibly do such a thing to her young child.
>
> Through the assessment process, you learn important information about the Vietnamese culture. The marks on this child were the result of the Vietnamese folk healing practice of "coining." It is conducted to alleviate congestion and fever. Skin on the chest and back is massaged with oil and then rubbed or stroked with the edge of a coin. The rubbing creates warmth to loosen up the congestion and can also create linear bruises.

Though this folk healing practice might not have been something you were familiar with, knowledge and understanding of both the practice and the parent's intent will allow you to respond to the reporting party and the child and family appropriately. If you are not familiar with a particular family's culture or beliefs, you may suggest measures or procedures that are not acceptable in the family's cultural setting. In addition, in treatment, you may run the risk of expecting the family to go further than their cultural limitations permit. You may also come up against taboos about certain topics and the ways they may be talked about.

Becoming culturally responsive is a lifelong goal. Ongoing education and experience will help you become sensitive to and aware of a family's culture and the strengths and challenges that the culture brings to your work with the family.

Becoming a culturally responsive professional. Regardless of your private beliefs, attitudes, and feelings, you must make every effort to be a courteous, culturally responsive professional. You should work to identify your main biases and prejudices so that they do not impede your delivery of appropriate and culturally sensitive services. Some typical errors made by workers who fail to clarify their own personal biases and prejudices include the following:

- In your eagerness to show you are culturally responsive, you may be overly friendly and accepting. This behavior is sometimes resented and may arouse immediate mistrust that can increase antagonism.
- In communicating with families for whom English is a second language, you may inadvertently talk down to them, assuming that their unfamiliarity with English means they are ignorant.
- You may assume that all members of a minority or cultural group are the same, ignoring their uniqueness and individuality.

You will be observed and judged carefully by the family; they can often quickly identify bias or less-than-objective casework practice. Some groups who may be disenfranchised and/or have experienced historical oppression have adapted by carefully observing the behaviors of those in positions of authority. The family will listen for the hidden meaning behind your words, will notice your mannerisms, and will judge your authenticity.

Understanding your personality and style of interacting with others. It is helpful to consider and analyze fully the effect of your personality on interactions. CPS is all about working with people and building relationships. It is important for you to consider your personality and style and how it might impact your relationships. Asking yourself the following questions may help you to understand better how you behave in your relationships with a family.

- Do you accept the family within the context of its unique characteristics, for example, race, culture, history, or religion? Are you able to identify strengths and resiliency in the family's way of being in the world?
- Do you find yourself putting words in a person's mouth?
- Do you say, "I don't quite understand" more frequently than you say "I understand?" (better)
- Do you find, on occasion, that you have reprimanded or reproached a person?
- Do you stay with a person's problem and follow his or her feelings as well as the words?
- Do you listen for themes to which a person repeatedly returns?
- Do you spot inconsistencies, such as a person's statement that he or she is "trying to find a job" when in fact the person cannot tell you specific places he or she has looked?
- Do you remember that your manner and the tone of your voice are as important as the wording of your question?

- Do you know whether you tend to ask too many or too few questions?

Analyzing your style with families is a prerequisite to effective casework, even though questioning your motives and admitting the need for improvement can be extremely difficult or even painful. Once you are more aware of yourself and your own style with families, several approaches may be helpful.

- Put yourself in the family's shoes. How would you feel if you were approached in negative ways? If you could, what would you tell the worker (yourself) to do differently? Would you ask the worker to listen—not so much to your words but to what you are trying to get across? Would you ask the worker to pay attention to you? Would you ask the worker to have more compassion for the reasons you are in your present situation?

- Ask for help from your supervisor and from other workers. Ask them how they would have responded to a specific situation.

- Be aware that although you cannot always change your values, you can modify the behaviors that are associated with your values. For example, say you have just received a referral alleging physical abuse by a father of his 6-year-old. The father spanked his son when the child ran out into the street to get a soccer ball. The child has bruises on the back of his legs. Personally, you do not believe in the use of physical discipline. You can tell yourself:

  > I would never use physical discipline on my child, and I certainly can't imagine causing an injury. I'm going to have to concentrate on keeping an open mind and not judging this father. I'm going to try to focus on the parents' intent behind the action—trying to teach his child how to stay safe.

- Be aware that you do not need to violate your values; you need to bring your values into play. For example, you may emphasize your belief that people can be helped and can change:

  > I really don't like these parents' behavior, yet this family needs to change. I will do what I can to help.

- Be aware that your emotional state can express itself in hidden, uncontrolled ways or in open, honest, controlled ways. Remember that understanding the meaning behind your behavior is a skill, and any skill is learned through practice.

☐ Self-Care

CPS work can take a heavy toll on mind, body, and spirit. The unrealistic expectations of the work, combined with the reality of secondary trauma as you listen to, think about, and intervene with children who have experienced painful and often devastating maltreatment combine to take a physical, mental, and emotional toll on you. Indicators of secondary trauma can include (Conrad, 2002):

- Distressing emotions.
- Intrusive imagery of a person's traumatic experience.
- Numbing or avoidance of work with the family or related material.

- Physical complaints.
- Addictive or compulsive behaviors.
- Impairment of day-to-day functioning and disharmony in personal and professional situations.

In an effort to mitigate the potential effects of CPS work, you must first commit to helping and taking care of yourself before you commit to helping others. Self-care includes both personal and professional strategies.

Personal strategies include the following.

> *"The most important strategy in your personal life is to have one"* (Saakvitne & Pearlman, 1996).

Do not make work the center of your life.

Create opportunities for fun and frivolity.

Embrace physical, emotional, and spiritual wellness.

Rest and play.

Professional strategies include (Conrad, 2002):

- Balancing your workload.
- Seeking group consultations with colleagues.
- Setting clear boundaries.
- Creating a safe and comfortable workplace.
- Regularly using supervision.

Supervision is a critical element in CPS work and should be a resource for support. You do not function within the agency as an independent agent. The use of supervision is an integral part of your work. Crucial decisions you make must be shared with your supervisor. No matter how articulate you are and how much experience you have in CPS work, the ideas and opinions of someone who is not directly involved with a particular case can offer an entirely different and perhaps more realistic perspective of the situation.

Supervisory consultation can help in the following ways:

- It will assist you in continuing to develop self-awareness.
- It will help you recognize and reinforce your need for self-care.
- It will give you guidance and direction.
- It will help you make certain decisions.
- It will broaden your understanding of a particular situation.
- It will help you with certain technical questions, such as how to complete documentation, and proper procedures.
- It will give you a sounding board for expressing feelings of frustration and discomfort.

With a commitment to self-awareness and self-care, you will be better able to assume the specific roles you are expected to play in relation to the child, the family, and other professionals. With self-awareness you will be better prepared to handle the challenges of CPS work.

■ The Challenges of CPS Work

Even with appropriate understanding of role, skills, and values, child protective work is challenging for the following reasons.

Hostility. You may encounter hostility, which is hard for anyone to deal with effectively. We all want to be liked. Our natural response is to defend ourselves in these situations, even sometimes wanting to react with the same level of hostility that has been directed toward us. However, a hostile response only creates an escalation of hostility and ultimately defeats the purpose of our profession.

Resistance. You also are likely to encounter resistance. Hostility may include resistance, which can pervade many aspects of the CPS process, especially at intake and during the initial investigation. Families may resist your intervention in a variety of ways. Generally, resistant behavior is either directive or manipulative.

Rejection. Rejection also makes CPS work difficult. Throughout our lives we seek positive, supportive responses from others, and we seek confirmation of ourselves. Because these are our natural tendencies, we are not psychologically or socially prepared to manage the rejection that often comes with CPS work.

Privacy boundaries. It is difficult to go into families' homes and to intrude in their lives, as privacy is an American value and a Constitutional right.

Difficult questions. The nature of the questions you must ask families makes the CPS process most challenging. You may appear to be questioning their worth, their value, and their rights. You are also questioning their capacity as parents or caregivers. And your intervention may elicit past traumas if the family or cultural group has an intergenerational history of involvement with child protection systems.

Difficult decisions. As a CPS worker you have a tremendous responsibility. Nowhere in social work are decisions more difficult than in CPS. You have the difficult task of identifying and rehabilitating abusing/neglecting families while protecting their children. You may have a greater workload than you are able to effectively manage. An immediate response may be essential because a child's life may be at stake. The decisions you make about a child's safety may involve life-or-death consequences. At the same time, you must make these immediate decisions regarding the child's safety on the basis of a relatively brief encounter, and you must decide whether to recommend that a family be separated or that a child be removed from his or her home.

Scope of knowledge. Your job may be difficult because you deal with other agencies and professionals, such as physicians and other hospital personnel, attorneys, the courts, and community service resources. You must be knowledgeable about their roles as partners in the CPS process and skillful and confident in dealing with them in the areas of their technical expertise as well as your own.

Role conflict. An additional aspect of CPS work that causes difficulty is the dilemma you face of balancing your role in providing help to the family in relation to your position of authority to invoke the legal process and remove a child from the home or impose other requirements on the family regarding their participation in services. Your work is with the family, not just the child within the family but also the parent or caregiver. However, you must also recognize the parent or caregiver as an alleged perpetrator who may be endangering the child's safety. These two roles may appear to be in conflict and may result in frustration. However, both roles are important, and they are compatible. While law and policy define your responsibility in terms of the expression of authority, authority can be invoked humanely. Consulting with supervisors and peers can help you to be more objective so that your compassion does not blind you, while at the same time you do not become punitive in your approach. Your helping in this way can empower a family.

While you want to help families reunify with their children, public policy has delineated stringent time frames for rehabilitating families with multiple, complex challenges. You are mandated to plan for placement outside of the family while working to reunify the family. This is a difficult balance: to maintain both optimism about family change and to plan for the reality that some families will not accomplish their goals in time to have their children returned to their care.

■ Dealing with the Challenges of CPS Work

Because CPS work is difficult, you are bound to experience discomfort. Your discomfort is the first and greatest barrier to effective service delivery. Discomfort and anxiety are normal emotions, and you must recognize and address them if you are to apply your knowledge and skills effectively. You should:

- Follow a defined process.
- Believe in the value of CPS, in your right to intervene, and in the efficacy of services available for families.
- Recognize that you are not making decisions alone. Rather, you are working in partnership with your supervisor and with the staff in your agency and the community.
- Maintain positive intentions. Remember that:

    You are there to help the family.

    You believe that people can change and thus are worth your time and effort.

    You respect and accept the parent or caregiver while not always accepting his or her behavior.

    You believe that the parent or caregiver is capable of participating in the helping process.

    Your primary work is to facilitate a safe and stable home for the child.

- Be prepared and ready to apply your knowledge, skill, and experience thoughtfully each time you become involved with a family.

■ Summary

Here is a summary of the important characteristics and competencies of the CPS worker:

1. You should be sensitive to people and the problems of family life and nonjudgmental in your work with families.

2. You should be committed to the value of partnering with families and the community to bring about changes that will lead to child safety, permanency, and well-being.

3. You should be direct in your interactions with families.

4. You should be capable of dealing with crisis constructively and able to work effectively under pressure.

5. You should be well organized and maintain accurate written and electronic records.

6. You should be able to use authority constructively without becoming controlling.

7. You should be committed to the maxim that, with help, most people can change.

8. You should understand the vital importance of the mission and goals of child protective services.

9. You should recognize that cultural responsiveness, along with all professional competencies, is a lifelong process requiring self-awareness and support.

10. You should pursue professionalism by acquiring additional knowledge and skill through experience and training.

11. You should practice self-awareness and self-care.

■ Summary of Competencies

The casework process is a specialized approach to working with families involved with CPS and incorporates key values, beliefs, and principles. Using an organized approach, workers help families address the issues that resulted in a referral to CPS to ensure that children are safe, permanency achieved, and the well-being of children and families improved.

Knowledge:

1. Philosophical bases of CPS as a specialized set of services intended to ensure safety while preserving families.

2. Values and framework for the casework process.

3. Knowledge of professional and ethical guidelines for worker behavior (e.g., National Association of Social Workers Guidelines for Practice).

4. Information about the different systems involved in child protection and the roles and responsibilities of these systems.

5. Knowledge of the effective case management techniques for coordination of services.

Skills:

1. Capacity to understand the basis for and purpose of CPS casework intervention and apply this understanding to all stages of the casework process.

2. Ability to be responsive.

3. Ability to develop self-awareness.

4. Ability to appropriately balance your authority to intervene to protect children with your responsibility to establish a helping relationship with the abusive or neglectful family.

References

Conrad, D. (2002, May). Secondary trauma prevention project. Presentation at the Kid's Brain Conference, Denver.

National Association of Public Child Welfare Administrators. (1999). Guidelines for a model system of protective services for abused and neglected children and their families. Washington, DC: American Public Human Services Association.

National Association of Social Workers. (1999). Code of ethics. Retrieved January 20, 2003, from http://www.socialworkers.org/pubs/code/code.asp.

Saakvitne, K. W., & Pearlman, L. A. (1996). Transforming the pain: A workbook on vicarious traumatization. New York: Norton.

4

Anne Comstock

Key Partners in Protecting Children and Supporting Families

- Partnering with the Family

- Putting It Together: Successful Partnerships

- Partnerships for Child Protection

- Summary of Competencies

Protecting children is about assessing their safety and then building a net of protection and support for them and their families. This net cannot be created or provided by you or your agency alone. The approach must be one of partnering—first and foremost among you, the family, and their informal networks of support; next with the other mandated systems, such as law enforcement and the legal system; and finally with the numerous other systems, service providers, organizations, agencies, tribes, or communities that can work together to accomplish the outcomes of child safety, permanence, and child and family well-being. The responsibility and privilege of protecting children is shared and requires a great deal of commitment and effort to work. As the CPS worker, you are often the cog in the wheel that keeps the partnerships turning.

The goal of this chapter is to identify and explore the myriad partnerships of CPS and the corresponding roles and responsibilities for protecting children. This chapter covers both challenges to and strategies for successful partnering.

■ Partnering with the Family

☐ Philosophy

Child protection intervention is based on the belief embedded within American culture that the protection of children is primarily the responsibility of parents. For some cultural groups, this responsibility also pertains to the extended family and community. When, for whatever reason, parents and/or families cannot keep their children safe, a CPS worker must intervene, providing assistance and support to strengthen the parents' ability to protect their children if at all possible.

An important partnership must be built between the family and the CPS worker to effectively protect children. This partnership then becomes the foundation for a collaborative effort with other community and professional partners.

The desired outcomes of CPS are child safety, permanence, and child and family well-being. Achieving these outcomes starts with a positive relationship between you and the family. In CPS, *family* is typically defined rather broadly to include all the persons living together in the same physical space, as well as any other persons outside this space whom the family designates as part of the family. Family strengths should be identified during initial contact. The family should be helped to assume responsibility for finding ways to assure the child's safety—safety that is assessed with the context of the family's culture and diversity (National Association of Public Child Welfare Administrators, 1999). This approach is referred to as "family-centered practice."

☐ Family-Centered Practice

As a worker, you are a key to providing this type of practice and intervention. It is important that you be aware of the basic assumptions that define this approach:

- *Most families want to do the best they can for their children.* While some families are not capable of keeping their children safe, many vulnerable families are quite motivated to provide quality care for their children and, with some form of support, are capable of providing a safe and nurturing home.

- Once safety is assured, *children do best when kept with their families* and in familiar situations.

- We know that *families function within the framework of formal and informal means of support,* including their extended families, friends, and neighborhoods (Day, Robison, & Sheikh, 1998; Matt & Berns, 1999). Strengthening these supports will ultimately strengthen the family and the likelihood that they can protect their children.

The family-centered perspective is a conceptual approach that is based on the belief that the best way to protect children in the long run is to strengthen and support their families, whether they be nuclear, extended, foster care, or adoptive families. This approach requires specialized knowledge and skills to build family capital and resources for strength and resilience by providing services to the family, extended family, and kinship group, as well as by mobilizing informal resources in the community ("A New Era," 2000).

Essential elements of family-centered practice include the following:

- The family as a unit is the focus of attention. Emphasis is placed on assessing and building on family strengths and on the capacity of families to function effectively.

- Families are engaged in designing all aspects of policies, treatment, and evaluation.

- Families are linked with more comprehensive, diverse, and community-based networks of supports and services.

- Family group decision-making is practiced; its approach exemplifies the family-centered philosophy.

☐ Family Group Decision-Making (FGDM)

This practice is based on the belief that extended family systems (broadly defined to include all persons designated by that family as family) should be engaged and empowered by child welfare agencies to make decisions and develop plans that protect their children from further abuse and neglect. Such engagement and empowerment is more likely to motivate families to address the situations that are putting their children at risk of maltreatment.

FGDM is primarily being used by child welfare agencies when maltreatment of a child has been confirmed. However, its use is expanding to address concerns of juvenile delinquency, truancy, and economic self-sufficiency, as well as to promote and support adoption and transitions for teens to young adulthood.

The principles of FGDM include the following:

- Families, communities, and the government must partner together to ensure child safety and well-being.

- Families, in collaboration with formal systems, can create safe plans that protect children and support their permanence and well-being.

- FGDM practice is family-centered, family strengths–oriented, and culturally and community based. The process emphasizes that families have the responsibility not only to care for but to provide a sense of identity to their children.

The FGDM process focuses on preparation and planning for a family group conference (FGC). A neutral coordinator works with the family and child to identify individuals who have personal relationships and connections with the child and family and a willingness to develop and support a plan to protect the child. Those involved can include parents, kin, children, tribal elders, and individuals whom the family considers to be supportive (e.g., neighbors, clergy). The coordinator spends considerable time working with the participants to create a climate of emotional and physical safety for all participants before, during, and after the FGC. The participants' roles are clearly defined and communicated.

The conference follows a specific structure, most typically including:

1. Introductions.

2. The sharing of information.

3. Private family time.

4. Decisions; the worker approves and other community partners contribute resources to the plan. The main purpose of the FGC is for the family (without professionals and nonfamily members) to develop a specific plan to protect the child from future harm.

Writing and distributing the plan, delivering services, and reviewing and monitoring the decisions are the activities that occur after the FGC. If necessary, follow-up meetings may be scheduled for case review. Common challenges include providing, organizing, and monitoring the services that the family and worker agree to in their plan. However, it is believed that family involvement in developing the service plan and identifying needed assistance directly correlates to their willingness to support and accept the services provided (Merkel-Holguín, 1996).

Whether using the FGDM model or other ways to engage the family in the process, it is important that both you and the family have a clear understanding of the different roles and some of the challenges that you both face in making the partnership work.

☐ **The Role of the Family**

The family has a number of roles as partners in child protection.

The family is a primary source of information. Even though you can obtain a great deal of information about the child and family and the possible nature of the abuse or neglect incident from many sources, such as the person who made the initial report, your primary information source is the family. In most cases, you cannot be certain about the nature of the problem without direct family contact. Your assessment must include contact with the parents and all of the children. In addition, the family can best describe the circumstances surrounding the incident.

To engage the family in a helping relationship, you need to know each member and understand his or her values and worldviews. Information must be obtained and evaluated within the context of the family's culture. Only the family members can tell you what their values are, how they see the world, and the nature of their problems and needs. You should be aware of how your own cultural biases could impede your ability to understand their worldviews. It is your responsibility to discern cultural variations in childrearing and child protection issues.

By recognizing the family as your primary information source, they become partners in the helping relationship.

The family as partner in the helping relationship. You rely on the family to provide information to assist in building the helping relationship, and you rely on family members' participation in the helping process.

There are a number of things you can do to facilitate the family's participation and cooperation. You should be sensitive to the family's schedule and commitments and try to plan accordingly. You should allow the family to make choices whenever possible, thereby returning some sense of control to them. Examples include deciding the location of meetings; deciding on particular people or individuals to involve in the plan; selecting a therapist from a list of approved treatment providers; and planning activities during family visits, if their children are in placement.

However, some families are unwilling or unable to participate in the process. If that is the case, even court orders may not assure this participation. You should be aware of the following:

- Some parents and caregivers will never change, no matter how well you do your job.
- You are ultimately responsible for seeing that the abused or neglected children are protected from further maltreatment.
- You must take aggressive action to obtain emergency in-home services, or remove children from the home, if the parents give you evidence that they cannot or will not change their behavior and the children are in danger.
- If children are not in immediate danger and the parents refuse to participate, case closure may be appropriate.

When the family is engaged in planning their own service program, their investment, commitment, and follow-through become much more likely. The family's participation will be enhanced if goals are realistic.

Depending on the age of children, they can be active participants in the process. They must always be seen, and if they are old enough to be verbal, they should be interviewed. If they are old enough, they should be involved in service planning.

The parent role in this helping relationship may be difficult. Maltreating parents often lack trust. A trusting partnership must be constantly renewed and strengthened. An example:

> Mrs. Jaramillo abuses alcohol and describes a sense of betrayal by her family. She says they had promised to help her with her 5-year-old daughter, Gina. Late one night, when Gina couldn't wake her mom, she got scared and called her grandmother, who lived in another state. Grandmother made the call to social services that resulted in Gina's removal from her mother's care.
>
> Mrs. Jaramillo is very skeptical of your statements that you will be helping her figure out what it would take to return Gina home to a safe environment. Mrs. Jaramillo doesn't believe she will see or hear from Gina again. The building of a trusting relationship between you and Mrs. Jaramillo starts when you quickly arrange phone calls between Gina and her mom. You also follow through on your promise to arrange for a supervised visit. Slowly, Mrs. Jaramillo begins to believe and trust that you really are trying to help.

The family may not initially succeed in their partnership role. They must be given the opportunity to continue to try. Effective concurrent planning can allow the parents to continue to work the plan while assuring permanency for the children by having an alternative, permanent, safe home in place.

You may be discouraged by the family's lack of progress. You should continually encourage the family to make an effort to become more in tune with their children's needs for protection and parental support.

Finally, parents often need to be guided in their role. You should not assume that parents know how to adequately parent. Assume that parents have many skills, and at the same time, could use your help in discovering what to do to better meet their children's needs and keep them safe.

Often explaining that you are going to do something not *to* the parents but *with* them, and letting them know what they are supposed to do, can constitute the first step toward building a trusting relationship. For example:

> Mrs. Jaramillo was expected to get an alcohol evaluation. She says she didn't know where to start and that "you guys" were just waiting for her to fail. You tell her: "It can be hard to get these evaluations arranged. When I'm at your home tomorrow, we can make the call together. I want you to get the evaluation completed because it will help all of us understand how your drinking is affecting your ability to keep Gina safe."

Be careful not to assume that good parenting is a universal process. Varying cultural norms and taboos may impact the family's ability to follow your guidance on parenting. If there are cultural differences between you and the family, take time to inquire about whether suggested techniques are comfortable or appropriate within the family's culture. Pay close attention to nonverbal cues that indicate that the family may not be accepting of your guidance regarding certain parenting approaches. For example:

When the worker arrived at the home of Mrs. Lone Eagle, an identified member of a Sioux tribe, he noticed that Mrs. Lone Eagle and the youngest child were sitting on the couch watching television. Two adolescent boys were in their separate bedrooms upstairs. One of the boys was working on the computer and the other was working on a craft project. Because the two boys had been in conflict with each other, as well as with their mother and younger brother, the worker thought it would be in their best interest to sit together and learn to communicate directly about their feelings. The worker asked the boys to join their mother and brother and say how they were feeling about their family. The older boys both put their heads down and refused to speak or make eye contact with the worker or their mother. Mrs. Lone Eagle had been involved with the child welfare system for 3 years. She had encountered a lack of cultural under-standing in previous workers. Because it was considered impolite to confront the worker, Mrs. Lone Eagle began telling a story. She told the worker about how she had to learn to make eye contact with teachers when she attended boarding school. The boys looked up briefly at their mother. The worker asked the boys to tell their mother about their anger at her drinking. Again, the boys refused to look up or speak. When the worker became frustrated, he asked Mrs. Lone Eagle why her sons would not talk to her or look at her. She explained that in their way, children were not to address their parents directly about their feelings but rather to listen and try to learn from the stories told by their parents or elders. To directly express feelings, especially in the presence of someone outside the family, would be a show of disrespect.

In this case, a culturally responsive worker might have asked the mother how conflicts were resolved in the cultural ways of the family. Time alone to think and calm down, rather than direct expression of feelings, may have been the healthy response from the family's perspective. In other words, the worker may have seen that things were going well rather than thinking there was a problem to which a solution needed to be applied. If the worker was confused by the mother's explanation, he might have tried to locate an agency affiliated with that culture to help understand the family's experience.

A good worker pays attention to his or her "gut feelings" when working with culturally different families. When confused, a worker may want to ask the family if they have a community ally or advocate who can work with them to build cultural understanding. It may also be helpful to discuss cultural differences with your supervisor.

Decision-making and partnering with the family. It is important that parents and caregivers commit to the helping relationship, as this partnership is intended to help strengthen the family unit and restore effective child protection. Parents and caregivers should understand that changing patterns of parenting might also alter other relationships both with their child(ren) and with other adults. Your primary objective for being involved is to help the parents become more able to protect and nurture their children. You will be working with the family to develop a plan that will allow the children to remain at home *safely*. If that is not possible, you may:

Seek court involvement to protect children through placement.

Make a diligent search for a suitable relative or family friend placement.

Organize a family group conference to create safety and permanency plans.

Should placement be necessary, your goal is to reunify the family at the earliest possible time, always considering the goal of permanence for the children. If all service provision fails, legal action may be essential to facilitate the finding of an alternative safe, permanent home.

You are attempting to develop a partnership based on trust with the family. Clearly you do have significant power over the lives of families involved with CPS. Your understanding of the implications of this power is crucial. You should remain aware that trust is not built through coercion, and that your work with the family is intended to achieve an honest partnership based on a mutual effort to protect children from further harm.

☐ Understanding Family Hostility and Resentment

Even as you make efforts to form a trusting relationship with parents, you will encounter anger, hostility, and resistance. The children and families on your caseload will represent a broad range of individuals from every social and economic class, race, culture, and religion. They will have their own unique lifestyles, childrearing practices, and beliefs. At the same time, they will be asked to share the intimate details of their unique lifestyles with someone who is unknown to them. Because some parents believe they have the right to manage and control their children as they wish, they may view any intervention by an outsider suspiciously as an intrusion on their parental rights. Consequently, they are likely to react to you in a hostile and resistant manner.

Hostility or anger could result from families having had a past negative experience with CPS or knowing of someone who has. Even without such prior involvement, it is human nature to be nervous with individuals who possess power and authority over oneself. Yet other families may be part of a culture that has a history of conflict with the CPS system. And some families may *appear* to "resist" intervention because of extreme hopelessness and a belief that no matter what they do, they will never get their children back.

Understanding the historical trauma of parents that contributes to their reactions is essential to forming trust. At the same time you must make clear that there are certain specific requirements of these parents and insist that the abuse or neglect cease, regardless of their feelings or attitudes. In addition, while parents may consent to the voluntary removal of the children, in extreme cases you may have to seek termination of their parental rights. You clearly have a great deal of power to significantly affect their lives. You must understand this authority and use it judiciously.

Despite the expression of hostile attitudes and feelings and despite resistance to your intrusion, you must intervene and continue your intervention until the abused and/ or neglected children are out of danger. Working with hostile and resistant reactions from parents may be difficult for you, but you must do it in order to achieve a successful partnership. For more information on understanding the source of the hostility and resistance and developing strategies for intervention, see chapter 6.

■ Putting It Together: Successful Partnerships

Prior to discussing all the partnerships that can and should be a part of protecting children and strengthening families, it is important to clarify what has to be in place in order for you to initiate, support, and maintain these partnerships on behalf of the children and families with whom you work.

☐ Agency/Organization Support

As a worker, you are encouraged to have conversations with your supervisor and administration about how they actively support your efforts to partner with families, professionals, service providers, and the community. Recommendations from the National Association of Public Child Welfare Administrators (NAPCWA, 1999) and the Child Welfare League of America (CWLA, 1989–99) regarding agency supports include the following:

You should participate in formalized relationships with agency and community partners. Find out if written protocols, agreements, or memoranda of understanding exist between your agency and others who intervene with children and families, including law enforcement, the legal system, schools, the medical community, and service providers. If these agreements are current and frequently reviewed and updated, they can help define roles, minimize conflicts, and assure availability and quality of services.

CPS agencies can also contract with particular providers for an array of services that are specifically designed to meet the needs of children and families in the CPS system. The costs, expected timelines, and outcomes should be clearly defined. This type of contractual agreement should assure you more readily available and appropriate services.

You will also develop informal relationships on behalf of families. In helping families build a support network, you will find yourself working with churches, schools, safe houses, resource centers, job placement agencies, community colleges, and numerous other individuals or organizations in efforts to keep children safe and strengthen families. (This is further explored later in this chapter.)

Your role as a child protection worker and support for your efforts can be approached and defined in different ways by your agency. For instance, some CPS agencies have collapsed worker roles and functions so that one worker provides the tasks of assessment and service delivery. Other agencies have developed assessment and service teams consisting of several types of specialists who can optimize their respective expertise. Areas of expertise can include sexual abuse, working with families from various cultural backgrounds, developmental disabilities, mental health, or juvenile justice. For example:

> Mr. and Mrs. Padilla were struggling with the out-of-control behavior of their 12-year-old son, Juan. He was getting into trouble while he was home alone after school. He set a fire and had charges pending. During an argument with his parents, Juan threatened to run away. Mr. Padilla grabbed Juan by the arm and left a small bruise. As a part of your intervention and service planning, you invite Mr. and Mrs. Padilla and Juan to attend a multidisciplinary, interagency team meeting at Juan's middle school. Team members include representatives from the school, social services, law enforcement, and mental health, housing, recreation, and health agencies. Mr. and Mrs. Padilla identified themselves as recent immigrants from Mexico. They were asked if a family or community support person could also be invited to assist with interpretation and provide advocacy for the unique cultural issues as first-generation Americans trying to adapt to the parenting norms of a new country. The plan will be to work with the Padillas to identify their needs and to develop a plan for both the appropriate service or intervention and the appropriate provider.

Some CPS organizations have trained workers to increase their skills in specific areas, such as substance abuse.

The colocation of providers from different systems (e.g., substance abuse and domestic violence) within CPS is another way agencies have tried to support a collaborative approach and assure ready access to particular expertise and interventions. For example:

> In gathering preliminary information regarding child neglect allegations of the Thomas family, you are advised by law enforcement that there have been past reports of domestic violence involving this family. The domestic violence specialist located in your office has offered to team cases with CPS workers. You decide this is a great opportunity to take the specialist up on the offer; you arrange to conduct the assessment together.

☐ Models and Approaches

There are many ways to facilitate partnerships among families, CPS, other systems, organizations, and the community. You might find yourself involved in any one of the following approaches.

Colocation of CPS and other professionals. Providers from other systems might be residing in your office or agency. Similarly, CPS workers have been located in mental health centers, courts, battered women shelters, or schools to make them available and accessible both to children and families, as well as to other professionals involved with the family.

Interagency multidisciplinary teams are another approach supported in national guidelines and recommendations (Day, Robison, & Sheikh, 1998; NAPCWA, 1999).

- Team membership should be inclusive, with representation from the family, systems, agencies, organizations, the community, and individuals who have both a formal and informal vested interest in the outcomes of child safety, permanence, and child and family well-being.

- These multidisciplinary teams should work together on referral, assessment, and service planning and/or service response.
- The team members should participate in joint planning. Accountability mechanisms for each major stakeholder should be developed. Intermediate and long-term outcomes should be identified and evaluated, in terms of both process and results.
- Mechanisms for collaborative approaches to sharing case information that maintain essential family privacy should be developed and maintained.

☐ Working Relationships

Positive working relationships with the different people who are serving as partners requires a respectful and patient approach. Though everyone shares the mutual goal of protecting children, the issue of how this is accomplished within the limitations and parameters to be identified can create challenges for productive working relationships. Lawson and Barkdull (2001, p. 253) reiterate, "Simply stated, every professional working with the same individual needs to be on the same page." That type of collaboration requires that all who will be involved do the following:

- Discuss desired outcomes, both common and different goals, and how the goals will be accomplished.
- Clarify roles, expectations, and responsibilities.
- Establish open and ongoing communication.
- Consider setting up regular opportunities for contact, such as conference calls or case meetings.
- Make it a priority to address and resolve problems as quickly as possible, acknowledging that in some circumstances, you may have to agree to disagree, and move forward on behalf of the children and families you are serving.
- Be proactive and build rapport. Allow time for staff concerns, priorities, and resources to be offered and to determine the next steps in the partnering process.
- Keep in mind possible cultural differences related to expectations around time, space, and structure involved in setting group norms. Engage the collaborative team in deliberate dialogue about possible differences.
- Learn more about the partnering agencies and their staff. Seek information about an agency's belief systems, protocols, services delivery system, sources of funding, policies, and roles of various staff members.
- Consider crosstraining with staff of partnering agencies.
- Assess the collaboration frequently.

☐ Confidentiality

Issues of confidentiality can be a barrier to achievement of successful partnerships, as agencies may use it as an excuse to block communication. However, confidentiality should not impede successful collaboration, as mechanisms do exist to share information that balance the interests of children and families with those of agencies who need to exchange information (Soler & Peters, 1993).

Confidentiality is often expressed in statutes, policies, memorandums, or other agreements. To understand a confidentiality provision, consider the following questions (Soler & Peters, 1993):

- What information is considered confidential?
- What information is not considered confidential?
- What exceptions are there to the confidentiality restriction? Who and for what purposes can information be shared?
- Can information be shared with the consent of the family? What information can be released with consent? What are the requirements for a consent release? Who is authorized to give consent for information related to children?

CPS agencies can successfully balance the privacy rights of families and their own needs to share information and find ways to exchange most necessary information. Some strategies for sharing information include the following (Soler & Peters, 1993):

- Obtain a signed release of information from the person who is the subject of the information. Do this on a routine basis, typically when assessments are conducted or services commence.
- Provide notices to the family of the agency's need to release information.
- Develop formal interagency agreements and memoranda of understanding.
- Develop and use multiagency release forms that satisfy the confidentiality mandates of each agency.

☐ Conflicts

It is utopian to think that all partnerships will be successful, and it is inevitable that conflicts will occur among yourself, agencies, and your community partners. When conflict does occur, strategies to successfully resolve it include the following (Strom-Gottfried, 1998):

- Avoid positional bargaining. Staking out a position means one party in the conflict digs in and refuses to give any ground in the negotiation, thus precluding a bargained resolution to the situation.
- Separate the people from this problem. You will need to untangle interpersonal issues from the real problem to be addressed. To do this, listen, and try to hear the other's perspective.
- Move from positions to interests. Try to find at least some areas of agreement and determine multiple interests.
- Refrain from rushing into premature solutions. It may be tempting to accept the first viable alternative to end the conflict, but that may not serve

your real purpose to help children and families. Instead, generate multiple solutions to resolve the problem.

- Select and use objective criteria to evaluate the viability of the options generated.

■ Partnerships for Child Protection

We have explored the critical partnership between you and the families with whom you work. The next step is to examine the other individuals, systems, or providers with whom you will be working to help build the net of safety and support described earlier.

☐ The CPS Agency

As previously described, CPS is legally mandated to receive and respond to reports of possible abuse and neglect. For many years, CPS agencies conducted investigations and assessments with a "one size fits all" approach. A number of states and counties are implementing a different approach. A dual track system, also known as an *alternative* or *differential response*, is designed to allow more flexibility in the agency's response to child protection. This approach recognizes both the variation in the nature of reports and the reality that one approach does not meet the needs of every case. Responses can vary from state to state in implementing this approach, but usually at least two categories exist:

1. Reports that are immediately recognized as presenting serious safety issues for children and/or potential criminal charges. This is sometimes known as the "investigation track."

2. Situations in which there are needs that, if addressed, could stabilize the family and enable the parents to better care for their children. Typically, there are no serious safety issues immediately present. This is often known as the "assessment track."

A dual track approach typically results in more appropriate interventions for the child and family, a better utilization of resources, and the hope that over time, this differential approach will solidify increased community responsibility for the protection of children (Schene, 2001).

Your involvement and response to reported concerns would depend on the specific approach your agency has in place. Whatever your agency's approach, at the point in time the report becomes your responsibility, you will begin to involve the other systems, agencies, and organizations that are a part of the *child protection partnership*.

☐ Partnering with Mandated Reporters

One of the keys to shared responsibility for child protection is people's awareness of child safety concerns and knowledge of what to do if they believe a child may need protection. People come into contact with children and families every day. The ultimate goal is for anyone and everyone to reach out to children and parents to offer support that prevents abuse and neglect from occurring at all. However, if any person identifies a child protection concern, they can contact child protective services to make a report.

States also require that individuals within certain professions are *mandated* to contact CPS if they know or have cause to suspect that a child is being maltreated. Mandated reporters are most typically those who come into contact professionally with children and families, including medical personnel, school staff, childcare providers, and therapists and social workers, to name a few. Those people who are mandated to report child maltreatment vary by state. You should check with your agency for a listing of people who are mandated reporters in your area.

This mandated reporting requirement is an important element of the idea of shared responsibility for child protection. The individual making the report is not required to conduct the assessment, and he or she is generally protected from liability if the report is made in good faith.

☐ Partnering with the Alternate Caregiver

When a child is placed out of the home due to safety concerns, a critical member of the intervention team is the foster parent or caregiver. It is imperative that a strong working relationship exist between you and the child's placement parents, for many reasons. You can support the caregivers as they provide for the child's safety and emotional well-being during placement. Even removal from an abusive or neglectful home to a place of safety can be frightening and traumatizing for a child. You can assist the caregiver in helping the child make the adjustment.

The foster parents or caregivers have the child in their care 24 hours a day, 7 days a week. They are the best source of information regarding the child's behavior, adjustment to placement, reactions to interventions, and responses to visits with parents and other family. However, you should be aware that the foster parents' values, beliefs, and attitudes may impact their perspective of the child-parent visits.

Foster parents or caregivers have an incredible opportunity to support the plan that has been formulated for the child's safety, permanence and well-being. To do this, the foster parents or caregivers need to have thorough and accurate information to be able to respond to the child's questions or concerns.

The foster parents or caregivers can support the service plan in many other ways, as follows:

- They can attend staffings or case review meetings.
- They can provide information regarding the child's behavior to be included in assessments and reports.
- They can ensure that the child gets to scheduled appointments, therapy sessions, or other service plan activities.

- They can be involved in the child's visitation with parents and other family. Foster parents or caregivers can transport the child, supervise the visits, allow the visits to occur in their home, model or mentor for the parent and the child, and provide feedback and information regarding the visits to you for planning purposes.
- They can also be trained and supported in providing for the child's cultural needs. In particular, when the foster parents or caregivers are not from the same cultural background of the child, the CPS worker can assist and encourage the foster parents or caregivers to assess and address behaviors that may be grounded in a child's unique cultural or ethnic background.

> Foster parent Mrs. Stewart has Ms. Ang's 6-month-old son in her home. Ms. Ang is very anxious to see her baby as much as possible. Mrs. Stewart agrees to allow Ms. Ang to come to her home and participate in parenting activities such as feeding, bathing, and playing with her young son. During these activities, Ms. Ang shares her traumatic history related to her childhood escape from the Khmer Rouge in Cambodia, her loss of her parents, and her subsequent adoption from an orphanage.

> Hopefully, Mrs. Stewart will report the disclosure of the traumatic events in Ms. Ang's life to the ongoing child protection worker. The worker may wish to explore the effects on Ms. Ang's ability to parent her infant due to the traumatic events that disrupted Ms. Ang's development. The worker's discussion of Ms. Ang's history with the child protection supervisor may help identify specific cultural resources for survivors of such profound trauma. Ms. Ang's parenting classes may also need to be provided by an agency that understands and specializes in healing such disruptions.

Sometimes maintaining this positive working relationship can be difficult. Historically, foster parents have been reimbursed for expenses related to the care of the child and not for their time, essentially working in a "volunteer" capacity. Given their willingness to volunteer their efforts and the fact that they live with the children, they come to expect that their input is valued. However, foster parents often report not being treated as a member of the team (Palmer, 1995). The CWLA indicates that 40% of foster families leave the system within 1 year of being licensed. While some of their issues focus on training, compensation, and validation by the agency, many speak to the relationship they have with their worker. Common concerns from caregivers include:

- Not being given enough information to make an informed decision about accepting the child into their home.
- Not understanding what was expected from them.
- Not being included in service planning or decision-making.
- Not having their input about the child seriously considered.
- Not being informed of changes in the plan.
- Not having enough quick and direct access to the worker when the need arises. This can create a crisis if the child's behavior has escalated and the

caregiver does not feel like he or she is being supported in trying to maintain the placement.

How can you create a strong working partnership? The National Foster Parents Association (Jorgenson & Schooler, 2000) identified the following needs from foster parents:

- *Communication.* This includes mutual sharing and ready access to the worker, within a framework of respect and positive regard.

- *Clear role definition.* Foster parents need a clear understanding of their role in the case of a particular child. They want to actively participate and to feel that their input is valued and needed.

- *Ongoing training.* Training needs should be assessed regularly and the training provided should be relative to their needs.

- *Ongoing support.* Foster parents want access to a support network of experienced foster/adoptive parents, caseworkers, and professionals when challenges and crises occur.

In some CPS agencies, the task of working directly with foster parents falls to a specialized worker. This may or may not be the circumstance in your agency. In any event, as the worker for the child and family who is coordinating the plan, you can contribute to a positive placement experience for both the child and the caregivers by making your best effort to be open, communicative, and attentive to the caregivers' needs and requests.

☐ Partnering with the Legal System

Like CPS, the legal system also has mandated responsibility to intervene with children and families in situations of child maltreatment. Law enforcement, the courts, attorneys, and advocates all have specific roles and responsibilities for intervention.

Partnering with law enforcement

This system works in close partnership with CPS. A joint, supportive effort between CPS and the police is most effective, especially in the investigative and assessment stages of a child protection case.

Law enforcement personnel have the responsibility to do the following (DePanfilis & Salus, 1992):

- Identify and report suspected child maltreatment.

- Receive reports of child abuse and neglect.

- Conduct investigations of reports of child maltreatment when there is a suspicion that a crime has been committed. This can be done independently or jointly with CPS.

- Determine whether sufficient evidence exists to prosecute alleged offenders.

- Assist CPS with any need to secure protection for the child, including taking the child into protective custody or removing the alleged perpetrator from the home.
- Provide protection to you during the course of your duties when your personal safety might be at risk.
- Support the victim through the criminal court process.
- Participate in multidisciplinary teams or service planning.

You will be working with law enforcement personnel in many ways, including:

- Reporting possible abuse or neglect to their agency.
- Determining (with the assistance of your supervisor and any agency protocols that are in place) the cases for which you need to have law enforcement involvement.
- Conducting joint investigations to best coordinate your efforts and to minimize the number of times a child will have to be interviewed.

> Your agency receives a report of possible sexual abuse of a 6-year-old boy by his grandfather, who lives in the home. You are assigned this referral, and per your agency's protocol, you contact the local law enforcement agency with jurisdiction to request a detective to accompany you to the school to begin the assessment process. Prior to the child's arrival, the two of you develop a plan for the interview, including such things as who will take the lead, what important questions need to be asked, and who will be taking notes or taping during the interview. You have both learned that this planning leads to a much more comprehensive and effective forensic interview.

Partnering with the Court System

In any given case, both the civil and criminal courts could play an essential role in the child protective services partnership. This role ranges from the ordering of cooperation in the investigation, to the actions taken to remove children and award temporary or permanent custody, to determining guilt or innocence of the alleged perpetrator and imposing punishment. (See chapter 11.)

Family or juvenile courts are expected to make sure a safe, permanent, and stable home is secured for each abused and neglected child. The National Council of Juvenile and Family Court Judges has outlined specific guidelines for those involved in these court proceedings (Grossman et al., 1995).

Victims of child abuse and neglect come before juvenile and family courts in need of protection from further harm and of timely decision-making for their future. Judges make critical legal decisions and oversee CPS efforts to maintain and rehabilitate families, or to provide permanent alternative care for children.

Decisions made by the court govern the lives and futures of the parties (e.g., child's emergency placement, issues of tribal jurisdiction or intervention, child's placement into extended foster care, parents' submission to evaluation or testing, parents' participation in treatment, schedule for parent-child and sibling visitation, termination of parental rights, and the child's adoption).

Actions of the court may include:

- Issuing protective orders.
- Assessing family circumstances.
- Ensuring parental responsibility.
- Adapting and monitoring appropriate service plans.
- Requiring accountability of all parties involved in the juvenile court action.
- Determining what parties may have the right to intervene in court hearings. For example, the tribes of American Indian children may file motions to intervene. In addition, some states may grant intervener status to grandparents or other relatives who have had a significant role in raising the children.

Other participants in the civil court process are attorneys, guardians ad litem (GALs), and court-appointed special advocates (CASAs).

Attorneys have specific responsibilities in these court proceedings. They are expected to:

- Actively participate in every critical stage of the proceedings.
- Thoroughly investigate the case at every stage of the proceedings.
- Determine what contacts the agency has made with the parents and the child, and what efforts were made to reunify the family, if the child has been removed from the home.
- Conduct full interviews with the parent or caregiver to determine what involvement the child welfare agency has had with the parents or child, what progress the parents and child have made, and what services the family (including the child, if age appropriate) believes would be helpful.
- Interview key witnesses; review all documents submitted to court, review agency's file and any pertinent law enforcement reports done in preparation for proceedings.
- Obtain or subpoena necessary records, such as school reports, medical records, and case records.
- Arrange for independent evaluations of children or parents when necessary.
- Stay in regular contact with the family, writing letters and making telephone calls when necessary.
- Continue to remain in contact with the agency and monitor case progress between court hearings.
- Notify tribes prior to removal, placement, adoption, or termination of parental rights hearings. In some states or counties, caseworkers may be designated to carry out this responsibility.

GALs and CASAs might also be involved in the court case. The Child Abuse Prevention and Treatment Act of 1974 requires any state receiving federal funds for prevention of child abuse and neglect to provide a GAL for every child involved in such proceedings. The federal act did not define the role or responsibilities of the GAL. Some jurisdictions appoint specially qualified and trained attorneys, and some appoint trained citizen volunteers (CASAs).

The GAL could be a person with formal legal training appointed by a judge to *represent the best interests* of an allegedly abused or neglected child. This attorney's role differs from the legal advocate for the child (a defense or respondent attorney) who specifically *represents the child's wishes* before the court.

CASAs are specially screened and trained volunteers appointed by the court to speak up for the best interest of abused and neglected children. They review records, research information, and talk with everyone involved in the child's case. They make recommendations to the court as to what is best for the child and monitor the case until it is resolved.

Both attorneys and trained volunteers play a significant role in providing GAL representation for children.

The *criminal court system* can also become involved in these cases. Criminal court action is initiated when the act or omission by the child's parent or guardian, or a non-family member, is serious enough to warrant the filing of criminal charges. The purpose of this action is to determine the guilt or innocence of the alleged perpetrator and to impose a punishment or sentence. Activities under this situation that are related to your work with the court systems include:

- Case conferences and planning.
- Report preparation.
- Court testimony.

☐ Partnering with the Medical Community

The medical community is critical in assessing, diagnosing, and reporting child abuse and neglect. Their responsibilities include:

- Identification and reporting of abuse and neglect.
- Consultation to CPS or law enforcement regarding the medical aspects of child abuse and neglect.
- Assessment, diagnosis, and direct treatment of child victims.
- Ongoing monitoring of at-risk children and vulnerable families.
- Participation on child maltreatment multidisciplinary teams.
- Provision of information and preventive parent education services to parents or caregivers and other professionals.
- Expert witness testimony in court proceedings.

Your activities that are related to your work with the medical community include:

- Receiving referrals from medical professionals.
- Making referrals to medical experts for diagnosis and treatment.

- Requesting consultation regarding a particular medical concern.
- Advocating and arranging for medical services.

> You have a particularly complicated medical case of a very young child who has unexplained injuries of different ages. Your supervisor lets you know of a medical consultation team at your local hospital. You and the police detective are invited to present the case information you have (reports, interviews, pictures) to their team of child maltreatment medical experts to assist you in your assessment, decision-making, and service planning.

☐ **Partnering with School System Personnel**

Principals, teachers, school counselors, and other school-related personnel play a critical role in protecting children and strengthening families. Their responsibilities include:

- Identifying and reporting suspected maltreatment.
- Developing a school/program policy for reporting.
- After reporting, keeping CPS informed of changes/improvements in child's behavior or performance.
- Providing input in diagnostic and treatment/remedial services for the child.
- Supporting the child through potentially traumatic events (e.g., court hearings and out-of-home placement).
- Providing treatment for parents such as school program–sponsored self-help groups.
- Developing and implementing prevention programs for children and parents.
- Serving on child maltreatment multidisciplinary teams.

You could be involved with the educational system in your role as a CPS worker. Your interactions and activities could include:

- Receiving referrals from school personnel.
- Collecting information from school personnel for your child protection investigation and assessment.
- Requesting information regarding the child's educational needs and services.
- Providing consultation and information regarding your role and the expectations of school personnel.
- Attending school staffings and conferences related to the child and family.

☐ **Partnering with Mental Health Providers**

Psychiatrists, psychologists, social workers, and other mental health professionals play an important role in the child protection partnership. Their responsibilities include:

- Identifying and reporting suspected cases of maltreatment.
- Conducting necessary evaluations of abused and neglected children and their families.
- Providing information to CPS for the child protection investigation and assessment.
- Providing treatment for abused and neglected children and their families.
- Providing clinical consultation to CPS.
- Providing expert testimony.
- Offering self-help groups or other services to parents who have maltreated their children or are at risk of maltreating their children.
- Developing and implementing prevention programs.
- Participating on multidisciplinary teams.

You will benefit from establishing collaborative relationships with various mental health professionals who can provide a wide range of services to the children and families with whom you work. Helpful ways to approach a productive working relationship include:

- Clarifying expectations regarding interventions and evaluation, such as timelines, reports or other work product, number of sessions, and payment.
- Working through issues regarding confidentiality between CPS and mental health providers. It is time well spent to discuss confidentiality expectations both with the mental health provider and the parent or caregiver. Releases of information are helpful to you and to the therapist or provider.

☐ Partnering with Substance Abuse Providers

An ever-present and growing number of children and families in the child protection system are struggling with the effects of alcohol and other drug (AOD) abuse. As a CPS worker, it is critical for you to develop partnerships with substance abuse providers to meet the needs of substance-abusing parents in order to ensure children's safety.

What is the common ground between CPS and AOD? Children of parents who are dealing with AOD abuse are almost three times more likely to be abused and more than four times likely to be neglected than children of parents who are not substance abusers (Kinney, Thielman, Fox, & Brown, 2001). Harmful involvement with AOD is a factor in as many as 80% of situations involving child maltreatment (Rogers & McMillan, 2000b). A 1997 CWLA study of state child welfare agencies estimated that 67% of parents in the child welfare system required substance abuse treatment services, but child welfare agencies were only able to provide for 31% of the families (Banks & Boehm, 2001).

These data suggest that as a CPS worker, you are quite likely to be intervening with parents who are abusing substances. You will be expected to assess how this abuse is affecting their ability to keep their children safe. This can be challenging for a number of reasons, as follows.

Barriers to working together. CPS workers are typically not trained experts in identifying and treating substance abuse. In addition, as a worker, you must meet the accelerated timelines required by the Adoption and Safe Families Act (Public Law 105-89) to ensure permanence for the child of a substance-abusing parent. This makes it imperative that substance abuse concerns be identified quickly, specific treatment be started as soon as possible, outcomes for success be identified, and the parent's participation be closely monitored (Kinney et al., 2001).

Though CPS and AOD workers have many clients in common, the two systems are quite different. Potential areas for conflict include:

- Differences in values and philosophies regarding whether the parent or the child is the primary client.
- Confidentiality issues regarding disclosure of information (stringent federal requirements for the AOD field make the sharing of information challenging).
- CPS and AOD have different ideas about anticipating and planning for relapse.
- AOD might not understand the time-frame requirements for CPS.
- CPS may not understand the rehabilitation process and consequently set unrealistic goals for recovery.
- AOD may not be aware of the need for continued interaction between the child and parent to support family attachment needs (Kinney et al., 2001).

While there is a need for CPS to be working closely with the AOD interveners on behalf of mutual clients, these barriers could prevent a strong working partnership. However, research and promising practices have identified a number of elements and ideas that can ease the way in working together.

Elements of a successful partnership. Your CPS agency can provide support by considering the use of a differential response in appropriate reports involving substance abuse and possible child maltreatment. If a report is placed in an assessment, as opposed to an investigative track, you would have the capacity to focus on providing services and interventions to prevent future maltreatment or harm, rather than conducting a child protection assessment and investigation and making an abuse or neglect finding.

Your CPS agency can also work with experts in the AOD community to develop or use an assessment instrument that addresses needs of both CPS and AOD.

You and the AOD treatment provider can partner more effectively by:

- Jointly identifying and using community agencies and resources for help in serving families at different stages of their recovery, with an array of services that meet their treatment and recovery support needs.
- Coming to an agreement to define the client within the context of the family (e.g., substance-abusing woman as a single parent of a 3-year-old child).

- Working together to locate gender and culturally specific substance abuse treatment. Treatment that is congruent with the family's religious, spiritual, or societal needs will be more readily received and utilized.

- Approaching interventions together in a holistic approach for the family (e.g., achieving a variety of goals, not just sobriety or custody of children). Examples of a variety of goals could include having a safe place to live, vocational training and employment, connection to the community, and developing a plan for future crises (Kinney et al., 2001).

- Rogers and McMillan (2000a, p. 252) suggest an "intelligent use of leverage and influence." You and/or an addiction counselor may be able to help parents or caregivers understand the consequences of choosing between accepting treatment for addiction and losing their rights or privileges involving their child.

A positive partnership can produce positive outcomes. Finding a way to work with substance abuse providers has been shown to have positive outcomes for children and their parents. Successful programs provide comprehensive services specific to the needs of substance-abusing parents and their children.

> Mrs. Adams and her 2-year-old son are successful graduates of her substance abuse program. Mrs. Adams received inpatient and follow-up outpatient drug abuse treatment. She also received parenting information and support, including child growth and development, nutrition, safety, and positive discipline. Mrs. Adams attended counseling and ongoing support groups. Her son was placed with her during her in-patient treatment; and while mom was busy in groups and individual sessions, he was supervised by program staff and participated in playgroups.

> Outcomes that defined Mrs. Adams's success included elimination of her drug use, no involvement with the criminal justice system, no subsequent CPS referrals, and stable employment and housing.

> Mrs. Adams and her son demonstrate how the outcomes of child safety and well-being can be achieved through a caring and supportive program.

Your efforts to familiarize yourself with the challenges of addiction and its impact on parenting, and to work productively with a substance abuse treatment provider, will benefit the children and families on your caseload.

☐ Partnering with Domestic Violence Providers

As is the case with substance abuse, many children and families who come to the attention of the child welfare agency face domestic violence issues. This is a serious form of violence that, again, is best responded to with a coordinated and collaborative approach between you and other professionals in the domestic violence community.

What is the common ground between child protection and domestic violence? The National Association of Public Child Welfare Administrators (2000) looked at the overlap of child protection and domestic violence cases and found that domestic violence is pervasive in child welfare caseloads; and the lack of proper and timely identification, assessment, and intervention in cases where there is domestic violence may compromise successful outcomes regarding child safety, stability, and permanence. In fact, more than 30 studies conducted regarding the link between domestic violence and child maltreatment show a 40% co-occurrence between these two forms of violence.

> Several studies indicate the presence of adult domestic violence correlates with an increased risk of physical abuse of children. In a national survey of 6,000 American families, researchers found that 50% of the men who frequently assaulted their partners also frequently abused their children (Straus & Gelles, 1990). Additionally, domestic violence has been linked to severe and fatal cases of child abuse. Studies from child protective services agencies in Oregon and Massachusetts found domestic violence in approximately 40% of families experiencing child fatalities and critical injuries (Felix & McCarthy, 1994; Oregon Children's Division, 1993). (NAPCWA, 2000, p. 13)

Schechter and Edelson (1994) also found the following: (a) Domestic violence and child abuse frequently occur in the same family. (b) Children who witness violence by their fathers may be at risk of developing a variety of problems. (c) Men who are perpetrating some of the most dangerous abuse of children are also assaulting women. (d) Child welfare and domestic violence programs serve an overlapping population of women and children.

As a child protection worker, you will be involved in cases of domestic violence. There are inherent challenges to a cooperative approach between professionals working within each area.

Barriers to working together. Most of the barriers between CPS and domestic violence stem from philosophical differences regarding the origins of family violence, the responsibility for violence, and the role of the intervener and CPS misunderstanding of a victim's actions.

CPS most often attributes family violence to family dysfunction, external stressors, ill-prepared parents, and/or poor parenting skills. Domestic violence providers most often attribute family violence to power/control dynamics, sexism and male privilege, and/or socially sanctioned beliefs and values about the use of violence.

When assessing who is responsible for the violence, CPS looks at the parents as being equally responsible. The nonabusing parent may be held accountable for "failing to protect." The safety of the child is paramount. Domestic violence providers believe that the abuser chooses violence and is solely responsible for this choice. The adult victim is never held responsible for the violence. The safety of victims (mother and children) is the priority.

Child protective service work is defined by law and public policy; CPS workers are responsible to work with both parents and are expected to be neutral. Domestic violence providers are social change oriented. They intervene in all forms of family violence. Domestic violence workers are not neutral, as they act as advocates on behalf of battered women and their children (Ludwig & Ganey, 1996).

Some actions taken by adult victims that are intended to increase protection are often misunderstood by CPS workers. These actions include:

- Minimizing and denying the violence to avoid harm and retaliation by the batterer.
- Fighting back and defying the batterer.
- Complying with and placating the batterer.
- Not leaving the batterer due to fear for her life or harm to the children by the batterer.
- Leaving the children with a relative or friend (NAPCWA, 2000).

CPS workers might interpret these steps as a victim's unwillingness or inability to protect herself or the children, while the victim has learned that these steps could be the only way to ensure some sort of safety.

The key to resolving these misunderstandings is open communication and discussion about *how* to reach the mutual goal of protection of both women and their children.

Recommendations for child protection interventions in domestic violence cases. NAPCWA (2000) said that child protection workers will be better able to protect children only if they know how to identify domestic violence; assess its nature, severity, and impact; plan for safety; and learn how to effectively use community services and legal protections. To accomplish this, NAPCWA developed a number of recommendations for child protection intervention. Some of these recommendations are:

- Domestic violence should be assessed within a cultural context. Services and interventions should be culturally sensitive and appropriate.
- Domestic violence is to be assessed as a risk factor during the investigation and assessment stage and must continue to be assessed at all phases of a case: opening, service plan development, placement decisions, services plan review, and case closure. CPS interventions need to be targeted toward removing the risks caused by the batterer, while assisting the adult victim in securing safety for herself and the children.
- CPS must accurately assess the protective factors that adult victims use in providing safety and stability for their children. Routine factors include seeking shelter, contacting the police, and obtaining a protective order. An adult victim's decision not to use these options has been misunderstood by CPS workers as "noncompliance" and evidence of "failure to protect."

Differential response should be considered for some domestic violence cases.

- Although many children suffer when they are exposed to domestic violence, not all children are in need of child protective services. It is unrealistic and intrusive for CPS to investigate every report of domestic violence involving children. The community should work together to offer these children a continuum of services contingent on the level of harm and risk they experience.

CPS should be involved in families whenever children have been physically, sexually, or emotionally abused as a result of exposure to domestic violence.

- In some cases, child protection efforts can be accomplished without a formal determination of abuse and neglect. On completion of a comprehensive investigation and assessment of the nature and severity of the domestic violence and its impact on the children, CPS may refer the family to the community for services and support rather than sustaining a CPS case.

- However, other cases will require ongoing child protective services due to presenting risk factors associated with potentially severe and lethal domestic violence cases.

CPS should hold batterers accountable for their violence. Workers should be wary of documentation practices that place blame on the adult victim by using words or phrases such as "domestic violence is occurring *between* the parents," "the mother *will notify* the father's probation officer or police when she is assaulted," or "the mother *will prevent* children from witnessing domestic violence." Alternative ways to describe batterer accountability include: "The batterer will not verbally or physically abuse the adult victim," or "the batterer will not use threatening or coercive tactics."

Separate safety plans should be developed for adult victims and children. This should be done in collaboration with a domestic violence advocate. Safety plans should be reviewed regularly. Psychological safety should be considered as well as physical safety. This may often involve separating parents during court hearings and child visits. Restraining orders may also need to be obtained to protect adult victims and children from contact with a perpetrator.

The CPS agency should provide safety support for workers. This could include cellular telephones, pagers, working in pairs, trauma debriefing, worker safety planning, and procedures for requesting assistance from law enforcement.

Working together. NAPCWA indicated that it was imperative to develop and support strong working relationships between CPS and domestic violence services. Much of this starts at the agency level. As a worker, you can discuss with your supervisor or administrator whether your agency has implemented any of the following ideas and recommendations:

- Incorporating domestic violence expertise within the CPS agency; for example, colocating domestic violence advocates with CPS workers.

- Encouraging cross-system collaboration and multidisciplinary practices. This involves developing interagency protocols to define how systems, agencies, and individuals will work together. Policies should also be developed that indicate how information can be shared between agencies. Multidisciplinary teams should be used to ensure the representation of differing agencies' perspectives and to clearly identify roles and expectations of those involved in planning and providing services.

CPS and domestic violence professionals working together can mean safer women and children. Data suggest that through the protection of mothers who are battered, many abused children are also kept safe. Finding strategies that help both women and children to be safe is a dilemma that challenges domestic violence advocates and CPS workers every day (Spears, 2000). A working relationship can begin between you and domestic violence providers by the following means:

- Establishing open and honest communication.
- Clarifying differences in beliefs, philosophies, and assumptions and striving to find "common ground."
- Maintaining regular and frequent contact to clarify expectations and outcomes that achieve the common goal of promoting safety for children and victims of domestic abuse.

☐ Partnering with the Community

One of the expectations of family-centered practice is that it takes place within the cultural and community contexts of the family. There are many best-practice examples of how a community can be mobilized to provide assistance for its families. The term "community" goes beyond geographical boundaries. As a worker, you can be looking toward a neighborhood, an ethnic or cultural community, an Indian child's tribe, a faith-based organization, a support group, or a civic organization—anywhere a child and family are connected—for help and support.

Successful programs have mobilized local nonprofit service providers, faith-based institutions, grassroots neighborhood organizations, and civic organizations (e.g., Boy Scouts and Urban League) to raise awareness of child safety issues and to formulate a community response ("Community Collaborations," 2000).

Actively involving some faction of a community to participate in CPS intervention and planning requires working with the family to identify the different communities of which they are a part and how and when to involve different community members in the plan. In addition, identify services or supports within the community that will strengthen the family and increase their capacity to keep their children safe. Increasing child safety and strengthening families can involve meeting the family's needs in many different areas, including childcare, after-school programming, housing, employment, education, health care, recreation, cultural and spiritual support, and culture-specific advocacy.

You, the family, and other individuals participating in their service plan will have to mobilize community services by:

1. Identifying the needs.
2. Assessing the community's capacity to help.
3. Identifying the provider.

4. Arranging logistics (e.g., payment, transportation, childcare).

5. Discussing timelines and expected outcomes.

> The Sandoval family came to your agency's attention because of lack of supervision of their three young children, ages 7, 3, and 2. Mr. and Mrs. Sandoval were leaving the children alone while one parent left for work before the other returned home (from about 7:00 to 9:30 p.m.) One evening, the oldest child awoke, became frightened, and called 911.
>
> You discover the parents are primarily Spanish speaking and have multiple needs. They are fearful of your intervention. Through the use of an interpreter, the parents shared that they had recently moved here from Mexico. They were feeling isolated since Mrs. Sandoval's mother had left their home and returned to Mexico. They were religious and had not found a church. They were very concerned about how their 7-year-old son was doing in school.
>
> The Sandovals live in a neighborhood where there is a family resource center. You contact an advocate there. He is Spanish speaking and offers to assist you in identifying needs and locating culturally appropriate services.
>
> Together, you are able to locate resources and services that will meet the Sandovals' needs and help them keep the children safe. The advocate is able to locate evening childcare for the children. You contact the school to request a meeting; you and the advocate plan to attend with the parents. The resource center is also starting a Hispanic parenting class that the Sandovals could attend. Finally, the advocate locates another resource center family who attends the local Catholic church. They invite the Sandovals to attend church with them.

You should educate your community about what child protection is and is not. For example, a community agency may want you to remove a child in order to give him or her a "better lifestyle." CPS investigates the situation and finds no safety concern necessitating CPS involvement. The agency may not understand the detrimental effects of removing a child from his home or the CPS mandate to keep families together when it is safe to do so. This community agency may think "CPS doesn't do enough!" You can help dispel these notions about CPS by effectively communicating CPS mandates and your role in helping families.

☐ Partnering with Animal Shelters

Studies linking violence to animals and humans found that between 30% and 65% of violent perpetrators had abused animals in childhood or adolescence (Ascione, 2001). Animal abuse and child abuse share common characteristics:

- Violence is directed toward a living creature.
- Both types of victim experience pain and distress.
- The perpetrator of both types of abuse is in a position of power over the victim.
- Both types of victim display physical signs of pain and distress.

- Both types of victim could be permanently disfigured or die as a result of the abuse.

Ways to partner with animal shelters include:

- Exchange information when an animal is in a home where violence has occurred or vice versa, when a child is in a home where an animal has been abused.
- Ask questions about the occurrence of violence toward animals in every assessment (Flynn, 2000).
- Reciprocate education programs to crosstrain CPS and animal shelter staff on the link between animal and child abuse.

■ Summary of Competencies

The CPS worker acts on behalf of the agency and must view effective child protection as an important partnership between the family and himself or herself. The worker must clearly understand the complex dynamics of families who maltreat children and the varying roles that the worker plays in facilitating a plan that enables families to protect children from maltreatment. In addition, the worker must be able to identify all of the potential partners who might intervene with children and families, and have the knowledge and skills to facilitate these partnerships effectively to further the goals of child safety, permanence, and child and family well-being.

Knowledge:

1. Knowledge of the methods of family-centered practice.
2. Familiarity with agency policies and procedures as they direct your interactions with children, families, other agencies, and members of the community.
3. Familiarity with interagency agreements, procedures, and guidelines.
4. Understanding of a family's strengths, needs, preferences, and ethnic/cultural background that will impact their participation in the service plan.
5. Knowledge of community resources, services, and contact persons.
6. Familiarity with the means to access resources and services for families.
7. Knowledge of techniques to facilitate communication and cooperation among involved partners and service providers.

Skills:

1. Be empathic to parents and children who are involved in abuse and neglect, even if you do not agree with their behavior.
2. Communicate effectively and listen attentively.
3. Think creatively about the development and use of community resources to help vulnerable families.
4. Solicit assistance from supervisors and/or multidisciplinary teams for broader based decision-making.

5. Communicate effectively with individuals and other professionals involved in the case.

6. Plan and coordinate service intervention, while remaining flexible and accommodating the needs of the child and family.

References

Ascione, F. (2001, September). Animal abuse and youth violence. *Juvenile Justice Bulletin,* 1–15.

Banks, H., & Boehm, S. (2001, September). Substance abuse and child abuse. *Children's Voice, 10*(5), 36–42.

Child Welfare League of America. (1989–99). *Standards for child welfare services.* (Rev. ed.). Washington, DC: Author.

Community collaborations. (2000, Fall). *Best Practice Next Practice, 1*(2), 1–3.

Day, P., Robison, S., & Sheikh, L. (1998). *Ours to keep: A guide for building a community assessment strategy for child protection.* Washington, DC: CWLA Press.

DePanfilis, D., & Salus, M. (1992). *The user manual series—a coordinated response to child abuse and neglect: A basic manual.* Washington, DC: Administration on Children, Youth and Families, U.S. Department of Health and Human Services, National Center on Child Abuse and Neglect.

Flynn, C. (2000). Why family professionals can no longer ignore violence toward animals. *Family Relations, 49,* 87–95.

Grossman, D., Gladstone, W., Grissom, P., Hall, S., McCully, S., Mitchell, D., Rouse, G., & Wohlford, P. (1995). *Resource guidelines: Improving court practice in child abuse and neglect cases.* Reno, NV: National Council of Juvenile and Family Court Judges.

Jorgenson, K., & Schooler, J. (2000, Fall/Winter). What makes foster parents come and stay: Understanding the keys to successful retention. *Permanency Planning Today, 1*(2), 3–5.

Kinney, J., Thielman, B., Fox, N., & Brown, A. (2001, October). *Connecting child protective services and substance abuse treatment in communities: A resource guide.* Washington, DC: American Public Human Services Association.

Lawson, H., & Barkdull, C. (2001). Gaining the collaborative advantage and promoting systems and cross-systems change. In H. Salee, H. Lawson, & K. Briar-Lawson (Eds.), *Innovative practices with vulnerable children and families* (pp. 245–265). Peosta, IA: Eddie Bowers.

Ludwig, S., & Ganey, M. (1996). *Crossing the bridge: A cross-training curriculum for domestic violence/child protection workers.* Denver: Colorado Department of Human Services. (Funded by Family Violence Prevention and Services Program, ACYF, USDHHS, Grant No. 90EV0050.)

Matt, R., & Berns, D. (1999). Partnerships in protecting children. In *Guidelines for a model system of protective services for abused and neglected children and their families* (pp. 35–42). Washington, DC: National Association of Public Child Welfare Administrators.

Merkel-Holguin, L. (1996). Putting the families back into the child protection partnership: Family group decision making. *Protecting Children, 12*(3), 4–7.

National Association of Public Child Welfare Administrators. (1999). *Guidelines for a model system of protective services for abused and neglected children and their families.* Washington, DC: American Public Human Services Association.

National Association of Public Child Welfare Administrators. (2000). *Guidelines for public child welfare agencies serving children and families experiencing domestic violence.* Washington, DC: American Public Human Services Association.

A new era of family-centered practice. (2000). *Best Practice Next Practice, 1*(1), 1–9.

Palmer, S. E. (1995). *Maintaining family ties: Inclusive practice in foster care.* Washington, DC: CWLA Press.

Rogers, R., & McMillan, C. (2000a). How do I protect children when caregivers have chemical dependency problems? In H. Dubowitz & D. DePanfilis (Eds.), *Handbook for child protection practice* (pp. 250–254). Thousand Oaks, CA: Sage.

Rogers, R., & McMillan, C. (2000b). How do I screen a caregiver's use and abuse of alcohol and other drugs and their effects on parenting? In H. Dubowitz & D. DePanfilis (Eds.), *Handbook for child protection practice* (pp. 105–108). Thousand Oaks, CA: Sage.

Schechter, S., & Edelson, J. (1994, June). *In the best interest of women and children: A call for collaboration between child welfare and domestic violence constituencies.* Briefing paper presented at the Wingspread Conference: "Domestic Violence and Child Welfare," Racine, WI.

Schene, P. (2001, Spring). Meeting each family's needs: Using a differential response in reports of child abuse and neglect. *Best Practice, Next Practice, 2*(1), 1–6.

Soler, M. I., & Peters, C. M. (1993). *Who should know what? Confidentiality and information sharing in service integration.* New York: National Center for Service Integration.

Spears, L. (2000) Building bridges between domestic violence organizations and child protective services. In *Building comprehensive solutions to domestic violence* (pub. No. 7, pp. 3–7). Harrisburg, PA: National Resource Center on Domestic Violence.

Strom-Gottfried, G. (1998). Applying a conflict resolution framework to disputes in managed care. *Social Work, 43*(5), 393–401.

5

Edward Nowak
Ingo Schamber
Charmaine Brittain

Interviewing Children and Families

■ The Purpose and Nature of Interviews

■ Preparing for the CPS Interview

■ Interviewing Adults

■ Interviewing Techniques

■ Interviewing beyond Intake and Investigation

■ Interviewing Children

■ Summary of Competencies

Effective interviewing is a composite of knowledge, skills, preparation, experience, attitude, and your own inherent competence, as well as your ability to build a relationship with the family. Some of your skills will develop naturally as you try various approaches. However, in learning to interview parents or caregivers successfully, it is important that you be aware that practice is indispensable and that competency will be achieved only if you are conscious of certain effective approaches and techniques in dealing with families involved with CPS. As you develop your capacity to interview, your confidence as a practitioner will increase and you will find that you are more likely to help parents or caregivers make positive changes as parents and individuals. The quality of the relationships you develop with parents or caregivers and their responsiveness to your help will depend to a great extent on your interviewing skills.

A family typically enters the CPS system when a report is made alleging abuse or neglect. Unlike a parent or caregiver who seeks voluntary assistance from an agency in order to solve a problem that they have identified, parents or caregivers who did not request help are often mandated to accept services involuntarily around an issue that they may not see as a problem. These parents or caregivers are often resistant to such services and are likely to be angry and hostile toward the interviewer. Learning to successfully conduct a CPS interview is a great accomplishment. These interviews are often conducted in circumstances where a child is at risk of further injury. Participants in these interviews are feeling a variety of powerful emotions and may express their anger, fear, and frustration during the interview. It is the intent of this chapter to assist you so that you can successfully cope with these complexities.

■ The Purpose and Nature of Interviews

An interview is not merely a conversation; it is a purposefully directed interaction between people. As an interviewer, you should constantly bear in mind the purpose or reason for talking with a particular person. Without a purpose, your interview will not be effective.

A professional interview is designed to meet certain specific purposes. It is designed to elicit and to impart information. It provides an opportunity for the parent or caregiver to express feelings and release tensions. It may be used to motivate the parent or caregiver to understand his or her own behavior and seek change. And it may promote understanding between you and the parent or caregiver.

☐ Factors Affecting the Interview

You should remember that your effort to understand parents or caregivers and their situations will be conditioned by a number of factors, as follows.

- *Intentionality* refers to the intent, reason, or purpose for seeing a particular parent or caregiver. You must keep in mind the intent or purpose of an interview in order to focus on those areas that will promote a purposeful and productive interaction between you and the parent or caregiver.

- *Self-awareness* refers to the understanding you have about your own feelings, attitudes, and prejudices toward the people to whom you talk. For example, lack of awareness of your prejudices toward a particular racial group may prevent you from being objective and will not enhance meaningful communication between you and a person from that racial group. (For more information regarding self-awareness, see chapter 3.) Being self-aware will make you more sincere and tolerant during the interview process.

- *Knowledge,* for the purpose of understanding a parent or caregiver and his or her situation, refers to knowledge of human behavioral dynamics.

- *Experience* refers to all of the direct or indirect knowledge about people and situations that you have accumulated.

- *Adaptability* refers to your ability to communicate in a responsive and flexible manner. Unless you can do so, you may not be able to achieve the goal or purpose of the interview.

- *Objectivity* refers to your ability to remain neutral in your thinking prior to and during the interview. Abuse or neglect may or may not have occurred. Allow yourself to be curious, gathering information to gain a better understanding of the family's situation. Without objectivity, the information you glean may be incomplete or inaccurate.

☐ Reasons for the CPS Interview

In your initial contact with the reporter or family, your purpose is to obtain and assess selected information in order to make decisions. You want to ask the reporter specific questions that will inform your investigation and assessment. For example:

> "Dr. Green, can you tell me why this injury is not consistent with the mother's story?"

> "Is there any possible way the child could have sustained this kind of fracture unless someone purposely hit her with an object?"

Interviewing to assess safety. There are several decisions that must be made in the early stages of the interviewing process. Most important, you must assess the immediate safety of all of the children in the home and determine if it is safe at this point for them to remain in the home. The interviewer must develop a plan of safety if the children are to remain in the home. Questions should be directed to determining whether the child can be "conditionally safe" in the home. A child will be conditionally safe as long as the safety issue is addressed and individuals follow through on their responsibilities as specified in the plan.

Interviewing to assess risk. You must also assess risk by doing a complete assessment of all adults and children in the home as well as the environment that they live in and the external supports that may exist.

Interviewing and communicating with the family. Interviewing occurs throughout the life of a service plan. You will continuously interview individuals to obtain and assess selected information in order to make decisions. You will interview to communicate information to parents and community partners, to develop a service plan, and to assess the family's ongoing situation.

Interviewing to assess the ongoing situation. In subsequent contacts your purpose is to further assess or identify problems and to assess strengths and needs, as well as evaluating progress toward case goals. At each contact, whether a child is in placement or continues to live at home, the Adoption and Safe Families Act (ASFA) requires you to have a plan of safety. This means that you must reassess the ongoing plan of safety and ask all participants how the plan is working and make any changes that are required to ensure success.

■ Preparing for the CPS Interview

The CPS interview can be a difficult part of your involvement with protective services families. You should be prepared in advance to apply a variety of important concepts and techniques. In addition, you will need to consider the most appropriate setting for the interview. Being prepared for your interview will increase your confidence by minimizing your level of anxiety, making you aware of certain feelings you might have that could become an obstacle during the communication process, and helping you deal effectively with unexpected behavior.

☐ Developing a Relationship with the Family

A relationship is the cornerstone of casework practice. Without a relationship very little can be accomplished during the helping process. It is important to recognize that a "relationship" is defined as resulting from a give-and-take process. It is unlikely to occur on your first contact with the parent or caregiver or during your first interview because of the highly emotional nature of the situation, parental resistance, and the possible need to remove the child. The first interview is the beginning of building a relationship. It may be unproductive and frustrating to expect to establish a "relationship" during the initial contact; instead, work to establish rapport.

Rapport consists of the positive feeling that you convey to the parent or caregiver by saying, in effect, "I want to help you." The following actions will help you to establish rapport:

- Place yourself in the parent or caregiver's "shoes" or position, that is, show empathy.
- Show your concern for the parent or caregiver.
- Be nonpunitive in your approach to the parent or caregiver.
- Focus on the here and now.
- Make sure that wherever possible and whatever decisions are made, the parent or caregiver is part of them.
- Focus on the parent or caregiver's current needs. Offer resources or assistance to the family.

- Try to respond honestly to what you see and hear. This does not mean that you should be judgmental and critical but that you should definitely express your opinion in a straightforward and, if possible, sympathetic and empathetic manner.
- Communicate understanding and respect for the parent's position, even if you do not agree with it.
- Make sure that the parent or caregiver understands the process that he or she is participating in, who will be interviewed, and why it is important for everyone to cooperate and engage in this process. For example, if you are investigating allegations of neglect that a 6-year-old child was home alone after school until the parent arrived home from work, you must let the parent know that in order to ensure that the plan of safety is workable, you will have to meet all substitute caregivers identified and make sure that they are appropriate and responsible.

☐ Deciding on the Appropriate Strategy for the Interview

First, determine who will be interviewed. In planning your interview you must develop a strategy that involves deciding whether to see the parents or caregivers together or separately. If the initial interview is being conducted and the purpose is to gather information about an allegation of abuse, the best-practice approach is to first interview children apart from their caregiver(s) and then interview other family members or caregivers. Many localities have policies saying that children should be seen first. Children usually have never met the investigative worker before and may be afraid of being removed from their caregiver's home. If the child is interviewed with their parent or caregiver present, he or she may follow nonverbal leads of that parent, and the interview may not yield accurate information. Thus every effort should be made to interview the child privately.

Attempt to interview parents or caregivers separately from each other first to obtain an understanding of the situation without influence from the other person. At a later time, try to arrange an interview with both parents or caregivers to give you a dynamic understanding of the family. You should not use joint interviews if you are forced into the role of referee or into taking sides, since your effectiveness as a worker will diminish.

Each interview must have a specific purpose, and therefore you may want to include the child in later interviews, for the following reasons:

- The child's presence may help to assess communication with the parents or caregivers. Any plan of safety that will allow a child to remain at home must include an assessment of the parent-child relationship. You may want to review the plan of safety with the parent and child together in order to observe how they relate and whether they understand and can carry out the plan.
- The child's presence may enable you to get a dynamic understanding of the parent or caregiver's knowledge about child development and whether his

or her developmental expectations of the child are appropriate for the child's age level.

If you have to conduct your interview in the presence of relatives and neighbors, you should remember the following points:

- Parents or caregivers should be consulted about the presence of others at interviews as confidential issues may be raised.
- Neighbors may be a source of family support.
- Because of the relatives' influence, if you exclude them, your efforts may be sabotaged, especially when working with families of different cultures.

Second, determine where the interview(s) will take place. You must decide whether to see parents or caregivers in their own homes or at your office. When investigating allegations of abuse or neglect, the immediate need to see the child might determine the location of the interview. Sometimes, for school-aged children, the school is the best and safest location. But the home should also be considered as a location for the interview, and in fact for younger children the home may be the only option. In addition, a home visit may be necessary to look at the condition of the home. In order to adequately develop a safety plan, the home will need to be assessed to ensure that any threats to child safety—for example, no heat, no hot water, exposed wiring—are repaired. Some of these problems may be identified in a risk assessment and will become objectives on a service plan to be completed over the next few months. The problems that pose an immediate threat to children must be addressed at the time of the safety assessment or another way to ensure safety must be found in order for the child to remain in the home. In some localities, parents or caregivers have the right to refuse access to their home. In those cases, you will need to involve law enforcement if seeing the home's condition is essential to the investigation.

Questions to consider include:

- Are the parents or caregivers likely to be more responsive in one location?
- Will there be distractions in the home that detract from your control over the interview? Would a neutral setting help you with this control? For example, is the parent or caregiver focused on the interview, or are they watching television or listening to music? Do activities around the parent or caregiver prevent him or her from focusing on the interview? For example, conducting an interview with a parent of three young children can be challenging. Prior to the interview, the worker and parent should brainstorm about how to ensure that the children are supervised during their conversation.
- Do the parents or caregivers have transportation to get to the office?
- Are there important scheduling considerations that make your office the best location for the interview when all of the benefits are weighed against the costs?
- Is your personal safety an issue? If family violence and/or substance abuse have been alleged, it may be necessary to have a law enforcement officer accompany you on the home visit.

Third, determine the time and duration of the interview. Time spent at the interview should be determined by your purposes. Does one parent or caregiver work during one part of the day? What are the attention spans of the children and parents or caregivers?

Finally, determine what content you will cover during the interview. Prior to the interview, think of the information you need to obtain and what questions you should ask to gather that information. You will decide what topics will be discussed, and the sequence in which topics will be covered is your prerogative. You are also responsible for deciding the focus within each topic to avoid parent or caregiver confusion.

■ Interviewing Adults

All content, activity, and feelings that present themselves during the face-to-face encounter that you have with the parent or caregiver are relevant in the interviewing process. It is important that you have a repertoire of approaches to use as you prepare to interview since your approach may vary, depending on each situation. The approaches you use in interviewing adults are different from those used with children. Considerations for interviewing children are discussed later.

☐ Conducting the Interview

The steps in the interview process with an adult are as follows.

1. Conduct introductions. In beginning of the interview, you should explain who you are, where you work, and why you are there and be specific and direct as to your purpose.

2. Determine the parent or caregiver's understanding of the purpose of the interview. Ask for his or her questions or concerns.

3. Build rapport. See the section later in this chapter for rapport-building techniques.

4. Use interviewing techniques to elicit the needed information. Classify and analyze the observed facts and the statements made by the parents or caregivers and ask yourself what conclusions can be drawn as a result. Remember that you are assessing the parent or caregiver and the situation as you follow this process in order to develop an understanding "on the spot."

5. Conclude the interview. Summarize the key points, decisions, and information that have been discussed. Ask the parent or caregiver for questions and respond honestly and directly. If appropriate, you should impart a feeling of accomplishment. Discuss future actions or next steps that will take place in the near future.

Improving the quality of the interview. You should recognize strengths, so as to highlight and emphasize the positive aspects of the family. When you do so, it allows the family to believe that change is possible and motivates them to make necessary changes to reduce the risk of future maltreatment. In addition, you should be sensitive to the parent or caregiver's feelings and pace your interview questions accordingly.

Avoid socializing. Because you want to be "nice," you may tend to make "small talk." This technique may be very useful at the opening of an interview. For example, you might ask the parent or caregiver how he feels or say that he looks well, that his garden is beautiful, or that the weather is lousy. However, you should not use this technique at the initial interview because it creates confusion and anxiety, since you have said you are from CPS and the parent or caregiver may wonder about your real agenda.

In general, you should follow a balanced approach, concentrating on both strengths and challenges.

Phrasing questions and content. Avoid words that convey blame or positive or negative judgments. Frequently CPS interviewers use words and expressions that irritate and anger the parents or caregivers and inhibit ongoing communication, for example,

> "I am here because we have received a report that you have abused your daughter."

The word "abused" can trigger all kinds of feelings, especially hostility, and this word indicates your judgment.

You should be descriptive rather than accusatory as you approach the parent or caregiver. You should always remember that the use of accusatory words could block effective communication and defeat your purpose. For example:

Accusatory:

> "Joshua was abused."

Descriptive:

> "On the basis of the report we have received, Joshua has two large bruises on his inner right thigh and a cut on his lip."

Avoid statements reflecting false reassurance. Often, in an effort to be "nice" to parents or caregivers, you may make promises and reassure the parent or caregiver that "everything will be all right." You may do this out of habit or because you are afraid of the parent or caregiver's hostility. This is a good point to do a "self-awareness check." For example, the parent or caregiver may wonder what will happen to the abused child, and you may want to say:

> "Do not worry—nobody's going to take the child away from you."

But you may later discover that it is necessary to remove the child because you have a valid case of serious physical abuse. When the parent or caregiver comes back to you and says, "But you told me that this was not going to happen," your credibility is jeopardized, and the parent or caregiver may not trust you in the future. Thus false reassurances may become a serious barrier to meaningful, effective communication and may set up a situation where you are determined to be dishonest or untrustworthy.

Avoid the use of technical terms or expressions. Frequently workers use terms and expressions that parents or caregivers do not understand. Workers may do this because they do not recognize that parents or caregivers do not understand the meaning of such terms or perhaps because they want to impress the parents or caregivers with their own importance. For example, you might say:

> "Yes, Mrs. Jones, it is obvious that this is a psychosomatic disorder" or "I must file a CHINS petition."

If parents or caregivers are embarrassed to ask you what you mean, despite not understanding, they may nod their heads. When you leave the family's home you may believe that they understood. It is often helpful to summarize at the conclusion of an interview and check with the parents or caregivers to see if they understood.

Understanding the cultural context of interviews. When interviewing parents of a different culture, you should be aware that they may view the offer of help by protective services in a different way. Do not assume that their discomfort with services is simply resistance; be aware that it may stem from how their culture views outside help. Not only will you need to show empathy to their feelings about being involved with protective services, but also you will have to navigate through the different approaches that each culture may take toward that involvement. It may be important to consult with a community expert prior to the interview to determine the best approach.

☐ Dealing with Difficult Situations

In your contacts with families, you will need to gather information from persons who may be openly hostile, passive, silent, or denying, or who may even have referred themselves to the agency. There are a number of specific approaches you may use to deal with these situations.

Hostility. The parents or caregivers may react aggressively to the fact that a report was made. Some families may be resistive, loud and hostile, and some may even order you out of their homes. It is important that you be alert and composed so you can interact with the family in a calming manner. Do not argue with the family. If that happens, you will lose sight of your purpose and your effectiveness as an interviewer will be minimized.

While some parents or caregivers may become angry when confronted by the allegations, you cannot ensure the safety of the children in the home unless you explore all of the issues that have been raised. For example:

> "You better get out of my home or I'll throw you out. You think you are better than me because you are white and you have a job. You don't know anything about raising kids or what my life is like."
>
> "You're really angry that I'm here."
>
> "That's what I said. Now get out."
>
> "Mrs. Thomas, we need to talk. I know you love Stacy, but she came to school with a black eye and I need to find out what happened."

"I don't want to talk about it."

"Can you at least tell me what happened between you and Stacy that made you so angry with her?"

"Well, yes, but then you have to leave."

A parent or caregiver's expression of hostility is common, especially at the initial contact. Hostility as a rule will not fade away because you ignore it. Unless you deal with it, your communication with the parent or caregiver will not be effective. You should handle hostility directly. For example, you could say to the parent or caregiver:

"I see that you are very angry, Mrs. Jones, and I can understand it. Why don't we sit down and talk about it?"

Allow the parent or caregiver to ventilate feelings and do not allow yourself to become defensive, argumentative, or angry.

You should be objective and demonstrate by your body language and speech that you are impartial, openminded, nonjudgmental, and willing to listen but also confident, determined, and not easily manipulated. Your questions and statements should reflect recognition and acceptance.

Confronting the parent or caregiver with his or her feelings is not always helpful and may not be interpreted by the parent or caregiver as accepting of those feelings. Deal with objective facts, not with how the parent or caregiver feels about them.

Once the parent or caregiver's level of anxiety is reduced, it is likely that hostility will also be reduced, and the parent or caregiver will be able to concentrate on what you say.

Passivity. Some families may show their passive resistance to your presence by appearing withdrawn or noncommunicative, directing their attention elsewhere. Some families may appear to be compliant by their attitude, but their seemingly compliant behavior may be more indicative of their own cultural values than a desire to comply with an investigation or other services. For example:

Mrs. Rosa Hernandez is the mother of two children who is being investigated for allegedly abusing her 5-year-old son. When the worker, Ms. Norris, arrives, Ms. Hernandez offers her something to drink. Ms. Hernandez is very respectful toward Ms. Norris and agrees to bring Ms. Norris all the information she needs about her children's health care to complete the investigation. However, Ms. Hernandez fails to give Ms. Norris the information. When Ms. Norris calls to remind her, she is respectful but never provides the information. Ms. Norris is confused by Ms. Hernandez's friendly and compliant attitude and her subsequent failure to give her the information.

You can deal with the passive or silent parent or caregiver by using specific approaches.

Be supportive. For example:

"I know how difficult it is to talk about personal and private family matters."

Let the parent or caregiver know directly or indirectly that you are knowledgeable about family problems and that you know how to be understanding and helpful.

Demonstrate your understanding by verbalizing your impressions of the home, children, parents or caregivers, and family interactions. For example, you might say:

> "It must be very tiring to have four small children to care for all the time—do you ever get a break?" Or: "I notice your child is very active and doesn't mind you very well. It must be very hard to be patient all the time." Or: "It must be hard to be getting up at night because of a sick child, and then have to get up in the morning and go to work or take care of the other children all day."

Try to lead the parent or caregiver tactfully by asking or talking about matters that are not directly threatening.

Don't suggest or imply that you can offer a cure-all, and do not deal with long-range objectives and goals. Keep suggestions or service offers oriented toward achievable goals that are practical and concrete. Silent and passive parents or caregivers may frequently feel that hope and optimism are only applicable to others.

Denial. Certain approaches are recommended for use with parents or caregivers who deny:

Respect the parent or caregiver's need to deny or "save face."

Let parents or caregivers know that you do not need to make judgments about whether they are good or bad. You are not there to criticize or blame, and you can accept them as people while not accepting their behavior.

Be extremely cautious in confronting the parent or caregiver with his or her denial or with lies or contradictory statements.

Instead, ask the parent or caregiver to repeat or restate what was said. This approach gives the person an opportunity to change an answer or explanation without being accused of lying.

Leave the door open for the parent or caregiver to come to you at a later date to clarify, ask for help, change his or her story; that is, be available.

Depression. Depression tends to isolate people, so attempt to reach out and show empathy to a person dealing with depression. Approach depressed parents or caregivers with questions and statements that reflect a supportive understanding. For example:

> "I can see, Mrs. Ling, how hard it is to raise three children." Or: "I do realize how difficult it is for you to talk about this, but we should discuss it."

Frame questions incrementally to help the parent or caregiver think through the areas you are exploring or needing information about. Persons dealing with depression may need additional help in solving problems and thinking through situations.

Anxiety. If the parent or caregiver is anxious, your questions and statements should convey reassurance. For example:

> "I want you to know that you are not the only parent with this kind of problem. But if we work together I hope we can find a solution."

Demonstrate empathy:

> "I sense that you feel real worried about this. What is it that you are worried about?"

Moderate your voice and affect so that you have a calming demeanor.

Sometimes anxiety has a biochemical basis, so you may want to explore in the interview whether the person has been assessed and is in treatment (either talk therapy or medication).

■ Interviewing Techniques

Techniques are specific methods that you, as an interviewer, may use to accomplish your purposes. These techniques may be used to stimulate discussion, clarify feelings and thinking, get information, help point up an error, or shift the focus of the interview to an important area. Interviewing techniques also promote parents or caregivers' participation in the CPS process.

The techniques you use will depend on the purpose of your interview and the type of parent or caregiver with whom you are dealing. Match the techniques to the situation; otherwise, a technique may be ineffective even if it is used correctly. For example, if your purpose at the initial contact with a parent or caregiver is to facilitate communication, the use of confrontation as a technique will not achieve the purpose. On the other hand, confrontation may be effective later to help direct the interview with parents or caregivers.

In addition, you should remember that the fact that you apply interviewing techniques correctly will not ensure that parents or caregivers will necessarily respond positively to you. However, you will have a better chance of breaking through defenses if you are prepared to use the following specific techniques than if you are unprepared and immobilized by the parent or caregiver's reactions or lack of reactions.

☐ Directive Interviewing Techniques

These techniques help you to have more control over the interview.

Questioning is the primary interviewing technique.

Open-ended questions are for the purpose of stimulating the parent or caregiver to talk. An example of an open-ended question is:

> "Could you tell me what happened?" Or "Could you describe for me how Joshua was injured?"

The parent or caregiver will most likely expand on answers and give you the opportunity to probe into the subject under discussion. This technique is useful with all parents or caregivers and especially with those who are hesitant to talk.

Closed questions restrict the parent or caregiver's response but may be useful in certain situations. For example, the answers to a question such as

> "Do you take him to the doctor?" will most likely be an affirmative "Yes" or a negative "No, I did not."

These questions do not stimulate further discussion yet may be necessary to obtain specific information.

You should try to use probing questions when a problem is being explored by continual examination at progressively deeper levels. For example, if Mrs. Pacheco tells you the story of Isaias's abuse and you cannot make any logical connections between the circumstances that she says precipitated the abuse, then you should ask probing questions until the whole matter becomes clear to you. For example:

> "A while ago you mentioned that Mr. Pacheco became upset because Isaias was not at the dinner table. What did he say?"

Clarification can be *immediate* or *retrospective*. You use immediate clarification in order to ask for information on the subject under discussion. For example:

> "You just said that you hurt Isaias with the broomstick. Tell me, what did you do when you saw Isaias bleeding?"

You use retrospective clarification in order to go back to a statement made earlier by the parent or caregiver and ask for additional information. For example:

> "At the beginning of our discussion you said that your boyfriend watched you spanking Steven. Did you say he tried to stop you?"

You should avoid asking leading questions when you already know the answer. These questions are problematic, particularly in court and with child victims of sexual abuse.

"Advice-giving" means letting the parent or caregiver know your opinions. Giving advice that is not asked for may be dangerous if the parent or caregiver decides to come back later and tell you that you gave bad advice. However, if a parent or caregiver is anxious, confused, and possibly disorganized and asks for advice, you should explore solutions with the family that best fit the family's situation.

Use recapitulation in order to go over topics you have discussed with the parent or caregiver and to summarize issues. Recapitulation is an important device for the following reasons:

- It is an indication that you have been listening and that you know what has been going on.
- You give the parent or caregiver the opportunity to see how you perceive the situation.
- Certain things expressed during the interview may need to be corrected.

You may use recapitulation during the interview and at the end of the interview. For example, you may say:

> "Before I leave, let's go over some of the things we talked about." Or, during the interview you may say, "Can we stop for a second and go over some of the things we have talked about up to this point? Tell me if you have any questions."

Confrontation occurs when you point out contradictions between what the parent or caregiver says and what he or she does. Confrontation should be done in a respectful way or your effectiveness as an interviewer and worker will be diminished. For example:

> "Mr. Wilson, I've heard your explanation of how your stepson broke his leg, but the medical report says that the injury could not have occurred in the way you describe. I need to know what happened so that I can assess his safety. I can't make a good assessment without knowing what happened. What really happened to Jamir?"

You use redirection to help parents or caregivers organize their thinking or to maintain focus. This can help some parents or caregivers keep from becoming overwhelmed by details. You can gently confront attempts to avoid sensitive issues by reminding the parent or caregiver why you are meeting. Redirection is also used to refocus the interview, for example, if the parent is talking incessantly about unrelated matters. If the parent's attention becomes directed at an issue that is not relevant to the purpose of the interview, you might say:

> "Mrs. Ling, hearing about your church is interesting, but we need to discuss the injury to your son and how we can ensure his safety." Or: "Mrs. Ling, I agree that everything costs more nowadays, but could we discuss how you are going to get clothes for Milo?"

Repetition may be used to make sure that the parent or caregiver grasps a situation intellectually. Some parents or caregivers may fail to understand because their emotions and anxiety levels are high. Others may have low levels of intellectual functioning that make repetition necessary.

Funneling is a technique that helps to focus the interview. The interviewer starts with broader, open-ended, and less threatening questions and moves to focused and more sensitive ones. It is best to start with questions in which you can express some empathy. For example:

> "You really seem frustrated with Sara's behavior. Tell me about what has been going on at home." Or: "I can see how angry you are that Nathan won't listen and talks back to you. What's been going on with Nathan during the summer?"

Generally, don't ask yes-no questions. Use some statement inquiries rather than just questions. Examples of statement inquiries are:

> "Tell me about your child."

> "I'm interested in getting your point of view about what has happened with Rueben over the past month."

Statement inquiries tend to make the interview an exchange of information rather than an "interrogation," as may occur with the use of too many questions. In addition, a good broad question would be "What would you like to talk about first?"

Sometimes, when interviewers try to use the funneling technique, people will invert the funnel on the interviewer, because of the nature of the issues being addressed. It is common for most parents or caregivers to want to deal with their feelings about the incident or about the fact that they are now involved with CPS.

You will have to deal with the parent or caregiver's feelings and concerns before you can reinvert the funnel back to the reason you are there. For example:

"Why are you here—I haven't done anything!"

"You sound angry."

"Yes, I am angry. All you people do is accuse me of hurting my kids."

"I can see where that can make you feel angry, but I really want to help you. Tell me about what has been happening with your children since school ended."

Funneling should be used in tandem with other interviewing techniques.

Partialization is helping families or caregivers deal with one problem at a time or breaking down complex problems into digestible issues. Many families are confused or overwhelmed by their circumstances. Partialization allows you to assist the family in setting priorities and dividing the problem into manageable portions.

Reframing is helping the family change their frame of reference in such a way that the problem can be approached in a positive way. It refers to the process of assisting the family in identifying a different framework for understanding and responding to a problem. For example, in a case of sexual abuse where the mother does not know whether to believe her daughter who has disclosed that her father has touched her inappropriately, rather than insist that the mother believe the child, you might say:

"It must be a lot to think about right now or to know what happened. Let's think of a way that we can protect every one. Let's come up with a plan to protect your daughter from future abuse or your husband from future allegations." This approach will result in a safety plan rather than a power struggle over whether the abuse did or did not occur.

Several other techniques are also likely to be useful.

- You may *give directions* to tell the parent or caregiver what to do.
- Use *focusing* to get the parent or caregiver to concentrate attention on a topic. This technique moves the content of the interview to the necessary topic. For example,

    "Let's talk about the discipline techniques you tried this week with Elle and Ben."

- You may use *explanation* to logically describe how you perceive a situation.
- *Universalizing* the parent or caregiver's situation may help reduce stigmatization and offer hope. For example,

    "At first, most parents I work with feel angry when they are reported for neglect or abuse. However, as we start to work together they realize I am just trying to get a better understanding of the family and that I can be helpful."

- *Use of self* can help build rapport and reduce the power dynamics that often lead to resistance. It can be used to reduce the emotional distance between you and the parent or caregiver, to increase his or her sense of familiarity with you, and to increase openness in your relationship. Like all techniques, the use of self or self-disclosure must be purposeful. If the technique is used incorrectly, it can shift the focus from the parent or caregiver to the worker or result in the parent or caregiver losing confidence in the worker.

☐   Nondirective Listening Techniques

These techniques help to keep parents or caregivers talking. They include:

- *Attending* to the parent or caregiver refers primarily to eye contact and body language but also includes following the parent or caregiver verbally. You should be sensitive to groups from some cultures that consider eye contact intrusive. Interpreting downcast eyes as evasive or deceitful is inappropriate for these populations.

- Various *verbal cues* encourage the parent or caregiver to continue speaking, for example, "right," "sure," "yes."

- *Reflection* refers to paraphrasing what the parent or caregiver has said (content) or identifying and verbalizing the parent or caregiver's feelings.

- Summarizing a parent or caregiver's concerns, both the content and the feelings, is a way of demonstrating that you as the interviewer have been listening.

- *Transition* or *bridging statements* can move the parent or caregiver smoothly from discussing one subject to another subject and are helpful when you, as an interviewer, realize that the discussion of a particular subject is useless or unproductive for achieving the purpose of the interview. An example:

  > "You have given me information regarding why you were reported to the agency, but now it would be helpful to explore this report in more detail. Tell me about that night when the kids were left alone in the apartment."

  You should use transitions more frequently at the initial contact when you are attempting to understand the various aspects of a particular situation and answer many questions in a short time and need to decide whether a referral is valid.

  You should not overuse transitions in later interviews. If you do, the parent or caregiver may become confused by what may appear to be jumping from subject to subject.

- *Silence* can also help to facilitate an interview. Parent or caregiver responses vary. Some parents or caregivers constantly talk, while others speak very little or may stare at you and say nothing. Silence can be an indication of fear and anxiety or a defense.

  Whatever the reason for silence, you should not try to break the silence prematurely. Give the parent or caregiver time to think and put his or her thoughts together. This may be especially true of those for whom English is not their first language. Even if proficient in English, in a stressful situation, individuals may retreat to thinking in an original language.

  If silence continues for too long, you should try to impress on the parent or caregiver your intent to help and try to show concern. These supportive techniques generally encourage silent parents or caregivers to respond. In such cases you should also consider the possibility of having a short interview, explaining that you will be back the next day.

☐ Telephone Interviewing

Not all interviews are conducted face to face; many are held via the telephone. Using the telephone as an effective means of communication is an essential skill that workers must develop in order to gain information and build their relationships with both parents or caregivers and others involved in their cases. Valuable information can be shared at any time. Considerable skill is required to maximize the information obtained and to properly present the mission of the agency and thereby effectively intervene for the benefit of the children and family.

The telephone is constantly used during the life of a case, and the skills required to communicate over the telephone are critical to achieving case goals. Each contact with a family should be seen as a continuation of the relationship-building process revolving around the purpose for the intervention. Information can be conveyed and received via telephone that can greatly facilitate the important work needed on a case. Because of the speed and immediacy of the telephone, you can often check in on how a safety plan is going or allow parents or children to update you as to the success of a plan or any barriers interfering with it. The telephone should not be used as a substitute for a face-to-face contact but as another resource for communication.

Poor telephone skills can heighten confusion parents may feel or increase resistance due to misunderstandings. Because the communication is only verbal, the important nuances that observing nonverbal behaviors affords you are missing and can confuse the communication process.

Despite the shortcomings of telephone interviews in providing visual information, some parents or caregivers may choose to reveal important information over the telephone that may have been more difficult to discuss in person at home. You must be prepared for the possibility of such events by remembering that the tone of your voice can make this easier for the caller.

For example, the nonoffending mother in a sexual abuse investigation may call the worker for support and reassurances at any time after the child's initial disclosure. This crisis counseling via telephone may provide a critical support to enable the mother to continue to protect, believe, and support her child in the face of the enormous pressures she faces that are typical with many child sexual abuse disclosures.

Another frequent occurrence is telephone calls from angry adults who are listed as alleged perpetrators during the initial phase of an investigation. You must be prepared for such a situation by realizing it is an important opportunity to gain valuable insight into the individuals' thinking and verbal expression and requires heightened alertness to using the best interviewing techniques at hand.

Any telephone contact with a family can potentially offer information that alters safety assessments currently in place, for example, when a father who is the perpetrator of sexual abuse and is court-ordered out of the home answers the home telephone, or a young child answers the telephone and indicates that she is alone. Both cases require immediate action.

The knowledgeable worker must be prepared for possible changes in family circumstances at any time. Handling apparent increased risk via telephone interviewing requires careful deliberation, as the connection can be broken at any time by the other person. It is critical that any information over the telephone that suggests that the safety of the children may be in question should result in an immediate visit with the child to accurately assess whether the child should remain in the home or whether the plan needs to be changed in order to ensure safety.

A great deal of contact with other service professionals occurs over the telephone. Information-gathering and negotiating over issues affecting children and families often takes place over the phone between workers and other key partners.

☐ Guidelines for Telephone Interviewing

You should always be polite and courteous in all your phone contacts. You are representing the agency and have a very important mission. Be prepared to explain your specific role and your agency function, not only to parents or caregivers but also to collateral individuals (teachers, medical personnel, etc.).

Be sensitive to individual personal and cultural issues as in any interview in someone's home. Ask permission to continue when an individual sounds emotionally distraught.

Consider the timing of your call. Gain the approval of the family to call them at home. Be considerate and refrain from calling before 10:00 a.m. and after 6:00 p.m. unless there is an emergency. Asking parents "When is the best time to call?" is always a good idea. Likewise, let everyone in the family know how to get in touch with you, best times, and so on, as well as emergency or after-hours telephones that your agency has available. Do not give out your home number to parents or caregivers.

Try not to call parents or caregivers at their place of employment unless prior approval is obtained from them. There are times when it may be necessary to call them at work to share important information regarding the child. However, at all times it is important to respect their privacy and confidentiality. When you call, explain to the person answering the telephone that you would like to speak to (name of the person) regarding his or her child. Do not identify yourself as a CPS worker. When the parent answers the telephone, briefly share the information or ask if he or she is in a position to discuss the matter now or would rather meet you during his or her lunch hour, after work, or at another time.

Don't leave messages on answering machines unless you have that individual's knowledge and approval ensuring privacy and security. You could be breaching confidentiality or privacy inadvertently and cause unforeseen difficulties if others also hear the message.

Return all calls to you within a day if possible. Assume that each message could potentially be important to the safety of a child.

Without visual cues to go by, you should assume that emotionally laden issues may be raised by the caller or by the worker in gathering information. Don't permit the caller to hear emotional responses from you that indicate anger or defensiveness. Remain calm and gather the facts. Assume that more information may be available if you raise the correct question in the most amenable manner. (All call-takers, whether they are agency hotline or intake staff or ongoing workers, should be trained on the agency's risk and safety assessment factors to professionally elicit the maximum information available from the source. New information impacting on the safety of a child or family can come from a variety of sources at any time.)

Confrontation over the telephone is the least desirable way to engage a parent or caregiver, yet in some circumstances it may be unavoidable. For example:

> A beleaguered parent desperately telephones the worker at 5:00 p.m. asking for help, as the perpetrating parent is back in the home. The worker needs to calm the one parent while carefully and clearly engaging the other parent in full cooperation.

> "Mrs. Douglas, you sound really frightened."

> "I am. You know he will hurt me or the kids if he stays here. What should I do?"

> "We talked about this with your husband. He agreed to stay with his mother until we have services in place. Can I talk to him?"

Waiting for a home visit may not be possible. Explaining options to each parent and further clarifying the agency's necessary responses to ensure the safety of the child may take considerable time.

> "Mr. Douglas, when we spoke yesterday you said that you were going to stay with your mother until everyone agreed that the children would be safe if you returned."

> "This is my home, and I don't like staying at my mother's house."

> "You will need to find another place to stay. I made an appointment with a counselor for you and you agreed to see the counselor and not return home until she met with you and your wife and me and we worked out a plan for your return. I'm asking you to see if you can stay with your mother for a while longer. I'll come out tomorrow and we can look at what other options you have."

> "Okay, I'll go back to my mother's house, but we need to talk about this tomorrow."

> The worker will need to follow up by telephone with Mrs. Douglas to verify that her husband has complied with the plan.

You should document all telephone interviews in detail, per your agency policy, realizing that information obtained over the telephone may be just as valuable as home visits. For example:

> Telephone calls at noon that appear to awaken a mother may warrant further exploration with the parent or caregiver. She may be ill, depressed, using drugs or alcohol, or just exhausted from raising her children. Her functioning is your concern and deserves your full attention to help.

Record all attempted telephone contacts with entries as to date, time, and number called, just as you would with attempted home visits that met no response at the door.

Phone interviews with apparently intoxicated persons, in which you observe slurred speech and altered mood, may also provide vital information about the safety of the children at home. The person should be fully engaged, if possible, so that an assessment for safety can be initiated over the telephone and followed with a home visit unless other reliable adults are available.

■ Interviewing beyond Intake and Investigation

□ Interviewing during the Service Provision Stage

Interviewing is most commonly associated with the intake and investigation stage of a case, but the reality is that interviewing should occur throughout the case. In cases where you are the ongoing worker, in the interview you will want to focus on the tasks at hand or refer the family to the service plan and the issues that you and they are working on.

Once a case is accepted for services, whether children remain at home or are placed in out-of-home care, it is the responsibility of the worker to continually assess the child's situation in terms of permanency, safety, and well-being. In counties where staff provide direct services, staff will take on the role of counselors and/or teachers of different skills. In counties where services are subcontracted, the provider worker will do the direct service provision and the county worker will monitor the service plan outcomes.

The safety plan that is put in place during the investigation process must be revisited at each contact. Interviews with all family members and their support network must occur in order to assess the level of compliance with the plan. If the plan is not working to ensure the child's *safety*, it must be revised, or the child may need to be placed in another setting until safety can be ensured. For example:

> At school a worker met with a 7-year-old girl and got important information.
>
> "Do you remember when we talked about your grandmother meeting your school bus and coming home with you?"
>
> "Yes, she does it most days, but sometimes she is late or I just go home by myself."
>
> After seeing the child at school, the CPS worker had the following conversation with the grandmother:
>
> "Mrs. Chang, you and your daughter agreed that if you couldn't pick your granddaughter up that you would call her and she would come home from work early."
>
> "I know, but I don't want her to lose her job. She really needs the money."
>
> "That's true, but we all agreed that your granddaughter's safety was more important. Is there any other family member who can be a resource?"
>
> "My son is not working since he left college. Maybe he can help."
>
> "I need to talk to him. Can you call him now?"
>
> "Okay, I'll ask him to come over right away."

In order to determine progress toward achieving *permanency*, the worker must:

- Meet with the parents or caregivers and children on a regular basis.
- Ask questions to determine if the parent is following through with the case plan, as this may be an important indication of whether the family is on track.

- Ensure that the plan focuses on the issues that led to the out-of-home placement and the services required to address those issues.
- Review, and if necessary, revise the service plan to ensure that the goal of permanency can be met.

For example:

> "Mr. Gonzalez, have you contacted the pediatrician to make an appointment for Juan?"
>
> "No, I keep forgetting."
>
> "If you don't get the appointment, Juan will not be able to go to kindergarten in September. You need to follow through on your agreement."

There are many dimensions to *child well-being*, including quality of health care, economic stability, education, and family stability. Depending on the specific issues of each case, the concerns around the well-being of each child must be addressed. This can only be done by interviewing children alone to determine what is really going on in their lives. The worker who has been involved with the family on an ongoing basis must develop a trusting relationship with the parents and children to ensure that they will be willing to present an accurate picture of what is happening. Here is an example of interviewing for well-being when a child is living in an out-of-home placement:

> Mario is a 13-year-old who has been in foster care for 2 months. His worker is seeing him for a regularly scheduled meeting.
>
> "Hi, Mario. How are you doing?"
>
> "Fine."
>
> "How are you doing in your new school?"
>
> "Okay."
>
> "What are your teachers like?"
>
> "They seem pretty nice so far. They are helping me catch up."
>
> "Great. Tell me about your friends."
>
> "Yes, I have a friend in school who comes over to my house on Saturdays."
>
> "Is there anything that is a problem for you at school?"
>
> "I wish I could take a different math class, but I can't 'cause I transferred after school started."
>
> "Why would you like a different class?"
>
> "I don't understand the math they are doing. There is an easier class."
>
> "Maybe I could go to the school and talk to your counselor."
>
> "That would be great. Can you get me into a different math class?"
>
> "I'll talk to the school counselor and see what can be done."

Here is an example of interviewing for well-being when a child is living at home:

> "Yvonne, your teacher tells me that you seem much happier at school. Is that true?"

"Yes, I like to go to school now that the kids don't laugh at me."

"I remember you told me that they gave you a hard time about your clothes."

"They made fun of me cause I wore torn clothes that smelled. I hated them all and tried to beat them up. But things are better now and I actually have some friends."

"That's great, and how are things at home?"

"Things at home are pretty good. My parents don't fight like they used to and those men don't come by at night to visit with my parents."

"I saw your mom making dinner when I came in."

"Yes, she likes to cook and I've been eating so good that I'm going to have to get new clothes soon."

"That's good. You're a young girl and need to eat in order to keep growing."

☐ Case Closing

The decision to close a case is one of the most complex decisions made by a CPS worker. Your interview will focus on the conditions that initially caused the CPS involvement. For example:

"Ms. Colon, I talked to your counselor and she reports that you have been drug free for a year now. You should feel very proud of yourself."

"I am, but I still need to go to counseling every week and attend my support group."

"I agree, and your counselor will let me know if there are any problems with your recovery."

"I know. She told me she would, and I signed the release form."

The decision to close assumes that the conditions that were present when the case was opened have been corrected, at least to a point where the children are now safe.

"Mr. Jefferson, we've been working together for about 10 months now and you seem much more comfortable with your children."

"Well if you mean I don't yell at them or hit them every time they make noise or cry, then you're right."

"When I talked with your children they said that they can't remember the last time that you hit them or threatened to hit them."

"I didn't like it when you told me that my kids were afraid of me, I love them and want to be a good father."

You must gather information to support the closing decision. The same factors that were looked at in assessing risk and safety must be reviewed. A safety plan must exist that will be monitored by the family system and other available supports in the community. It is critical to base this safety plan on the strengths of the individual family members and their ability to monitor their own behavior if the plan is to succeed. Each part of the plan must be reviewed.

You should use your relationship with the children and parents to gather specific information about what is happening.

"Ms. Edwards, as we discussed I'll be closing your case. I just want to go over one more time your plan for the children when you're working late."

"Well, my sister isn't working, so she will be home when they get back from school. She will give them a snack and make sure they do their homework. If I'm really working late she will feed them dinner and stay till I get home."

"And what if she isn't available?"

"Her teenaged daughter says she will help. She needs money for clothes, and I will pay her to watch the kids."

In talking with the child alone, you must be sure that the abusive or neglectful situation has been resolved.

"Nadia, how are you getting along with your sisters?"

"Better now that I don't have to watch them or tell them what to do. We used to fight all the time because they told me I wasn't their boss."

"Well you aren't. You're their sister. Are you helping out around the house?"

"Not like before. I clean my room and Emily's with her, but Mommy cooks and cleans the rest of house."

"Your teachers tell me you're doing great and come every day."

"Yes, I go to school every day now unless I'm sick and then Mommy stays home with me."

When you are confident that no more safety issues exist, it is time to close the case.

■ Interviewing Children

There are a number of specific considerations that are important when interviewing children. You cannot interview a child who is a victim of maltreatment in the same way you would interview an adult. For example, you will need to specifically take into account children's dependency on their parents, their developmental level, and the trauma experienced as a result of the abuse and/or neglect. Many of the techniques that you use to interview adults will be applicable to the child, but these techniques will have to be modified and adjusted on the basis of the factors just noted. To effectively interview children also requires a high degree of flexibility, sensitivity, and knowledge of child growth and development. For all of these reasons, interviewing children is a challenging task. (See chapter 8.) This section will focus primarily on interviewing a child during the initial stage of a case to gather information about the child's safety and to verify or disprove the initial allegation.

□ Dynamics of Interviewing a Child Who Has Been Abused or Neglected

Children in general are used to being tested by adults (e.g., "Have you cleaned up your room?") but are seldom treated by adults as unique sources of otherwise unavailable information. In addition, children may be shy with adults they do not know;

or, in contrast, a child may put up a facade of self-confidence or pseudomaturity in an effort to hide his or her real feelings and impress on you that there is nothing wrong.

Children have an allegiance to their parents or caregivers, in spite of the fact that they may have been abused or neglected. If, as an interviewer, you start blaming the parents, this may cause the child to withdraw and become defensive. Therefore, you should convey neutrality about the parents. You should also reassure children that you understand their anxiety.

You should be prepared for all kinds of resistance from a child who has been abused or neglected. Such resistance may be manifested in the form of stubbornness, withdrawal, and even aggression. You may experience difficulties in discussing the abuse/neglect incident with the child. The child may be distrustful and uneasy; may have fears of rejection by friends and relatives; may have been threatened with additional abuse; may fear removal to a foster home; or may fear that the parent will be removed from the home or punished. In addition, the child may have actually found comfort in the abuse since it involved getting attention.

The interview experience will depend on how the interview is conducted and the child's psychosocial developmental level and cognitive abilities.

You can expect that a child's accuracy in relating a specific historical event will decline over time and that the level of accuracy in recall is directly related to the child's age, the types of questions you ask, and the importance of the event to the child (Poole & Lambe, 1998).

Because of a child's thought processes, a child may be likely to assume that the adult asking questions already knows the relevant information and is just looking to confirm it. For example, a child might assume that he or she should answer the question "What did *he* hit you with?" with a man's name, even if the child was not hit by a male (Poole & Lamb, 1998).

☐ Interviewing Children as Opposed to Interviewing to Adults

Children's perceptions and capacities differ from those of adults. Children are much more literal and concrete in their thought processes. For instance, consider this typical exchange between an adult and a child. An adult calls a home and asks, "Is your mother there?" The child says "Yes," but then there is silence. She's not going to go and get her mom until the adult says, "Please go get her and let me talk to her."

Children often mix reality and fantasy. It is important to not confuse them. All interview questions should be clearly based on reality. Therefore, avoid statements such as:

> "Pretend you were there again and tell me what happened."

Or:

> "Tell me your story."

Younger children have a limited attention span. You will need to be comfortable using a variety of ways to interview younger children. You may want to move from formal interviewing to "play" type methods, since you will not be able to gather information with younger children in the same way you do with older children or adults.

Children's time orientation is limited in terms of the meaning of the length of time or past and future. Their time orientation is better when it is geared around specific events (e.g., when you started third grade, right before the show *Arthur* came on TV). This is critical when doing an investigation and trying to get specific information.

Children have poorer linguistic skills than adults and have a limited vocabulary. They speak in shorter and simpler sentences. They are also less able to deal with abstract terms.

Children's memories are not as good as those of adults; however, the amount of information remembered does gradually increase with age.

Children are concerned about different things. For instance, they tend to think about short-term versus longer term consequences. They are not familiar with societal systems for help and punishment; they tend to think about these in terms of what they know from experience, including TV. Therefore, "help" means teachers and preachers, whereas "punishment" means police, judges, and jail.

Children of various cultures have different social norms about communicating with adults. Avoidance of eye contact and of direct expression of feelings may be construed as disrespectful in some cultures. In such situations indirect assessment such as play therapy or art therapy is more likely to yield information than a direct approach.

The pace of the interview will differ from that of one with an adult. The tempo of the interview should be slower. Questions should be less rapid or abrupt.

☐   Developing a Strategy for Interviewing Children

Depending on circumstances, the mandates of your law, and agency procedure, you will have to decide whether a child should be interviewed at school, in your office, in the hospital, in the child's home, in a child advocacy center, or in some other community location. If you are interviewing a child in the home, you must create an environment that will allow the child to feel safe enough to discuss honestly the allegations or ongoing circumstances that are safety concerns.

Minimize the amount of time spent interviewing, as a child's attention span is short. If all issues cannot be explored in one interview, make arrangements for another or several subsequent interview(s).

The choice of interviewing techniques is highly dependent on situation factors, such as the child's developmental level, the child's overall functioning, and safety and risk concerns.

Prepare yourself to be open to hearing the child's explanation of the incidents. Do not judge, qualify, or limit what you are willing to hear with such statements as: "Tell me a little bit about what happened." This statement may suggest you are uncomfortable with some part or the whole story. It may suggest you do not have time to listen or the entire story is not important.

Upon first meeting the child you should be prepared to assess his or her condition by observing nonverbal expressions and physical, emotional, and behavioral symptoms. Some children may be fearful, show little affect, or appear detached and withdrawn, while other children may be aggressive. Being aware of these behaviors as an interviewer will help you to decide how to approach a particular child in order to facilitate communication.

Make an effort to understand the differences in children on the basis of their stages of development, as these distinctions are of enormous consequence in thoroughly and accurately gathering the information you need from the child. (See chapter 8 on *child development*.) Be prepared to establish rapport with the child, just as you would with an adult. Make sure the child has an understanding of who you are and your role.

During the initial investigative interview, focus your questions not just on the allegation but also on areas of inquiry that will inform your assessment of the child's current safety and future risk of harm.

Script some questions in advance; preferably ones that are open-ended and that can serve you as a mental checklist during the interview. Review the list of question "frames" that can be quickly adapted (e.g., "You said _____. Tell me about that."). See the box for sample question frames.

Whenever possible, interview in an uncluttered environment with as few distractions as possible. When that's not possible, make an effort to create a physical space for yourself and the child; for example, clear off the desk, and move two chairs to a quieter corner of the room.

Avoid wearing formal attire or uniforms that may suggest a specific role to the child, especially if this will be a joint interview with law enforcement. Dressing more casually will help to differentiate your role from that of any accompanying law enforcement personnel.

Keep the following considerations about your behavior and demeanor in mind as you begin the interview:

- Appear businesslike yet sensitive.
- Be gentle, reassuring, and supportive.
- Avoid any indication of becoming a parent surrogate or undermining the parent or other family members, because this may create resistance. You can discuss unacceptable behavior without blaming or judging the parent. Focus on the need for help for all family members and the child's need and right to be safe.
- Do not expect children to rebuke their parents, no matter how much they have been abused or neglected.
- Recognize the difficulty of dealing with the subject for you and the child.
- Minimize the need to verbally "control" the child's behavior by focusing on what is permissible behavior. Instruct the child (during the interview) about what the child is allowed to do rather than what the child cannot do. For example, if you hold an interview with a child in the office, it is better

Sample Question Frames

Familiarity with a list of flexible question frames can help interviewers ask follow-up questions that are not leading.

Elaboration

"You said _____; tell me more about that."

"And then what happened?"

"Sometimes we remember a lot about sounds or things that people said. Tell me all the things you heard (when that happened, in that room, etc.)."

"Sometimes we remember a lot about how things looked. Tell me how everything looked (when that happened, in that room, etc.)."

Clarification

Object or action: "You said _____; tell me what that is."

Ambiguous person: "You said _____ (Grandpa, teacher, Uncle Bill, etc.). Do you have more than one _____?"

"Which _____?"

"Does your _____ have another name?" (or "What does your [mom, dad, etc.] call _____?")

Inconsistency

"You said _____, but then you said _____. I'm confused about that. Tell me again how that happened."

"You said _____, but then you said _____. Was that the same time or different times?"

Repeating Conversational Breaks

"Tell me more about that."

"And then what happened?"

Embarrassed Pause

"It's okay to say it."

"It's okay to talk about this."

Inaudible Comment

"I couldn't hear that. What did you say?"

Single or Repeated Event

"Did it happen one time or more than one time?"

If child says "Lots of times":

"Tell me about the last time something happened. I want to understand everything from the very beginning to the very end."

"Tell me about another time you remember."

Source: Poole and Lambe (1998). Copyright © 1998 by the American Psychological Association. Reprinted with permission.

for you to say: "Joshua, you can play over here with these toys while we talk," instead of "Joshua, while we talk you are not supposed to climb on the windows or play with my papers."

☐ Phrasing of Questions

You should raise clear questions and carefully select words that are within the child's vocabulary range in order to avoid misunderstandings. This means avoiding words or phrases that are either well below the child's developmental level or way too advanced. Ask only one question at a time. Avoid words or terms that are not appropriate for the child's age.

Allow for pauses and avoid interruptions (Milne & Bull, 1999). For example, to slow down the pacing of the interview, use a 10-second pause between the child's response and your next comment or question (Poole & Lamb, 1998).

Use open-ended questions that will result in narratives rather than close-ended questions that more often will lead to the child's brief one- or two-word responses. Use a variety of question types, with a hierarchy of questions that move from open-ended to direct. Once you have gone down the hierarchy of questions, try to move back up into open-ended questions. See the table for a description of the hierarchy and question types.

Use the information already provided as the basis for asking for more information. For example: "You said your mom left you alone before. Tell me more about that." Avoid the use of leading questions. Important considerations are:

- Leading questions suggest an answer. For example:

    "Daddy left you alone, didn't he?" "Mom slapped you on the face with her hand, right?"

- A more neutral question would be:

    "Tell me about Saturday night." Or "How did you get the bruise on your cheek?"

- Leading questions may affect the accuracy of the child's reply.

- Leading questions are problematic legally and may make your testimony regarding the child's out-of-court statement inadmissible.

A progression or hierarchy of questions is suggested (see the table). Open-ended questions are preferable to closed-ended questions to facilitate information gathering, especially at the initial stages of the interview. For example:

    "What did he say to you about telling other people?"

allows a broader range of responses than

    "Did he tell you not to tell?"

Move to specific or focused questions once the child has exhausted his or her free recall. For example:

    "Where did it happen?"

    "Has this happened one time or more than one time?"

Questioning Typology

Most Preferred Questions

Question Type	Description	Example
General question	Open-ended inquiry about the child's well-being or salient issues; it does not assume an event or experience.	How can I help you? How are you feeling today? Is there something I can help you with?
Invitational question	Open-ended inquiry that assumes there may be an event or experience.	Can you tell me everything you remember about going to the doctor? (Saywitz et al.) I heard something might have happened to you. Tell me about it as best you can (Boychuk).

Preferred Questions

Question Type	Description	Example
Focused question	One that focuses the child on a particular topic, place, or person but refrains from providing information about the subject (Myers, Goodman, & Saywitz).	Can you tell me about daycare? Tell me about your dad. (Are there things you like about him? Are there things you don't like about him?) Can you tell me about penises? (Who has one? What are they for? Did you ever see one? Whose did you see?)
Follow-up strategies	Strategies that encourage continued narrative.	
Facilitative cue	Interviewer gesture or utterance aimed at encouraging more narration.	Uh-huh (affirmative). Anything else? And then what happened?
Specific question	Follow-up inquiry to gather details about the child's experience.	Do you remember where it happened? What were you wearing? Were any clothes taken off? Did anything come out of the penis? *(continued)*

Questioning Typology *(continued)*

Less Preferred Questions

Multiple choice question	Presents the child with a number of alternative responses from which to choose.	Did he do it one time, two times, or lots of times?
		Did it happen in the daytime or night or both?
Externally derived question	Relies on information not disclosed in the child interview.	Do you remember anything about a camera?
		Did John say anything about telling or not telling?
Direct question	A direct inquiry into whether a person committed a specific act.	Did John hurt your peepee?
		Was your father the one who poked your butt?
Repeated questioning	Asking the same question two or more times.	Did anything happen to your pecker?
		Do you remember if anything happened to your pecker?

Least Preferred Questions

Presumptive question	A question that takes for granted facts.	
Leading question	A statement the child is asked to affirm.	Isn't it true that your brother put his penis in your mouth?
Misleading question	A question that assumes a fact that is not true and that the child is explicitly or implicitly asked to confirm.	What color scarf was the nurse wearing? (when she wasn't wearing one)
		Show me where the doctor touched you. (when he didn't touch)
Coercion	Use of inappropriate inducements to get cooperation or information.	If you tell me what your father did, we can go for ice cream.
		Don't tell my boss that I was playing. (And gives the child a piece of candy.)

From *Maltreatment in Early Childhood: Tools for Research-Based Intervention,* by K. C. Faller, 1999, Binghamton, NY: Hawthorne Maltreatment and Trauma Press. Reprinted with permission from Haworth Press.

Avoid yes-no questions, as children by nature try to please adults and may say yes to please an adult rather than provide an accurate response.

☐ Using an Interview Protocol

Several organizations have developed research-based, validated interview protocols to improve the quality of interviews with children about abuse or neglect. A protocol is simply a structured format for the interview and includes both the different stages and the kinds of questions to ask children. These protocols are intended to provide operational guidelines in order to gather more complete and accurate information that will help determine the veracity of an allegation as well as more thoroughly assess the child's safety and risk (Orbach, Hershkowitz, Lamb, Sternberg, Esplin, & Horowitz, 2000). Most protocols were originally developed to address sexual abuse allegations. Many of the components of the protocol presented below suggest an allegation of sexual abuse, but they can and should be applied in cases of allegations of all types of maltreatment.

Characteristics common to various interview protocols (Poole & Lambe, 1998) are as follows:

- The initial stage explains the nature of the interaction and the goals of the interview.
- You should build rapport with the child before launching into the substantive portion of the interview.
- You should establish some ground rules with the child, such as the importance of telling the truth, and the child's right to ask for clarification, to say "I don't know," and to correct any misinformation. Even young children are less likely to answer questions that might be misleading if you begin with a discussion of the ground rules.
- Questions should progress from open-ended to specific and avoid reference to details of the allegations until the child volunteers them.
- You should try to clarify the child's comments and elicit legally relevant information about actions and persons.

A Sample Interview Protocol

The following protocol combines recommendations from several formal protocols. Its use should be adapted to fit the situation, including the stated allegation, the child's developmental level, and safety and risk concerns. Depending on agency policy, structured interviews may be conducted jointly with law enforcement, a child advocacy center, or some other agency, and the person who takes the lead role during the interview may also vary. Check with your agency for your local policy and protocol.

The introduction phase:

1. Allow plenty of time for introductions, to help the child feel comfortable with the room, you, and the interview process.

2. Give the child your name and ask the child for his or her name. Respect what he or she prefers to be called and explain your own preferences for what you should be called. Be sure to respect the child's family and cultural norms. For example:

> "My name is Terry Jones. In your family what do kids call grownups? First names? Mr. or Mrs.?"

3. Explain the nature of your job. You should tell the child that your job is to help children who might not be safe and, if not, figure out how to make sure the child is safe. For example:

> "My job is to find out if children are not feeling safe. If they're not, I help find ways to protect them."

Use an example with a pet or some other special object to help to explain safety to the child. For example:

> "Have you ever had to make sure your dog was safe? Like maybe you make sure the dog is on a leash when you go for a walk so he doesn't run into the street and get hit by a car."

4. Ask the child about his or her perceptions about today's interview. Use an open-ended question such as:

> "What have you been told about seeing me today?" Or "Tell me what you know about what we'll be doing here today."

5. State the purpose for your presence and the interview. For instance:

> "Remember how I said earlier my job is to find out if children feel like they're not safe? Someone asked me to talk to you because they were worried that you might not be safe. I'd like to get to know you better."

6. Build rapport with the child before discussing the allegation. Without such a foundation, children may not feel comfortable disclosing abuse or neglect. You should use open-ended questions to engage the child. For example:

> "Tell me about school."

> Or "Tell me about your last field trip?"

Do not forget that this child's trust in an adult may have been shaken because of what may have happened, and the development of a working relationship with him or her may be a slow process. It often helps to explore the child's interests, hobbies, pets, or school.

7. Explain to the child that you have worked with many children who have been hurt and afraid, but you have been able to help them work out problems.

8. Ask the child for the names and relationships of everyone who lives in his or her household. You should establish all household members and clarify everyone's name and relationship. One technique to do this is by asking for any other names that adults call Daddy, Mommy, Grandpa, and so on.

9. Discuss the importance of telling the truth in a way that is developmentally appropriate for the child's level. You should explain that your job is to find

out what, if anything, has happened, and the child's job is to answer the interviewer's questions truthfully.

10. Engage the child in a developmentally appropriate discussion of *truth* and *lie*. Be sensitive to the child's anxiety during the discussion, and ask the child for multiple examples of both *truth* and *lie* to ensure understanding. Be sure to ask the child about the consequences for not telling the truth in his or her home.

11. Set the ground rules for the interview. Explain to the child that he or she should say "I don't know" if the answer to a question is not known, or even if he or she thinks it is so but is not quite sure. Explain to the child that he or she should not guess. For example:

> "In school, when the teacher calls on someone and he says 'I don't know,' the teacher may ask him to guess. If I ask you a question and you don't know the answer, please don't guess. Instead, say 'I don't know,' and that is the right answer."

12. Make a mutual agreement to tell the truth with the child. For example:

> "I agree to tell you the truth today and I need you to agree to tell the truth as well. Okay?"

The target event discussion:

1. Transition to the target event using a statement such as:

> "Someone had a worry that you weren't safe. Tell me about that."

Or if the target event was brought up or discussed during the initial portion of the interview, use a statement such as:

> "Remember when you said your mom went out Saturday night and left you at home with your baby sister? I want to talk with you more about that now."

2. Avoid mentioning a particular individual or action during this phase of the interview and avoid words such as *hurt, bad,* or *abuse* or other terms that project adult judgments onto the situation or imply harm. If the child does not respond to the initial open-ended prompt, you may need to try progressively more directive questions or statements (Poole & Lamb, 1998).

3. Ask the child open-ended questions that allow him or her to provide free recall and narrative about the target event in his or her own words. Information volunteered in response to open-ended questions is more accurate than information gathered with specific questions. Responses to open-ended questions are also longer and richer than responses to more specific questions (Poole & Lambe, 1998). For instance:

> "Tell me what happened when you were in the bedroom."

> "Tell me how you got that black eye."

Gather what factual information you can with open-ended questions and then ask for the specifics of the target event. Then proceed with emotional considerations, such as:

"How do you feel?"

"What do you hope will happen next?"

4. Determine exactly what happened, including what was done to the child and what the child was made to do to the perpetrator (if sexual abuse is alleged). Ask the child about it in such a way as to help him or her visualize the incident, much like describing the events in a movie.

5. Establish whether the child experienced a single event or multiple events. You could ask directly or follow the child's lead. For example, if the child says, "Sometimes he does," or "Sometimes he doesn't," you could say, "You said 'sometimes'—so this happened more than once?"

6. Assess the child's current safety by obtaining information on the following:

- Any other individuals who may have been present when the abuse last occurred.

- The name and relationship of the alleged perpetrator.

- Names and relationships of all possible perpetrators who might have participated with the perpetrator discussed, either in the target event (e.g., "Who else was there when this happened?") or other target events without that perpetrator (e.g., "With some kids I've talked to before, this has happened with other people too. What about you?")

- Whether the alleged perpetrator made a threat of harm. This could be done with a series of questions, beginning when a child who has divulged that the perpetrator "told me not to tell." For example, you would then ask, "How did he or she get you to keep it a secret?" and then fully explore the threat of harm. Ask questions to specifically determine whether the child is fearful of the alleged perpetrator. You should follow up on any statements made by the child that suggest he or she was threatened (or whether any threats were made to harm the child's toy, pet, or another person), in order to adequately assess the child's degree of fear toward the perpetrator.

- How the child was coerced and/or manipulated into cooperating (relevant for sexual abuse). You should find out how the child was made to participate and how the child was made to keep the incident(s) a secret. For example, "You said he made you take your clothes off. Tell me more about that."

- Whether there is another person in the house who will help protect the child in the immediate future.

7. Conclude the interview:

- Summarize the child's version of events and verify that you have understood the child and clear up any misunderstanding. Ask the child to comment on your version and amend or correct as necessary.

- Ask questions about the child's fears or concerns. For instance:

    "What are you worried about?"

    "What are you afraid would happen?"

- Ask the child if he or she has any questions. For example:

  "What questions do you have for me?"

- Assure the child that he or she has done the right thing in telling. For example:

  "You have done the right thing to talk with me today."

  "I believe you."

  "You did the right thing to tell."

- Identify the immediate, appropriate next steps for you and the child. For example:

  "You will be going back to class while I make some decisions about what to do next."

☐ **Interviewing Skills**

Effective interviewing takes lots of practice. The following tips will help to ensure the quality of the interview, keep the child talking, and minimize trauma to the child during the interview process.

- Appear relaxed and do not react with surprise to disclosures of physical or sexual abuse.

- If, during the interview, you get stuck, take some time to look at your notes and reflect on missing information and how to ask questions. For example:

  "Let me think about this for a minute. I want to be sure I ask the right questions to understand exactly what happened."

  Typically, children will be quite patient with adults as they take some time to collect their thoughts. And you can always ask the child if he or she would like to get a drink of water and use the time to formulate where you want to go next with the interview.

- Avoid confirmatory bias by maintaining an open mind throughout the interview about whether the abuse or neglect occurred and if so, by whom. Explore alternative explanations, especially with younger children, and avoid any comments or questions indicating that you already knew what had happened.

- Avoid touching the child during the interview.

- Do not ask the child to demonstrate events that require the child to remove clothing.

- Avoid asking the child questions that would require the child to guess about or analyze the abusive situation. For instance: "Why do you think he asked you to come into the room?" or "Why did your dad hit you?" or "What made your mom want to leave you alone that morning?" Or "What do you think your mom will say when she finds out?"

- Avoid asking "why" questions about the target event. Instead, start questions with "How did." For instance: "How was he able to get you to play the game" rather than "Why did you play the game?"

- Do not make any promises, as you may not be able to keep them. A promise—such as "Do not worry, you will return to your parents"—can be very risky if you are not able to keep it and may contribute to the child's increased mistrust of adults.

- Do not make comments about the feelings or actions of another, such as: "Don't worry, your dad won't be mad," as Dad might be quite angry at the child for disrupting family life, even though the child has been hurt in some manner. Such comments will weaken your credibility in the long term.

- Do not criticize the child or a parent. Criticism or judgments will alienate the child and block communication.

- Use reflective listening skills to keep the child talking and pace the interview. Reflections can focus on content, feeling, or a combination of the two.

- Use appropriate minimal encouragers, such as "Um hm," "Yes," or "I see," throughout the interview. Inappropriate encouragers include the raising of your voice ("Oooh"), showing surprise, judgmental comments, or the use of "okay").

- Always use the child's own words for objects, events, body parts, and people during the interview, and again, make sure that you are clear about what words the child uses for body parts. If a mistake is made, or you are not sure, you should immediately clarify whether your use of words reflects the child's meaning for that word and correct yourself if you've used a word mistakenly.

- Address the child's questions using responses that are honest and straightforward. For example:

  "Lots of children ask me whether the person who hurt them will be going to jail. I don't know if that will happen. You need to understand that whether or not that happens is not something that you or I get to decide. Other people will make that decision."

  "Lots of children have this worry that their moms will be mad for telling. I don't know about your mom, but many of the parents of children I talk to are angry. They are angry because of what has happened to their children. Sometimes they are upset that you told what happened, that you were able to tell me rather than them, or other reasons. My job is to help your parents understand that you have done the right thing to tell."

  The child may ask a question you are not prepared to answer at this time, such as if they are going to get to go home. For example:

  "I don't yet know the answer to that. Remember when I said that my job was to find out if you need to be protected? If you can go home and be safe, you will do that. You need to know that if that happens it will not be a surprise. You and I will talk about it before that decision gets made."

- Use active listening skills throughout the interview. Listen to the child; reflect the content of what the child has already said. In addition, use good body posture and make natural eye contact with the child. Follow the child's lead in making eye contact; this will ensure that the child's cultural norms regarding eye contact are respected. Remember that some children are auditory rather than visual in their perceptual orientation. Allow for children to look away if they are more comfortable. Do not assume that children are not telling the truth if eye contact is not sustained.

- Direct the child to continue the interview when he or she pauses or seems stuck. Use phrases such as "I know this is hard, but continue telling me about this." You may want to allow the child some silence to experience emotion. Use reflection to identify what is known and what are gaps in understanding.

- Use developmentally appropriate questions or explanations throughout the interview. A common mistake is to ask questions or explain in a manner that is way beyond the child's developmental level, resulting in confusion and anxiety for the child.

- Direct any reinforcement (when used) toward the child's effort rather than what the child says. Avoid comments such as "Good girl" that might be interpreted as selective reinforcement of specific types of answers. For example:

    > "I've asked you many really hard questions and you've answered them all with the truth."

    > "Even though you're scared about his finding out, you did the right thing by letting me know about what has been happening."

- Avoid questions that ask why the perpetrator or child behaved in a particular way (e.g., "Why didn't you tell your mother that night?"). Such questions are difficult for children to answer and may communicate a belief that the child is at least partially responsible for what happened.

- Avoid questions that start with the phrase "Can you tell me" or "Can you show me," as children can be quite concrete and they just might answer "No, I can't."

- Avoid use of the words *pretend* or *imagine* or other phrases that suggest a fantasy or play mode.

- Diffuse the situation by focusing on less stressful topics when a child becomes visibly upset and emotional until the child regains composure. Avoid extensive comments about what the child is or should be feeling. Such comments project adult expectations onto the child and may provide an excuse for the child to avoid talking.

☐ Interviewing Young Children

Points to consider when interviewing young children are as follows:

- As soon as children become verbal they can communicate about their environment and experiences they have had, although this information may be challenging to gather and understand (Poole & Lambe, 1998).

- Younger children are more susceptible to false suggestions, although they are more often resistant to such inquiries than not. Like adults, children may have difficulty distinguishing between events they thought about or heard discussed, thus making it more important to establish the child's ability to distinguish reality from fantasy and truth from falsehood. Even young children can provide accurate information, as long as adults do not try to purposely usurp their memories through repeated suggestions over a long period of time (Poole & Lambe, 1998).

- Children often resist suggestions about significant events that involve their own bodies better than they resist suggestions about other details or events.

- Young children may feel obliged or forced to answer questions affirmatively.

- When young children are asked open-ended questions (e.g., "What happened?") they generally provide limited information, but what they do provide tends to be highly accurate (Ceci, Leichtman, & Bruck, 1995).

- Specific or misleading questions are more likely to produce inaccurate responses.

- Memory may be impaired when there is a significant delay between the target event and the questioning of that event.

- Suggestibility varies as a function of a child's age, the timing of misleading information, the importance of an event to a child, and the types of questions asked.

Strategies to improve the recall of young children include the following:

- Use specific questions or cues (Milne & Bull, 1999).

- By age 4, children's understanding of *truth* and *lie* improves dramatically. Establish *truth* and *lie* by asking concrete questions (e.g., "If I said this pen was a banana would that be a truth or a lie?").

- For sexual abuse allegations, use dolls with anatomically correct body parts. When used properly, anatomical dolls can help children provide more details about the touching than approaches without the dolls (Ceci et al. 1995).

- Spend more time helping a young child feel comfortable, especially when he or she needs to describe intimate and possibly embarrassing events.

- Be sure that the child understands that you do value what he or she has to say.

- Be aware that preschool children may not stay on a topic or answer a specific question even when specifically asked, as they may be focusing on an entirely different event or topic. To address this, be clear that you are switching topics and check for the child's understanding. Even if the child begins talking about the target event, he or she may shift the focus as questioning continues.

- To avoid planting suggestions, test alternative hypotheses to explain the target event (Ceci & Huffman, 1997). For example, find out if there could be other explanations for the bruise, like falling off a bike or fighting with a sibling.

- Consider modifying your language to make it easier for children to understand. This is called adult-to-child language (ACL), and adults do it all the time when speaking to younger children. Generally ACL is simpler, and its use will promote greater understanding between you and the child. To practice ACL (Poole & Lambe, 1998):

> Speak in short and simple sentences and try to minimize use of pronouns and modifiers.

> Focus on objects currently visible and events that are currently happening or recently happened. (For instance, if the interview is occurring during the month of January, ask about Christmas, not the Fourth of July. This also helps to establish a child's ability to sequence).

> Speak more slowly and exaggerate enunciation.

☐ Interviewing Issues Specific to Sexual Abuse

It is estimated that only about 5% to 8% of sexual abuse allegations are false (Poole & Lambe, 1998). Accuracy in a child's account of an event depends on many factors, such as how long ago the event took place, the circumstances surrounding the recall, and emotional and social factors such as the child's motivation to tell the truth and to please the interviewer (Poole & Lambe, 1998). Contrary to some prevailing attitudes about children's allegations of sexual abuse, children are highly resistant to suggestion, do not typically lie, and in fact are as reliable as adult witnesses about acts perpetrated on their own bodies (Ceci et al., 1995).

General Guidelines for the Sexual Abuse Interview

There is no prescribed questioning protocol or strategy that works every time in every situation. Instead, use the strategy or protocol that works best for you *and* that situation. Whatever strategy or protocol you do use, be sure it is based on research and you can answer questions about your choice.

Use open-ended questions whenever possible, but to some extent focused or closed-ended questions may be necessary and are permissible if asked properly.

Keep in mind that the use of leading or suggestive interviewing can direct the interview to *confirm or disconfirm* abuse even when the child is naturally inclined to tell the truth. If you believe that abuse occurred or did not, the interview can lead to that outcome without careful attention to the use of good interviewing techniques.

Preparation for the Interview

(While indicated for sexual abuse, these preparations may also be helpful for more severe cases of abuse or neglect that may result in criminal prosecution.)

Determine whether and how law enforcement should be involved. Check to see if your agency has a memorandum of understanding detailing the protocol. It may be necessary to call on law enforcement assistance to gain access to the child for an interview. Children should be interviewed apart from their parent or caregiver, as the parent's or caregiver's verbal or nonverbal interference may inhibit the child's sharing of information (Faller, 1999). Determine whether you or law enforcement will ask the questions, who will observe, and what will happen at the interview's conclusion.

Explore whether a child advocacy center is available to host the interview. Child advocacy centers usually have special interview rooms with one-way mirrors and audiovisual equipment available to record the interview.

Consider recording the interview. Policies regarding audio and video recording vary significantly from agency to agency, so find out your local agency's policy. The information gathered in this interview with the child might be the only evidence available if there is a criminal trial. Recording this interview is key to being accountable. If video and/or audiotaping is done, it needs to meet the mandate of state law and agency procedure (Faller, 1999).

Determine the setting for the interview. The ideal setting for interviewing all child victims of abuse and neglect, including sexual abuse, has the following characteristics:

- A neutral and/or familiar setting so that the child does not feel pressured or intimidated.
- A room with a one-way mirror or space in back of the room for other professionals who may otherwise have to interview the child again.
- Child-sized furniture (tables and chairs, or pillows and rugs for sitting on the floor) so that you can sit at the child's level.
- Toys such as playdough and Legos and props such as anatomical drawings and dolls. The interview room should be child-friendly, with a few toys, but still be uncluttered and free from too many distractions.

Determine whether multiple interviews may be necessary to elicit information. The age of the child and his or her attention span should be considered in making the decision regarding additional interviews. Multiple interviews may increase the amount of information obtained and afford interviewers a second chance to clarify a child's accounts.

Conducting the Interview with the Child

You should interview the child alone if possible. If a trusted adult is available and necessary, be aware of the power and control he or she might have over any disclosure the child might make.

Review the protocol for interviews, which facilitates the gathering of information and evidence when sexual abuse is alleged. See the protocol presented earlier in this chapter.

The interview should be conducted at the child's developmental level and pace. (Refer to suggestions made earlier in this chapter and to chapter 8.)

Be sure to ask the child to differentiate between truth and a lie and elicit his or her agreement to tell the truth. Tell the child to reply with "I don't know" or "I can't remember" if he or she does not know an answer.

Conduct a brief developmental assessment. Establish the child's ability to distinguish same and different objects, to logically sequence events, and to differentiate between abstract and concrete terms. Determine the child's language for body parts and sexual terms.

Explore possible sexual abuse. When asking about the sexual abuse, begin with open-ended questions; for example, "Tell me about the 'fresh' game." If necessary to clarify the child's response, follow up with forced-choice questions—for example, "Were your panties on or off?" The child's development level will determine how much he or she will be able to freely recall. Using props such as anatomical dolls may increase the amount of recall. Anatomical dolls should be used judiciously, and only:

- When a child gives indications of sexual abuse.
- For the primary purpose of establishing rapport with the child.
- When the child is verbally unable to provide more specific details of the victimization.

Anatomical dolls should be used in conjunction with law enforcement to prepare for any potential shortcomings that may occur as a result of using those controversial tools. Because they are controversial, you should be aware that use of anatomically correct dolls may create difficulties in the criminal prosecution of offenders.

Gather information to answer the following questions:

- Who is the alleged perpetrator(s)? Clarify his or her relationship to the child.
- What specifically happened in the most recent incident? Determine what specific body parts on the child were involved. Determine what body parts on the perpetrator were involved.
- When did it start? When was the most recent incident?
- How many incidents were there?
- Where did it (they) occur?
- Is there any evidence (e.g., sheets, weapons, lubricant), and where is it now?
- Who else, if anyone, knows? Specifically evaluate whether or not the nonabusing parent or caregiver has been told.
- Who is able to protect, believe, and support the child? Determine if the non-abusing parent or caregiver is willing and has the capacity to protect the child.

In closing the interview, the child should be told that revealing information was the right thing to do. It is wise to explore what the child would like to see happen next. Follow up by discussing immediate next steps.

The interview process should have a reassuring effect on the child. Techniques to enhance this may include the following:

- *Universalizing* refers to attempts to bring about understanding that the child's problems are shared by others. For example, you may say: "You are feeling alone now, but it is important for you to know that I talk to lots of children who feel the same way you do right now."

- *Empathic* responding involves the ability to perceive accurately and sensitively the inner feelings of the child and communicate understanding of these feelings in language attuned to the parent or caregiver's experience of the moment (Hepworth & Larson, 1986).

Conducting Other Interviews

You should interview siblings separately; interview the nonoffending parent or caregiver alone; and interview the alleged perpetrator alone and/or with law enforcement.

☐ Ongoing Interviewing of Children

In ongoing contacts with children, you must continually reassess safety and the safety plan to understand what is happening in the home. The child's age, location, and other factors may have an impact on who is present, and interviewers need to be able to factor into their assessment the impact of interviewing children when the caregiver is present. However, there may be times when joint interviews are preferable in order to assess how the adult(s) and children interact in order to evaluate their relationship.

■ Summary of Competencies

Interviewing is one of the key competencies that you as a child protection worker must have, as it is so pervasive in all the work you do. To develop and enhance this competency as you grow professionally, the following knowledge and specific skill areas must be developed and strengthened.

Knowledge:

1. Familiarity with crises intervention techniques.

2. Understanding of communication theory and techniques.

3. Knowledge of the wide variety of cultural, ethnic, and religious values held by individuals.

4. Knowledge of how to prepare for interviews including determining who will be interviewed, where it will occur, the duration of the interview, and the content to be covered.

5. Knowledge of how to respond appropriately to specific situations such as angry, hostile, or depressed clients.

6. Knowledge of different interviewing techniques.

7. Knowledge of how to interview children and what types of questions are most effective.

8. Knowledge of interpersonal relationship theory and techniques.

Skills:

1. Ability to establish rapport and develop a working relationship with a family.
2. Ability to ask appropriate questions to guide an interview and to gather information in a neutral, supportive, nonjudgmental manner.
3. Ability to recognize a family's strengths when interviewing.
4. Ability to assess the safety and well-being of children at each contact with the family.
5. Ability to be supportive, empathetic, and understanding.
6. Ability to be culturally responsive during interviews.
7. Ability to effectively interview children using a variety of techniques.
8. Ability to use an interview protocol with children.

References

Ceci, S., & Huffman, M. (1997). How suggestible are preschool children? Cognitive and social factors. *Journal of American Academy of Child and Adolescent Psychiatry, 36*(7), 948–958.

Ceci, S., Leichtman, M., & Bruck, M. (1995). The suggestibility of children's eyewitness reports: Methodological issues. In F. Weinert & W. Schneider (Eds.), *Memory performance and competencies: Issues in growth and development.* Mahwah, NJ: Erlbaum.

Faller, K. C. (1999). *Maltreatment in early childhood: Tools for research-based intervention.* Binghamton, NY: Hawthorne Maltreatment and Trauma Press.

Hepworth, D., & Larson, J. (1986). Direct social work practice: Theory and skills. Chicago: Dorsey Press.

Milne, R., & Bull, R. (1999). *Investigative interviewing: Psychology and practice.* Chichester, England: Wiley.

Orbach, Y., Hershkowitz, I., Lamb, M., Sternberg, K., Esplin, P., & Horowitz, D. (2000). Assessing the value of structured protocols for forensic interviews of alleged child abuse victims. *Child Abuse and Neglect, 24*(6), 733–752.

Poole, D. A., & Lamb, M. E. (1998). *Investigative interviews of children: A guide for helping professionals.* Washington, DC: American Psychological Association.

6

Janine Tondrowski

Intake and Investigation: Initial Stages of the CPS Process

- The Intake Process

- The Investigation Process

- Assessing Safety

- Assessing Risk

- Final Steps in the Investigative Process

- Summary of Competencies

The CPS process begins with the referral. Your evaluation of the referral through intake sets in motion the rest of the process. It is critical for you to maintain your focus on child safety and engage the family in ensuring that safety. If you focus on collecting information that is balanced and fosters cooperation among all of the involved parties, your chances of helping the family to a successful resolution of concerns will be greatly enhanced.

For the purposes of this chapter, the term *investigation* will refer not only to the traditional CPS investigation but also to any of the differential responses that agencies may use when responding to a valid CPS referral or complaint.

Intake and investigation have been characterized traditionally as the most difficult practice areas in CPS because of an intense emotional climate and the immediacy of serious decision-making. Despite these challenges, experience in the field demonstrates that greater difficulties arise when CPS workers are not adequately prepared for the job. For the most part, effective intake and investigation result from the worker's comfort, knowledge, skill, and experience.

The *intake process* involves the identification of cases of child abuse and neglect. For purposes of this chapter it is made up of the activities that take place as a result of a referral of child maltreatment. These activities include assessing whether the referral is a valid report of child abuse or neglect, determining the agency response, and determining the urgency of that response.

The *investigation process* includes the activities that follow the intake process in order to assess the safety of the child, initiate the appropriate intervention with the family, make a decision on the substantiation of the report if an investigation is conducted, and identify and initiate services for the child and family. Some locales use the term *assessment* for this stage in the casework process, but to avoid confusion with the process of assessment, the term *investigation* will be used here. Furthermore, throughout the chapter, intake and investigation are described as two discrete functions for purposes of simplification. In actual practice, there is a significant level of overlap and variation in the activities that occur, depending on the organization of your agency.

■ The Intake Process

□ Definition

The term *intake*, as used here, refers to all of the activities necessary to receive referrals alleging child maltreatment, assess whether a referral will be accepted as a report of child abuse or neglect, and determine the agency's response and the urgency of that response.

□ Purposes of the Intake Process

Intake provides a means by which the community can report its concern for children whose safety is in question. Intake is the initial point of contact between the

CPS agency and the community and determines the perception of expertise and professionalism with which the person making the report regards the CPS agency.

The emphasis is on helping. As a CPS worker, your role is not one of law enforcement but a helper. The focus of the intake is to promote safety of the child and to identify ways the family can ensure that safety. You need to maintain your focus on the concrete ways you can help the family and leave other functions to the community partners that are involved.

The intake process should be child centered, family focused, and culturally responsive.

☐ Receiving the Referral

When you receive a referral, you have a responsibility to the community and reporter, as well as the family involved, to begin the process of determining a child's safety. Effective, skillful work at the point of intake is critical. You must be aware of not only your responsibilities to a child who may be in danger of abuse or neglect but also your responsibility to the community, especially the reporter. In addition, thorough information gathering and assessment are essential, since you must decide whether the referral is a valid report of abuse or neglect and, if it is, determine its urgency and the type of response indicated.

You, as the intake worker, have a responsibility to assist the reporting caller through the difficult job of reporting. For example, you might say:

> "I know this must be difficult for you, but you are doing the responsible thing by sharing your concerns with us."

You can help the reporter by responding to his or her referral in a thoughtful, respectful, and professional manner, keeping in mind your responsibility to the family's confidentiality rights, as well as the reporter's confidentiality rights to remain anonymous to the family. For example:

> "My supervisor and I will review the information you have provided and we will follow up with an appropriate response to your concerns."

Many states require that reporters be contacted once the investigation is completed to let them know a response has been made. How this contact is made and what the content is depends on the role of the reporter and his or her need to know the information, weighed against the confidentiality rights of the family.

Thoroughly gather and examine relevant information. You should always remember that it is better to have too much information than too little, since the more comprehensive the information provided by the reporter, the better able you are to decide to accept the referral and provide follow-up. You should encourage the reporter to provide specific information on the family situation that is prompting the reporter to contact the agency, the family composition, alleged abuse/neglect and perpetrators, children involved, and other persons or agencies having knowledge of or contact with the family. Many agencies use standardized intake forms. Much of the information outlined here is incorporated into such forms, whether used on a computer or as hard copy.

Information on the family and factors prompting contact with the agency should include:

- The nature of the referral (why the family is being referred for protective services; the incident that precipitated the referral).
- The source of the reporter's information. For example, was the reporter a witness to the incident? Did the reporter hear about the incident from someone else? Was a rumor the source of information? What is the reporter's relationship to the family?
- What types of previous incidents of abuse or neglect have been known to the reporter.
- Whether the family knows of the referral.
- Identifying information on all persons involved.
- Specific facts, dates, and descriptions related to the condition of the children.
- How long the situation has been going on.
- If the situation has worsened or remained relatively constant.
- Any efforts that have been made to resolve the situation and their results.

Information on the family, parents, and the alleged perpetrator should include:

- The family's cultural and ethnic background information, including an assessment of American Indian/Alaska Native tribal affiliation or ancestry.
- Any associated family problems such as substance abuse or domestic violence.
- Parents' or caregivers' employment.
- Names, ages, addresses, and phone numbers of parents, guardians, and/or the alleged perpetrator, if different from the parent or caregiver.
- Other information about the alleged perpetrator.
- Where parents or caregivers, guardians, and the alleged perpetrator can be located if different from home—for example, work address, relative's home, including directions for finding these locations.
- Parents' or caregivers' explanations of conditions or injuries (if the reporter knows).

Information on children who may be involved should include:

- Name, age, sex, birthdate, and address of the involved children.
- Siblings of the involved child(ren) or other children in the home whose safety may also be in question—for example, names, ages, and gender.
- Specifics of present condition of the involved child(ren)—for example, injured, alone, or in potential danger.
- Current location of the child(ren).

Information to be obtained from other persons or agencies familiar with the family should include:

- Names, addresses, and phone numbers of other individuals who may be aware of current or previous safety concerns, including persons who have a general knowledge of the involved child, or the family's ongoing situation.
- Identifying information on extended family or other personal relationships.
- Names, addresses, and phone numbers of individuals or agencies that have had contact with the family in professional or helping roles—for example, schools and social services agencies—and their willingness to become involved or possibly testify.

This in-depth information is necessary for a number of reasons. Most important, it helps you determine if the child is in a situation that puts him or her in immediate danger that might require emergency removal from the home. Second, it enables you to identify the child and parents, caregivers, and/or alleged perpetrators and how to locate them so that an assessment can be conducted. Third, it enables you to identify other possible sources of information about the child and his or her family that will help you assess the possibility of past, current, or future abuse or neglect. Finally, it enables you to determine if the identified child is the only person whose safety is in question.

Listen and respond to the reporter and assess his or her motivation for reporting. When speaking with the reporter, listen carefully. Pay close attention to how the he or she describes the problem and do not interrupt to question at this point. Take notes on a notepad or the computer as you listen. Save your direct questioning for the last part of the conversation. Use listening techniques that encourage the reporter to continue, such as "I see," "Go on," "Sure," "Mm-hm."

It is important for you to assess the reporter's motivation, for it becomes a part of the information you will use to decide whether the referral should be assigned for further assessment or screened out.

There is a higher degree of credibility among referrals in which the reporter's motivation is positive. The reporter is positively motivated when he or she demonstrates an appropriate concern for the child and the family, is not punitive, recognizes the responsibility to report, wishes to see the family situation improve, demonstrates an appropriate emotional response, reports as a part of his or her job, and has nothing to gain personally from reporting.

The intake worker should view all referrals with an open mind. Do not start out by automatically assuming either that the reporter is genuinely concerned or that the referral is being made maliciously. Listen, ask questions, and make your judgment after you have the necessary facts.

Usually, as you converse with the reporter, the information you need to determine the reporter's motivation will surface. However, assessing motivation is largely a matter of judgment. There are a number of areas you should be attentive to that will assist directly with this; although no list is complete, the following considerations will be helpful in identifying the reporter's motivation. If you must ask direct questions, ask them respectfully and professionally. Open-ended questions are recommended and generally yield the best information.

- Is the reporter willing to give his or her name, address, and phone number?
- What is the reporter's relationship to the child and family—for example, relative, neighbor, friend, or employer?
- If the reporter knew of previous neglect or abuse, what happened to make him or her decide to report at this time?
- Does the reporter stand to gain anything from reporting or by the report being validated—for example, custody of children? (This would not, of course, be reason enough to question the credibility or the need to further assess the referral.)
- How well does the reporter know the family?
- As shown in agency records, has the reporter made previous referrals that were invalidated (on this family or others)?
- Would the reporter be willing to talk with you or another worker at a later time to discuss the referral further and give additional details if the situation warrants such contact?
- Is the reporter drunk, unusually bitter or angry sounding, or exhibiting unusual behavior that would give you reason to question his or her judgment, accuracy, or competence?
- How does the reporter know about the alleged maltreatment?
- Is the referral based on the reporter's own knowledge or what has been heard from other sources?
- Can or will the reporter take any responsibility beyond the referral—for example, testifying in court if necessary?
- Can or will the reporter provide information leading to others with information about the allegation?

While anonymous referrals may have somewhat less credibility, workers should make the same attempt to gather extensive information as with a known reporter and follow through to the greatest extent possible. If the content of the referral could be true (some are patently ridiculous), then an effort should be made to document the allegation through other records and agencies but within a context of confidentiality. Individuals such as neighbors or employers should *not* be contacted before the family is advised that the agency has received a referral. It is preferable to search agency records to determine if the agency or other child welfare agencies have had previous contact with the family. This could be accomplished through a search of the child abuse/neglect database if available and, if appropriate, a search of a criminal database.

When in doubt, accept the referral for further assessment and make a home visit to share the report with the family. It is always possible to withdraw if the facts do not warrant further assessment.

In some cases, both lay and professional reporters may demand that you "remove that child." There are several ways that you can effectively respond to such demands. In general, reporters should be made aware of agency limitations, responsibilities, and procedures. You should do this without being defensive or sounding overly bureaucratic. Often acknowledging the caller's concern first and then trying to help him or her understand the role of the agency will help. Thank him or her for the referral and the concern; assure the caller that your agency will do everything possible to ensure that the children are safe; sympathize with any strong feelings; and accept criticism and attacks in a professional manner without becoming angry, defensive, or retaliatory.

Some specific ideas to keep in mind that may be helpful to you in these situations:

- All reporters should be given support and recognition for reporting.
- Sometimes when reporters make demands, such demands are defensive expressions of fears that the alleged perpetrator may retaliate against them. In such instances, the reporter should be reassured that his or her identity will be protected should the reporter's testimony not be needed in court and if the report was made in good faith.
- Reporters should be informed honestly that the agency must assess the report before action can be taken, that the agency must operate within legally defined boundaries, and that removal of children can only be made when the child's safety demonstrably requires removal and the court agrees.
- Reporters can be told that you must not, by law, disregard a family's rights.
- Reporters can be told that your professional and legal mandate (Adoption and Safe Families Act, Public Law 105-89) is to determine if children can be maintained safely in their own home.

☐ Screening the Referral

You must first determine whether the referral is a report of child abuse or neglect as defined by state law and agency policy. If you determine that it is a credible report, you then must decide what the agency's role with the family will be. Will there be an investigation or will the report be handled with a differential response?

Evaluate the reported condition of the child and the description of the alleged abuse or neglect. Does it meet state and agency guidelines? For example, reports not meeting state guidelines might include a report involving an 18-year-old developmentally disabled youth (because, despite developmental level, an 18-year-old is considered an adult) or a report that indicates that the child was maltreated by someone who was not a caregiver (e.g., a neighbor's son).

The reporter's description of the circumstances will help you to decide whether the referral is a report of abuse or neglect.

You must also weigh the importance of family conditions, the home, and other problems and social relationships, as described by the reporter. You should attempt to assess the following:

- Is there misuse of drugs or alcohol?
- Is there disability or illness present?
- Is the family socially isolated?

- Are the parents or caregivers described as mentally ill?
- Are the parents or caregivers described as angry or dangerous?
- Is there domestic violence in the home?

Your agency policy and state law should be your guideline as you accept referrals.

In the event that intervention by CPS is not indicated, you should consider the need for referral to other services. Such services might include referral to the local food bank, the health department, or another agency that provides immediate concrete services to meet the needs of families. It is important that you know what resources your community has to offer families in need. Families may be more responsive to agencies with services that are culturally specific, so a good working knowledge of culture-specific family resources is important.

If the referral falls within the definition of child neglect and abuse, you must determine whether the agency has an appropriate role with the family, on the basis of agency guidelines such as:

- Does the family reside within the jurisdictional boundaries of the agency? If not, you must ensure that the information is transferred to the appropriate jurisdiction. This would include children who are wards of Indian tribal courts or who are temporarily residing off their reservation, but whose permanent residence is on the reservation. In these instances, jurisdiction would rest with their Indian tribe. Your immediate supervisor or agency legal department may be able to answer procedural questions regarding situations involving the unique requirements for Indian children and families who are referred for child abuse or neglect.
- Will a worker be able to locate the child and family to conduct an investigation?

A report may raise serious safety concerns but otherwise offer limited information on the whereabouts of a child. In this situation, the worker should be creative about finding ways to locate the child (e.g., surrounding school districts, motor vehicle records, telephone searches).

You should always provide feedback to the reporter about what will happen next with the referral. (Your agency may also require contact after the investigation to let the reporter know whether or not the agency will follow up with the family. This is agency dependent, and you need to be informed of your agency's policy.) Considerations include:

- From a public relations standpoint, this procedure provides you with an opportunity to explain the agency's service and to express your support for the reporter's performance of his or her civic duty on behalf of a child.
- The reporter needs to be told only that the agency will or will not proceed beyond intake. Confidentiality will not be breached by the simple message: "Our agency will follow up."
- When the reporter is another agency having a continuing role with the family, information sharing, interagency planning, and mutual reporting can be accomplished at agreed-on intervals. This information sharing is

often guided by a formal agreement between the two agencies, a "memorandum of understanding," or may be described in the code or law that defines and outlines child protection in your state.

☐ Determining the Urgency of the Report and the Level of Response

Once you determine that the report has met the necessary criterion for acceptance, you must determine the *urgency* of the response. Your agency may provide written guidelines and/or utilize a safety assessment tool or a decision tree to help prioritize the agency's response. A report may be considered to be urgent if the child's condition is described as critical. More specifically, consider:

- What is the age of the child? This is a primary piece of information when considering urgency. The urgency of any case increases as the child's age decreases.
- Is the child injured and in need of medical care? A child who has been injured and whose injury is untreated needs an immediate response. Even though some children may suffer from what appear to be relatively minor physical illnesses (such as a 6-year-old who has strep throat), they may die or be seriously disfigured if the parents refuse to seek treatment. Other cases are urgent not because of the immediate problem but because subsequent problems may arise if treatment is not provided.
- Is the child alone? Any child who is alone and is under 10 years of age or has special needs is at best only conditionally safe. The longer the child has been alone, the more urgent the case.
- Does the alleged perpetrator have access to the child?
- Is the child fearful of his or her circumstances? Children usually know when they are not safe. Whether situations are real or imagined, no child should face them alone. For example:

    One teacher referred a situation to child protection in which a 6-year-old girl refused to go home, fearing that she would be beaten. Subsequently, it was determined that the child was beaten frequently for such things as forgetting her lunch.

- Does the child show signs of repeated abuse and neglect? Since repeated abuse suggests a pattern of ongoing danger, the need for protection is urgent.
- Is the problem *acute* or *chronic*? Chronic cases of neglect may also be urgent if new, specific, and possibly dangerous circumstances are also present. For instance, a child who is physically neglected for his entire life may not need *urgent* attention, since he has managed to survive, yet he does need attention. However, if the report on the same child also said that the caregiver had not been home in several days, this fact would suggest an urgent response.
- Are there concerns about developmental disabilities, mental health, or medical fragility? These issues may impact urgency as well.

A report may be considered to be of less immediate concern or urgency if you can answer the following questions positively:

- Is the child's behavior appropriate?
- Does the child appear healthy and properly nourished?
- Is the child attending school?
- Does the child's development seem normal?
- Is the child dressed appropriately for the weather?
- Is there a parent or caregiver available to protect the child from the alleged perpetrator?

You must also determine the agency's *level of response*:

- Will the report be investigated by the agency?
- Will the report be responded to through a differential response system?
- Will the report be referred to another community agency for follow-up assessment or information?

☐ Worker Safety Concerns

There are a number of things you must keep in mind when preparing to respond to a complaint that is accepted for further investigation. Your own safety is one of those things. If you find yourself in a situation where your safety is an issue, you will, in all likelihood, not be able to be effective in determining the safety of the child. Here are a few things to be mindful of:

- Always be aware of (1) your surroundings; and (2) anything unusual in the neighborhood or home.
- Check with others (coworkers, law enforcement) about the neighborhood.
- Pay attention to information provided by the caller regarding animals in the home and obvious safety hazards such as drugs, alcohol, or firearms.
- Be comfortable about leaving the situation if that is warranted—call for assistance if needed.
- Utilize the availability of a coworker or law enforcement personnel if the situation suggests that assistance may be needed.
- Be smart—being professional does not mean putting yourself unnecessarily at risk.

Decision Point

Questions to Ask

1. Is the referral a report of child neglect or abuse?
2. Will the agency complete an investigation or will there be a differential response?
3. How urgent is the report?

Safety to Assess

1. Is the child currently safe?
2. Do the safety concerns pose imminent danger to suggest the need for out-of-home placement?
3. Is the child in immediate danger?

■ The Investigation Process

Many states have differential responses or multitrack systems where the referral is not necessarily investigated but the agency responds. For the purposes of this chapter, the word *investigation* will be used to describe all of these types of response. Much of the information applies to all of the interventions; some, such as making dispositions, may only apply to investigations. The investigation of (or, if appropriate, a differential response to) a report of child abuse or neglect sets the stage for problem identification, validation, service planning, and the continuation of a helping relationship. This is probably the most discomforting and difficult part of the CPS process. However, when conducted with an open mind, a caring orientation, and a desire to build trust, not establish guilt, the initial assessment is an integral and positive part of the helping process. During the investigation you should attempt to answer certain basic questions by collecting information from families and collaterals; evaluate the information, help the family identify issues and strengths that impact the safety of the child(ren), and work with the family to decide the most appropriate intervention strategy.

☐ Definition of the Investigation Process

The investigation consists of those activities undertaken in order to evaluate the safety of the child, determine whether the report of neglect or abuse can be substantiated, and initiate services for the child and family.

☐ Purposes of the Investigation and Key Activities

Several decisions are made as a result of the investigation. You must first decide the safety of the child. You must attempt to substantiate or not substantiate the allegation of maltreatment. And you must determine if there is future risk of abuse or neglect to the child. In order to do this, you must be prepared to answer the following questions:

1. Is the child currently safe?
2. Has the child been abused or neglected, or is he or she likely to be abused or neglected?
3. Who has abused or neglected the child?
4. What action is to be taken?

The parents or caregivers are given the opportunity to discuss the allegation of abuse or neglect (however, the worker must not reveal the identity of the reporter). The role of the CPS agency in the intervention is shared with the parents or caregivers. The agency's plan for future involvement with the family—for example whether the agency will continue to work with the family or whether its involvement may end after the investigation is completed—are communicated. (This may change as the case progresses. Inform the family at each stage what they can expect next.) You must involve the family in the safety planning process and in identifying how to address any issues that may impact safety and future risk.

In order to accomplish these purposes and answer essential questions, you must gather and evaluate information during the investigation that will be the basis for the decisions you make. Attempting to make decisions without adequate information or knowledge of how to assess this information could be disastrous. It could endanger a child, unnecessarily destroy a family, or both. For example:

> A worker determined that a child had been abused (a correct assessment based on sufficient information). The worker also determined that the very young mother had abused the child (an incorrect assessment based on insufficient information). With the best intentions the worker attempted to help the mother with her problems. But the worker soon became very discouraged by her lack of progress with the family. The husband began to threaten to leave his wife and take the child because the wife continued to deny the abuse and seemed to be making no progress with her problem. The child's mother angrily denied what everyone pointed out to be her problem and began to suspect her husband of the abuse. Only after the child was abused a second time did the worker discover that the babysitter was responsible for the abuse.

A complete investigation includes gathering all pertinent information and engaging the parents in the process before cases are substantiated.

☐ Methods Used to Gather Information during the Investigation

Your first contacts should be with the child (if the situation is appropriate), parents or caregivers, and other siblings. If necessary, neighbors, relatives, friends, and other involved community representatives can also be interviewed. Several interviewing techniques are appropriate during this phase. (See chapter 5.) Considerations about who should be interviewed first are outlined hereafter. (Your agency may have guidelines or protocols about the specific order of investigation.)

You should observe the child, the family, and the home situation. The purpose of observation is to collect and document current and historical information relevant to the case.

You should specifically focus on looking closely at the child's physical and emotional condition.

☐ Important Considerations Prior to Contacting Families

Before contacting the family, you should be clear about the purposes of the contact and the goals to be accomplished by the interview. Remember that safety is the reason for your intervention. For example:

- Are you trying to determine if the alleged victim is in immediate danger?
- Are you trying to determine if the report is substantiated?
- Are you trying to gather historical information of maltreatment?

You should be clear about your own position, attitude, confidence, and skills before beginning the family interview. This self-awareness will greatly influence your approach, the success you have in engaging the family, and the degree to which you will accomplish your goals. Ask yourself the following questions:

- Are you already convinced of the parent's guilt, are you approaching the parent with an open mind, or will you believe everything the parent says?
- Are you afraid for your own safety?
- Are you able and prepared to confront the parents or caregivers with the information you have even if they make contradictory statements?
- Are you prepared to enlist the help of the parents or caregivers in identifying what, if any, concerns there are for the child's safety? Can you do this in a helpful, sympathetic, and understanding way? Can you use the authority you have in a helpful and nonthreatening manner when needed?

You must be prepared to acknowledge and respect the culture and lifestyle of the family that may be different from your own. It may be helpful in the interview if you acknowledge that the family's culture and lifestyle are unlike your own and ask for help in understanding the differences. Fear of the unknown, of dealing with different cultures, or residual fears due to racial prejudice or cultural misconceptions will limit your ability to engage the family and ensure the safety of the child(ren). The laws and policies that guide your decisions reflect a community standard of parental care and child safety yet may conflict with your own cultural background. Unless you are aware of and respect the positive aspects of cultural differences that exist, you will overlook unique opportunities to engage the family.

You should be thinking of helping and planning how to immediately engage the family. Be open and honest about the allegations and your agency's statutory role in the situation. Listen carefully to the family and let them know that you have heard what they are saying to you about their circumstances. Acknowledge your understanding that this intervention is anxiety producing. Be empathetic and sympathetic to the family's feelings and encourage them to express their feelings. Remind the family that your interest is in making sure that the child is safe and that you intend to be helpful. Ask the family for input on how you can be helpful. Go into the interview with the outlook that you are trying to help the family identify the strengths that they have to solve whatever problem(s) are identified. Use techniques that encourage family involvement and participation in the solution of the problem. (See chapter 10.)

Your knock on the door and subsequent informing the family that you are investigating an allegation of abuse/neglect is enough to initiate a crisis in the family. You should be familiar with the nature of *crisis intervention*, the relationship between the report of child abuse or neglect and a family crisis, parental or caregiver response to the crisis, and the proper way for you to respond to the crisis. Your efforts should be directed toward moving the family from the emotional to the rational or problem-solving level, as follows:

- You must actively explore and clarify with the family the elements of the crisis: the report, the safety concerns for the child, the child's condition, and the family's perceptions.

- Discuss with the family how safety issues have been addressed in the past and whether the methods have been successful.

- Let the family tell you what they consider to be a reasonable outcome and what changes are necessary to ensure the child's safety. Help the family understand the necessity for change.

- The effectiveness of crisis intervention resulting from the assessment will determine the ongoing relationship between the family and the agency. Here are some points to remember:

  Be observant, quick, and ready to act in any situation because crisis situations call for immediate assessment and assistance.

  Engage the family in problem solving and guide the situation when necessary.

  Be sensitive and understanding, and provide warmth and support to the family.

  Recognize that cultural differences may have an impact on how the family is reacting and identify what approaches will be most productive.

  Model appropriate behavior by remaining calm and rational.

  Be flexible with regard to schedules, preparation, approaches to the problem, methods, and techniques for solving problems.

  Be able to seek consultation and support from your supervisor and peers, since crisis intervention is stressful and sometimes threatening.

  Focus on current and future behavior.

  Maintain your focus on child safety and be objective.

  Be fair and understanding of the behavior or feelings of the person in crisis.

  Be aware of what the person's behavior is telling you.

  Use the crisis as an opportunity for constructive changes.

(These guidelines are from the National Center for Comprehensive Emergency Services to Children, 1975).

Do not leave notes for the family if they are not at home when you arrive. Notes raise anxiety, and they can be damaging. For example:

> Because a report seemed routine and not too serious, John, a new worker, decided to leave a note when he did not find a parent at home. He believed that this approach would save him time and reduce the chances of the parent not being home when he returned the next day. Later, on finding the note, the parent panicked. She knew that she had been neglecting her child and also had been

using and dealing in drugs. Her fear of being caught overpowered her and she left the community. No one knew what happened to the child.

Since John was an efficient, well-organized worker who never missed a deadline, he usually looked for ways to save time. Leaving notes was his normal practice. Another note that he left on a neighbor's house read: "Mr. Gill, I need to speak with you about your 4-year-old son, Donny. I'll stop by tomorrow afternoon. Please be here. I am enclosing my card, John Lee." The card identified John as a CPS worker. Later Mr. Gill called the agency, incensed since he was a policeman and felt that John's indiscretion could seriously hurt his reputation. Incidentally, the report was subsequently determined to be unfounded.

On entering the home for the first time, you should anticipate the possibility of certain reactions by the parents or caregivers.

- Continued denial or unwillingness to accept that there is a problem is a typical response.
- Parents or caregivers may minimize or deny the seriousness of child maltreatment and hint at other problems.
- Parents or caregivers may admit being involved in the reported incident but deny that the problem is serious enough to warrant intervention or has the potential for continuing. With regard to such denials, you must remember that you do not need to have a confession and that the focus is having the parent accept that change is needed in order to ensure the child's safety. Keep in mind that:

    Parents' or caregivers' denial tells you something about their perception of reality, their recognition of the problem, and the likelihood that they will work to change.

    When parents or caregivers deny, do not challenge them. Accept their denial, but then interpret reality as you perceive it in a calm, non-accusatory manner. An example of how you might handle such a situation:

    "I understand you say that Sarah bruised her face by banging it against the crib; however, a child her age cannot roll over hard enough or fast enough to bruise her face. You see, it is very unusual for a baby to bruise her face, and that's why I'm so concerned about the injury that Sarah has."

- Parents or caregivers may express fear that the child will be removed.
- They may also fear that their autonomy will be jeopardized and feel intimidated. It is your job to reassure them that your concern is making sure that the child is safe and helping the family find a way to accomplish that. Discussing the purpose and philosophy of CPS and its legal mandate may be helpful.
- As previously mentioned, you should be prepared to encounter hostility toward you and/or the reporter.
- Parents or caregivers may aggressively protest the agency's right to intervene. This aggressiveness is designed to throw you off balance. Do not

respond defensively toward them. Show respect for their right to privacy and an understanding of their strong feelings. If you are calm and gentle and keep the purpose of the intervention foremost in your mind, their hostility will often defuse. Simply state the agency's purpose and cite the state statute that gives you the authority and the responsibility to be there.

- You should be prepared for the fact that the parents or caregivers may blame others for their problems.

- Extreme politeness, compliance, projection, or manipulation may be used to avoid dealing with the real issues. These devices enable parents or caregivers to not face up to or take responsibility for their actions. Reality-orienting techniques, such as confrontation, can help them to face the issue. (See Chapter 5.)

- Parents or caregivers may be silent and offer nothing.

- You may observe apathy and depression.

- Parents or caregivers may make themselves unavailable. This type of behavior may be either a means of avoiding the reality of their problems or a means of avoiding you. You must be careful to give space to these parents or caregivers. Be reassuring and supportive. Recognize them individually and express your awareness of the difficulty of the situation they are facing. This type of parent may be surprised and more cooperative as a result of your helping orientation and reassurance that you are not there to punish or persecute.

- Cooperation may also be evident.

- In some cases, the parent or caregiver may in fact not have abused or neglected a child and can provide a reasonable explanation for an injury. Therefore, in all cases you should listen without judgment until all facts can be fully considered.

☐ **Initial Contact with the Family**

Typically, your first contact will be with the alleged child victim. The exception to this might be cases where the child is nonverbal because of age or disability. (Refer to Chapter 5 for specific guidance on how to interview children.) The second contact will generally be with the parents or caregivers.

Generally the best approach to introducing yourself and your function is honesty. For example:

> "I am (name) from (agency). We have received a report concerning injuries your child has received [your children being left alone, and so on]. Our agency is required to look into all reports such as this to make sure that the children are safe. I need to talk to you about this report. May I come in?"

The importance of a good introduction is that it will help to establish the kind of rapport in which the parents or caregivers will be willing to share information. It will also give them a sense that you or your agency can be helpful.

You should begin the initial contact by communicating in a nonaccusatory, courteous manner.

- You should be clear that you are there to make sure that the children are safe, not to make inferences or establish guilt.
- You should not be deterred by attempts by the parents or caregivers to blame others (or express negative feelings toward you or others) for the report or for their own problems. You can do this by continuing to return the conversation to the issue of the child's safety as the concern.
- Your role as a helper should be stressed.
- You should continue to be aware of your own values, feelings, positions, and attitudes toward the family. (See Chapter 3.)
- As an outsider in the home you should be courteous and respectful of parents' or caregivers' rights.
- You should seek to understand and respect cultural differences.

The course of the initial family contact will depend on how the parents or caregivers respond. The important factors are:

- How do they react to the report and your assessment of its validity?
- How do they react to the agency's intervention?
- Do they admit that the report is true or do they deny its truth?
- Do they understand the importance of the safety of the children and their responsibility to keep the children safe?

Be prepared to encounter anger, hostility, and a variety of immediate defensive reactions. If the parents or caregivers respond in this way, it may be helpful to acknowledge that you realize that your contact is distressful and frightening. Dealing with anger and hostility is discussed in further depth in the next section.

Parents or caregivers who refuse to speak with you should, if possible, be gently advised that you must assess the report and determine whether the child is safe. Helping them understand that you need to hear their side of the story before going to other available sources of information suggests that you are not accusing them and are willing to be openminded and fair. Many families will appreciate honesty, clarification of your responsibility, and your ability to allow them to react emotionally, as opposed to disguising the purpose of the visit and being vague about your responsibility and mandate to assess reports.

However, if you are ordered out of a home, you should (while being careful not to endanger yourself) try to make a full statement of your purpose in making the visit and express your concern before your departure. If the situation is such that you believe the child is unsafe, you should inform the parents or caregivers that, in order to ensure the child's safety, the help of law enforcement might be enlisted.

When admitted into a home, you should share reported information in detail with due consideration to protecting a reporter's identity.

- Vague or emotionally charged words, such as "abuse" or "neglect," should be avoided, for example, if the allegation is of physical abuse, use the words "injury," "bruises," and so on.

- Be frank and specific about allegations. Avoid using vague words like "problem" and "help."

- Do not ask questions in which the answer is already known. Avoid trapping a family in lies. If some points have already been corroborated, mention them briefly but avoid identifying the source.

- Encourage the family to respond. Use phrases such as: "Why do you think someone would express such concern?" "Are you surprised that a complaint would be made about you? Has anyone ever mentioned these concerns before?"

- After you state the allegations honestly and directly, the parents or caregivers are then in the immediate position of having to admit, explain, or deny the allegations, or prove that they are false.

- The parents' or caregivers' response, and the degree to which they try to rebut, deny, counteraccuse, and so on, may indicate a potential for change.

- Their response, even when very angry and aggressive, is usually not directed toward you personally and, therefore, should not be reacted to in a personal way. (However, a threat to harm you should be heard. Don't discount the possibility that the threat is real!) Comments such as "It is certainly understandable that you are upset. Such statements are bound to make one upset," are designed to show your ability to understand without backing away from the need to talk about what is wrong. These comments are useful in reducing the tension during the early part of the interview. If you do not respond defensively, there can be no "fight."

- Once the parents or caregivers offer to prove that the allegations are false or to explain how the alleged maltreatment occurred, you are in a good position to view the evidence and/or seek clarification or elaboration of their explanation. For example:

  "Can you show me exactly where and how he fell?" "It looks like he has four marks on his back, all of the same age, but you said he fell on his head. Can you explain how the marks on his back occurred?"

- It is frequently a good technique to relate immediately to the parents' or caregivers' feelings. Emphasize that you realize that they may be upset, angry, and so on, and the importance of their feelings, and that you can sympathize with and relate to them on a feeling level.

- When discussing the specifics of the referral, give the family the opportunity to identify problems without being accused. This will provide you with more information to assess how they may view issues such as discipline and children's needs and to assess their judgment, values, and amenability to help or treatment.

- You can also begin interviews by telling the family that although your function includes assessing complaints, you are most interested in making sure that the child is safe and helping the family address any issues that might get in the way of the child's continued safety. You are not there to accuse, and you are talking to them first because what they have to say and how they feel are important to you.

- One technique frequently used successfully is to begin by asking the parents or caregivers about the child's normal or routine behavior. Such an approach can serve to inform the parents or caregivers that you sympathize with their difficulties and that you can be supportive.

- Open-ended questions are generally preferable to questions to which the parents or caregivers can respond with a yes or no answer. For example:

    "Please tell me how your child was injured" is better than "Did you hit your child?"

- In general, your questions should be as supportive and nonaccusatory as possible. Parents or caregivers are usually going to be braced for criticism, especially implied or direct judgments. You need to be able to get around these feelings and defenses.

- However, it is generally true that a worker who appears to believe everything the parents say and tries to be totally agreeable and nice sets up a false basis for relating to the parents. Objectivity is a preferred position. Appearing to be too agreeable and later taking action against the family justifiably creates an atmosphere of distrust. This inconsistent behavior obviously will hinder the development of trusting relationships between the parents and any helping professional in the future.

No amount of skill or experience can completely remove the sense that the relationship between you and the parents or caregivers is an adverse or potentially adverse relationship. In the initial interview the most you should expect is a lessening of the parents' or caregivers' fears so that you can obtain the information you need to make an initial judgment and decision regarding the child's safety and to set the stage for whatever future contacts may be required for your continuing assessment, service planning, and service provision.

As your interview with the parents or caregivers continues, it is important that you direct your discussion toward the parents or caregivers, reassure and show your concern for them, and encourage their involvement from the beginning of your initial contact. If you show concern only for the injured or neglected child, you will probably alienate them. It is essential to the CPS process that the parents or caregivers be involved in the identification and solution of any safety-related problems that exist. You can demonstrate your concern and encourage their involvement in the following ways:

- Discuss the parents or caregivers' lives; their history; how they were raised; how much of a social life they have; if they feel alone as parents or caregivers. What makes them happy? How do they make important decisions in the household? How do they show their support for one another?

- Encourage them to talk about their attitudes toward parenting. Have them describe what their child is like. What does their child add to their life? What do they expect of their child?

Intervention with self-referred parents or caregivers needs to take into consideration some additional dynamics. The cooperative, motivated parent or caregiver should also be responded to promptly. Some issues for you to consider are as follows:

- Although the self-referred parent or caregiver perceives the situation as needing intervention, and this is a major step toward change, it does not assure change.
- The fact that they may feel less than adequate as parents certainly does not indicate a capability to protect the child.
- The self-referred parent or caregiver may be motivated, but incapable. Your focus must remain the safety of the child. Though self-reporting, the parent or caregiver may not be able to ensure the child's safety.
- Self-referral should be framed as a strength and as an important step in making the changes necessary for the parent or caregiver to best support and protect their child.

In almost all investigations, the parents or caregivers will ask you who has reported them. In most states, this is considered confidential information. Although you may use numerous approaches and responses to deal with the issue of reporting, you must keep in mind that your primary function is to ensure the safety of the child and assess the allegations of abuse or neglect and not to be distracted by a prolonged discussion with the family regarding the source of the referral. Consequently, your approach should be based on your judgment of the type of response that will most effectively satisfy the family without distracting you from your purpose. Points to keep in mind include the following:

- You should always anticipate that the family will want information about the reporter. Plan in advance how you will respond to their questions.
- No matter how the parents or caregivers threaten or manipulate, you must not be persuaded to reveal the source of the complaint. In particular, be aware that you must not confirm that the parents or caregivers have correctly identified the reporter.
- Honesty is frequently key. It is often safe and best simply to be truthful. For example:

  "I am not able to share that information with you."

- In declining to identify the reporter you should be sympathetic to the parents' or caregivers' anger and frustration at not being able to identify and directly confront their accuser.
- Usually a comment about the motives of the reporter is helpful in softening the blow to the family. For example:

  "The law requires that anyone who suspects that a child is being abused or neglected must report this concern to the child protection agency or to law enforcement."

Continue to keep in mind that throughout the initial contact with the family you should make the following observations in order to assist in assessing the situation for future risk to the child.

- What are the parents' or caregivers' appearance and behavior?
- How do the parents or caregivers relate to the reality of their situation?
- What kind of affect is present?
- Is there resistance?
- What are the physical and mental states of the parents or caregivers?
- What situational factors are present—for example, home and financial circumstances, illness, domestic violence, or substance abuse?

Ask the family who else might have information that would be helpful in the investigation. When possible, interview the individuals the parents or caregivers recommend. Contact other community representatives when it appears that they might have information that would be useful in the investigation and maintaining the safety of the child. Contact individuals who have firsthand knowledge of the incident. Interview the siblings of the child.

Keep these interviews focused on the safety issues and strengths of the family.

- Do they have any safety concerns now or have they had them in the past?
- Do they have knowledge of the incident or circumstances that initiated the investigation?
- What are the family's strengths?
- Are they aware of any factors—for example, substance use, domestic violence, etc.— that would impact the child's safety?

☐ **Dealing with Anger, Hostility, and Resistance**

You will be more effective if you understand the source of the anger, hostility, and resistance and develop strategies for intervention.

The causes and manifestations of anger. Anger is first a physiological response to a dangerous situation—real or perceived. It is triggered by increased levels of the hormones that regulate heart rate, blood pressure, perspiration, muscular tension, and so on. Anger occurs in preparation for either one of two basic reactions to a threatening situation: "fight" or "flight." The body is made ready to defend itself to survive.

Anger does not subside until the physiological response subsides. This occurs only when real or perceived danger is minimized. Anger is also a psychological reaction to a threat to one's well-being. It is an intense emotion that tends to build quickly as the physical response increases. The emotion of anger subsides only as the threat is seen as subsiding.

The emotional component of anger. This component usually lasts much longer than the physical response. Hostility is one outward expression of anger. Hostility may be verbal, physical, or both. The intent of hostility is to minimize the threat or danger to which the individual is reacting. It is meant to put the threatening individual on the defensive; to demonstrate power or strength; and to protect the self. Hostility on the part of an angry parent or caregiver may represent the "fight" reaction and may consist of verbal or physical abuse. Hostility on the part of an angry parent or caregiver may also represent the "flight" reaction and may consist of refusing to cooperate, literally running away, or denying the allegations of abuse or neglect.

The causes and manifestations of resistance. Like hostility, resistance is another outward expression of anger. In fact, resistance can be viewed as stemming from hostility. However, resistance entails a broader spectrum of behavior. Resistance can be a conscious effort on the part of the parent or caregiver to avoid changing his or her abusive or neglectful behavior. Resistance can be an effort to exert control into a situation in which the person feels powerless.

Resistance can also be unconscious and may be a self-preservation mechanism that prevents self-incrimination. Resistance of this type can be manifested through behaviors such as forgetting to keep an appointment; unknowingly changing the topic of discussion; or not being able to see contradictions in a conversation. These behaviors may stem from a deep-rooted, hidden strategy to avoid dealing with reality because it is too painful or threatening. Dealing directly with this kind of resistance is extremely difficult because the person has no idea he or she is resisting. This kind of resistance should begin to subside as a trusting relationship is established.

Conscious resistance takes many forms. The parent or caregiver may openly refuse to cooperate with you. The parent or caregiver may deny that the abuse or neglect occurred, despite evidence to the contrary, or blame someone else for the maltreatment. The parent or caregiver may appear to be extremely helpful or cooperative but prove otherwise in his or her actions. The family may even leave the community.

Reasons for a parent or caregiver's anger, hostility, and resistance. Anger, hostility, and resistance may be a result of your intervention in the family's life. Your very presence suggests that the parent or caregiver has done something wrong— that the parent or caregiver has abused the child. You are invading the parent or caregiver's privacy. You are proposing that the way the parent or caregiver treats the child is "wrong." There is the chance that the parent or caregiver may be subject to court proceedings as a result of your intervention.

A parent or caregiver's anger, hostility, and resistance may be the result of other problems. The parent or caregiver could be under considerable stress as a result of other problems within the home or the family circle. Problems could include health or financial issues or relationship difficulties resulting from conflict or criticism. As the result of life experiences, the parent or caregiver may have acquired hostile attitudes toward authority in general. You may be the "last straw" among multiple stressors. You are the perceived threat, and only you can minimize the parent or caregiver's anger and hostility by minimizing the threat you represent.

Anticipating the possibility of hostility and resistance. With careful and thoughtful advance preparation, you will be in a stronger position to overcome the parent or caregiver's negative feelings and attitudes. With an understanding of human behavior, you can make some assumptions:

- The parent or caregiver may question your right to intervene and resent it.
- The parent or caregiver may resent being reported for mistreating the child.
- The parent or caregiver may be fearful about what may happen as a result of this behavior, either personally or to the child and may be relieved that some help is offered.

You must assert your firm conviction that the intervention is both necessary and required by law. While being willing to hear and understand the parent or caregiver's perspective, you must be determined not to retreat or back away from your responsibility.

Before your contact with the parent or caregiver, plan a strategy by considering the following:

- What is the nature of the allegation of abuse or neglect?
- How are you likely to be received by the parent or caregiver?
- What are some of the reasons the parent or caregiver may become hostile?
- What are some ways the hostility might be reduced?
- How can you exercise your authority in a nonthreatening way and be perceived as a helpful person?

You must be prepared to relate to the parent or caregiver in a professional manner that communicates care and concern. If the parent or caregiver shows anger, raises his or her voice, or uses abusive language, you must remain unruffled and composed. In your ordinary, day-to-day relationships, you may have the tendency to retaliate in like fashion to those who attack you. In CPS, such a response would be unacceptable and would likely only cause the parent or caregiver to get angrier.

Remember that constructive interaction cannot take place until the parent or caregiver's anger subsides. Anger will block meaningful communication; reduce the parent or caregiver's ability to "hear"; and interfere with rational thinking.

If the parent or caregiver resists your intervention, you must explain your concern for the family, both for the parents and the children, as well as your desire to be helpful. However, you cannot back away from your task.

Responding professionally to hostility and resistance. Just as you have expectations of parents or caregivers in terms of how they will relate to you, they will have expectations of how you will relate to them. Your first task is to dispel parents' or caregivers' negative expectations. You must act in such a way that you could be perceived as accepting and authentic rather than judgmental and authoritative. Keep in mind that sometimes, no matter what strategy is tried, some parents or caregivers will be unable to reduce their hostility or resistance without the help of other services. For example, if a parent is detoxifying from drugs or alcohol or has been diagnosed with a bipolar illness and is not taking the prescribed medication, "rational" interventions may prove fruitless.

The courtesy you extend, your calm rational explanation of your purpose, and your sense of inner strength, professional competence, and confidence may facilitate the deescalation of the parent or caregiver's hostility toward you. Although the parent or caregiver may be inclined toward anger, he or she will be more than likely disarmed by this kind of response.

Parents' resistance will diminish if:

- The intervention is viewed as a means of reducing rather than increasing present stress in the parent or caregiver's life.
- The intervention is respectful of the family's culture and worldviews.
- The intervention builds on strengths identified with the family and incorporates the use of their support systems.
- The parent feels that his or her autonomy and security are not threatened.
- You are able to recognize valid disagreements and relieve unnecessary or unrealistic fears.
- You keep the relationship clear of most value judgments and evaluations.
- You provide the family with a new and constructive experience in human relationships.

As you listen to the family's expression of anger, look for the reasons behind the anger and respond to these reasons, not to the anger itself. Consider:

- Is the anger based on the belief that you have no right to intervene? If so, indicate that you are concerned about the child and the family; that you want to see if there is some way you can help to make things better for both; and that you have no intention of taking over the child or the family's life.
- Is the anger about being reported by someone for the treatment of the child? If so, recognize those feelings and indicate that the community members also care about parents, and that reporting shows their concern.
- Is the anger aimed at your authority and based on previous experiences with authority that have been unpleasant? If so, show that authority can be human, personal, nonthreatening, and helpful.
- Is the anger about your threat to the parent or caregiver's self-esteem, or the parent or caregiver's feelings about himself or herself? If so, show your acceptance by being nonjudgmental and noncritical.

Use of yourself to elicit cooperation by demonstrating unconditional regard and empathy. Unconditional positive regard or total acceptance of the parent or caregiver as a person may be difficult at times, but it is important. Total acceptance of the parent or caregiver as a person is not the same thing as approving of unacceptable behavior. Your goal is to be able to accept the parent or caregiver as a *person*, who has behaved in an unacceptable way. You will be letting the parent or caregiver know that abusive or neglectful behavior will not be tolerated, but that you believe he or she can and will make changes to ensure the child's safety and well-being.

Unconditional positive regard means putting aside your own preconceived notions, attitudes, and beliefs to allow yourself to really listen to parents or caregivers and to allow them to present themselves to you as they really are, rather than as you want to see them or as they want to see themselves.

Empathy should also pervade your perception of the family. Empathy is being able to put yourself in the parent's shoes, to feel what he or she feels, to view the world from his or her perspective.

Having unconditional positive regard and empathy for the parent or caregiver does not mean that you give up your own sense of self. You cannot lose sight of your primary responsibility, which is to safeguard the well-being of the child involved. You cannot allow the child to continue to be at risk due to abusive or neglectful parental behavior. You *can* allow the parent or caregiver to trust you and to believe that his or her welfare, as well as that of the child, are your concern.

Having unconditional positive regard and empathy for parents or caregivers who mistreat their children is extremely difficult and requires a conscious, continued effort on your part. If you are able to be sensitive, aware, and accepting of your own feelings, you have moved a significant step forward in being able to have unconditional positive regard and empathy for the parent or caregiver.

The following case illustrates how you may use yourself to help the parent or caregiver feel better about him or herself:

> Ms. Thornton is struggling with her fears about being able to parent. You decide it might be helpful for Ms. Thornton to know she isn't alone in her fears and worries about parenting. You share that you were also a young, single parent who struggled with self-doubt and worry. You describe how you reached out to others for support and that you plan to help Ms. Thornton do the same.

By sharing a small bit of your history and generalizing Ms. Thornton's common concerns, you accomplish several things:

- You continue to build a trusting, caring relationship.
- You provide her with the chance to see that you are not only a caseworker, but a human being with real fears, worries, and similar experiences.
- You help her to see she is not alone in her doubts about parenting.
- You demonstrate that everyone can use the support of others.

It is essential that you know what and how much you should share regarding your personal life. Although a small amount of self-disclosure can assist in building a caring relationship, too much disclosure may lessen your credibility as a professional. Use supervision to discuss what kind of information you should share with families.

Reflection of the parent or caregiver's feelings should complement your instructions or explanations. Reflection of feelings does not mean repeating the words a person says. It does mean that you identify and state to the parent or caregiver the meaning of what he or she is saying. For example:

Parent:

> "All I get is criticism."

Inappropriate worker response:

> "All you get is criticism."

Appropriate worker response:

> "You can't seem to please anyone and it's so frustrating. You feel like you're not getting anywhere."

Parent:

> "Who are you to barge in on me like this?"

Inappropriate worker response:

> "You wonder who I think I am to barge in on you."

Appropriate worker response:

> "You're angry that I dared to violate your privacy, like I'm better than you."

You will find that being nonjudgmental and accepting will help dissipate the parent or caregiver's anger and hostility; and that the appropriate reflection of feelings will open the way for continued discussion and provide the basis for a trusting relationship.

Handling a dangerous parent or caregiver. There may be occasions when a parent or caregiver who represents a threat to your physical safety confronts you. Such individuals may behave in aggressive, uncontrolled ways. Their anger, rage, and hostility will be seen in their eyes, posture, mannerisms, and movements. Some individuals may seem to be completely out of touch with reality—unable and unwilling to be reasonable or unwilling to permit any kind of cooperative relationship. In some cases this may be related to the use of alcohol or drugs. If the reporter has indicated the use of alcohol or drugs or lack of touch with reality, you may need to request that someone from law enforcement accompany you.

Do not behave in a way that will increase this parent or caregiver's angry feelings. Remain calm. Speak softly and maintain your composure.

Protect yourself, but do not fight back. If you are in the parent or caregiver's home, leave and obtain the assistance of law enforcement officials. If you are in your office, seek the assistance of others in calling for help or use deescalating techniques to calm the parent or caregiver.

An encounter with a truly dangerous parent or caregiver is quite frightening. However, you have invested a great deal of effort in developing your skills and knowledge and have the capacity to really help a great number of children and families. You must not let such experiences deter you from continuing your efforts to provide important protective services to abused and neglected children. Just make sure to plan accordingly to assure your safety. See page 162 for strategies on how to increase your personal safety.

■ **Assessing Safety**

There are several decisions that must be made in the early stages of the investigation process. When a report is received alleging physical, sexual, or emotional abuse or neglect, it is critical that a decision is made to assess the immediate safety of the child(ren) living in the home. Depending on several factors—the allegations made, the vulnerability of the children, the history of both the adults and children and perpetrator access—the immediacy of the response to these allegations will be determined. In looking at *safety* and *risk*, it is important that a clear distinction is made between these two types of assessments and subsequent issues around interviewing to make those assessments. A safety assessment considers the *immediate* safety of the child, while the risk assessment considers the *long-term* potential risk of maltreatment. However, in both types of assessment the worker must look at all of the children in the home and not just the subject child of the report. In both risk and safety assessment, consideration should be given to the individual culture of the family, and emphasis should be on identifying individual and family strengths and building on those strengths. The worker must develop a plan of safety if any children are to remain in the home.

☐ Determining Safety

Before the end of your initial contact with the family, you will need to determine if the child is safe. This determination is often made with the help of a prestructured decision-making tool. A number of factors are important in developing the safety plan. (See Chapter 7 for a detailed look at safety assessment factors.) The factors often focus on the behaviors and characteristics of the parents or caregivers, as safety depends on what they do or refrain from doing. The overriding questions to consider when determining child safety include six basic elements. The factors generally provide the information that is needed to answer these questions.

- *Threat:* what is the immediate threat of harm to the child?
- *Harm:* does the nature or type of harm impact the child's immediate safety?
- *Severity:* how severe is the possible consequence to the child's safety?
- *Vulnerability:* what is the child's level of vulnerability? Is the child very young or disabled, thus increasing the safety concerns?
- *Imminence:* how imminent is the possibility of harm to the child?

You must balance the factors that negatively impact the child's safety and the factors that serve as protective measures against the negative. For example, if there is an allegation of sexual abuse, there must be someone in the home who can be counted on to protect the child from having contact with the alleged abuser during the course of the investigation, considering as well the elements just outlined.

☐ The Safety Plan

The safety plan is what has to happen *now* to protect the child from abuse or neglect. If safety concerns are identified and the child is to be left in the home, a safety plan must be completed to identify how the child will be kept in the home in spite of the safety concerns. The safety plan, in order to truly address the safety of the child, must be clear and specific to each child and each situation and specify what has to be done, why, and by whom. The plan must also include how the plan will be monitored by the supervising agency and must take into consideration the parent's willingness and ability to follow through with the plan.

The worker must ask questions that will determine if a plan can be developed that will ensure *conditional safety*. This term refers to the concept that the child is safe as long as the "condition" or parts of the plan are adhered to by all participants. The worker must be aware of and understand the values and beliefs as well as the cultural context within which each family operates in order to develop the most workable plan. For example:

> "Ms. Gomez, what will you do if your husband comes home smelling of alcohol and begins to yell at and threaten your son?"
>
> "My husband is a good man and did not mean to hurt Felipe last night."
>
> "When I spoke with Felipe he told me that this has happened many times before. I don't want to remove Felipe from your care, but I will need to know what you will do if he needs your protection."
>
> "I guess I will tell Felipe to go to his grandmother's house."
>
> "I will need to speak to his grandmother to see if she is able to cooperate with this plan. I also will need to speak to your husband about this plan."
>
> "Mr. Gomez, I have talked with your son and your wife, and we have decided that when you come home angry and smelling of alcohol she will send Felipe to her mother's home."
>
> "What do you mean? He is my son, and she does not have the authority to make these decisions without talking to me first."
>
> "I apologize for not speaking to you first. Can we talk about how we can make sure your son will be safe?"

Assessing strengths in relation to the safety assessment. When assessing strengths or mitigating factors in a safety assessment, the strengths must be specific to those things that contribute to controlling the safety factors. For example, if a parent is out of control or violent, the fact that the parent has realistic developmental expectations of the child does not mitigate that safety concern. A mitigating strength in this situation might be that there is a person in the home who is willing and able to protect the child and will ensure that the child is not left alone with the out-of-control parent. If a caregiver is under a great deal of stress and has previously harmed the child when administering discipline, it may be a strength that the caregiver takes responsibility for the harm and feels bad about what happened. It would not, however, mitigate the safety concern if the stressful situation still exists, the caregiver has poor coping skills, and it is likely that he or she will be faced with administering discipline again. In this situation, mitigating factors might be the presence of another protective adult or daycare for the child so the caregiver gets a break from childcare responsibilities.

Safety plans involving substance abuse issues. If a safety concern for a family is the caregiver's inability to care for the child due to the use of drugs or alcohol, the safety plan must include a way to keep the child safe while the parent or caregiver addresses his or her addiction. The plan may include the stipulation that the parent using substances not be left alone with the child and that there is always supervision by another approved adult. A worker might monitor this plan through frequent and regular contact with the supervising adult in the home, and with unannounced home visits. A service or case plan will also be created to address the longer term issues of the caregiver's substance abuse treatment. (See Chapter 10 for more information on developing service plans.)

Safety plans involving medical issues. If the safety concern is that the caregiver is unable to meet the medical needs of the child, the safety plan may involve visits by a home health nurse and regular doctor appointments. Monitoring this plan would include frequent contact with the home health nurse and doctor, as well as assurances from these providers that they will notify the supervising agency if there are any concerns about the welfare of the child. Unannounced home visits by the worker, especially if the home health nurse is not available on a daily basis, would also be advised.

Safety plans involving conditions of the home. When the safety concern is the hazardous conditions of the home, the safety plan would include specifics about what needs to be remedied in the home and a time frame for the remedies. If the home cannot be made safe immediately, the safety plan could include voluntary placement of the child with a friend or relative until the home no longer poses a safety concern. Home visits by the worker to assess the living environment would be critical prior to the child returning home and then on a regular basis once the child returns home.

You will need to check in with each of the adults and children regularly to ensure that they are continuing to comply with the agreement, or the child's safety may be compromised. The plan of safety is reviewed each time you have contact with the family on the telephone, at the family's home, or during any other interaction with family members. It may involve telephone calls and face-to-face contact, and it must be fluid enough to be revised at each contact in order to ensure that the child can remain in the home.

☐ Physical Abuse: Interviewing and Developing a Plan of Safety

Assessing for safety in physical abuse cases requires that you determine the severity of any injury the child may have suffered. If there are injuries, a medical exam and treatment may be necessary. Some children require immediate medical attention; other children in the household also warrant full assessment. Photographing of injuries is required in some states.

Understanding how the injuries occurred is essential in determining safety from future harm. Full comprehension of what occurred may not be readily apparent on the first contact with the family. Interviewing to understand what occurred requires separate interviews in private for each child and adult who may have information about the alleged incident.

Children may often be the best source of information of what transpired in cases where adults may be reluctant to assume responsibility for causing the injuries discovered. Wherever possible, children should be interviewed in detail. The key safety factors to explore in the subject child's interview are:

- Has the child suffered a moderate or high level of harm, or experienced threatened harm?
- What actually did the child experience?

    "Tell me all about what happened. How did you get hurt?"

- Does the child have information about the caregiver's behavior being violent or out of control? For example:

    "What happens when your dad or mom get mad?"

- Is the child fearful of anyone who is living in or frequenting the home? For example:

    "Are you afraid of anyone at home?" "What makes you feel afraid?"

- Does the child have information about anyone using drugs or alcohol that may seriously affect or impair that person's functioning to the detriment of those around them? For example:

    "What do you know about drugs or alcohol? What do they say about it at school? Have you ever seen anyone in your own life use drugs or alcohol?" "Some adults like doing things that kids aren't allowed to do, like drinking and doing drugs."

- Does the child have information about anyone having mental health or disability concerns or conditions? For example:

    "Earlier you told me that Uncle Eddie scares you. What does he do?"

- Does the child have information about how parents or caregivers manage their behaviors?

    "Andrew, when you do something wrong or make a mistake, what happens?"

- Does the child have information about previous incidents about being harmed him or herself in the home? For example:

    "Did anyone hurt you or your sister before? Has anyone at your house ever been hurt by someone hitting?"

The same safety factors need to be explored with each adult in the home.

The alleged perpetrator may be the least reliable source of information about what transpired in cases where moderate or severe harm occurred to a child. Interviewing the alleged perpetrator last whenever possible permits the worker to assimilate all the data gathered and determine credibility. Information gathered from earlier interviews with children and nonoffending adults permits far more refined questioning about the alleged incident.

The parents' or caregivers' reactions to the information gathered and presented by the worker are essential for safety intervention.

In cases where injury or harm of a moderate or severe level have occurred, the worker needs to determine how the safety of the child will be assured once the worker leaves the home. For example:

"Mr. Schwartz, do you understand that you went too far in punishing your son physically? If he gets you angry again, how will you control your temper and not hit him?"

In cases of suspected physical abuse of young children or infants who are not yet verbal, special safety concerns must be considered. Babies with unexplained bruises may be at high risk of harm. A complete medical assessment is essential to determine if there are other injuries and if treatment is warranted. The medical exam is critical in attempting to determine if the explanation for the injury is plausible or if there are old injuries that may not be identified by nonmedical personnel. Determining who had care of the infant may not be straightforward in some households. Frequently no one may come forward to admit responsibility for the inflicted injuries.

Preverbal children who have been hospitalized cannot be safely returned to their homes without a full understanding of the causal factors.

The safety intervention may typically require use of alternate caregivers while the assessment of the family continues. For example:

"Mrs. Adams, I have spoken with you and your husband at length about what happened to baby Quincy. Neither of you can tell me how he got the fractured ribs. And you told me no one else was caring for him. The medical experts believe the injuries were inflicted. Before we use foster care I would like to see if there are family members outside of your home who could care for Quincy, and guarantee his safety while we continue assessing what happened in your home."

☐ Chronic Child Neglect: Interviewing and Developing a Plan of Safety

Assessing for safety in chronic child neglect cases may be very challenging for workers to pursue with full confidence because often there is no precipitating incident, event, or injury to scrutinize as in physical abuse cases.

In cases where neglect is alleged, parents and any other caregivers, if in the home, must be considered as responsible parties for possible neglect.

As with allegations of abuse, safety must be immediately assessed at the first visit. However, a full assessment of the parent's functioning and the children's well-being may take some time to make accurately. For example:

A report was received alleging that Maria Lopez and her husband, Esteban, were neglecting their five young children. The allegations included concerns about medical neglect, lack of supervision, lack of food, poor school attendance, and suspected illicit drug use in the house.

The reporting source was the school counselor, who confirmed that the oldest child, Antonio, had attendance problems and poor hygiene. The classroom teacher was concerned about Antonio, a second grader, because he was fighting with other children. Immunization records were not completed.

Before meeting the family at home, the worker was able to interview the reporting source over the telephone, as follows:

"Mrs. Delgado, I'm the caseworker from Child Protective Services and I'm calling about your report on Antonio Lopez. You said that Antonio is stealing."

"Yes, it is so sad. He seems to be a nice boy, but he has taken school supplies out of other children's desks. When they find out they argue and begin to fight."

"You also reported that his immunizations were not completed."

"Yes, he is behind on several immunizations and we really shouldn't let him remain at school. His attendance is so poor. He only comes here once or twice a week."

"What about his siblings?"

"He has two siblings who attend our school and they both are behind in their immunizations."

"Thank you. You have been a big help and have done the right thing by making a report. Do you know anything about Antonio's parents?"

"Not much. I know they recently moved here from Puerto Rico. I sent several notes home with Antonio, but they never responded to them."

The worker discussed the case with the supervisor, and the possibility of a language barrier with the parents was discussed. At the initial contact with the family, the worker would assess whether language could be an issue.

At the first home visit with the family, you should introduce yourself, explain your purpose, establish rapport, and develop a relationship with all members of the family. In addition, you must assess the safety of all the children in the home at each visit. This may be most difficult at the first visit. To continue the example:

The home visit found Maria Lopez with all five of her children. Mr. Lopez was not home. While she was bilingual in Spanish and English, her language of preference at home was Spanish with her children. She spoke English to the worker and then switched to Spanish when she addressed her children. The worker asked to talk with her in private.

"Mrs. Lopez, I'm here because we received a report alleging that Antonio comes to school hungry and steals from the other children. His immunizations are behind, and he is absent from school several days each week. I am also concerned about his brother and sister and their coming to school hungry. The report also said that there was drug use in your house."

Mrs. Lopez became very angry. "Who told you this? It's a lie. My neighbors don't like me because I'm Puerto Rican."

The worker explained that the reporting information was confidential and could not be released. She added: "We get lots of reports; some are true, some are false, and some are half and half. All that matters is what is going on in your home and with your children. If the allegations are true it is our job to help your family. It must be very hard to live in a new country with different ways and a place where you feel discrimination because you are Puerto Rican."

Mrs. Lopez blurted out her feelings: "You're so young. How could you help me?"

"I'm young, but I know how difficult it is to care for five children. I've had specialized training, and I think together we can find out what is needed for your children and the resources to make sure your children are safe. In order to find out if your children are safe, I need to take a close look at where they sleep, eat, and play. So I need to do a 'walking tour' of your home. Could you please show me around the entire house?"

"What for?"

"I need to see if the children are living in a safe environment, having a place to sleep and enough food to eat. Sometimes I find unsafe conditions."

During the walking tour, the worker learned that Mrs. Lopez's brother was staying in the basement and was making methamphetimines in a makeshift meth lab. The worker immediately recognized the situation, explained to the family about the potential danger, and called law enforcement. It was a dangerous situation that had to be immediately addressed by CPS and law enforcement.

Assessing whether the physical living conditions are hazardous for the children is an important process to ensure safety. Having an adult give you a "tour" is necessary if you are to actually observe the conditions throughout the house. You must determine whether community living standards are met, noting such items as whether the utilities are functional, the home has hot water, the plumbing works, and there is a functioning heater. You are also looking for safety hazards such as exposed wiring, broken glass, and unsanitary conditions. Only by observing each room in the home can you assess if there are obvious structural problems that pose a hazard.

Actual visual observations are required and should be done sensitively, as this will always be experienced by the family as an intrusion.

While the walking tour is intrusive and many parents will initially resist, it is better to be honest about your need to see the home then try to "guess" about the conditions from the parts of the house you do not see. Honesty is a critical component in developing the helping relationship.

Visiting the kitchen and actually looking for food in the refrigerator and pantry are necessary in making a complete assessment of well-being.

Some families may not have enough money to purchase the necessities of life but may be too proud or too embarrassed to talk openly about their situation. In some cases, parents or caregivers may be diverting the family's resources to buy drugs or alcohol, thus leaving less money for food or payment of utility bills.

In order to complete the assessment and develop a plan of safety, the worker must interview all of the children and assess for both abuse and neglect.

There were two immediate safety concerns for the Lopez children. (1) *Physical living conditions were hazardous* and could have caused serious harm to the children. The existence of a meth lab in the basement created a threat to the lives of all the adults and children living in the home. (2) *The child was fearful* of people who were living in or frequenting the home. Antonio was afraid of his uncle, who had chased him from the basement. In addition, if the uncle was selling the meth, it was likely that there was a good deal of traffic of strangers going in and out of the home.

The safety plan for the Lopez family addressed these two concerns.

Safety Concern: Physical conditions in the home are hazardous.

Safety Plan:

a. Children will live with a cousin until conditions in the home have been corrected.

b. The meth lab will be shut down and all hazardous chemicals removed.

c. The entire home shall be cleaned and its safety assessed by industrial hygienists before inhabitation resumes to ensure that any remaining chemicals or drugs cannot pose a threat of harm.

d. Worker will return to the home, inspect the basement, and take another tour of the home to ensure that the meth lab has been shut down.

Safety Concern: Child is fearful of people living in or frequenting the home.

Safety Plan:

e. The uncle is currently in jail, but if he is released on bond, he will be asked to stay elsewhere.

☐ Child Sexual Abuse: Interviewing and Developing a Plan of Safety

Allegations of sexual abuse present a unique situation for the worker. In most situations there will be an interview by law enforcement officials. Some departments have specialized units or refer to community agencies that specialize in child sexual abuse assessment in order to not contaminate a court proceeding with information gained in an inappropriate manner.

Depending on the practice in your local agency this may be done separately or concurrently with your work. At any rate, you must assess the safety of the child while the rest of the interviewing goes forward. It is strongly suggested that workers have specific training in interviewing for child sexual abuse prior to engaging in the process.

In order to make the most accurate assessment of the situation and the child's safety, it is important to interview the child alone. For example:

> A report was received alleging that Mr. Williams had sexually abused his 4-year-old stepdaughter, Latrice. Per agency protocol, a report was made to law enforcement. The worker met with Mrs. Susan Williams, the mother, and Latrice immediately. There were no other children in the home.
>
> "Mrs. Williams, I would like to meet with Latrice alone to discuss the allegations."
>
> "Okay, why don't you two sit in the kitchen?"
>
> After several minutes the worker noticed that Latrice kept looking up at the ceiling. Pronounced sounds of footsteps from the room above appeared to be distracting to the 4-year-old.
>
> "Mrs. Williams, is there another place that Latrice and I can talk in private?"
>
> "Yes, you can use the sun porch."

In states or counties where a forensic interview will be conducted by law enforcement authorities, the worker should end the interview with the child by thanking him or her for talking and then explain what will happen next. If this is not the protocol, then the worker must complete an in-depth interview. (See the section on interviewing children in Chapter 5.)

Interviewing the nonoffending parent or caregiver. In assessing safety in sexual abuse cases, the capacity of the nonoffending parent or caregiver to believe, support, and protect the child is a critical concern that must be analyzed in determining if the child can remain in the home. In many cases, this capacity will change over time. While the nonoffending parent or caregiver may initially believe the child's story, subsequently his or her opinion may be changed when he or she hears the alleged offender's version. In some cases, nonoffending parents face economic pressures that may cause them to side with the offenders and pressure children to recant rather than face the uncertainties that may result from the relationship ending.

A comprehensive interview should be conducted with the nonoffending parent. Continuing with the example:

> The worker interviewed Mrs. Williams alone and shared the allegations with her. Mrs. Williams appeared to be in shock in response to the allegations. The worker explained to her that it is quite normal to react this way in cases of child sexual abuse. The worker gathered information about Mrs. Williams's life by asking open-ended questions.
>
> "Mrs. Williams, what was it like for you when you were growing up? I know that your family was involved with our agency when you were a child."
>
> "My father hit me once when I was twelve, and it was reported to your agency. Things between my parents didn't go that well, and my father left us a few years later. We went on welfare and things were rough."
>
> "How do you and your husband get along?"
>
> "He is a good man, and we get along real good, but sometimes he gets angry. He gets mad when I drink my wine. He's a bourbon man himself."
>
> "I saw the empty gallon bottles of wine in the bin. Why does he object to you drinking wine?"
>
> "He doesn't want me to spend his money, and he's afraid I might scratch up the car. I only have a glass or two to calm my nerves."
>
> "How does your husband act toward you when he is angry?"
>
> "Sometimes he can get pretty physical, but he hasn't touched me in over a month. He really loves me, but I wish he would help out with the housework and with Latrice."
>
> "How does your husband help with "Latrice?"
>
> "He watches her sometimes while I am working, fixes her dinner, that kind of thing."

The worker will need to determine if Mrs. Williams has noticed anything different about Latrice's behavior. She should ask questions like:

"Tell me about your daughter. What does she like to do? What does she like to do least? Are there any relatives and friends that she has a close relationship with? Has she been sleeping well lately? Has she complained about any nightmares? What about her behavior at preschool, daycare?"

Motivation to suppress damaging information is common not only for offenders but also nonoffending parents and other household members.

Many cultures are loath to present family problems to outsiders. In particular, some cultures have specific taboos against openly discussing sexual matters. Nonetheless, most cultures also have very strong taboos against child sexual abuse. It may be important to consult with a community expert prior to the interview to determine the best approach. Otherwise, you will want to bring any taboos out into the open and try to find a way to focus on the immediate safety and long-term effects of sexual abuse for the child.

All cultural groups have grave concerns about problems that result in law enforcement involvement. This issue may need to be explored in terms of fears, beliefs, or prior history with the legal system.

Members of cultural minorities may have heightened anxiety based on an established history of oppression manifested through police action and court decisions.

As with the interview with Latrice, if a forensic interview with law enforcement is part of your agency protocol, you may choose not to gather specific information about the alleged incidents at this point from either Mrs. Williams or the alleged perpetrator, Mr. Williams.

At the conclusion of the interview with Mrs. Williams and Latrice, information had been gathered that raised several concerns that would impact the decision about whether Latrice could remain in the home, as follows:

- Assuring safety in child sexual abuse cases requires total separation of the alleged perpetrator and the child victim until a determination has been made that no abuse occurred.

- Child victims can easily be intimidated by adults to suppress their disclosures and thus may recant even when the allegation is true.

To this point the worker has gathered information from the child victim and the nonoffending parent or caregiver to help decide if the child is safe in the home. There are three major issues in the Williams case example at this point:

1. *Child sexual abuse is alleged, and circumstances suggest that child safety may be an immediate concern.* Latrice has identified her stepfather as the perpetrator and said that he touched her "kitty cat" (Latrice's word for her genital area).

2. *The parent or caregiver may be a victim of domestic violence, which affects his or her ability to care for and/or protect the child from imminent moderate to severe harm.* Mrs. Williams has told the worker that he hasn't hit her in the past month, clearly indicating that there is a history of physical abuse by her husband.

3. *The parent's or caregiver's drug or alcohol use may seriously affect his or her ability to supervise, protect, and care for the child.* Mrs. Williams told the worker that she enjoys drinking wine to "calm her nerves"; evidence suggests that she

may be drinking more than she realizes or will admit. The crisis of the investigation will not help her "nerves."

Techniques for interviewing the perpetrating parent or caregiver. Coordinate your assessment with law enforcement, according to your local policies and protocols. In cases of sexual abuse or criminal investigations, many protocols restrict CPS workers from interviewing the alleged offender. In areas that allow you to interview the alleged offender, consider the following techniques:

- Remain calm, objective, courteous, and matter-of-fact about the process.
- Present the allegations fully without revealing the source of any reports.
- Explain the rights of parents or caregivers to confidentiality, and the process for involvement with CPS, as well as the agency's responsibility to help the family in the areas of need.
- Inform both parents or caregivers that a report was made to law enforcement about the allegations of child sexual abuse.
- Be prepared to explain at length the ramifications of the investigation. The potential of arrest and incarceration will loom over this discussion.
- Do not discuss details at this point, as you may inadvertently affect the law enforcement investigation that follows.

Here is the safety plan for the Williams case.

1. The worker asked both parents if there were relatives available to care for Latrice during the investigation phase—possibly for several weeks.

> *Note:* In other cases where the nonoffending caregiver is stronger in his or her capacity to believe, protect, and support the child and the other safety factors are not present, the alleged perpetrator is asked to leave the home. In such cases, close scrutiny and supervision are required, as the alleged perpetrator may return suddenly to try to maintain control of the family or squelch testimony.

2. The Initial Safety Intervention is for Latrice to stay with her maternal grandmother, Mrs. Phillips. The worker accompanies Mrs. Williams and Latrice to Mrs. Phillips's home. The worker must assess Mrs. Phillips's ability to protect and support her granddaughter. Mrs. Phillips must be able to assure the worker that no one will discuss the sexual abuse allegations with Latrice and that the alleged offender will not be permitted contact with Latrice either in person or by phone or mail. In addition, a general safety assessment as to the condition of the home and the ability of Mrs. Phillips to care for Latrice is made. Both Mrs. Williams and Mrs. Phillips are urged to come to the Child Advocacy Center to support Latrice during the forensic interview and medical evaluation. The safety plan includes the following provisions:

- Latrice is conditionally safe in the home of Mrs. Phillips.
- The forensic interview with law enforcement will be arranged for quickly in order to secure evidence, uncover wrongdoing, or determine that no sexual abuse took place.
- The medical evaluation will follow the same day.

■ Assessing Risk

You must evaluate all of the information you have obtained to assess the degree of *risk to the child* and to develop an initial plan of services for the child and family.

The amount of information on which you will base your decisions will always be limited by time and resource constraints. The use of structured decision-making tools may assist you if your agency employs such a model. You will have to rely mainly on impressions or limited information regarding parental or caregiver perceptions, potential for change, and effects of maltreatment on the child. However, you must seek out enough information to decide: Is the child's safety in question? Six critical areas to consider are:

1. The nature, extent, and seriousness of what is happening to the child must be established.

2. The effect of the maltreatment on the child must be determined.

3. You must consider the family's awareness of the problem.

4. An assessment of the potential for change with intervention must be made.

5. The next immediate steps must be considered.

6. The initial plan for ongoing services should emerge.

You must assess whether or not the child is at risk. There are a number of methods that you can use to gather the information necessary to make this assessment and to establish a working relationship with the family. (For more information on this topic, see Chapter 7.) Some of these methods include:

- Physical examination of the child by you or other lay or professional people to establish the degree, if any, of abuse or neglect, and to document the physical effects of abuse or neglect.

- Interviews with parents or caregivers, the child, and collaterals. You may refer the child for a psychological evaluation. Occasionally you may need to interview medical providers. It is not the medical provider's responsibility to label something abusive or neglectful. Develop your questions in a way that leads to an obvious conclusion but does not put the medical provider in the position to have to make the determination. For example:

    "Could you describe the injury to the child?"

    "How serious is the injury?"

    "Do you see many injuries of this type?"

    "How unusual is this injury for an 18-month-old?"

    "How do such injuries occur?"

    "Is it possible that this could be a nonaccidental injury?"

(See Chapter 9 for information on medical evaluation of abuse and neglect.)

A number of criteria that focus on the strengths and needs of the child and family may be used, or you may be required by your agency to use a specific risk assessment tool. (See Chapter 7.)

Formal risk assessment models, protocols, and structured decision-making tools are useful in improving the consistency of case decision-making and case documentation. These tools are not a substitute for your professional judgment or training.

Keep in mind that most assessment and decision-making tools have not been normed with various cultural groups and may contain some degree of bias that has not been examined.

There are four generally recognized categories of factors that are considered in assessing the risk to the child. They are the child characteristics, parent or caregiver characteristics, family characteristics, and environmental characteristics. (See Chapter 7 for a detailed description of risk assessment factors to consider.)

Decision Point

Questions to Ask

1. Have you obtained enough information from the child, family, and collateral contacts to adequately assess the child's safety and reach a determination about the alleged abuse or neglect?

2. Is your decision on substantiation based on a clear understanding of state laws and agency policies?

3. Have you assessed the need for other agency or community services when CPS intervention is not warranted?

Risks to Assess

1. Have you carefully considered all of the factors and their interaction to determine if the child is at continued risk of abuse and neglect?

2. Have you evaluated the strengths and resources of the family and child and how they support the protective needs of the child?

■ Final Steps in the Investigative Process

☐ Evaluation of the Information Obtained during the Investigation to Determine Whether the Report Is to Be Substantiated

You must determine the *disposition* of the report on the basis of state laws, agency guidelines, and the information you have gathered. Agencies use different terms for disposition categories, such as *substantiated, confirmed, founded, unsubstantiated,* or *unfounded.* The definition of "substantiated" that has been adopted by many states bases the decision on "credible evidence" that abuse or neglect has occurred. In some states, the standard of proof is a "preponderance of evidence that abuse or neglect has occurred." "Unsubstantiated" is frequently defined as those reports where "no credible evidence of abuse or neglect has been identified" (National Association for Public Child Welfare Administrators, 1988).

Avoid making the disposition on the basis of considerations other than those related to the question "Did it happen?" Such considerations may include:

- The family is likeable/unlikeable.
- There are potential media or influential community persons involved.
- There is a need to complete the investigation.
- The abuse or neglect does not seem "that serious."
- You want to use substantiation to send a message to the parents or caregivers about their parenting style.
- Any reason other than that the facts meet the required standard of proof.

When evaluating the facts that you have collected, consider the following:

- Is the explanation of how the injuries/condition occurred consistent with the documented evidence? The parents' or caregivers' explanation of the child's condition and how it occurred should be a significant factor influencing your decision.
- Did the parents or caregivers describe the child as doing something of which the child is not physically or chronologically capable?
- Are the injuries inconsistent with the parents' or caregivers' explanation?
- Do the parents or caregivers acknowledge they did not see what happened or do not know what happened?
- Are the parents or caregivers hesitant to provide any explanation, or does the parent or caregiver who was not present provide all of the information?
- Do the parents or caregivers tell you that they are responsible for the injuries or condition of the child but view their behavior as normal and appropriate?
- What was the condition of the home when you visited? Were the conditions such that the safety of the child was a concern?
- What did the parents or caregivers say about the fact that the child was found home alone in circumstances that were inappropriate?
- What information was provided by collaterals to support/refute the circumstances?
- What other observations were you able to make of the home situation that are pertinent to the concerns of child safety?

In some cases where the report is unsubstantiated, you may find that the child or family is in need of services other than child protective intervention, and these families should be referred to other services within the agency or the community.

☐ Key Decisions Following Your Investigation and the Disposition of the Report

After assessing the risk to the child and substantiating the report, you and the family must make certain decisions regarding the agency response to the child and family.

A determination must be made as to whether the agency will continue to work with or be involved with the child and family and/or if the child and family will be referred to another agency for services. Consideration must be given to the child's and family's cultural background and circumstances and what resources will best serve their needs. Consideration must be given to the adequacy and the availability of treatment resources in your agency and your community. Agency response must be based on the guidelines established by your agency.

A decision must be made about whether emergency services are needed to protect the child from further harm while in the home. Available emergency resources, including extended family and friends, must be assessed in terms of adequacy, accessibility, and appropriateness. Determine whether the family is receiving services from another agency.

It must be determined whether court action should be pursued. If the child is to be removed from the home, a petition must be filed in the court. You must understand the differences between the different types of court systems and the circumstances under which you become involved with any of them. Crucial decisions involving the case will involve your supervisor and your agency's legal counsel. Your decisions will be based on the results of your assessment and the mandates of federal and state law and agency policy. (See Chapter 11 for information in legal issues in CPS.)

You must decide whether removing the child from the home is indicated. Criteria for making this decision include:

- The present or potential maltreatment in the home is such that the child has suffered or could suffer physical or mental injury if left there.
- The child needs immediate medical or psychiatric treatment that the parents refuse to obtain.
- The child's physical or emotional injuries require a special environment for treatment and recuperation that the family cannot or will not provide—for example, a hospital or therapeutic residential treatment facility.
- The child's age, sex, physical, or mental condition makes him or her incapable of self-protection, or for some reason his characteristics or condition are intolerable to the parents.
- The evidence suggests that the parents or caregivers have been systematically resorting to disciplinary methods that are completely inappropriate responses to the child's behavior—for example, extreme verbal or physical punishment of a child who makes a simple age-appropriate request.
- The parents or caregivers acknowledge being abusive and think that they will probably continue to be abusive if the child remains in the home.
- The physical environment in the home poses an immediate threat and danger to the child—for example, extremely unsanitary, a total absence of food, and/or inadequate protection from the weather.
- There may be hazardous consequences for the child as a result of your assessment; therefore, you should evaluate whether potential danger signs are evident:

Is the child extremely provocative; for example, is the child blatantly disrespectful or manipulative of the parent or the system?

Is the parents' or caregivers' anger extreme?

Is the child fearful?

Is there any member of the family or some other person available to maintain contact with the family and observe the parent- or caregiver-child interaction?

Is parental or caregiver pathology or scapegoating of the child evident?

- If the parents or caregivers cannot be located, the decision to identify an alternative placement is automatic. Consideration must be given to a relative or kin placement if there is enough information available to identify such a placement.

Even if you have the legal authority to remove a child, you should always try to obtain a court order prior to your action or immediately thereafter in cases of emergency removal. Removal of the child should involve, to the extent possible, the parents or caregivers. Include them in the preparation for the placement. Keep the parents or caregivers in the parental role by exploring their concerns and by obtaining information and items about and for the child that will help the child, once in placement. Ask them to talk to the child about the placement and tell him or her that it will be okay. Ask them if the child has any allergies or medical conditions that may need attention while the child is in alternate care. Ask if there are specific cultural or spiritual needs of the child and ask the parents for information on resources to meet these needs.

Children should be prepared for placement. You should talk to the child about the reason for the placement, emphasizing the need to keep the child safe. Ask the child what would make him or her feel safe. Maintain a calm demeanor even though the situation may be far from calm. Listen to what concerns the child has. Respond as honestly as you are able. Make only promises you can keep.

Tell the child about the family with whom he or she is going to stay. Ask the child what questions he or she has. Ask the child to help gather his or her clothes and personal items to be taken with him or her to the placement. Be sure to include a special toy such as a stuffed animal or doll.

Law enforcement personnel should be involved in dangerous situations where there is resistance and/or when the law requires their participation.

You should understand the philosophy and requirements of the Adoption and Safe Families Act and, for Indian children, the Indian Child Welfare Act prior to removing the child. Public Law 105-89 (ASFA) focuses on meeting the safety, permanency, and well-being needs of children. One of the primary ways of meeting those needs is to identify the safety issues as well as the strengths of the family and supplement them so the child can safely stay in his or her own home. This is often referred to as *reasonable efforts.* Such services could include emergency daycare in a situation where supervision is an issue, or intensive in-home family services to provide immediate hands-on parenting skills training to a new and inexperienced parent who does not understand child development. It is the goal to identify and provide services that will allow the child to stay in his or her own home so that placement is not necessary. In some instances, no services can be put in place to ensure the child's safety, and placement becomes the only option.

Public Law 96-608 (ICWA) requires active remedial and rehabilitative efforts prior to removal of Indian children and culturally appropriate services to prevent the breakup of the Indian family. Evidence must be of a clear and convincing nature that the child is at immediate risk and that active efforts to prevent the Indian family's breakup have failed.

Public Law 105-89 (ASFA) clarifies that safety is of the utmost concern and must be paramount in every decision. "Reasonable efforts" to preserve families are not required under aggravated circumstances. States have the authority to define what constitutes "aggravated circumstances." Examples of such circumstances include:

- A child has been abandoned.
- A child has been tortured.
- A child has suffered chronic abuse.
- A child has been sexually abused.
- A parent or caregiver has murdered another of his or her children.
- A parent or caregiver has committed voluntary manslaughter against another of his or her children.
- A parent or caregiver has aided or abetted in attempting, conspiring, or soliciting to commit the murder or manslaughter of another of his or her children.
- A parent or caregiver has committed a felony assault that resulted in a serious bodily injury to the child or another child of the parent or caregiver.
- A parent's or caregiver's rights to a sibling have been terminated involuntarily.

If the child is of American Indian heritage or has a tribal affiliation, a courtesy contact should be made with the tribal authorities to allow an opportunity to request transfer of jurisdiction to tribal court and to facilitate the appropriate placement of the child with an extended family member or other tribally approved home or treatment facility. In addition, a formal written notification must be made to the tribe to allow an opportunity to transfer the case to tribal court or to intervene in the state court proceeding. However, if the child is domiciled off the reservation and is not a ward of the tribal court, the state court has concurrent jurisdiction with the child's tribe. In this case, CPS must proceed with an emergency removal if the court deems that active efforts have failed and the clear and convincing evidence burden of proof is met that there is an immediate risk to the child's safety. (See Chapter 11 for more details about the Indian Child Welfare Act.)

Whether the removal is an emergency or with prior court approval, you must document why services could not be provided to prevent placement without endangering the child.

Services must be initiated to remediate the situation whenever possible so that the child can return home. If placement is necessary, a clearly developed service plan must be developed for parents or caregivers so that problems leading to the abuse or neglect can be resolved and the child can safely return home.

Consideration must be given to family members when identifying appropriate placement resources.

Decision Point

Questions to Ask

1. Can the child be maintained safely at home?

2. Have all service alternatives to out-of-home placement been considered?

3. What resources in the agency or community will best serve the child and family's needs?

4. Is court action warranted or mandated?

5. Are there relatives who could care for the child in a safe, secure environment?

6. Is the child subject to the provisions of the Indian Child Welfare Act?

Risks to Assess

Is the immediate safety of the child threatened if he or she is left at home? (See the previous section on the criteria for removal.)

Families must be involved in the entire CPS process if they are to be empowered to protect the child and reduce long-term risk. Parents or caregivers should be advised of the decisions regarding the substantiation of the report, your assessment of the situation, psychological evaluations, removal of the child or court action, and possible next steps.

Parents or caregivers should be given all the answers that you can supply. Promote a dialogue. Ask:

- How do they feel about the decision? (Also share with them how you feel about the decision.)
- Do they disagree?
- What are their suggestions?
- How do they plan to comply?

If you discuss matters openly, the parents or caregivers should not be surprised by your decisions. Be specific when you talk with families. Answer questions related to where, what, how, when, and why. Clear up misconceptions or fears about decisions, such as the fear that going to a psychiatrist means that a person is crazy.

When the decision is made to remove a child, the natural family, the Indian child's tribe and Indian guardians, the child, and the foster family should be prepared and kept informed.

You should share as much information with the child as he or she is able to accept. This information should include not only what is happening regarding a foster home but also what is happening with the natural family. The child must understand why the agency is involved with the family and why he or she is being placed.

You should explain your decisions to children, particularly with regard to removal. Because the child's guilt is immense, it must be dealt with explicitly. Children must be assured that they are not the cause of the placement or family breakup. However, you should recognize that no matter what is done, separation and the effects on children are real and will be evident. By consciously remembering that children have emotions too, you will be more aware of their feelings and behaviors and better able to deal with them. The following are feelings and behaviors frequently experienced by children:

- When children are separated from their parents or caregivers, they usually experience feelings of abandonment.
- Children often feel as though they are totally responsible for being abandoned by their parents or caregivers.
- Blaming self for the abandonment usually helps children deny anger at the parents or caregivers.
- Children usually believe that the separation is caused by some problem they are having within a particular stage of development they are going through. For instance, a 3-year-old child might believe the parents or caregivers abandoned him because he was not successful in learning to be toilet trained as quickly as the parents or caregivers wished.
- Separated children, as a result, tend to fear punishment for misdeeds. The younger child may expect to be totally abandoned by parents or caregivers and then to die, while the older child may fear being physically attacked and mutilated (National Center for Comprehensive Emergency Services to Children, 1975).

To assist the child and limit separation effects, it is important to provide the child with information about the foster family when out-of-home placement occurs. There should be preplacement visits if the situation allows.

- The child should know about the members of the foster family.
- The child should be introduced to the foster family's routines, such as mealtimes and bedtimes and social and recreational activities.
- The child should know where the foster family resides.
- The child should be familiar with the new school situation.

The child's family should be involved in the placement as much as possible. This involvement should help to maintain the link between the child and his or her family.

Information should be shared with the foster parents to assist them in better dealing with the child's feelings and behaviors.

Since reunification with the family is the plan in most situations, the placement needs to be as similar to the child's natural family as possible. Understanding the cultural context of the child and family is necessary to make adequate decisions about placement. If foster parents are encouraged to work with the natural family toward reunification, your services to the child and family will be strengthened.

☐   **Strategies for Minimizing Placement Trauma to Children**

When a child's safety is at stake and out-of-home placement cannot be avoided, strategies and interventions should be put in place to minimize the trauma to children and to reduce the long-term negative effects of separation from their family. By understanding the magnitude of changes a child experiences in out-of-home placement and children's developmental limitations in handling stress, you can contribute to the child's well-being by helping him or her cope with the challenges of foster care.

Recognizing and dealing with stages of a child's grieving process when separated from the parent or caregiver. The behavioral responses of children in foster care can best be interpreted by examining them in the context of the stages of grieving set forth by Kubler-Ross (1972) and Fahlberg (1979); as cited in Rycus & Hughes (1998).

Shock/denial. After the initial separation from their parents or caregivers, children may appear to be adjusting to foster care. They may seem indifferent in affect and behavior and appear to take the change in placement in stride. This is often known as the "honeymoon" period and may last from several days to several weeks. In this stage children may go through the motions of play in a "robotlike" manner but lack the exuberance of regular child play; or they may appear quiet, be quick to please, and not show any emotional reaction to the move. Children often deny a loss by thinking "I'm going home tomorrow." Infants may have physical symptoms, including sleeping or feeding disturbances or intestinal upset.

You should not mistake the child's compliant behaviors of this first stage to mean that the separation from home was easy or the child handled it well. Otherwise, when the anger of the second stage sets in, you may misinterpret it to mean the child is "misbehaving."

In a few cases a child may not react at all to being separated from his or her parent or caregiver. In cases like these, the child may not have attached, and the ability to form relationships may be damaged. Therapeutic interventions will need to be put in place to assist the child in developing future relationships.

Anger/protest. During this stage children display anger in many different ways. For example:

- Infants and young children may have physical symptoms that manifest in difficulties with sleeping or eating patterns.
- Some children may tantrum, have emotional outbursts, bully other children, break toys, lie, or steal.
- Other children at this stage may withdraw and isolate themselves, refusing to participate in activities.
- Children may also make comparisons between their own home and the foster care home, pointing out that their own home was better. For example:

    "My mother makes better macaroni and cheese than this."

- When you are able to identify these behaviors as an expression of grieving, you are able to support the children through this process, allowing them an opportunity to appropriately express their feelings of anger while gently setting limits for their behaviors. Although angry feelings are also characteristic of children who have been abused or neglected, separation from their family usually exacerbates these feelings.

Bargaining. School-age children go through this stage more frequently because they have the cognitive abilities to understand "cause and effect." During this stage children may try to negotiate agreements with you or the foster care provider such as "If I don't get in trouble I can go home." Although most foster parents welcome the compliant behavior that children demonstrate in this stage, it does not mean these behaviors are long lasting or the children are indeed changing. It only means they are desperate to control or change their environment and to defend against their fear of loss.

Depression. During this stage children appear to have lost hope and experience the feelings of ultimate loss. Infants or young children may appear forlorn or detached while still clinging to a temporary caregiver.

Older children may isolate themselves. They may seem listless or distracted, and although they play, their actions may appear mechanical. Usually they are unable to concentrate, which may influence their school activities. Children in this stage are easily frightened, frustrated, and overwhelmed by minor events and stresses. Often they are more vulnerable to accidents and are easily hurt. They may cry for little or no reason. Some children may regress at this stage, with thumb sucking, toileting accidents, and so on.

It is important to give the child assurance, be patient, and recognize these expressions as part of the evolving grief process.

Resolution. Ultimately the depression and other behaviors give way to acceptance and constructive attempts to adapt to the new placement. Children may begin to identify with their new family and may express that they want to stay with the new family. Normal childhood play and pleasure returns, and they reach out to others, displaying positive interactions. When the permanency goal is reunification, the resolution stage may be difficult for a child, as he or she is expected to reunify. Separation from the foster family may create additional stress that will need to be addressed.

Strategies that assist a child with out-of-home placement (Rycus & Hughes, 1998). The most appropriate placement should be selected. You should:

- Commit to placing siblings together unless it may be harmful to one or both. A child should be placed in an environment that is as homelike and as close to the child's own home as possible. Relatives, friends, and neighbors should be assessed to determine their willingness and ability to care for the child. This may reduce some of the "cultural shock" that accompanies placement.
- Caregivers should be chosen according to their ability to best meet the needs of the child.

- The number of changes in lifestyle and environment should be minimized. It is important to select a family, whenever possible, with an ethnic, socioeconomic, and cultural background that is similar to that of the child's original family.

- In choosing a placement, consider the importance of connections to kin, school, church, community, and friends. The importance of proximity for frequent visitation between parents, siblings, and other kin should also be factored in.

The foster parents or relative caregivers need detailed information to reduce stress and provide continuity in the child's life (Rycus & Hughes, 1998).

- Routines regarding the child's care should be communicated—for example, eating, sleeping, bathing habits, food preferences, whether the child sleeps with the light on, if he or she has a favorite blanket.

- A substitute caregiver needs to know how the child likes to be comforted when upset. He or she also needs to know what fears and anxieties the child might have.

- Facts regarding the child's medical history should be communicated. Who is the family's doctor? What are the family's expectations around medical care? Does the child take medication? Has he or she had immunizations?

- A caregiver needs to know what behavior problems the child has and how they have been handled in the past.

- The child's academic performance should be discussed, as well as his or her interests and hobbies.

- Culturally specific practices should be discussed in order to assist the child in maintaining his or her cultural identity.

- Any past history of abuse or neglect should be disclosed.

Assist the child in knowing what to tell others about his or her change in placement (Rycus & Hughes, 1998). Children are often embarrassed and do not know what to say about why they are in foster care. Likewise, it may be hurtful to hear their foster family or relatives talk about it to others. You can help children deal with this situation by helping them prepare and practice an honest statement of why they are no longer living with their parents. For example:

> "I'm staying with the Smith family for a while until my mom gets better and can take care of me."

Preferably the foster family can use the same statement.

Allow children to express their feelings about separation from their family and the new placement. If children can express rather than repress their feelings, they are less likely to experience long-term negative effects from the separation. Some feelings children may need to discuss are as follows:

- Children in alternate care worry about their parents. They wonder if the parents are surviving without them.

- If visitation is infrequent, young children may also think their parents have abandoned or left them.
- Some children may think they are personally responsible for the family disruption.
- Adolescents may reject a foster family's support and may not remain in the placement. Their identity may remain with their biological family, and they may be unwilling to accept another family as more than a temporary place to stay. Individual counseling is often helpful to them in sorting out their feelings regarding their history of abuse and neglect, the separation from their family, and their fear of the future.

Make sure that foster families or relative caregivers receive adequate support to ensure stability of the placement and meet the foster child's needs. Foster families and relative caregivers need to be able to access you or someone at the agency that can answer questions or assist in a crisis. Prompt return of phone calls and frequent visits with the foster family communicate that you are there for them. At times foster families may need respite to regenerate and focus on their own needs. Foster family or relative support groups allow families the opportunity to talk with other caregivers, exchange ideas, and receive encouragement.

A child's need for stability and connections. Other than safety, the American Academy of Pediatrics says that "paramount to the lives of children is their need for continuity with their primary attachment figures and a sense of permanence that is enhanced when placement is stable" (2000, p. 1146). Interruptions in the continuity of a child's caregiver can be detrimental to the child's development. However, there are children who cannot be protected at home, even with intensive services, and must be placed in alternate care for their protection. In an alternate care setting, repeated moves from one home to another compound the adverse effects that initial stress and inadequate parenting have on a child's development and his or her ability to cope (American Academy of Pediatrics, 2000). Therefore, when safety necessitates placement, every consideration must be made to preserve the stability of the placement and of the child's previous connections.

Some ways to preserve connections include:

- Placement with siblings and frequent visitation with parents or caregivers, extended family, friends, or siblings who could not be placed together.
- Attendance at the same school, church, and neighborhood activities.
- Continuation of the same interests, such as soccer, basketball, or softball.
- Visitation or allowing children to take their pets, toys, or other personal belongings to foster care.

■ Summary of Competencies

Intake and investigation represent the initial points of contact between the CPS worker, the community, and the involved child and family. Your intervention sets the stage for all of the CPS activities that follow, and your competence in the following areas of knowledge and skills will largely influence a successful and safe outcome for the child and family.

Knowledge:

1. Knowledge of your state statutes defining child abuse and neglect.
2. Knowledge of agency policies and procedures and responsibilities regarding acceptance of referrals of child maltreatment.
3. Knowledge of the time frames mandated by state law or agency procedures for responding to reports of child abuse.
4. Knowledge of the safety factors that necessitate emergency placement.
5. Knowledge of communication methods and interviewing techniques.
6. Knowledge of community resources and family eligibility criteria.
7. Knowledge of the agency's policies and procedures regarding the CPS assessment.
8. Knowledge of the information required in order to complete an investigation and reach a disposition decision.
9. Knowledge of child development and the dynamics of human behavior.
10. Knowledge of the variety of cultural and lifestyle contexts in your community.

Skills:

1. Ability to utilize effective communication and listening techniques in order to elicit factual information.
2. Ability to solicit and record pertinent information in an organized, clear, and coherent manner.
3. Ability to deal with anger and manage hostility, while remaining calm during tense situations.
3. Ability to analyze and sort relevant from irrelevant information.
4. Ability to communicate and coordinate service activities with other community professionals.
5. Ability to interview children.
6. Ability to interview parents or caregivers and families.
7. Ability to utilize sound interpersonal relationship skills and communication techniques.
8. Ability to confront anxious or resistant parents or caregivers while remaining supportive.
9. Ability to convey respect for and respond with sensitivity to families with varied cultural, educational, or racial backgrounds.
10. Ability to remain rational and objective during stressful circumstances.
11. Ability to interpret complex medical, legal, or agency documents.
12. Ability to utilize supervision and share decision-making.

13. Ability to evaluate and summarize complex and potentially conflicting information.
14. Ability to work effectively within designated, and often limited, time frames.
15. Ability to complete required written documentation.
16. Ability to be aware of personal emotions and "triggers," as well as biases and prejudices.

References

American Academy of Pediatrics. (2000). Developmental issues for young children in foster care. *Pediatrics, 106*(5), 1145–1150.

National Association for Public Child Welfare Administrators. (1988). *Guidelines for a model system of protective services for abused and neglected children and their families.* Washington, DC: National Association for Public Child Welfare Administrators.

National Center for Comprehensive Emergency Services to Children. (1975). *Comprehensive emergency services.* Nashville, TN: Under contract to the Children's Bureau, U.S. Department of Health, Education, and Welfare.

Rycus, J., & Hughes, R. (1998). *Field guide to child welfare: Placement and permanence.* Washington, DC: CWLA Press.

7

Carol A. Wahlgren
Linda Metsger
Charmaine Brittain

Assessment

- Conducting an Assessment

- Safety Assessment

- Risk Assessment

- Family Assessment

- Summary of Competencies

Assessment is an essential ingredient for appropriate and adequate intervention with families. The goal of assessment is to gather and analyze information that will support sound decision-making regarding the safety, permanency, and well-being of children and to determine appropriate services for the family. This chapter contains practical suggestions regarding how to approach assessment, including recommended issues to address and examples of key questions to ask in order to understand how to conduct comprehensive and accurate safety, risk, and family assessments. Information from this chapter should be used in tandem with that in chapter 5.

■ Conducting an Assessment

□ The Purposes of Assessment

Assessment is based on the principle that all families have strengths that must be used to resolve the issue of concern. For services to be relevant and effective, workers must systematically gather information and continuously evaluate family members' strengths and their ability to address their problems. This information is used to engage parents and caregivers in a culturally responsive working relationship that builds on their strengths to resolve the problems that endanger their children and families.

Assessment begins with the first contact with a family or the person who first tells the worker about the family, and it does not end until a case is closed. Working with families is a dynamic process that calls for frequent and flexible decision-making as new information becomes available. On the basis of assessment activities, decisions are made, plans for services are developed, and conscious, planned intervention takes place that may change problem situations through empowered parents or caregivers.

The following are some of the ways that the CPS worker may apply the information gathered through a comprehensive assessment (Colorado Department of Human Services & American Humane Association, 2001).

- Assessment is a direct link to and basis for service planning and decision-making.
- Assessment helps CPS staff explain their decision-making to others.
- The assessment process can create rapport between the worker and family through increasingly better understanding of the family.
- Assessment provides an opportunity to engage the family to set and achieve goals.
- Assessment offers a practical way to utilize family strengths in a service plan to offset, control, or reduce risks.
- Assessment encourages the worker and family to explore family resources for placement, if necessary.
- Assessment provides important information to a new worker if cases are transferred.

☐ Building a Relationship with the Family

In order to conduct assessment in a way that builds positive relationships, you will increase the likelihood of success if you employ a few strategic tactics. It is important to: (1) treat the family with respect; (2) instill a sense of hope by approaching the family from a strengths-based perspective; (3) maintain a professional and nonjudgmental attitude; and (4) learn about and value what is important to the family.

Develop a "tool kit" of practical tips that are helpful in engaging families. Interaction with families is a learning process. Use a family-centered approach that recognizes the family as the expert regarding themselves. The family, more than anyone, knows their own history, culture, strengths, and needs. Some practical tips include the following:

- Be organized.
- Develop an introduction that fits your style.
- Address the parent or caregiver as *Mr.* or *Mrs.* This shows respect and maintains the appropriate professional boundaries between you and the family.
- Listen to the family. Allow family members to talk about themselves and their family situation. Validate the family's experience with the process.
- Observe and mirror the body language, pace of conversation, eye contact, and physical space set by the family.

☐ Methods for Conducting Assessment

Workers rely on three main sources for gathering information for the safety, risk, and family assessment:

1. Interviews
2. Reviewing records
3. Observations

Interviews. You will interview parents, caregivers, children, relatives, community support individuals, and professionals, as well as any other individuals identified as significant by the family. See chapter 5 for more information on this topic. Much of your information will come from these interviews.

Reviewing records. This is an important source of information for conducting any type of assessment. Often records will include information about family and individual functioning. Records may be recent information (e.g., from an interview conducted by law enforcement, another family services agency, a substance abuse or mental health agency, a school, or a healthcare provider). Records may also include prior CPS involvement. Unless you have reason to believe that the information is wrong or misinterpreted, you can use it as part of your assessment, citing the source in your narrative. Clearly, you will also conduct your own interviews and make your own observations. But written records can fill in gaps on an assessment. Older records may help you understand patterns over time, such as history of child maltreatment or substance abuse.

Observations. Observation helps confirm, question, or refute the information you receive from interviews. Observations can also direct the course of the interview.

Some information is best obtained from observation, although interviews may help give some additional perspective about what is observed. For instance, observing injuries is more accurate than hearing them described. Common indicators can best identify some safety and risk factors (such as current substance use). Dangerous environmental factors are best identified by observation.

Observations can assist in directing the assessment. Consider: What do you see or hear? What more should you do to verify your observations (e.g., ask the client, neighbors, or landlord: "Is this the way it is most of the time?")? Remember that your own observations may be limited by the "lens" of your personal history and culture. When drawing conclusions about what you observe, ask yourself about the influence of your personal biases and values.

☐ Safety and Risk Assessment and Decision-Making

Risk assessment is a structured process that is used to assist in determining the future risk of harm to a child and to assist in key decision-making processes regarding child abuse and neglect situations. *Safety* refers to a subset of risk, that is, *immediate* or *short-term* risk of *moderate to severe harm.* It is important to assess safety because some abuse/neglect situations are currently dangerous to the child. If you were to attend only to longer term risk, signs of present danger might be overlooked or minimized. Effective risk assessment models focus on the strengths and needs of the family environment. Successful implementation of a risk assessment process has value for the children and families as well as workers, supervisors, and management. For example, safety and risk assessment models also serve as a vehicle for communicating agency activities to the court system, other agencies, advocacy groups, and lawmakers.

The rationale for the use of safety and risk assessment is as follows:

- Safety and risk assessments are standardized screening processes that clarify the agency's responsibilities in the protection of children.
- They assist workers in gathering information by helping workers focus on certain factors that must be addressed in order to complete the assessment instruments.
- They define the parameters of the agency's intervention, so that children who are vulnerable to abuse and neglect are identified and at the same time CPS does not become unnecessarily involved in the lives of families where risk and safety are not an issue.
- Safety and risk assessment guides the casework process by keeping the focus on child safety and well-being.
- Safety and risk assessment focuses critical decisions (such as whether children need to be removed, what services are needed, whether sufficient progress has been made, whether reunification can occur, and whether a case can be closed) back on the key concern: "Will children likely be safe from harm?"

- Safety and risk assessment establishes a baseline of risks. This enables everyone to better assess change over time—for example, whether services are helping the family to create a safe environment for children.

- Safety and risk assessment may also address risk factors unique to population groups or geographic areas. Some models address substance abuse or domestic violence. Specific models may also identify and respond to cultural and ethnic differences. It is wise to find out if assessment tools for specific groups are available within your agency. If not, questions should be asked regarding the cultural relevance of standardized tools, and modifications may be necessary. While most cultural groups would agree about basic safety and well-being of children, there may be considerable variation in how these are accomplished. When in doubt, cultural experts within the child's community or primary reference group are a valuable resource in discerning culture-based differences.

Safety and risk assessment is an organized process that assists in the development of risk reduction strategies.

- The number of reports to CPS has increased dramatically, making it difficult to prioritize services. The use of safety and risk assessment instruments aids in establishing priorities for investigation and service delivery.

- Formal safety and risk assessment helps organize case data and facilitates service planning and decision-making about safety, placement, and reunification.

- Safety and risk assessment instruments provide a vehicle for communicating and clarifying agency activities and decisions in child protection, thereby focusing resources of other agencies in a common direction for increased safety and risk reduction for children.

Well-constructed assessment models assist in managing accountability. The factors articulate the information that is needed to assess maltreatment reports and document case dispositions. The instruments provide verification that responses to all maltreatment reports are systematic, comprehensive, and legally sufficient. The models promote accuracy and error reduction in all phases of intake, service delivery, evaluation, and case closure.

Safety and risk assessment models are not sufficient for understanding every family's unique situation and cultural context. Although safety and risk assessment instruments are excellent tools in gathering and documenting standardized information regarding child abuse and neglect, the factors on the assessment instruments were not designed to be used as a checklist for interviewing families, nor are they the only measure on which decisions about risk should be based. Interview questions regarding the factors on the assessment tools should be respectfully worded according to the interviewing principles presented in chapter 5.

Assessment is an ongoing process and is conducted throughout the life of a case both formally and informally. Every time you meet with parents or caregivers, you are assessing the current situation to determine children's current safety and progress or lack thereof toward case goals. You do this formally by conducting and docu-

menting three main types of assessments—safety, risk, and family assessment. As is depicted visually in the diagram, these assessments are conducted at distinct times in a case and for different purposes, but the information gathered from each overlaps and informs subsequent assessments.

Safety assessment is distinct from but also related to risk assessment. Safety assessment is concerned with the present and very near future. Thus, the time frame for safety is a *subset* of all future risk. Risk assessment builds on the safety assessment and occurs during the first stage of the case, for most states typically within the first 60 days. The family assessment then incorporates information on both the safety and risk assessment to more fully understand the family's situation.

The diagram below depicts the timeline of safety assessment, risk assessment, family assessment, and reassessment. Starting immediately or now, the worker will assess the current safety situation. Over the course of time, subsequent assessments determine risk, assess the family's situation, and then reassess the risk to the child. Each assessment builds upon the information gathered from previous assessments to understand the current situation and make decisions.

Each type of assessment is discussed in this chapter. The information from each of the assessments informs and builds upon the others. At all times, the paramount concern is to assure the children's safety.

☐ **Application of Safety and Risk Assessment**

Safety and risk assessment may be used at all critical decision points in referrals of child abuse and neglect, beginning at intake, continuing through service provision, and ending at case closure. Safety and risk assessments inform decision-making

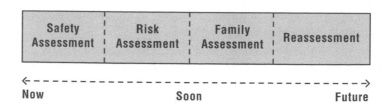

throughout the stages of the casework process and are conducted at both formal and informal points throughout the case, as follows.

Intake and investigation. This process encompasses several activities in an agency's initial response to reports, including:

- *Report taking,* or the process of collecting sufficient information to assess the nature of the report, evaluate the source, and explain the agency's statutory responsibilities and resources. It also includes assessing the urgency of the situation.

- *Screening,* or determining if the report fits within the scope of statutory responsibility or if CPS staff should refer the matter to another service agency. It also includes assessing the seriousness of the report and prioritizing the agency's response.

- *Investigation,* or assessment, is the actual point of gathering information to assess the child's immediate safety and level of risk of harm and includes contact with the child, the caregivers, and individuals with corroborating information. This activity typically involves extensive use of safety and risk assessment tools.

Crisis intervention or brief services. This entails the immediate provision of services to some children and families. As information is gathered it is often necessary to take immediate action to protect the child or to intervene to stabilize a family crisis.

Service planning. This includes assessment for ongoing services and embodies a set of decisions that can be supported by risk assessment as well as a more thorough family assessment. Risk assessment helps to identify factors that contribute to the child's future safety and guide staff in service planning with the family to address and ameliorate specific risk factors. It also serves as an instrument to assess components of family functioning and assists in decisions about court referral. Consistency is aided in such activities as removal, placement, and reunification.

Periodic evaluation and case closure. These occur when the agency continues to assesses a family to determine if the parents are willing and able to keep the child safe and protect the child from risk of harm, or the agency assumes responsibility for assuring another permanency option. Use of risk assessment provides one type of measurement to assess observable results against the stated goals set for the family during service planning.

Prior to using any safety or risk assessment tools, it is important to understand the specific decisions that are made on the basis of the instruments. Specific uses of both the safety and risk assessments vary from state to state. The supervisor should help the worker to understand the specific policies of the agency and state regarding safety and risk assessment instruments. For instance, is the safety assessment used only for founded cases of abuse or neglect, or is it used for all cases that are investigated? Is the safety assessment used to help determine the need for out-of-home placement, or are there other decisions that are generated by the safety assessment? Is the risk assessment used to determine if a case is opened for services, or is it used to determine the level of contact between the worker and the family? These questions should be answered before a worker begins to use the safety or risk assessment instruments.

Because they help to structure and organize a worker's thinking and decisions about safety and risk, safety and risk assessments allow the supervisor to better assess how a worker reached specific conclusions about a family and to ask questions about the behaviors the worker observed or the information he or she received that led to that specific conclusion. If a worker struggles with a particular factor, the supervisor can use this as a teachable moment and perhaps direct the worker to ask different questions, talk with a different collateral, or observe something different in the family interaction to clarify issues around that factor. The next time the worker does a safety or risk assessment he or she will have a better idea of the information that is needed to make more accurate assessments.

■ Safety Assessment

□ Safety Defined

There are two parts to the decision about safety: (1) Is the child currently safe? And (2) If not, what needs to happen to ensure safety?

A safety concern is about the potential harm to the child that could be:

- *Immediate* or in the *near future*. Immediate is defined as (1) having recently occurred or occurring now, or (2) likely to occur in the very near future.
- *Serious* (moderate to severe) if an intervention is not made to control the situation. Moderate to severe harm means that there is a threat of one or more of the following:

   Danger to the child's health or life.

   Impairment to his or her physical or mental well-being (including emotional abuse).

   Disfigurement.

   Severe developmental impairment.

☐ **Examples of Safety Concerns**

> Jamal, age 8, is reported by his teacher, who suspects he is being sexually abused. She says that just after participating in an abuse prevention program, Jamal revealed that Uncle Wayne molests him. Jamal lives with his grandmother and her son Wayne. Grandmother is immobilized by the allegation; she says that she just can't believe it, but if it happened she thinks it's due to Wayne's run of hard luck with jobs and drugs. Wayne denies the allegation. Grandma says she can't keep Wayne out of his own house, but that she will have Jamal sleep in her room.

This scenario presents a safety concern because the grandmother is immobilized and may not be able to protect Jamal. Having Jamal sleep with her is not a feasible safety plan because Uncle Wayne has access to Jamal during the time he is not asleep in grandmother's room.

> Ahmad, age 13, is reported by his teacher as abused. He has bruise marks on his face, and one eye is swollen shut. His grandfather, who lives at his house, beat the boy after he found Ahmad's stash of X-rated magazines. Ahmad's mother was able to stop her father but said it was very difficult. Although Ahmad is a big boy for his age, he did not fight back because he has been taught to respect his elders. She said the grandfather has repeatedly hit Ahmad and cursed him. Grandfather shouts at the CPS worker, saying that it is his job to teach his grandson right from wrong, that Ahmad will be disciplined, and that he is not finished with him yet.

Ahmad is considered unsafe in this example because of the grandfather's harsh attitude toward disciplining and his statement that implies in the near future he will continue to hit Ahmad. Repeat maltreatment is likely, since Ahmad's mother is not able to stop her father from hitting her son. While it is clear that Ahmad is at immediate risk, the interview also reveals strengths that can help the family redirect behaviors in a less destructive way—behaviors that may have a positive intent.

☐ **Key Factors Common to Most Models**

The following factors are commonly found on safety assessment instruments:

Factor: Caregiver behavior is violent or out of control.

Description: The caregiver uses extreme physical or verbal outbursts, brutal punishment, or weapons or otherwise exhibits a serious lack of self-control. A caregiver may use harsh punishment that results in physical or emotional injury to the child.

Factor: Caregiver describes or acts toward child in predominantly negative terms or has unrealistic expectations.

Description: The caregiver describes the child in a degrading manner, attacks the child's self-esteem, or requires the child to perform in a way that is beyond the child's developmental capabilities. For example, if a parent expects an 8-year-old child to provide care for an infant as well as another younger sibling while the parent is at work, these unrealistic expectations may create a safety concern for all of the children.

Factor: Caregiver has caused harm or made a plausible threat of harm.

Description: The caregiver has caused serious injury to the child, has tortured the child, or plans to retaliate against the child for the investigation, or the caregiver threatens to abuse and/or neglect the child in the future. Workers must assess how the parent will react to the CPS investigation. If the worker suspects that the child will be severely punished by the caregiver, this may become more of a safety concern than the reason for the original referral.

Factor: Caregiver refuses to give access to child, or there is reason to believe the family may flee.

Description: The family has previously fled during an investigation, has isolated the child from outsiders for extended periods of time, or will not disclose the current location of the child.

Factor: Sexual abuse is suspected, and circumstances suggest the child's safety is of immediate concern.

Description: The alleged perpetrator will continue to have access to the child or the caregiver is unable/unwilling to protect the child. This factor may involve a caregiver who does not believe the child's allegations and therefore will not attempt to protect the child from the alleged perpetrator who lives in the home or elsewhere.

Factor: Caregiver is unable or unwilling to provide sufficient supervision to the child to protect him or her from moderate to severe harm.

Description: The caregiver leaves the child alone, makes inadequate babysitting arrangements, or is unaware of the child's whereabouts even though the caregiver is at home with the child. The child can wander outdoors alone, handle dangerous objects, play on an unprotected window ledge, or be exposed to other serious hazards. The length of time a child may be left alone will depend on local laws and will vary with the age and developmental stage of the child. The worker must assess the caregiver's willingness or ability to provide supervision. Mental illness or substance abuse may prevent adequate supervision. Included in this risk factor are situations where the caregiver may leave the child with another person who is incapable of providing supervision. Younger children are more vulnerable to this factor.

Factor: Caregiver is unable or unwilling to meet the child's immediate need for food, clothing, and/or shelter.

Description: Food for the child is not available, and the child appears malnourished, clothing is not minimally protective, or no adequate shelter is available to protect children from the elements.

Factor: Caregiver has not or is unable to meet medical needs of the child that may result in moderate to severe harm.

Description: Child has specific emotional or behavioral needs that are unmet by the caregiver, and the caregiver does not seek treatment for the child's dangerous medical condition or does not follow through with prescribed treatment for a serious medical condition.

Factor: Caregiver has previously abused or neglected the child, and the severity of the past maltreatment or the caregiver's response to the incident suggests that child safety may be an immediate concern.

Description: Based on the seriousness of past maltreatment and the caregiver's response to a prior investigation, it is believed that the child's current safety is of concern. The worker should check records to see if the caregiver previously retaliated against the child after a CPS investigation or if there appears to be a pattern of abuse that presents a current safety threat.

Factor: Caregiver's alleged or observed substance use affects his or her ability to currently supervise, protect, or care for the child.

Description: Caregiver is unable to care for the child due to substance use, substances are accessible to the child, or the child was exposed to substances in utero.

Factor: Caregiver suffers from severe and/or chronic mental or physical illness that jeopardizes the child's safety.

Description: Caregiver has a distorted sense of reality that interferes with his or her ability to care for the child, is unable to physically care for the child, and/or is unable to provide for the child's basic needs due to a physical or mental illness. Services and/or adaptive supports are not in place to ensure child safety.

Factor: Caregiver is unable or unwilling to protect the child from moderate to severe harm from others.

Description: The caregiver is unable to protect the child from others in the home. He or she is unable to protect the child from verbal or physical outbursts by others. The worker must assess everyone who is in the home, including adult siblings, roommates, or other relatives. If one of these people has recently verbally or physically assaulted the child and the caregiver is unable to offer protection, this would be a safety concern.

Factor: Domestic violence in the home affects the caregiver's ability to protect the child from imminent moderate to severe harm.

Description: The child was previously injured during a domestic violence incident, or the child's own behavior during an incident increases risk, or weapons have been used during domestic violence in the home. The worker should assess the child's proximity to the domestic violence. If the child is often in the room during incidents of domestic violence or attempts to intervene to protect a caregiver, the child may be hurt, and a safety concern exists. Emotional harm should also be considered when assessing this factor.

Factor: Physical living conditions are hazardous or immediately threatening.

Description: Child has access to dangerous objects or substances, lack of utilities, exposed wires or broken windows, spoiled food that poses a health hazard, animal or human waste throughout the residence, or unlocked guns. The age of the child needs to be considered when assessing this factor. A toddler who has access to exposed wires or may eat spoiled food is more vulnerable than an infant who is unable to get around on his or her own.

If safety concerns are identified, the worker then looks at factors that may mitigate the concerns or puts a safety plan in place to ensure safety. If these options still do not appear adequate to keep the child safe, placement should be considered. If the safety factors can be addressed and the children can remain in the home, the children are said to be "conditionally" safe in that they are safe so long as the safety plan components are working.

☐ Assessing Safety for Specialized Issues

When assessing safety, CPS workers often see the same issues over and over again. Mental illness, substance abuse, domestic violence, and cognitive developmental disabilities are pervasive in CPS practice and can substantively impact safety decisions. For each of these issues, the following lists of safety factors should be considered. Like other safety factors, these should be assessed by determining whether they are present or not. (This list of specialized safety factors is based on Murphy and Harper, [2001]).

Mental Illness Safety Factors

- The parent or caregiver shows bizarre/delusional thinking about the family/child.
- The parent or caregiver involves the child in psychotic/bizarre behaviors/actions (e.g., cuts own body, hides/withholds food).
- The parent or caregiver has thought about harming child or self in last 3 months.
- The parent or caregiver does not take medication that has been prescribed for his or her own mental illness condition.
- The parent or caregiver frequently does not respond to child's interactions or stated needs (i.e., is "off in own world" at times).
- The parent or caregiver is diagnosed with severe/chronic mental illness but does not receive or use services or supports.
- The child is afraid of the parent or caregiver due to the caregiver's behavior(s).
- The child is diagnosed with severe/chronic mental illness but does not receive or use services or supports.

Substance Abuse Safety Factors

- The parent or caregiver has experienced blackouts while with the child due to alcohol/drugs in the last 3 months.

• The parent or caregiver has driven with the child in the car while drunk/ high within the last 3 months.

• The parent or caregiver has left children unsupervised while obtaining or ingesting alcohol/drugs within the last 3 months.

• The parent or caregiver has been physically/sexually inappropriate or violent while drunk/high in the last 3 months.

• Drug/alcohol paraphernalia is in a location where children can get it.

• The parent or caregiver is diagnosed with a substance abuse problem but does not receive or use services or supports.

• The child was born with a positive toxicology from alcohol/drugs in the last year.

• The child has found and taken, or may have been given, alcohol/drugs by the caregiver within the last 3 months.

• The child has been diagnosed with a substance abuse problem but does not receive or use services or supports.

Domestic Violence Safety Factors

• The parent or caregiver has physical signs of abuse (e.g., multiple injuries, bruises, bites, burns, lacerations, broken bones).

• The parent or caregiver has experienced physical violence from his or her partner (e.g., has been pushed, punched, kicked) within the last 3 months.

• The parent or caregiver's frequency and/or intensity of violence have escalated in the last 3 months.

• The parent or caregiver is unable to protect child from harm due to the batterer's violent acts and/or threats against the caregiver.

• The batterer has assaulted the caregiver while he or she is holding the child.

• The batterer has used or threatened to use a weapon during a domestic violence assault.

• The parent or caregiver has been identified for domestic violence problems but does not receive or use services or supports.

• The child has been used as a shield or been forced to participate in domestic violence in the last 3 months.

• The child has physically attempted to stop a domestic violence episode in the last 3 months.

• The child is afraid to leave the caregiver alone with the partner.

Cognitive Developmental Disabilities

• The parent or caregiver has been assessed with an IQ of 70 or less.

• The parent or caregiver does not know how to perform daily living activities (e.g., preparing meals, personal hygiene).

• The parent or caregiver does not show adequate problem-solving skills during crisis or emergency situations.

- The parent or caregiver is diagnosed with cognitive developmental disabilities but does not receive or use services or supports.
- The child has unsuccessfully tried to assume the caregiver role of providing basic necessities (food/clothes/shelter).
- The child has jeopardized the safety of others in the last 3 months due to his or her own cognitive impairment.
- The child has been diagnosed with cognitive developmental disabilities but does not receive or use services or supports.

☐ Cultural Considerations in Safety Assessment

Typically, the factors that make a child unsafe in a home are the same across all cultures. Culture guides people's interpretation of life experiences and the development of coping strategies for day-to-day living. Generally, cultural considerations have less impact on evaluation of safety than on the development of safety plans. Unsafe situations are generally such regardless of culture. However, cultural behavior can sometimes be misinterpreted when assessing safety factors. Examples include verbal threats, the parenting responsibilities given to children, living and sleeping arrangements, and physical markings and healing practices. When writing and implementing safety plans, it is important to look toward supports and resources that meet the family's needs and are culturally relevant to the family. This will increase the likelihood that the interventions will be successful. Examples of cultural considerations may include the following:

- When assessing sexual abuse as a safety concern, it is important for the worker to understand that in some cultures, children may share a bed with other children past an age that the worker may feel is appropriate, or the child may even share a bed with an adult past the age most American children sleep with their parent or caregiver. Nonetheless, whatever the culture, it is never safe for a small child to sleep with an adult when the parent or caregiver is under the influence of drugs or alcohol or is obese (as rolling on the child may endanger him or her).
- When assessing whether supervision poses a safety concern for the child, the worker should also consider cultural factors. Some cultures teach young grade-school-age children to care for siblings and to take responsibility for household chores such as cooking. They may also teach safety skills at an earlier age than most American children, and there also may be easy access to extended family members.
- When assessing the adequacy of medical care, cultural healing practices and religious beliefs must be considered. Instead of taking a child to a doctor to treat an illness, a caregiver may rely on a spiritual healer such as a medicine man or woman—a shaman or curandero. The worker needs to assess the child's medical condition, as opposed to the caregiver's choice of treatment. Religion may also influence the caregiver's choice of medical treatment, as some religions do not believe in the use of Western medical technology or

practice. In these situations, a true safety concern may exist that requires intervention, but all consideration must be given to respecting the caregiver's religious and spiritual beliefs.

- Culture may also influence day-to-day activities that might appear to be harsh or even abusive to individuals outside of a culture. For example, Tibetan Buddhists practice prolonged periods of meditation requiring sitting or kneeling for many hours. Children as young as 5 are taught to contemplate and may spend many hours a day sitting still and practicing their religion, which may be perceived by others outside the culture as abusive. Whenever you are uncertain about a situation, seek a cultural guide to help you understand the context.

■ Risk Assessment

□ Risk Assessment Defined

Risk is the likelihood of any degree of long-term future harm. Risk assessment does not predict when the future harm might occur but rather the likelihood of it happening. It also does not predict the level of harm that might occur.

Risks for future harm to children can be chronic or exist when certain conditions recur in the family, such as a parent relapsing due to drug or alcohol abuse or mental illness.

A formalized risk assessment tool helps to reduce instances in which significant risk factors are unintentionally overlooked or minimized. Using the risk assessment tool as a guide, workers can gather specific information from the child, parent, or caregiver and collateral contacts that will assist them in completing the risk assessment. If a worker is talking with a medical professional who has been involved with the child, he or she should ask specific questions about how the parents have followed through with the child's medical needs in the past to help determine if the parents are willing and able to meet the child's current medical needs. If the family has had previous involvement with a CPS agency, it is important to talk to previous workers about how the family responded to involvement with the agency.

The generally recognized risk factors are broadly categorized into child, parent or caregiver, family, and environmental factors. Many risk assessment models share risk factors in common. Almost all risk assessment models also contain some unique factors that are regarded as important by a particular state or local CPS agency.

If your agency uses a specific risk assessment tool, weights may be assigned to each factor in each category—for example, child factors, caregiver factors, family factors, and environmental factors. The weights are then added to arrive at a predetermined level of risk to the child. Some agencies use an approach that is less quantitative, and the level of risk is determined by reviewing and considering them all together and determining one overall rating.

Risk assessment tools are used as guides and *never* as a substitute for worker judgment that is based on a more comprehensive knowledge of family dynamics and culture.

☐ Key Factors Found in Most Models

Child Factors

Factor: Child's age, physical, and/or mental abilities.

Considerations: How do the child's age, physical, and/or mental abilities make him or her more or less vulnerable to future abuse/neglect?

- The premise of the age factor is that younger children are more vulnerable to maltreatment by the caregiver, are less able to protect themselves, and are at more risk of harm because of their fragile physical condition. Infants and toddlers do not have language skills that allow them to verbalize abuse/neglect. Preschool children may be socially isolated with their caregivers and may be without the observation of others who could report abuse/neglect.

- The child's ability to care for himself or herself is influenced by his or her chronological and mental age.

- Certain children are considered to be at greater risk because of physical handicaps or mental retardation, prematurity, behavioral problems, or chronic illnesses. Children with these conditions require extra care and may place additional financial or emotional stress on a family.

- Additional factors to consider: Does the alleged perpetrator have access to the child? Are the parents or caregivers willing to protect the child by preventing or supervising contact with the alleged perpetrator?

Factor: Severity, frequency, and type of abuse/neglect.

Considerations: How does the severity/type and frequency of the abuse make the child more or less vulnerable?

- Severity relates to the seriousness of harm. Bodily injuries from abuse or neglect that result in disfigurement or impairment are more severe.

- Frequency is the incidence of actual harm perpetrated on the child, not the incidence of reports of harm; more frequent harm creates higher risk.

- The type of abuse may impact risk. For example, in sexual abuse cases, the risk of recurring abuse is significant if the perpetrator continues to have access to the child.

Caregiver Factors

Factor: Conditions of the caregiver, which may impede his or her ability to care for the child.

Consideration: How do the conditions or handicaps of the caregiver make the child more or less vulnerable?

- *Physical functioning* includes mobility and flexibility and is usually easily observed.
- *Mental abilities* include the ability to make sound judgments, the ability to make use of resources to care for the family, and awareness of time and location.
- *Emotional functioning* includes impulse control, anger control, level of apathy, frustration tolerance, and ability to cope with stress.
- Additional factors include:

  The expectations regarding the children's role in providing them with emotional support and sustenance.

  The presence of domestic violence or of volatile or conflictual relationships in the home or in the caregiver's history.

  The presence, as well as the extent, of mental illness.

  The degree of substance use/abuse.

  The presence and extent of cognitive developmental delays that may interfere with parenting.

Factor: Caregiver's level of cooperation/response to the investigation.

Considerations: How does the caregiver's level of cooperation/response to the investigation make the child more or less vulnerable?

- How willing is the caregiver to protect the child by recognizing the problem or being motivated to change? This may include willingness to participate in treatment or willingness to remove the perpetrator from the home.
- How willing is the caregiver to take responsibility for the maltreatment or failure to protect the child?
- How does the caregiver respond to the investigation? Although emotional responses should be expected, caring parents or caregivers may also express some understanding of your involvement, demonstrate some concern about the child, and perhaps show an interest in seeking a resolution to the referral.
- The parents or caregivers may feel strongly that you are infringing on their rights. Reluctance to cooperate should not always be interpreted as an intention to hide something.
- You should not be strongly influenced either by cooperation or lack of cooperation. You need to understand and acknowledge that the parent's or caregiver's reaction may be as a result of longstanding negative history with

the system you represent. Resistant parents or caregivers may need time to test out your intentions and understand the meaning of your involvement. When they no longer feel intimidated, they may be more open to you.

- Does the family have a history of hiding the child from outsiders? For example, keeping the child home from school frequently, not letting the child have playmates, not letting the child have medical treatment when it is clearly necessary and available.

Factor: Caregiver's motivation to improve parenting skills.

Considerations: How does the caregiver's understanding of his or her parenting skills and role in the abuse/neglect make the child more or less vulnerable?

- Does the caregiver understand and accept that his or her action/inaction is not safe for the child?

- You should consider the caregiver's level of motivation and ability to improve parenting skills if necessary.

- Are the parents or caregivers aware of the normal developmental stages and abilities of children? Are their expectations reasonable and appropriate, given the child's age and level of development? Is a 2-year-old always expected to keep quiet? Is a 9-month-old expected to walk or be toilet trained? (These expectations are unrealistic.)

- Do caregivers describe a variety of alternative means of disciplining and controlling the child, or are they tied to one method, such as physical punishment? When you suggest alternatives, do they reject them immediately, or only try them once or twice and then revert to their old methods?

- Do the parents or caregivers normally provide for the child's basic needs, such as food, clothing, shelter, supervision, medical care, and education?

- Do they feel their methods of providing for the child's needs are adequate? Are they defensive about their methods? Does the evidence suggest that their childcare practices are in fact not adequate when the family believes they are?

- Is the primary caregiver willing and able to work with the agency on identifying strategies to reduce the risk within an established time frame?

Factor: Previous history of abuse/neglect.

Considerations: Does the caregiver have a history of victimization? There is a higher risk of maltreatment when a caregiver was a victim of abuse/neglect and there was little or no resolution. Placement of the caregiver out of the home in childhood is another factor to be taken into consideration.

Factor: Substance abuse.

Considerations: Substance abuse may interfere with the caregiver's ability to care for the child. The child's basic needs for adequate clothing, food, shelter, supervision, or medical care may be neglected while the caregiver is obtaining and/or using drugs or alcohol. In addition, a child's emotional needs may not be met by a parent or caregiver who has difficulty bonding with or nurturing a child due to drug/alcohol use.

- The chronicity and type of substance used by the caregiver are key factors in the assessment. Often chronic substance abuse problems result in a chaotic lifestyle, criminal behavior, loss of employment, and poverty.

- Keep in mind that in many families with substance abuse, the extended family has developed a network of safety for the children during episodes of the caregiver's substance abuse. It is not appropriate to assume that a substance-abusing parent comes from a family that also uses substances or could not provide for the safety of the child.

Family Factors

Factor: Strength of family support system.

Considerations: How does the strength of the family support system make the child more or less vulnerable?

- How do the composition, characteristics, and behavior of the family as a whole impact on future risk?

- The presence of resources, including individuals, agencies, and professionals who are available to caregivers in times of crisis, should be determined. Risk can be mitigated if support systems are constructive and accessible and resources are effectively used.

- Families who live in rural and remote areas may be geographically isolated and may have a difficult time accessing resources and thus be less able to protect children; likewise, people living in urban areas may be socially isolated and less able to access resources because of their social isolation.

Factor: Interaction between the child and the parents or caregivers.

Considerations: What is the nature of the interaction among family members?

- How do the parents or caregivers behave toward the child? Is there affection? Are the parents or caregivers capable of providing sympathy and comfort to the child when the child is hurt, angry, sick, or confused?

- Do the parents or caregivers exhibit a lack of guilt or remorse about the child's condition? Are they critical of the child and unconcerned with the injuries? For example: "It's his own fault; he's so clumsy."

- Parents' or caregivers' anger and discomfort with the assessment may be directed toward the child, using some form of retaliation, if they believe, for example, that the child is responsible for the report.

Factor: Domestic violence.

Considerations: Risk is determined by assessing the level of violence in the home and the ability of the parent or caregiver to protect the child from the violence. This includes readiness of the adult victim of domestic violence to receive high levels of specific support and/or education to help break the very complex cycle of dependency on the perpetrator.

Environmental Factors

Factor: Stressors.

Considerations: Are the stressors chronic or short-term, and how does this relate to the caregiver's response to stress?

• Sudden and continual changes add stress. Situations causing stress frequently occur together, such as a divorce, relocation, and loss of income.

Factor: Environmental conditions of the home.

Considerations: How might the family's environment be affecting their functioning, keeping in mind cultural differences of cleanliness, use of space, and tidiness?

• Are the conditions of the home a factor in the report? Is the report a result of conditions of poverty, such as substandard housing or homelessness?

Factor: Strength of the community support system.

Considerations: How can the community support the family?

• Do the parents or caregivers have any social supports such as relatives, friends, or neighbors? Do they have access to community or professional resources?

• Are the parents or caregivers able to utilize outside resources for problem solving, or do they feel that they must always solve their own problems? Do they reject outside resources because they feel that outsiders would infringe on their rights to privacy or their right to parent their children in any way they see fit? Or do they reject outside resources because of a long history of negative interaction with such resources? You may need to help the family develop a more positive relationship with resources in order to ensure the safety of the child.

Factor: Availability of treatment resources.

Considerations: What services are needed to protect the child and strengthen the family? Needed resources must be available and accessible in order to protect the children and strengthen families. Is the family willing and able to utilize the resources? Are the available resources appropriately culturally responsive?

☐   Completion of Risk Assessments

Typically risk assessment instruments are completed toward the end of the investigation process. This enables the worker who is assessing risk to gather information from a variety of sources. Using the risk assessment as a guide, the worker can obtain information from the family and from collateral resources such as schools, childcare providers, treatment providers, agency records, and previous workers.

■   Family Assessment

Comprehensive family assessment uses information gathered from the initial screening, safety assessment, and risk assessment. It takes a broader look at the

family and is not as specifically focused as the risk assessment that results from an investigation into a specific incident involving an identified child. The family assessment seeks to understand family connections and capacities to nurture and keep children safe. Throughout the assessment process, family strengths as they relate to the presenting concerns should be identified, and you should exhibit responsiveness to and respect for the family's culture and uniqueness. Family assessment considers everything already collected during the safety and risk assessment, as well as more comprehensively assessing family interactions and relationships, strengths and supports, and, as appropriate, developmental issues, physical and mental health, educational history, social adjustment, substance use or abuse, domestic violence, the culture and the community, and any other factors that affect a specific family's ability to resolve concerns that led to their involvement with CPS (Colorado Department of Human Services and American Humane Association, 2001). Assessment of these factors must recognize the strengths of the family, as well as areas needing improvement.

☐ Methods and Sources

As is true for risk and safety assessment, there are three main methods for collecting information: interviewing, reviewing records, and observation. The most direct way to gather information is to meet with the family. Allow the family members to be the primary source of information if they are capable and available. Other methods include talking with relevant professionals involved with the family (doctors, teachers, therapists, for instance) and obtaining copies of evaluations and reports about family members, when permission for this has been obtained in compliance with confidentiality laws. Talking with members of the extended family, or "kinship network," whom the family has identified as important to them provides another perspective about the family that is equally significant. Consider the following sources of information:

- Physical examination of victims, depending on the protocol and procedures in your agency and state law.

- Observations that will yield information about family functioning and capacity to care for and protect children. Observations may include the home environment, individual behaviors, interactions among family members, and other environments in which the family members function (school, job, church, etc.).
- Objective tests, such as intelligence tests, personality tests, psychological tests, and aptitude tests.
- Specific types of tests or assessment instruments (e.g., substance use assessments) may be administered by a qualified professional.
- Validated family assessment instruments. These instruments have the capacity to measure change in family functioning from the time CPS first intervenes to the conclusion of the provision of services.
- Assessment tools for gathering information, such as ecomaps, genograms, family timelines, cultural genograms, strength cards, and culturegrams.
- Current and historical documents (medical records, police records, social service and counseling records, school records, employment records, and immunization records).

☐ **Framework**

Whether talking informally with the family or others or using specific assessment instruments, an assessment framework is recommended that routinely gathers information in the following areas:

- Child assessment.
- Parent or caregiver assessment.
- Family assessment.
- Environment assessment.

Workers and other providers are encouraged to use various types of assessment tools to explore the different dimensions of this framework. It is sometimes thought that when everyone who works with the family speaks in the same basic assessment framework language, it allows important information to be easily shared and built on (Seden, Sinclair, Robbins, & Pont, 2001). However, this philosophy should not cause the exclusion of providers who bring new insights and frameworks to bear on the family's uniqueness or culture. Social workers should always seek to "start where the client is" and "respect individual worth and dignity." Social work practice is improved by exposure to and integration of theories and practices that are outside the mainstream body of knowledge.

As you assess these areas, it is important to identify *strengths* as well as problems. The shift to a strengths-based approach has been the outstanding change in family-centered practice in the last 30 years (Walton, Sandau-Becker, & Mannes, 2001). What family members have learned about themselves and others in overcoming abuse and neglect, trauma, oppression, or confusion is also a source of strength

(Saleebey, 1992). Family survival through difficult times often is a measure of a family's creativity, resilience, and cohesiveness. With the family, assess the strengths the parents or caregivers have that will help empower them to make positive choices. Ask the family to tell you stories of past times or previous generations where the family overcame struggles and challenges. A strengths-based approach includes assessment of the following capacities:

- Does the family take pride in the accomplishments of individual family members?
- Is there a commitment to sticking together in difficult times?
- Does the extended family have a connection and commitment to help each other in difficult times?
- Is there a belief that family relationships will outlast material possessions?
- Is there a sufficient capacity to learn, participate in problem solving, and gain some insight?
- Is there capacity to find the "bright side" of or even a sense of humor about a bad situation?
- Is there motivation to change and a sense of hope?
- Is there a sense in the family that life could be better or different? Is there a vision of the future (Holder, 1996)?
- Do family members keep busy in order not to dwell on situations beyond the family's control?
- Do family members have ways of seeking help from others when needed?
- Are there informal supports to help in a crisis?
- Does the family talk about or demonstrate different ways of dealing with problems?
- Do family members find time to be together?
- Are there mechanisms for individual expression within the family?
- Are family members willing to get things done that are important to them (Dunst, Trivette, & Mott, 1994)?
- What meaning does the parent or caregiver give to the problem situation?
- What does the parent or caregiver want in relation to the problem situation?
- What does the parent or caregiver expect by seeking assistance?
- What would the parent's or caregiver's life be like if the problem was resolved (Cowger, 1997)?
- Does the family have a sense of pride in their culture and history?

Remember, you interpret information you receive from an assessment through your own cultural lenses. To be effective, you will want to be careful with that interpretation. For example, what you may have come to understand as a deficit may be considered a strength, depending on a family's history and level of power and privilege.

☐   **Assessment Areas**

Explore the different dimensions of child, parent or caregiver, family, and environment assessment areas with family and collateral contacts. Consider all of them when making recommendations regarding a level of intervention and planning for services. Each assessment area and its corresponding factors are described below.

Child Assessment

Your most important task will be assessing whether the child is being adequately safeguarded from significant harm and what actions are required to keep the child safe and promote the child's well-being.

Factor: Self-protection skills.

- To what degree can the child protect him or herself from a condition or behavior?
- Is the child under 5 years of age?
- Does the child demonstrate the ability and willingness to protect him or herself from abusive treatment by fighting back, escaping, or getting assistance?
- Does the child demonstrate the ability and willingness to feed him or herself or seek help in an emergency?
- When mental illness is a factor, are there protective factors that might have existed and continue to exist in the child's environment?
- What are the child's behavioral style, temperament, and current competencies?
- What supports are or could be put in place for this child? Does the child have a teacher, a relative, a neighbor, or other member of the community to whom the child can turn for assistance?

Factor: Current situation.

- Does the condition or behavior endanger the child's life or health? If so, how?
- Will the child experience developmental delays or die if feeding does not become more adequate?
- To what extent are the child's basic needs for food, clothing, and shelter currently being met?
- To what extent are the parents able to respond appropriately to the child's needs in the areas of health, education, emotional and behavioral development, identity, family, and social relationships?

Factor: Child development. Assess the child's developmental level in the following areas:

- Physical health and well-being.
- Cognitive functioning.
- Academic achievement. (Does it match the child's cognitive functioning?)

- Emotional functioning.
- Motor skills.
- Social development.
- Stress management and anger control capacities.
- Self-regulation.

Factor: Interaction between the child and parent or caregiver.

- If the child has special needs, what is the parent's or caregiver's attitude toward the child?
- How does the parent or caregiver react to the child?
- How are the child's behavior and developmental stage affecting the family?
- What are the parent's or caregiver's expectations for children, and are they appropriate for the child's level of development?
- To what extent is the child compensating for parent inadequacies? For instance, a highly engaging child might rouse a depressed parent and get his or her needs met despite the parent's mood state, whereas a passive child may be unable to do so.
- To what extent is the parent or caregiver aware of and accepting of the children's emotional needs?
- What is the parental knowledge of the care needs of the child?
- What is the parental knowledge of the role adjustments required on his or her part? (Parenting styles and behaviors may need to be adjusted, depending on the child's needs, developmental level, or temperament.)
- Is the parent or caregiver able to acknowledge limitations in parenting skill or personal unmet needs that interfere with the capacity to attend to the child's needs?
- Is there a willingness to receive information, support, or education to improve parent-child interaction or to resolve unmet dependency needs that interfere with parenting? (Keep in mind the access to culturally appropriate parent education and support).

Factor: Child characteristics.

- What is the child's behavioral functioning? Use scales like the Child Behavior Checklist as well as parents' and teachers' reports. Keep in mind cultural variances in what is considered normal and appropriate behavior.
- What is the child's overall level of dependency?
- How does the child communicate?
- What is the child's temperament?
- What is the child's mobility?
- How are the child's social skills?
- Does the child have any behaviors, such as withdrawal, exaggerated compliance (almost too eager to please), aggression, or bedwetting?

- What is the child's "cuddability," or physical attractiveness (as this may impact the parent's or caregiver's response to the child)?

Factor: Physical and/or developmental disabilities. Certain children are more vulnerable to certain forms of maltreatment; for example, the battered child syndrome, shaken child syndrome, or failure to thrive. Children who are perceived as "different"—for example, a child with a disability—are at greater risk for abuse and neglect (Jaudes & Diamond, 1985; Soeffing, 1975). Areas to explore include the following:

- What kind of kind of physical demands result from the child's disability?
- What is the financial impact of the child's disability?
- How do family members react to the child's disability (e.g., rejection, guilt, jealousy, feelings of inadequacy)?
- Are there cultural or religious factors that would shape family perceptions (Wayman, Lunch, & Hanson, 1990)?
- To what/where/whom does the family assign responsibility for their child's disability (Wayman et al., 1990)?
- How does the family view the role of fate in their lives (Wayman et al., 1990)?
- How does the parent or caregiver respond to the child with special needs?
- How does the family view their role in intervening with their child? Do they feel they can make a difference, or do they consider it hopeless (Wayman et al., 1990)?

Parent or Caregiver Assessment

It is important to be alert, when assessing parents' and caregivers' behavior patterns, to those rare situations in which parents are, for all practical purposes, "untreatable" (Jones, 1987). These include parents and caregivers who, with premeditation, painfully abuse their children, and those families with a history of prior serious injury or child abuse death. The Adoption Safe Families Act refers to these instances as "aggravated circumstances," and in situations like these a judge may find that no reasonable efforts need to be made to reunify the family.

Factor: Parent or caregiver characteristics.

- What does the parent or caregiver say others would say are his or her best qualities and what they do like best about him or her?
- What is the nature of the parent's or caregiver's overall emotional functioning (e.g., depressed, apathetic, satisfied)? This can be assessed on an informal or more formal basis depending on the person's presenting situation.
- What is the parent's or caregiver's temperament?
- Does the parent or caregiver use defense mechanisms (unconscious psychological processes that enable all of us to make sense of the world) in order to avoid taking responsibility for making the changes to keep the child safe? (See box.)

Common Defense Mechanisms

- *Acting out.* A mechanism in which the person acts without reflection or apparent regard for negative consequences.

- *Denial, minimization.* Refusing to accept or reducing the importance of a real circumstance because of its emotional implications; for example, responding to an intervention by not cooperating, being preoccupied with other things, or saying an incident "just did not happen."

- *Devaluation.* A mechanism in which the person attributes exaggerated negative qualities to self or others.

- *Displacement.* Transferring the feelings from one relationship or situation into another; for example, the battered wife who batters her children may be displacing her own hostility toward her husband onto someone less dangerous.

- *Dissociation.* The separation of a thought or feeling from consciousness; for example, when a sex abuse victim "pulls away" from the cognitive and emotional experience of the abuse. A most severe and rare outcome of dissociation is the clinical diagnosis of *multiple personality disorder.*

- *Idealization.* A mechanism in which the person attributes exaggeratedly positive qualities to self or others, for example, the child who idealizes the absent and abusive parent.

- *Identification.* The psychological process of feeling affinity with and like someone else and then behaving like the person. For instance, an abusive person may identify with her mother, who abused her as a child.

- *Intellectualization.* Thinking and talking about behavior from a perspective so as to avoid the emotional implications; for example, attributing a child's withdrawal to his developmental age rather than to the fact that he has been abused.

- *Passive aggression.* A mechanism in which the person indirectly expresses aggression toward others.

- *Projection.* Blaming others for one's problems or the actions (such as the abuse); for example, the noisy, meddling teacher; the bad child; the uncooperative spouse or worker.

- *Rationalization.* Justifying behavior to get oneself socially and psychologically "off the hook"; for example, "My son's behavior warranted the beating."

- *Reaction formation.* A mechanism in which a person substitutes behavior, thoughts, or feelings that are diametrically opposed to his or her own unacceptable ones; for example, the parent who feels guilty about her lack of bonding with her child and overindulges him.

- *Repression.* A mechanism in which the person is unable to remember or to be cognitively aware of disturbing wishes, feelings, thoughts, or experiences.

(continued)

Common Defense Mechanisms (*continued*)

- *Somatization.* A mechanism in which the person becomes preoccupied with physical symptoms disproportionate to any actual physical disturbance (common among sex abuse victims).

- *Splitting.* A mechanism in which the person views himself or others as all good or bad, failing to integrate the positive and the negative qualities into cohesive images. Often the person alternately idealizes and devalues the same person; for example, the parent or caregiver who is either defiant or compliant with the CPS worker with little apparent provocation.

- *Suppression.* A mechanism in which the person intentionally avoids thinking about disturbing problems, desires, feelings, or experiences.

- *Undoing.* A mechanism in which the person engages in behavior designed to symbolically make amends for, or negate, previous thoughts, feelings, or actions; for example, a child who feels responsible for his abuse, attributing the abuse to his angry feelings, becomes a very good or model child.

- What is the parent's or caregiver's overall level of intellectual functioning—for example, is he or she cognitively delayed, of average, or superior intelligence?

- What is the parent's or caregiver's memory and recall?

- What is the parent's or caregiver's ability to maintain concentration or attention on a task or activity?

- Does the parent or caregiver have the capacity to perceive the immediate situation accurately?

Factor: Background and history of parent or caregivers.

- What kind of family does the parent or caregiver come from?

- Is there any abuse or neglect in the parent or caregiver's history?

- What kind of upbringing did the parent or caregiver have?

- In the parent's or caregiver's family of origin, what were the family roles?

- In the parent's or caregiver's family of origin, how were children disciplined?

- In the parent's or caregiver's family of origin, how were children viewed?

- What family-of-origin scripts may be present that will allow the parent or caregiver to improve on the errors of the past?

- What evidence is there that the parent or caregiver has attempted to do things differently from his or her own parents or family of origin?

- How does the parent or caregiver feel about the way he or she was raised? Does he or she have a hope of doing better?

Factor: The parent's or caregiver's behavior patterns.

- To what extent is the parent or caregiver impulsive (reacts immediately, without planning, reflection, or regard for the consequences of the action)?
- To what extent is the parent or caregiver flexible (able to change behavior to fit different situational demands or expectations)?
- To what extent is the parent or caregiver compulsive (seems driven to do things)?
- How is anger directed (e.g., at a particular person or situation, or generalized and indiscriminate)?
- What is the parent's or caregiver's capacity to self-reflect on his or her behavior?
- What is the parent's or caregiver's ability to express empathy to all family members?
- To what extent is the parent or caregiver aggressive (physically or verbally intrusive)?
- To what extent is the parent or caregiver submissive (allows others to lead and influence behavior)?
- To what extent are these characteristics a function of personality, and how much of these behaviors could be contributed to situational stresses associated with the CPS process?

Factor: Social interaction.

- What is the parent's or caregiver's contact and involvement with others?
- Are the parent's or caregiver's relationships characterized by "splitting," in which the parent or caregiver sees individuals as all good or all bad, often designating one professional as the good one and another as the bad one? Parents and caregivers with this pattern of perception also usually do this within their families. They are often intensely and inappropriately angry. Their children may experience parenting as a roller coaster. They usually do not know what will happen next.
- Is the parent or caregiver dependent (expects and seeks help for things he or she can or should be able to do)? Role reversal is likely to characterize such caregivers' relationships with children.
- What is the parent's or caregiver's ability to form trusting relationships with others?
- What are the social support networks, either formal or informal (political, fraternal, religious, community)?
- What are the parent's or caregiver's outside sources of recreation or relaxation?
- How do others respond to the parent's or caregiver's behavior in social situations?

- What is the parent's or caregiver's attitude to normal social or legal rules, laws, limits, and guidelines?

Factor: Reasons for intervention and the conditions that caused the abuse or neglect.

- Were the conditions or characteristics beyond the parent's or caregiver's ability to control? For example:

  Does the parent or caregiver have a disabling disease or injury?

  Does the parent or caregiver have a mental illness?

  Is the parent or caregiver developmentally delayed, and are supports unable to reduce the future risk of child abuse or neglect?

  Was unemployment a recent occurrence?

  Was domestic violence present in the home, with the parent or caregiver in the victim role lacking information about protective resources?

- Could the parent or caregiver have the ability to prevent the conditions or circumstances but was unable to do so, and why? For example, was the parent or caregiver unemployed because of a failure to perform on a job or pursue job opportunities?

- What could the parent or caregiver do to effectively prevent the conditions or circumstances from continuing?

- When does the parent or caregiver usually become abusive or neglectful— for example, when drinking, or only when other stresses are also present?

- Is the problem caused by something the parent or caregiver or child does (a commission) or something the parent or caregiver or child does not do (an omission)?

Factor: Parental and caregiver roles.

- How do the parents or caregivers support each other?

- To what extent are philosophy and practices regarding parenting similar or different between parents or caregivers?

- What is the parents' or caregivers' dependence/independence balance in their relationship?

- What is the quality of communication between the parents or caregivers (how do they deal with problems, individual needs, concerns, and frustrations)?

- If the parents or caregivers are married or in some other committed arrangement, is the union what each expected it to be?

Family Assessment

Factor: Family composition (Wayman et al., 1990).

- Who are the members of the family system?

- What is the living arrangement of the family?

- What is the relationship of friends to the family system?
- What is the hierarchy within the family? Is status related to gender or age?
- Who is the primary caregiver?
- Who participates in the caregiving?
- Does the family system cooperate to assure that the child is cared for and protected?
- What are the cultural norms about multiple caregivers and amount of time spent with different caregivers?
- What is the degree of connection between family members?

Factor: The nature of the condition or characteristics that contributed to abuse or neglect.

- Was the abuse or neglect a result of unintentional actions or circumstances?
- Was the onset of the problem sudden or the result of multiple stressors suddenly converging on the family? For example, did it result from the sudden illness of the only income-earning parent? Did it result from a child's negative reaction to a move or change of schools? Did the parent or caregiver lose a job and need surgery, and did the unemployment check get lost, all about the same time?
- Did the problem result from unrealistic expectations? For example, did the parent or caregiver become angry because the baby cried when teething
- Did the parents or caregivers physically punish the child for having an accident?
- Did the abuse or neglect develop as a result of deliberate intent?

Note

The issue of intentional versus nonintentional is not the same as accidental versus nonaccidental. Sometimes children are hurt by an act that the perpetrator did not intend to result in injury to the child. The act may still be abuse or neglect because the parent or caregiver's actions were not prudent. Whether or not a parent or caregiver intended to hurt a child is not relevant in determining whether abuse or neglect occurred. Thus, assessment of intent probably will not affect the decision about substantiation of maltreatment but will affect decisions about risk, protection, and intervention. This distinction between intentional and unintentional harm is relevant in deciding the level and type of services that are appropriate in each individual situation.

- Does the abuse or neglect affect only one or many aspects of the family's functioning or circumstances?
- How consistent is the behavior or characteristic that contributed to abuse or neglect?

- What is going on with the family when the abuse or neglect occurs?
- What is or has been the duration of the condition or characteristic that contributed to abuse or neglect?

Factor: Dynamics of family interaction and functioning.

- What characteristics describe how the family functions as a unit?
- What is the predominant mood of the family as a whole?
- Who are the key decision-makers (Wayman et al., 1990)?
- Is decision-making related to a specific situation (Wayman et al., 1990)?
- Is decision-making individual or group oriented (Wayman et al., 1990)?
- How are family finances handled, and are they adequate and stable to meet the family's basic needs?
- How is money budgeted and managed, and who is responsible for these tasks?

Factor: Interaction styles (Wayman et al., 1990).

- Do family members communicate with each other in a direct or indirect style?
- Does the family tend to interact in a quiet or a loud manner?
- How do family members share feelings when discussing emotional issues?
- What cultural norms or taboos influence family communication?

Factor: Problem-solving skills.

- Are family members able to recognize a problem when one arises?
- Can they determine when a behavior or condition is currently or potentially abusive or harmful to a child?
- How do they relate to feelings of discomfort, such as pain and confusion?
- To what extent can they identify the cause or origin of problems?
- How are problems perceived?
- To what extent can they identify the consequences or effects of the problem on individuals or the family as a whole?
- To what extent have they made specific efforts to solve, remove, or deal with problems?
- To what extent have their efforts been successful?
- To what extent can they identify how their method of dealing with the problem helped to solve it or whether their efforts had no effect or made the problem worse?
- What alternative methods do family members use to solve problems, or do they use a single method to solve all problems?
- Do they demonstrate optimism about being able to change their behavior or circumstances?

Factor: Child rearing practices.

- What form of discipline is used on children?
- To what extent is the type or severity of discipline or punishment appropriate for the situation/cultural group? Is discipline intended to help or correct rather than hurt? Is there an overall balance in correction within a context of support and nurturing?
- What is the parent's or caregiver's intent when disciplining, teaching, or punishing?
- What are the parameters of acceptable child behavior?
- Who metes out the disciplinary action?
- To what extent do parents or caregivers understand the developmental stages of children; for example, the children's physical, social, emotional, and intellectual abilities at different ages? (See chapter 8.)
- To what extent are the parents or caregivers consistent in their approach to parenting?
- To what extent do parents or caregivers perceive children either as independent beings with their own personalities or as small carbon copies of themselves?
- To what extent do parents or caregivers recognize each child as an individual?
- To what extent do the parents or caregivers enjoy their children, or do they see them as a burden?
- Were the children planned or unplanned?
- How are children encouraged, acknowledged, and comforted?
- What is the family's response to disobedience and aggression?
- What is the family's response to a crying infant?
- How long is it before the parent or caregiver picks up a crying infant?
- How does the parent or caregiver calm an upset infant?

Factor: Family feeding practices (Wayman et al., 1990).

- What are the family feeding practices?
- What are the mealtime rules?
- What types of foods are eaten?
- What are the beliefs regarding breastfeeding and weaning?
- What are the beliefs regarding bottle-feeding?
- What are the family practices regarding transitioning to solid food?
- Which family members prepare food?
- Are there any taboos related to food preparation or handling?
- Which family members feed the child?
- What is the configuration of the family mealtime?

- What are the family's views on independent feeding?
- Is there a discrepancy among family members regarding the beliefs and practices related to feeding an infant/toddler?

Factor: Family sleeping patterns (Wayman et al., 1990).

- Does the infant sleep in the same room/bed as the parents?
- At what age is the infant moved away from close proximity to the mother?
- Is there an established bedtime?
- What is the family response to an infant when he or she awakes at night?
- What practices surround daytime napping?

Factor: Family's perception of health and healing (Wayman et al., 1990).

- What is the family's approach to medical needs?
- Do they rely solely on Western medical services?
- Do they rely solely on holistic approaches?
- Do they utilize a combination of these approaches?
- Who is the primary medical provider or conveyer of medical information? Family members? Elders? Friends? Folk healers? Family doctors? Medical specialists?
- Do all family members of the family agree on approaches to medical needs?

Factor: Family's perception of help seeking and intervention (Wayman et al., 1990).

- From whom does the family seek help—family members or outside agencies/individuals?
- Does the family seek help directly or indirectly?
- What are the general feelings of the family when seeking assistance— ashamed, angry, demanding it as a right?
- With which community agencies does the family interact?
- What barriers are there to accessing services?
- How are these interactions completed (face-to-face, telephone, letter)?
- Which family member interacts with other agencies?
- Do family members feel capable of navigating through and interacting with other systems?

Environment Assessment

Child abuse often occurs as a result of multiple forces impacting families. It needs to be emphasized that this does not mean that the presence of these factors will always result in child abuse and neglect.

Factor: Stress level of family.

- What are the family's income and other resources? Are they sufficient to meet their basic needs?

- Have there been any changes in marital status, health, or employment?
- How does the family cope with stress?

Factor: Physical, environmental, and economic conditions that affect the individual or family.

- What are the environmental conditions in the surrounding community and on a national level?
- What is the housing situation? What are the community norms regarding adequate housing?
- What is the employment situation?
- What is the general mood in the community? How does the community perceive or interact with the family?

Factor: Integration with the community.

- What community does the family affiliate with?
- What kinds of support do they have from their community?
- What community resources does the family have available?
- What is the parent's or caregiver's description of the needs and the barriers that interfere with needs being met?

Specialized Assessment Areas

Substance abuse. Assess whether the use of chemical substances, including alcohol and drugs, affect the individual's ability to keep children safe.

The Cage Test

The following are recommended questions to ask in order to do initial screening for alcohol abuse.

Have you ever felt you should cut down on your drinking?

Have people annoyed you by criticizing your drinking?

Have you ever felt bad or guilty about your drinking?

Have you ever had a drink first thing in the morning to steady your nerves or get rid of a hangover?

If the respondent answers yes to at least two of these questions then a more comprehensive assessment should be considered.

Source: J. A. Ewing (1984). Detecting Alcoholism: The CAGE Questionnaire. *Journal of the American Medical Association, 252,* 1905–1907.

Domestic violence. Witnessing domestic violence may put children at risk for increased emotional problems. Child witnesses of domestic violence have been found to show increased aggressive and antisocial behavior, as well as more anxiety, depression, and temperamental problems and lower self-esteem than other children (Schechter & Edelson, 1994).

The following questions are recommended in doing initial screening for domestic violence. It is important for the worker to arrange to speak to the adult who is a potential victim alone. Integrate these types of questions into your routine screening practices in order to lessen the discomfort and defensiveness they may cause for that person. Explain that asking these types of questions is a routine agency practice.

Ask general questions about the presence of a spouse, partner, boyfriend, or girlfriend, and about the nature of the relationship; for example: "Tell me about your relationship and how decisions are made." "What happens when the adults disagree?" "Is force used?" If appropriate to what the parent or caregiver has already told you, it may be effective in getting the parent or caregiver to disclose more information to say: "Sometimes when people feel the way you do, it is because they may have been hurt or abused at home. Is this happening to you?"

Ask:

- Does your partner act jealous or possessive? Please tell me about that.
- Are you afraid of your partner? Please explain why.
- Has your partner physically hurt you, for example, by hitting, slapping, or kicking?
- Has your partner forced you to have sex?
- Are you afraid that your partner may harm your children? If so, why?
- Has your partner prevented you from going to school or work or seeing friends or family?
- Has your partner followed you?
- Does your partner control or steal your money?
- Has your partner called you degrading names, emotionally insulted you, or humiliated you at home or in public?
- Has your partner destroyed your possessions, broken furniture, pulled the telephone cord out, or punched holes in walls or doors?
- Has your partner threatened to injure you, him or herself, your children, or other family members?
- Has your partner threatened to use or used a weapon against you, or threatened to kill you or to commit suicide? Does your partner have a gun or rifle at home?
- Has your partner hurt your pets?
- Has your partner recklessly endangered you or your children by driving too fast with you and the children in the car, or driving when drunk?
- Has your partner hurt you in front of your children or while you were holding your children?
- Has your partner touched your children in ways that made you feel uncomfortable?
- Do your children behave in violent ways similar to those of your partner?
- Have your children exhibited physical, emotional, or behavioral problems at home, school, or daycare?

- Have your children tried to stop violence by your partner, protect you in violent situations, or been fearful of leaving you alone?
- Have your children overheard violence against you?

Mental illness. Determine the effect of the mental illness on the person's life.

- Does the parent or caregiver's mental illness interfere with holding a job?
- Does the illness make caring for the children and managing the household unlikely?
- Has the mental illness been diagnosed or treated?
- Does the caregiver recognize that he or she suffers with a mental illness and its impact on his or her relationship to the children?

Psychotic Conditions. These are the most severe type of mental illness and may substantially interfere with an individual's ability to safely parent a child. Psychotic conditions include schizophrenia and paranoia and typically result in extreme thought disorders, emotional withdrawal, and possibly hallucinations or delusions.

Personality Disorders. Every situation involving a child of a parent or caregiver with personality disorders needs to be evaluated on its own merits. Factors to assess include the severity of the personality disorder, coexisting problems, the family situation, the vulnerability and needs of the child, the parent's or caregiver's view of his or her problems in functioning, and the availability of social supports and resources. The following reactions described below should alert workers to the possibility of a personality disorder.

- The parent or caregiver persistently puts his or her needs before the child's, even when the parent or caregiver's needs are inconsequential.
- The parent or caregiver equates the child's needs with his or her needs and does not think of the child as someone with his or her own needs.
- The parent or caregiver repeatedly casts responsibility for problems in his or her life or in the family on someone else such as a spouse, a boss, the child, or professionals.

Mood Disorders. These disorders affect the individual's moods and include depression and bipolar disorders. Like other mental illness, mood disorders may interfere with parenting and should be assessed by a professional.

Cultural Issues. Understanding the influence of culture on patterns of parenting and family roles is important to the assessment of child abuse and neglect. Culture is embedded in the values and attitudes of the family that govern social behavior and relationships. As in mainstream American culture, behavior does not always match values. Cultural norms should be understood so that interventions do not impose solutions that are inappropriate. If a family has recently immigrated from a foreign country, some acceptable forms of discipline or medical treatment in their home country may be considered abuse or neglect in the United States.

Conducting a culturally responsive family assessment means that the worker seeks to understand the family's ideas, even when they seem unusual to the worker who is from a different culture from that of the parent/caregiver family. For example:

> A traditional Navajo couple practiced the use of the cradleboard with their infant. The cradleboard is used by numerous American Indian tribes and may vary slightly in design but generally consists of a board or frame on which an infant is secured by wrapping in a blanket and binding the child tightly to the board. It is a portable cradle and carrier. It also provides the infant with security and warmth. Other cultural teachings regarding the benefits to the child in terms of the infant's orientation to the world vary from tribe to tribe. In this case, the child was customarily placed in the cradleboard for his nap at the daycare center. A health inspector cited the center with a violation and informed the parents that this practice was child abuse. With the help of a cultural rights advocate at a state university, the health inspector was informed that the couple's cultural rights under both federal and international law were being violated. The state licensing agency eventually allowed for an "exception" in allowing the child to sleep in the cradleboard. Nonetheless, the approach of the state agency caused emotional upset to the parents, disruption of the child's routine, and confusion to the childcare center staff. (Prins, 2000)

Social workers should always seek to understand the history and context of current family patterns of functions, including the history of immigration, interaction with the child welfare system, and effects of racism and oppression. Culturally responsive workers learn about other communities, whether they represent differing classes, geographic locations, family variations, ethnicities, races, religious beliefs, or sexual orientations. They also employ partnerships with cultural resources or cultural guides who can assist in interviewing and supporting the change or healing processes occurring in the family (Walton, Sandau-Becker, & Mannes, 2001).

The cultural belief and intention behind the behavior must be considered in determining the intervention and approach to the family. It is important to assess whether the type or severity of discipline, punishment, or some other situation is considered appropriate for the situation within a particular cultural group. However, some disciplinary or medical methods from other cultures are technically considered abuse by state children's codes. For example, there is the practice of "coining" by some Southeast Asian groups whereby a child's chest is rubbed with hot coins to cure colds; it leaves physical marks on the child. During the safety and risk assessment, gathering information about cultural practices can inform the child welfare and legal system in determining the approach taken during legal and service intervention.

☐   Assessing the Family's Motivation to Change

As part of the assessment process, it is helpful to determine how motivated the family is to change and their level of readiness for change. Families change at different rates, depending on how they perceive their situation and how they embrace the change process. The *transtheoretical model* assumes that changing behavior is a dynamic process and that people progress through a series of stages in trying to modify their behavior. It is helpful to assess the individual family members' stage of change to select the most appropriate interventions and link families to services. If a parent or caregiver is in the initial stage of change, some interventions may be ineffective, inappropriate, and unsafe.

The transtheoretical model of change describes five discrete stages of readiness for change (Prochaska & Prochaska, 2002):

1. *Precontemplation.* There is initial resistance to change. Characteristic statements from family members in this stage include:

    "I have done nothing wrong and resent CPS's involvement."

    "It's the babysitter's (someone else's) fault."

    "I am who I am and I shouldn't have to change."

2. *Contemplation.* A family member becomes aware of the problem but has not yet made an effort to change. He or she may say:

    "I know I should clean up this messy house and handle the kids better." Sometimes an individual gets stuck in this stage because of the amount of work it may take to change. He or she may also anticipate a loss in making the change and may not want to make that sacrifice.

3. *Preparation.* A family member is intending to take some action to change. For example, in this stage a family member may ask you for information regarding a resource or a referral.

4. *Action.* A family member changes his or her behavior and/or environment. The attitude of an individual in this phase is:

    "I am working real hard to change."

    Or: "I am doing things about the problem that got me involved with child protection."

5. *Maintenance.* Family members work to prevent relapse and maintain the gains they have made during the change process.

The following questions may be used to help identify the parent's or caregiver's stage of readiness for change (Prochaska, DiClemente, & Norcross, 1992):

Stage 1: Does the parent or caregiver believe that the consequences of the problem are insubstantial and see no reason to make a change at this time?

Stage 2: Does the parent or caregiver begin to recognize that there might be a problem and consider a need for change? The parent or caregiver typically feels ambivalent and is weighing the pros and cons of making the change. He or she is in a decision-making process but has not yet resolved to make a change. The individual may see the change as likely to occur within the next 6 months.

Stage 3: Does the parent or caregiver experiment with change and consider options for change? The treatment options, social supports, and barriers to each option are considered. The parent or caregiver usually thinks of change as occurring in the immediate future—some time in the next 30 days.

Stage 4: Is the parent or caregiver taking action-oriented steps toward making a change? Does he or she consider the effects of the steps toward change on his or her life and consider how the change affects the social support network? If the steps are not successful, does he or she modify the plan until it works for him or her? In this stage, the parent or caregiver has typically worked on taking action to change behavior for anywhere from 1 day to 6 months.

Stage 5: Does the parent or caregiver maintain the behavior change for more than 6 months? Relapse may occur during this stage and is seen as a normal part of obtaining ongoing change. Relapse is considered a temporary repeat of the first three stages, through which skills gained in understanding what has contributed to relapses can lead to permanent maintenance.

Progression through these stages is not a linear process. In fact, it is frequently cyclical, with regression to previous stages likely during the change process. Certain strategies or processes of change can be tailored to the stage of readiness the parent or caregiver is currently exhibiting. One such technique is *motivational interviewing.* It focuses on strategies such as reflective listening, summarizations, open-ended questions, and affirmation-eliciting self-motivation statements and has been used at the early stages of engagement to reduce barriers for individual family members in their change process (Miller & Rollnick, 1991).

Motivation for change also should be considered in the context of family history with the child welfare system. Some families have come to believe that no amount of effort will help them get their children back. Their "noncompliance" may not be an effect of motivation but rather a sense of powerlessness and discouragement. When children have been removed from parents, it is good to assess the parents' belief about their ability to influence the process.

☐ Reassessment

Many states have protocols that require reassessment of risk at certain junctures in a case. A reassessment may be conducted at the following times:

- Prior to returning a child to his or her caregiver from foster care.
- Prior to filing a petition to terminate parental rights.
- Prior to case closure after a case has been opened for services.
- When a CPS worker, supervisor, or court wants to determine the degree of risk reduction since the last risk assessment was completed or to determine the significance of one or more issues and/or the level of current risk in response to significant changes that have recently occurred in the family.

Reassessment is beneficial in that it provides contemporary documentation of risk and strengths, helps assess progress, refocuses your service plan to address current risk and family needs, and helps justify permanency decisions or requests.

☐   **Assessment Documentation**

Assessment information is recorded in a variety of different formats and instruments. Frequently, the formal family assessment document that you prepare will only have the capacity for a summary of each of the main assessment areas. Nonetheless, the summary is based on a thorough understanding and detailed information from each of these assessment areas. The level of detail provided by the worker in a written report will vary, depending on the requirements of the agency or the court and the purpose for which the document will be used.

The assessment information gathered will become an important part of many documents you develop as part of your work with families, such as a report to the court, service and/or case plans, and a social history that is used as a referral to other agencies.

Tips for Successful Documentation

- Be specific and concise.
- Record pertinent facts, impressions, and conclusions.
- Distinguish between documented and unverified information.
- Avoid judgments that are vague, inconsistent, or unsupported.
- Clearly identify strengths and problems.
- Categorize and document information in a way that will assist with compliance with required agency and court mandates and service and/or case plans.
- Distinguish fact from opinion.
- Document the basis for opinions by giving examples.
- Disregard irrelevant information.
- Distinguish between strengths and weaknesses of parent or caregivers. Focus on strengths for problem solving.
- Distinguish between worker perceptions, opinions, and judgments and those of the parent or caregiver.
- Document specific situations or examples to illustrate risks, strengths, and needs.
- Identify patterns of behavior, problems, and attitudes.
- Make rational judgments (based on documentation) concerning the causes, the nature, and the consequences of the problem, or parent or caregiver characteristics.
- Seek the opinion of supervisors or other resources regarding conclusions.

Tying the Assessment to the Service Plan

The assessment information will be tied to service needs and serve as the basis for the service plan. For instance, what services and resources are needed to support family continuity as well as to achieve or maintain safety, which is always of paramount concern? If placement outside of the home is necessary, determine the plan that is most likely to result in fulfilling the child(ren)'s need for a safe, permanent home within legally required time frames. The formal family assessment information is gathered from all of the areas previously discussed and should include the following components:

- Reasons for intervention and/or conditions giving rise to the abuse or neglect.
- The effect of the abuse or neglect.
- Safety needs of the child(ren).
- The family's view of the problem, including its understanding of why CPS is involved.
- The family's perception of its previous efforts to meet needs and solve problems and its identification of what it needs to change.
- Family strengths.
- Family system and other social supports.
- The child(ren)'s role in the family.
- The parent-child relationship and discipline methods.
- The living situation and environment.
- Education and employment.
- Cultural issues such as language, ethnicity, and religion.
- History of abuse and neglect.
- Mental health needs and/or history of treatment of the child(ren) and/or parent(s).
- History of substance abuse by any family member.
- Medical condition and medications (including a former history of use) of child(ren) and/or parent(s).
- Legal history of child(ren) and/or parent(s).
- Any other additional information that is relevant to the individual case.

■ Summary of Competencies

Assessment builds the foundation for further intervention. In order for a relevant and useful service plan to be constructed that targets and prioritizes the most needed services and builds on the family's strengths, a foundation of information that relates to the reason for agency involvement is necessary regarding the family as a whole and regarding its individual members. Even if there are no further services provided with a family following the initial involvement, the act of any type of assessment is an intervention in and of itself. Whenever a worker comes into contact with a family or any of its members, his or her interaction with the family is an intervention that holds the possibility to help create change in the family, even when the worker is primarily asking questions and gathering information rather than providing new information or assistance to the family. The worker must be competent in the following areas.

Knowledge:
1. Knowledge of assessment methods that facilitate obtaining pertinent information on which to base your decisions.
2. Knowledge of methods for conducting an assessment.
3. Knowledge of the different purposes and uses of safety and risk assessments.
4. Knowledge of key factors common to safety assessments.
5. Knowledge of key factors common to risk assessments.
6. Knowledge of key factors common to family assessments.
7. Knowledge of your state's requirements for reassessment.

Skills:
1. Ability to work effectively with children, parents or caregivers, and families.
2. Ability to conduct skillful family and individual interviews.
3. Ability to secure information needed to complete an assessment in a manner that minimizes the family's resistance.
4. Ability to be culturally responsive when conducting all types of assessments.
5. Ability to recognize a family's motivation to change.
6. Ability to factually document an assessment.
7. Ability to use information from the assessment to develop a service plan.

References

Colorado Department of Human Services & American Humane Association. (2001). *Colorado child welfare practice handbook*. Englewood, CO: American Humane Association.

Cowger, C. (1997). Assessment of client strengths. In D. Saleeby (Ed.), *The strengths perspective in social work practice*. New York: Longman.

Dunst, C., Trivette, C., & Mott, D. (1994). Strengths-based family-centered intervention practices. In C. Dunst, C. Trivette, & A. Deal (Eds.), *Supporting and strengthening families*. Cambridge, MA: Brookline Books.

Ewing, J. A. (1984). Detecting alcoholism: The CAGE questionnaire. *Journal of the American Medical Association, 252*, 1905–1907.

Holder, W. (1996). Services under certain circumstances equals success (SUCCESS). Unpublished study. Charlotte, NC: ACTION for Child Protection.

Holder, W., & Corey, M. (1996). *Child Protective Services Risk Management System: A decision-making handbook*. Charlotte, NC: ACTION for Child Protection.

Jaudes, P. K., & Diamond, L. S. (1985). The handicapped child and child abuse. *Child Abuse and Neglect, 9*, 341–347.

Jones, D.B. (1987). The untreatable family. *Child Abuse and Neglect, 11*, 409–420.

Miller, W.R., & Rollnick, S. (1991). *Motivational interviewing: Preparing people to change addictive behavior.* New York: Guilford Press.

Murphy, K. C., & Harper, C. J. (2001). Specialized safety assessment tool. Unpublished assessment tool, American Humane Association.

Prins, H. (2000, November 20). Cradleboard cultural rights issue. *People's Voice.*

Prochaska, J. M., and Prochaska, J. O. (2002). Transtheoretical model guidelines for families with child abuse and neglect. In A. R. Roberts and G. J. Greene (Eds.), *Social worker's desk reference* (pp. 379–384). New York: Oxford University Press.

Prochaska, J. O., DiClemente, C. C., & Norcross, J. C. (1992). In search of how people change: Applications to addictive behaviors. *American Psychologist, 47,* 1102–1114.

Saleebey, D. (Ed.). (1992). *The strengths perspective in social work practice.* New York: Longman.

Schecter, S., & Edelson, J. (1994, June). In the best interests of women and children: A call for collaboration between child welfare and domestic violence constituencies. Briefing paper prepared for the Wingspread Conference: "Domestic Violence and Child Welfare," Racine, Wisconsin.

Seden, J., Sinclair, R., Robbins, D., & Pont, C. (2001). *Framework for the assessment of children in need and their families.* London: The Stationery Office.

Soeffing, M. (1975). Abused children are exceptional children. *Exceptional Children, 42,* 126–133.

Walton, E., Sandau-Becker, P., & Mannes, M. (Eds.) (2001). *Balancing family-centered services and child well-being: Exploring issues in policy, practice, theory, and research.* New York: Columbia University Press.

Wayman, K. I., Lunch, E. W., & Hanson, M. J. (1990). Home-based early childhood services: Cultural sensitivity in a family systems approach. *Topics in Early Childhood Special Education, 10,* 65–66.

8

Kimberlee C. Murphy

Child Development

■ How Children Develop

■ Challenges for Parents or Caregivers:
Normal Development

■ Challenges for Parents or Caregivers:
Beyond Normal Development

■ Developmental Problems Often Associated with
Child Maltreatment

■ Attachment and the Separation of Children from
Their Caregivers

■ Resiliency and Coping

■ Summary of Competencies

In order to work effectively with families, you need to become well versed in child development. Every aspect of a worker's job, from assessment to decision, is influenced by the needs of the child. When you are required to go into a family's home to assess the safety of a child, you will need to understand the child's developmental stage and how that stage may reduce or exacerbate current and future risk of maltreatment. When you are faced with the decision of whether to remove a child from a parent's or caregiver's home temporarily to assure child safety, you will need to weigh safety concerns against the potential consequences to the child of such removal. When you work toward helping a family assure child safety and well-being, you will need to assess and make efforts to meet any unmet needs related to the child's level of development that may be contributing to the safety concerns. Finally, if you determine that a child must be removed from the home to assure safety, you will need to understand normal grief reactions and know how to help that child cope with separation and loss. Therefore, in order for you to work effectively with families and children, you will need to have a good working knowledge of child development.

In this chapter, you will learn about the stages and progression of child development and the accompanying challenges a parent or caregiver may anticipate. In addition, you will learn about some of the challenges that are associated with atypical patterns of child development, including mental illness and developmental disabilities, and how those challenges can adversely impact the behavior of otherwise loving and caring parents or caregivers. You will learn about children's attachment to their families and how child abuse and neglect adversely affect attachment. In addition, you will learn about the risk of out-of-home placement and its effect on attachment. Finally, you will learn about resiliency, children's coping, and how to help children deal with the challenges they encounter, so that they can experience positive outcomes in functioning and development, despite the stressful events they encounter.

■ How Children Develop

As you work with families to identify and address the safety concerns resulting in their involvement with CPS, you will need a working knowledge of how children develop, including the developmental skills, behaviors, and characteristics that are typically observed at various ages. This information will assist you as you conduct ongoing family assessments and make decisions regarding the need for services. It will also help you to educate families about what to expect from their children.

□ Definition of Development

Over time, children go through changes in their physical characteristics (e.g., height and weight), neurological makeup (e.g., changes in brain functioning), behaviors (e.g., learning new skills), and personality traits (e.g., empathy, social skills). These changes that occur over time are considered to be "child development" (Papalia & Olds, 1996).

Changes in physical characteristics, neurological makeup, behaviors, and personality traits progress in a similar manner for most children. When changes occur, they tend to last. Changes typically build on one another, making them accumulative in nature. Changes are generally linked to chronological age; and the younger the child, the more frequent the change.

☐ Stages of Development

The development that is observed in physical characteristics, neurological makeup, behaviors, and personality traits can be grouped into three general domains: physical, cognitive and language, and psychosocial.

The *physical* domain includes changes over time in the body, brain, sensory capacity, and motor skills (gross motor skills involving the torso and limbs, and fine motor skills involving hands and hand-eye coordination [Papalia & Olds, 1996]). The *cognitive and language* domain includes changes over time in mental abilities (e.g., ability to acquire and use knowledge), activities, and organization. The *psychosocial* domain includes changes over time in the style of behaving, feeling, and reacting. Moral development is often included in this domain.

Development in all three domains occurs in a series of stages that are tied closely to chronological age. Thus, for example, a child will gradually gain more fine motor skills, learn increasing numbers of words, and display more maturity as he or she ages. Stages of *physical* development are reflected by specific skills, behaviors, and characteristics that are displayed at various ages (see table).

Stages of *cognitive* development, reflected by specific skills that are gained over time, include (e.g., Piaget, 1929, as cited in Papalia & Olds, 1996) the following:

- *Sensorimotor.* Between 0 and 2 years of age, infants and toddlers learn through sensory and motor activity. They go from responding primarily through reflexes to organizing activities in relation to the environment.

  For example, 14-month-old Angelica is into everything. She is learning about her environment by touching and trying everything. She has learned in the last few months that an object or person continues to exist even when it is out of sight—no more "out of sight, out of mind." She is also beginning to understand the idea of cause and effect—now that she has discovered that flipping the light switch up and down makes the light turn on and off, she enjoys playing with the light switch in the middle of the night. Unlike 4-year-old Calvin (in the *preoperational* stage), she doesn't yet know that the name "Grover" stands for her pet dog. She also hasn't figured out yet that if she has one apple and her mom has two apples that her mom has more apples than she does; and unlike 9-year-old Antone (in the *concrete operations* stage), who understands identities, she is far from understanding that even if she was dressed in boys' clothes, she would still be a girl.

- *Preoperational.* Between 2 and 7 years of age, children develop a representational system, using symbols such as words to represent people, places, and events.

- *Concrete operations.* Between 7 and 12 years of age, children solve problems logically if they are focused on the current scenario. Long-term thinking is difficult.
- *Formal operations.* From 12 years of age and beyond, young people can think in abstract terms, deal with hypothetical situations, and think about possibilities.

> For example, 9-year-old Antone is able to understand the concepts of time and space. He knows the difference between fantasy and reality and can group things into categories. He thinks in concrete terms about "what is" rather than "what could be." He hasn't gotten to the point yet where he can hypothesize about what does not actually exist, as 14-year-old Samantha can do.

Stages of *psychosocial* development, reflected by thoughts and behaviors, include (Erikson, 1963) the following:

- *Basic trust versus mistrust.* Between 0 and 12 months of age, infants develop a sense of whether the world can be trusted.

> For example, 10-month-old Robert has come to learn that when he has a need, his caregiver will take care of it. When he's hungry, she feeds him. When he's wet, she changes him. When he's upset, she holds him. He has learned that he can rely on her to take care of his needs. Unlike 16-month-old Jocelyn, however, he doesn't yet venture out on his own. He hasn't reached the emotional maturity to know that he can now crawl around without her constant presence.

- *Autonomy versus shame and doubt.* Between 12 and 18 months of age and up to 3 years of age, children develop balance of independence over doubt and shame.
- *Initiative versus guilt.* Between 3 and 6 years of age, children develop initiative when trying new things and work toward not being overwhelmed by failure.
- *Industry versus inferiority.* Between 6 years of age and puberty, children learn skills of the culture or face feelings of inferiority.
- *Identity versus identity confusion.* Between puberty and young adulthood, adolescents determine their own sense of self by incorporating the mores of the family and expressing them in a unique way.

> For example, 4-year-old Timmy is quite energetic and independent. He seems willing to try anything and is not easily discouraged when things don't work out. Unlike 10-year-old Little Foot, however, he does not yet understand the social skills of his culture and occasionally gets into trouble when he interrupts people and forgets to use his "indoor voice" while inside. Little Foot, while understanding and abiding by the expectations for behavior in her culture, is still feeling her way in finding out who she is and what she stands for. She is significantly more influenced by what other people think than is 18-year-old Kim-Yung, who, while still respecting the opinions of his elders, now has a strong sense of his own opinions and values.

Although development typically follows the same stages of progress, it does not always occur at equal rates across all children or all domains. For example, a child may be on target for physical development but delayed in cognitive, language, or psychosocial development.

To determine how children are progressing in each domain, professionals have summarized "milestones" in development that represent characteristics, behaviors, and activities that are typically observed for a given age. Many of the milestones can be observed directly (e.g., an 8-month-old infant who learns to sit; a 4-year-old preschooler who prints her name). Others, such as the psychosocial tasks, are indirectly observable (e.g., a 2-year-old toddler who is comforted by his caregiver's presence is likely to be securely attached to his caregiver and therefore able to trust people later on; a 13-year-old adolescent who is preoccupied with her reflection in the mirror, irritable, and sensitive to criticism is most likely going through self-discovery and identity formation).

As a way to determine whether a child is "on track" developmentally, it is common to compare what he or she is doing against the milestones for the child's age. Keep in mind that there may be cultural variation in how children are viewed at various stages and that approaches to meeting developmental needs may also vary. Such information can help you determine whether a professional assessment of a child's development is needed or whether services should be provided.

Primary milestones and experiences observed at various ages include:

- *Infancy.* During the first year of life, an infant's development changes quickly. Physical development proceeds from head control to mobility. Cognitive/language development proceeds from reflexive responses to recognition and early communication. Psychosocial development entails building a sense of safety, security, and trust in parents or other caregivers.

- *Toddler years.* During the first 12 to 36 months of life, a toddler separates emotionally from parents or caregivers. Self-confidence and self-esteem develop as the toddler makes a move toward greater autonomy. Key milestones include locomotion, toilet training, and verbal communication.

- *Preschool years.* During years 3 to 5, a child attains proficiency in simple self-care within the home and begins to form important relationships with peers and adults in nursery school or childcare settings. The child shows continued growth in individuation and independence. Identification and attachment to the family is strong. The child is egocentric and prone to magical thinking.

- *Elementary school years.* During years 6 to 10, a child shows successful mastery of the world outside the family unit. He or she is involved in academic learning, social interactions with same-sex peers, and developing motor skills. As the child matures, there is a strong need to learn more about personal history and incorporate this knowledge in the growing sense of self-identity.

- *Adolescence.* During years 11 to 18, the tasks of adolescence are similar for the male and female. Asymmetrical development (e.g., cognitive development before physical growth) is common. Normal development often involves swings in mood and reliability, vacillation between dependence and independence, self-absorption, impulsivity, and control conflicts with adults. The primary tasks are (1) exploring personal identity and roles; (2) lessening dependence on family and renewed emphasis on separation and individuation (the notion of independence may vary—in some cultures, youth remain connected and are not expected to separate); (3) exploring relationships with peers; (4) exploring sexuality; and (5) exploring ways to feel competent, important, and accomplished.

Table 8.1 beginning on page 257 provides a summary of milestones in the physical, cognitive and language, and psychosocial domains that are typically observed at various ages.

Successful progression from one stage of development to the next depends on the completion of the tasks, experiences, and milestones of the earlier stages. Without corrective experience, disruptions at one stage of development could result in additional challenges throughout other stages.

> For example, a 15-month-old infant who does not learn to trust people because his caregivers were unresponsive or inconsistent in responding to his needs is likely to have difficulty achieving a balance between attachment and autonomy at age 2 and beyond. This in turn may impede his ability to develop relationships with peers during his school-age years and beyond.

The ages at which children develop skills, behaviors, and characteristics is determined, in part, by their cultural background.

> For example, while you are observing an American Indian child interacting with her parents, you notice that she is quiet and does not show eye contact as they interact. Although your first thought is that the child is shy or even reluctant to interact with her parents, you realize that this child is showing deference to her parents—something that reflects respect, a valued behavior in the family's tribe.

☐ Factors That Affect Development

Child development is thought to be affected by physical and mental predispositions (characteristics predetermined by genetic makeup), as well as the conditions in the environment. In essence, development comes down to a combination of "nature" (genetics) and "nurture" (environment). Children start with the genes they inherent from their parents, genes that influence many characteristics. Their predispositions (determined by genes) are then modified by other sources such as environmental experiences.

Some environmental experiences happen to most people within the cultural reference group (e.g., attending school, going through puberty), thus leading children to develop in similar manners. Other environmental experiences happen to a subgroup of people, giving that subgroup much the same experiences that will affect them similarly. However, because each subgroup can have different experiences, each subgroup's development will be unique (e.g., a boy will encounter experiences that most boys encounter, leading that boy to develop similarly to other boys. However, that boy will develop differently from a girl, who has developed on the basis of her experiences as a girl). Still other environmental experiences include unexpected events that do not happen to most people (e.g., an abusive episode, death of a parent during childhood), thus influencing children in ways that most children will not be influenced.

Environmental influences over development include experiences that range from intimate to global settings. Examples of these can include:

- *Intimate*: experiences from family, peers, teachers, and classmates.

- *Surrounding*: experiences from extended family (although in some cultures, extended family would be classified as an "intimate" source), neighbors, the workplace, and the community (e.g., available resources, the education system, the laws and customs, and the media).

- *Global*: experiences from society (e.g., economic status of the country, medical advances, available technology).

Although a child's development is influenced by a variety of experiences, those that come from the family and extended family have significant and long-lasting impact. In essence, these experiences set the stage for how the child will develop in all areas. Therefore, preservation and enhancement of family ties are critical to child development.

☐ Your Role in Helping Families

One of the most important things you can do for families is to make sure that parents or caregivers are knowledgeable about child development. This information will provide them with an accurate picture of what the children can be expected to do at various ages, possibly leading to less parental frustration resulting from unrealistic expectations.

To *assure that parents or caregivers have the information they need* about their child's development, you can:

- Share information with parents or caregivers on what their child can be expected to do. As you share information, remember to listen to and observe parents, caregivers, and the child so that you can provide the information that will best fit the philosophy, cultural worldview, and current patterns of the family.

- Encourage a connection with other family members and friends who have childrearing experience.

- Find a mentor for parents or caregivers who can provide individualized education (e.g., home visitors program, a caring adult from the family's church or neighborhood).

- Arrange for parents or caregivers to take parenting classes, connect them with parent support groups, and/or enroll them in parent-child playgroups.

- Connect parents or caregivers with community groups or resource materials (e.g., videos, audiotapes) that can provide information on parenting and child development.

- Model appropriate interactions and reasonable expectations for the child.

Consider referring the child to appropriate professionals (e.g., private therapists, medical practitioners, hospital clinics, school districts) *for a thorough assessment,* if you have concerns about possible developmental delays. Consider utilizing professionals from the family's cultural reference group or getting a subsequent cultural consultation regarding the results of an assessment.

> In a contested custody hearing, a psychologist assessed an 8-year-old American Indian child who had been raised primarily by her Indian aunt and Hispanic uncle as being "overly passive and dependent." The attorney of the aunt and uncle, who were seeking to adopt their niece, challenged the psychologist's findings. The attorney questioned whether the psychologist believed that there could be cultural biases in the assessment tools or if he had ever evaluated an American Indian child. The psychologist denied cultural bias in either the tool or in his ability to determine "what was normal for all children." An expert cultural witness who was also a licensed mental health professional countered the testimony, saying that the "passivity" was a more cultural approach to learning, being quiet and observing rather than aggressively engaging in a process without knowledge of potential consequences. The "dependence" was reinterpreted as being connected to and respectful to the adults in the family, which was a cultural expression of appropriate child development.

Find as many possible avenues for maintaining family and cultural connections as possible, if a parent or caregiver is not able to safely raise a child over the long run. Contact with siblings and other relatives, creation of life books, opportunities for culturally based learning and experiences, and other avenues will help to prevent or minimize damage to the child's developmental foundation.

■ Challenges for Parents or Caregivers: Normal Development

Not surprising to anyone who has been around children is the fact that caring for them can be both enjoyable and challenging. Challenging phases of development may be normal for children but may pose significant tests of patience for parents or caregivers. For families who already face numerous social, environmental, and/ or psychological stresses (e.g., loss of a job, death in the family), encountering the challenges associated with normal child development may be enough to overwhelm parents or caregivers and may possibly contribute to the occurrence of child abuse or neglect.

☐ Normal Challenges

Colic. Typically observed from 0 to 3 months of age, this includes fussy, intractable crying (20 minutes to 2 hours at a time), one or more times per day, in absence of hunger or physical symptoms. Caring for a baby who has colic can lead to frustration at not being able to pacify the baby. It may also lead to a feeling of insecurity about one's ability to parent effectively. If colic becomes a chronic problem, it can jeopardize the formation of a healthy caregiver-infant attachment.

Table 8.1 Developmental Stages

Infancy: 0–6 months old

Physical development	Cognitive/language development	Psychosocial development
0–4 Weeks	**0–4 Weeks**	**0–8 Weeks**
Proceeds from head to foot and central part to extremities.	Smiles selectively at mother's voice.	Gazes at faces (birth).
Sucks reflexively.	Shows startle reflex to sudden noise.	Smiles responsively.
Visually tracks to midline.		Uses vocalization to interact socially.
Lifts head when held upright.	**3–6 Months**	**3–4 Months**
	Babbles and coos, squeals and gurgles (by 3 months).	Distinguishes primary caregivers from others and will react if removed from home.
3–4 Months	Anticipates food with vocalization.	
Prone: lifts head momentarily—rolls from stomach to back.	Laughs.	
Pulls to sit without head lag.		Smiles readily at most people.
Grasps rattle.		Plays alone with contentment.
5–6 Months		
Reaches for objects.		
Inspects objects with hands, eyes, and mouth.		

Infancy: 6–12 months old

Physical development	Cognitive/language development	Psychosocial development
Gross motor	**6–9 Months**	**6–9 Months**
6–9 Months	Smiles and vocalizes to own mirror image.	Discriminates strangers (e.g., frowns, stares, cries).
Creeps.	Says "ma-ma," "da-da" (nonspecific).	Stranger/separation anxiety begins.
Sits without support.	Shakes head "no-no."	Actively seeks adult attention; wants to be picked up and held.
Pulls to stand to cruise furniture.	Imitates playful sounds.	
9–12 Months	Responds to name with head turn, eye contact, and smile.	Plays peekaboo.
Crawls on all fours.		Rarely lies down except to sleep.
Attains sitting position unaided.	**9–12 Months**	Pats own mirror image.
Stands momentarily.	Recognizes voices of favorite people.	Chews and bites on toys.
Takes first steps.	Responds to verbal request such as "Wave bye-bye."	Begins to respond to own name.
	Calls parent Mama or Dada.	

(continued)

Developmental Stages (*continued*)

Infancy: 6–12 months old

Physical development	Cognitive/language development	Psychosocial development
Fine motor	Repeats performances that are laughed at.	**9–12 Months**
6–9 Months	Plays peekaboo.	Social with family, shy with strangers.
Transfers objects hand to hand.		Begins to show sense of humor.
Bangs with spoon.		Becomes aware of emotions of others.
Finger feeds part of meal.		
Shakes bell.		
9–12 Months		
Holds, bites, and chews a cracker.		
Grasps string with thumb and forefinger.		
Beats two spoons together.		
Begins to use index finger to point and poke.		

Toddler years: 12–18 months old

Physical development	Cognitive/language development	Psychosocial development
Gross motor	**12–15 Months**	**12–15 Months**
12–18 Months	Jabbers expressively.	Shows strong dependence on primary caregiver with increasing difficulty separating.
Walks alone.	Communicates by gesture.	
Stoops and stands up again.	Vocalizes more than cries for attention.	Shows difficulty quieting and relaxing into sleep.
Climbs up on furniture.	Understands word "no."	Wants to have caregiver nearby all the time.
Walks up stairs with help.	Shakes head to indicate *no*.	
Fine motor	Says 2–3 "words" other than "Ma-ma" or "Da-da"	Gives toy to adult on request.
12–18 Months	Looks in appropriate place when asked (e.g., "Where is book?").	Shows sense of "me" and "mine."
Builds tower of 2 cubes.		
Scribbles spontaneously or by imitation.	**15–18 Months**	**15–18 Months**
Holds cup.	Vocalizes "No."	Begins to distinguish "you" and "me."
Puts raisin or pellet in bottle.	Has vocabulary of 10–15 words.	Imitates adult activities.
Turns book pages, 2–3 at a time.	Fluently uses jargon.	Interested in strangers but wary.
Holds spoon.	Points and vocalizes to indicate wants.	Does not respond well to sharp discipline.
Self-help		
12–15 Months		
Feeds self with fingers.		

(*continued*)

Developmental Stages

Toddler years: 12–18 months old (*continued*)

Physical development	Cognitive/language development	Psychosocial development
Removes hat, shoes, and socks.		Does not respond to verbal persuasion and scolding.
Inhibits drooling.		Expresses autonomy through defiance.
15–18 Months		Plays alone or beside other children.
Chews most foods well.		
Opens closed doors.		Strongly claims "mine."
Holds cup and drinks with some spilling.		Follows simple requests.
Imitates housework.		
Brings familiar object upon request.		

Toddler years: 18–24 months old

Physical development	Cognitive/language development	Psychosocial development
Gross motor	Points to pictures in books.	Moves about house without constant supervision.
Runs stiffly.	Points to one body part on request.	
Pushes and pulls large objects.		Plays primarily alongside children but not with them.
Carries large teddy bear while walking.	Has vocabulary of 20 words—mostly nouns.	
Comes downstairs on bottom or abdomen.	Understands "yours" versus "mine."	Has temper tantrums in situations of frustration.
Seats self in small chair.	Uses words "me" and "mine."	Is conscious of family as a group.
Fine motor	Enjoys simple stories.	Enjoys role playing.
Builds tower of 4–6 cubes.	Speaks in 2–word sentences (e.g., "juice gone").	Mimics real-life situations during play.
Tries to fold paper imitatively.		Claims and defends ownership of own things.
Wiggles thumb.		Begins to call self by name.
Places rings on spindle toy.		Discriminates between edible and inedible substances.
Turns pages singly.		
Turns knobs (television).		
Self-help		
Helps dress and undress self.		
May indicate wet or soiled diapers.		

(*continued*)

Developmental Stages (*continued*)

Toddler years: 18–24 months old

Physical development	Cognitive/language development	Psychosocial development
Pulls person to show.		
Asks for food and drink by vocalizing and gesturing.		
Uses spoon with little spilling.		
Replaces some objects where they belong.		

Toddler years: 24–30 months old

Physical development	Cognitive/language development	Psychosocial development
Gross motor	Often calls self by first name.	Initiates own play activities.
Jumps in place.	Speaks 50 or more words.	Want routines "just so."
Walks on tiptoe (imitation).	Has vocabulary of 300 words.	Does not like change in routine.
Walks up and down steps, both feet on each step.	Uses phrases and 3- to 4- word sentences.	Cannot wait or delay gratification.
Walks backward.	Understands and asks for "another."	Does not share.
Runs headlong.	Points to 4 body parts.	Knows identity in terms of sex and place in the family.
Fine motor		Observes other children at play and joins in for a few minutes.
Holds pencil with thumb and forefingers.		
Zips and unzips.		
Builds tower of 6–8 cubes.		
Self-help		
Learning to use buttons, zippers, and buckles.		
Pulls on socks.		
Pulls on pants or shorts.		
Drinks from cup without spilling.		
Helps put things away.		
Toilet training in progress.		

(*continued*)

Developmental Stages   *(continued)*

Toddler years: 30–36 months old

Physical development	Cognitive/language development	Psychosocial development
Gross motor	Verbalizes toilet needs.	Begins playing "with," as opposed to "next to," others.
Builds tower of 6–8 cubes.	Uses plural.	
Completes 3-piece form board.	Increases use of verbs.	Names or points to self in photos.
Fine motor	Begins using adjectives and prepositions.	Joins in nursery rhymes and songs.
Turns book pages singly.	Has vocabulary of 900–1,000 words (36 months).	Likes praise.
Builds tower of 6–8 cubes.	Uses verbal commands.	Dawdles.
Holds pencil with thumb and forefingers.	Gives full name when asked.	Has auditory fears (noises).
Can zip and unzip.	Asks "What's that?"	Shows sympathy, pity, modesty, and shame.
Self-help		
Toilet training in progress.		
Dresses with supervision.		
Eats with fork and spoon.		
Pours from one container to another.		
Gets drink unassisted.		
Avoids simple hazards.		

Preschool years: 3 years old

Physical development	Cognitive/language development	Psychosocial development
Gross motor	**Receptive language**	Is ready to conform to spoken word.
Gallops.	Follows two unrelated commands.	Begins to take turns.
Balances on one foot (1–5 seconds).	Has concept of 2 or 3.	Plays simple group games.
Catches large ball, arms flexed.	Identifies same versus different with pictures.	Toilets self during the day.
Hops on one foot (3 times).	Responds to verbal limits and directions.	Shows fear (visual fears, heights, loss of parents, nightmares).
Turns somersaults.	Identifies 2–3 colors.	Uses language to resist.
Shows lack of coordination (3½ years)—stumbling, falling.	Listens attentively to short stories.	Is able to bargain with adults.
Fine motor	Chooses objects that are hard/soft, heavy/light, big/little.	Tries to please.
Copies circle.		May masturbate openly.
Imitates cross.		

(continued)

Developmental Stages *(continued)*

Preschool years: 3 years old

Physical development	Cognitive/language development	Psychosocial development
Builds with Legos, bristle blocks, etc.	**Expressive language**	May have imaginary playmates.
Builds tower of 10 cubes.	Converses in sentences.	Plays most often "with," as opposed to "next to," others.
Spontaneously draws.	Speaks intelligibly.	Shares upon request.
Handedness may shift.	Answers simple yes/no questions.	
Imitates snipping with scissors.	Rote counts to 5.	
	Repeats nursery rhymes.	
	Counts 2–3 items.	
	Has 50–75% articulation of consonants.	
	Has vocabulary of 1,500 words (age 4 years).	
	Tells age using fingers.	
	Cognitive	
	Uses words for ordering perceptions and experiences.	
	Understands past versus present.	
	Shows curiosity; asks endless questions.	
	Matches colors (2 or 3).	
	Completes 6-piece puzzles.	
	Answers sensibly to "Why do we have stoves?" etc.	
	Tells a simple story.	

Preschool years: 4 years old

Physical development	Cognitive/language development	Psychosocial development
Gross motor	Understands opposite analogies.	Is dogmatic and dramatic.
Runs smoothly, varying speeds.	Follows 3-stage commands.	Shows urge to conform/please is diminished.
Hops on one foot (4–9 times).	Listens eagerly to stories.	May have control issues.
Balances on one foot (8–10 seconds).	Follows directions with prepositions (e.g., "above," "under").	May be physically aggressive.
Bounces ball with beginning control.	**Expressive language**	Is self-sufficient in own home.
	Uses all parts of speech correctly.	Has nightmares.

(continued)

Developmental Stages (*continued*)

Preschool years: 4 years old

Physical development	Cognitive/language development	Psychosocial development
Throws ball overhand.	Has vocabulary of 2,000-plus words.	May argue, boast, and make alibis.
Handles stairs with alternating feet using rail.	Uses color names.	Calls attention to own performance.
Fine motor	Defines words in terms of use (e.g., *car*, *pencil*).	Bosses and criticizes others.
Copies cross and square.	Asks many questions (e.g., why, what, how).	Rarely sleeps at nap time.
Attempts to cut on straight line.	Has 100% production and use of consonants.	Separates from mother easily.
Has established hand dominance.	Corrects own errors in pronunciation of new words.	Often has "special" friend.
"Writes" on page at random.		Prefers peers to adults.
May try to print own name.	Has sense of humor and self-laughing.	Washes face, brushes teeth, and dresses self.
Draws person—arms and legs directly from head.	Loves silly songs, names.	Uses bathroom unassisted.
	Increasing use of imagination.	
	Enjoys dress-up play.	
	Is interested in time concepts (e.g., yesterday, hour, minute).	
	Identifies several capabilities.	
	Rote counts to 10.	
	Counts 4 items.	
	Categorizes animals, food, toys.	
	Matches geometric forms.	
	Identifies missing part.	

Preschool years: 5 years old

Physical development	Cognitive/language development	Psychosocial development
Gross motor	**Receptive language**	Enjoys small group cooperative play—often noisy.
Balances on one foot.	Listens briefly to what others say.	
Skips smoothly.	Understands 6,000 words.	Listens and participates in 20-minute group activity.
Uses roller skates.	Categorizes words.	
Rides bicycle with training wheels.		Knows when certain events occur.
Balances on tiptoes.		

(*continued*)

Developmental Stages *(continued)*

Preschool years: 5 years old

Physical development	Cognitive/language development	Psychosocial development
Fine motor	Guesses object by attribute or use of clues (e.g., "What bounces?").	Accepts adult help and supervision.
Handedness firmly established.	Points to first and last in a line-up.	Is serious, businesslike, and self-assured.
Colors within lines.		Wants to help and please adults.
Cuts on line.	**Expressive language**	Enjoys competitive exercise games.
Copies circle, square, and triangle.	Has vocabulary of 2,500-plus words.	Fears parental loss, thunder, and scary animals.
Is not adept at pasting or glueing.	Repeats days of the week by rote.	More conscious of body, wants.
Draws within small areas.	Defines words and asks for word meanings.	Respects peers and their property.
Ties knot in string after demonstration.	Acts out stories.	
	Gives rhyming word after example.	
	Cognitive	
	Is often ready to enter kindergarten.	
	Appreciates past, present, and future.	
	Can count 6 objects when asked "How many?"	
	Begins to enjoy humorous stories and slapstick humor.	
	States address, age, name, and ages of siblings.	
	Acts out stories.	
	Learns left from right.	
	Matches 10–12 colors.	
	Predicts what will happen next.	
	School milestones	
	Prints first name and simple words.	
	Writing is mostly capital letters.	
	Frequently copies left to right.	

(continued)

Developmental Stages (*continued*)

Preschool years: 5 years old

Physical development	Cognitive/language development	Psychosocial development
	Reversals are common (e.g., writes *b* as *d*).	
	Reads letters in sequence.	
	Recognizes first name.	
	Recognizes several or all numerals on clock, phone, calendar.	
	Counts and points to 13 objects.	
	Writes 1–10 poorly—many reversals.	
	Adds and subtracts using 5 fingers.	
	Is capable of self-criticism.	

Elementary school years: 6 years old

Physical development	Cognitive/language development	Psychosocial development
Gross motor	**Receptive language**	Has poor ability to modulate feelings.
Is constantly active.	Uses picture dictionary.	Enjoys performing for others.
Shows smooth and coordinated movement.	Knows category labels.	Has difficulty making decisions.
Stands on one foot, eyes closed.	Defines and explains words.	Dawdles in daily routines, but will work beside adult to complete tasks.
Has good balance and rhythm.	**Expressive language**	
Bounces ball with good control.	Identifies likeness and differences between objects.	Shows jealousy of others; very competitive.
Hops through hopscotch course.	Identifies consonant sounds heard at beginning of words.	Plays simple table games.
Fine motor	Gives category labels.	Often insists on having own way.
Ties own shoes.	Likes to use big words.	Is easily excited and silly.
Makes simple, recognizable drawings.	Shows increasingly symbolic language.	Persists with chosen activities.
	Cognitive development	Goes to bed unassisted, but enjoys good night chat.
	Names all colors.	Frequently frustrated— may tantrum.
	Knows what number comes after 8.	May return to thumb sucking, baby talk, etc.
	Understands quantity up to 10.	

(*continued*)

Developmental Stages *(continued)*

Elementary school years: 6 years old

Physical development	Cognitive/language development	Psychosocial development
	Identifies similarities and differences among pictures.	Responds better to praise of positive behaviors, as opposed to focus on negative behaviors.
	School milestones	Often takes small things from others and claims found them.
	Begins to recognize words.	
	Matches words.	
	Identifies words by length or beginning sound/letter.	Begins to distinguish right and left on self.
	Rereads books many times.	
	Prints first and last name.	
	Invents spelling.	
	Reverses two-digit numbers (e.g., writes "13" as "31").	
	Rote counts to 30 or higher.	
	Adds amounts to 6.	
	Subtracts amounts within 5.	
	Uses simple measurement.	
	Names coins, states, values of penny, dime, and nickel.	
	Writes slowly and with effort with mixed capital and lowercase letters.	

Elementary school years: 7 years old

Physical development	Cognitive/language development	Psychosocial development
Gross motor	Speaks fluently.	Shows independence in completion of routines.
Shows variability in activity level.	Uses slang and clichés.	Is learning to screen out distractions and focus on one task at a time.
Rides bicycle.	Understands cause-effect relationships.	
Runs smoothly on balls of feet.	Recites days of week and months of year.	Becomes quiet and sullen when angry.
Fine motor	Talks about own feelings in retrospect.	Has better control of voice and temper.
Has well-developed small muscles.	Often seems not to hear when absorbed in own activity.	Sets high expectations for self; frequently disappointed by own performance.
Has well-developed hand-eye coordination.	Shows concrete problem solving.	
Draws triangle in good proportion.		

(continued)

Developmental Stages (*continued*)

Elementary school years: 7 years old

Physical development	Cognitive/language development	Psychosocial development
Copies vertical and horizontal diamonds.	Organizes and classifies information.	Is anxious to please others; sensitive to praise and blame.
	Learns best in concrete terms.	Has not learned to lose games; will cheat or end game abruptly.
	Shows interest in issues of luck and fairness.	May have little sense of humor; thinks others are laughing at him/her.
	Internal sense of time emerging.	Is considerate of others.
	School milestones	Is concerned about right and wrong.
	Shows increasing reading vocabulary.	
	Shows greater speed with writing.	
	Begins to self-monitor reversal errors (e.g., writing *b* rather than *d*).	
	Learns to solve addition and subtraction combinations.	
	Learns to tell time.	

Elementary school years: 8 years old

Physical development	Cognitive/language development	Psychosocial development
Gross motor	Easily expresses and communicates.	May be selfish and demanding of attention.
Shows rhythmical and somewhat graceful movement.	Is often out of bounds verbally (e.g., boasting, exaggerating, sharing private information).	May be cheerful.
Has frequent accidents due to misjudging abilities (e.g., broken arm).	Likes to use big words.	Is curious about activity of others.
Holds pencil, toothbrush, and tools less tensely.	**Reading**	Learning to lose at games.
Enjoys exercise of both large and small muscles.	Shows variable enjoyment of reading.	Is sensitive to criticism, especially in front of others.
	Likes humor in stories.	Shows strong interest in own past (e.g., stories, baby books, life books).
	Reads new words through context and phonics.	Begins to have sense of humor for own jokes or riddles.
	Stops and talks about what he or she reads.	May be snippy and impatient in talk with family members.
	Omits words and reads out of order.	
	Prefers silent reading.	

(continued)

Developmental Stages *(continued)*

Elementary school years: 8 years old

Physical development	Cognitive/language development	Psychosocial development
	Arithmetic	
	Knows addition and subtraction combinations—some by heart.	
	Learning to carry in addition.	
	Learning to borrow in subtraction.	
	Knows a few multiplication facts.	
	Knows ½ and ¼.	
	Interested in money.	
	Written language	
	Writes sentences.	
	Begins cursive writing.	
	Shows few reversal errors.	
	Uses capital and lowercase letter forms.	
	Tries to write neatly.	

Elementary school years: 9 years old

Physical development	Cognitive/language development	Psychosocial development
Gross motor	Gains proficiency in reading, writing.	Appears emotionally more stable.
Becomes interested in competitive sports—social aspects of sports.	Works and plays hard.	Experiences quick, short-lived emotional extremes.
Apt to overdo physical activities.	Frequently discusses reproduction with friends.	Mostly cooperative, responsible, and dependable.
Shows poor posture (e.g., slouches, head close to work).	Associates scary daytime events with frightening dreams.	Capable of concentrating for several hours.
Works purposefully to improve physical skills.	Enjoys school; wants to operate at optimal level, and may relate fears and failure more strongly to subject than to teacher.	Likes to plan ahead.
May have somatic complaints (e.g., stomachache, dizziness, leg pains).	Can describe preferred methods of learning.	Is increasingly attentive to peer pressure.
	Likes to read for facts and information.	Begins to subordinate own interests to group purpose.
		May take up collecting hobbies.
		Learns to lose at games.

(continued)

Developmental Stages (*continued*)

Elementary school years: 9 years old

Physical development	Cognitive/language development	Psychosocial development
	Enjoys keeping a diary and making lists.	Begins to be neater about own room.
	Prefers to read silently.	Chooses member of own sex for special friend.
	Usually prefers written to mental computation.	Overtly criticizes opposite sex.
	Worries about doing well in school.	Makes decisions easily.
		Responds relatively easily to discipline.

Elementary school years: 10 years old

Physical development	Cognitive/language development	Psychosocial development
Girls and boys tend to be even in size and sexual maturity (early in 10th year).	Participates in discussion of social and world problems.	Seems relaxed and casual; describes self as "real happy."
Girls' bodies undergo slight softening and rounding at 10½.	Interest in reading varies greatly by child.	Boys show friendship with physical expression (e.g., punch, shove, wrestle).
Has decreasing somatic complaints.	Shows humor that is broad, labored, and often not funny to adults.	Girls show friendship with note writing, gossip, and hand-holding.
Is increasingly fidgety—more common for girls.	Repeats "dirty" jokes to parent but often does not understand them.	Enjoys sharing secrets and discussing mysteries with friends.
Shows little awareness of fatigue.	Is interested in his or her future as a parent and how will treat own child.	Believes friends over parents.
Strongly refuses bathing.	Rarely interested in keeping a diary.	Does not respond well when praised or reprimanded in front of friends.
Loves outdoor exercise play (e.g., baseball, skating, jumprope, running).	Mostly interested in material possessions, health and happiness for self and others, and personal improvement.	Shows infrequent and soon-resolved anger.
	Enjoys memorizing.	Yells and calls names.
	Prefers oral to written work in school.	Rarely cries except with hurt feelings.
	Shows short interest span—needs frequent shift of activity in school.	Tends to have sincere, trusting, and physically affectionate relationship with mother.
	Is decreasingly interested in movies and television.	Tends to have positive, adoring, admiring relationship with father.

(*continued*)

Developmental Stages (*continued*)

Early adolescence: Beginning age, 11–13 years old

Physical development	Cognitive/language development	Psychosocial development
Females Pubic hair pigmented, curled. Auxiliary hair begins after pubic hair. Height growth spurt. Breast development continues. Labia enlarged. Increase in subcutaneous fat. Menstruation begins. **Males** Prepubescent physical development. Beginning growth of testes, scrotum, and penis. Downy pubic hair. Consistent height growth.	Begins to move from concrete toward abstract thinking (reasoning based on hypotheses or propositions rather than only on concrete objects or events). Increasingly interested in ideas, values, social issues; often narrow in understanding and dogmatic. Is very interested in music and personal appearance— especially common for females. Has increasing conflict with family—however, most place strong value on family and involved parents.	Is anxious about peer acceptance. Is concerned with self-identity. Depends on family but increasingly tests limits. Establishes independence through conflicts with peers and family.* Is egocentric. Has abrupt mood and behavior swings. Females highly concerned with body image, physical changes. Increasingly interested in peers and peer culture. Changes in friends are common. Has same-sex relationships most often, although has concerns, anxiety, and experimentation with opposite sex. Has strong needs for achievement and recognition of accomplishment, although may be masked by feigned indifference.

Mid-adolescence: Beginning age, 13–15 years old

Physical development	Cognitive/language development	Psychosocial development
Females Pubic hair fully developed. Auxiliary hair in moderate quantity. Continued breast growth. Menstruation well established. Decelerating height growth.	Shows fully developed abstract thought (usually by age 15) and can apply in more situations. Anxiety, major distractions interfere with abstract thinking. Has continued interest in ideas, ideals, values, social issues.	Increasingly independent from family; less overt testing.* Females somewhat more comfortable with body image and changes. Males highly concerned with body image and changes as puberty begins.

(continued)

Developmental Stages (*continued*)

Mid-adolescence: Beginning age, 13–15 years old

Physical development	Cognitive/language development	Psychosocial development
Ovulation (fertility). Moderate muscle growth and increase in motor skills. **Males** Pubic hair pigmented, curled. Auxiliary hair begins after pubic hair. Penis, testes, and scrotum continue to grow. Height growth spurt. Seminal emissions but sterile. Voice lowers as larynx enlarges. Mustache hair.		Shows increase in relationships with opposite sex; same-sex relationship continues to dominate. Is reliant on and anxious about peer relationships. May experiment with drugs. Enjoys achievement, experiences, feelings of accomplishment, receiving recognition.* Continues to be interested in appearance, music, and other elements of peer culture.

Late adolescence: Beginning age, 15–16 years old

Physical development	Cognitive/language development	Psychosocial development
Females Full development of breasts and auxiliary hair. Decelerated height growth (ceases at 16 years ± 13 months). **Males** Facial and body hair. Pubic and auxiliary hair denser. Voice deepens. Testes, penis, and scrotum continue to grow. Emissions of motile spermatozoa (fertility). Graduated deceleration of height growth (ceases by 17¾ years ±10 months). Muscle growth and increase in motor skills.	Shows well-established abstract thinking. Makes applications to own current and future situations and to broader issues (e.g., social concerns, academic studies).	May show increase in anxiety and avoidance behaviors as a major emancipation step becomes imminent (e.g., graduation, moving out of the house, going to college, partial or total self-support).* Increasingly concerned and interested in movement toward independence; generally not prepared emotionally or logistically for complete emancipation.* Maintains more stable relationships with peers and adults. Has reasonably well-established body image, especially among girls.

(continued)

Developmental Stages (*continued*)

Late adolescence: Beginning age, 15–16 years old

Physical development	Cognitive/language development	Psychosocial development
		Has more realistic and stable view of self and others and nature of problems, and is better at problem solving.
		Has continued need for achievement and recognition for accomplishment.

Post adolescence: Beginning age, 17–18 years old

Physical development	Cognitive/language development	Psychosocial development
Females Uterus develops fully by age 18–21. Other physical maturation complete. **Males** Full development of primary and secondary sex characteristics; muscle and hair development may continue.	Ability for abstract thinking and for practical problem-solving skills is increasingly tested by the demands associated with emancipation and/or higher education.	Is partially or fully emancipated, although often with difficulty. Shows decreased concerns about autonomy and increased concerns about resources. Often has less conflictual relationships with family; existing conflict tends to revolve around emancipation issues. Still directs attention toward peers and self-identity.*

*Given cultural differences in the development of "independence," it is important not to ascribe pathology to families and youth who may emphasize continuing connection to the family throughout adolescence and adulthood. In such families, rather, the focus may be on increasing responsibility and competence in performing a variety of roles for the benefit of the whole rather than individuation and spearation.

Night crying/awakening. Typically observed at 4-plus months of age, this continues after the infant has given up middle-of-the-night feedings. This can also occur following an acute illness that has involved nighttime contact with parents or caregivers. If night crying/awakening becomes an ongoing experience, parents or caregivers can become sleep deprived, leading to frustration and low energy for carrying out daily household, employment, and caregiving responsibilities.

Separation anxiety. Typically observed from 6 months to 2½ years of age, this includes crying, clinging, and fearfulness when the parent or caregiver is not present.

From 6 to 12 months of age, this anxiety can occur when the parent or caregiver is out of the infant's visual field. Parents or caregivers with multiple tasks to complete in a given day may become frustrated by the child's need to be close. They may also perceive the child as spoiled and punish harshly to "train" the child.

Exploratory behavior. Typically observed from 9 months to 2½ years of age, the child "gets into everything" repeatedly, out of normal, healthy curiosity. This interest in the environment can be physically dangerous for the child, provocative to parents or caregivers when valued possessions are touched (e.g., TV or DVD), and embarrassing when displayed in front of others who may not understand and may become impatient with the normalcy of exploratory behavior.

Negativism. Typically observed from 1 to 3½ years of age, a child delights in refusing most adult requests or suggestions, often becoming generally argumentative. The child's "no" is a healthy sign of developing self-identity and independence but can tax parent or caregiver tolerance.

Poor appetite. Typically observed from 1½ to 3 years of age, poor appetite is normal because the child's growth rate has slowed. Poor appetite can often lead to battles at the dinner table and conflict among the parents or caregivers. Concern about the child's nutrition or frustration at a failed attempt to teach the child to follow directions may lead parents or caregivers to force-feed or engage in power struggles—things that often make matters worse.

Toilet training. Typically observed from 1½ to 5 years of age, this is the process by which a child learns to be independent in using the toilet. Readiness for daytime training usually occurs by 24 months of age, since sphincter control is typically achieved between 18 to 24 months. Nighttime bladder control may not be achieved for several years. Pressure around toilet training can occur when parents or caregivers feel the need to toilet train early (e.g., due to requirements of childcare settings that children be toilet trained; due to money constraints that could be helped by "getting out of diapers"). Pressure can also build when parents or caregivers incorrectly conclude (due to a lack of knowledge about child development) that their child is developmentally behind or just being resistant.

Lack of compliance with parental or caregiver expectations. Typically observed from 6 to 11 years of age, this often occurs as a result of self-assertion, control conflicts, or simple lack of attention or forgetfulness. This is a natural part of a child's development and is important for the formation of independence. Parents or caregivers trying to keep their child safe or teach respect for authority may see noncompliance as a lack of discipline and respect, possibly leading them to "turn up the heat" as they discipline. The reverse may also occur—parents or caregivers may conclude that their child is capable of self-care, possibly leading them to provide inadequate supervision and caregiving. Cultural ethnic groups and other groups that value interdependence above independence may show variations in their approaches to training of children at this stage (e.g., military families, African Americans). For such children, "belonging" would be the essence of "identity" and thus would be the healthy resolution of this stage of development (Joe, 1989). For example:

> The intricate relational dynamics that characterize American Indian family systems are reinforced by cultural norms. American Indian children's sense of belonging is rooted in an understanding of their place and responsibility within the intricate web of kinship relationships. (Red Horse, Martinez, Day, Day, Poupart, & Sharnberg, 2000)

The sentiments expressed in this quotation may also apply to other cultural groups.

Attempts at independence, vacillations in mood, lack of responsibility and compliance, and experimentation with behaviors that anger or frighten adults. Typically observed from 12 to 18 years of age, the young person's capacity for self-care, coupled with the desire to make his or her decisions and a tendency to avoid responsibility, may lead to lack of supervision on the parent's or caregiver's part or an inability to control youth behaviors that are particularly problematic. Any of these behaviors may lead to confrontations with parents or caregivers that result in physical or emotional abuse. This can be a particular issue for recent immigrants (e.g., immigrants from Latin America, Hmong) or American Indian families that have recently migrated to urban areas for the first time. As youth become more acculturated to mainstream expectations for adolescents to be increasingly autonomous and even rebellious, parents from indigenous populations may interpret such behavior as highly disrespectful and struggle to regain a sense of parental authority.

☐ Your Role as a Resource

Your role as the worker is to help the parents or caregivers know what to expect and understand that these developmental phases are considered normal. If they are able to accept this, they will not take their child's behavior personally or assume that the child is trying to anger them or that the behavior is a result of the parents' or caregiver's failure. It is also important for you to work with the parents or caregivers to identify safe ways of coping when their child taxes their patience. This work will help you to promote child safety and well-being.

Work closely with families whose children are going through challenging phases of development. Offer specific information or connect families with resources that can educate them about child development, parenting challenges, and positive parental responses. Beyond the information presented in this chapter, you can obtain information on child development from places such as pediatricians' offices, local hospitals, and early childhood education clinics. Also look for community resources that specialize in providing culturally responsive family services.

- Conflicts with younger children that are related to developmental phases often involve parental attempts to change bodily functions that the child cannot control (e.g., eating, sleeping, elimination).
- Conflicts with older children related to developmental phases often involve parental expectations of a child's behavior or ability that may be excessive or unreasonable, given the child's current development.

For example, a parent may become annoyed or impatient with a child, believing that he or she is not behaving or performing out of laziness or an attempt to make the parent mad.

- Conflicts may also result when youth behavior is particularly difficult and parents are unable to control it as they attempt to ensure youth safety and well-being.

For example, a youth who is regularly using drugs and alcohol, staying out all night, and is physically violent when his parents try to get him to hand over his drug paraphernalia is taxing his parents' ability to handle him. Out of frustration and a lack of ideas of how to handle their son, the parents may decide that they can no longer handle their son and decide to call the CPS agency.

- Physical and emotional abuse may be prevented if you and the parents or caregivers recognize and respond to difficult phases in a way the child is developmentally ready to respond to.

Connect families to an outside resource for parenting information and support. Parenting classes are often used as a way to provide general information on child development to the family. Keep in mind, however, that not all parents or caregivers respond to the same type of setting for learning. While some parents or caregivers may benefit from a group learning setting (as is used by many parenting classes), others may benefit more from individualized work.

Use the family's natural support system as a way to help parents or caregivers deal with challenging developmental behaviors. In many cultural groups, including African American, American Indian, and Hispanic populations, the extended family may be very involved in the ongoing caregiving of children.

Assist the family in identifying and implementing specific alternatives to violence within the home, including steps for coping when frustration builds (e.g., calling someone when they need a break; seeking reassurance and help from a friend, mentor, or professional; setting up a reward at the end of the day—a hot bath, a good book).

- Make sure to include the parents, caregivers, and older children and youth in developing the plan for alternatives to violence. Solutions dictated by workers often have a poor rate of compliance. Provide a copy of the plan to family members as appropriate.
- Develop a plan with the parents or caregivers that takes into account the child's developmental needs. Regularly review the plan for needed revisions.
- Use concrete terms and examples that are based on the family's experiences. Vague suggestions have little behavioral impact. Talk about or note examples of appropriate parent or caregiver responses used in the past and then build on their strengths.

For example, rather than saying "Samuel will display anger in an appropriate manner," leaving the definition of "appropriate" unclear, concrete examples could include "Samuel will talk in a calm voice when angry" or "Samuel will not touch anyone or anything while angry" or "Samuel will leave the room when angry and return to discuss the problem once he has calmed down."

Continue to see the parents or caregivers and check on the child regularly until the problems that place the child at risk for maltreatment have been resolved.

Model the desired caregiving behavior.

Get feedback from the parents or caregivers and older children on how their plans for nonviolent responses and coping are working. Meet with the parents or caregivers regularly and refer to the written plan. Ask the parents, caregivers, and older children:

- How do you feel about the plan?
- Have you been able to use the plan?
- How well has the plan been working for your family?
- What aspects of the plan have worked for your family?
- What aspects of the plan have not worked for your family?
- How does the plan need to be modified to better meet your needs?

Realize that progress may be slow. Problems did not develop overnight and therefore will not be resolved overnight. Reinforce any degree of progress.

Help parents or caregivers to change the plan as needed. Developing a plan in which they have contributed their knowledge and ideas will go a long way to assure that the plan is followed.

■ Challenges for Parents or Caregivers: Beyond Normal Development

In addition to the normal developmental behaviors that provide challenges for parents or caregivers, some families will encounter challenges that go beyond normal development. The most common such challenges that are faced by parents or caregivers are those associated with mental health issues and developmental disabilities. Caring for a child on a daily basis who has special needs can require a great deal of energy and support. Some parents or caregivers may have neither, making their parenting demands extremely difficult. Parents or caregivers who love and take care of their child (along with all the other responsibilities involved in working and running a household) may reach the point where their psychological resources are gone. When this happens, child maltreatment may result. Your ability to spot potential mental health issues and developmental disabilities will help you to make necessary referrals for needed assessments and services, thereby preventing subsequent abuse or neglect.

□ Mental Health Issues

Children who experience abuse or neglect are more likely to show problems with mental health issues than children who do not experience maltreatment (Manly, Kim, Rogosch, & Cicchetti, 2001). Although there are a number of mental health issues that children and youth can display (e.g., autism, eating disorders, conduct disorder, and early signs of schizophrenia and bipolar disorder), the two mental health issues often observed in maltreated children and youth are depression and anxiety. There is growing interest and research regarding bipolar disorder in children (Papolos & Papolos, 1999). In many cases, attention deficit hyperactivity disorder is misdiagnosed. Posttraumatic stress disorder, too, is confused with bipolar illness. Many children with fetal alcohol exposure also have bipolar illness. (The information presented in this section was obtained from National Alliance for the Mentally Ill [2001].)

Major depression is a serious medical illness that affects a person's mood, concentration, sleep, activity, appetite, social behavior, and feelings. Young people who experience depression cannot simply "snap out of it" because it is a persistent condition (unlike normal emotional experiences of sadness, loss, or changing moods) that can significantly interfere with thoughts, behavior, mood, activity, and physical health.

Psychological, biological (e.g., chemical imbalance of neurotransmitters, genetics), and environmental factors may all contribute to the development of depression. Life events, such as the death of a loved one, a major loss or change, chronic stress, and alcohol and drug abuse, may also trigger episodes of depression.

Approximately 12.5% of adolescents and 3% of children in the United States may have depression. Nearly twice as many females as males experience major depression each year. Major depression can occur at any age. Although depression occurs in all ethnic, racial, and socioeconomic groups, it is particularly evident in low-income families. Left untreated, depression can lead to suicide. Suicide is the third leading cause of death for 15- to 24-year-olds (approximately 5,000 per year) and the sixth leading cause of death for 5- to 15-year-olds.

The symptoms of major depression represent a significant change from how an adolescent or child functioned before the illness and include:

- Persistent sadness and hopelessness.
- Withdrawal from friends and from activities once enjoyed.
- Increased irritability or agitation.
- Anger.
- Missed school or poor school performance.
- Changes in eating and sleeping habits.
- Indecision, lack of concentration, or forgetfulness.
- Poor self-esteem or guilt.
- Frequent physical complaints (e.g., headaches, stomachaches).
- Lack of enthusiasm, low energy, or low motivation.
- Drug and/or alcohol abuse.
- Thoughts of death or suicide.

Anxiety disorders are conditions that cause children and young people to feel excessively frightened, distressed, and uneasy during situations in which most others would not experience such symptoms. Anxiety disorders can lead to poor school attendance, low self-esteem, deficient interpersonal skills, alcohol abuse, and adjustment difficulty.

The most common anxiety disorders include:

- *Panic disorder.* Results in sudden feelings of terror (panic attacks) that strike repeatedly and without warning.

- *Obsessive-compulsive disorder (OCD).* Is characterized by repeated, intrusive, and involuntary thoughts, ideas, urges, impulses, or worries (obsessions), and/or behavioral rituals that have no real purpose (except to relieve tension) and seem impossible to control (compulsions). Children may hide their rituals and become mentally exhausted from the strain. Other children find their rituals so time-consuming that they are too tired to play with friends or concentrate in school.

- *Posttraumatic stress disorder.* Occurs after experiencing a trauma such as abuse, natural disasters, or extreme violence. It includes persistent memories of the trauma that get in the way of daily functioning.

- *Phobias.* Disabling and irrational fears of something that poses little or no actual danger. The fear leads to avoidance of objects or situations and can cause extreme feelings of terror, dread, and panic, which can substantially restrict one's life. Phobias center around particular objects (e.g., certain animals) or situations (e.g., enclosed spaces).

- *Generalized anxiety disorder.* Chronic, exaggerated worrying about everyday, routine life events and activities (lasting at least 6 months). Children and youth with this disorder usually anticipate the worst.

- *Other anxiety disorders.* These include agoraphobia, acute stress disorder, anxiety disorder due to medical conditions, and substance-induced anxiety disorder.

Although biology (e.g., genes, biological imbalance of the brain chemical serotonin) may play a role in the development of anxiety disorders, environmental factors have also been associated with anxiety.

Approximately 1 in 10 young people have an anxiety disorder, making anxiety disorders one of the most common mental illnesses in the United States; OCD is as prevalent or more prevalent than many other childhood ailments, affecting approximately 1 million children and adolescents in the United States.

High levels of anxiety or excessive shyness in 6- to 8-year-old children may be indicators of a developing anxiety disorder. Other symptoms of anxiety disorders are based on the type of disorder.

- *Panic disorder.* Physical symptoms include chest pain, heart palpitations, shortness of breath, dizziness, abdominal discomfort, feelings of unreality, and fear of dying. Children and youth with this disorder may experience unrealistic worry, self-consciousness, and tension.

- *Obsessive-compulsive disorder (OCD).* Symptoms can occur as early as 3 to 4 years of age and can include counting, arranging and rearranging objects, and excessive hand washing. At school, children may repeatedly check, erase, and redo their assignments—possibly resulting in work being late or incomplete.

  Common *obsessions.* Symptoms include fear of contamination or a serious illness, fixation on lucky/unlucky numbers, fear of danger to self and others, need for symmetry or exactness, and excessive doubt.

  Common *compulsions.* Symptoms include repetitive rituals such as cleaning or washing, touching, counting, repeating, arranging or organizing, checking or questioning, and hoarding.

- *Posttraumatic stress disorder.* Symptoms include nightmares; flashbacks; numbing of emotions; depression; feeling angry, irritable, and distracted; and being easily startled.

- *Phobias.* Symptoms with "social" phobia commonly include hypersensitivity to criticism, difficulty being assertive, and low self-esteem.

- *Generalized anxiety disorder.* Symptoms include frequent complaints of fatigue, tension, headaches, and nausea.

☐ Developmental Disabilities

Children who have developmental disabilities are at greater risk of child maltreatment than children who do not have such disabilities (Sullivan & Knutson, 2000). Therefore, your attention to the resources that families require to sufficiently meet the needs of their children with disabilities will help families assure child safety and well-being. (Unless otherwise noted, the information presented in this section was obtained from Developmental Disabilities Resource Center, n.d.)

A developmental disability is a disability that is observed before the person reaches 22 years of age, which constitutes a substantial disability to the affected individual, and is attributed to mental retardation or related conditions (including cerebral palsy, epilepsy, autism or other neurological conditions) when such conditions result in impairment of general intellectual functioning or adaptive behavior similar to that of a person with mental retardation. (Developmental Disabilities Resource Center, n.d.)

The disabilities may be biological or the result of an accident (e.g., head trauma, lack of oxygen for an extended period).

- "Impairment of general intellectual functioning" means that the person has been determined to have an IQ of 70 or less (equivalent of two or more standard deviations below the mean, assuming a scale with a mean of 100 and a standard deviation of 15).

- "Adaptive behavior" means that the person has overall adaptive behavior that is significantly limited in two or more skill areas (communication, self-care, home living, social skills, community use, self-direction, health and safety, functional academics, leisure, and work).

- "Similar to that of a person with mental retardation in regard to adaptive behavior" means that a person's adaptive behavioral limitations are a direct result of or are significantly influenced by the person's substantial cognitive deficits and may not be attributable to only a physical or sensory impairment or mental illness. (Developmental Disabilities Research Center, n.d.)

Some children do not have a developmental disability but show developmental delays in one or more areas. A "developmental delay" can be defined in three ways:

1. It can refer to the slowed or impaired development of a child who is under 5 years of age and who is at risk of having a developmental disability because of the presence of one or more of the following:
   - Chromosomal conditions associated with mental retardation.
   - Congenital syndromes and conditions associated with delay in development.
   - Metabolic disorders.
   - Prenatal and perinatal infections and significant medical problems.
   - Low birth weight infants weighing less than 1,200 grams (2.65 pounds).
   - Postnatal acquired problems known to result in significant developmental delays.

2. It can refer to a child less than 5 years old being delayed in development by at least 1.5 standard deviations on assessment instruments in one or more of the following areas: communication; self-help; social-emotional, functioning; motor skills; sensory development; and cognition.

3. It can refer to a child less than 3 years of age who lives with one or both parents or caregivers who have a developmental disability and do not receive supportive services.

Children with disabilities show significant difficulties in one or more of the following areas: cognition, speech and language, motor skills, vision, hearing, emotions and behavior, and self-help skills. Accurate diagnosis, careful assessment, and appropriate medical management are important in helping parents, caregivers, educators, and health personnel to work together effectively on behalf of a child with a disability.

Children with disabilities, particularly children with multiple disabilities, are at greater risk for child maltreatment than children without disabilities (Sullivan & Knutson, 2000). However, if appropriate assessments and services are provided, risk to these children can be reduced.

The reasons children with disabilities are at greater risk for child maltreatment, compared to children without disabilities, seem to center around two areas:

1. Parent or caregiver psychological feelings and adjustment to having a child with a disability. These feelings and the adjustment occur for children born with disabilities as well as for children who later develop disabilities (e.g., through an accident).

   When a child is born with a disability, the parents or caregivers often experience the loss of the "dream child" they fantasized about during pregnancy.

   Parents or caregivers go through a grieving process (e.g., anger, denial, guilt) that is neither orderly nor time bound. New stages of child development and societal expectations bring new challenges that can rekindle stages of grieving.

   Some parents or caregivers experience a state of "chronic sorrow," burdened by pervasive sadness and feelings of guilt for the way they feel or for their possible contribution to the disability (e.g., drug or alcohol exposure during pregnancy).

   Parents or caregivers tend to experience grief and adjustment differently.

   > One parent or caregiver may be responsible for direct day-to-day caregiving. Demands of the physical care coupled with potentially lowered child responsiveness (associated with some disabilities) can result in emotional withdrawal and depression for this parent or caregiver.

   > Another parent or caregiver may be more focused on long-term problems such as financial pressures, the child's likelihood of occupational success, and ability to eventually care for himself or herself.

   > One parent or caregiver may experience relief in talking about the situation, while another may tend to deny the disability and her or his own emotional reactions to it.

   Sometimes parents or caregivers are drawn closer together by the experience of caring for a child with disabilities. However, unresolved differences in coping styles, cumulative stress on the relationship, and loss of intimacy may lead to marital conflict and divorce.

   Siblings are also affected by a child with disabilities. Often they experience loneliness or even neglect as the parents or caregivers focus attention on the child requiring extra attention.

   The potential for child abuse and neglect may increase when:

   - The parents or caregivers are overwhelmed and have little or no respite from caring for their child.
   - Families are emotionally and socially isolated.
   - The child is emotionally unresponsive or hypersensitive to touch.

2. Challenges associated with providing care for a child with disabilities. Parents or caregivers experience tremendous stress and pressure as they simultaneously deal with their psychological reactions and make decisions regarding the medical treatment of their child.

Day-to-day care for a child with disabilities can be extremely demanding (e.g., special diets, medical treatments, additional laundry, therapy appointments, social restriction and isolation, financial pressures, anxiety about the future, and ongoing loss of sleep).

The risk of child abuse and neglect may be reduced if parents or caregivers receive appropriate support, such as:

- Opportunities to talk openly with nonjudgmental peers and professionals.
- Participation in day programs or summer camps for children and youth with disabilities.
- Provision of respite care as needed.
- Assistance with financial demands associated with the disabilities.

☐ Types of Developmental Disabilities

Although there are several types of developmental disabilities (e.g., mental retardation, visual or hearing impairment, cerebral palsy, language problems), two disabilities often observed in maltreated children include attention deficit disorder and learning disabilities.

Attention deficit disorder (ADD) and attention deficit hyperactivity disorder (ADHD). These are thought to be neurochemical disorders that interfere with attention. ADD is a condition characterized by inattention and impulsivity. If children show these symptoms along with hyperactivity, they are considered to have ADHD. Most children identified as having ADD are also hyperactive and restless (ADHD), have poor impulse control, and are prone to outbursts of anger and aggression. Often they are emotionally labile and immature and are resistant to discipline. (Unless otherwise noted, the information presented in this section was obtained from the National Alliance for the Mentally Ill [2001] and Children's Disabilities and Special Needs [2001].)

Causes of ADD and ADHD do not include dysfunctional parenting, lack of intelligence, or poor discipline. ADD and ADHD are thought to be biologically based disorders; compared to individuals without these disorders, those with them show lower levels of the neurotransmitter dopamine in critical regions of the brain; and lower metabolic activity occurring in regions of the brain that control attention, social judgment, and movement. These disorders also seem to have a genetic component, running in families. Other causes of these symptoms include central nervous system diseases, prenatal drug exposure, and serious emotional disturbances. These disorders are rarely caused by diet. However, there is evidence that diet may positively or negatively affect the management of these disorders.

Approximately 3% to 10% of all school-aged children in the United States (over 1 million) have ADD or ADHD (Children's Disabilities and Special Needs, 2001), making it the most commonly diagnosed behavior disorder in young persons. ADHD is significantly more prevalent than ADD, although the higher incidence of ADHD may be due, in part, to the fact that parents, caregivers, and teachers recognize it more frequently than ADD alone. Boys are about three times more likely than girls to have ADHD.

The symptoms of these disorders vary, depending on the type of disorder observed. *Predominantly inattentive* involves:

- Failure to pay close attention to details (e.g., makes careless mistakes).
- Difficulty sustaining attention to tasks or leisure activities.
- Inattention when spoken to directly.
- Tendency to be easily distracted.
- Failure to follow through on instructions and finish tasks.
- Forgetfulness.
- Difficulty organizing tasks and activities.
- Tendency to lose things necessary for tasks or activities.
- Avoiding, disliking, or being reluctant to engage in tasks that require sustained mental effort.

Predominantly hyperactive/impulsive includes:

- Being fidgety.
- Difficulty sitting still.
- Difficulty engaging in leisure activities quietly.
- Being "on the go," acting as if "driven by a motor."
- Talking excessively.
- Blurting out answers before questions have been completed.
- Interruption of or intrusion on others.
- Low tolerance for frustration.
- Temper tantrums.

Combined is the most common type of disorder; it has a combination of the inattentive and the hyperactive/impulsive symptoms.

Learning disability. Broadly defined as a disorder in which there is a significant discrepancy between a child's achievement (in reading, spelling, written language, mathematics, and/or language skills) and his or her ability. The discrepancy between actual and expected achievement is not the result of lack of educational opportunity, emotional disturbance, physical disability, or health impairment. These children have difficulty with information processing because of perceptual, memory, attention, and language defects. (The information presented in this section was obtained from the American Academy of Child and Adolescent Psychiatry [1997].)

Learning disabilities are thought to be caused by a difficulty with the nervous system that affects receiving, processing, or communicating information. These disabilities may also run in families. Some children with learning disabilities are also hyperactive, unable to sit still, easily distracted, and have a short attention span. Learning disabilities may also occur as a result of chromosome disorders (e.g., fragile

X, Turner's syndrome), traumatic brain injuries, or a history of recurrent ear infections.

Approximately 10% to 15% of school-aged children have a learning disability. Specific reading and written language disorders (dyslexia) are more common than a specific mathematics disorder (dyscalcula) or handwriting disorder (dysgraphia).

Symptoms of a learning disability can include:

- Difficulty understanding and following instructions.
- Trouble remembering what someone just said.
- Failure to master reading, spelling, writing, and/or math skills.
- Difficulty distinguishing right from left, identifying words; tendency to reverse letters, words, or numbers.
- Lack of coordination in walking, sports, or small activities such as holding a pencil or tying a shoelace.
- Easily losing or misplacing homework, schoolbooks, or other items.
- Inability to understand the concept of time—confused by "yesterday," "today," and "tomorrow."

☐ Your Role in Helping Families

Children with developmental disabilities often have multiple needs that can be overwhelming. Parents of children with one or more disabilities may face challenging child behaviors that are sometimes associated with the disability. Stress may be associated with ongoing work that goes far beyond typical caregiving responsibilities, frequent contacts with and trips to multiple professionals who supervise various aspects of the needed care, and financial responsibilities that can quickly tax the family budget. Children with disabilities often have multiple caregivers (all of whom may pose a risk for maltreating them) and may not be able to verbalize what is happening to them. Therefore, to address issues of child safety and well-being, it is critical for you to make sure that families have sufficient support.

Although you may not be able to provide treatment for mental health issues and developmental disabilities, you can help parents, caregivers, and children by developing a plan to address their needs and connecting them with appropriate resources for proper diagnosis, treatment, and support. Coming up with a plan to address family needs often includes working with a team of service providers and family members who can decide together the issues to be addressed and how to address them. Depending on the cultural background of the family, you may also need to include extended family and community supports in the planning process.

The *individualized family service plan* is often seen for children with disabilities; it is developed by service providers and family members and is designed to enhance the family's ability to meet the needs of the child (Cruz, Meredith, Park, & Slay, 1999). Such plans will outline:

- The child's present level of development (strengths and areas of concern).
- The family's resources, priorities, and concerns.

- The outcomes or goals the family would like to address within a given timeframe.
- The supports and services to be used to achieve the outcomes/goals.

The *primary service coordinator* is the person who will assist the family in developing a plan and looking for services and supports. This person will:

- Coordinate evaluations and assessments.
- Facilitate and participate in the development of the individualized family service plan.
- Assist in identifying available service providers.
- Coordinate and monitor delivery of services.
- Inform the family of availability of advocacy services—useful for settings such as school.
- Coordinate with medical and health providers.
- Facilitate development of a transition plan to preschool services or independent living, if appropriate.

A transition plan will provide for transitioning into supports and services for young children when they turn 3 years old.

You should connect families with resources for proper diagnosis and treatment. In case of mental health issues, diagnosis and treatment is most often carried out by mental health professionals. Some conditions (e.g., depression) may also be treated by primary care physicians who use medication but often require supplemental work with people qualified to provide therapy.

In the case of developmental disabilities, diagnosis and treatment typically are done by private therapists (e.g., speech language pathologist for language problems), medical practitioners, hospital clinics, or school districts. Multidisciplinary teams can often be used to develop a comprehensive plan for enhancing current functioning. Early intervention is thought to be key to maximum effectiveness of treatment and outcomes.

Treatment for disabilities is specified in an *individual education plan* (IEP), an educational plan for a specific student that is written by a multidisciplinary team (consisting of school personnel, parents or caregivers, and other appropriate professionals, perhaps including you as the CPS worker). The IEP outlines learning objectives and steps to meet the objectives within a given time frame (Developmental Disabilities Resource Center, n.d.). The IEP is mandated by Public Law 105-17 (the Individuals with Disabilities Education Act), which requires local school districts to provide appropriate educational services for 3- to 21-year-olds who have disabilities (IDEA Practices, n.d.).

Your agency will probably have a list you can use to connect families with resources for diagnosis and treatment of mental illness and developmental disabilities.

You should connect families with sources of support that are beyond those of traditional service providers. Because social support is important for families facing stress, particularly if the stress is ongoing, it is important for you to make sure that families have a sufficient support system. Such supports can include, but are not limited to (1) family—immediate and extended; (2) friends; (3) neighbors; and (4) community support groups, which can provide families with the opportunity to meet other people who deal with similar issues. These groups (e.g., Parent to Parent) often provide emotional support and information on available resources, and "lessons learned" from personal experiences.

■ Developmental Problems Often Associated with Child Maltreatment

Children who have been maltreated often display a variety of problems that may require special services. Although much of the relevant research has not determined whether maltreatment "causes" poor developmental outcomes to occur, the fact of the matter is that these children can present multiple needs. As a worker, you will want to look out for potential developmental problems in maltreated children, so that you may better address their safety and well-being through appropriate service provision.

Because research cannot determine whether maltreatment "causes" the problems that maltreated children display, you cannot automatically conclude that children who have developmental problems are being maltreated. If children display a developmental problem, what you can conclude is that they have specific needs that should be evaluated and appropriately addressed.

☐ Problems Seen in Fetuses

Trauma to the fetus can have severe and long-term developmental consequences. The most common trauma to a fetus that potentially leads to harmful long-term developmental problems is exposure to alcohol and illicit drugs, which is being defined by more and more professionals as a form of maltreatment. When women use alcohol and illicit drugs during pregnancy, the substances pass through the human placenta and can affect the developing fetus (Ornoy, 2002). Fetuses that are exposed to alcohol and illicit drugs can have major organ malformation, growth retardation (Stratton et al., 1996, as cited in Autti-Ramo, 2000), and facial and congenital anomalies. Fetuses are also at increased risk for being stillborn (Ornoy, 2002).

Infants exposed to alcohol or illicit drugs before birth are called "drug-affected babies." The effects of alcohol on fetuses are described as "fetal alcohol syndrome" (FAS) for more recognizable and severe effects and "fetal alcohol effects" (FAE) for more subtle indicators. (See Chapter 9 for more information.)

Fetal exposure to alcohol and illicit drugs can result in damaging effects across all developmental domains. For example, in the physical domain, alcohol and drug-exposed fetuses have physical manifestations such as facial anomalies (e.g., eyes droopy or far apart, thin upper lips, asymmetrical ears), small heads, small body size and/or weight, poor weight gain, and failure to grow. Fetuses exposed to crack cocaine and other illicit drugs often experience varying levels of withdrawal symptoms at birth and may exhibit physical and behavioral problems similar to those seen in FAS babies. (See chapter 9.)

The developmental effects on the fetus depend on the type of substance, dose, duration of exposure, and the age of the fetus. For example, the fetal developmental stage is related to the effects observed (e.g., drinking in the first trimester is associated with physical malformations, whereas drinking in the second trimester is associated with impaired infant growth). Children with fetal alcohol exposure often display uneven development in various domains. For example, an adolescent with FAE may do well in school but show dramatic immaturity and impulsiveness in social relationships.

Increased awareness and ability by healthcare professionals (e.g., OB/GYN staff) to identify alcohol/drug use by pregnant women (through blood and urine testing and social history) increase the chance that infants will be diagnosed.

Many identifiable drug-affected babies are at risk of abuse and neglect because the alcohol/drug involvement of the parents or caregivers makes it difficult to care for the babies while under the influence. There are few alcohol/drug in-patient treatment programs that serve pregnant women and fewer still that serve mothers and their children.

The role of CPS in cases of fetal alcohol/drug exposure is not the same in all states. Some states have mandatory reporting and investigation laws that include fetal exposure to alcohol/drugs; others do not. Evidence of alcohol/drug exposure at the time of birth may or may not be seen as a mandatory reporting and investigation condition. In some states, parental neglect or abuse beyond the evidence of exposure is the only reason for a mandated report and investigation.

☐ Problems Seen in Infants

Maltreated infants can show delays in achieving developmental milestones in any of the developmental domains. These lags may become more exaggerated over time, given the speed with which infants develop. The types of developmental problems seen in maltreated children will sometimes vary, depending on the type of maltreatment experienced.

- *Physical abuse.* Because physical abuse at an early age can affect the development of the central nervous system, children who are physically abused may show problems in the areas of cognitive, speech/language, and learning development. In turn, these problems can hinder opportunities for experiences and interactions with peers and adults, leading to challenges in the psychosocial area of development.
- *Neglect.* This can place infants at risk for similar developmental consequences, since all domains of development (physical, psychosocial, and cognitive/language) are highly dependent on the opportunities (provided by caregivers and the surrounding environment) to develop. Two forms of severe developmental problems often seen with child neglect are failure to thrive and psychosocial dwarfism. (See Chapter 9 for more information.)

Infants who are maltreated may also show problems in the psychosocial domain, although these problems often do not become pronounced until later years. The most readily apparent psychosocial problem observed in infants has to do with their quality of attachment to their primary caregivers. Infants who are maltreated are at risk for not developing a secure attachment to their primary caregivers. Having an attachment that is not secure can put children at risk for a variety of psychosocial problems later on. (For a more detailed description of attachment, see the section that follows.)

☐ Problems Seen in Preschool- and School-Aged Children

Aside from the developmental consequences associated with damage to the central nervous system (sometimes seen in severe abuse or neglect), children who are maltreated often endure psychological damage that can, in turn, affect other areas of their development (Garbarino & Garbarino, 1986). Although children can often move beyond their traumas, the experience of abuse and neglect does not occur without a cost; and with these children, the cost is often seen in their behavioral, social-emotional, and cognitive functioning. Table 8.2 on page 290 includes a summary of behavioral, social-emotional, and cognitive problems that are often observed in abused and neglected children.

As mentioned earlier, problems in behavioral, social-emotional, and cognitive areas are problems that maltreated children, compared to nonmaltreated children, are more likely to display. The problems are not necessarily a result of child abuse or neglect but are often observed in children who have been abused or neglected. They should not be used as a way to determine whether children have been maltreated, but rather to alert you to the potential needs of these children. Efforts to look for these potential needs and then address them through services or other activities will help you better address safety and well-being issues.

- *Behavioral.* Abused and neglected children can display a variety of behavior problems, many of which get in the way of social functioning. Perhaps the most common behavioral problem seen in maltreated children is *aggression.* Abused children, compared to nonabused children, are more likely to be aggressive toward peers, adults, animals, and objects in their environments.
- *Social-emotional.* Abused and neglected children, compared to non-maltreated children, display greater and more problems, which run the gamut from low self-esteem and depression to poor social interactions with and rejection from peers.
- *Cognitive.* Compared to nonmaltreated children, those who are abused and neglected are more likely to show impairments in learning, problem solving, concentration, and reality testing. This is particularly true for neglected children. Not surprisingly, these children are more likely to experience failure at school (e.g., below grade level performance, repeating a grade).

Abused and neglected children, compared to nonmaltreated children, are more likely to have problems in school, which include performance below grade level, greater behavioral problems, greater delinquency, and poorer social adjustment with classmates. Maltreated children, compared to nonmaltreated children, are more likely to receive special education classes, repeat a grade in school, and drop out of school before graduation.

Children whose maltreatment continues into adolescence are often at greater risk for danger, because they may place themselves in dangerous situations that result in victimization. This can increase their risk of significant impairments and failure in experiencing interpersonal relationships and accomplishing emancipation tasks.

Children who experience developmental delays as a result of maltreatment may tend to behave in ways that elicit further maltreatment. In effect, this behavior doubles their victimization and their risk for further developmental delays.

☐ Factors That Influence Observed Developmental Problems in Maltreated Children

A variety of factors can serve to exacerbate or diminish the developmental problems observed in maltreated children. Such factors include (Manly, Kim, Rogosch, & Cicchetti, 2001), but are not limited to:

- *Nature of the maltreatment act.* Emotional and physical abuse is more often associated with problems such as depression, aggression, and poor social interactions. Neglect is more often associated with problems in cognitive development.
- *Frequency and duration of the maltreatment.* The more often the maltreatment occurs and the longer it lasts, the more problems children display (e.g., depression).
- *Severity of the maltreatment.* The more severe the maltreatment, the more problems children display (e.g., anxiety, behavior problems).
- *Developmental stage of the child at the time of maltreatment.* The younger the child when the maltreatment starts, the more problems he or she is likely to display—possibly because children who experience maltreatment at younger ages are more likely to experience more maltreatment over time.
- *Interpersonal relationships.* Children who have social support (e.g., friends, a teacher, extended family, or neighbor) show fewer problems than children who do not have social support.

It is important to remember that some behavior problems observed during out-of-home placement and in supervised visitation with parents may be related to long-standing patterns of neglect and abuse or may be situational to the grief and anxiety associated with separation from the familiar environment.

☐ Effects of Child Maltreatment on Brain Development

The process of brain development, particularly in the early years, is constantly modified by environmental influences (Glaser, 2000). Because child abuse and neglect function as an environmental influence, the occurrence of child maltreat-

Table 8.2 Developmental Problems Observed in Maltreated Children

Behavioral	Social-emotional	Cognitive
Aggression	Problems with peers: lower peer popularity, fewer prosocial interactions, greater negativity in interactions, less peer interaction	Low academic achievement
Physical violence (to people, animals, objects)		Poor problem solving
Impulsiveness		Poor reasoning skills
Hyperactivity		Poor listening comprehension
Out-of-control behavior	Poor attachment to caregiver	Easy distractibility
Noncompliance		Low average to borderline levels of intellectual functioning
Negative verbal interactions	Deficits in empathy and social sensitivity	
School discipline referrals and suspensions	Unfriendliness	Impaired social and moral reasoning
	Withdrawal	
Juvenile delinquency and criminal behavior	Avoidance	External locus of control orientation
	Fearfulness	
Conduct disorder	Anxiety	Poor understanding of social roles
Self-destructive behavior: suicide, self-mutilation	Negative emotions	Poor receptive and expressive language
Enuresis, encopresis	Unhappiness	
Substance abuse	Low self-esteem	Less creativity
Psychosomatic symptoms	Sense of worthlessness	
Sexual acting out	Hopelessness	
Perpetrator behavior with other children	Mental health disorders: depression, posttraumatic stress disorder	
	Low ego control	

Note. Information in this table comes from Angold, 1988; Cicchetti, 1987; Dubowitz, Harrington, Staff, Zuravin, & Sawyer, 1994; Eckenrode, Laird, & Doris, 1993; Famularo, Kinscherff, & Fenton, 1990; Haskett & Kistner, 1991; Hochstadt, Jaudes, Zimo, & Schachter, 1987; Kiser, Heston, Millsap, & Pruitt, 1991; Koverola & Foy, 1993; Kurtz, Gaudin, Howing, Wodarski, 1993; Salzinger, Feldman, Hammer, & Rosario, 1993; Sawyer & Dubowitz, 1994; Shonk & Cicchetti, 2001.

ment may affect how the brain develops—ultimately affecting the physical, cognitive and language, and psychosocial development of children. Although there are multiple ways in which maltreatment may be linked to brain development (a discussion well beyond the scope of this chapter), two of these ways involve the *environmental stimulation* received by the child and the amount of *chronic stress* the child might experience as a result of maltreatment.

- *Environmental stimulation.* During the first two years of life, there is a genetically determined overproduction of axons, dendrites, and synapses in different regions of the brain. (Synaptic connections allow brain signals to flow to appropriate areas.) However, not all synaptic connections survive. During this period, the determination of which synaptic con-nections will persist is regulated by the environment and is dependent on the environmental information received by the brain. Neglect and the limited environmental stimulation that are often associated with neglect may lead to changes in brain development (the elimination of certain synaptic connections and the failure to develop other connections) that may result in permanent deficits in cognitive abilities (Glaser, 2000).

- *Acute stress.* When children respond to stressful events, they experience a physiological coping response that involves the sympathetic nervous, neurotransmitter, and immune systems. The reactions and operations of these systems can alter the development of multiple neurotransmitter systems and promote structural and functional alterations in brain regions (Kaufman & Charney, 2001). A child who encounters one or more episodes of child maltreatment will experience these psychological responses, which over time will have an effect on brain development.

Although research in this area has not conclusively determined a direct link between child maltreatment and brain development, studies are finding differences in brain structure between people who have been maltreated and those who have not. These studies show, among other things, differences in the size of various regions of the brain (De Bellis et al., 2002). The differences in brain structure and chemical processes are also being linked to problems in the cognitive and psychosocial domains (e.g., the link between maltreatment and depression described earlier). Unfortunately, because many of these studies involve people who also have mental health or other related issues, it is hard to know for sure if the maltreatment itself or some other issue has led to the differences noted.

■ Attachment and the Separation of Children from Their Caregivers

When you are faced with the decision of whether to remove a child from his or her family, keep in mind that when you separate children from their parents or caregivers, you put them at risk for tremendous stress and psychological trauma. Parents or caregivers are often the people children have known their entire lives; and despite the maltreatment children may have experienced, they are attached to these people. Separation from them, particularly in the infant and toddler periods, can have long-term negative consequences on their subsequent attachment to caregivers and significant others. Therefore, weigh the risks to child safety against the possible psychological consequences of removal. Keep a child in the home if you can ensure safety. If foster care placement must occur, it is imperative that it be done in a way that minimizes the erosion of existing attachments, offers the child an experience in making a positive attachment to temporary caregivers, and provides the opportunity to maintain family attachments. Placement with relatives whom the child knows may help to minimize the damage to the child–parent/caregiver attachment, as the child may have a better chance of seeing the parent or caregiver more often.

☐ Definition of Attachment

Attachment is an "active, affectionate, reciprocal, enduring relationship between two people" (Papalia & Olds, 1996, p. 272), the infant and the primary caregiver. Attachment is thought to be critical to the formation of trust and the development of future relationships. How attachment is established between an infant and primary caregiver is based on how well the caregiver responds to the infant's needs for physical care, nurturing, and social interactions. When the caregiver responds to the infant's needs, the infant comes to realize on some level that he or she can count on the caregiver to meet any needs, thus developing a secure attachment to the caregiver.

At times, parents or caregivers may not respond to the infant's needs out of a lack of awareness. They may not understand the infant's needs or may have difficulty reading the cues for hunger, sleep, and other necessities. Information to parents or caregivers on child development, how to spot cues, and what their infant needs at various ages will help them better meet infant needs, thus facilitating the development of attachment.

Parents or caregivers may also not meet their infant's needs due to multiple demands that overwhelm them: for example, (1) multiple stresses that tax parent or caregiver ability to handle caregiving demands; (2) other responsibilities which demand the parent's or caregiver's time; and/or (3) lack of resources.

In addition, parents or caregivers may have trouble meeting their infant's needs because of their own problems and challenges. Such problems and challenges that can benefit from your identification and support include:

- Physical or mental illness.
- Substance abuse.
- Poor self-esteem.
- Depression.
- Immaturity.
- Poor impulse control.
- Anxiety.
- Parents' or caregivers' neediness and fears.
- Difficulty forming helpful and supportive relationships with other adults.
- Impaired empathy for the child.

Infants and toddlers show different types of attachment to their caregivers that are thought to reflect the degree to which they are securely attached. Because of early experiences, some infants are more attached to their caregivers than are others. The different types of attachment in infants listed here are based on the "strange situation" test of attachment. During this test, infants and toddlers are observed for their reactions to their caregivers when their caregivers leave them alone in a room (with and without a stranger) and then return several minutes later (Ainsworth, Blehar, Waters, & Wall, 1978). The key to determining the type of attachment to the caregiver is to watch the infant's behavior once the caregiver returns. The types include:

- *Secure attachment.* Infants separate readily from their caregivers when they leave but then happily greet them when they return. Infants use their caregivers as a secure base, leaving them to explore but then returning to them for occasional reassurance.

- *Avoidant attachment.* Infants rarely cry when their caregivers leave, and avoid them upon their return. They do not reach for their caregivers in time of need.

- *Ambivalent or resistant attachment.* Infants become anxious even before their caregivers leave but then show ambivalence toward them when they return (seeking them out and then resisting contact with them). These infants do little exploring and are hard to comfort.

- *Disorganized-disoriented attachment.* Perhaps the least secure attachment. Infants show inconsistent contradictory behavior. They greet their caregivers, but then turn away or approach them without looking at them. They seem confused and afraid.

Attachment patterns normally persist over time, but can change to a more or less secure attachment. For example, parents who gain skills in parenting over time and begin to show positive emotions as they care for their children have children who become more securely attached.

Many abused and neglected children experience some degree of insecure attachment because their parents or caregivers have had trouble meeting their needs due to limited knowledge of the child's needs, excessive environmental stresses, or their own psychological challenges.

Attachment theory is based on psychodynamic notions that place emphasis on the infant's or toddler's relationship to a single caregiver (usually the mother). It is important to recognize that attachment assessments were derived from research with a limited population and may not be valid for some groups. Attachment theory may differ for indigenous populations that value the infant's attachment to multiple caregivers. When attachments are based on a broader communal network, assessments should be modified accordingly. For example, if multiple attachments are a cultural and social norm, you would expect to see children easily moving between adult caregivers rather than experiencing trauma from such an event. For example:

Navajo children have multiple mothers and fathers. Joe (1989) describes aunts and uncles as "little mothers and fathers." In addition, children belong to paternal and maternal clans. Adult women of the mother's clan may be referred to as *Mother* or *Grandmother*, whereas adult men of the father's clan may be referred to as *Father* or *Grandfather*. An extensive kinship system usually exists for most tribal groups, and older cousins may also be referred to as *Grandmother*, *Uncle*, and so on. Sometimes nonblood kin are also referred to as relatives.

An African American couple who are foster parents are also godparents by choice to 16 African American single mothers and their children. Being a godparent for this couple in this culture means that any time the mothers feel stress or are afraid, they can call on their godparents at any time to take care of their children and give them respite. These godparents are referred to as *Aunt* and *Uncle* by all their godchildren.

Researchers at Lakehead University School of Social Work in Canada are challenging the universality of attachment theory and its application to aboriginal child welfare. The preliminary research replicated the "strange situation" within an indigenous First Nation in a remote community of 1,200 people. The pilot study showed that issues that would be applicable to urban children, such as the aspect of danger, the child getting lost, or reactions to a stranger, did not apply. The reactions of those studied focused on the responsibilities of the parent rather than the "internal working model" of the toddler. For example, the respondents asked such questions as "Why would a parent leave a child alone in a waiting room and not with relatives?" Or "Why doesn't the child just go home?" More research is needed to determine if the conclusions supported by the original "strange situation" test research apply differently to other populations. In many indigenous cultures, then, multiple attachments are both desirable and necessary for healthy child development. Children from cultures where multiple attachments are the norm may thus erroneously be given a negative assessment of their attachment to their primary caregivers, most likely the typology "Avoidant Attachment" of the "Strange Situation" model. Rather, not crying when caregivers leave and not necessarily reaching for them upon return may show a toddler's strong internal model of trust and security (Brownlee, Miller, Jourdain, & Neckoway, 2002).

☐ Long-Term Effects of Attachment

Securely attached children become older children who have a strong and secure foundation. Compared to children who are less securely attached, those who are securely attached are more likely to show:

- Self-esteem.
- Independence and willingness to explore on their own.
- Social and academic competence.
- Trust in people.
- Willingness to ask for help when they need it.
- Success in their relationships with peers and significant adults.

Insecurely attached infants often become older children who have an unsteady and sometimes compromised emotional foundation. These are children who are not secure in themselves and more vulnerable to environmental stressors. Compared to children who are securely attached, insecurely attached children are more likely to show:

- Delays in any of the developmental domains.
- Unusual fears for their age in leaving the parent or caregiver—they are less likely to have developed an age-appropriate sense of autonomy.

- Unusual ease in appearing to attach to another adult, with no signs of missing the parent or caregiver.
- Aggression, withdrawal, or anxiety-based hyperactive behaviors.
- Conflictual or superficial relationships with peers and significant adults.

☐ Effects of Separation from Family

Separation from a parent or caregiver, especially under stressful circumstances or for prolonged periods of time, negatively affects most children, regardless of their attachment level. Children may be frightened, withdrawn, or aggressive. However, children who are not securely attached to their caregivers are particularly vulnerable to separation. Insecure attachments are more fragile than secure attachments. This means that children with insecure attachments, compared to those with secure attachments, have fewer positive emotional, cognitive, and social resources for coping with a disruption in the caregiver-child relationship. Thus removal of these children from their home has the potential for further eroding an already fragile attachment, impairing their ability to make attachments to other caregivers, and to gain the developmental skills that are built on the foundation of a secure attachment.

☐ Your Role in Preserving Attachment

You can do things to help preserve or prevent erosion of a possibly shaky attachment, should children need to be removed from their homes. *Arrange for as much family contact as is possible* and appropriate (including in-person, phone, and letter contact). For infants and toddlers, frequent in-person contact is critical for the maintenance and continued development of the attachment. Opportunities for the parent to respond to the child's needs during visits will allow the child to continue learning that when he or she has a need, the parent will meet it.

Research studies consistently show that children who have regular contact with parents have better outcomes in foster care than do children who do not have such contact (e.g., less depression, less anxiety, and better self-esteem).

When children were asked what they wanted most for their workers to do for them, the large majority wanted more contact with their families. When asked what they wanted most for the judge to do, family contact was again most often mentioned (Johnson, Yoken, & Voss, 1995).

Do not forget sibling contact. Unless children in foster care are placed with one or more of their siblings, they may experience limited sibling contact. Such contact is important, particularly if in-person contact with parents or caregivers is not possible.

Of equal importance is contact with extended family and adults important to the child.

Place children with their kin (relatives, other family members, close friends) when possible. For some infants and toddlers, kin placement will not necessarily replace attachment to the primary caregiver. However, it may facilitate easier visitation between the caregiver and the child, so that the attachment is minimally disrupted.

For all children, placement with kin allows children on a daily basis to maintain ties, in environments that are more similar to their home, to the family, culture, and community.

Do not criticize parents or caregivers as you discuss with children the family status and issues to be addressed, because when you attack the family, you attack the child. Remember that the child is a member of the family. Despite a child's own potential anger with parents or caregivers, the child will defend them. If you criticize the parents or caregivers, you may lose the relationship you have established with the child.

Do not assume that a child's expressed anger at his or her parents is related to the severity of neglect or abuse. Anger is often seen in young children as a result of the grief process related to separation from their families.

■ Resiliency and Coping

Children who are maltreated experience a variety of stressors that may tax their ability to function and develop well during or after the maltreatment. Along with these stressors, children who are placed in an out-of-home placement often experience new challenges (e.g., separation from families, multiple placement changes, new schools) that may contribute to their already stressful lives. Despite these challenges, some children are able to function and develop well; these children are considered to be *resilient.* As in the case of your role with attachment, you are not responsible for or able to control whether children will be resilient. However, in your attempt to look out for child well-being, there are things you can do to increase the likelihood that the children with whom you work are resilient.

Resiliency is defined as the process of, capacity for, or outcomes of successful adaptation, despite challenging or threatening circumstances. Psychological resiliency pertains to the behavioral adaptation (usually considered to be driven by psychological well-being) and/or effective functioning in the environment (Masten, Best, & Garmezy, 1990). Resiliency can represent:

- good outcomes, despite high-risk status;
- sustained competence under threat;
- recovery from a trauma.

Resiliency is something that is not necessarily constant or that covers all areas of daily functioning. Children may be resilient during some stages of their lives but not others.

> For example, 7-year-old Sonya showed no ill effects from her physical abuse while she was in elementary school, but once she reached junior high, she started having problems with depression, low self-esteem, and anxiety in social settings. Sonya was resilient in elementary school but not in junior high.

Children may be resilient in some areas of their lives but show problems in other areas (Herrenkohl, Herrenkohl, & Egolf, 1994).

For example, despite Rasheed's experience with sexual abuse in the last year, he excels in his school work (making good grades and scoring above average on standardized achievement tests). However, Rasheed is having problems with aggression and cruelty to animals, showing poor social-emotional development. Rasheed can be considered resilient in terms of cognitive but not psychosocial functioning.

Sometimes children will adapt to a particularly stressful situation by acting "normal" while feeling quite vulnerable inside. Using magical thinking that is characteristic of children's natural narcissism, a child may think it is his or her fault that he or she was removed from home. The child may think, "If I behave really well, perhaps they will let me go home." Sometimes parents instruct children to "be good" in their foster homes, and children, in an attempt to help the parent, fail to express some of the normal grief related to the situation.

☐ Factors Associated with Resiliency

There are characteristics in children themselves, and in the situations children encounter, that are often found in children who are resilient. These characteristics and situations are called "protective factors." These factors appear to alter the perception of the challenge faced so that the psychological stress associated with the challenge is decreased (Hockenberry-Eaton, Kemp, & Dilorio, 1994). Protective factors moderate the effects of children's vulnerability so that their development and functioning are not adversely affected (Masten et al., 1990).

Protective factors include individual and environmental characteristics and surrounding setting and experiences.

Individual factors include good cognitive and social skills, a positive self-perception, and a willingness to seek out support.

Environmental factors include support from family and friends, stability of the living environment, positive interactions with others, and a connection to the community.

Table 8.3 provides a summary of factors associated with resiliency.

Although you cannot influence all factors associated with resiliency, you can do a variety of things to facilitate the existence of protective factors. For example, to promote individual protective factors, you could:

- Connect children with needed school services to promote cognitive performance.
- Obtain appropriate mental health services for children, as needed, to promote better self-perception.
- Assure that children are engaged in activities and hobbies that will allow them to experience success, thus promoting self-confidence.
- Make sure children are connected to activities outside of the home to promote the opportunity for social interaction.

- Identify a passion or area of interest for children so that they can engage in an enjoyable activity that can serve as an outlet for them.
- Help children connect with mentors or other supportive individuals, and help them seek out their own supports as needed.
- Link children with groups that will help them stay connected with their culture.

To promote environmental protective factors, you could:

- Assure that children get as much contact as possible with family and friends.
- Make sure children are in a setting that provides them with the structure they need.
- Limit the number of times children must change placements.
- Find a new placement within the same school district so that children at least experience stability in their school setting, if a placement is necessary.
- Help children get involved in community and cultural activities so that they feel a sense of connection with their community.

Table 8.3 Protective Factors Associated with Resiliency

Individual characteristics		Environmental characteristics
Good cognitive skills and styles: intelligence, a reflective as opposed to impulsive way to respond to problems	A sense of autonomy	Support from family and friends
	Goal-directed behavior	Stability of the family
	Enthusiasm	Quality of caregiving before and after the stressor(s)
Above average IQ	Eagerness to learn	
	Curiosity	
Good reading and reasoning skills	Multiple interests and hobbies	Home with rules
Good social and communications skills	Flexibility	Peer acceptance and support
Active and sociable involvement with others	Skill in identifying and relating to positive models	Positive school experiences
		Institutions that foster ties to the community
Positive responsiveness to others	Willingness to seek support from adults in the community	
Self-perception based on sense of power, self-regard, positive cultural identity, and belief that one's social attributes are positive	Faith or religious beliefs	
Higher self-esteem		
Internal locus of control		
Belief in one's effectiveness in handling situations		

Note. Information in this table comes from Garmezy, 1991; Herrenkohl, Herrenkohl, & Egolf, 1994; Hockenberry-Eaton, Kemp, & Dilorio, 1994; Masten, Best, & Garmezy, 1990.

☐ Children's Coping with Stress

A significant part of a child's ability to function and develop well despite life stressors (resiliency) involves how well he or she *copes* with the experiences encountered. *Coping* is defined as the thought process and behavioral strategies people use to manage the demands of their environment or their reactions to those demands (Folkman & Lazarus, 1980). Coping occurs continuously and involves the stressful event, the person's appraisal of the event, the strategies he or she uses to deal with it, and the degree to which the coping efforts are effective (Rosenthal & Levy-Shiff, 1993).

General coping strategies used by children include two main types.

1. *Problem-focused coping strategies.* First seen during preschool years, these strategies involve efforts to act on or influence the situation. This type of general coping strategy is used more often in situations that are thought to be potentially changeable (Compas, Banez, Malcarne, & Worsham, 1991) and are more effective when people know the demands of the situation, the probable consequences, and the strategies that will lead to effective outcomes (Armstrong, Lemanek, Pegelow, Gonzalez, & Martinez, 1993).

   The use of problem-focused strategies is often associated with fewer poor outcomes; children who generate alternative solutions for handling challenging situations display fewer problems (Spivack & Shure, 1985, as cited in Compas, Malcarne, & Fondacaro, 1988).

2. *Emotion-focused coping strategies.* First seen in later childhood and early adolescence, these strategies involve efforts to manage or regulate the negative emotions associated with a stressful situation in an attempt to minimize discomfort with the situation as it is (Band & Weisz, 1988). This type of general coping strategy is more often used in situations in which children have no control. The use of this strategy is often associated with poorer outcomes; children who generate fewer alternative solutions for handling a challenging situation (showing an emotion-focused as opposed to problem-focused coping strategy) display more problems.

Although children will use both types of coping strategies, they have individual *coping styles* that reflect a tendency to use one type over another. Some children cope actively, making attempts to change the situation and showing a preference for problem-focused strategies. Other children cope passively, opting to regulate their negative emotions rather than attempting to change the situation and showing a preference for emotion-focused coping (Garbarino, 1993).

There may be cultural expectations and preferences for coping. Regulating of emotions may be highly valued in populations that have experienced high levels of trauma (genocide, war, historical oppression, extreme poverty) over generations. Under these conditions, children may have learned to sacrifice individual emotional comfort for the good of the whole.

The more active children are in their attempts to cope, the better they do. For example, children who actively cope display sustained high motivation, persistence at problem solving, increased concentration, and enhanced performance. Those who cope passively show low levels of effort, high levels of discouragement, and deteriorating performance (Garbarino, 1993).

The types of coping strategies children use are determined, in part, by the degree to which they think they have control over a situation. If children think they do not have control, they are less likely to use problem-focused coping strategies (Compas et al., 1988). The perception of control plays a significant role in how well children cope with stress. Control can reduce the effects of stress by allowing the person to ensure that the situation will not become intolerable, or by allowing the person to prepare for the situation. Children who believe that they have some control in their lives (compared to those who see themselves as passive recipients to whatever life hands them) seem to fare better under stress (e.g., they display fewer psychological problems such as depression [Moran & Eckenrode, 1992]).

Despite the positive influence that control has on coping, the match between perceived and actual control is important. When perceptions of controllability are matched with situations in which no control is feasible, children are more likely to see their attempts to remedy the uncontrollable situation fail. These failed attempts can lead to problems (Thompson & Spacapan, 1991). A study of 6- to 12-year-olds exposed to varying levels of stress and conflict in their homes (physically violent, discordant homes) supports this idea. The more children thought they could control the family conflicts, the more feelings of incompetence they had, because they saw their attempts to control an uncontrollable situation fail (Rossman & Rosenberg, 1992).

☐ Your Role in Helping Children Cope

The children with whom you work will encounter significant stressors that may tax their ability to function and develop well. Although you will not have total control over how children handle the experiences they encounter, you can work toward ensuring children's well-being by helping them cope with the experiences they encounter and promoting experiences that will help them to be resilient.

Prepare children for the events they will encounter. For older children, giving them information so that they can anticipate and prepare for upcoming events may go far in helping them feel that they have at least some control in how they will get through the events. For example, if you need to remove children from their homes, prepare them for separation from their families, to the extent possible.

Be honest with children about why they are being removed from home. Your message to them is that their parents or caregivers love them but have issues that make it difficult to provide the care they need right now. Do not fudge or talk in vague terms. (For more information on this topic, see Chapter 6.) Providing this information in an honest manner is extremely important because:

- Children will look for answers about why they have to be removed from home; and if they do not have them, they will imagine what those answers could be, often to their own detriment (e.g., blaming themselves).

- Children cope better with stressful events when they have information. Among other things, having information allows them to prepare themselves for what to expect.

- If children ask you why they are being removed from home and you are not honest with them, they are likely to realize it and conclude that you cannot be trusted.

Keep in mind that the idea of child neglect being "not okay" is a difficult concept for children to understand, since they often do not know another way of life. Point to concrete things about neglect that are not experienced by other children and should not be experienced by them.

> For example, "Most kids don't have to ask their neighbors for food. We need to help your parents so that you don't have to do that anymore."

Familiarize the children with their temporary placement. Take them to the placement before they are placed, if at all possible. If you cannot have children do a preplacement visit, describe the placement to the children *before* they get there. If siblings are to be placed into separate placements, tell the children *before* they arrive at the placement. Address children's visitation concerns with siblings and parents or caregivers in age-appropriate language and detail. For older children and youth, you will also need to address their school and peer concerns.

Do not make up answers. For example, as tempting as it is, do not tell children that they will get to return home soon. The truth is that you will rarely know how long children will remain in foster care; and if you tell them something that turns out to be wrong, they will often conclude that you are not being honest and will then not trust you.

Be prepared to explain the same information repeatedly and during times when children are less stressed. Children, particularly young children, require repeated messages before information sinks in. When children are under tremendous stress, they often do not fully process the information being provided. Therefore, giving information during periods when children are less stressed (e.g., before removing them, after they have a chance to adjust to new surroundings, outside of attending court) will be more effective in giving them the messages they need.

Use foster parents or placement staff as a way to inform children. The more they know about the children's situations, the more the children know (Murphy, 1997). Therefore, work with foster parents or placement staff so that together you can make sure children have sufficient information.

Include older children and youth in developing the plans that involve them. Such involvement can help them have a sense of control over at least some aspect of what is happening to them. It can also promote their "buy-in" on things they may need to change in order to remedy the problems that have led to CPS involvement (e.g., when children are in foster care primarily due to their own behavior problems).

Invite older children and youth to meetings in which you are developing the plan, and get their input on things they think need to happen and things they think they may need. For youth who are in an out-of-home placement due to their own behavior problems, this involvement is critical for their willingness to make necessary changes.

As you give older children and youth a voice in the decision-making process, make sure to keep their decisions to things that they will actually be able to control (e.g., their participation in an after-school anger management program). Giving them a choice about other people's actions over which they have no control will only set them up for a sense of failure if the other people do not accomplish what is needed.

Check in with children and youth regarding their opinions about family visitation, their current placement, and the family plans. If nothing else, they will feel that you value their input, giving them a sense of a little control over an otherwise uncontrollable situation.

Bring remembrances of home with children as they enter new placements. This is important not only when you remove children from their homes but when you must change placements once they are in foster care. Taking transitional objects that are familiar (e.g., clothes, toys, bottles, cups, music tapes, and pictures of family members) can give children a sense of comfort when they miss their family or are afraid of the unknown.

Encourage children and youth to express their feelings and concerns. This might include nonverbal expressions using play or creative methods. This could be especially important when the cultural norm of direct expression of emotion was not encouraged or allowed in the home. You should:

- Accept their feelings without judgment.
- Give them permission to miss their families.
- Connect older children and youth with peer support groups or activities that include other children and youth in similar situations.

Help children explain why they are no longer living with their families. Children in foster care often struggle with how to explain their out-of-home placement to other people, sometimes due to an unclear understanding of the reason, other times due to embarrassment. Help them to find their own words so that they are comfortable with the explanation they may have to provide. For example, "I'm staying with my grandma 'til my mom can take care of me."

■ Summary of Competencies

Your work with families will be determined, in large part, by the needs of the children. Therefore, it is important for you to have a working knowledge of child development so that you can better serve parents, caregivers, and children. You should be competent in the following areas.

Knowledge:

1. Knowledge of the developmental changes that children experience over time in their physical characteristics (e.g., height and weight), neurological makeup (e.g., hormone changes), behaviors (e.g., developing new skills), and personality traits (e.g., becoming more empathetic).
2. Knowledge of the physical, cognitive and language, and psychosocial developmental domains.

3. Knowledge of how child development unfolds in a series of stages, each of which is characterized by critical tasks in the physical, cognitive/language, and psychosocial domains.

4. Knowledge of the factors from nature (genetics) and nurture (environment) that affect development.

5. Knowledge of the effect of culture on development and of cultural resources to guide understanding.

6. Knowledge of the difficult phases of normal development that are especially difficult and may bring about control conflicts and frustration between parents or caregivers and children.

7. Knowledge of children's mental health issues or developmental disabilities that can present significant challenges to their families, beyond the challenges experienced from normal development.

8. Knowledge of potential developmental problems in maltreated children, so that CPS may better address their needs through appropriate service provision.

9. Knowledge of attachment and how insecure attachment may have long-term effects on child development.

10. Knowledge of resiliency and how the factors that are associated with children's resiliency include a combination of individual characteristics (e.g., good social skills) and environmental characteristics (e.g., security in the living environment).

11. Knowledge of children's coping strategies.

Skills:

1. Ability to access resources to assess children's development.

2. Ability to educate parents on their children's development.

3. Ability to develop a plan with a family and connect them to resources to address their children's developmental needs.

4. Ability to work with children in a developmentally appropriate manner.

References

Ainsworth, M. D. S., Blehar, M. C., Waters, E., & Wall, S. (1978). *Patterns of attachment: A psychological study of the strange situation.* Hillsdale, NJ: Erlbaum.

American Academy of Child and Adolescent Psychiatry. (1999). Children with learning disabilities. Retrieved November 7, 2002, from http://www.aacap.org/publications/factsfam/.

Angold, A. (1988). Childhood and adolescent depression: Research in clinical populations. *British Journal of Psychiatry, 153,* 476–492.

Armstrong, F. D., Lemanek, K. L., Pegelow, C. H., Gonzalez, J. C., & Martinez, A. (1993). Impact of lifestyle disruption on parent and child coping, knowledge, and parental discipline in children with sickle cell anemia. *Children's Health Care, 22,* 189–203.

Autti-Ramo, I. (2000). Twelve-year follow-up of children exposed to alcohol in utero. *Developmental Medicine and Child Neurology, 42,* 406–411.

Band, E. B., & Weisz, J. R. (1988). How to feel better when it feels bad: Children's perspectives on coping with everyday stress. *Developmental Psychology, 24,* 247–253.

Brownlee, K., Miller, L., Jourdain, L., & Neckoway, R. (2002, April). *Attachment theory: Developing an Aboriginal model of attachment.* Presentation to the National Indian Child Welfare Association, at "Protecting Our Children: National American Indian Conference on Child Abuse and Neglect," Duluth, MN.

Children's Disabilities and Special Needs. (2001). ADD/ADHD FAQ. Retrieved November 7, 2002 from http://www.comeunity.com/disability/adhd/add-adhd.html.

Cicchetti, D. (1987). Developmental psychopathology in infancy: Illustration from the study of maltreated youngsters. *Journal of Consulting and Clinical Psychology and Psychiatry, 26,* 85–96.

Compas, B. E., Banez, G. A., Malcarne, V., & Worsham, N. (1991). Perceived control and coping with stress: A developmental perspective. *Journal of Social Issues, 47,* 23–34.

Compas, B. E., Malcarne, V. L., & Fondacaro, K. M. (1988). Coping with stressful events in older children and young adolescents. *Journal of Consulting and Clinical Psychology, 56,* 405–411.

Cruz, V., Meredith, C., Park, L., & Slay, R. (1999). *Assessment of young children for developmental delays.* Denver: Colorado Department of Human Services, Office of Human Services, Division of Staff Development, and Division of Child Welfare.

De Bellis, M. D., Keshavan, M. S., Shifflett, H., Iyengar, S., Beers, S. R., Hall, J., & Moritz, G. (2002). Brain structures in pediatric maltreatment-related posttraumatic stress disorder: A sociodemographically matched study. *Biological Psychiatry, 52*(11), 1066–1078.

Developmental Disabilities Resource Center. (n.d.). What is a developmental disability? Retrieved November 4, 2002, from http://www.ddrcco.com/dddef.htm.

Dubowitz, H., Harrington, D., Staff, R., Zuravin, S., & Sawyer, R. (1994). Children in kinship care: How do they fare? *Children and Youth Services Review, 16*(1/2), 85–106.

Eckenrode, J., Laird, M., & Doris, J. (1993). School performance and disciplinary problems among abused and neglected children. *Developmental Psychology, 29*(1), 53–62.

Erikson, E. H. (1963). *Childhood and society.* New York: Norton.

Famularo, R., Kinscherff, R., & Fenton, T. (1990). Symptom differences in acute and chronic presentation of childhood post-traumatic stress disorder. *Child Abuse and Neglect, 14,* 439–444.

Folkman, S., & Lazarus, R. S. (1980). An analysis of coping in a middle-aged community sample. *Journal of Health and Social Behavior, 21,* 219–239.

Garbarino, J. (1993). Children's response to community violence: What do we know? *Infant Mental Health Journal, 14*(2), 103–115.

Garbarino, J., & Garbarino, A. (1986). *Emotional maltreatment of children.* Chicago: National Committee for the Prevention of Child Abuse.

Garmezy, N. (1991). Resiliency and vulnerability to adverse developmental outcomes associated with poverty. *American Behavioral Scientist, 34*(4), 416–430.

Glaser, D. (2000). Child abuse and neglect and the brain: A review. *Journal of Child Psychology, Psychiatry, and Allied Disciplines, 41*(1), 97–116.

Haskett, M. E., & Kistner, J. A. (1991). Social interactions and peer perceptions of young physically abused children. *Child Development, 62,* 979–990.

Herrenkohl, E. C., Herrenkohl, R. C., & Egolf, B. (1994). Resilient early school-age children from maltreating homes: Outcomes in late adolescence. *American Journal of Orthopsychiatry, 64*(2), 301–309.

Hochstadt, N. J., Jaudes, P. K., Zimo, D. A., & Schachter, J. (1987). The medical and psychosocial needs of children entering foster care. *Child Abuse and Neglect, 11*, 53–62.

Hockenberry-Eaton, M., Kemp, V., & Dilorio, C. (1994). Cancer stressors and protective factors: Predictors of stress experienced during treatment for childhood cancer. *Research in Nursing and Health, 17*, 351–361.

IDEA Practices. (n.d.). Laws and regulations: IDEA '97 laws & regs. Retrieved December 21, 2002, from http://www.ideapractices.org/law/index.php.

Joe, J. (1989). Values. In E. Gonzales-Santin and A. Lewis (Eds.), *Collaboration: The key* (pp. 13–29). Tempe: School of Social Work, Arizona State University.

Johnson, P., Yoken, C., & Voss, R. (1995). *Foster care placement: The child's perspective* (Discussion Paper No. 36). Chicago: University of Chicago, Chapin Hall Center for Children.

Kaufman, J., & Charney, D. (2001). Effects of early stress on brain structure and function: Implications for understanding the relationship between child maltreatment and depression. *Development and Psychopathology, 13*(3), 451–471.

Kiser, L. J., Heston, J., Millsap, P. A., & Pruitt, D. B. (1991). Physical and sexual abuse in childhood: Relationship with post-traumatic stress disorder. *Journal of the American Academy of Child and Adolescent Psychiatry, 30*(5), 776–783.

Koverola, C., & Foy, D. (1993). Post-traumatic stress disorder symptomatology in sexually abused children: Implications for legal proceedings. *Journal of Child Sexual Abuse, 2*(4), 119–128.

Kurtz, P. D., Gaudin, J. M., Howing, P. T., & Wodarski, J. S. (1993). The consequences of physical abuse and neglect on the school age child: Mediating factors. *Children and Youth Services Review, 15*, 85–104.

Manly, J. T., Kim, J. E., Rogosch, F. A., & Cicchetti, D. (2001). Dimensions of child maltreatment and children's adjustment: Contributions of developmental timing and subtype. *Development and Psychopathology, 13*, 759–782.

Masten, A. S., Best, K. M., & Garmezy, N. (1990). Resilience and development: Contributions from the study of children who overcome adversity. *Development and Psychopathology, 2*, 425–444.

Moran, P. B., & Eckenrode, J. (1992). Protective personality characteristics among adolescent victims of maltreatment. *Child Abuse and Neglect, 16*, 743–754.

Murphy, K. C. (1997). Foster care from the child's perspective: Knowledge and attitudes about foster care and their relationship with developmental functioning and the foster care environment. Unpublished manuscript. University of Kansas.

National Alliance for the Mentally Ill. (2001). The nation's voice on mental illness. Retrieved November 4, 2002, from http://www.nami.org/Hometemplate.cfm.

Ornoy, A. (2002). The effects of alcohol and illicit drugs on the human embryo and fetus. *Israel Journal of Psychiatry and Related Sciences, 39*(2), 120–132.

Papalia, D. E., & Olds, S. W. (1996). *A child's world: Infancy through adolescence* (7th ed.). New York: McGraw Hill.

Papolos, D., & Papolos, J. (1999). *The bipolar child: The definitive and reassuring guide to childhood's most misunderstood disorder.* New York: Broadway Books.

Red Horse, J., Martinez, C., Day, P., Day, D., Poupart, J., & Sharnberg, D. (2000). *Family preservation: Concepts in American Indian communities.* Seattle: Casey Family Programs.

Rosenthal, M. K., & Levy-Shiff, R. (1993). Threat of missile attacks in the Gulf War: Mothers' perceptions of young children's reactions. *American Journal of Orthopsychiatry, 63*, 241–254.

Rossman, B. B. R., & Rosenberg, M. S. (1992). Family stress and functioning in children: The moderating effects of children's beliefs about their control over parental conflict. *Journal of Child Psychology, Psychiatry and Allied Disciplines, 33*(4), 699–715.

Salzinger, S., Feldman, R. S., Hammer, M., & Rosario, M. (1993). The effects of physical abuse on children's social relationships. *Child Development, 64,* 169–187.

Sawyer, R. J., & Dubowitz, H. (1994). School performance of children in kinship care. *Child Abuse and Neglect, 18*(7), 587–597.

Shonk, S. M., & Cicchetti, D. (2001). Maltreatment, competency deficits, and risk for academic and behavioral maladjustment. *Developmental Psychology, 37*(1), 3–17.

Sullivan, P. M., & Knutson, J. F. (2000). Maltreatment and disabilities: A population-based epidemiological study. *Child Abuse and Neglect, 24*(10), 1257–1273.

Thompson, S. C., & Spacapan, S. (1991). Perceptions of control in vulnerable populations. *Journal of Social Issues, 47*(4), 1–21.

9

Kathryn M. Wells
Andrew Sirotnak

Medical Evaluation of Abuse and Neglect

■ The CPS Worker and the Medical Evaluation

■ Components of the Medical Examination
for Child Abuse or Neglect

■ Child Physical Abuse

■ Child Abuse Fatalities

■ Child Sexual Abuse

■ Physical Neglect

■ Emotional Abuse and Neglect/Psychological Maltreatment

■ Summary of Competencies

The medical evaluation of a suspected child abuse or neglect victim may be of great assistance in establishing the presence and nature of the maltreatment. The medical provider's primary goals are the identification of trauma or illness in need of treatment and assisting in the restoration of health. Secondarily, the medical provider can assist in establishing the presence or absence of additional injury as well as other relevant medical conditions. This evaluation may help determine a course of action and the need for placement of the involved child or other children. Clear communication between the worker and the medical provider is essential as you share a mutual goal of enhancing the child's health. Throughout this chapter, the term *medical provider* is inclusive of any medical professional, including pediatricians, general practitioners, family physicians, nurse practitioners, physician's assistants, and child health associates. Because interaction with medical professionals can be an intimidating process, this chapter will increase your professional knowledge base so that you can effectively work with medical professionals to assist your clients.

■ The CPS Worker and the Medical Evaluation

It is important for the CPS worker to be able to appropriately identify situations in which a medical evaluation is necessary. When a medical evaluation is deemed necessary, the worker must provide all pertinent history available regarding the client to the physician to assist in developing a complete evaluation. When reviewing information already provided in a medical evaluation, the worker must be able to determine whether available information is sufficient or if there is need for additional information.

The CPS worker should be familiar with the top ten "red flags" for child abuse or neglect:

Ten "Red Flags" for Child Abuse and Neglect

1. Injury unexplained by history or incompatible with the developmental age of the child.

2. Absent, changing, or evolving history.

3. Delay in seeking care or injuries that appear older than the history given for them.

4. Inappropriate affect of caregiver or a child being brought to medical care by a caregiver unrelated to the incident prompting the need for medical care.

5. Triggering event causing loss of control in caregiver.

6. Unrealistic expectations for the child.

7. Crisis or stress in child's environment.

8. Social or physical isolation of child or family.

9. Pattern of increasing severity or escalation of event over time.

10. Prior history of abuse of caregiver as a child.

The CPS worker should also be familiar with the following situations, which are considered medical emergencies:

- Any infant or child less than 2 years old with a history or suspicion of shaking or other inflicted head trauma.
- Any infant with bruises (anywhere, but especially head, face, neck or abdomen), fractures, or burns.
- Any child with suspected inflicted or suspicious trauma to the abdomen.
- Any child with genital, stocking/glove pattern, branding, or extensive burns on the body.
- Any child with a disclosure of sexual assault within the past 48 to 72 hours.

When requesting a medical evaluation of a child, you need to integrate your knowledge of abusive patterns with the specific history of the child; this should help you formulate specific concerns to express to the medical provider to address in the course of the medical examination. The multidisciplinary approach, with CPS workers, medical professionals, law enforcement, cultural advisors or community advocates, and any other involved personnel working together and providing collegial support, helps to ensure the best possible outcome in these difficult cases.

When obtaining the *history* and subsequently relating it to the medical provider, remember to include the following:

- What child was involved in the incident? What is the child's developmental maturity?
- When exactly did the act occur? If there was a delay in seeking treatment, why? Is the delay in care reasonable or not?
- Who had access to the child?
- If the child is verbal, what does he or she say happened?
- Were there any other adult witnesses and, if so, what does he or she say happened?

The worker should understand the findings in the *medical provider's report*, along with their significance in determining abuse. Do not be afraid to ask specific questions or to request explanations. Remember, the role of the medical provider, in addition to caring for the medical needs of the child, is also to assist you in your assessment of the case. The medical provider's experience and knowledge can be one of your most important resources in providing a safe and secure plan for the child.

As the intermediary between the medical provider and the parent or caregiver, it is crucial that you understand any *medical and treatment recommendations* so that you can help the parent or caregiver follow through on treatment.

As the worker, it is also imperative that you assess for any *cultural considerations* in the apparent abuse, and seek understanding or support from cultural allies or community advocates who are familiar with medical taboos or disciplinary practices that may appear to create common indicators of "abuse." Engaging a cultural ally in explaining medical treatment recommendations may avoid misunderstandings regarding "noncompliance."

■ Components of the Medical Examination for Child Abuse or Neglect

The medical exam should include all of the following. If the exam is felt to be unsatisfactory, it may be necessary to schedule a second appointment to complete the evaluation or arrange for another evaluation by a medical provider who is more skilled in the area of child abuse and neglect.

1. General observations must be made of the child and his or her *interactions* with the caregivers. A complete history should include:
   - The current complaint.
   - The history of present illness (HPI)/complaint, including timing, duration, associated symptoms.
   - The past medical history, including prenatal and birth history, previous hospitalizations, previous injuries, and immunization status.
   - The child's developmental history.
   - A social/family history of the child, including cultural and religious differences regarding preventive care and medical treatment.
2. Measurements must be made of *height, weight, and head circumference.*
3. A complete *physical exam*, including assessment of all organ systems, should include:
   - Skin.
   - Head including eyes, ears, nose, and mouth/throat.
   - Neck.
   - Chest/heart/lungs.
   - Abdomen.
   - Back.
   - Genitalia/anus.
   - Extremities.
   - Neurologic.
   - Development/behavior.
4. *Laboratory/diagnostic studies*, as indicated by the history and physical exam, must be done.
5. *Diagrams or photos* must be made of the physical injury, as indicated, to document evidence of abuse.

■ Child Physical Abuse

Physical abuse is a large category that contains many types of maltreatment. There are also many different presentations of physical abuse. Child physical abuse may present as external skin lesions, for example bruises, abrasions, pattern injuries, lacerations, burns, or scars, or it may be more internal, for example fractures. Abusive head trauma may present as a child with vomiting, irritability, lethargy, seizures, coma, or unexpected death. Abusive abdominal or chest trauma may also present with vomiting, shock, or death. But physical abuse may also be subtler, as it is in cases of poisoning, asphyxiation, starvation, and factitious disorder (Munchausen's syndrome by proxy).

☐ Skin Trauma

Cutaneous (skin) manifestations of abuse are injuries such as bruises (contusions), abrasions, lacerations, pattern injuries, burns, frostbite, and scars. One study that examined injuries of 616 children who were felt to be the victims of abuse showed that at least 80% of the 775 primary injuries involved the skin. The study revealed that bruises accounted for 56% of the injuries, marks or erythema (redness) 9%, burns 8%, and abrasions/scratches 7% (Johnson & Showers, 1985). It has been shown that skin injuries are often the earliest and most common manifestations of physical maltreatment and may signal more severe underlying injuries, so it is important to recognize these indicators and address them promptly (O'Neill, 1979). To help distinguish unintentional injuries from abusive ones, a detailed, concise history is crucial. Examples of necessary details include the height of the table from which the child allegedly fell, or what he was playing when he bruised his legs and buttocks.

Bruises

Normal bruising in childhood.   Bruises are known to be common childhood injuries, depending on the location of the bruise as well as the age and developmental status of the child. Once children begin exploring their environment by cruising along furniture items, followed by walking independently, they may occasionally sustain minor bruises. Typically accidental bruises are located on overlying areas of bony prominence such as the forehead, chin, knee or elbow. Often the caregiver is able to provide a history for the fall or bump that preceded the bruise. Bruises that occur outside this typical childhood pattern should raise suspicion for child abuse or neglect.

Pathophysiology of bruises.   Bruises result from the application of a blunt force to the skin surface, which results in damage to the underlying blood vessels. Blood then leaks out of the vessel to the surrounding area, which includes the overlying skin (Wilson, 1977). Many factors contribute to the size, color, and extent of the bruise, including the force of the impact, the size and fragility of the affected blood vessels, and the density of the injured tissue. Sometimes the injured vessels of a bruise are located so deeply under the skin that it takes days for them to become visible. These deep underlying bruises may remain dark for days or weeks. Bruises generally fade from the edge inward.

Dating of bruises.   Current literature does not support attempting to date bruises (Schwartz & Ricci, 1996). Although there are detailed color changes that occur as bruises progress through different stages of healing (Richardson, 1994), it is difficult to accurately predict the order of color progression. This process depends on the depth and location of the bruise, the amount of bleeding into the skin, the blood

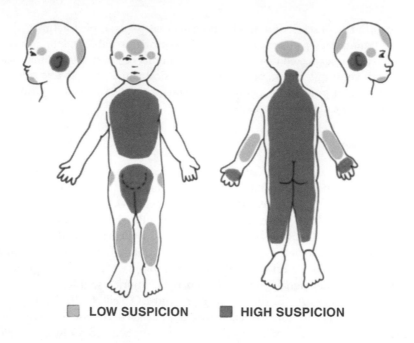

☐ **LOW SUSPICION**   ■ **HIGH SUSPICION**

Low Suspicion/High Suspicion Bruises. From J. Brier, L. Berliner, J. A. Bulkley, & C. Jenny, & T. Reid, *The APSAC Handbook on Child Maltreatment.* Thousand Oaks, CA: Sage Publications, p. 211. Copyright 1996 by Sage Publications. Reprinted with permission.

supply to the area, the effect of gravity in dependant areas of the body, the child's normal pigmentation, and whether or not there was reinjury to the affected area. Studies have shown that from impact until resolution the bruise may be a deep red, blue, or purple (Langlois & Gresham, 1991) and swelling commonly persists for about 2 days following the injury (Richardson, 1994). Bruises that are yellow in color are generally older than 18 hours. In addition, bruises of identical age and cause on the same child may not appear as the same color and may not disappear at the same rate (Langlois & Gresham, 1991).

Documentation.   All bruises should be documented clearly by a description of their location, size, color, and shape. When possible, bruises should be addition-ally documented with color photographs that show their location, size, and color. These should be taken within the first few days of the incident. A reference scale, such as a ruler, should be included in the photograph to indicate size of the mark. Because some bruises may not appear on the skin until a few days after the injury, a second set of photos may need to be taken at that time. It may be helpful to con-tact the local police department or ask the medical personnel if an experienced pho-tographer is available to obtain the photographs.

Differential diagnosis of bruising.   The following nonabusive medical conditions may cause bruising. These other conditions constitute the differential diagnosis and must be considered and rejected as implausible by the medical provider.

- *Accidental trauma.* Bruises are common childhood injuries and are frequently caused in an accidental manner. A thorough history is critical in differentiating accidental from nonaccidental bruising.
- *Bleeding disorders.* A child whose blood does not coagulate properly will have an abnormal amount of blood released from injured vessels. This may occur in:

    Hemophilia. In this inherited disorder, blood fails to clot adequately and abnormal bleeding can occur.

    Von Willebrand's disease. A rare inherited disorder that affects the blood's ability to clot due to platelet abnormality.

    Vitamin K deficiency. Can affect the liver's production of clotting factors.

    Leukemia. In this form of cancer there is a tremendous increase in the number of immature white blood cells that are unable to fight infection and an associated marked decrease in the production of platelets and red blood cells, often causing a child to "bruise easily."

    Idiopathic Thrombocytopenic Purpura (ITP). This bleeding disorder is characterized by marked decrease in the number of platelets in the system, resulting in multiple bruises.

    Anticoagulant ingestion. This affects the body's ability to clot blood.

    Severe infections (viral or bacterial).

- *Dermatologic conditions.*   Naturally occurring skin marks that are often confused with abuse include:

    Mongolian spots. Grayish-blue, clearly defined areas of increased skin pigmentation that are most commonly found on the buttocks or the back. They are present at birth and usually fade after the first few years of life. These are most commonly found in darker pigmented children.

    Salmon patches/"stork bites." Pink marks that are commonly seen on the nape of the neck, the eyelids, above the nose, and the midforehead of newborns.

    Strawberry marks (hemangiomas). Red marks that are usually not present at birth but appear during the first 4 to 6 weeks of life. These marks represent blood vessel growth just below the surface of the skin.

    Eczema. Allergic skin condition that causes reddened, dry areas on the child's skin and may be mistaken for abuse.

    Erythema multiforme. Skin condition that produces red, targetlike lesions.

    Phytophotodermatitis. Skin reaction to psoralens (chemical compounds found in citrus fruits). Skin in contact with psoralens manifests red marks that may look like bruises or burns if exposed to sunlight (Coffman, Boyce, & Hansen, 1985).

"Tattooing." Discoloration of skin from fabric dye, giving the appearance of a bruise (Tunnessen, 1985).

- *Vascular inflammation* include the following:

  Henoch-Schönlein purpura (HSP). Vascular inflammation that causes areas of distinctive rash, particularly on the lower extremities and buttocks, abdominal pain, and joint symptoms. The rash may resemble bruising. This illness is most commonly found in children between 3 and 10 years of age.

  Infections. May cause a vasculitic rash that may be mistaken for abusive bruising, e.g., rickettsial disease or severe bacterial infections that may result in disseminated intravascular coagulation (DIC) and purpura fulminans.

- *Collagen Synthesis Defects* include the following:

  Ehlers-Danlos (ED) syndrome. A rare inherited disorder of collagen, which is characterized by skin laxity, hyperextensible joints, and skin fragility. The skin of these children is extremely fragile. The diagnosis of this syndrome is made with the help of genetics.

  Osteogenesis imperfecta (OI). A group of rare, inherited connective tissue disorders that are characterized by bony fragility and skeletal deformity. The incidence of this disorder is 1 in 25,000 to 30,000 live births, and it is diagnosed with the help of a geneticist (Hurwitz, 1993).

- *Folk healing practices.* Normally, these practices should not cause concern about child abuse; however, adherence to such practices when a child is seriously ill with refusal to seek medical care may raise a concern of medical neglect. Every effort should be made to secure a medical opinion from both a traditional healer and a Western medical professional with substantial experience in treating various immigrant and indigenous people. Such practices include:

  Coining (cao-gio, pronounced "cow zow"). Vietnamese folk medicine practice in which the skin is massaged with oil and stroked with the edge of a coin, causing linear bruises of the chest and back (Yeatman & Dang, 1980).

  Cupping. Asian or Mexican practice of warming a cup and placing it on the skin, creating a vacuum as the cup cools and ultimately a bruise as well as a burn (Sandler & Haynes, 1978).

Medical assessment of bruising. The history, physical examination, and laboratory assessment are critical to the inclusion or exclusion of all potential differential diagnoses and for that reason guide the assessment and workup. Usual laboratory evaluation to exclude bleeding disorders includes a complete blood count, including a platelet count, a prothrombin (PT), a partial thromboplastin time (PTT), and a bleeding time.

It may be necessary for the medical provider to perform other tests, including more specialized bleeding tests, blood cultures, or genetic evaluation, depending on the presentation and history obtained.

Pattern Injuries

Bite marks. Bites are common pediatric injuries, but they may also be indicators of abuse or neglect. Bites typically produce a pair of elliptical, crescent-shaped bruises or lacerations, often containing individual teeth marks. The most common areas where bites occur are on limbs, abdomen, and cheeks.

The first step in the evaluation of a bite is to identify whether it was caused by a human or an animal. Typically, animal bites tear the flesh and puncture the skin, while human bites usually cause compression of the skin, causing contusions.

Documentation of a bite mark may be of great assistance in identifying the perpetrator of the bite. Photographs should be obtained and should contain multiple views of the bite. A reference scale such as a ruler should be included in the photograph to indicate the size and length of the mark. The medical provider may also choose to attempt the collection of salivary samples for DNA evidence from the wound site.

A dental specialist may be able to match the pattern of the bite to a mold of the alleged perpetrator's teeth.

Circumferential wounds are injuries around wrists and ankles from the restraint of a child's limbs during abuse (Kornberg, 1992). Often these injuries are in the form of rope burns or other friction burns, appearing as blisters or scars that encircle the extremity.

Grab marks may occur when a child is grabbed. These marks have a characteristic oval shape, and they are most commonly located on the upper arm, shoulder, and extremities. The characteristic pattern for this kind of injury is one or two thumb prints on one side of the body, with as many as eight finger marks on the other side.

Loop marks are made by flexible objects such as belts, electric cords, or clotheslines.

Strap marks are usually 1 to 2 inches wide and linear. The end of the strap usually hits the hardest, sometimes breaking the skin and leaving a loop-shaped mark (Johnson, 1990).

Marks from Instruments. From R. E. Behrman, R. M. Kleigman, & H. B. Jenson, *Nelson Textbook of Pediatrics, 16th ed.* (p. 112). Philadelphia: Saunders. Copyright 2000 by Elsevier. Reprinted with permission.

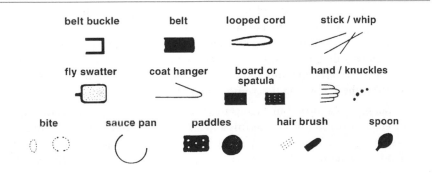

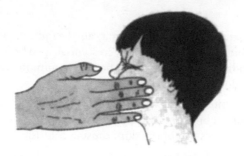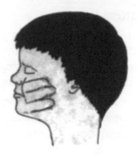

Slap Marks.

Slap marks are characterized by linear, parallel bruises similar to the outline of the fingers. It may be possible to see the entire hand outlined, including the creases of the perpetrator's fingers (Kessler & Hyden, 1991).

Burns

Although burns are a common result of unintentional injury in children, approximately 10% to 25% of pediatric burns are a result of abuse (O'Neill, 1979; Purdue & Hunt, 1992). About 10% of children who are hospitalized for burns are believed to have sustained them in a nonaccidental manner (Feldman, 1987; Meagher, 1990; Purdue, Hunt, & Prescott, 1988). The patterns that most typically are associated with abuse are immersion burns, splash burns, and contact burns.

Classification of burns. The *severity* of burn injuries is divided into four categories, depending on the number of layers of skin injured or the depth of the skin injured. Historically this was described as degrees (first-, second-, third-, and fourth-degree burns). Currently, the terms *superficial, superficial partial, deep partial,* or *full thickness* are used to describe the depth of the burn (Giardino, 1997b). To better understand burns, it is helpful to understand that the skin is divided into three layers. The outermost or most superficial layer is the epidermis. The layer directly beneath (deeper than) the epidermis is the dermis, and this layer contains the hair follicles, sweat glands, and nerve endings. The subcutaneous tissue layer makes up the deepest layer of skin. This layer serves as an underlying support structure of the skin (Giardino, 1997b).

- *Superficial burns* (considered analogous to a first-degree burn) are the least severe. They are of minimal depth and only extend into the outermost layers of the epidermis. These injuries are characterized by redness, tenderness, and swelling (e.g., sunburn). Blisters do not form in superficial burns. Within a few days, the injured skin may slough, and the injury is expected to heal without scarring (Giardino, 1997b).

- *Partial thickness burns* (analogous to second-degree burns) extend through the epidermis and into the dermis and are characterized by vesicles (blisters) on the skin's surface. They may have a beefy red appearance caused by blood vessel damage. These injuries are painful because the nerve endings are exposed. Depending on the depth of the injury, these lesions may be further classified as *superficial partial thickness* (only minimally involving the dermis) or *deep partial thickness* (more extensive involvement of the dermis). If no infection occurs, these injuries may take 14 to 28 days to heal and may produce scars (Giardino, 1997b).

- *Full thickness burns* (analogous to third- and/or fourth-degree burns) are the most serious kinds of burns and destroy the entire thickness of the skin, including the hair follicles. These burns extend through the epidermis and the dermis and into the underlying subcutaneous tissues. If the burn extends into the muscle or bone, it is considered equivalent to a fourth-degree burn. Because blood vessels and nerve endings are destroyed, these lesions present as white and painless. These injuries require hospitalization and often skin grafting. Scarring and disfigurement are always present (Giardino, 1997b).

The size of the burn is another important factor in determining severity. The size of the burn is calculated as a percentage of body surface area involved. A superficial burn that covers a large part of the body may be more serious than a third-degree burn that covers a small part of the body. Physicians describe burns in terms of percentages of total body surface area covered.

A detailed history is vitally important in determining the etiology of a burn. It will be important to determine the following (Giardino, 1997b):

- Does the history adequately explain the burn, on the basis of the child's development, age of burn, and/or pattern of burn?
- Was the child reported to be "found" with the burn (injury not witnessed)?
- Was the caregiver responsible for the child at the time of the burn present with the child at the time of the medical evaluation/presentation?
- Was the burn attributed to a sibling or playmate?
- Are there patterns of injury that imply restraint during the burn injury?
- Was there an unexplained delay in seeking care?
- Are there other suspicious injuries, such as bruises or scars of various age or stages of healing?
- Is there evidence of neglect, such as poor hygiene or malnutrition?
- Is there a history of previous injury?

The temperature of the liquid that caused the burn is important. In hot water burns, the temperature of the tap water determines the amount of time of exposure it takes to cause a burn and the severity of the burn (Baptiste & Feck, 1980).

The research that has been done in this area only shows the temperatures and duration of exposure needed to cause burns in adult skin (Moritz & Henriques, 1947). Adult's skin is thicker than a child's skin, creating a greater risk for scalding injuries in children from various household sources. Adult skin can tolerate higher temperatures for longer periods of time than a child's skin.

Below 120°F, hot water is unlikely to inflict major injury. Adult skin placed in water that is 127°F can sustain full thickness burns in approximately 1 minute. At 130°F,

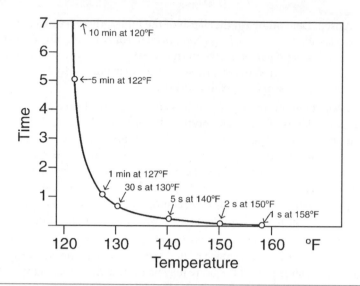

Relationship between Water Temperature and Full Thickness Skin Burns. From A. P. Giardino, C. W. Christian, & E. R. Giardino, *A Practical Guide to the Evaluation of Child Physical Abuse and Neglect* (p. 85). Thousand Oaks, CA: Sage Publications. Copyright 1997 by Sage Publications. Reprinted with permission.

full thickness burns of adult skin will occur within 30 seconds, and at 150°F within 2 seconds (Feldman, 1987; Moritz & Henriques, 1947). Most homes have hot water heaters set between 120°F and 150°F, but it is recommended that home water heaters be set to 120°F to reduce the risk and severity of accidental burns (Erdman, Feldman, Rivara, Heimbach, & Wall, 1991).

Burn injuries are typically classified into scalds (hot liquid), flame, contact (hot solid object), electrical, and chemical (Meagher, 1990).

Scalding is the most common cause of childhood burns, both accidental and non-accidental or inflicted. It also accounts for 45% of all pediatric burn admissions (Ahlgren, 1990). Scalding occurs when a child's skin comes in contact with a hot liquid. Scald burns are further classified into the following three categories (Giardino, 1997b):

- *Splash/spill burns* occur when a hot liquid falls, is poured on, or is thrown at the child. These usually appear as several small, scattered burns, or "satellites." Frequently the pattern is an "arrowhead" configuration, decreasing in severity toward the bottom edges as the liquid cools as it runs down the body. Accidental splash/spill burns are most likely to occur on the front of the head, neck, trunk, and arms. Those found on the back of the head, neck, chest, extremities, and genitalia are rarely self-inflicted.

- The history and physical should be compatible in terms of the amount of liquid involved. In the case of suspected splash burns, the following information should be obtained:

How far did the liquid travel in the air before hitting the child? (Across the room? From the stove to the floor?)

What was the exact position of the child's body when the incident occurred?

What clothes was the child wearing when the incident occurred? Were the clothes removed immediately?

What was the nature of the splashed liquid? Was it greasy?

- *Immersion burns* occur when a child falls into or is placed into hot liquid. These burns may be accidental or abusive, and although they may occur at any age, they are most common in infants and toddlers. In the case of suspected immersion burns, the following information should be obtained:

  What was the container in which the child was immersed? (Tubs produce areas of sparing, pots on hot burners do not.)

  How deep was the liquid in the container?

  What was the exact position of the child's body when the incident occurred?

  What was the estimated temperature of the liquid?

- *Forced immersion burns* occur when parts of the body are forced into a hot liquid, usually water from a running tap or a filled tub. When the restrained child cannot move in the liquid, the burns often leave clear lines of demarcation on the skin. Splash marks are either not present or are limited.

Contact burns (dry burns) are often seen in child abuse cases but may be accidental. This injury occurs when the child's skin is placed in direct contact with a hot object such as an iron or a heating grate (Feldman, 1987). The shape of the burn frequently resembles the shape of the object being touched. The burn tends to be more geometric in shape if inflicted and less geometric if accidental because of the glancing and briefer nature of the contact (Feldman, 1987). See further examples in the following section.

Abusive patterns of burns. Certain patterns of burns should raise suspicions for inflicted injury. *Full thickness burns* (deep second and third degree) *to the hands and feet* should raise suspicion of abuse. These usually appear as "stocking" or "glove" patterns that are uniform in depth. *Scalds of the perineum* (the buttocks, genital, or rectal area) may be inflicted as a form of punishment for the child who is not yet toilet trained.

- *Doughnut-hole burns* are created when a child is forced into a porcelain or fiberglass tub with his or her buttocks resting on the cooler bottom, thus creating a patch of unburned skin in the center of the burn.

- *Flexion burns* have a "zebra-stripe" appearance, in which there are stripes of unburned skin in the middle of the burned area. These "stripes" occur in folds of skin that were protected as the body came into contact with the liquid and are typically caused by abuse.

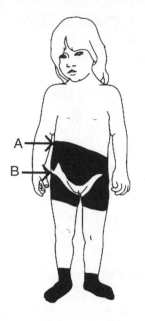

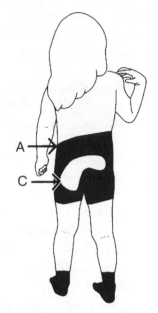

Forced Immersion Burn. As the child's buttocks are plunged into the hot liquid and held against the porcelain tub, the child instinctively flexes the hips. The burn is well demarcated (A). The crease between the thigh and abdomen is spared (B). From A. P. Giardino, C. W. Christian, & E. R. Giardino, *A Practical Guide to the Evaluation of Child Physical Abuse and Neglect* (p. 83). Thousand Oaks, CA: Sage Publications. Copyright 1997 by Sage Publications. Reprinted with permission.

Forced Immersion Burn. The area of the buttocks that is held against the relatively cooler tub is less severely burned and gives rise to the "doughnut-hole" pattern (C). The child's heels may come in contact with the hot liquid, and the burn is well demarcated (A). From A. P. Giardino, C. W. Christian, & E. R. Giardino, *A Practical Guide to the Evaluation of Child Physical Abuse and Neglect* (p. 84). Thousand Oaks, CA: Sage Publications. Copyright 1997 by Sage Publications. Reprinted with permission.

- *Parallel lines* occur when a distinct line separates the skin area that has been exposed from that which has not. These lines can be made parallel by positioning the body into the estimated position of the child at the time of immersion.

- *Cigarette burns* are usually difficult to diagnose with certainty. They typically measure about 1 centimeter in diameter and are often found in sensitive areas on the trunk, external genitalia, and extremities. Accidental cigarette burns occur when the child brushes up against a lit cigarette, which causes a glancing contact. This results in an irregularly shaped, superficial burn.

- *Contact burns by objects*, such as irons, stove burners, heater grates, radiators, electric hot plates, and hair dryers may create typical patterns that can help in determining the etiology of the burn.

Parallel Line Burns. From E. Lenoski, & K. Hunter, "Specific Patterns of Inflicted Burns in Children," *Journal of Trauma, 17.* Copyright 1977 by Lippincott Williams and Wilkins. Reprinted with permission.

Differential diagnosis of burns. The following nonabusive medical conditions may involve burns or mimic burns.

- *Accidental injury.* An accidental *cigarette burn* is usually more elongated than round, with a higher degree of intensity on one side. Accidental *contact burns* have irregular shapes and are deeper and clearer on one edge. Often in the hot summer months children will sustain second and third degree burns caused by vinyl upholstery, seat belts, infant backpack carriers, or seat belt buckles, as these objects heat up in cars or other enclosed places. History and physical examination should support the caregiver's explanation of the cause of the burn.

- *Dermatologic disorders. Epidermolysis bullosa* is a group of blistering skin disorders that may mimic burns. Blisters may develop in response to mechanical trauma. *Dermatitis herpetiformis* is a chronic, recurrent papular

Burn Marks. From R. E. Behrman, R. M. Kleigman, & H. B. Jenson, *Nelson Textbook of Pediatrics, 16th ed.* (p. 113). Philadelphia: Saunders. Copyright 2000 by Elsevier. Reprinted with permission.

hot plate	light bulb	curling iron	car cigarette lighter	steam iron
knife	grid	cigarette	forks	immersion

skin condition that is usually symmetric. Lesions are usually small, clustered in groups, very itchy, and seen on the extremities, buttocks, back, and abdomen. This condition may be mistaken for cigarette burns. *Dermatitis* may be seen in severe diaper rash that mimics a scald burn.

- *Infections. Impetigo* is a superficial bacterial infection of the skin typically caused by *Staphylococcus aureus*. This condition produces lesions that appear as pustules and then later form crusts. These lesions are of different sizes and may produce blisters similar in appearance to cigarette burns. These usually do not leave scars, whereas cigarette burns may (Richardson, 1994). *Group A beta-hemolytic strep infection* also causes blisters of varying sizes. The blisters usually have a clear fluid. Suspicious blisters will generally be cultured by the medical provider for staphylococcal or streptococcal infections and treated with antibiotics. Burns can become infected with impetigo and obscure the diagnosis.

- *Several folk medicine treatments* tend to cause burns that may appear abusive. *Cupping*, defined earlier in the bruises section, may also leave a burn. Southeast Asian children will sometimes exhibit burns or scars, usually ½–1 centimeter in diameter, located randomly around the lower rib cage or in a definite pattern around the umbilicus, or "belly button." These are created by a practice in which pieces of burning string are lowered onto the child's skin, in an attempt to cure abdominal pain or fever.

Other types of burns.

- *Chemical burns* may come from contact with irritating chemicals such as medicated creams. It is important to try to find the source of the chemical to verify the cause of the burn.

- *Drug reactions/eruptions* may have the appearance of a burn.

- *Phytophotodermatitis* may also have a blisterlike appearance.

Medical assessment of burns (Giardino, 1997b). The history, along with the physical examination, are very important in determining the cause of a child's burn. As diagnosis is usually made clinically, laboratory and diagnostic testing are usually not necessary. Specific laboratory and diagnostic testing may be indicated, depending on the severity of the burn or other diagnostic possibilities suggested by the pattern of the burn.

☐ **Skeletal Injury**

It is estimated that the frequency of fractures in physically abused children varies from 10% to 50% depending on the population and age of the children studied, as well as the type of diagnostic imaging used to detect the fractures (Cooperman & Merten, 2001; Ebbin, Gollub, Stein, & Wilson, 1969; Herndon, 1983). Abusive skeletal injuries occur more commonly in infants and young children than in older children (Akbarnia, Torg, Kirkpatrick, & Sussman, 1974). The majority of fractures occur in children below the age of 3 (Johnson & Showers, 1985). The frequency, type, location, and healing of pediatric fractures are directly affected by the anatomic and physiologic characteristics of the immature skeleton. Because developing bone is more porous than mature bone, the extent and type of fractures seen in children is different from that in adult bones (Giardino, 1997b). Bone healing is also much more rapid in infants than in children and in children than in adults.

History of Skeletal Injuries

Suspicion of abuse should be raised in any of the following cases:

- Unsuspected fractures are "accidentally" discovered in the course of an examination.
- There is either no history, or the history given is not compatible with the type or location of the fracture.
- There are multiple fractures and/or fractures that are in different stages of healing.
- Skeletal trauma is accompanied by other injuries, such as burns or bruises, to other parts of the body.

Description of Skeletal Injuries

A medical provider's first step in evaluating a skeletal injury is determining its location and type and attempting to date it.

Location of fracture. The following skeletal diagram outlines the locations of particular bones.

What part of the bone is involved? *Long bones,* the bones of the arms and legs (e.g., humerus, ulna, radius, femur, tibia, and fibula), have special anatomy, as shown in the following illustration.

The *diaphysis* is to the shaft, or midportion, of a long bone. The *epiphysis* is either end of the bone, the parts of the long bone that are developed from the center of ossification. In a growing child, the epiphysis is separated from the shaft by a layer of cartilage, called the *epiphyseal plate,* or "growth plate." It is often not seen on x-rays of infants and young children because it is not yet ossified. The *metaphysis* is the area between the epiphysis and the diaphysis. It borders the growth plate. On the x-ray it is identified as the flaring portion of the long bone.

Types of fracture (Giardino, 1997a):

- *Closed fracture.* A fracture of the bone with no skin wound.
- *Compound fracture.* Open fracture; a fracture in which the bone is broken and protruding through the skin.
- *Depressed skull fracture.* Skull fracture in which part of the skull is inwardly displaced.
- *Diastatic fracture.* Fracture with significant separation of the bone fragments; a term often used in the description of skull fractures.

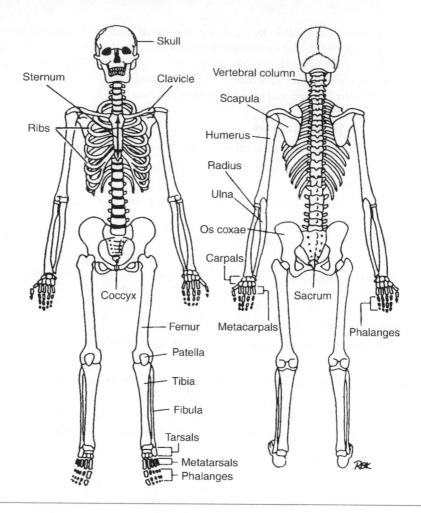

Human Skeleton. From R. Bruck-Kan, *Introduction to Human Anatomy*. New York: Harper and Row, 1979. Reprinted with permission of the author.

- *Greenstick fracture.* Incomplete fracture; fracture in which the compressed side of the bone is partially bent/bowed and the other side is partially broken, as when a green stick breaks, but not completely fractured. Caused by compression and angulation.
- *Hairline fracture.* A minor fracture in which all the portions of the bone are in perfect alignment.
- *Linear fracture.* Fracture that resembles a line; a term used in description of some skull fractures.
- *Metaphyseal fracture.* A micro fracture through the growing end of a bone at the metaphysis (Kleinman, Marks, & Blackbourne, 1986).

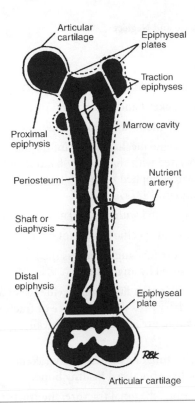

Long Bone. From R. Bruck-Kan, *Introduction to Human Anatomy*. New York: Harper and Row, 1979. Reprinted with permission of the author.

Metaphyseal Fracture. From J. C. Leonidas, "Skeletal Trauma in the Child Abuse Syndrome." *Pediatric Annals, 12.* Copyright by SLACK. Reprinted with permission.

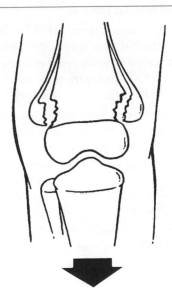

This type of fracture:

> Is highly specific for child abuse (Kleinman, 1987a).
>
> May appear as "bucket-handle fractures" or corner fractures.
>
> Usually is found in infants and young toddlers.
>
> Usually involves as the mechanism of injury the acceleration-deceleration forces associated with shaking or shaking and impact or torsional and tractional forces applied to the bone when the extremity is twisted or pulled (Kleinman, 1987a).
>
> Usually is not associated with significant swelling or external bruising.
>
> Usually heals without specific treatment or need for immobilization.

- *Oblique fracture.* Fracture line angled across the long axis of the bone. This fracture is typically caused by angulation.
- *Occult fracture.* Clinical, not radiographic, evidence of a fracture. The x-rays repeated a few weeks later may show evidence of fracture healing; may also be used to describe a fracture seen radiographically but without clinical manifestations.
- *Pathologic fracture.* Fracture of a diseased or weakened bone, produced by a force that would not have fractured healthy bone.
- *Spiral fracture.* A slanting, diagonal fracture; the fracture line is oblique and encircles a portion of the bone. This injury is caused by a torsional force.
- *Torus or buckle fracture.* A minor fracture that only affects one side of the bone and is typically caused by compression.
- *Transverse fracture.* A fracture in which the fracture line is at right angles to the long axis of the bone. Usually caused by impact with a hard object.

Medical Assessment of Skeletal Injuries

In the evaluation of a fracture, the medical provider will examine any soft tissue damage, such as bruises or lacerations; the visibility of the fracture line on an x-ray; the presence of a periosteal reaction; and the presence of changes in the periosteal new bone, or callus. Subtle fractures or hairline fractures may be difficult to discern on x-ray immediately because the bone has not yet had time to form a callus.

The diagnosis of skeletal injuries is made by history and physical examination and confirmed by radiographic imaging. Skeletal radiography (x-ray) is used to assist in the determination of the location, age, and cause of a suspected fracture. It is important to try to avoid exposing the child to unnecessary radiation by keeping records of all x-rays obtained. If it is necessary to take a child to another medical provider, request that all prior medical records, including x-rays or copies of the x-rays, be sent. Types of radiographic procedures include:

- *Skeletal Survey.* A series of x-rays taken of the child's entire skeleton to look for indications of new or old injury. Includes the skull, chest, spine, and extremities. Should be done in cases of suspected physical abuse for all infants and children under 2 years of age; rarely used in children over 5 years of age.

- *Bone Scan.* A process in which a small amount of radioactive phosphorus is injected into the bloodstream. The radiation, or "heat" from this injection is then photographed. Those areas of bone that are growing will demonstrate radioactivity. Can detect fractures within 48 hours after they occur. Does not allow for dating of injuries.

Dating of skeletal injuries. The radiographic appearance of fractures is used in conjunction with historical information and physical findings to approximate the dating of injuries when possible (Chapman, 1992; Merten, Cooperman, & Thompson, 1994). Dating is based on the radiographic appearance of the periosteum, soft tissues, callus formation, and fracture line (Merten et al., 1994). It is possible to differentiate new from old injuries and sometimes estimate the age of a fracture in days, weeks, or months.

Skeletal Injuries and Abuse

Fractures of the extremities. These are most likely to occur in the long bones of the arms and legs, and are not as common in the hands and feet. Accidental injury accounts for the majority of long bone fractures, as this is a common type of childhood injury (Rivara, Parrish, & Mueller, 1986). Abusive injuries account for only a small proportion of long bone fractures and are most common in infants.

A direct blow to the shaft of the bone may cause a transverse fracture, while a twisting force may cause a spiral fracture. While spiral fractures in a child who cannot yet walk should always raise suspicion, the diagnosis of a transverse fracture should not rule out abuse.

Metaphyseal fractures should always be investigated for abuse, for they do not occur from falling down but rather from having a jerking force applied to the extremities or from rapid swinging movements of the extremities, as are seen in shaking injuries.

Skull fractures. These are caused by direct impact of the head with a solid object. These injuries are the second most common form of skeletal injury in abuse (Merten et al., 1994). Description of the fracture includes the name of the bone(s) involved and the type of fracture. The immobile joints that separate the bones of the skull are called *sutures.*

Linear skull fractures and fractures of the parietal bone are the most common skull fractures seen in both abusive and accidental injuries (Leventhal, Thomas, Rosenfield, & Markowitz, 1993).

The child may or may not have evidence of external trauma such as bruising or swelling.

Skull fractures do not predict brain injury. In addition, the absence of a skull fracture does not exclude the possibility of a significant underlying brain injury.

Further information on skull and brain injuries can be found in the section on abusive head trauma.

Rib fractures. Because the rib cage is compliant under mild pressure, fractures of this area are uncommon in infants and children and should be considered the product of major trauma. Several studies have confirmed the association between rib fractures and child abuse (Cameron & Rae, 1975; Leventhal et al., 1993; Schweich & Fleisher, 1985). It is estimated that rib fractures account for between 5% and 27% of all skeletal injuries in physically abused children, and almost 90% in children younger than age 2 (Cooperman & Merten, 2001).

Blows occurring from the side or squeezing may create fractures in the back of the rib cage, near the spine, which are called *posterior rib fractures*. Blows onto the front of the chest, or *sternum*, as well as squeezing, may create fractures on the sides of the rib cage, which are called *lateral rib fractures*. Although rib fractures commonly occur during cardiopulmonary resuscitation (CPR) in adults, CPR has not been found to be a cause of rib fractures in infants and children (Feldman & Brewer, 1984; Spevak, Kleinman, Belanger, Primack, & Richmond, 1994).

Vertebral fractures.   Although uncommon, vertebral fractures or fractures of the spinous processes along the spine may also be seen in abuse. These injuries are probably more common than is generally realized because they are often not symptomatic (Kleinman, 1987b). They can result from forced bending of the spine, or hyperflexion/hyperextension, as well as torsion of the spine. Vertebral injuries may be associated with shaken baby syndrome. Excessive force from above downward to the child's head or spine can also cause these injuries (e.g., slamming the child into a chair or a car seat). Symptoms of neurologic injury may include vomiting, weight loss, irritability, and slowed development. However, frequently no neurologic signs of injury exist, and the spinal lesions frequently go unrecognized. Plain x-rays may detect these injuries during a skeletal survey.

Accidental Trauma and Organic Abnormalities

In a differential diagnosis of a skeletal injury, the medical provider may consider accidental trauma as a cause of fractures. The medical provider should also consider the following organic abnormalities as possible causes for the radiological findings. These conditions are quite rare, and the presence of the following conditions does not preclude the possibility of abuse, as both may be present.

- *Birth trauma.* Difficult deliveries of infants may cause a variety of different skeletal injuries. The most common skeletal injuries seen as a result of birth trauma due to large infants, malpresentation, or instrumentation are clavicle, humerus, femur, and skull fractures.

- *Congenital syphilis.* Causes bone irregularities as a result of a weakening of the bone. Radiographic findings are usually diagnostic, but affected infants also have many other clinical findings that suggest the disease. The diagnosis is confirmed by serologic testing.

- *Osteogenesis imperfecta.* Rare, inherited disorder of connective tissue with variable expressions and severities. Symptoms may not become apparent until months or years after birth. Genetic testing assists in confirming this diagnosis.

- *Osteomyelitis.* A bacterial bone infection that may produce bone weakness and subsequent fractures.

- *Rickets.* Bone disease—caused by vitamin D deficiency, renal and hepatic disease, and/or certain medications—which may cause bone irregularities similar to those caused by trauma. The radiographic findings in this disease are specific to the disease and usually not confused with abuse. The diagnosis is confirmed by laboratory studies.
- *Scurvy.* Rare condition resulting from vitamin C deficiency, may cause irregularities and fractures of the bones.
- *Infantile cortical hyperostosis (Caffey's disease).* Rare disorder present in infants up to 2 to 3 months of age as red, painful, swollen extremities.
- *Menke's kinky hair syndrome.* Very rare syndrome resulting from a deficiency in copper metabolism, results in symmetrical problems in the shaft (diaphysis) and the ends (metaphysis) of the bones.

Abusive Head Trauma

Whenever there is suspected trauma to the head or face, a medical provider should examine the child immediately. Trauma to the skull and brain is the primary cause of mortality in abused children today (Billmire & Myers, 1985; Duhaime et al., 1992; Gotschall, 1993). Although hard to quantify because of underrecognition and underreporting, inflicted head injuries are believed to account for about 25% of hospital admissions for head injury. In addition, these children's injuries are disproportionately more severe than for those children who suffer accidental injuries (Duhaime et al., 1992). Children under 2 years of age are at the greatest risk for this type of trauma. It is estimated that 80% of deaths from head trauma in children less than 2 years of age are from child abuse.

Head Injuries

Types of head injuries include the following:

- *Scalp.* Trauma of the scalp, the skin and soft tissues that cover the skull, can cause lacerations, bruising, or hematomas. Bruises are often missed

Bilateral Subdural Hematomas.   Subgaleal Hematomas.

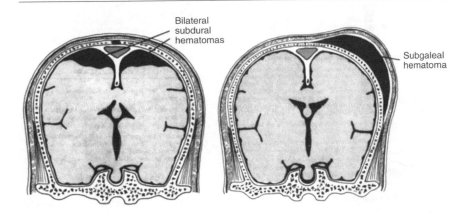

because of the overlying hair. Deep scalp injuries are often identified first at autopsy.

- *Subgaleal.* Bleeding or hemorrhage into the space just underneath the scalp and overlying the skull causes a hematoma. This is usually associated with blunt injury but can also arise from hair pulling (Hamlin, 1968).

- *Subperiosteal.* Bleeding into the layer of fibrous tissue that immediately overlies the skull, called the periosteum; causes a cephalhematoma.

- *Skull.* The skull consists of eight cranial and facial bones that are joined by immobile joints called sutures. Skull fractures cannot be accurately dated. In the skull of the newborn infant there are "soft spots," or areas not covered by bone, called fontanelles. When these eventually close they leave sutures. The immaturity of the newborn skull and brain make it more susceptible to trauma. Because the infant brain floats in a relatively larger space of cerebrospinal fluid than the adult brain, it has room to move around and sustain injury. There may be fractures of the skull bones, but serious injury may also underlie an area that is not fractured.

- *Epidural.* The epidural space is located between the skull and the dura membrane, and bleeding into this area causes an epidural hematoma/ hemorrhage. This injury is frequently the result of accidental trauma but has been seen in abused children (Merten & Osborne, 1984). Because these injuries are usually due to the tearing of an artery that traverses this space, they are considered surgical emergencies and may be life-threatening.

- *Subdural.* The subdural space is located between the dura and the arachnoid membranes. Bleeding into this space causes a hematoma and is called a subdural hematoma/hemorrhage. This injury results from tearing of the

Fontanelles of Infant Skull. From R. Bruck-Kan, *Introduction to Human Anatomy*. New York: Harper and Row, 1979. Reprinted with permission of the author.

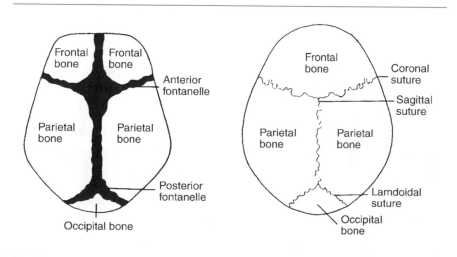

bridging veins that extend from the surface of the brain to the dura. This usually occurs as the result of a severe acceleration/deceleration/rotational injury and is therefore frequently seen in shaken baby syndrome. This bleeding may extend along the surface of the brain and into the posterior interhemishperic fissure. Severe motor vehicle accidents account for most of the accidental trauma that causes this injury.

- *Subarachnoid.* The subarachnoid space is located between the arachnoid membrane and the surface of the brain. This injury may result from many different mechanisms that may or may not be associated with abuse.

- *Parenchymal.* This space is located within the brain tissue. Injuries here may or may not be related to abuse. These injuries include shearing tears, infarctions, axonal injuries, cerebral edema, encephalomalacia, and herniation.

- *Intraventricular.* The *ventricles* are the very central spaces in the brain through which the cerebrospinal fluid flows. Bleeding in this area, known as intraventricular hemorrhage, may arise from newborn problems, vascular malformations, bleeding disorders, trauma (accidental or inflicted), or as a complication of surgery.

Medical assessment of head injuries. All growth parameters should be obtained and compared. Measurement of head circumference that is over the 90th percentile for age and/or a child whose head is growing faster than expected often prompts the need for evaluation of possible injury.

A complete physical examination, including close evaluation of the skin and nervous system, should be performed. Special attention should be focused on the eyes, and if possible a pediatric ophthalmologist should be consulted to do a complete dilated eye examination, including indirect ophthalmoscopy.

Several laboratory studies are usually obtained, including blood counts (assessing for anemia), bleeding studies (assessing for bleeding tendencies), and liver function tests, amylase, and urinalysis (all assessing for indicators of abdominal trauma). If there is concern for the possibility of infection such as meningitis causing the presenting symptoms, a lumbar spinal tap may be done. In this procedure, a small amount of the fluid that surrounds the brain and spinal cord (cerebrospinal fluid) is withdrawn from the lower portion of the spine and evaluated for signs of infection. The presence of blood in this fluid may signal that bleeding has occurred.

Radiographic studies play a significant role in assessing children who present for evaluation of possible head trauma, including the following:

- *Skeletal survey.* Should always be done in an infant suspected of having abusive head trauma as it may identify skull fractures as well as subclinical fractures of other bones. Special attention needs to be given to the skull, the ends of long bones, and the ribs. The examination may need to be repeated in 2 to 4 weeks to assess for healing injuries that may not have been identified initially. The age of skull fractures cannot be estimated accurately.

- *Computerized tomography (CT).* Commonly used for initial evaluation of a child suspected of having an abusive head injury. Can detect hemorrhages, or pockets of blood, which might exist in any of the locations inside the cranium. This examination is very useful in evaluating for acute injury. It may also detect fractures of the skull or widening of the sutures caused by brain swelling or bleeding. It identifies the location and extent of the injury.

- *Magnetic resonance imaging (MRI).* Useful in demonstrating small injuries, as well as showing different stages of resolution. It may also assist in evaluation for vascular lesions that may cause hemorrhage.

Shaken baby syndrome. This is a frequently recognized mechanism of head injury in abused children. This type of abuse involves infants who are held by the arms or trunk and violently shaken. There may or may not be impact with an either hard or soft surface in addition to the shaking. Commonly, infants with this identified form of injury are less than 2 years of age and are usually less than 6 months of age.

Presenting symptoms are often irritability, poor feeding, and lethargy. The child may present for medical attention with a history of apnea (not-breathing spell), seizures, or visual impairment or as an unexplained infant death. The history given at the time of presentation is often vague or nonexistent.

Common features of shaken baby syndrome are as follows:

- *Subdural hematoma.* Occurs when the cerebral veins that bridge the subdural space are injured. In children these vessels are fragile and poorly supported and can be easily damaged when the head undergoes acceleration/deceleration/rotational forces, as in shaking. The subdural blood often extends to the interhemispheric space and may or may not be accompanied by cerebral edema and/or skull fracture(s). These injuries can cause permanent brain damage, seizures, developmental delays, and possibly death.

- *Retinal hemorrhages.* Occur in 50% to 80% of infants with shaken baby syndrome and frequently correlate with the severity of the child's neurologic status (Wilkinson, Han, Rappley, & Owings, 1989). They occur only very rarely as a result of other causes, such as severe accidental trauma (Duhaime et al., 1992). They may occur as a result of birth trauma, but such hemorrhages are usually resolved by 6 weeks of age. Other uncommon causes are ruled out by history and the physical. Retinal hemorrhages cannot be dated (Levin, 1990). See the section on eyes for further description.

- *Diffuse cerebral edema* is frequently present with this syndrome. This is felt to be the result of the cascade of events initiated by the apnea that frequently follows a shaking event. This apnea causes a period of lack of oxygen to the infant brain, which results in this swelling of the brain tissue. This can be life-threatening.

- *Diffuse cerebral edema* refers to swelling of the cerebrum, one of the largest portions of the brain. This type of injury is life-threatening. *Infarction*, lack of blood to the brain, can cause necrosis (death) of the brain tissue. *Posttraumatic hypopituitarism*—injury to a part of the brain that secretes hormones affecting growth—can result in delayed growth of the child and may be detected through laboratory tests.

- There may be *bruising of the head, thorax, or extremities*, but usually there are no external signs of trauma. There also may be associated *rib or extremity fractures.*

Hair and scalp injuries. *Traumatic alopecia* (loss of hair) occurs in children who have been pulled or yanked by the hair. The scalp may be tender or even bruised at the site where the hair was pulled. *Subgaleal hematomas* occur when the scalp separates from the skull, causing blood to pool under the skin, creating a soft, "boggy" area. Children with pigtails or braids are often victims, as their hair provides accessible "handles" for an angry caregiver.

Differential diagnosis of head injuries. Certain nonabusive conditions should be ruled out. Benign subdural fluid collection of infancy, or an *effusion,* is a condition that appears at birth. The appearance of this condition on CT scan differs from that of subdural hematoma. In addition, this condition is not accompanied by any signs of intracranial injury other than increased head circumference.

Skull fractures result when a child receives a direct impact injury to the head. A common history given for head injuries is that the child "fell" from a bed, changing table, or sofa. Past studies have suggested, however, that children who fall from heights of 90 centimeters (about 41 inches) or less very rarely sustain serious head injury. It is important to consider the child's developmental maturity and whether the child is capable of performing what the parent or caregiver has reported.

A *cephalhematoma*—a swelling under the scalp containing blood—may appear on a newborn infant's scalp several days after birth when forceps or vacuum suction are utilized in the delivery. This swelling disappears within months.

Tinea capitis (ringworm), a fungal infection, may produce round areas of baldness on the scalp. Diagnosis is usually made by fluorescence under a Wood's lamp.

Accidental injury is frequently given as the explanation for an abusive head injury. Although accidents such as falls may cause minor head injuries, child abuse should be suspected when serious injury results from unwitnessed accidents such as falls. Serious head injuries are extremely rare when children fall from short heights such as beds, cribs, or couches (Lyons & Oates, 1993). Death is unlikely to result from injuries sustained in a fall from less than 20 feet, unless it has resulted in an epidural hematoma (Chadwick, Chin, Salerno, Landsverk, & Kitchen, 1991). Stairway falls have also not been shown to result in life-threatening injury.

Prognosis in abusive head injuries. The developmental and neurologic outcomes in children who are victims of abusive head trauma are not good. Approximately one-third of these children will die, one-third will suffer severe disability, and of the remaining one-third who appear normal for the short term, another one-half will develop late findings of the injury such as microcephaly, hydrocephalus, seizures, developmental delay, learning disabilities, and psychological and/or behavioral difficulties. The outcome in children who suffer retinal hemorrhages as the result of abusive head trauma usually parallels their neurologic outcome. Two-thirds of these children will have some form of visual impairment, and of these one-fourth will be blind.

Eye Injuries

Whether from accidental or nonaccidental causes, these are common in childhood.

Medical assessment of eye injuries. A detailed evaluation should be made of the external surface of the eye, as well as its mobility and the movement of the pupil. The medical provider may use a direct ophthalmoscope to visualize the retina in the back of the eye. There may be a need for examination by an ophthalmologist using indirect ophthalmoscopy if there is concern about injury of the internal parts of the eye (e.g., retina, lens). If possible, given the developmental and physical status of the child, the medical provider may measure the visual acuity and the field of vision of the eyes.

Descriptions of eye injuries follow.

- *Lens detachment.* Direct blows to the eye may cause the lens to actually detach and become dislocated in the eye. This injury not only affects the child's ability to focus but may cause the formation of a cataract, or an opacity of the lens.

- *Subconjunctival hemorrhage.* The conjunctiva is a mucous membrane that forms the inner surface of the eyelid and covers the front part of the eyeball itself. Subconjunctival hemorrhage occurs when a small blood vessel in this membrane breaks, causing the eyeball to appear dark/bruised or the lid to appear swollen. This may be the result of direct trauma or increased intrathoracic pressure, as in a child who is coughing excessively. These "bruises" usually clear within 2 weeks; they go through the usual stages of resolution of color from dark red through yellow. They may occur quite easily with little trauma.

- *Corneal abrasions.* The cornea, the transparent layer of the front of the eye, may reveal lacerations or abrasions that can occur as a result of direct trauma

- *Hyphema.* This is a collection of blood in the anterior chamber of the eye (in front of the lens) resulting from the rupture of blood vessels in that area. This also occurs as the result of direct trauma.

- *Retinal hemorrhages.* The retina is the delicate innermost surface of the eye and is composed of many layers. Injuries to this portion of the eye are described both by their location and their extent. The location and extent of the hemorrhages are very helpful in differentiating their cause. They cannot be used to date an injury (Levin, 1990).

  Differential diagnosis: Infants who have suffered abusive head trauma, such as in a shaking, often present with this condition, as do those sustaining direct impact force to the skull. The presence of retinal hemorrhages in conjunction with unexplained fractures, bruises, or burns is a strong indicator that abuse has occurred.

  Newborn infants may exhibit retinal hemorrhages as a result of a traumatic delivery. These hemorrhages are generally mild and resolve within a few days. They have not been described beyond 6 weeks of age (Sezen, 1970).

  Retinal hemorrhages can result from severe accidental trauma such as a significant motor vehicle accident or a fall from a high window (Duhaime et al., 1992). They may occur rarely as a result of nontraumatic causes such as coagulopathy, meningitis, severe hypertension, endocarditis, vasculitis, sepsis, and carbon monoxide poisoning (Rosenberg, Singer, Bolte, Christian, & Selbst, 1994). These can all be ruled out by the medical evaluation.

Retinal hemorrhages rarely occur as a result of cardiopulmonary resuscitation (CPR) and when present are not extensive. They are highly correlated with abuse in this population of infants.

- *Periorbital ecchymosis.* Bruising around the eyes that may be associated with underlying ocular damage. Injury to both eyes should arouse suspicion, for accidental injuries usually occur on one side of the face. Sometimes trauma to the nose or mid-forehead causes bleeding that collects in the areas under both eyes, producing "raccoon eyes." Allergic conditions can produce the appearance of bruising under the eyes, known as "allergic shiners."

Ear Injuries

Ears are another area of the head that may reveal injury in an abused child. Direct blows to the ear may result in bruising of the outer ear (*pinna*), perforation of the eardrum, or a collection of blood in the inner ear. This area is relatively protected from accidental injury by a triangle formed from the top of the head and the shoulder to the neck. Therefore, injuries of the pinna should always be considered suspicious.

Injury to the middle or inner ear can only be achieved by inserting a sharp, pointed object into the ear. Such injuries are commonly the result of either an adult's innocent attempt to clean a child's ear with cotton swabs or an infection of the middle ear.

Nose Injuries

Injuries of the nose are also occasionally seen in victims of child abuse. The most common injuries to the nose involve the nasal septum, the partition that divides the nasal cavity into two sections. The insertion of foreign bodies into the nose is common in the normally developing, curious child.

Direct trauma to the nose may cause bruising, abrasions, or bleeding. History and developmental age is important in determining the accidental or nonaccidental nature of this injury.

Mouth Injuries

The physical significance in both feeding and communication make the mouth an easy target for physical abuse. The history of injury to the mouth is important in determining the nature of such injuries. Types of injury include:

- *Frenulum tears.* The frenula are the small folds of skin that connect the lips to the gums and connect the tongue to the floor of the mouth. Injuries to these areas can occur from a direct blow to the face or from the jamming of a spoon or bottle into a resistant child's mouth.

- *Lip injuries.* Most often seen as lacerations, bruises, abrasions, and burns. Bruises on the external corners of the mouth suggest that the child may have been gagged.

- *Dental injuries.* Traumatic injury to the teeth of young children is very common. These injuries include avulsion, fractures, intrusions, and luxations. An *avulsion* refers to the total removal of a tooth from the socket. Treatment of these injuries should be sought immediately to avoid losing the tooth. *Intrusions* occur when the teeth are forced back into the supporting bone around them. Teeth will usually reerupt within 3 to 12 months. Teeth that are loosened in the mouth but have not left the socket are referred to as *luxated.*

- *Jaw injuries.* Fractures of the upper jaw are relatively rare in children and are the result of severe trauma. Fractures of the lower jaw are much more common. Immediate treatment, often by an oral or plastic surgeon, is necessary to avoid disfigurement.

☐ Abdominal and Thoracic Trauma in Child Abuse

Injuries to thoracic and abdominal organs due to child abuse are frequently underreported. Trauma to the thoracic area is less common than trauma to the abdominal organs. Although less than 1% of child abuse cases involve internal injuries (Cooper et al., 1988), when present, they have a mortality rate around 50%. Therefore, any child who is suspected to have sustained internal injury should immediately be taken for emergency treatment. These injuries require a high index of suspicion for detection. The high mortality rate with these injuries relates to the severity and nature of the injuries often sustained and the organs affected (they often bleed rapidly), delay in medical care, delay in correct diagnosis because of incomplete or completely lacking history for the injury, and the young age and noncommunicative nature of the victim.

Abdominal Trauma in Child Abuse

Demographics. Most commonly, children who sustain severe nonaccidental abdominal trauma are between the ages of 6 months and 3 years of age (Cobb, Vinocur, Wagner, & Weintraub, 1986; Cooper et al., 1988). Children who suffer accidental abdominal trauma tend to be a little older (Ledbetter, Hatch, Feldman, Linger, & Trapper, 1988).

Prevalence. When comparing accidental and inflicted abdominal trauma, Ledbetter et al. (1988) found that 11% of all abdominal trauma was attributed to abuse. However, the same study found that child abuse accounted for 44% of all abdominal injuries seen in children under 4 years of age.

Mechanisms. Blunt trauma accounts for most abusive abdominal injuries, although deceleration forces may cause injury to these organs as well. When a blow is administered to the abdomen, the solid organs (liver, spleen, pancreas) may be crushed against the vertebral bodies or the bony thorax. Rapid deceleration, as when a child is thrown against a wall, may cause shearing of the attachments of the organs or their vascular supply.

Specific organ injuries. These include:

- *Liver (hepatic) injuries.* Commonly found in abusive abdominal trauma. These consist of lacerations of the organ or bleeding forming a hematoma underneath the liver capsule (subcapsular hematoma).

- *Pancreas injuries.* Common abusive injuries. When this organ (a gland that aids in digestion) is injured, usually by a crushing mechanism, pancreatitis, or inflammation of the pancreas, often develops. A pancreatic pseudocyst, which is a cystlike nodule on the pancreas, may also develop after injury of this organ.

- *Small intestine (duodenum, jejunum and ileum) injuries.* Common among abusive abdominal injuries. The duodenum is particularly vulnerable because of its fixed position near the vertebral column. Injuries to these organs take the form of hematomas or perforations.

- *Spleen injuries.* Less common in nonaccidental trauma, as this organ is partially protected by the overlying ribs. This injury is more common as a result of accidental trauma. Injuries to this organ cause internal bleeding that can be life-threatening.

- *Kidney injuries.* Rarely seen in abusive trauma, as these organs are protected well by surrounding tissues.

Signs and symptoms. There are often no external signs of injury. The presentation of the child is dependent on the type and severity of the injuries, the length of time since the injury, and the rate of bleeding. The child may present for care in shock or cardiac arrest. Most commonly, the symptoms are subtle and nonspecific, for example vomiting, fever, abdominal pain, and lethargy. Examination *may* detect abdominal tenderness, abdominal distention, decreased bowel sounds, external bruising, tense abdominal muscles, and/or labored breathing.

Medical assessment of abusive abdominal trauma. Children who are thought to have sustained abusive abdominal trauma need to be evaluated by medical personnel emergently. Because external signs of trauma are frequently absent, the presence of abdominal bruising also presents a medical emergency.

The medical provider will obtain a detailed history of any possible injury to the abdomen, if possible. Because history of the actual cause of the injury may not be forthcoming, the provider will also work to clarify when the symptoms began and the course of the symptoms. The provider will complete a thorough physical examination after the child's clinical stability is ensured. This examination includes serial evaluation of vital signs, examination for external signs of trauma, and careful assessment for evidence of underlying injury.

A laboratory evaluation assesses for any sign of underlying trauma. The medical provider will usually obtain a complete blood count (CBC) (to assess for signs of bleeding, infection, or nutritional deficiency), bleeding studies (prothrombin time and partial thromboplastin time to assess for bleeding tendencies), chemistry panels

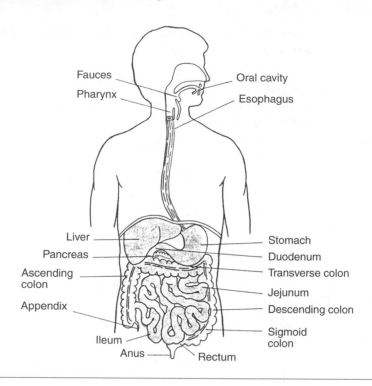

Digestive System. From R. Bruck-Kan, *Introduction to Human Anatomy*. New York: Harper and Row, 1979. Reprinted with permission of the author.

(to assess for metabolic abnormalities), liver studies (AST, ALT to assess for liver injury), urinalysis (to screen for kidney or bladder injury or infection), and serum amylase and lipase (to screen for pancreatic injury).

Regarding radiologic evaluation, several radiologic studies may be helpful in the evaluation of abusive abdominal trauma. Plain abdominal radiographs may reveal evidence of intestinal obstruction or perforation as well as foreign bodies or surrounding bony injury. An abdominal CT scan assists in the evaluation for solid organ injuries, while upper GI series and barium enema both assess for esophagus, stomach, duodenum, intestine, or colon injury. Other evaluations such as abdominal ultrasound, radionuclide scans, and intravenous pyelography may be utilized.

Thoracic (Chest) Trauma in Child Abuse

Abusive injuries to the chest are less common than abdominal injuries. This is in part because of the protection of these organs by the rib cage, as well as suspected underreporting. Like abdominal injuries, chest injuries result from direct trauma as well as deceleration forces. Abusive chest injuries involve the lungs and the heart.

Pulmonary injuries. Injuries to the chest are dangerous because broken ribs can puncture or damage the lungs, causing a *pneumothorax*, a collection of air in the pleural cavity (the sac-enclosed area surrounding the lungs). A *hemothorax* refers to blood or fluid in the pleural cavity caused by ruptured blood vessels. *Pulmonary contusions* are bruises to the lungs.

Cardiac injuries. Injuries to the heart consist of bruising or contusions. These injuries may cause electrical conduction abnormalities as well as cardiac muscle damage.

☐ Poisoning in Child Abuse

In recent years workers in both the medical and CPS field have become increasingly aware of poisoning as a less obvious but frequently underreported form of abuse. It has been reported that 17% to 33% of intentional or abusive cases of poisoning result in death, compared to 0.04% of the accidental cases (Bays, 1994). Twenty percent of the cases reviewed (Bays, 1994; Dine & McGovern, 1982) were also associated with physical abuse.

Impulsive acts under stress are probably the most common cause of nonaccidental poisoning. In these situations, a parent or caregiver administers drugs to a child with the intent to sedate the child. Sedatives such as alcohol, barbiturates, or antihistamines are most commonly used in these situations. Parents or caregivers may use drugs that have been prescribed for them, or they may use those prescribed for the child (e.g., colic medication). When this problem is recognized early and when the family is capable of learning the hazards of medication in children, the results of appropriate intervention are usually good. When parents or caregivers are under continually high stress, are unable to change their behavior, or are drug abusers themselves, protecting the child from harm may be more difficult.

Parents or caregivers may poison their children through intentional or unintentional poisoning. Sometimes they are well intentioned yet misinformed. Poisioning may also intentionally be used as a form of punishment. In addition, poisoning may be the result of living in an unsafe environment.

Parents or caregivers who are using drugs and alcohol often leave their drugs within the reach of children, posing a risk of accidental ingestion. If the parent or caregiver is manufacturing illegal drugs such as methamphetamine, additional risk is posed for the child. The chemicals used in the clandestine manufacture of drugs such as methamphetamine are very toxic themselves, and furthermore, when mixed in the manufacturing process, they create dangerous chemical reactions. This increases the risk as the child may accidentally drink some of these chemicals, be burned by skin or eye exposure, inhale dangerous vapors, ingest contaminated food, or be hurt or killed in a fire or explosion.

In Munchausen's syndrome by proxy, a child maybe given a medication or chemical in an attempt to create a fictitious illness (see the section later in this chapter).

Varieties of Unintentional Poisoning

Some parents or caregivers may unintentionally poison their children by giving them toxic doses of vitamins, minerals, or herbs in an attempt to cure an illness or to ward off disease. Many indigenous cultural groups utilize traditional herbal remedies for healing. It is important to assess with the family, traditional healer, or cultural ally the reason for and usual dose of administering remedies. A possible explanation for accidental poisoning would be the attempt to substitute locally available herbs or ingredients when indigenous remedies were not available. Alternatively, a parent or caregiver might feed a baby an improperly diluted formula, resulting in either water or salt intoxication.

Supervisional neglect can result in unintentional poisonings as a result of improper storage of household chemicals such as bleach, charcoal, lighter fluid, furniture polish, or kerosene and lack of appropriate supervision resulting in the poisoning.

Varieties of Abusive Ingestion

Parents or caregivers may punish children by forcing them to ingest toxic amounts of chemicals or food. Others may give their children drugs to initiate them into the drug culture. Both practices can cause severe damage to the child, both physically and psychologically. Substances reported in this type of abuse include the following:

- Table salt is a common form of forced ingestion. The resultant hypernatremia (excess sodium in the blood), causes dehydration, seizures, and vomiting.

- Forced water ingestion is another frequently reported form of abuse. The resulting hyponatremia (a decreased amount of sodium in the blood) can lead to seizures, convulsions, confusion, lethargy, and comas. Other causes for this condition are metabolic disorders and inappropriate mixing of baby formula.

- Hot peppers and their derivatives, when force-fed to children, can damage the mucous membranes of the mouth and stomach as well as injure the nervous system.

- Ground black pepper has a powdered consistency, which can be inhaled into the lungs, leading to apnea (cessation of breathing).

- Laxative ingestion, and the resulting diarrhea, may lead to severe dehydration, fever, and bloody stools.

- Household products reported in this type of abuse include lye derivatives (toilet bowl cleaner), hydrocarbons (lighter fluid), detergents, and oil. Many of these products may be found in homes where the caregivers use them to manufacture drugs such as methamphetamine (i.e., clandestine laboratories). Ingestion or exposure to these chemicals should always prompt a thorough evaluation of the home.

- Drugs reported in abusive ingestion include anticoagulants (blood thinners), insulin, barbiturates, Quaaludes, antidepressants, sedatives, tranquilizers, and painkillers.

☐ Munchausen's Syndrome by Proxy (MSBP)

This is an abusive parenting disorder that is still frequently unrecognized in the CPS field. In 1977 Dr. Roy Meadows used the term *Munchausen's syndrome by proxy* to describe a form of child abuse in which the parent or caregiver reports a fictitious illness in his or her child after either inducing or fabricating the signs or symptoms. As a result, the child may be subjected to extensive medical tests and hospitalization. It is estimated in some medical literature that about 10% of all recognized MSBP cases have resulted in death. All of these deaths occurred in children under 3 years of age. The definition of MSBP includes the following criteria:

- An illness in a child is fabricated and/or produced by the parent or caregiver.
- The parent or parental figure persistently presents the child for treatment of an illness, often resulting in multiple medical procedures.
- There is denial by the perpetrator of knowledge as to the cause of the illness. Acute symptoms abate when the child is separated from the parent.

Boys and girls are equally reported as victims of MSBP. Although infants and toddlers are at the age of most common victimization, cases have been reported in older children. A child may develop an actual illness as a result of being subjected to the parent or caregiver maltreatment or as a result of an invasive medical investigation. Children who have been victims may develop Munchausen's syndrome or be hypochondriac adults.

The actual existence of a disease should not exclude the possible diagnosis of MSBP. Careful consideration must be given to any actual medical diagnosis the child has. The mother may view the child as vulnerable (vulnerable child syndrome) and be anxious about the child's health. For example, the case of a premature infant who almost died at birth and whose mother is always worried about the health of the child would not be considered a case of MSBP.

In almost every literature-reported case of MSBP, the perpetrator has been the mother or foster mother of the victim. The father is often distant and uninvolved with the family; often he appears completely unaware of the problem that exists. Though quite rare, fathers have been reported as perpetrators as well. The mothers are frequently:

- Intelligent and articulate, with friendly, socially adept personalities.
- Capable of forming a close but insincere rapport with the hospital staff.
- Extremely close and attentive to the child, sometimes claiming that the child will eat or take medication "only for her."
- Isolated and emotionally distant from spouse, family, and friends.

Although psychiatric treatment is recommended for these parents or caregivers, the treatment in literature-reported cases has rarely been successful and fails to produce any specific psychiatric diagnosis for the parent or caregivers. The most common condition that has been recognized is depression.

Keep in mind that *simulated* illnesses are fictitious, while *produced* illnesses are those whose symptoms really do exist. An example of the latter would be a child presenting with chronic diarrhea produced by unnatural causes, such as poisoning with laxatives.

The following guidelines are suggested in the evaluation of suspected MSBP:

- Separate the child from the mother to see if there is an occurrence of symptoms and signs in her absence. Check the relationship in time between symptoms, signs, and the presence of the suspected caregiver.
- Obtain detailed family psychosocial history and check its veracity. The suspected perpetrator's medical history should be examined for fabricated symptoms of his or her own and to determine whether he or she has ascribed to the child symptoms and signs of his or her own history.
- Engage a psychiatric consultant immediately for the suspected caregiver. This may need to be court ordered.

The primary care physician or consultant should be responsible for the review of all pertinent medical records of both the child and caregiver. Release of medical records from any reported site of medical care may need to be court ordered. It is not unusual for such a parent or caregiver to falsify records, claim they are missing or destroyed, and fail to comply with a requested voluntary release of records.

The CPS worker should obtain a social history of the child, the parent or caregiver, and immediate family. These histories should be verified, since they may be falsified or unreliable. The history should include:

- Any unusual illness or hospital admission of siblings.
- Previous psychiatric illness of the parents or caregivers.
- A list of all drugs available to the parents or caregivers.

In the decisions regarding placement of the child, the CPS/medical team will need to closely consider each case on an individual basis. In many cases, the diagnosis of MSBP is unclear or needs further detailed review of medical information. The focus should be on whether there is clear evidence that the disease or illness is fabricated, whether the child is in medical danger of serious complication or death, and whether the parent or caregiver appears to be unsafe or dangerous for the child. An initial removal of the child may allow time to assess the parents or caregivers and evaluate the success of initial intervention. Children should not return home if the perpetrator is unresponsive to treatment or denies the problem entirely. Placement in the home with the perpetrator, even under the spouse's supervision, is not generally considered a safe alternative.

Obstacles in the treatment of MSBP include the following:

- Because of general lack of knowledge of MSBP, both the medical provider and CPS worker will need to educate others, such as attorneys and courts, about this form of child abuse.
- Often the parents or caregivers will befriend the medical staff, CPS staff, attorneys, and courts. Their attempts to "charm" people into believing their innocence are often successful and can be a hindrance in the treatment of MSBP.
- In a constant search for sympathy from the medical profession or for confirmation of the child's illness, such perpetrators will often "doctor

shop," moving from hospital to hospital, sometimes even leaving the state to do so. The scattered locations of these professionals often make the collection of medical records and histories a laborious, lengthy process.

■ Child Abuse Fatalities

The death of a child as a result of abuse or neglect often represents the tragic failure of our society to identify at-risk families and to protect vulnerable children. Yet even in the most well designed and well delivered community system of child protection, children will die from abuse or neglect. Your role, and the involvement of your agency, will vary depending on state statutes, agency policy, and whether you had prior contact with the child or family. Reports involving a child fatality may also come to your attention because as a CPS worker you must assess the safety of other children who will either remain in a home or be placed out of home until an investigation is completed. CPS workers also play a crucial role in both local and state child fatality review teams.

Each year, between 1,000 and 1,200 children will die from abuse or neglect in the United States. These numbers are estimated to be unchanged in national reporting data over the last decade. Inconsistent state reporting, uninvestigated suspicious child deaths, and deaths misidentified as accidental or SIDS are factors in this number being an estimate only.

Children under 6 years old account for 85% of all child abuse deaths, and children aged 1 year and under account for 44% of all child abuse deaths, according to the 2000 U.S. Department of Health and Human Services report (2002). Most are killed by a parent or caregiver; often both parents or caregivers are responsible; and both genders of victims are equally victimized. Despite the high-profile cases in recent years, the national data reports that only 12.5% of these families had received services in the 5 years prior to the deaths, and 2.1% of these deaths occurred in foster care.

All child abuse deaths should be considered preventable. Through a multidisciplinary child fatality review process, system problems can be addressed, coordinated protocols for death investigations can be developed, and agencies can work together to both identify children at risk and prevent severe injury and death.

□ Investigation of Child Abuse Deaths

In each state an individual or agency is usually responsible for the completion of an investigation of all suspicious deaths. The professional role of the coroner/medical examiner and his or her education will vary by state and county. For example, this individual may be a physician (or have additional forensic pathology training), a mortician, a law enforcement official, or even an elected or appointed citizen with no medical training whatsoever. It is not your role to determine the medical cause of death; however, it is important to understand the mechanics of a pathologist's investigation of a child's death. A pathologist's investigation of the circumstances leading to the child's death may also provide you with clues in assessing the living conditions and environment of the child that died, the parent or caregiver, and, most important, those children who are still living in the home. An autopsy, or "post-mortem" examination, should be performed by an appropriate medical examiner, such as a forensic pathologist, on the child in every case of an unexpected or unexplained death or of suspicion of intentional injury.

The pathologist, through an autopsy, will attempt to determine if:

- There was any natural disease process which could have caused the death.
- The child has any anatomic and/or pathological finding that is not consistent with the history given by the parent or caregiver.
- The injuries are consistent with any other possible explanations.

A thorough exam would include the following:

- A meticulous examination of the external appearance, noting and photographing any bruises, abrasions, burns, or signs of blunt trauma, strangulation, malnutrition, or neglect.
- A complete post-mortem x-ray, noting any old or healing fractures, their location, age, and number. For example, fractures often seen in physical abuse, such as the metaphyseal chip fracture and rib fractures, might be seen on post-mortem x-ray.
- Cultures for various infections that might have caused the death.
- Investigation for head injuries, the most frequent cause of child abuse death in infants and young children. In the investigation the pathologist will look for fractures of the skull, any external or scalp hemorrhages, subdural hematomas, or other injuries from blunt force trauma or shaken baby syndrome.
- Investigation for chest trauma, for example, broken ribs, punctured lungs, or traumatic bleeding in the internal chest cavity.
- Investigation of gastric contents to help estimate the time of death.
- Investigation of the internal organs such as the liver, spleen, pancreas, bladder, kidney, or gastrointestinal tract for any lacerations or bruises caused by blows to the abdomen.
- Investigation of sexual abuse, including examination for signs of trauma and possibly forensic evidence kit collection.
- Analysis for signs of starvation or malnutrition, including testing of blood components such as electrolytes, urea nitrogen, creatinine, and glucose. When a finding of starvation is expected, the doctor will need to investigate the child's previous medical records to look at growth patterns prior to illness or death. Analysis is made of body fluids or tissues for the presence of drugs or toxic substances.

It is important to understand what the final autopsy report means to the investigation. National standards for the death certificate exist and are reported to the county and state health departments to track these vital statistics. The coroner or medical examiner will dictate a report of an autopsy and its findings. The cause and manner of death will be listed in the report and on the death certificate.

The cause of death is defined as the chain of events or disease process that led to the death. For example, cause of death in a child could be sudden unexplained cardiac failure, pneumonia, blood infection, complications of leukemia, extreme prematurity, brain swelling due to blunt force trauma, or SIDS. The cause will list some specifics about the chain of events leading to the final determination of the manner of death.

The manner of death is defined as the circumstances of the death. These are *natural, suicide, homicide, accidental*, or *undetermined*. For example, for a 4-month-old baby who dies from abusive head injury, the cause could be listed as "subdural hematoma, brain edema and herniation from brain trauma" and the manner as "homicide." For a murdered, battered child, cause might be listed as "multiple contusions, fractures, and liver laceration from blunt force trauma."

Often, however, deaths that may be related to neglect are not recognized as such, and the worker investigating may still need to address family issues. For example, the case of a toddler who is left home alone by the parent or caregiver and starts a fire and dies of smoke inhalation would be considered a case of neglect.

☐ Sudden Infant Death Syndrome (SIDS)

The cause of SIDS is still unknown, and research is being performed to try to discover it. Most infants who die of SIDS are under 1 year old, and the majority of those are under 6 months old.

The usual presentation is that a previously healthy infant is fed or bathed, put to bed, and later found dead. There may be foamy discharge in the infant's mouth or nose, and if the infant has been dead overnight, lividity and rigor (dependent pooling of blood and stiffness) may be present. An autopsy may be completely normal or show petechiae in the lungs or heart tissue. There is usually no other autopsy finding. The autopsy findings in suffocation deaths can be identical. A physical exam or autopsy exam that shows physical trauma, signs of neglect or malnutrition, or other disease immediately excludes the diagnosis of SIDS.

The evaluation of SIDS must include a scene investigation, complete medical and social history. The family investigation must not indicate or identify risk factors for abuse. The coroner or medical examiner may call the CPS worker to inquire if any such information exists regarding the family and children in the home.

The family of a SIDS infant needs immediate support services and grief counseling. Families should not be confronted with the fact that child abuse needs to be ruled out. A coroner protocol may exist in the county or state, and you need to be familiar with the local or state SIDS investigation protocol.

The incidence of SIDS has been decreasing in the United States in the past decade. The "Back to Sleep Campaign" of the American Academy of Pediatrics has directed education efforts during primary care about placing infants to sleep on their back. There has been a demonstrated decrease in SIDS incidence rates with this campaign. Current research is still looking at why SIDS may occur more frequently in infants who are placed on their stomachs and if other environmental factors are involved. This is important to remember, as some families may have limited access to primary care and may not receive this SIDS education.

■ Child Sexual Abuse

In most states, the legal definition of the sexual molestation of a child is typically defined as *an act of a person (adult or child) that forces, coerces, or threatens a child to have any form of sexual contact or to engage in any type of sexual activity at his or her direction*. This includes inappropriate touching of genitalia, buttocks, or breasts (clothed or unclothed), oral-genital contact, penetration using any body part or an object, and forcing sexual activity between children for the sexual gratification of the perpetrator.

Statutes vary from state to state regarding definitions of sexual offenses, but the guiding principles are usually the age of the victim who cannot developmentally and/or legally consent to sexual activity, the perpetrator's abuse of power and/or authority over the child, and often the age difference between the victim and perpetrator. *Incest* offenses include both biological and nonbiological relatives of a child (stepparent or adoptive parent) and clearly violate the social taboos of family roles.

Statutory rape laws also vary by state but refer to a legal-age adult engaging in sexual relationship with a minor, regardless of that minor's ability to consent. For example a 35-year-old male having a relationship with a 14-year-old is considered statutory rape or assault regardless of the adolescent having consented to sex.

Some circumstances serve to aggravate a sexual offense in criminal codes—for example habitual offending, kidnapping, physical assault, or torture. Federal laws also address transmitting and receiving child pornography. *Sexual exploitation* includes asking a child to view, to read, or to pose for pornographic materials or engaging a child in prostitution. The development of computer technology and the Internet has led to an alarming growth in the sexual exploitation of children both in the United States and internationally.

☐ The Incidence of Child Sexual Abuse

The number of reports for child sexual abuse increased steadily in the late 1980s and early 1990s but in the past several years has declined slowly but steadily. The most recent data from the U.S. Department of Health and Human Services (2002) show that the incidence rates for child sexual abuse declined steadily between 1995 and 1999. In 1999, only 11.3% of all confirmed victims of child abuse were reported as child sexual abuse. The reasons for the decline are being researched but may point to both better prevention and education efforts or possibly to a relaxation in reporting of cases. In general, it must be emphasized that it is still true that more children will be sexually abused by persons known to them in positions of trust or by relatives than by strangers.

☐ Physical Examination for Child Sexual Abuse

When a child shows either behavioral or physical symptoms of sexual abuse, he or she should have a complete physical and genital examination from an experienced examiner. Many parents and caregivers do not realize that the pediatric genital and anal examination for sexual abuse is very different from that performed on adults either for routine healthcare or for sexual assault. For example, only in rare cases will the medical provider use a speculum or perform an internal examination, as is done in adult cases or sexual assault.

You should remember that a hospital emergency department, adult medicine physician, or obstetrician-gynecologist may not have pediatric training or experience with children in general and may have little or no training in the evaluation for child sexual abuse. The medical providers who are best qualified to perform such evaluations include pediatricians, child health associate–physician assistants (CHA-PAs), pediatric nurse practitioners (PNPs), sexual assault nurse examiners (SANEs), and physicians or nurses who have had forensic training in sexual assault evaluation or child abuse medical fellowship training. Finally, the evaluation of child sexual abuse is not simply an exam. It includes knowledge of child development, how to interview a child correctly, and the examiner having both the comfort level and the sensitivity to address the crisis of child sexual abuse with both the victim and the supporting family member or legal guardian.

If the abuse or assault has occurred or may have occurred within the past 48 to 72 hours and there is a disclosure or allegation of possible penetration or ejaculation by a perpetrator, the child should be seen immediately. Preferably, the child or adolescent should not bathe, change clothes, brush teeth, gargle, or use the bathroom before examination. The majority of cases reported to human services will not be acute rape or assault, however, and most such cases will present to a medical facility, physician, or police department.

The reasons for this 48- to 72-hour time frame for acute sexual assault examination are important to understand. Forensic evidence kit collection may need to be completed. These kits will collect swab specimens from the skin externally, and from the vaginal, anal, and oral cavities internally, and will collect samples of saliva, hair, and blood from the victim. These can be used to identify a possible perpetrator and to show that any foreign hair, saliva, semen, blood, or other DNA evidence deposited during an assault is from that assailant and not the victim. Many steps may not be needed with child victims (for example, pubic hair cannot be collected from a very young child, who does not have any yet), and several steps that involve swabs may be uncomfortable to a child. This is why an experienced pediatric examiner is best qualified to evaluate these cases.

Documentation of acute trauma to the genital and anal areas should also occur within this time frame, as these areas of the body may heal quickly, especially when minor trauma such as a bruise, an abrasion, or redness may be the only finding.

In the older child and adolescent, issues of sexually transmitted disease testing and treatment, HIV prophylaxis, and pregnancy prevention counseling, in the setting of acute assault with transmission of blood or semen, may need to be addressed in this period of time.

If the child has pain, bleeding, or discharge from the urethra, vagina, or rectum; painful urination (dysuria); painful defecation; obvious bruises, lacerations, or abrasions externally on or near these parts of the body; or if the child complains of pain when walking or sitting, the child should be examined immediately.

Children who have been abused weeks or months earlier should be examined when and where they can be seen by an experienced examiner, preferably within a few days. These children should have a forensic interview by an experienced interviewer prior to the examination to get the best possible understanding of the nature of the abuse, as this may also direct the physician's examination. For example, a child disclosing chronic penetration with ejaculate contact may need a sexually transmitted disease workup, while a child disclosing fondling and exploitation with pornography may not need such testing.

Children with repeated complaints of abdominal pain, urinary tract infections, genital rashes, or vaginal irritation or infection, with no other symptoms, should be considered as possible sexual abuse victims. They may need both an interview and physical examination as soon as possible.

☐ Behavioral Changes Indicating Child Sexual Abuse

The first indicators of sexual abuse may be not physical signs or complaints but behavioral changes or abnormalities. These are different at various ages and are not necessarily seen just in sexually abused children, and the absence of any or all of them does not rule out sexual abuse.

A knowledge of general child development should guide the worker when behavioral or emotional symptoms are either reported or directly observed. Normal sexual behavior, like other behaviors and developmental milestones, occurs at predictable ages. Children under age 3 will have normal self-exploration of private parts and discovering of the genital area. Preschool-age children will become playfully curious about peers, and gender differences will be discovered through curiosity and "playing doctor." School-age children will become modest about their bodies and learn to respect others' privacy and modesty. Preadolescent children will have a period of disinterest in the opposite sex, establishing stronger same-sex peer relationships. Adolescents will strive to develop healthy self-image and self-esteem, closely tied to their interests in developing socially acceptable friendships, relationships, and partner intimacy.

Key concepts to remember in evaluating sexualized behaviors in children include the following. Who initiated the behavior and how it was initiated (with playful curiosity or mutual consent versus with one child being aggressive and controlling)? Is there secrecy that is coerced or threatened? Are there threats of or actual physical harm? Is the behavior itself exploratory or is it graphic in nature (are the children looking at private parts or are they simulating an adult sexual act)? Is there language or drawing that suggests adult knowledge or graphic exposures?

Today's society, with an ever-present emphasis on sex and with frequent images of sexuality, exposes children and adolescents to an increasingly aggressive and easily accessible amount of sexualized material and may suggest to them the need to reach an earlier age of sexual awareness. With peer pressure, adolescent risky behavior and experimentation, and lack of parental or family guidance, children may be at risk for earlier sexualized activity or for victimization. Questions about what children are exposed to in the home, in school, and in their community should be asked when evaluating children who display developmentally age-inappropriate sexual knowledge or behaviors for sexual abuse.

The following behavioral symptoms have been observed in sexually abused children.

- *Toddlers and young children (ages 2 to 5):*

  Fear of a particular person or place.

  Regression to earlier forms of behavior such as bed wetting, stranger anxiety, separation anxiety, thumb sucking, baby talk, whining, fear of abandonment, and clinginess.

  Sexualized behaviors with other children.

  Unusual mood swings, temperament changes, excessive sadness, or loss of interest in age-appropriate activities.

  Feelings or expressions of shame, low self-esteem, or guilt.

  Excessive masturbation.

  Cruelty to animals.

  Fire setting.

- *Children ages 6 to 8.* Any of the preceding symptoms or changes and/or:

  Nightmares and other sleep disturbances.

  Sexualized behaviors with other children or directed toward adults.

  Sexually inappropriate or graphic language or drawings.

  Phobias about specific school or community activities, places, or people.

  Withdrawal from family and friends and previously enjoyed activities

  Regressive behaviors.

  Eating disturbances.

  Physical complaints such as abdominal pain or urinary or bowel difficulties.

- *Preadolescents (10 to 12 years).* Any of the preceding symptoms or changes and/or:

  Depression, anxiety, mood swings, unusual anger or aggression.

  Poor school performance.

  Promiscuity.

  Pregnancy.

  Use of illegal drugs or alcohol.

  Fear that the abuse will recur (posttraumatic stress disorder symptoms).

Eating disturbances or disorder such as anorexia.

Suicidal thoughts, gestures, or attempt.

- *Early adolescents (13 to 15 years).* Any of the preceding symptoms or changes and/or:

Running away from home.

Depression.

Promiscuity or prostitution.

Recurrent physical complaints.

School truancy.

Anger and rage about being forced into a situation beyond one's control or with attempted disciplinary action by a parent or caregiver.

☐ History

When requesting an examination for child sexual abuse, the following history provided to the physician or nurse is helpful. *Any information about the alleged or disclosed assault obtained by you, police, a witness, parent, caregiver, or guardian may be helpful, so inform the examiners that you have information and would like to share it with them.*

- What history has been provided to you by the child or guardian that raises concern about sexual abuse? Has the child or guardian reported genital or anal pain? Has there been any genital or anal bleeding or discharge? Has there been any difficulty or pain reported with urination or defecation? Has someone seen a rash, bruises, or other trauma to the genital, anal, or surrounding areas? Has there also been a physical assault to the child? Has the child's behavior been abnormal?

- In what way was the child sexually abused? What type of contact has been alleged or disclosed? (Oral-genital; genital-genital or genital-anal contact; digital, genital, or object penetration of any part of body?) Was there ejaculation? Was a condom used? Was there any evidence at the site of the assault that you have been informed of by police such as blood, semen, lubricants, illegal drugs, or alcohol? Did the child or adolescent report having been given anything to eat or drink that made him or her sleepy or incoherent?

- What did the child say in a forensic interview with you, therapist, or police?

- When was the last suspected incidence? Is this an acute assault within the last 48 to 72 hours or is this a remote or chronic event? Has the child been sexually abused in the past? When, how, and by whom? If there is a history of sexual abuse, has the child and/or family been in counseling for this abuse? With whom and has therapy been helpful? Are there new disclosures or concerns discovered during therapy?

- Is there anyone that you know of in the family's living environment who currently has, or previously had, a sexually transmitted disease? Has anyone in the child's family or living environment been sexually abused?
- Has the child ever been examined for any type of child abuse or neglect?
- Is the parent or caregiver applying any ointments or creams to the child's genitals and is this a prescribed or required medication?
- Is the child toilet trained? Does the child wipe herself or need assistance? What is the bath and hygiene routine in the child's family, living environment, and childcare setting?
- If there is concern of an offending parent, caregiver, or companion of parent, is the other parent protective and supportive of the child? Is there any concern of false allegation through the parent or caregiver or coaching of the child? Is there a custody dispute complicating or precipitating the investigation or concern of sexual abuse?
- Were there any witnesses to the abuse?

☐ Physical Exam

During the physical exam, the child may want to have you, the mother, or another person who has a close relationship with the child to remain in the examining room. Your presence may not only help calm the child but may also allow you to hear firsthand the physician's interview and any immediate findings. Depending on the age and gender of the child, the presence of the opposite gender parent might be uncomfortable for the child. It is never appropriate to have a suspected offending parent or caregiver present for a sexual abuse evaluation or examination of a child.

Do not expect to always leave the examination knowing for certain if a child has been sexually abused. The majority of sexually abused children have normal findings on their genital exams. A normal physical exam and negative laboratory results do not rule out the possibility of sexual abuse. The child's delayed disclosure may have allowed for healing of past trauma if it was present, or the child may have been sexually abused in such a manner as to not leave physical trauma (fondling, oral contact, exploitation). *The child's disclosure in the context of the medical examination, interview, or therapy becomes the most important aspect of the overall evaluation for sexual abuse.*

The physician should begin with a general physical examination of the child. The physician should strive to make the genital exam as nontraumatic as possible by taking plenty of time to explain each step. In cases in which the child seems excessively fearful of the exam or has already been severely traumatized, or if acute trauma is present that needs urgent examination and treatment, the physician may need to sedate the child.

☐ Examination for Forensic Evidence

If a child has been sexually abused within the past 48 to 72 hours, the physician will look for signs of both physical trauma to the child's body and sexual trauma to the child's oral, genital, and anal areas. Procedures include the following:

- In appropriate cases the examiner will use a cotton-tipped swab to obtain specimens from the skin, mouth, genital area, vagina, and anus of the victim.

- The doctor may pass an ultraviolet light, called a Wood's lamp, over the child's clothing and body. Substances, which fluoresce a green color under this light, may indicate seminal fluid and will be collected for analysis.

- The doctor may obtain specimens from the vagina, mouth, and rectum when indicated, for examination under a microscope, to detect the presence of motile or nonmotile spermatozoa (sperm).

- If ejaculation is suspected or confirmed by history, the physician will collect specimens from the mouth, skin, vagina, or anus for a forensic lab to analyze for sperm or semen fluid chemicals such as acid phosphatase and P30 glycoprotein from the male prostate gland. Other laboratory tests such as hair and fiber analysis, and blood type (ABO typing) and DNA typing of body fluids, may also help determine the identity of the assailant. These will not be recovered if the assailant wore a condom.

- Hair may be pulled—not cut—from a victim's head and pubic area to identify hair from an assailant by comparing with the victim's hair. This is painful and is usually done as a last step in the process of the forensic kit. In many children who have not started puberty, there will of course be no pubic hair to collect.

Rape Kit. From A. P. Giardino, M. A. Finkel, E. R. Giardino, T. Seidl, & S. Ludwig, *A Practical Guide to the Evaluation of Sexual Abuse in the Prepubertal Child* (p. 77). Thousand Oaks, CA: Sage Publications. Copyright 1992 by Sage Publications. Reprinted with permission.

- Blood is drawn and saliva samples are obtained for the kit for ABO blood typing. Many adults secrete the protein of their blood type in saliva, and this may identify a perpetrator.

It should be cautioned that for most cases of sexual abuse of children, even when acute in a 48- to 72-hour period, a forensic evidence kit collection might not be warranted. Such collection may be requested inappropriately by uneducated police officers who conceive of "evidence" as being the same for both adults and children. Inappropriate collection of such kits may be traumatizing and painful to a child.

Multiple swabs are obtained so that the lab has them in storage if a specimen is needed for repeat analysis or is requested by a defense attorney representing an identified perpetrator and they want repeat, independent testing.

Finally, there may be evidence at a scene of an assault that could recover forensic evidence, such as semen on sheets or towels, blood evidence, or other material, objects, or surroundings described by the victim, that could confirm the assault.

In every examination the physician will look for physical trauma to the genital and anal areas, test for sexually transmitted diseases (STDs) if indicated, and test for pregnancy when appropriate. Often bloodwork is needed for bloodborne STDs. Chemistry tests may be needed as baseline function tests—for example, liver enzymes—as medications for HIV may have side effects that are monitored by these tests.

The young child is often most comfortable when examined seated in someone's lap, with knees apart (the "supine frog-leg" position). Another position may be the "knee-chest" position, in which the child rests one side of her head on her folded arms and supports her weight on her bent knees and buttocks are pointed upward. This position is helpful for the examiner to visualize the posterior parts of the hymen tissue and the anus. It is, however, difficult at times to sustain, and some children may have been assaulted in this position (from behind). Careful monitoring of the child's affect and emotional state by the examiner and the support person is important.

The physician will examine the vagina and anus for signs of acute, healing, or chronic trauma and for signs of STD. Areas of tissue disruption, scarring, or absence of hymen tissue will be indicative of abuse trauma. Assessment of the condition of the hymen, the size of the hymenal ring, and the condition of the vaginal introitus (the vaginal opening) should be described in a medical report. The actual diameter of the hymenal opening is not as important as previously hypothesized in the medical literature. What is more important is the appearance of the tissue, its amount and distribution, and if there is any disruption in the hymen and surrounding tissues.

☐ Examination of Female Genitalia

In relation to the female genitalia, the exam covers the following:

- *Cervix.* The lower portion, or "neck," of the uteruan internal structure should be examined in adolescent and adult sexual assault victims.

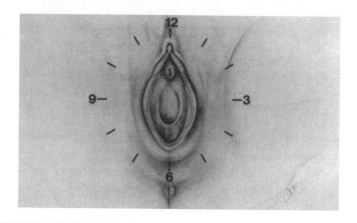

Female Genitalia, Clock Orientation with Patient in Frog-Leg Supine Position. From A. P. Giardino, M. A. Finkel, E. R. Giardino, T. Seidl, & S. Ludwig, *A Practical Guide to the Evaluation of Sexual Abuse in the Prepubertal Child* (p. 33). Thousand Oaks, CA: Sage Publications. Copyright 1992 by Sage Publications. Reprinted with permission.

External Structures of the Female Genitalia. From A. P. Giardino, M. A. Finkel, E. R. Giardino, T. Seidl, & S. Ludwig, *A Practical Guide to the Evaluation of Sexual Abuse in the Prepubertal Child* (p. 32). Thousand Oaks, CA: Sage Publications. Copyright 1992 by Sage Publications. Adapted with permission.

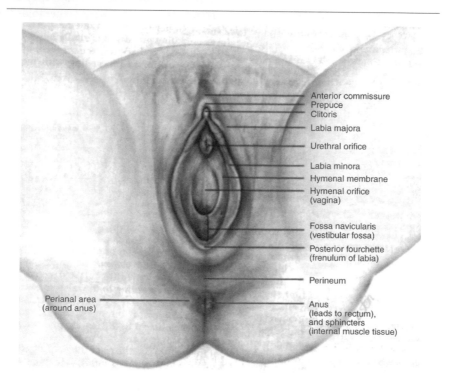

- *Clitoris.* The highly sensitive, erectile organ of the female vulva. Children will also masturbate by touching this area.
- *Hymen.* The membrane that partially surrounds the vaginal opening. The physician will look for any unusual injuries or scars, attempting to differentiate what may be a naturally occurring variation (normal variant finding like a tag or cleft) from those caused by child sexual abuse trauma. Accidental injuries to this internal ring of tissue are extremely uncommon and usually involve penetration or an impaling trauma. The hymen is *not* injured by horseback riding, straddle accidents that usually cause anterior and external trauma to the genitalia, or tampon use in adolescents.
- *Labia.* Folds of skin, or "lips," that surround the hymen and the vaginal opening. The labia minora are the smaller, more internal folds that directly surround the hymen and vaginal opening. In young girls these are completely hidden by the larger, more external labia majora.
- *Perineum.* A general term referring to the area between the male or female genitalia and the anus, along with the surrounding area.
- *Vaginal introitus.* The vaginal opening. Beyond the opening is the *vaginal canal.* In children or adolescents who have not had penetration or sexual intercourse, the vaginal introitus is partially covered by the hymen, which usually has a central, oval or crescent-shaped opening.

Tears occurring from attempted or completed penile penetration often occur in the posterior part of the hymen or introitus, between the three and the nine o'clock position, most often in the midline six o' clock position.

The physician will examine the width of the hymenal ring and vaginal opening. Some literature has suggested that transverse measurements exceeding 4 millimeters in children less than 10 years of age are highly suggestive of abuse; however, this standard is no longer considered valid. No measurement of hymenal opening size should be used to diagnose or rule out sexual abuse. Use of such a limited and highly variable (with age and patient size, as well as examiner technique) examination finding has not been supported by the latest medical literature. It also gives a false sense of reliability in the finding, as many children are sexually abused in ways that do not traumatize the hymen.

- *Vulva.* The female external genitalia.
- *Urethral orifice.* The opening of the urethra, which connects the bladder to the external genitalia, through which the child urinates.

☐ **Male Genitalia**

In relation to the male genitalia, the exam covers the following:

- *Glans penis.* The cone-shaped head of the penis, which contains the urethral orifice, or the opening through which the child urinates.
- *Testis.* The reproductive glands located under the penis (the plural is *testes* or *testicles*), enclosed in a sac-like pouch of skin called the scrotum. Boys

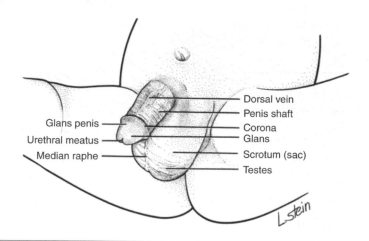

External Structure of the Male, Circumcised. From A. P. Giardino, M. A. Finkel, E. R. Giardino, T. Seidl, & S. Ludwig, *A Practical Guide to the Evaluation of Sexual Abuse in the Prepubertal Child* (p. 33) Thousand Oaks, CA: Sage Publications. Copyright 1992 by Sage Publications. Adapted with permission.

begin to make active sperm and seminal fluid in early adolescence after puberty begins. Ejaculation can occur before active sperm are made, however, and the beginning of and progression through puberty is genetic, race, and age dependent.

- *Penis shaft.* The shaft of the penis contains the urethra and the erectile tissue that engorges with blood to become erect. This erectile tissue functions even in infancy and throughout childhood. Redness, bruises, "hickeys," and cuts on the shaft or glans of a boy's penis may indicate forceful sucking by a perpetrator—the sexual act called fellatio. Bite marks, ligature marks, and bruises from pinching can be seen resulting from assault or from discipline of young boys by an angry caregiver. Bruises or chafing may also occur from excessive handling of the shaft of the penis. Bruises are not normally seen as a result of masturbation, which can however cause chafing to the penile skin if lubricant is not used.

- Boys should also be tested for sexually transmitted disease if any discharge from the urethral opening is noted by the examiner or if symptoms are reported by the child.

☐ Trauma to the Anus and Rectum

Current literature suggests that boys and girls are at similar risks for this type of abuse, although the literature supports the finding that boys will often disclose sexual abuse much later than girls. Male victims report shame and sexual identity concerns as a result of sexual abuse.

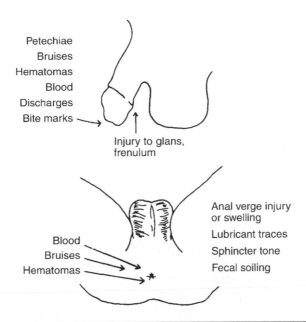

Male Genitalia Trauma.

The degree of injury caused by anal penetration depends on many factors, including the size of the penetrating object, the amount of force used in the incident, the use of lubricant, and the frequency of penetration. Once the abuse has stopped, the gross physical signs of trauma can heal fairly quickly, within days or weeks. The genital and anal areas are mucous membranes with a blood supply and tissue type that allows for rapid healing of minor traumas such as abrasions, small cuts or lacerations, or areas of chafed tissues. Chronic penetrating trauma to either the anus or the hymen and vaginal area in a prepubertal child may leave diagnostic findings of sexual abuse, mainly the absence of healthy appearing tissue, development of scar tissue, or change in tone of the anus.

The following terms are often used in describing the anal exam:

- *Anal verge.* The skin surrounding the anus. The *anal rugae* are the puckered folds of tissue that give the anus the starburst appearance on external examination. Flattened or smoothed rugae may indicate repeated anal penetration.
- *Anal sphincter.* The circular muscles that closes the anus. There is one external and one internal sphincter.
- *Perianal region.* The region around and close to the anus.
- *Rectal canal.* The end portion of the large intestine; its external opening is the anus through which defecation occurs.

Depending on the size of the child, the size of penetrating object, the amount of force, and the use of lubricant, injury following penetration may vary from small cuts or bruises to actual tears of the perianal skin, rectal canal, or anal sphincter.

Fissures or lacerations around or in the anal canal may be caused by fingers, a penis, or foreign bodies inserted into the anus.

Penile penetration may cause anal hematomas, swellings, or collections of blood in the anal tissue. When anal injuries heal, they may leave anal tags, small flaps of skin on the anus. Anal tags may also occur naturally, usually in the midline at twelve or six o'clock, and may not be an indicator of abuse.

Another frequent indicator of penetration is anal dilatation, an expansion or stretching of the anus. Immediately following abuse the anal sphincter may spasm, causing the opening to become very small and tight. In cases of repeated penetration, the anal sphincter may lose its tone, or ability to close properly. In the relaxed state, the anal opening may appear lax or loose, or excessively large, causing the child to unintentionally soil underwear. Sexual abuse is one cause of childhood encopresis. This may lead to itching, irritation, and poor hygiene.

"Reflex anal dilatation," or an opening of the anus after stimulation of the surrounding skin, has been reported as a sign of sexual abuse. Some investigators have reported seeing this in cases of chronic constipation, so its finding on physical examination alone is not indicative of sexual abuse.

Occasionally children may suffer unintentional trauma to the perineum or the anus through play or from sitting on sharp objects. The history should clearly reveal this unusual form of trauma, and in a nonverbal child, sexual abuse trauma should still be considered. Finally, physical abuse trauma to the genitals and anal area can also occur, often when a caregiver is angered by a toileting accident and injures the child intentionally.

☐   Differential Diagnosis

Medical conditions or illnesses, including the following, can cause changes in the genital or anal areas or cause symptoms that can be mistaken for sexual abuse. A careful medical history should be obtained by the physician.

- Severe constipation with the passage of a very large bowel movement can create fissures in the anus. The parent or caregiver and/or child can usually give a clear history of this problem.

- Children with excessive diarrhea may present with swelling, redness, or chapping in the perianal and genital area.

- Vulvovaginal irritations—from lack of proper hygiene, bubble bath and lotions, or allergy or reaction to nylon in underwear—are all frequent causes of irritation and itching in the genital and anal areas.

- Children may contract a parasite known as "pinworms." These small white worms live in the upper part of the large intestine, and the females lay their eggs on the skin surrounding the anus. Their movements cause itching, and the child usually scratches, causing irritation, redness, or swelling. Often a piece of tape on the anus attracts the eggs (the "scotch tape test") and oral medication clears the infection.

☐ Accidental Genital or Perineal Trauma

In all children, this type of injury is often very painful and frightening. In such situations most parents or caregivers will not hesitate to bring the child immediately to a physician or the emergency room, providing unsolicited, detailed explanations of the injuries.

Straddle injuries resulting from horseback riding, gymnastics, monkey bar trauma, rope climbing in gym class, bicycle bars, or sometimes climbing naked over the side of a tub are not uncommon. These injuries do not cause trauma to the internal hymen tissue or the anus. Accidental penetrating trauma to these areas is uncommon but does occur and has a clear history and usually no delay in care, as it is painful and may cause bleeding. For example, a toddler falls backward and straddles a plastic toy protruding in the tub at bath time. In these cases, just as in all cases of suspected abuse, you should consider the developmental maturity of the child, the time elapsed before treatment, and the compatibility of the history and injury.

☐ Examination Tools

The physician may use various magnifying instruments and examination techniques in his examination of the child, the most common of which include the following:

- An *otoscope* is a small instrument commonly used to examine the ears; it may be used to magnify and illuminate the genitalia as well.
- The *coloposcope* is like a set of binoculars mounted on a stand. It does not touch the child. It provides a magnified and illuminated view of the genitalia; it is used to detect extremely small injuries, and to magnify the often very small area being examined. Often there are findings not seen with the naked eye. This instrument can be equipped with cameras, which can produce magnified photographs, slides, or a video of the genital and anal examination. Some colposcopes now can take digital images and store them in a secure computer attached to the instrument.
- Another technique used in detecting small tears of the anal and genital areas is the use of a dye called *toluidine blue*. When the dye is swabbed onto the vulva or anal areas, small, previously unnoticed lesions appear as darker, deeply stained regions.

☐ Vaginal Discharge, Infection, or Irritation

The presence of vaginal discharge in the preadolescent girl usually suggests infection, irritation, or a sexually transmitted disease. The physician may refer to irritation as vulvovaginitis or vaginitis, meaning inflammation of the vagina and surrounding vulva area. The cause of the vaginitis can be nonsexual infections such as group A streptococcus, or irritations from chemicals or soaps and bubble baths, as well as sexually transmitted disease.

Normal discharges. Most newborn baby girls will experience a vaginal discharge, possibly with traces of blood, during the newborn period. This is the result of stimulation of the infant's vaginal mucosa by the mother's estrogen. It should disappear within 7 to 10 days. One other instance of normal preadolescent discharge occurs in the months just prior to menarche (the beginning of menstruation). Once a girl has reached adolescence, a small amount of gray-white, non-foul-smelling discharge is normal and healthy.

Vaginal discharge due to nonspecific infections. Most cases of nonspecific vulvovaginitis result from poor genital hygiene. One of the most frequent causes of infection in children is back-to-front wiping, which causes fecal contamination of the vagina.

Other common causes of irritation and discharge are chemicals, clothing, or cosmetics. Soap products used in both bathing and laundry may cause irritation, as may bubble bath and perfumes. In the older adolescent, douches and "feminine hygiene deodorants" may cause a similar problem. Noncotton underwear, as well as tight-fitting jeans, pantyhose, tights, ballet leotards, rubber pants, disposable diapers, or sanitary pads may all have a similar effect.

Foreign bodies may be the cause of vaginal irritation in a child, and are often accompanied by a persistent, sometimes bloody, foul-smelling discharge. The most common foreign body is a piece of toilet tissue. Very young children may innocently insert objects like a penny or a tiny toy in the area, just as they would place something in the nose. However, as children get older, insertion of objects into the vagina or anus should prompt concern for sexual abuse. Children do not masturbate or seek pleasurable sensation from insertion of objects, and this may be a sign of an event that was witnessed or perpetrated.

Specific infections that are not sexually transmitted. These usually arise from a previously existing infection located elsewhere. These can be either from an illness or from naturally occurring bacteria. Common infections include the following:

- *Parasites.* Pinworms, for example, are small white worms that live in the large intestine and lay their eggs on the perianal skin. Sometimes worms may actually be recovered from the vagina.
- Bacterial inoculation from the gastrointestinal tract. For example, salmonella, shigella, and E. coli from the child's intestinal tract or anus.
- Bacterial inoculation from the respiratory tract, such as group A streptococcus.
- Bacterial inoculation from the skin, such as *Staphylococcus aureus.*
- Fungal infections such as *Candida albicans* (common yeast infection).

☐ Sexually Transmitted Diseases

In some cases of suspected sexual abuse, the physician will assess the child for such diseases. The guiding principles to remember in determining the need for STD assessment in the sexually abused child are:

- The type of sexual abuse involving genital or anal contact that is alleged or disclosed.
- The presence of acute trauma on examination.
- The presence of any complaints or symptoms that may indicate an infection.

- Contact with ejaculate, particularly with the mouth, vagina, anus, and any open area of trauma or wound.
- The risk of an STD in the perpetrator such as promiscuity, bisexual or homosexual activity, intravenous drug use, and the current presence or past diagnosis of an STD.
- The risk of a preexisting infection or illness in an older child or adolescent that could predispose to STD infection.
- The epidemiology and presence of an STD in the child's living environment or community.

In addition to these, parental anxiety about STD, especially hepatitis and AIDS, may be an indication for the physician to test a child even if not medically indicated and the child is at low risk.

Cultures may be obtained from the vagina, the rectum, penis, and/or throat, depending on disclosure, reported symptoms, or exam findings.

It is important to realize that many diseases can be transmitted both sexually and nonsexually. Mothers may pass infections to their children by placental blood transfer, as in the case of syphilis, hepatitis B and C, or HIV infections, or by passage through the birth canal. The actual passage through the birth canal transmits diseases such as herpes type 2, gonorrhea, chlamydia, and human papilloma virus (HPV). Infants delivered through a Ceasarean section should not contract these diseases from the mother.

In rare cases, a disease may be transferred through *fomites*, that is, objects such as toilet seats, washcloths, or water. Some diseases may be innocently transferred from one person's hands to the vagina, anus, or mouth of another. Studies are clear on which specific infections can and cannot be transmitted in this way.

The presence of a sexually transmitted disease in the preadolescent child and beyond the immediate newborn period is highly indicative of sexual abuse. However, the physician must also consider other modes of transmission in certain infections.

In some cases, it is helpful to know the *incubation time* of a particular organism. This refers to the amount of time that elapses between the child's first contact with a bacterium or virus and its initial appearance with either symptoms or examination findings. For example, a child who has been sexually abused the day before her exam may have a negative culture for a bacterial or viral STD that has an incubation period of 3 days or 2 weeks. The physician may want to reculture a child who initially has a negative culture for any STD or give prophylaxis (preventive) antibiotic therapy for certain diseases, more commonly in adolescents who report vaginal rape.

The main types of STD include the following:

Chlamydia trachomatis. This bacterial STD can cause pelvic inflammatory disease and/or lifelong infertility if not treated. Children or adolescents with this disease should also be tested for gonorrhea and *Trichonomas vaginalis*. Doctors may test for this disease with immunologic tests or chlamydial cultures. The latter is preferred in sexual abuse cases, since some immunologic tests have been shown to have some false positive results, particularly from the rectum. Newer DNA amplification tests, identifying bacterial DNA from a tissue swab, have been developed for both chlamydia and gonorrhea, with nearly equal ability to accurately detect the organism without these false positives. Cultures are still considered the "gold standard" until studies are completed comparing the performance of these new techniques with cultures.

Incubation is 1 to 2 weeks. Transmission can occur as a baby is born through the birth canal of an infected mother. Chlamydia can cause eye infections and pneumonia in newborns. Infants and very young children under 1 year of age can carry the organism (be "colonized") in the throat, vagina, and rectum with or without becoming symptomatic.

This STD in children and adolescents is always considered to be sexually transmitted. No cases have been reported of transmission via fomites.

Human papilloma virus (HPV), or Condyloma acuminata. This virus causes venereal warts, which can appear as either flat fleshy or cauliflower-like lesions, either singly or in clusters, in the anorectal, perineal, or genital regions. The warts can also appear in the larynx, pharynx, or mouth. Certain types of HPV cause hand and foot warts, while other types cause genital and anal warts. These types are identified by numbers and genetic typing in a lab. The genital types have been associated with abnormal PAP smears and cervical cancer in women, but there are no studies yet to determine if the presence of HPV in a child will lead to any predisposition to cancer later in life.

Incubation time is 6 weeks to 1 year or up to 2 years. Therefore, the current general recommendation is that any child under 3 years may have contracted HPV from the birth canal, and that any newly identified warts in a child over 3 years of age warrants a screen for sexual abuse risk factors, and possibly for other STD. Any child old enough to be interviewed should have this screen completed as well. Medical records of the child and mother should be reviewed by a physician in order to investigate whether a lesion was noted previously that could have been a wart or if the mother has a history of HPV or abnormal PAP smears.

Transmission can occur through vaginal births, sexual encounters, or close but nonsexual encounters from the hands to the mouth, genital, or anal region.

Treatment is removal with chemical topical medications, freezing, or surgical excision. Removal is indicated when a large number complicate hygiene, cause discomfort, or are internal in the vaginal or anal canal. Warts have a high recurrence rate after removal. Treatment is usually done by a pediatrician or dermatologist.

Gardnerella vaginalis. This STD is usually accompanied by a white, gray, or yellow malodorous discharge. It does not appear frequently in non–sexually abused prepubescent children. Its presence in the prepubertal child should raise suspicion of sexual abuse. It is diagnosed by the positive "whiff test," where a positive fishy odor is given off when a swab of discharge is treated with a few drops of potassium hydroxide. The infection is treated with a short course of antibiotics.

Herpes simplex virus (HSV). Genital herpes is caused by herpes simplex virus and is one of the most frequently diagnosed STDs in adolescents and adults. Painful blister lesions (vesicles) develop on the genitalia, anus, or mucous membranes of the mouth. The disease may be confused with chicken pox or shingles.

Incubation is 2 to 20 days, with an average of 6 days. Herpes simplex type 2 is the common genital infection, and type 1 is the cause of oral blisters/cold sores. Type 1 can be transmitted from the mouth to the genital area by hand contact or oral-genital contact.

Transmission can occur through vaginal birth, oral-genital contact, genital-genital contact, or by the hands from the mouth to genitals. Fomite transmission has not been reported. Diagnosis is made by the appearance of the vesicles and by laboratory culture or rapid DNA tests. Symptomatic infections are treated with acyclovir to decrease the duration of outbreaks, which are recurrent, as medication does not eradicate the virus from nerve cells, where it lies dormant.

Human immunodeficiency virus (HIV). Acquired immune deficiency syndrome (AIDS) is a disease that breaks down the body's immune system, or its ability to fight disease. The virus infects white blood cells (T-cells) and uses these cells to replicate in the infected human. Antiviral medications are used to suppress the virus replication. Other medications may be given to prevent opportunistic infections that occur when the immune system is severely compromised. These infections, along with malignancies, are the usual cause of death in AIDS patients. The overall diagnosis and treatment for AIDS has changed dramatically in the past decade, and the prognosis for the disease has shifted from quickly terminal to controllable and chronic.

There are still misunderstandings about the transmission of HIV, even with better education about risk factors and the disease itself. The issues of confidentiality and stigma surrounding the diagnosis of HIV and AIDS are still important to remember when discussing the disease in patients and in human services clients.

The virus can be transmitted through:

- Sexual contact in which the body secretion (such as saliva, blood, feces, semen, or vaginal secretions) of an infected person comes into contact with the mucous membrane or open wound of another person.
- Shared needles of drug abusers, accidental needle sticks in healthcare or other settings, and contaminated blood or blood products used in blood transfusions or medical care. However, the incidence of transmission by blood products has decreased significantly since the implementation of universal screening of blood in the United States.
- Transmission by mothers who are infected to their infants either during pregnancy or childbirth. Medication can be given to a mother during pregnancy and delivery to prevent transmission.
- Risk factors for HIV disease include promiscuity, intravenous drug abuse, homosexual or bisexual activity, and the presence of another bloodborne STD such as hepatitis or syphilis.

The virus has never been shown to be spread through kissing (unless an open sore exists in the mouth), sneezing or coughing, hugging or touching an infected person, mosquitoes, or fomites, such as toilet seats or door handles.

Testing for AIDS can determine if a person has been exposed to the virus (is "HIV positive"). Because of the time it takes for the virus to manifest itself in the body, these antibody tests do not always indicate the presence of the virus. Newer tests can detect HIV DNA, can determine the viral load (how many particles of virus are in the blood), and can culture the virus from tissue, white blood cells, or blood. The routine HIV test that is ordered in cases of sexual assault is either an ELISA or a Western Blot and will be reported as reactive or nonreactive.

In cases of acute sexual assault in which there is transmission of blood or body fluid, especially with tissue damage during assault, preventive (prophylaxis) medicine can be given within hours of the rape to decrease the chance of acute HIV infection. This is very important in cases of both child/adolescent and adult rape.

If you encounter cases involving AIDS, it is crucial that the family be referred to the proper medical and supportive resources for medical treatment, education, and counseling. Families may ask for HIV testing in cases of sexual abuse that might not need testing. Refer to a medical provider for counseling. Request that the family sign a consent to allow discussion with a medical provider if needed. Know your agency's internal policy on HIV testing and confidentiality.

Know the prevalence of HIV in your community. More detailed information about AIDS can be obtained from the federal Centers for Disease Control (CDC) or your local health department.

Molluscum contagiosum. This virus is relatively common among both adults and children. The signs of infection are the formation of flesh-colored, dome-shaped papules with central dimples on the skin. Incubation time ranges from 2 to 7 weeks and up to 6 months. Therefore, contact can occur long before the lesions appear.

Transmission occurs either sexually or nonsexually, via fomites or with contact with the skin of an infected person. When determining the mode of transmission, it is helpful to consider the site of the disease. Sores on the trunk and extremities may occur easily from play, while genital sores (genital molluscum contagiosum) should raise the suspicion of sexual abuse. Although the disease in children and infants is usually caused by nonsexual contact, the presence of molluscum contagiosum does not rule out the possibility of sexual abuse. Treatment is by either mechanical or chemical removal of the lesion.

Neisseria gonorrhea. The signs and symptoms of gonorrhea include purulent vaginal, penile, anal, or pharyngeal discharge, genital or anal swelling, painful urination, and redness, although patients may also be asymptomatic. Children who present with this disease should also be tested for syphilis and chlamydia.

Incubation time is 2 to 7 days. Transmission can occur through vaginal birth and usually causes severe eye infection, but can also cause blood, joint, and spinal fluid infection. Infants receive eye ointment as a routine precaution at birth. Diagnosis is made by culture of the discharge.

Beyond the immediate newborn period, *Neisseria gonorrhea* is always considered to be sexually transmitted. No cases have been reported of transmission via fomites.

Antibiotic treatment must be provided. Complications of untreated gonorrhea in adolescent females include pelvic inflammatory disease, which, like untreated or recurrent chlamydia, can affect fertility later in life.

Syphilis (Treponema pallidum). This disease occurs in three stages. In the primary stage, the patient has small painless ulcers (chancres) of the skin and mucous membrane where contact has occurred, usually the genital, penile, or anal area. Open, ulcerous lesions, or *chancroids*, can pass the disease when they are rubbed against another person. The secondary stage occurs 1 to 2 months later and causes a characteristic rash that includes hands and feet, headache, joint pain, or fever. A period of latency occurs between this stage and the tertiary stage, in which patients have blood antibodies but no external signs of disease. Relapses of the secondary stage are common. The tertiary stage occurs a variable number of years later and affects the heart muscle, bone, and brain.

The screening laboratory tests used in detecting these diseases are the VDRL and RPR. Other tests, called the treponemal tests (FTA-ABS and MHA-TP), are more specific and are used to confirm the diagnosis.

Incubation time is typically 3 weeks and can range from 10 to 90 days. Syphilis is sexually transmitted when the diagnosis of birth transmission can be ruled out by medical history. Any child or adolescent diagnosed with syphilis should be tested for other STDs, including HIV and hepatitis B and C. Treatment will depend on the stage of disease and might include either intramuscular or intravenous penicillin.

Trichomonas vaginalis. This STD is relatively uncommon in prepubescent children. The presence of the organism should raise concern for sexual abuse. A frothy vaginal discharge with burning and itching is present, but both females and males can be asymptomatic. Tests for the presence of this disease is made by examination of the smear of the vaginal discharge or by culture.

Transmission can occur through vaginal birth and, in rare cases, through fomites, for example a wet washcloth. However, transmission occurs most commonly through sexual contact. The incubation period is from 1 week to 1 month. Treatment is an oral antibiotic of both the patient and, if in a sexually active adolescent, the partner.

Pubic lice. These organisms are spread by direct body contact. Body and hair lice in children are common pediatric conditions. Lice attach to specific body hair areas and pubic lice are specific to the genital area. A lab can look at the lice under a microscope to determine the type. If pubic lice are diagnosed, evaluation of caregivers in the home should be done, and the possibility of sexual contact needs to be evaluated.

Hepatitis B and C. This is a liver disease caused by viruses that are transmitted through birth, blood, or body fluids, including semen, cervical secretions, and saliva, and through intravenous drug use or accidental needle sticks in the healthcare environment. Although children are immunized against hepatitis B during childhood, there may be some children who do not adequately respond to the immunization, or there may be decreasing levels of protection during adolescence.

The physician will do bloodwork for levels of antibody to the virus and for the presence of the virus in the patient as well. Acute hepatitis infection has an incubation period of 45 to 160 days. An acutely infected person then becomes a chronic carrier of the virus, and the virus predisposes that person to chronic liver disease and possible liver cancer later in life. Immunoglobulin can be given to acutely exposed individuals to prevent development of the disease. There is no effective treatment for the chronic stage of the disease, and chronic liver failure may lead to the need for liver transplant or cause death.

Sexual assault victims should be screened for their antibody level of protection and offered repeat immunization for hepatitis B. Child sexual abuse victims who have contact with blood or body fluid or have severe physical tissue trauma should also be screened. Because the type of screening is often dependent on the type and timing of the exposure, a physician will need to determine which testing is needed.

☐ Medical Treatment for Sexual Abuse

This will vary according to the extent and nature of the injury and whether the child is either at risk for or has contracted an STD. Sexual partners of adolescents may need to be evaluated and treated for STD.

A child who has undergone severe acute genital or anal abuse may need to be evaluated by a surgeon or gynecologist for repair of injury. These severe cases will be evident to both the physician and worker.

Children may be prescribed antibiotics orally for STD treatment. Some topical creams or ointments for minor irritation might be needed. Sitz baths will aid discomfort in children with vaginitis.

☐ Psychological Effects of Sexual Abuse

These can range from minor and brief trauma-related symptoms to severe psychological trauma that is life altering. All children who experience any type of sexual abuse should receive some form of counseling. Some cultural groups have specific healing ceremonies for children who have been sexually abused. Psychotherapy is not always considered an appropriate approach to healing. It is important to explore the cultural meaning of sexual abuse and learn about the approaches to healing that are appropriate within the family and child's cultural or spiritual beliefs. For example, some cultures may view the victim differently, as changed or not virginal, and this can affect the child's future emotional development.

A healthy outcome depends on both a protective, supportive environment and caregivers and on the access to age- or developmentally appropriate mental health services. Unless cultural taboos are discovered, or there are culturally appropriate alternative treatment methods in place, a caregiver who does not follow through with either recommended medical or mental health services for a sexually abused child should be considered neglectful, and consideration of a court-ordered treatment plan for the family is warranted.

■ Physical Neglect

□ Definition of Physical Neglect

Cases of neglect, still the most frequently reported form of child maltreatment in the United States annually, are difficult not only because of their frequency but also because of the widely variable scope of definition that sometimes overwhelms treatment needs. Neglect as defined by both civil and criminal statutes also varies widely by state.

Most commonly, neglect has been narrowly defined as parental or caregiver acts of omission such as inadequate supervision. More appropriate might be a broader definition that includes all circumstances in which a child's major needs are not met by either parental or caregiver acts of omission or commission, otherwise out of their control, including basic food, shelter, clothing, education, safety, emotional nurturing, and protection. (A family that is homeless, for example, due to loss of employment or natural disaster would not be overtly neglectful, but an evicted parent or caregiver who is homeless due to loss of income from severe drug addiction and refusing treatment could be considered neglectful.) The definition of neglect should take into account severity, chronicity, actual or potential harm to the child or family, and the willingness of a parent or caregiver to accept the services that society can offer to improve the well-being of the family and children.

Cultural differences and biases may present misunderstandings regarding neglect. For example, most CPS workers come from a more privileged background than most CPS clients and may have different values and standards regarding cleanliness, use of space, and tidiness.

Finally, in our society, neglect may be incorrectly confused with poverty or ignorance, or associated with parents or caregivers who are overwhelmed with other life problems.

Whether neglect of a child involves a common or serious medical condition and care needs, or leads to growth failure, injury, or developmental disability, your role as a CPS worker is to understand normal growth and development, well child care, and currently recommended schedule for care health visits, as well as to develop a working knowledge of a child's medical condition that is reported to you by both parent or caregiver and medical provider. The medical provider should work with you not only in treating the child's immediate problem, but also in monitoring the child's growth and development through the course of any required treatment. Finally, you should emphasize to medical providers who are reporting neglect or medical neglect that it is only with their time and help that you will gain a better understanding of the child's condition or medical needs. This is often not easy, given the time constraints of medical practice, but it can be accomplished with focused persistence.

□ Failure to Thrive

Failure to thrive (FTT), sometimes referred to as pediatric growth failure, is a nonspecific term applied to infants and young children who are failing to grow according to commonly described normal parameters. A medical provider may report that an infant is not gaining weight or height according to standard growth curves or developing according to normal milestones for age. The CPS worker should be familiar with standard growth curve for weight, height, and head circumference, as well as with the commonly used Denver Developmental Screen that assesses age-appropriate milestones. This instrument is typically available at pediatrician offices and hospitals.

Failure to thrive may be *organic,* meaning that the growth failure is caused by an underlying disease, or *nonorganic,* meaning that the cause is psychosocial or environmental in origin and not due to underlying disease. Many children present with failure to thrive and an underlying medical condition complicated by a dysfunctional or maladaptive interaction with the parent or caregiver.

Ultimately, inadequate caloric intake or the body's processing of the calories may be the cause of FTT. Sufficient calories are not being offered to the child, the child is not taking the offered calories because of lack of appetite or maladapted behavior, the child is using calories at an increased rate, or the calories are not being absorbed into the body from the gastrointestinal system.

Medical and psychological evaluations are needed to identify and clarify the abnormal growth pattern and cause for each child.

There are many medical and psychosocial causes of FTT, and a child may have any number of causes for FTT. Disorders of attachment (bonding) between the parent, usually the mother, and the child typically manifest themselves after the first 3 months of age. Maternal postpartum depression; underlying mental illness; an unwanted pregnancy; circumstances surrounding conception such as rape; untreated substance abuse; a young, inexperienced, or overwhelmed parent; or a premature baby whose mother had little physical contact after birth due to medical condition and care are all examples of situations that could affect healthy maternal attachment.

The child, by nature or temperament, may be a contributor to the parental response. Babies with colic or babies who sleep excessively and never cry, even when hungry, may play a significant role in the way that the parent responds to them.

Other contributing factors may include marital stress, financial distress, or family violence. Any adverse situation or occurrence that affects the parent or caregiver should carefully be evaluated as a factor in the parent-child attachment or interaction that has become unhealthy dangerous to the child, or that is affecting the growth and development.

Later in the first year of life, children will begin to organize their own behaviors and develop more independence. It is developmentally appropriate for children to "battle" their parents or caregivers and assert control in those few areas open to them. Appetite and feeding behavior are two areas where a child can assert such independence. In situations already exacerbated by abuse or neglect, "battles" between the child and parent or caregiver about eating may lead to problems with weight gain and growth. The typical 2- or 3-year-old who refuses to eat something can recognize that a parent or caregiver clearly is distressed over the situation, for example, and the battle to "eat this or that" may ensue leading to the child developing adverse reactions to food beyond what is developmentally appropriate and thus aggravating an already stressed parent-child relationship.

The consequences of FTT can be severe. A child deprived of an adequate intake of calories will break down (metabolize) fat and muscle to maintain growth of the brain. With continued poor caloric intake, the brain growth will also start to slow and eventually plateau.

A child who is failing to thrive usually has low weight gain first, often falling across several growth percentiles on curves. Subsequently, the child will slow in height growth.

Small head size and delayed growth of the brain is seen as a manifestation of either severe or prolonged FTT.

Long-term consequences, in addition to small stature, include global developmental delays, including motor, speech and language, and higher learning. In addition, because the environment may be neglectful in terms of nurturing and healthy emotional attachment, the child's psychological and emotional development can be adversely affected as well.

The warning signals of potential neglect and subsequent FTT may be apparent before the baby is ever born. The medical providers involved with pregnant women, family members, and the CPS worker should be alert to signals that may be risk factors for later neglect. A mother may need special attention if she:

- Denies the pregnancy or fails to seek any prenatal care until she is near term.
- Has attempted or seriously considered an abortion. An unwanted pregnancy may be the product of rape or incest, and this possibility must always be explored.
- Fails to exhibit normal "nesting" behavior in the home in preparation for the child. Nonetheless, you should recognize that some cultures purposely may refrain engaging in any preparation for a child's birth to thwart any potential bad luck.
- Refuses to hold, touch, feed, name, or interact with infant after birth. Calls the infant something inappropriate or acts verbally or emotionally in a negative way toward the infant. Wishes the infant dead or never born or implies or threatens the infant.
- Considers putting the child up for adoption, then changes her mind at the last moment.
- Has an alcohol or drug use problem or addiction, either treated or untreated.
- Has or has had a psychiatric disorder.
- Has no emotional support from a partner, family, or friends. Is socially or physically isolated either by circumstances beyond her control or by control of another person, the latter raising concern for domestic violence.
- Has either limited or no financial support.

- Has a history of abuse or neglect as a child himself or herself, has abused or neglected a previous child, or has allowed abuse or neglect to occur previously.
- Is not able to hold, feed, or care for the child for an extended time following the birth for medical reasons; this might affect attachment.

Once the mother has given birth to her child, observe her behavior around the infant. Does she handle the baby roughly, like a package, or hold him close to her body? Does she talk and smile at him, or does she ignore him?

Once the baby has returned home with the mother, the baby, or eventually an older child, may show any of the following symptoms over time.

- Weak, pale, and listless appearance. Instead of smiling, cooing, and maintaining eye contact, the baby stares vacantly or is not interactive at all.
- Sleeping in a guarded-appearing, curled-up, fetal position, and with fists tightly closed.
- Engaging in self-stimulatory behavior, such as rocking back and forth or banging own head repeatedly against the crib.
- Presence of dirt under long, ragged fingernails, severe diaper rash, a dirty face, hands, feet, or body—may be overt signs of physical care neglect.
- Obvious delays in developmental and motor function.

It is imperative that all malnourished children be examined by a medical provider. The medical provider will not only treat the existing malnourishment but also be able to monitor the child's growth and development closely. Both the medical provider and the CPS worker should physically see the infant or young child when there is concern of FTT. A description over the phone or by report of someone else should never be relied on as that can be falsified or minimized. A physical examination of the infant or child, and weight measurement, completely unclothed, must occur immediately. Physical abuse or sexual abuse signs might be seen on examination.

One of the most important tools in determining the course of treatment for FTT is obtaining a detailed, accurate medical and social history. The medical provider may ask specific questions about the feeding of the infant:

- Is the child breastfed? If so, the medical provider needs to assess the quality of the feeding by asking questions to determine if the child is latching on properly and whether the mother is producing enough milk to satisfy the child's appetite.
- If the child is not breastfed, what formula is used? Is this mixed correctly or diluted? Can the parent or caregiver read the formula instructions? How often is the child fed? Is the family receiving or refusing food assistance through a public health or welfare agency?
- How exactly is the child fed? (Propping the bottle on a pillow in the crib not only suggests a lack of maternal contact but also the possibility that the child is not getting enough food.) Does the family have bottles and nipples? Is anyone else responsible for or not feeding the infant?

- How is the infant's appetite? How do you know when the baby is full? Does the infant burp well or spit up a lot? (Infants who drift to sleep during feeding may be listless and apathetic from lack of stimulation, or malnourishment, or may simply sleep a lot naturally.)
- Has the child experienced any diarrhea or vomiting? How do the child's stools look?

In addition, the history should look for any factors other than FTT that might be the cause of the child's malnutrition, including the following:

- How large are the biological parents? (Genetics are often a contributing factor to a child's short stature but not to severe weight loss or poor weight gain during the first year or two of life.)
- Were there any problems in the pregnancy? Was the child born prematurely? Did the mother receive adequate prenatal care? (A detailed review of the mother's records is needed and should be done by the medical provider.)
- Is the child on any medications? Are these prescribed and needed, or is a parent or caregiver inappropriately giving them to the infant or child? If so, why? Are there any cultural or alternative substances that are being given and why?
- Are there any documented allergies to food types, medicines, or environmental allergens in child and/or family history?
- Has the child had any serious illnesses requiring medical care, hospitalization, surgery, or medicines? If care was not obtained, why? Are there any concerns of adult eating disorders in the parent or caregiver?
- How often does the child sleep and nap? Is the child active during waking hours?

If the doctor does not have access to the infant's mother or caregiver, your history and report to the medical provider should try to include this information. This may require contacting previous physicians, public health nurses, or clinicians. A parent or caregiver who is not cooperating should be court-ordered to have these records released.

The medical provider will want to know of any factors in the psychosocial history that may indicate maternal difficulties. In addition to the high-risk factors just listed, the doctor and CPS worker should attempt to determine the nature of the relationship between mother and child. For example, ask the mother to describe a typical day with her infant. How often does she hold the baby? Do they play together? Is he or she a difficult child? What does the mother do when the child cries? How has the family adjusted and developed with the new infant in the home?

In the initial medical assessment, the medical provider should obtain all previous measurements of height, weight, and head circumference and plot these on a standard growth curve. These curves can compare the infant's weight and length to standardized curves of healthy infants nationwide. These growth curves are a standard of care and should be done at each routine well child visit.

The history and physical are the most important tools in assessing the cause of FTT. Laboratory studies can be kept to a minimum, and an observation feeding trial, either in the hospital or as an outpatient, can begin. Most infants who are FTT and not severely malnourished will not be hospitalized unless there are clear child safety concerns identified by CPS, and even then out-of-home placement rather than hospitalization will be recommended. The minimum studies might include:

- Complete blood count to assess for anemia.
- Analysis of electrolytes, kidney function, and glucose in the blood.
- Urinalysis for infection and kidney function and, in older children, for glucose and protein that might indicate diabetes or other disease.
- Stool examination for blood and fat to look for infection or malabsorption.
- Thyroid test, as hypothyroid can cause poor growth.
- Test for cystic fibrosis, if indicated.

In addition, the medical provider should check the infant's newborn screen to assess for any inherited metabolic diseases that can affect growth. The diseases screened for will vary by state, so know which are tested for in your state. Additional tests or radiology studies (x-rays, barium studies of swallowing function or gastrointestinal anatomy or function) might be ordered if the initial screening shows something abnormal, if a specific examination finding raises suspicion for a certain disease or physical or sexual abuse, or if the infant continues not to gain weight after initial interventions.

The CPS worker and/or dietician should interview the family about feeding and mealtime behavior as soon as the medical workup has been done. This interview can occur in the hospital or clinic setting. The worker should obtain the detailed psychosocial family information that a medical provider or dietician may not pursue. Throughout this process, emphasize the team evaluation approach to FTT.

It is not uncommon for new mothers to inadvertently feed babies incorrectly, perhaps giving the wrong dilutions of formula or not feeding them enough. Although these cases are a type of nonorganic FTT, they are not necessarily intentional neglect. It is crucial that these mothers work closely with a nurse or other clinician to learn correct feeding techniques and overall care of the baby.

As in all abuse and neglect evaluations, one of the medical provider's primary concerns will be to rule out any other conditions, organic or nonorganic, that may be causing the infant's or child's FTT. Problems in the following organ systems can all lead to organic failure to thrive:

- *Lungs* (chronic infection, cystic fibrosis, congenital malformation).
- *Kidney* (loss of protein, sugar, or other chemicals in urine; diabetes; failure of the kidneys, or chronic infection).
- *Intestines and stomach* (structural abnormality causing chronic vomiting or functional abnormality causing poor absorption of nutrients).
- *Liver* (hepatitis, defect in using or processing nutrition, inherited metabolic diseases effecting processing of nutrition, structural abnormality causing jaundice, or improper liver function or liver failure).

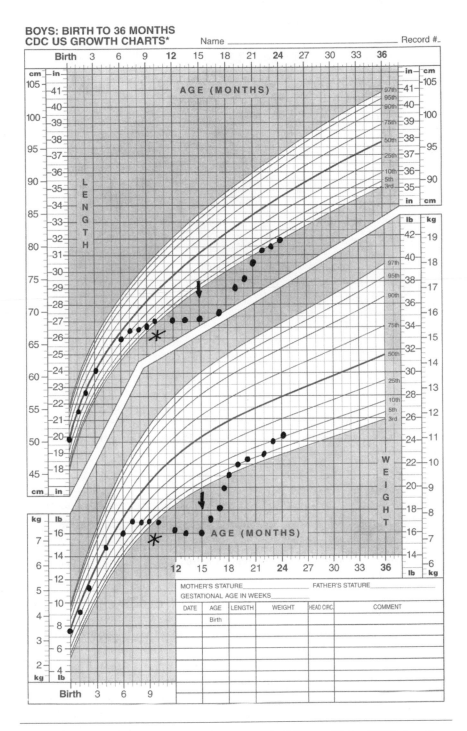

Growth Chart for Child Diagnosed with Nonorganic Failure to Thrive (FTT): Length and Weight.

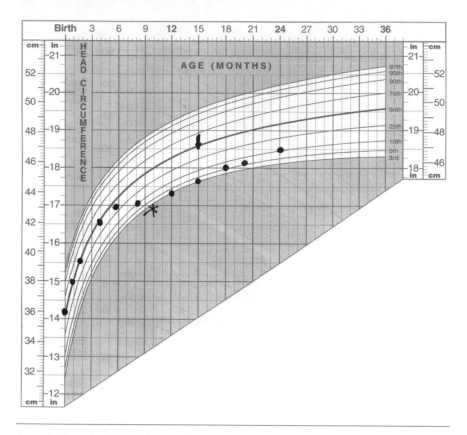

Growth Chart for Child Diagnosed with Nonorganic Failure to Thrive (FTT): Head Circumference.

- *Hormone system* (thyroid, pituitary, gonadal, or adrenal gland dysfunction).
- *Cardiac* (structural or functional heart disease with chronic failure or infection).
- *Blood and lymphatic systems* (anemia, leukemia, lymphoma and other cancers, AIDS).

The first step in treating the FTT infant is determining the need for immediate hospitalization. In cases involving severe malnutrition, dehydration, or suspected physical abuse, the doctor should probably hospitalize the child. Sometimes the hospitalization is a routine part of determining whether another serious medical condition exits. Unfortunately, many nonorganic FTT children may not gain weight until the second or third week of hospitalization. In fact, some might actually lose weight during hospitalization, perhaps due to the various testing procedures requiring fasting, a change in the diet required for the child, or maladaptive behaviors that cannot be corrected immediately during a hospitalization, along with the actual trauma of hospitalization and exposure to a new, foreign environment. If the infant is fed a high-calorie, high-protein diet and given lots of nurturing and stimulation yet still fails to gain weight, the child may have underlying medical problems other than nonorganic FTT.

If nonorganic FTT is diagnosed, the goals of treatment include the following:

- *Correct the malnutrition.* This is usually achieved by feeding the child a high-calorie, high-protein diet, with a set feeding routine and a close monitoring of weight, height, and head circumference. Detailed observation of feeding behaviors and caregiver technique, recording of intake and output, and weighing of the infant on the same scale daily and then weekly or monthly is needed.

- *Provide nurturing and care.* This should be done either by the parents or alternative caregivers who demonstrate understanding of the infant's or child's FTT, developmental needs, and any additional medical diagnosis. The parents or caregivers will need support and assistance in adapting to the change in parenting style or feeding regimens required for the baby. For example, a dietician may recommend adding a high-calorie snack food or formula additive for increased nutrition, or a home evaluation might show that eating a meal as a family has been difficult because of the work schedules of the parents or caregivers. Support should be provided from whatever source can correct the identified problem or aberrant parenting behavior.

☐ Psychosocial Dwarfism

Growth failure accompanied by varying degrees of intellectual, developmental, and emotional impairment can result in the most severe form of nonorganic FTT: psychosocial dwarfism. This is a condition occurring in older children rather than infants. Whereas FTT occurs secondarily to inadequate nurturing and mothering, psychosocial dwarfism is the result of adverse mothering and aberrant parenting behavior. Food often plays a pathologic role in the disturbed relationship between caregiver and child. Psychosocial dwarfism is characterized by:

- Severe growth failure (less than the third percentile for height and weight). The height may be more severely affected than the weight, particularly in the older child.
- Delay in skeletal maturation ("delayed bone age").
- An appearance of infantilism because the facial features and head size tend to be consistent with the reduced height age.
- Stereotypic behavior, either passive and withdrawn or aggressive and feral, including self-abusiveness.
- Delayed, immature, and often indistinct speech, night wandering, and severe temper tantrums.
- Ravenous appetites and bizarre eating habits such as eating from garbage cans and food hoarding.

- Excessive or abnormal drinking habits such as drinking from toilet bowls.
- Large, malodorous, and watery stools.
- Developmental delays or arrested developmental stages.
- In addition, physical abuse is not uncommon in psychosocial dwarfism.

Psychosocial dwarfism has been related to endocrine abnormalities. The medical provider may want to perform tests to check the levels of the child's growth hormone. Typically, however, administration of growth hormone will not change the growth pattern or increase the child's size.

These cases are usually treated in the same fashion as severe FTT cases, with a multidisciplinary team approach. Mental health evaluation and care will be an important part of treatment. More often than not these children will require an immediate permanency plan and reunification with the parent or caregiver may never be possible, as the unhealthy environment and aberrant parenting behavior have led to the child's condition.

☐ Medical Neglect

When a child with a treatable serious chronic disease or handicap has frequent hospitalizations or significant deterioration because the parents or caregivers ignore medical recommendations, court-enforced supervision, or even foster placement on the grounds of medical neglect may be required. Medical care neglect occurs when a child's medical or healthcare needs are not appropriately met, resulting in either potential or actual harm to a child. Broadly organized into failure or delay to seek health care or treatment refusal, these categories can include serious or life-threatening acute illnesses, chronic or disabling diseases, handicapping chronic diseases or conditions, and routine well child care.

Cases involving serious, acute life-threatening illness are usually considered emergencies. Examples are parents or caregivers who refuse to allow a blood transfusion to save a child in shock or who refuse to admit a severely dehydrated child to the hospital. When parents or caregivers refuse to sign a consent form in these circumstances, the court must intervene quickly. Diseases that endanger the public safety, such as treatment for a life-threatening communicable disease, may require a court order if the parents or caregivers refuse treatment. Other examples are the following:

- A parent or caregiver refusing antibiotics for bacterial meningitis is endangering both the child's life and potentially those of others in contact with the child.
- A parent or caregiver refusing insulin for a diabetic with severely high blood sugar level is likewise neglectful and endangering the child.

Certain religious reasons to refuse medical care are routinely addressed by hospital settings, such that policy and procedures exist for these scenarios, the most common being refusal of blood transfusions. Court-ordered treatment may be required but can be ordered and provided with the additional community or religious support that the family needs. Other scenarios may meet state both civil and criminal statutes for child abuse or neglect and are quite different. For example, refusing medical care for diabetic shock or a newborn who is turning blue or has a high fever is again life threatening and warrants emergency custody and court-ordered treatment.

End-of-life decisions in which a parent or caregiver wishes to withdraw life support or basic nutrition, or in which a parent or caregiver cannot understand the futility of life support (that the child will have no good outcome, and persistent medical intervention is futile, harmful, or painful), may sometimes need emergency CPS and court involvement. All hospitals have strict policies and procedures regarding such situations, and these situations can usually be resolved with open, sensitive, and team communication with the family.

Life-threatening chronic diseases, such as asthma or diabetes mellitus, that require continual monitoring, medication, or therapy and are not treated require immediate intervention. If parents or caregivers are not capable of caring for their children even after warning and instruction, you may need to request a court order for the child's treatment or removal from the home. Parents or caregivers might minimize the severity of the condition or the child's symptoms or try to convince you that the medical provider is wrong. Careful documentation of what the medical provider communicates to you and the parent or caregiver about the disease or condition is crucial. Your role is to understand the disease or condition, ask questions about this to the medical provider, investigate and understand why the parent or caregiver refuses treatment or fails with follow-up care, and assess the safety of the children in the current environment.

For example, in the case of a child with a poorly controlled diabetes blood sugar level, a parent or caregiver not checking the blood level or giving insulin because he or she does not like needles, or is otherwise clearly incapable of performing the procedures, is not a safe caregiver for the child. Moreover, if the parent or caregiver cannot understand the disease and complications of inadequate treatment, or either minimizes or cannot accurately read the child's symptoms, that caregiver is not safe.

Disabling or handicapping chronic diseases involve children who will develop permanent disfigurement or disability if they do not receive treatment. Examples are children with congenital glaucoma or cataracts, which will eventually develop into blindness if surgery is not performed. Although parents or caregivers eventually can be persuaded about the need for surgery in these conditions, those who cannot will eventually need to be taken to court and will need to be educated by the medical provider and CPS worker about the disease and the need to intervene.

For example, a child with severe cerebral palsy might need corrective spine or orthopedic surgery to prevent further disfigurement or paralysis, to decrease pain, and increase quality of life. A parent or caregiver may be simply scared about surgery or resistant for no apparent reason. A CPS worker or court-appointed guardian could assess the caregiver and help reach an understanding of what is in the best interest of the child. A nonemergent court order or hearing may be indicated as soon as possible.

The American Academy of Pediatrics (AAP) sets recommended standards for well child care. The local health department and medical provider should try to help caregivers meet the minimal standards set forth in these guidelines. This involves five visits before 24 months of age allowing for well child care and full immunization. The minimal AAP recommended standards for preventive pediatric care (well child checkups) include:

- Newborn nursery examination and reexamination in 2 to 4 days if discharged less than 48 hours after delivery.

- Visits at 1, 2, 4, 6, 12, 15, 18, and 24 months, which coincide with current recommended immunization schedule (see charts). These visits also are scheduled to assess developmental milestones at these ages from infancy through childhood.

- After 24 months, children are seen annually for routine preventive care and immunization boosters between 4 and 6 years, 11 and 12 years, and then between 13 and 18 years.

- Different assessments may be required at certain ages, depending on the level of risk, for example, lead screening, cholesterol screening, and tuberculosis skin testing. All visits include a health history, examination, and anticipatory guidance on behavior, development, educational progress, injury prevention and safety, and sexuality during adolescence.

Immunization. Unfortunately, some families are uninformed about the immunization process. They may delay taking the child to a clinic, thinking they can "catch up" missed shots later, or simply get them all at one time. If parents or caregivers do not understand this process, it is the responsibility of the medical provider, public health nurse, home visitation contact, or the CPS worker, to attempt to educate the parent or caregiver about the routine health and immunization needs of the child. A medical professional should be the one to explain the benefits and risks of the actual immunizations to the family.

Because the shots are free or are available at reduced costs in most public health departments or clinics, financial problems should not interfere with this process. Some clinics may have budget constraints, may not have enough of a certain vaccine available, or may not have the staff or ability to track all children. The CPS worker should know the public health clinic system in the county or state and know what resources are available to children needing immunization assistance.

If a child has not received any shots by the first 1½ years of age, the health department might intervene and help the family, but this responsibility falls to the medical provider or clinic to track the family and contact them for follow-up. The most current 2003 recommendations for immunizations for healthy children are shown in the following chart; those who have not received shots will require a special "catch-up" schedule, which is listed in the two tables that follow.

The tables give catch-up schedules and minimum intervals between doses for children who have delayed immunizations—those who are starting late or who are less than 1 month behind. There is no need to restart a vaccine series, regardless of the time that has elapsed between doses. Use the table that is appropriate for the child's age.

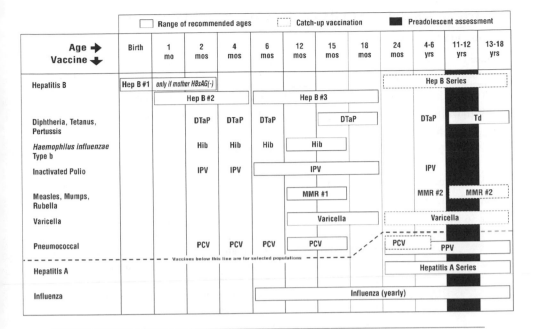

Age ➜ Vaccine ⬇	Birth	1 mo	2 mos	4 mos	6 mos	12 mos	15 mos	18 mos	24 mos	4-6 yrs	11-12 yrs	13-18 yrs
Hepatitis B	Hep B #1	*only if mother HBsAG(-)*									Hep B Series	
			Hep B #2			Hep B #3						
Diphtheria, Tetanus, Pertussis			DTaP	DTaP	DTaP		DTaP			DTaP	Td	
Haemophilus influenzae Type b			Hib	Hib	Hib	Hib						
Inactivated Polio			IPV	IPV		IPV				IPV		
Measles, Mumps, Rubella						MMR #1				MMR #2	MMR #2	
Varicella						Varicella				Varicella		
Pneumococcal			PCV	PCV	PCV	PCV			PCV	PPV		
Hepatitis A										Hepatitis A Series		
Influenza						Influenza (yearly)						

Range of recommended ages ☐   *Catch-up vaccination* ⠒   *Preadolescent assessment* ■

Vaccines below this line are for selected populations

Recommended Childhood Immunization Schedule United States, 2003. This schedule indicates the recommended ages for routine administration of currently licensed childhood vaccines, as of December 1, 2002, for children through age 18 years. Any dose not given at the recommended age should be given at any subsequent visit when indicated and feasible. The dotted line bars indicate age groups that warrant special effort to administer those vaccines not previously given. Additional vaccines may be licensed and recommended during the year. Licensed combination vaccines may be used whenever any components of the combination are indicated and the vaccine's other components of the combination are not contraindicated. Providers should consult the manufacturers' package inserts for detailed recommendations. Sources: The Centers for Disease Control, the Advisory Committee on Immunization Practices, the American Academy of Pediatrics, and the American Academy of Family Physicians.

Some parents or caregivers may refuse treatment on the basis of religious grounds. Others are simply anxious and afraid of a disease and treatment they do not understand. In such circumstances a primary goal is identifying and addressing the parents' concerns about the procedure, treatment, and/or hospitalization. Although the medical provider will be the most knowledgeable source of information, the parents or caregivers may also relate comfortably with you. As a liaison between them and the medical provider, you may play an important role in this process.

There are also parents and caregivers who have carefully researched and considered both the pros and cons of immunization. There is some debate about the constitutional rights of parents or caregivers and children in the issue of forced immunization. Consultation with the legal staff of the agency is important when working with parents or caregivers who refuse immunization even after education.

Catch-up Schedule for Children Age 4 Months through 6 Years

Minimum Interval between Doses

Dose 1 (minimum age)	Dose 1 to dose 2	Dose 2 to dose 3	Dose 3 to dose 4	Dose 4 to dose 5
DTaP (6 wks)	4 weeks	4 weeks	6 months	6 months
IPV (6 wks)	4 weeks	4 weeks	4 weeks	
HepB (birth)	4 weeks	8 weeks (and 16 weeks after first dose)		
MMR (12 mos)	4 weeks			
Varicella (12 mos)				
Hib (6 wks)	4 weeks: if first dose given before 12 mos 8 weeks (as final dose): if first dose given at 12–14 mos No further doses needed: if first dose given at or after 15 mos	4 weeks: if current age is less than 12 mos 8 weeks (as final dose): if current age is 12 mos or older and second dose is given before 15 mos No further doses needed: if previous dose given at or after 15 mos	8 weeks (as final dose): this dose only necessary for children 12 mos–5 yrs who received 3 doses before 12 mos	
PCV (6 wks)	4 weeks: if first dose given before age 12 mos and current age is under 24 mos 8 weeks (as final dose): if first dose given at or after 12 mos or current age is 24–59 mos No further doses needed: for healthy children if first dose given at age or after 24 mos	4 weeks: if current age is less than 12 mos 8 weeks (as final dose): if current age is 12 mos or older No further doses needed: for healthy children if previous dose given at or after 24 mos	8 weeks (as final dose): this dose only necessary for children 12 mos–5 yrs who received 3 doses before 12 mos	

Catch-up Schedule for Children Age 7 through 18 Years: Minimum Interval between Doses.

Done 1 to dose 2	Dose 2 to dose 3	Dose 3 to booster dose
Td: 4 weeks	Td: 6 months	Td: 6 months: if first dose given before or at 12 mos and current age is under 11 yrs 5 years: if first dose given at or after 12 mos and third dose given before 7 yrs and current age is 11 yrs or older 10 years: if third dose given at or after 7 yrs
IPV: 4 weeks	IPV: 4 weeks	IPV
HepB: 4 weeks	HepB: 8 weeks (and 16 weeks after first dose)	
MMR: 4 weeks		
Varicella: 4 weeks		

Sources: The Centers for Disease Control, the Advisory Committee on Immunization Practices, the American Academy of Pediatrics, and the American Academy of Family Physicians.

A worker may encounter an American Indian or African American parent or caregiver who refuses immunization or treatment that is considered in the mainstream community to be routine. This may be due to historical trauma resulting from forced experimental medical procedures. In earlier centuries, American Indian people have experienced deliberate exposure to biological agents that led to widespread death in certain communities. These types of experiences have led to a certain amount of distrust of Western medical practices.

Cases in which the child's health is at risk should be given strict attention, but usually the course of action is that of education, both for the parents or caregivers and the child.

Any conditions such as severe diaper rash, lice, impetigo, scabies, or severe insect bites should be examined by a medical provider who can not only treat the child, but also help educate the parent or caregiver.

☐ Safety and Supervisional Neglect

This may be defined as any situation where an injury occurs because of gross lack of supervision. This might involve, for example, leaving poisons, adult medications, illegal drugs or alcohol, open space heaters, knives, or guns within a child's reach.

Every child will sustain minor injuries or traumas during the childhood years. No parent or caregiver can watch an infant or young child every minute of the day.

However, when accidents are repeated and severe, then medical providers and workers should become concerned about safety and supervisional neglect.

Parents or caregivers will need education on child safety, and this should be provided by the primary health care provider. They may need financial help in making their home "accident proof"—for example, placing screens around open heaters, putting plugs in electrical outlets, or installing safety latches on cabinets.

One warning sign of safety and supervisional neglect is the parent's or caregiver's concern for the child. Observe how the parent or caregiver handles the child and reacts to the injury. If a baby who has fallen off a changing table at home is brought to the doctor and left unattended on the examining table, you should be concerned about the parent's or caregiver's ability to understand simple safety information that a prudent parent or caregiver knows will protect the child.

If a medical provider reports an injury that he or she considers a result of gross safety or supervisional neglect, you should investigate whether any other hospitals, doctors, or clinics have records of previous accidents, just as you would investigate previous reports of physical or sexual abuse. If the child is new to your agency, you may need to look beyond the county or state for this information.

☐ Substance Abuse and Child Maltreatment

Parental addiction to alcohol, marijuana, heroin, cocaine, methamphetamine, and other drugs has led to one of the more complex and devastating problems in child neglect and abuse. Data from the 1996 National Household Survey on Drug Abuse (NHSDA) reveals that an estimated 8.3 million children, 11% of all children in the United States, live with at least one parent who is in need of substance abuse treatment (Huang, Cerbone, & Gfroerer, 1998). Furthermore, research has confirmed a strong connection between substance abuse and child maltreatment (Child Welfare League of America & North American Commission on Chemical Dependency and Child Welfare, 1992; Jost, 1991; White, 1995). In one study that controlled for many variables, children whose parents were abusing substances were found to be 2.7 times more likely to be abused and 4.2 times more likely to be neglected than other children whose parents were not substance abusers (USDHHS, 1998; White, 1995).

The added stresses of substance abuse and demands of the routine care of infants and children create a volatile or otherwise vulnerable environment in which physical neglect or abuse can occur. Parents or caregivers who are high on drugs or alcohol will not respond appropriately to the cues an infant or child gives for both physical nurturing and social interactive nurturing. A parent or caregiver who is abusing substances has impaired judgment and priorities and is unable to provide the consistent care, supervision, and guidance that children need. Therefore, substance abuse is a critical factor in child welfare (USDHHS, 1999). These children have poorer outcomes (behaviorally, psychologically, socially, and physically) than children whose parents or caregivers do not abuse substances.

The impact of maternal substance abuse is even more profound because it affects the infant's health before birth and in the immediate neonatal period. These children are often not identified because their mothers do not disclose their substance abuse for fear of prosecution as well as of losing their children. However, this may be the best time for intervention, as motherhood is often the only legitimate social role that is valued by drug-dependent women, and most women in treatment are quite concerned about how their substance abuse had affected their children. Therefore, pregnancy and motherhood are times of increased motivation for treatment. Data from one survey of 36 hospitals were extrapolated to arrive at an estimate of 375,000 infants exposed in utero to illegal drugs each year in the United States, or 11% of all births.

Pregnant women who are substance abusers are at far greater risk for a range of medical problems. They are at risk for many different kinds of infections, including HIV, sexually transmitted diseases, tuberculosis, hepatitis, syphilis, endocarditis, and pulmonary infections. In addition, they may display nutritional deficiencies and anemia, as well as toxin-induced organ damage to the heart, lungs, liver, or kidneys.

Additional *obstetrical complications* include infections of the amniotic fluid and sac, premature rupture of the membranes (which protect the fetus from infections), abruptio placenta (an early separation of the placenta that leads to loss of blood and oxygen supply to the fetus), intrauterine growth retardation, and premature birth.

Frequently women who are using substances do not seek out adequate prenatal care, which places the infant at increased risk. Mothers who do not receive prenatal care are more likely to give birth to low-birth-weight infants, which places them at increased risk of death and other complications during the first 4 weeks of life. *Neonatal complications* of maternal substance abuse include immune system abnormalities, jaundice, blood sugar difficulties, brain bleeds, growth abnormalities, neonatal withdrawal syndrome (neonatal abstinence syndrome), pneumonia, infections, and increased risk for SIDS.

Because these infants are often born prematurely, have low birth weights, and frequently acquire infections at birth and prenatally from the mother, they are at increased risk for all the problems related to these conditions. These complications may include the need for mechanical ventilation and oxygen, bleeding into the brain from rupture of small fragile blood vessels, overwhelming infections requiring antibiotics, and poor feeding, often requiring artificial feeding assistance.

Prenatal substance abuse can lead to specific medical and developmental problems for the child in addition to the overall obstetrical and neonatal complications.

The potential effects of maternal substance abuse on the infant depend greatly on the substance being used. Often, women use multiple chemicals, placing the infant at even further risk.

Alcohol ingested by the pregnant woman does cross the placenta to the fetus. Therefore, any amount of alcohol ingested during pregnancy may harm the infant. Alcohol-related birth defects (ARBD) occur in 1 out of 200 births worldwide and account for 5% of all congenital anomalies, as well as 10% to 20% of all cases of mental retardation. *Fetal alcohol syndrome* (FAS) is a constellation of physical characteristics, as well as the behavioral and developmental problems that children exposed to alcohol in utero may display. The unique infant traits associated with this syndrome are as follows:

- Facial characteristics, including an abnormally small head, a low nasal bridge, small eyes, a flat midface, a short nose, and a thin upper lip.
- Irritability in infancy.
- Low birth weight and/or sustained smallness in size for age.
- Moderate intellectual impairment.
- Frequent hyperactivity and attentional impairments in childhood. Commonly these children also have developmental delays, hypotonia, and motor problems. They may also develop a seizure disorder.

Fetal alcohol affect (FAE) is the disorder displayed by children who are alcohol exposed and display the behavioral and developmental difficulties without the physical/facial characteristics of FAS.

Heroin and methadone addiction are also associated with all the prematurity and low-birth-weight problems just described for prenatal exposure to alcohol and drugs. In addition, these infants can experience life-threatening withdrawal symptoms shortly after birth.

The effect of prenatal exposure to cocaine and methamphetamine are both the subject of numerous studies. Some of the specific problems found in cocaine-exposed babies are similar to methamphetamine-exposed babies and include:

- Prenatal problems such as early separation of the placenta in labor, irregular heartbeat, prematurity, and growth retardation while in utero.
- Problems identified at birth, such as brain abnormalities with areas of no blood or oxygen supply, and a variety of birth defects (particularly gastrointestinal).
- Poor sucking and feeding difficulties after birth.
- Cocaine-exposed infants are noted to be very irritable, to have a shrill cry, and to be very difficult to console. Methamphetamine-exposed infants are sleepy and lethargic for the first few weeks, to the point of not waking to feed. After the first few weeks, they resemble cocaine-exposed infants, becoming very jittery, having a shrill cry, and often startling at the slightest stimulation.
- Sudden infant death syndrome is reported to be higher in cocaine- and meth-exposed babies. Most researchers acknowledge the controversy that exists in this area.
- These children display long-term delays in development. Although research is being done in this area, it is difficult to separate the effects of cocaine or methamphetamine prenatally from the poor family functioning and environmental conditions that are likely to occur in these families.

Alcohol and drug-related cases are more likely to result in foster care than are other child welfare cases. Of children prenatally exposed to drugs, 10% to 20% enter foster care at birth and another one-third within 1 year. Once in foster care, children with parents or caregivers who have substance abuse problems tend to remain in care for longer periods of time. Many infants born to substance-abusing mothers become boarder babies (left with caregivers such as friends or relatives for extended periods of time) and are often essentially abandoned. In some cases, their mothers die early from problems related to their substance use such as organ failure, infections such as HIV or hepatitis, or violence.

Those infants who do go home with a parent are at an increased risk from medical neglect because of their special medical needs. These children are often fussier and more difficult to console and may easily frustrate any caregiver. If this situation is coupled with the caregiver's use of a substance to deal with the stress, the risk to the child is further increased.

For all the preceding reasons, safety and support plans utilizing extended family and community members are essential to the continuing safety and well-being of the infant and the continuing recovery of substance-abusing parents who are reunified with their child.

Studies of the families of substance abusing mothers point out the vicious cycle of parents being neglected or abused as children and then perpetuating the neglect and abuse with their own children. As with other aspects of child neglect and abuse, the prime concern is protection of the child. Comprehensive programs that can identify the addicted mother, offer drug addiction education and treatment, and provide necessary support services are most likely to meet the unique needs of substance-abusing mothers.

Substance abuse treatment programs that are culturally responsive, immediately available, and include full wraparound services are the key to offering the mother the best chance at recovery and the child the best possible outcome. These services would include family group planning meetings with the extended family and community support providers, adequate housing, counseling for sexual and domestic violence, child care, health care (including family planning and well child care, in addition to prenatal care), mental health care assistance if needed, education, training, and employment.

One bias in child welfare regarding substance-abusing parents is that a parent who is a substance abuser is always the victim of childhood abuse or neglect or the product of substance-abusing parents. In other words, a child's grandparents may automatically be "blamed" for producing a substance abuser now turned parent. Therefore, grandparents or other relatives of a substance-abusing parent are often overlooked as kin caregivers. Since time limits for reunification are more difficult to accomplish when substance abuse is involved, consideration of placement with relatives becomes an even more critical issue if the child is to remain connected with family and not be unnecessarily adopted outside of the extended family. It is still important, however, to carefully evaluate any placement options before exercising them.

Most drug treatment programs have focused on males and not on the different issues of women and their special needs during pregnancy. Some of these issues include the need for childcare assistance, transportation, and job skills training. Many of these women also need assistance with issues related to domestic violence, infectious diseases (such as HIV, hepatitis, tuberculosis), and mental health. Many more treatment programs where mothers reside with their children are needed. In addition, front-loading services and expanded family and community support can be an effective means of keeping children in the home while parents recover from substance abuse and cooccurring mental health concerns, or receive other needed remedial or rehabilitative services.

■ Emotional Abuse and Neglect/Psychological Maltreatment

Emotional abuse and psychological maltreatment remain the most difficult type of abuse or neglect to define, to assess when reported to human services, and to design appropriate service plans for. National data for 2000 reported that just 7.7% of the reported cases of abuse were for emotional abuse alone, and the victimization rate reported each year from 1996 to 2000 has remained at approximately 1.0 per 1,000 children (USDHHS, 2002). It should be emphasized that emotional abuse and psychological maltreatment underlie all types of abuse and neglect and that better recognition of and treatment for this form of abuse is needed. Care must be taken to identify culture-specific parenting styles that may be judged outside the cultural context and thus labeled emotionally abusive or neglectful when in fact the practice may be a culturally appropriate response to a child's behavior. For example, a 13-year-old African American boy is caught stealing at a local store, and the parent or caregiver screams at the child that he is going to "tan the child to within an inch of his life," among other loud threats and verbal admonitions. While this parent or caregiver never physically assaults the child, he or she is heard clearly by neighbors, who make a report to CPS. Within the African American community such loud and angry reactions are not uncommon, particularly since historically, failure to comply with societal rules may result in extreme consequences for youth, such as winding up in jail or even dead. Cultural groups may vary in expression of affection, direct praise, or use of threatened consequences. Knowledge of these different cultural practices and seeking information to educate oneself as a worker are helpful in the family assessment process.

□ Defining Emotional Abuse and Psychological Maltreatment

The definitions of emotional abuse and psychological maltreatment and neglect that are most referred to are those that have separated abuse and neglect components (Garbarino, Guttman, & Seeley, 1986; O'Hagan, 1993). However, in reality, the abuse and neglect may overlap. Emotional abuse and psychological maltreatment includes verbal or emotional assaults, threatened harm, and emotional abuse. Psychological neglect includes inadequate nurturance, inadequate affection, refusal to provide basic care, or knowingly allowing maladaptive behavior such as delinquency or substance abuse.

A more helpful definition (by the same researchers, Garbarino, Guttman, & Seeley, 1986; O'Hagan, 1998) emphasizes that emotional maltreatment is not an isolated event but rather a pattern of destructive behavior that may include:

- *Rejecting.* The caregiver refuses to acknowledge (whether verbally and directly or nonverbally and indirectly) the child's worth and the legitimacy of the child's needs.

- *Isolating.* The caregiver isolates the child from typical social experiences, prevents the child from forming friendships or relationships, and makes the child believe that he or she is alone in the world.

- *Terrorizing.* The caregiver verbally assaults the child creates a climate of fear, bullies, and frightens the child.

- *Ignoring.* The caregiver deprives the child of essential stimulation and responsiveness, impacting typical childhood emotional growth and/or intellectual development.

- *Corrupting.* The caregiver directs or stimulates the child to engage in destructive or antisocial behavior, inhibiting the child's typical social experiences. Such emotional abuse and/or psychological maltreatment involves acts of commission or omission that jeopardize the development of self-esteem, social competence, capacity for intimacy, and positive and healthy interpersonal relationships.

☐ Cultural Considerations

When working with families of various cultural groups, the interpretation of emotional or psychological abuse should be carefully evaluated with assistance from a cultural expert.

☐ Other Considerations

Two commonly evaluated family situations that should be considered when emotional abuse is a concern are divorce/custody situations where the child may become a pawn in the parental battle and homes with domestic or interpersonal violence that the child may be exposed to or witness.

☐ Physical or Behavioral Indicators for Emotional Abuse or Neglect

Characteristics of the emotionally/psychologically abused or neglected child include feelings of inadequacy, isolation, low self-esteem, and being unwanted or unloved. Children can become hostile and aggressive or turn these feelings inward and become self-destructive, withdrawn, depressed, and/or suicidal, and/or develop somatic complaints (headaches, bellyaches, nervous habits) or sleep problems.

☐ Providing Treatment

The treatment needs of such children and families can be both complex and overwhelming. The basic principle in developing treatment should be to address any other obvious underlying forms of abuse (physical, sexual, neglect) as well as the family or caregiver issues that have led to the emotional abuse and psychological maltreatment (e.g., mental illness, domestic violence, poor parenting skills, substance abuse). Typically, parents or caregivers who are emotionally abusive *may be* repeating intergenerational patterns or are demonstrating frustration over their own unmet needs for self-esteem, nurturing, or bonding. Finally, it is important that the worker addressing this form of abuse that impacts normal emotional growth and development has an understanding of the basic development milestones of infancy and childhood, and that cultural norms and values are considered.

■ Summary of Competencies

Interaction with medical providers can sometimes be intimidating to the worker because of a lack of familiarity with medical terminology and procedures. Your knowledge and skills in the following areas will not only enhance your ability to communicate more effectively with medical providers but, more important, will provide essential information for developing a safe plan for the child and family.

Knowledge:

1. Knowledge of common patterns of physical abuse and neglect such as shaken baby syndrome, abdominal trauma, burns, bruises, and broken bones, and failure to thrive.

2. Knowledge of the patterns that the medical examination would most likely find consistent with abuse, based on their severity, physical appearance, and location on the body.

3. Knowledge of Munchausen's syndrome by proxy and the specific approach to diagnosis.

4. Knowledge of common differential diagnoses for different types of child maltreatment, including common pediatric diseases, accidental trauma, and cultural folk practices.

5. Knowledge of diagnostic tests for physical and sexual abuse, including the names of particular x-ray techniques, blood tests, and cultures for sexually transmitted diseases.

6. Knowledge of the conditions that require emergency treatment by a medical professional, for example, suspected head or abdominal trauma or acute sexual abuse occurring within the previous 48 to 72 hours.

7. Knowledge of current literature on sexual abuse, including diagnostic techniques, behavioral indicators in children, behavioral and psychiatric outcomes of sexual abuse, sexually transmitted diseases, and differential diagnoses for genital or anal irritation.

8. Knowledge of the primary indicators of medical neglect, safety and supervisional neglect, and lack of well child care, and the cultural variations of the populations with which you work.

9. Knowledge of the causes of child abuse death, unexpected child death, and the coroner's role in determining cause and manner of death.

10. Knowledge of the essential components that should be included in a complete medical examination.

Skills:

1. Ability to utilize your knowledge of abusive patterns to seek medical examinations in a timely fashion and understand the medical report information.

2. Ability to work efficiently with medical providers by asking specific questions concerning the suspected child abuse and neglect, providing a detailed and helpful history to help the medical provider in diagnosis, and providing follow-up reports to medical providers as part of maintaining an open dialogue and working relationship with the medical providers.

3. Ability to utilize your understanding of the medical provider's report or other information in order to make placement decisions and treatment planning for the family and the child.

4. Ability to utilize your understanding of the medical provider's report or correspondence to instruct parents or caregivers about appropriate follow-up medical and mental health care for the abused or neglected child.

5. Ability to interview in a culturally responsive manner, including being open to differences, being willing to ask questions with sensitivity to history and possible taboos, and the inclusion of cultural experts or traditional healers in making determinations about abuse and neglect.

References

Advisory Committee on Immunization Practices (2002). Retrieved September 1, 2002, from http://www.cdc.gov/nip/acip.

Ahlgren, L. S. (1990). Burns. In S. S. Gellis & B. M. Kagan (Eds.), *Current pediatric therapy* (13th ed., pp. 682–683). Philadelphia: Saunders.

Akbarnia, B., Torg, J. S., Kirkpatrick, J., & Sussman, S. (1974). Manifestations of the battered-child syndrome. *Journal of Bone Joint Surgery, 56A*, 1159–1166.

American Academy of Family Physicians (2002). Retrieved September 1, 2002, from http://www.aafp.org.

American Academy of Pediatrics. (2000). Active immunization. In L. K. Pickering (Ed.), *2000 Red Book: Report of the committee on infectious diseases* (25th ed., pp. 24–25). Elk Grove Village, IL: American Academy of Pediatrics.

Baptiste, M. S., & Feck, G. (1980). Preventing tap water burns. *American Journal of Public Health, 70*, 727–729.

Bays, J. (1994). Child abuse by poisoning. In R. M. Reese (Ed.), *Child abuse: Medical diagnosis and management* (pp. 69–106). Philadelphia: Lea & Febiger.

Billmire, M. E., & Myers, P. A. (1985). Serious head injury in infants: Accident or abuse? *Pediatrics, 75*, 340–342.

Cameron, J. M., & Rae, L. J. (1975). The radiological diagnosis. In *Atlas of the battered child syndrome* (pp. 20–50). London: Churchill Livingstone.

Chadwick, D. L., Chin, S., Salerno, C., Landsverk, S., & Kitchen, L. (1991). Deaths from falls in children: How far is fatal? *Journal of Trauma, 31*, 1353–1355.

Chapman, S. (1992). The radiological dating of injuries. *Archives of Diseases of Children, 67*, 1063–1065.

Child Welfare League of America & North American Commission on Chemical Dependency and Child Welfare. (1992). *Children at the front: A different view of the war on alcohol and drugs.* Washington, DC: Child Welfare League of America.

Cobb, L. M., Vinocur, C. D., Wagner, C. W., & Weintraub, W. H. (1986). Intestinal perforation due to blunt trauma in children in an era of increased nonoperative treatment. *Journal of Trauma, 26,* 461–463.

Coffman, K., Boyce, W. T., & Hansen, R. C. (1985). Phytodermatitis simulating child abuse. *American Journal of Diseases in Children, 139,* 239–240.

Cooper, A., Floyd, T., Barlow, B., Niemirska, M., Ludwig, S., Seidl, T., O'Neill, J., Ziegler, M., Ross, A., Gandhi, R., & Catherman, R. (1988). Major blunt trauma due to child abuse. *Journal of Trauma, 28,* 1483–1487.

Cooperman, D. R., & Merten, D. F. (2001). Skeletal manifestations of child abuse. In R. M. Reece & S. Ludwig (Eds.), *Child abuse: Medical diagnosis and management* (pp. 123–156). Philadelphia: Lippincott Williams and Wilkins.

Dine, M. S., & McGovern, M. E. (1982). Intentional poisoning of children—an overlooked category of abuse: Report of seven cases and review of the literature. *Pediatrics, 70,* 32–35.

Duhaime, A. C., Alario, A. J., Lewander, W. J., Schut, L., Sutton, L. N., Seidl, T., Nudelman, S., Budenz, D., Hertle, R., Tsiaras, W., & Loporchio, S. (1992). Head injury in very young children: Mechanism, injury types, and ophthalmic findings in 100 patients younger than 2 years of age. *Pediatrics, 90,* 179–185.

Ebbin, A. J., Gollub, M. H., Stein, A. M., & Wilson, M. G. (1969). Battered child syndrome at the Los Angeles County General Hospital. *American Journal of Diseases of Children, 118,* 660–667.

Erdman, T. C., Feldman, K. W., Rivara, F. P., Heimbach, D. M., & Wall, H. A. (1991). Tap water burn prevention: The effect of legislation. *Pediatrics, 88,* 572–577.

Feldman, K. W. (1987). Child abuse by burning. In R. E. Helfer & R. S. Kempe (Eds.), *The battered child* (4th ed., pp. 197–213). Chicago: University of Chicago Press.

Feldman, K. W., & Brewer, D. K. (1984). Child abuse, cardiopulmonary resuscitation, and rib fractures. *Pediatrics, 73,* 339–342.

Fischler, R. S. (1983). Poisoning: A syndrome of child abuse. *American Family Physician, 28*(6), 103–108.

Garbarino, J., Guttman, R., & Seeley, J. W. (1986). *The psychologically battered child.* San Francisco: Jossey-Bass.

Giardino, A. P. (1997a). Fractures and skeletal injuries. In A. P. Giardino, C. W. Christian, & E. R. Giardino (Eds.), *A practical guide to the evaluation of child physical abuse and neglect* (pp. 97–126). Thousand Oaks, CA: Sage.

Giardino, A. P. (1997b). Skin: Bruises and burns. In A. P. Giardino, C. W. Christian, & E. R. Giardino (Eds.), *A practical guide to the evaluation of child physical abuse and neglect* (pp. 61–95). Thousand Oaks, CA: Sage.

Gotschall, C. S. (1993). Epidemiology of childhood injury. In M. R. Eichenberger (Ed.), *Pediatric trauma: Prevention, acute care, rehabilitation* (pp. 16–19). St. Louis, MO: Mosby Year Book.

Hamlin, H. (1968). Subgaleal hematoma caused by hair pulling. *Journal of the American Medical Association, 205,* 314.

Herndon, W. A. (1983). Child abuse in a military population. *Journal of Pediatric Orthopedics, 3*(1), 73–76.

Huang, L., Cerbone, F., and Gfroerer, J. (1998). Children at risk because of parental substance abuse. In Substance Abuse and Mental Health Administration, Office of Applied Studies, *Analyses of substance abuse and treatment need issues* (Analytic Series

A-7). Rockville, MD: U.S. Department of Health and Human Services, Substance Abuse and Mental Health Services Administration.

Hurwitz, S. (1993). Congenital dermal defects. In *Clinical pediatric dermatology: A textbook of skin disorders of childhood and adolescence* (pp. 191–192). Philadelphia: Saunders.

Johnson, C. F. (1990). Inflicted injury versus accidental injury. *Pediatric Clinics of North America, 37,* 791–814.

Johnson, C. W., & Showers, J. (1985). Injury variables in child abuse. *Child Abuse and Neglect, 9,* 207–215.

Jost, K. (1991). Foster care crisis. *CQ Researcher, 1*(20), 707–727.

Kessler, D. B., & Hyden, P. (1991). Physical, sexual, and emotional abuse of children. *CIBA Foundation Symposium, 43* (2).

Kleinman, P. K. (1987a). Skeletal trauma: General considerations. In P. K. Kleinman (Ed.), *Diagnostic imaging of child abuse* (pp. 5–28). Baltimore: Williams and Wilkins.

Kleinman, P. K. (1987b). Spinal trauma. In P. K. Kleinman (Ed.), *Diagnostic imaging of child abuse* (pp. 91–102). Baltimore: Williams and Wilkins.

Kleinman, P. K., Marks, S. C., & Blackbourne, B. (1986). The metaphyseal lesion in abuse infants: A radiologic-histopathologic study. *American Journal of Radiology, 146,* 895–905.

Kornberg, A. E. (1992). Skin and soft tissue injuries. In S. Ludwig & A. E. Kornberg (Eds.), *Child abuse: A medical reference* (2nd ed., pp. 91–104). New York: Churchill Livingstone.

Langlois, N. E. I., & Gresham, G. A. (1991). The aging of bruises: A review and study of the color changes with time. *Forensic Science International, 50,* 227–238.

Ledbetter, D. J., Hatch, E. I., Feldman, K. W., Ligner, C. L., & Trapper, D. (1988). Diagnostic and surgical implications of child abuse. *Archives of Surgery, 123,* 1101–1105.

Leventhal, J. M., Thomas, S. A., Rosenfield, N. S., & Markowitz, R. I. (1993). Fractures in young children: Distinguishing child abuse from unintentional injuries. *American Journal of Diseases of Children, 147,* 87–92.

Levin, A. (1990). Ocular manifestations of child abuse. *Ophthalmology Clinics of North America, 3,* 249–264.

Lyons, T. J., & Oates, K. (1993). Falling out of bed: A relatively benign occurrence. *Pediatrics, 92,* 125–127.

Meagher, D. P. (1990). Burns. In J. G. Raffensperger (Ed.), *Swenson's pediatric surgery* (5th ed., pp. 317–337). Norwalk, CT: Appleton and Lange.

Merten, D. F., Cooperman, D. R., & Thompson, G. H. (1994). Skeletal manifestations of child abuse. In R. M. Reese (Ed.), *Child abuse: Medical diagnosis and management* (pp. 23–53). Malvern, PA: Lea and Febiger.

Merten, D. F., & Osborne, D. R. S. (1984). Craniocerebral trauma in the child abuse syndrome: Radiological observations. *Pediatric Radiology, 14,* 272–277.

Moritz, A. R., & Henriques, F. C. (1947). Studies of thermal injury: The relative importance of time and surface temperature in the causation of cutaneous burns. *American Journal of Pathology, 23,* 695–720.

O'Hagan, K. (1993). *Emotional and psychological abuse of children.* Toronto: University of Toronto Press.

O'Neill, J. A. (1979). Burns in children. In C. P. Artz, J. A. Moncreif, & B. A. Pruitt (Eds.), *Burns: A team approach* (pp. 341–350). Philadelphia: Saunders.

Purdue, G. F., & Hunt, J. L. (1992). Burn injuries. In S. Ludwig & A. E. Kornberg (Eds.), *Child abuse: A medical reference* (2nd ed., pp. 105–116). New York: Churchill Livingstone.

Purdue, G. F., Hunt, J. L., & Prescott, P. R. (1988). Child abuse by burning: An index of suspicion. *Journal of Trauma, 28,* 221–224.

Richardson, A. C. (1994). Cutaneous manifestations of abuse. In R. M. Reece (Ed.), *Child abuse: Medical diagnosis and management* (pp. 167–184). Philadelphia: Lea and Febiger.

Rivara, F. P., Parrish, R. A., & Mueller, B. A. (1986). Extremity injuries in children: Predictive value of clinical findings. *Pediatrics, 78,* 803–807.

Rosenberg, N. M., Singer, J., Bolte, R., Christian, C., & Selbst, S. M. (1994). Retinal hemorrhage. *Pediatric Emergency Care, 10,* 303–305.

Sandler, A. P., & Haynes, V. (1978). Nonaccidental trauma and medical folk belief: A case of cupping. *Pediatrics, 61,* 921–922.

Schwartz, A. J., & Ricci, L. R. (1996). How accurately can bruises be aged in abused children? Literature review and synthesis. *Pediatrics, 97,* 254–256.

Schweich, P., & Fleisher, G. (1985). Rib fractures in children. *Pediatric Emergency Care, 1,* 187–189.

Sezen, F. (1970). Retinal hemorrhage in newborn infants. *British Journal of Ophthalmology, 55,* 248.

Spevak, M. R., Kleinman, P. K., Belanger, P. L., Primack, C., & Richmond, J. M. (1994). Cardiopulmonary resuscitation and rib fractures in infants: A postmortem radiographic-pathologic study. *Journal of the American Medical Society, 272,* 617–618.

Tunnessen, W. W. (1985). The girl with the blue hands. *Contemporary Pediatrics, 2,* 55.

U.S. Department of Health and Human Services, Administration on Children, Youth, and Families. (2002). *Child maltreatment 2000.* Washington, DC: U.S. Government Printing Office.

U.S. Department of Health and Human Services, Administration for Children, Youth, and Families, Substance Abuse and Mental Health Services Administration, Office of the Assistant Secretary for Planning and Evaluation. (1999). *Blending perspectives and building common ground: A report to Congress on substance abuse and child protection.* Washington, DC: U.S. Government Printing Office.

U.S. Department of Health and Human Services, Public Health Service, Substance Abuse and Mental Health Services Administration, & Office of Applied Studies. (1998). *National household survey on drug abuse: Main findings, 1996.* Rockville, MD: Substance Abuse and Mental Health Services Administration, Office of Applied Studies.

White, W. L., Illinois Department of Children and Family Services, & Illinois Department of Alcoholism and Substance Abuse. (1995). *SAFE 95: A status report on Project Safe, an innovative project designed to break the cycle of maternal substance abuse and child neglect/abuse.* Springfield: Illinois Department of Children and Family Services

Wilkinson, W. S., Han, D. P., Rappley, M. D., & Owings, C. L. (1989)Retinal hemorrhage predicts neurologic injury in the shaking baby syndrome. *Archives of Ophthalmology, 107,* 1472–1474.

Wilson, E. F. (1977). Estimation of the age of cutaneous contusions in child abuse. *Pediatrics, 60,* 750–752.

Yeatman, G. W., & Dang, V. V. (1980) Cao gao (coin rubbing): Vietnamese attitudes toward health care. *Journal of the American Medical Association, 244,* 2748.

10 Shirley Alexander

Intervention with Families

■ Intervention Strategies in Child Maltreatment

■ Service Planning

■ Monitoring the Service Plan and Evaluating the Family's Progress

■ Concurrent Service Planning to Reach the Goal of Timely Permanency

■ Strategies in Service Provision

■ Understanding the Stages and Process of Change in Selecting Interventions

■ Effective Interventions Strategies in Child Maltreatment

■ Termination of the CPS Casework Process

■ Summary of Competencies

Intervention is an act that modifies the behavior of an individual or a family system. In child protection services, intervention strategies are not meant to create an ideal family. Rather, the overall goal of intervention is to change the conditions or behaviors causing risk to the child(ren) so the child(ren) is (are) protected from future maltreatment. Intervention can begin with the initial contact of the CPS worker and continue through a series of carefully planned steps that help family members identify and make important changes to safely care for their child(ren).

Meaningful intervention can take place through the informal process of the CPS worker making effective use of self-engaging families through a professional relationship while providing guidance, support, and encouragement toward positive change. Intervention should be the focus of all casework activities, including assessment, service/case planning, monitoring, and evaluating outcomes. You are the professional—who facilitates change through continual assessment, case management activities, and referrals to services.

In some areas, a differential approach is used in responding to reports of child abuse and neglect. Whether a CPS report is assigned to a local community agency for a "noninvestigatory tract" to determine if the family is in need of services or to a traditional child protection agency, best practice intervention techniques remain the same. For optimal results, intervention with families who abuse or neglect their children should be carefully planned and linked to information gathered through the initial and ongoing assessment process.

■ Intervention Strategies in Child Maltreatment

Although many intervention models have been developed to reduce the risk of child abuse and neglect, studies have attributed the most positive case outcomes to the relationship between the CPS worker and the family. Your relationship is the vehicle of change. Your engagement techniques, how you interact with families and build rapport, and the manner in which you serve families may have greater impact on the outcomes of your CPS cases than any other intervention strategy.

You are using the professional relationship as an intervention tool. As you work with families and help them identify their problems, strengths, and goals, you are in fact providing services. These services can have a therapeutic effect if you become skilled in the casework relationship.

☐ The Purpose of the Casework Relationship

The casework relationship sets forth the principles of who you are as a person. It demonstrates your ability to relate to another person in a nonthreatening, nonevaluative manner. For example:

> "I think most people really care about their children and want them to be safe. I am interested in hearing what you think you can do to show others that your child will not be at risk of being home alone again."

It lays the foundation that you are honest, trustworthy, dependable, and consistent. For example:

> "I imagine you don't trust me yet because we have just met. I will do my best to be honest in my communication with you, letting you know all your options so you can choose for yourself. I will also follow through with the things that I tell you I will do."

Your words must be congruent with your actions, for example, keeping the family informed of the CPS process, keeping appointments, and making referrals for services when you say you will.

A genuinely caring attitude lets the family know they do not have to navigate the CPS process alone. You are willing to serve as an honest guide by explaining what the agency does, what assistance can be provided, and what the family can expect to happen next.

The casework relationship can help to motivate and engage the family in the change process. Your positive attitude can communicate hope to a family who may otherwise be feeling extremely overwhelmed, insecure, immobilized, or even angry. Often a family needs to know that change is possible. You can assist families in enhancing their own problem-solving skills and developing a sense of self-sufficiency by:

- Providing support, understanding, and encouragement to families in crises.
- Allowing families an opportunity to talk.
- Assisting families in learning alternate ways to solve problems and make decisions.
- Offering families a reality-based perception.

If a family feels comfortable with you as a person, they will be more willing to accept the services and suggestions you offer.

The casework relationship allows you to break through resistance by normalizing the family's feelings of anger. For example:

> "I know you must be really upset and perhaps feel we are intruding in your life. Most people I work with feel that way initially, but after a while they realize the services we offer can be helpful."

If you communicate an attitude of genuine acceptance and support, the family will be more willing to share information and solutions regarding the abuse or neglect. For example:

> "It is important for you to be involved in making decisions about your child and your family because you know your child and understand your situation much better than I do. If you think about it, you probably know what changes you need to make in your family so your child will not be injured again."

A strong casework relationship is built on clear communication that allows the family to make informed decisions.

An effective casework relationship serves multiple functions. You will be a teacher, an empathetic listener, a motivator, or someone who can offer an honest objective perspective. You will be a liaison in establishing linkages to other resources by providing information, making referrals, and assisting families in accessing services. You will be a mediator or facilitator between families and other agencies. You will be a broker who acts as an agent for families by locating service resources, providing necessary information about resources to families and service providers, and developing services where none exists. Finally, you will be an advocate for families.

Results of studies show that families involved in the CPS system rated workers most helpful when they (Dawson & Berry, 2002):

- Were willing to help and join with the family.
- Were supportive and nonpunitive.
- Listened to families and encouraged them.
- Provided concrete services.

Research in this area has found that a worker can influence the process of family engagement and compliance by increasing the amount of time they spend in direct contact with the family. Specifically, MacLeod and Nelson (2000, pp. 1130–1131) found that "interventions which were more intense, requiring a greater number of hours, resulted in fewer children being removed from their homes because of child maltreatment."

☐ Principles That Promote an Effective Family/Worker Relationship

The family/worker relationship can be enhanced, as outlined by the Biestek Principles (1957), if you:

- Demonstrate respect for the family by acknowledging trust when warranted and by encouraging self-sufficiency.
- Respect the family's rights.
- Always seek out the family's point of view and recognize their right to have a point of view.
- Are honest and genuine with the family.
- Keep promises and commitments you make to the family.
- Express concern for the family's well-being.
- Keep confidences the family may share, if these are not detrimental to the child and to the case. When you cannot keep a confidence, discuss this with the family.
- Seek out areas of shared concern.

Many families in the CPS system have been rejected by their families and communities and are not given the basic considerations and civilities that most people enjoy. Therefore, families often appreciate your use of simple respectful gestures such as:

- A smile and eye contact if it is culturally appropriate.
- A positive greeting with the person's name repeated in the conversation once in a while.

- A handshake if the family seems willing and ready and if it is culturally appropriate.
- The avoidance of labels and words that might seem offensive to the family, such as "alcoholic" or "drug addict."

Developing a positive, meaningful casework relationship takes time. You can measure the progress and depth of the relationship as you proceed by asking yourself the following questions:

- Does the family employ fewer defenses?
- Can the family attempt to share important and sensitive aspects of their life and/or can they discuss painful concerns?
- Does the family openly express intense feelings with you?
- Is the family willing to use your help?

☐ **Cultural Considerations in the Casework Relationship**

Cultural differences can often present barriers to establishing a casework relationship. The following attitudes and strategies can help with engaging families and cultures with different backgrounds (Rycus & Hughes, 1998):

- You should become familiar with the attitudes, values, traditions, and rules of each social group that your agency serves and abide by them.
- You should openly acknowledge that there are cultural differences and seek to clarify any misunderstanding that might occur. Encourage the family to point out cultural issues so misunderstanding can be avoided.
- If lack of cultural knowledge leads to a "social blunder," apologize and assure the family that it was a mistake and not intentional.
- You should communicate interest in understanding things from the family's perspective. It is important to do a lot of listening and to ask clarifying questions. For example,

    "I'm not sure I understand because I grew up very differently. Please tell me more about it so I can learn what you mean."

- Never assume that you know what the family means or that the family understands your intentions. Ask for feedback from the family to clarify meaning.
- Language can create barriers. If you are not fluent in the language the family speaks, seek the support of interpreters or cultural allies, such as close family friends or advocates from within the cultural community of the family. A family has the right to be clearly understood and to understand all that is happening in the CPS process.
- When possible, families should have services provided in the language in which they are most fluent.

■ Service Planning

In many agencies the service plan may be called a case plan, a treatment plan, or an intervention plan. For the purposes of this chapter the process and the final document shall be referred to as a service plan.

Before formally providing services and applying interventions, it is necessary to strategize and create a plan that will guide the case. Service planning is the bridge or link between assessment and intervention. In CPS, service planning is one of the most essential elements of intervention for protection, risk reduction, and successful treatment. Although some CPS agencies may refer to the service plan as the document that is completed to outline the goals, objectives, and tasks that the family is expected to accomplish, in practice, service planning is much more. A service plan is the outcome of the cognitive process whereby you and the family "sort things out" together, to help the family make sense of what is happening and come to a common understanding of what everyone needs to do to make the situation better. While it may be impossible to engage the family in this process, it should always be attempted, because it is an important part of the family's change process and should not be minimized. The result of service planning is a document that formally records the agreed-on action plan that guides you, the family, other service providers, and casework activities toward well-defined goals and outcomes. Regarding family intervention, the service planning is to case management as the steering wheel is to a car. Without a detailed service plan, the case, like a car without direction, can be out of control. You need the plan to steer the case.

☐ The Purpose and Value of Service Planning

The service plan, along with ongoing assessment, provides a guide for measuring the family's progress in reducing or eliminating risks. A service plan defines and documents the methods and activities for reaching the desired goal and the benchmarks that indicate positive change and readiness for case closure. The service plan provides a framework for case decision-making as you evaluate the family's progress.

The service plan provides a vehicle for communication. A clear purpose and plan help you communicate clearly with the family, your supervisor, service providers, the courts, and other agencies involved in the case. The service plan is a way to communicate issues and solutions. Jointly, you and the family identify intervention strategies and services that can change the conditions contributing to abuse and neglect.

Service planning provides accountability for the family, the agency, and you by clarifying roles and responsibilities. Service planning reduces a "trial and error" approach that is costly in time and effort.

The service plan models an effective method of issue resolution that may be useful to families as they encounter future challenges. Families are strengthened as they see the relationship between planning and positive change. The service plan communicates the belief that change is expected and desired. It sends an optimistic, hopeful message that change is possible.

☐ The Process of Service Planning

There are five principles to follow when developing and implementing a service plan with the family: (1) actively involve the family in the service planning process; (2) identify and prioritize the issues of child abuse and neglect; (3) identify family strengths on which a plan can be built; (4) formulate a plan to include goals, objectives, and tasks that will reduce maltreatment; and (5) monitor or evaluate the family's progress. Further discussion of the first four principles follows. Monitoring is discussed in the next section.

Actively involve the family in the service planning process. The service plan is more likely to be successful if the family participates in its development. Like the assessment process, a service plan is developed with, not for, the family. The family will be more invested in accomplishing the tasks outlined in their service plan if their concerns have been heard, respected, and considered. Involving the family in the service planning process increases the likelihood that the agency and the family are working toward the same goals.

At times, engaging the family will not be possible. Following are some reasons families may resist involvement:

- Family members may feel threatened.
- Family members may feel that if they cooperate in the service plan development it is an admission of guilt regarding child abuse and neglect. Some attorneys may advise a family member to not attend meetings or discuss any aspect of the case unless the attorney is present. In situations like this, involve the attorney in the planning process as well as the family.
- A parent or caregiver may have issues that prevent him or her from being actively involved in the case. For example, if a parent is heavily using drugs or alcohol, the drugs may affect the parent's ability to keep appointments or think of solutions that are integral to the service planning process. If a parent or caregiver does not participate in the service planning process, clearly explain the purpose and consequences of not following the plan, as in the next two examples.

It is important that the family understand the purpose of the service plan and how it will be used. You should explain the importance of the service plan to the family, free of agency jargon and in words familiar to the family. For example:

> "We need to make an appointment to develop a service plan. Let me explain what it's about so you can be thinking of what you'd like it to say. A service plan is a written agreement between you, me, our agency, and the court. It will include the reason our agency is involved with your family and tasks that you agree to complete in order to safely care for your baby. The plan will also include services you think will help you be a better mother/father. Please be thinking of what you need to do to demonstrate that your usage of drugs will not interfere with your ability to take responsibility for your baby. Please also think of what we can do to provide services to help you."

In addition, explain that the service plan is an important part of the case record, that progress toward plan objectives will be monitored and reviewed, and lack of progress will have consequences. For example:

> "The plan we create together will be sent to the court and will be used to measure your progress. Every month we will review the plan with you to see what you have accomplished. If for some reason you don't follow the plan, the court may not return the baby to your home."

Some CPS workers shy away from speaking honestly with families because they feel it will alienate the family and become a barrier to engaging the family in the CPS process. The opposite is true. Family-centered practice includes respectful candid communication with the family. It is not the message or subject matter that exacerbates family resistance; it is the manner and attitude with which the message is delivered. Honest communication builds trust and allows families to make informed decisions.

The family should understand that the plan may change during the life of the case, depending on the family's progress and other circumstances. The family should be reassured that if the plan changes, they will be consulted and the reasons for the change will be explained.

Prior to convening the family to develop the service plan, it is helpful to ask the parents or caregivers if they would like to invite other family members, community support people, or friends who can help them think of solutions. Various family involvement models can be employed to develop a service plan at this juncture in a case. (For more information on the family group conference model, see chapter 4.)

As you initially meet to develop the plan, it is important to gain an understanding of why the family thinks CPS is involved with them.

Identify and prioritize the issues or risk factors of child maltreatment. One of the purposes of assessment is to guide the service plan by focusing directly on the problem areas that are causing risk. A thorough assessment is, therefore, the foundation of service planning. Since many family situations have multiple, interrelated factors that contribute to the risk of future child maltreatment, it is tempting to develop "overeager" service plans, addressing all risk factors identified through the assessment process. For the following reasons, you must help families set priorities in dealing with the most critical needs first (Christensen, Todahl, & Barrett, 1999).

- Addressing too many risk factors may overwhelm the family with appointments to keep and objectives and tasks to accomplish.
- Selecting multiple risk factors may overwhelm you because of having to monitor and document progress over a wide range of issues.
- Overeager service plans level the objectives of the service plan so that critical issues are given the same weight as less significant issues.
- Ultimately, the service plan can collapse over time, due to lack of focus or the real issues being diluted.

In prioritizing issues or risk factors that need to be addressed in a service plan, the family and you should ask: "What would be the worst possible outcome if this issue is not addressed?" (Rycus & Hughes, 1998, p. 340). If the answer is "not much," it is a low priority. If the answer is "it would benefit the child but it is not essential to the safety of the child," it is a low priority. If the answer is "it may put the child at risk of future maltreatment," it is a high priority. In CPS, service planning objectives and tasks related to the reduction of risk have the highest priority. Activities of low importance should not be performed at all.

Identify strengths and positive aspects on which a plan can be built. From the assessment, you and the family should identify strengths that can be maximized to reduce the likelihood of future maltreatment. For example:

> Mom and dad have protected their child in the past and want to do so again.

> The parents have relatives who are willing and capable in assisting in the care and protection of the children.

When a family is overwhelmed by problems, it is often difficult for them to believe change is possible. By pointing out positives, you can help the family feel a sense of hope and acknowledge the family's ability to make necessary changes.

Due to multiple problems within a family, there are times you may feel as overwhelmed as the family in identifying strengths that can be used in service planning. Look closely for strengths in the categories of the parent-child relationship, the parental support system, the family's past support system and history, the parent's self-care and maturity, and the child's emotional, cognitive, and social development.

Formulate a plan to include goals, objectives, and tasks or activities that will reduce maltreatment. Although the names of the elements of the service plan may differ from one CPS agency to another, they should correspond to the following:

- Issue/problem identification
- Goal
- Objective
- Task

Writing effective service plans takes practice and skill. It is important to clearly understand the definition of each of these four elements and how they complement each other.

Issue/problem identification. The *issue* or *problem identification statement* gives the reason CPS is involved with the family. It states the concerns of the referral or the reason the child is in CPS custody. For example:

> "*Issue*: While Mr. Sandoval was disciplining 10-year-old Maria, he hit Maria repeatedly, bruising her lower back and legs."

In the service planning process, a family does not have to admit to causing abuse or neglect. The CPS worker should take care to frame the issue in such a way that the family and CPS system do not enter into a power struggle over wording. This can best be accomplished by writing substantiated facts. For example:

"*Issue*: Two-year-old Jason was found wandering downtown unsupervised. His parents, Mr. and Mrs. Baca, were found 1 hour later sleeping in their car."

If facts cannot be clearly substantiated in the case, issues can be addressed through community concerns expressed in the child protection referral. For example:

"*Issue*: Allegations have been made that Mr. Jackson has inappropriately touched 8-year-old Jonathan."

A family can be successful in the change process even if they deny the validity of the issue. Initially a family may feel too threatened to take responsibility for the abuse or neglect of their children. However, as the family begins to work their service plan, behavioral changes may take place that will protect the children from future maltreatment.

Goals. A goal is the statement of the desired outcome toward which all case activities are directed. Goal statements are usually broad and express the child welfare outcomes of safety, permanency, and child and family well-being. An example of a goal involving safety is:

"*Goal*: Maria will be safe at home, protected from physical injury."

If the child cannot be protected at home, the goal may be "*Maria will return to her home when she can be safe from injury.*"

The case goal may change during the time the case is open. For example, the initial goal may be to safely maintain the child in his or her own home. If that effort is unsuccessful, the child may be removed to ensure his or her safety. The goal will then be changed to reunification. If reunification is unsuccessful, the goal will reflect an alternative permanency option. The permanency goal and the plan for the child should, however, reflect what is best for the child rather than what is convenient for the case.

Results of the federal Child Family Service Reviews find the permanency goal is often substantially influenced by the available placement. For example, if a child had adoption as a goal and a resource of long-term foster care became available, then the plan might change accordingly. This is even more evident with older children.

The case goals will direct the specific case objectives and tasks that are the components of the plan.

Objectives. The terms *goal* and *objective* are often used interchangeably. They do not, however, have the same meaning. An objective is more specific than a goal; in a service plan, an objective is what must be done in order to achieve the desired goal.

An objective should be stated in positive terms. In writing objectives, describe what the family member will do rather than what the family member is not to do. Examples of using positive terms are "remain drug free" versus "not use drugs" or "make arrangements to leave the child" versus "not leave the child alone." Stating objectives in positive terms allows the family to envision the desired behavior or outcome.

The language used to state the objective should be geared to the family member's level of comprehension, vocabulary, and cultural background. Agency jargon and words with obscure meaning should be avoided. For example, the following means something to a CPS worker but is unclear to a family: "*According to ASFA, the transition team works on resolving familial issues using concurrent planning to consider reunification, TPR, or other alternative permanency solutions.*"

Words that do not specifically state an end result should not be used, for example, "attempt," "work on," "try," or "make an effort."

Objectives must be clearly and directly related to the issue that is to be changed or corrected. The family should see the relationship between the issue or problem statement and the solution or outcome. For example, if the problem is that the parent or caregiver leaves very young children unsupervised, an objective of attending counseling sessions for 6 weeks does not establish a clear relationship between the issue and the solution. It is difficult to measure or communicate the importance of an objective that only indirectly relates to an issue or problem area.

Objectives should be time limited. With no timelines, agency case records get larger, and there may be no incentive for the CPS worker or the family to work on tasks consistently or determine when, in fact, the work is completed and the case record can be closed. To the family, indefinite time frames may imply that the objective is not obtainable. Often the family and CPS worker lose sight of what the objective really is and what the benefits of attaining the objectives will be. When this occurs, the family is apt to lose whatever incentive or motivation they originally had.

An objective is more specific and more limited in scope than a goal. Objectives that are vague are subject to interpretation and may become a source of dispute between the family and the CPS worker. For example:

Vague statement:

> Father will use safe methods of disciplining his children.

Specific statement:

> Father will give his child a "time out" or use an alternate method of discipline he has learned from his parenting class rather than hitting or slapping his child.

Vague statement:

> The house will be clean and sanitary.

Specific statement:

> Mrs. Sert will put the food in the refrigerator immediately after breakfast, lunch, and dinner. The floor will be free of trash and debris.

Vague statement:

> Mother will leave her child with appropriate caregivers.

Specific statement:

> Mother will leave her child with an adult who has a drug-free history and no prior child protection referrals.

An objective is observable and measurable. This allows the family and CPS worker to know when the objective has been accomplished. Objectives must be clear to both you and the family. Each objective must have some criteria by which you can measure achievement.

Global or vague objectives cannot be measured. For example, how can you measure objectives that use words such as "adequate," "safe," or "appropriate"?

Objectives stated in behavioral terms using action verbs (what the family will do) are easier to understand and easier to measure than vaguely stated objectives that do not guide the family member. *Behavioral* implies an action or activity that is observable and not subject to varied interpretations. Examples of behaviorally stated objectives include:

Vague statement:

> John will look for a job.

Behavioral statement:

> John will submit at least four completed job applications before July 1.

Vague statement:

> Doris will spend quality time with her child.

Behavioral statement:

> Doris will spend 20 minutes a day reading Joey stories, practicing his ABCs, and holding him on her lap.

To assist the family in developing an objective, ask the family, "What will it look like when the issue isn't an issue anymore?" For example:

> "*Objective*: During the next three months, Mr. Sandoval will demonstrate ways to discipline Maria that will allow her to be free from injury. He will use one or several methods of correcting her behavior that he has learned during his seven sessions of parenting classes."

Tasks. These are specific, incremental activities designed to move family members toward their service plan objectives. Criteria for stating task assignments are:

- Include clearly stated activities that must be performed.
- State who in the family will be involved or responsible for each task.
- Will the task be your responsibility or the responsibility of a community provider? Who performs a particular task should be determined by how well the task fits that person's role. For example, Do you have time to observe the parent or caregiver in the home three times a week practicing infant feeding techniques learned in a childcare skill class? If not, can you find a volunteer or other family member who could perform this task? Or can the class teacher report his or her observations of the progress the parent or caregiver is making on a weekly basis, unless a major problem is observed, at which time the teacher will report the problem to you immediately?

Include time frames for beginning and ending each activity/task. Time frames provide structure and boundaries for the risk reduction effort. Not all tasks should begin or end at the same time in the service provision process. Some will come into play only after another task has been completed. For example, a parent or caregiver should not be expected to attend a job preparation class until the task of finding a reliable babysitter for the children is complete.

Complex tasks requiring multiple steps should be partialized, with each step listed as a separate activity. An example follows of a service plan containing partialized tasks:

Issue: While Mr. Sandoval was disciplining 10-year-old Maria, he hit Maria repeatedly, bruising her lower back and legs.

Goal: Maria will be safe at home, protected from physical injury.

Objective: During the next 3 months, Mr. Sandoval will demonstrate ways to discipline Maria that will allow her to be free of injury. He will use one or several methods of correcting her behavior that he has learned during his seven sessions of parenting techniques.

Task: Mr. Sandoval will enroll in and attend all seven sessions of the parenting class held at the community hall. Start date _____ End date _____

Task: Mr. Sandoval will compose a list of ways to discipline a child that do not involve hitting, slapping, or shaking the child. Start date _____ End date _____

Task: Mr. Sandoval will keep a journal and report times he managed Maria's behavior using one of the methods from his list. Start date _____ End date _____

Tasks and objectives should be flexible. Task development should reflect your awareness and acceptance that circumstances are subject to change and are based on continuous assessment and monitoring of the plan. Rigidly set tasks often set the family up for failure and are unfair. Changes in the family's life and/or environment may make the objective inappropriate or unattainable.

Tasks to achieve objectives should be culturally appropriate. Involving the family in the service planning process will increase the likelihood that the tasks are consistent with the family's culture or values.

Differentiating goals, issues, objectives, and tasks. The following summary may be helpful in clarifying the structure and content of the service plan agreement:

Issue: Addresses why we are involved with the family.

Goal: Involves a general statement regarding the child's safety, permanency, or well-being.

Objective: Describes, in measurable terms, how the situation will look when the issue isn't an issue anymore.

Task: Specific activities planned to make the objective happen.

Several objectives may be necessary to accomplish a single goal. Likewise, in order to achieve a single objective, a family may need to complete numerous tasks.

Avoiding pitfalls in writing service plans. Watch out for the following:

- Writing objectives that do not accurately reflect the desired change in behavior; for example, "compliance with court orders," "attendance at counseling," "attendance at parenting classes," or "participation in a drug treatment program." Although each of these activities may be beneficial, all measure attendance. They do not identify the behavior that must change that contributes to the risk of maltreatment. The parent may achieve the objective, but the risk may not be reduced or eliminated.

- Developing service plans that address the parent's or caregiver's needs but do not assess or include the child's needs. The needs of children must also be addressed in the service plan.
- "Cookie cutter" plans that do not consider the individualized needs of children and families. Too often we match service plans to the services the CPS agency has available rather to services that would be most helpful to the family.

Some agencies incorporate the goals, objectives, and tasks of the service plan into a formal agreement or contract. In addition to providing a document with the steps clearly defined, signature lines are often provided for parents, the child (depending on his or her age), and other individuals named in the service agreement or contract.

It is generally assumed that a contract implies agreement of all parties. However, when allegations of abuse are involved, some family members may not agree with all the terms and may refuse to sign the plan. Some people may feel afraid not to sign for fear of additional repercussions. Later the feeling of being coerced may create resentment and provide a rationale for not following through. In such cases, the goal of negotiating a service agreement/contract is for the family member to understand the plan and possible consequences, whether they sign or don't sign the agreement/contract.

■ Monitoring the Service Plan and Evaluating the Family's Progress

The primary purpose of evaluating family progress is to measure what changes have occurred involving the most critical risk factors identified during the initial child and family assessment. In monitoring the service plan or evaluating the progress of the overall case, the following points should be considered.

Identify the family's progress or lack of progress in achieving objectives and tasks. If the objectives and tasks established in the service plan were specifically stated in positive behavioral terms and written in clear, understandable language, evaluating the level of accomplishment should be straightforward. Evaluating the family's progress should include a point-by-point description of the progress being made toward each task and objective.

Reviewing each service plan task allows the family to see that their efforts are "paying off." It reinforces change, encourages families to "keep up the good work," and builds hope for the future. Remember that families can be quite discouraged and overwhelmed. Look for the positive changes and note these with the family before identifying things that have not progressed as well.

Careful review of the service plan identifies problems related to the delivery of services and the family's participation in these services, allowing for needed changes to be made to the service plan. For example, some problems are procedural or logistical. An outpatient substance abuse group may have a waiting list. Designated services may not be culturally responsive or may be perceived as not welcoming or inaccessible. At other times, lack of progress is related to client issues such as avoiding participation in the treatment process. If services are not being provided or utilized according to the service plan, find out why, and then support and encourage implementation, enforce consequences, and/or modify the plan.

In all cases, compliance or lack of compliance with the service plan should be communicated to the family, the court (if there is court involvement), and your supervisor. The reasons for lack of compliance should also be explored.

Verify the level and quality of services that have been provided. Verification can be accomplished by obtaining periodic written and oral reports from service providers and the family. You should consider whether the type and frequency of the service should be changed by exploring the following questions (DePanfilis & Salus, 1992):

- Has the family member participated in services as planned?
- What is the family member's level of participation?
- Have the services been helpful to the family in achieving their service plan objectives?
- Have the services been provided in a timely manner?
- Has the family's service provider developed a reasonable degree of rapport with the family?
- Is there a need to alter the plan of service based on changes in the family?
- What barriers prevented the family from participating in the service plan?

Monitoring and evaluating the family's progress helps focus discussions between the family, service providers, the court (in some instances), and you. It provides an opportunity to communicate clearly with the family by identifying problems related to not achieving the objectives identified in the service plan and the consequences if these objectives are not achieved.

Information acquired through monitoring should be shared among key service providers and with the court if there is court involvement. Obtain written consent to release and share information as defined in your agency's policies.

The process of monitoring and evaluating a family's progress. Monitoring and evaluation is a continual process that takes place during each family and service provider contact. However, research suggests that formal case evaluation should take place at 3-month intervals. The following steps are used in the evaluation process (DePanfilis & Salus, 1992):

- Reviewing the service plan.
- Collecting information from all service providers regarding the progress toward achieving service plan goals.
- Engaging the child (if age appropriate) and the family in a discussion to review progress in relation to objectives and tasks established in the service agreement.

- Evaluating changes in the conditions and behaviors felt to be most critical to the risk of maltreatment.
- Collecting information regarding the child's well-being and treatment.
- Considering any changes in family dynamics during the last evaluation period.
- Documenting the results of the evaluation process for reference in future decision-making.

■ Concurrent Service Planning to Reach the Goal of Timely Permanency

The Adoption and Safe Families Act emphasizes moving children safely and quickly from the uncertainty of foster care to the security of a safe and stable permanent family. In order to achieve timely permanency for children, the law requires CPS to develop, communicate, and work simultaneously on two types of plans. Concurrent planning is the process of working toward reunification while at the same time establishing an alternative or contingency backup plan. The family service plan is designed to make reasonable efforts to reunify a child with his or her family. For the Indian Child Welfare Act, the standard is "active efforts." The contingency plan assists you in meeting the federal mandate to provide an alternate permanent home for the child.

According to the National Resource Center for Foster Care and Permanency Planning (NRCFCPP, 2001), the purpose of concurrent planning is to:

- Achieve early permanency for children.
- Decrease children's length of stay in foster care.
- Reduce the number of moves and disruptions of relationships that children experience in foster care.
- Develop a pool of resource families (relatives or nonrelatives) who can work toward reunification while also being available to serve as a permanent placement for the child.
- Maintain continuity in family and sibling relationships.

☐ Steps in the Concurrent Planning Process

The following steps in concurrent planning were developed by Linda Katz (1999), as well as the NRCFCPP.

1. *Within the first 30 to 90 days of the case, you should examine the family's strengths as well as poor prognosis indicators to evaluate the challenges the family might have in achieving reunification.* If the issues or problems are significant, a concurrent service plan should be developed with the family.

2. *Early on, inform families about the goal and process of concurrent planning.* Educate them about the detrimental effects of out-of-home care on children and the urgency of reunification or an alternate permanent plan such as legal guardianship or adoption. Explain the shortened time frames for reunification (for

younger children) and the consequences of not meeting the time frames. This knowledge may help motivate parents to make more effective use of services by actively working toward the changes necessary to regain custody. It will allow them to make informed decisions.

Be very clear about the importance of the involvement of the family and extended family in the case.

Use language that is free of jargon to communicate the principles of concurrent planning. It is extremely difficult, so you may want to rehearse or role play in order to find your "own" words. For example:

> "It is very important to understand that your child must have a permanent home within 15 months (12 months in some states). Once your child is removed from your home, the clock starts. This clock is controlled by federal and state laws. Our first goal is for you and your child to be reunified. We have talked about the things that need to change for your child to be safe in your home. If you are unable to provide a safe and permanent home for your child within 15 months, by law we will move forward with another plan for your child. This could be adoption or being placed permanently with a relative or other guardian.

> In order for your child to have a permanent home within the 15-month time frame we will develop what is called a concurrent plan. In this plan you will work on two things at once. Number one is making your home a safe and stable place so your child can return. Number two is helping prepare your child for another permanent home in case you are not successful with efforts to bring the child home."

3. *Meet with the family (all interested extended family members, relatives, or close family support persons) and formulate a concurrent plan for permanency for the child.* Family involvement models, including family group decision-making strategies, allow for parents, extended family members, and other family resources to be involved early in identifying possible solutions to achieve permanency, safety, and well-being for children. Concurrent permanency planning encourages adults to work together cooperatively as they plan where the child will grow up.

4. *Within the first 3 months, conduct an immediate, diligent, and continuous search* for possible noncustodial parents and other family members, tribal or community members, or customary kin and friends who are able to commit to participation in a permanent plan.

5. *Determine if the child has American Indian tribe affiliation and make appropriate tribal contacts so the tribes can be involved in the permanency planning process.* Even if the tribe is unable to formally intervene in the court proceedings, there are often cultural and family resources available to assist in the long-term permanency planning. Tribal family or representatives may be able to participate by telephone conference if the cost of travel is prohibitive.

6. *Place the child with a family who is willing and able to work cooperatively with the biological parents toward reunification but also willing to become the child's permanent family if needed.* This could be a kin or a foster family, or one designated by

the family that is able to pass a home study. A child needs to hear "You're either going to go home or remain with us."

7. *Make "reasonable efforts" to help the family reunify.* For families eligible under the standards of the Indian Child Welfare Act, "active efforts," including culturally appropriate services, are required.

Provide immediately accessible, focused, intensive services to families while working on the tasks of an alternate permanent plan.

Mediation is used in some instances to resolve disputes about permanency planning and child welfare issues. It may also prove beneficial in resolving adversarial family relationships, thereby offering the family additional supports or placement options.

Ensure the availability of opportunities and supports needed for meaningful visitation. Visitation is so vital to family reunification and case decision-making that the final subsections of this section are devoted to it.

8. *Clearly document the family's progress and hold frequent informal and formal reviews.* The concurrent service plan should be included as part of the family's service plan. Monitoring of the plan can be a way to assess the efficacy of the services being provided to assist the family in achieving the service plan goals. An example follows of a concurrent plan that has a contingency goal other than reunification. It is important to actively pursue a backup plan for permanency while working toward reunification rather than wait until the family has exhausted their reunification options. Otherwise, concurrent planning would be not concurrent but "serial" or "linear."

> *Issue*: Jeremy needs a safe permanent place to live. Currently, Jeremy is living in a foster home, and foster care is a temporary living arrangement.
>
> *Goal*: Jeremy will have a safe permanent home.
>
> *Objective*: Mrs. Sarnoff (Jeremy's mother) will accomplish the tasks and objectives that are identified in this service plan so it will be safe for 5-year-old Jeremy to return to Mrs. Sarnoff's home. An alternate permanent home will be identified, and plans will be in place by May 15, 20__, in the event a return to Mrs. Sarnoff home is not possible.
>
> *Task*: The CPS worker will contact the parent locator service to search for Mr. Boatwright (Jeremy's father) to see if he or his family can serve as a resource to his son. Start date: ____ End date: ____
>
> *Task*: A family group conference will be held the week of May 9, 20__ (at a time and place convenient for the family), to consider ideas for another permanent home for Jeremy. Options for Jeremy to permanently live with a relative or another person will be explored. The legal status of guardianship or adoption will be selected. Mrs. Sarnoff will make a list of all persons who should be invited to the meeting by April 11 so Mr. Mason, the FGC coordinator, can conduct the many activities necessary to prepare for the meeting. Start date: ____ End date: ____
>
> *Task*: The CPS worker will gather information from Mrs. Sarnoff and compile a social history and life book for Jeremy. Start date: ____ End date: ____

Task: Jeremy will be placed in an alternative permanent placement with a person who can commit to both reunification and permanency. Start date: ___ End date: ___

9. *When reunification seems unlikely, use "options counseling"* so the family can consider voluntary surrender, directed consent, kinship care, guardianship, adoption, or independent living.

10. *Continuously discuss the concurrent case with your supervisor.* Cases that require concurrent planning are extremely difficult, and it is helpful to get another perspective regarding the case progress.

☐ Avoiding Pitfalls in Concurrent Planning

Experience in implementing concurrent plans has identified the following mistakes that are frequently made in concurrent planning (Katz, 1999).

Equating concurrent planning with adoption and minimizing reunification efforts. You need to actively and objectively pursue reunification efforts while implementing the alternate permanency options of concurrent planning.

Failing to accommodate cultural differences. In designing plans and making service referrals, cultural differences must be acknowledged. For example:

> An American Indian mother's children have been in foster care for the past 15 of 22 months. When asked early in the process, the mother was unable to identify relatives who could care for her children. The tribe was notified and made a decision not to intervene in the case. The mother made several attempts to engage in treatment and to seek employment that had not proved successful. When the proceedings were moving toward termination of parental rights, and the foster parents (non-Indian) expressed a desire to adopt the children, the mother's older sister came forward and voiced willingness to have the children placed with her and her husband. Under the Indian Child Welfare Act, adoptive placement preferences (extended family, other tribal family, other Indian family) must be exhausted before children can be placed in a non-Indian home. The judge ordered a home study. The worker and court personnel were very frustrated. They argued that bonding had occurred with the foster family and did not want to consider another option. A cultural consultation with a local Indian advocacy center revealed that in the tribal customs of the family, it was inappropriate to ask for help from other family members until making every effort to regain custody. In addition, family members would be considered intrusive if they appeared before giving the mother a chance to succeed. In addition, it was explained that if the sister had identified herself as a permanency placement option, she would have been seen as "wishing bad luck" on the mother's ability to reunify. Since involvement of multiple caregivers is a common childrearing practice for many tribal people, having children in foster care is not necessarily seen as a reason to intervene. It may be culturally inconceivable that children would not be returned because of "bonding" to a foster family.

Subtle cultural differences involve meaning and values. Therefore, early exploration with families of various cultural backgrounds regarding the meaning of asking for help, family intervention, and a clear explanation with the extended family and other tribal support people regarding "concurrent planning" is critical. It may be necessary to engage cultural consultants and community allies when working with families of a different cultural group.

Assuming that assessment tools will infallibly predict case outcomes. Even though poor prognosis indicators may suggest that the possibility of family reunification is unlikely, parents or caregivers may rally and be successful regarding reunification efforts. Unless the child's safety cannot be ensured due to a finding of aggravated circumstances, families deserve an opportunity to succeed.

Investing in one particular outcome, either reunification or not, rather than allowing the results to evolve from the family's decisions and actions. Case progress sometimes stands still because a CPS worker or judge continues to wish for an outcome that it seems unlikely the family will achieve.

Defining staff as primarily enforcers, rather than social workers with case management responsibilities. It is difficult to engage families by using a "policing approach." The principles of family-centered practice are much more effective in guiding families through the change process.

Designing service plans that are not family centered. Concurrent planning supports parents' rights and responsibilities to visit and be involved in planning for their child's future.

Interpreting 15 months as an absolute limit on reunification, regardless of parental progress. Although you should avoid giving parents "one last chance" if they make a last-minute effort, you should consider their motivation, their incremental progress, and a foreseeable reunification.

Failing to train and support kin and foster parents. Temporary caregivers need specialized training to help them support the child's biological parents and to understand the cultural practices and viewpoints that affect the care of the child and to understand long-term planning for permanency. In all cases the relatives and foster parents must support the service plan of reunification. If the foster parents or relative placement work against the parents, it is your responsibility to intervene.

☐ The Importance of Family Visitation in Concurrent Planning

Wright (2001) lists the following benefits of visitation.

Visitation can ease the family's pain of separation and loss. It helps both the parent or caregiver and the child express and deal with the pain. Visitation reassures the child of the parent's or caregiver's well-being. It lets the child see that the parent or caregiver is all right. It assists the family in dealing with changing relationships and supports the family in coping with changes. It can support the child's adjustment to the foster home. Children who regularly visit their parents can "settle in" more easily and ultimately have fewer behavior problems.

Visitation allows the parents or caregivers to stay current with the child's development and activities. It provides a regular time that everyone in the family can meet and exchange information about changes that affect the child(ren) and family.

Regular visitation has been shown to increase the likelihood of reunification and reduce time in out-of-home care. Therefore, visitation maintains and strengthens family relationships. The parents' or caregivers' motivation is enhanced when there is ongoing contact with the child and they feel that they still play a meaningful role in the child's life.

Visitation helps older children avoid self-blame for the placement and reassures the child that his or her parents or caregivers still want him or her.

Visitation can be a powerful factor in case decision-making. Family visits can be used as interventions in which family members learn new behaviors and can practice and demonstrate progress in the areas of parenting that are related to the reason for placement. Likewise, when a parent or caregiver does not attend or participate in regularly scheduled visitation, this lack of participation can demonstrate parental ambivalence, discouragement, or not being able to meet the child's needs.

Visitation helps the parents or caregivers and the child deal with reality. There is a great deal of distortion when a child comes into care. The child and parent may both create a fantasy of how it was prior to placement or what it may be like after placement. Regular visitation gives all participants a more realistic perspective.

Well-documented visitation can be a great source of information to support decision-making.

Visitation can assist with the transition to reunification and reduce the likelihood of disruption after reunification has occurred.

☐ Considerations in Scheduling Visitation

Visitation can carry the pain of the past but also the hope for the future. The emotions that accompany visitation are often difficult for parents, children, relative and nonrelative foster parents, service providers, and you. Nevertheless, you can help all participants to understand how visitation fits with concurrent planning and to tolerate the mixed emotions and accompanying behaviors that may result before and after visitation.

The visitation experience changes during the life of the case (McCart Hess & Ohman Proch, 1988). Early visitation is characterized by a great deal of emotion because the pain is so new and coping strategies are not yet in place. After children and families have adjusted to the out-of-home situation, it is easier for participants to settle into visitation. At this stage many families can focus on service plan implementation. During the final period, whether the family will be reunited or another permanency option has been chosen, new emotions emerge related to the transition.

You have an important role in helping all participants to understand their reactions to visitation, as well as the reactions of others. There may be anxiety prior to seeing family members, as well as disappointment in how the visit went. Often it may fall short of the family members' expectations. Saying goodbye often brings back the emotions of the initial separation. Therefore, children may become angry or withdraw before the visit is over. Parents or caregivers often feel rejected. During the initial phase of visitation, children may regress (e.g., whining, wetting, nightmares, or acting out) due to their intensified feeling. Foster parents and even some service providers may view the behaviors of the children as indications that the visits are not good for the children and should be discontinued. Despite these reactions, visitation is a right of the parent and the child that can expedite reunification or another permanency option.

Scheduling Visitation

Visitation plans should be individualized. Generously schedule as many visits as the family and other parties can reasonably attend. Visitation should be scheduled at times and locations that work for the family, the child, and other involved parties. Visitation can occur at different places such as the child's home, a foster home, the agency visiting room, a park, or a visitation center. It is optimal for visitation to occur in natural settings with opportunities for comfortable parent-child interaction. All participants in the visitation need to have a copy of the visitation plan so they know exactly where and when the visits will occur.

Each visit should have a purpose. Consider the following questions in scheduling meaningful visits (McCart Hess & Ohman Proch, 1988):

- How can visits reinforce cultural identity? For example, can the visit allow the child to attend an event related to his or her culture, such as a religious service or cultural-oriented festival?

- How can visits provide ways for parents or caregivers to attend to the child's developmental tasks?

- How can visits facilitate their involvement in the child's daily care and special events?

- How can visits be structured to provide a forum for parents or caregivers to demonstrate increasing competence as caregivers or their progress toward service plan objectives?

- In what ways should visitation activities change to reflect the family's progress or needs?

- What do the child's and the parent's or caregiver's reactions to visits thus far indicate about the family's potential for reunification?

- What aspects of the visits need to be documented in order to develop and support case recommendations?

■ Strategies in Service Provision

After a family's problems, needs, and strengths have been assessed and you have developed a service plan, it is time to help the family access services to meet their needs. At times you will provide direct service as you interact with the family. You will also provide indirect services as you select and/or arrange for the most appropriate, accessible, and culturally relevant services to address the objectives and goals of the service plan. To be effective in service provision you must be familiar with your own community and its service resources.

☐ Referring the Family to Service Providers

When selecting services and/or providers, consider the following (DePanfilis & Salus, 1992):

- Will the selection of services address the factors contributing to the risk of maltreatment? Is the service best suited to deal with the particular problems identified through the assessment process?
- Will the services be culturally appropriate?
- What skill or experience is required of the service provider? Does he or she have competency in dealing with the issues that must be addressed?
- What factors will enhance or prohibit the family's participation and cooperation?
- Can you provide the services yourself? Is it more appropriate to have another service provider? Does your agency expect you to personally deliver services, or to contract for services?
- Can various methods of service delivery be used concurrently, and how might this benefit the family?
- How soon are the services available? Findings suggest that agencies should invest the most intensive resources during the initial months of treatment to engage the family and begin altering behavior as close to the point of initial referral as possible.

☐ Communicating and Collaborating with Service Providers

Obtain agency-required "release of information" forms so you can share pertinent information regarding the family with the provider. The provider must also be able to share information regarding the family's progress with you. (For more information on bridging confidentiality issues, see chapter 4.)

Educate the service provider about the reason the family is being referred. To be effective, the service provider needs the results of the family assessment, including identification of the most critical risk factors that you want the service provider to address. The service provider should have a copy of the service plan with his or her role clearly identified.

Talk with the service provider regarding the purpose of the referral and expectations regarding the type, scope, and extent of services needed. Communicate the expectations of the agency regarding the service provider's role in reporting the family's progress. Identify how often and in what manner the information will be shared. Be specific in identifying how the family's progress will be measured and how the service delivery will be evaluated.

Since families often have more than one service provider, coordinate services and share family progress. Periodic team meetings that monitor progress may be helpful. In using a family-centered approach, it is most respectful to involve the family in the meetings.

Assure that services are accessible to the family, the service provider is delivering them according to your agreement, and the family is participating. Negotiate any issues between the family and the service provider that may interfere with the provision and success of services.

■ Understanding the Stages and Process of Change in Selecting Interventions

There are five stages during the process of change. They include precontemplation, contemplation, preparation, action, and maintenance (Prochaska & Prochaska, 2002). (See chapter 7 for a thorough description of assessing stages of change within families.) In order to facilitate parents or caregivers through the stages of change, you should assess each family member's stage of change. Where is he or she in the process?

Assist family members in moving through the stages of change, one stage at a time. The "change-based child protection intervention model" describes how you can facilitate the family's passage through the change process. After assessing where each person is with respect to the stages of change, the model suggests the following actions for each stage (Holder, 2000):

Precontemplation. You need to raise awareness of the problem and consequences and discuss the possibility of change. Assist the parent or caregiver in looking at his or her self-defeating defenses that get in the way of change. In working with "precontemplators," avoid pushing, nagging, or giving up on them. It is preferable to ask questions that allow the family member to evaluate his or her behavior. For example, you may pose the questions "What effect do you think your use of drugs has on your child?" or "How do you think your life would be different if you were not using drugs?"

Contemplation. Encourage the family to think about change, support change, elicit reasons for change, and consider the risks of not changing. "Contemplators" may need your assistance in recognizing the benefits of change. You might ask: "What would the benefits be in change?" "What will happen if you don't change?" "How would your life have been different if your parent had become sober?"

Preparation. Strengthen the family's commitment to change. Collaborate with them in designing a change strategy.

Action. Affirm and support the family's commitment, reinforce necessary steps, and provide supports and resources. For example, if a person who has stopped drinking is beginning to feel like a relapse is about to happen, you could ask, "What helped you get through the last time you felt this way?"

Maintenance. Affirm the family's commitment and effort; reinforce positive benefits, identify potential pitfalls, and develop strategies to prevent relapse (Nelson, 2000).

Select the right intervention at the right time. Avoid treating all family members as though they are in the "action" stage of change. Usually family members will not participate in services if they are still "precontemplating" change.

If a CPS referral is assessed to have a high level of risk and the family members are in the precontemplation stage, home-based services may be not ensure the child's safety. However, families who have high levels of risk but are in the action stage may benefit from family preservation services with close monitoring (Gelles, 1996).

■ Effective Interventions Strategies in Child Maltreatment

There are no miracle interventions in the child protective system. The formula for success includes many variables, such as your skill in linking the family to a combination of services that will strengthen their ability to safely care for their children and the family's ability and motivation to change. Working together, however, the family and you can create changes that will improve their lives while ensuring the safety, permanence, and well-being of their children. The interventions and services discussed here are those that have proven to be most effective in dealing with child maltreatment.

☐ Interventions That Are Fundamental in CPS

Solution-focused therapy is often used by CPS workers because it lends hope to families who are otherwise overwhelmed and discouraged. It assumes that families have tried to solve their problems but have been unsuccessful. However, solution-focused therapy also assumes that families have not always failed. It is these moments, these successes or exceptions to the problem, to which solution-focused approaches direct their attention. Solution-focused therapy asks families questions to assist them in discussing concerns, talking about options, and crafting solutions.

- *Exception-finding questions* formulate solutions by building on strengths and past successes. For example:

  "Has there ever been a time you were angry with John but did not hit him? What did you do instead?"

- *Miracle questions* allow the family to envision a future time when the problem is solved and they can savor their success.

  "If tomorrow morning a miracle happened, and you knew exactly how to handle your temper and John's difficult behaviors, what would be different? What would you notice?"

- *Scaling questions* assess where a family is in relation to their problem. These types of questions can also be used to measure a family's motivation and degree of change.

> "If a ten means you spend every minute of the day with your child and a one means you spend no time at all, pick a number that describes how much time you currently spend with your child. What number would you like it to be? What will it look like when you are at that number?"

- *Coping questions* allow family members to get in touch with internal resources to discover what they must do more of to create a foundation for future success.

> "There are so many stressors in your life! How are you doing as well as you are?" or

> "It sounds like things are really tough. How do you get through each day?"

Solution-focused therapy assumes that change is constant and inevitable and that small changes can lead to bigger changes.

Family therapy can be a useful intervention if family members are willing and able to articulate their feelings, if the children are old enough to participate, and if the level of anger and frustration is not overwhelming. Usually the most gains from family therapy are made within the first 6 weeks. The outcome of family therapy should be to prevent future maltreatment, which can be accomplished with the following treatment objectives (DePanfilis & Salus, 1992):

- Confront the maltreatment openly as a family.
- Define the patterns of maltreatment within the family system.
- Discuss rules and roles to enhance a safer level of family functioning.

Group therapy can be beneficial as well. Since many parents or caregivers who abuse or neglect their children are unorganized about keeping appointments, most therapy interventions need special supports such as transportation and daycare. *Group interventions* can provide the following benefits:

- Groups can be used to reduce isolation and improve self-esteem in recognizing that other families struggle with similar issues.
- Groups create an environment where peers can assist each other in confronting defense mechanisms such as denial and thinking errors.
- Group therapy is most often used with situations involving sexual abuse, domestic violence, alcohol or other drug abuse, and anger management.

Individual therapy is not effective in dealing with all categories of child maltreatment because some individuals do not have the capacity for self-reflection. Caution should also be taken with individual therapy to not allow an individual to introduce other ideas, thereby diverting the focus of the therapy. Issues to be addressed in individual therapy may include past history of abuse, managing stress, patterns of thinking, attitudes toward violence, and sexuality.

Home-based visitation services can reduce incidences of maltreatment (McCurdy, 2000). To be effective, home-based services need to occur frequently enough so the home visitor gets to know the family and the family can develop a therapeutic relationship with the visitor. The home visitor may include a CPS worker, a community service provider, a paraprofessional, or volunteer. The home visitor can watch for potential maltreatment and provide services or create a safety plan to prevent a future occurrence.

If home visiting is going to have an impact on the occurrence of serious physical abuse, strategies will need to be developed to include fathers, boyfriends, partners, or coparents as well as mothers.

The home visitor should model all aspects of effective parenting. Like all services, home visiting should be individualized to fit the family's needs.

Home-based services and *family preservation services* consist of intensive, short-term programs that offer a range of tangible, supportive, and therapeutic services. Home-based and family preservation services have shown success in preventing out-of-home placement in 40% to 95% of participating families. Consequently, they are often used to demonstrate reasonable efforts to prevent placement in order to receive federal reimbursement for foster care (Dawson & Berry, 2002).

Studies also document positive results in using family preservation services to reunify children with their families. For example, 70% of the children in families receiving intensive family preservation services were reunited with their families, compared to only 47% of the children in a control group (Nelson, 2000).

Research shows that intensive family preservation services are more effective in dealing with cases involving physical abuse than cases involving neglect. These findings may indicate a need for longer term services with neglect cases. See later in this chapter for more information regarding interventions involving physical abuse and neglect (Nelson, 2000).

Family preservation services attribute success to small caseloads that allow workers to have frequent (sometimes daily) contact with families. Interventions from these models rely heavily on behavioral models and skill building. Services are delivered in the home setting where the new skills or behaviors will be used.

Support services are usually community-based activities designed to strengthen families and promote the well-being of vulnerable children. However, "family support" reflects a set of values about having a nonjudgmental attitude rather than a clearly defined program strategy.

Examples of support services include parent educational services, employment counseling and training services, budget management, legal services, homemaker services, respite care, temporary shelter and housing services, referrals to food banks, and transportation.

A review of six family support programs found that "well conceptualized and implemented" family support programs have the ability to (Tracy, 2000):

- Improve family functioning.
- Improve parent-child interaction by providing a more educationally stimulating home environment.

- Provide a higher level of parental knowledge of child development and less strict attitudes toward child rearing.
- Improve a child's school performance and attendance.

Paraprofessional parent aides and volunteers are often used in the intervention process to enhance family supports. Although they cannot replace the trained professional helper, with clearly defined roles and tasks they can supplement services to families. Many paraprofessionals serve as mentors, teach childcare and nurturing or home management skills, and help with problem solving.

Wraparound services is a term that developed from the goal of integrating services into a "system of care" to support family members and keep children in the least restrictive placement in their home communities. However, there is no consistent definition of what combination of services qualify as wraparound services. Wraparound service is not a program but a philosophy that requires services to be community and strength based, individualized, culturally responsive, and requiring parent involvement. Wraparound services also require interagency collaboration and the ability of agencies to access flexible funding.

Wraparound teams for children with special needs usually consist of representatives from mental health, law enforcement, CPS, education, developmental disabilities, and community groups. Families may invite others who are involved in their life to be part of the team.

Although outcome studies regarding wraparound services are limited, existing studies suggest that children served by wraparound services are more likely "to succeed in foster care, reenter regular education, complete their GED, or transition to independent living" (Skiba & Nichols, 2000, p. 24). Children receiving wraparound services have been found to have fewer behavioral problems and abuse-related behaviors such as sexually acting out, cruelty to animals, and self-injury.

Mediation is used with families in child protective services to resolve disputes between family members. This often enlarges placement options for children or allows family members to put aside "differences" so they can assist in planning for the best interest of their children.

Full-time support models have been developed in which the parent and child live in foster care together and the foster parent acts as a "coparent" in *shared parenting.* Most agencies struggle with resources to fully implement this model.

When formal services do not exist or do not meet a family's needs it is necessary to *create your own.* Often a neighbor, a teacher, a landlord, a volunteer, a girls' or boys' club, a church group, or a member of the extended family can serve as a mentor or provide an informal service that can meet the family or child's needs. This may be particularly valuable in areas where minority populations are underserved or where culturally based services are not available.

The strategies and services just presented are the core of child protective services. In the following sections, the application of these interventions is discussed more specifically within each category of child maltreatment.

☐   **Interventions Specific to the Well-Being of Children**

The American Academy of Child and Adolescent Psychiatry reports that about 30% of children in foster care have severe emotional, behavioral, or developmental problems. Therefore, you need to continually assess and refer children for services as follows (American Academy of Pediatrics, 2000). Each child in the foster care system should have a *comprehensive physical* and *dental examination* to identify and meet the child's physical needs. Young children should have early *developmental screenings* to assess gross motor skills, fine motor skills, cognition, speech and language function, self-help abilities, coping skills, relationship to person, emotional well-being, and behaviors. Due to the impact of abuse and neglect as well as the potentially negative effects of separation from a child's family, each child should be *screened and treated for mental health issues.*

Children in foster care often experience delays in academic functioning. Therefore, it is important to collaborate with the schools in assessing children's *educational needs.* You should be aware of how each school-age child is performing and monitor his or her educational progress.

Other intervention strategies or services to consider in addressing the well-being of children are as follows:

- *Group therapy* provides a safe place for children to talk and sort out their feelings regarding individual and family problems. In this setting they can relate to other children who have had similar experiences while learning protective strategies and social skills.
- Children benefit from short-term *individual therapy* that is sequenced over time so that it is responsive to developmental milestones rather than one uninterrupted period of therapy.
- *Play therapy* serves as a diagnostic tool for very young children who do not yet have the verbal skills or introspection to express their feelings. This type of therapy works best when it is coupled with concurrent parent treatment (not jointly with the children).
- *Special educational programs* provide individualized training plans intended to raise the child's level of academic functioning. Tutors and peer mentors can also be used to bring a child's functioning up to his or her grade level.
- *Early childhood programs* assist children by establishing structure and limits, providing time away from a potentially stressful home environment, and offering children an opportunity to interact with adults and other children. Early childhood programs often allow children to "catch up" to age-appropriate developmental levels.
- *Childcare* can serve as a support and prevention of child maltreatment, as well as an intervention, by teaching children positive ways of interacting with other children and providing a safe environment to develop self-esteem and coping skills.
- *Supportive services and activities* are a great way to supplement a child's treatment plan. Services provided by organizations such as Big Brother/Big

Sister or the YMCA or adopted grandparents can provide children with consistent role models, mentors, support, and nurturance. High-quality one-on-one mentoring can make a difference in the lives of children. In one study, youth who participated in a well-organized mentoring program were compared to youth who did not. The results showed (Tierney & Grossman, 2000):

> Mentored youth were 46% less likely to use drugs during the study period. Mentored minority youth had even stronger prevention rates.

> Mentored youth were one-third less likely to hit someone than youth who were not mentored.

> Mentored youth skipped half as many days of school and showed modest gains in grades.

> Relationships between mentored youth and their parents and peers improved as well.

Church and community activities also broaden a child's support network. Cultural activities and access to positive role models from the child's broader cultural community can assist a child in remaining connected to his or her identity within the biological family.

- *Meeting the needs of adolescents* involves some specific considerations. Adolescents may reject a foster family's support by "acting out" or running away from the placement. Their identity may remain with their biological family, and they may be unwilling to accept another family as more than a temporary place to stay. Individual counseling is often helpful in sorting out their feelings regarding their history of abuse and neglect, the separation from their family, and their anxiety about the future.

If a youth is 16 years of age or older, his or her service plan should include independent living skills to assist in transitioning from foster care to independence. Included in the plan should be educational goals, life skills development, employment training, and preparation for living on his or her own.

The youth should have relationships that he or she can turn to after reaching the age of majority. Lifetime connections should be cultivated, whether it be parents, relatives, foster parents, teachers, church members, or neighbors.

Wraparound services are being implemented for youth in transition, with the youth designating the services, supports, and providers to be involved. This may or may not include parents.

- A child's well-being is enhanced by *maintaining meaningful connections* through:

> Placement with relatives whenever possible, with siblings, and frequent visitation with parents, extended family, friends, or siblings who do not live in the same foster home.

Attendance at the preplacement school, church, and neighborhood activities.

Continuation of the same interests, such as sports, hobbies, or clubs.

Being allowed to take his or her pets, toys, or other personal belongings to foster care.

- Youth who are maltreated are at increased risk of abusing alcohol or other drugs. Therefore it is advisable to involve youth in school-based substance abuse prevention programs or treatment programs for substance-abusing youths.

The aforementioned services and interventions are basic tools in the child welfare arena. Situation-specific interventions are discussed in the sections that follow.

☐ Interventions in Families Where There Has Been Physical Abuse

An understanding of the factors contributing to child physical abuse influences the selection of prevention and treatment strategies. Since contributing factors to physical abuse may be different for every person, interventions must be closely linked to a comprehensive assessment and individualized according to the risk factors identified during the assessment process. For example, some parents or caregivers may have totally unrealistic expectations regarding a child's crying, eating difficulties, or toilet training. In situations like these, educational and supportive approaches may be most effective.

Other parents or caregivers may understand the developmental levels and needs of a child but lack skills in self-control and managing their own anger. Parenting education probably will not reduce the risk of future maltreatment if the cause of physical abuse is lack of impulse control. Anger management or therapy to address underlying issues related to anger is the appropriate intervention.

Sometimes a parent's or caregiver's anger is a symptom of untreated depression or substance abuse. Even with treatment, some medications may have an adverse effect, including increased agitation or anxiety that is expressed as inability to handle the normal stresses of parenting.

Therefore, the type of intervention used should be linked to the underlying cause of abuse. No single intervention approach will be universally effective for all individuals.

The following interventions promote change in families where lack of parenting skills is identified as a cause of child physical abuse.

- Programs offering instruction in specific parenting skills such as discipline methods, basic childcare, and infant stimulation.
- Child development education.
- Local support services and linkages to other parents in the community. The content and structure of these programs may vary from in-home visitation programs to community-centered services. However, to be effective, services should include the following goals (Pecora, Whittaker, Maluccia, Barth, & Plotnik, 2000):

Increasing the parent's or caregiver's knowledge of child development and the demands of parenting.

Enhancing the parent's or caregiver's skill in coping with the stresses of infant and childcare.

Enhancing parent-child bonding, emotional ties, and communication.

Increasing the parent's or caregiver's skills in coping with the stress of caring for children with special needs.

Reducing the burden of childcare.

Increasing access to social and health services for all family members.

Parents or caregivers should also be educated regarding child abuse law, child safety, and the role of CPS in preventing future maltreatment.

- Studies suggest that family therapy reduces violence by providing a forum for teaching communication and noncoercive problem solving, establishing mutually respected family rules, and facilitating more positive future interactions (Berliner & Kolko, 2000).

The following interventions promote change in families where a lack of anger management and self-control skills are identified as a cause of child physical abuse (Pecora et al., 2000).

- Anger control training aimed at recognizing "triggers" and reducing anger-arousing behaviors.
- Relaxation training that seeks to short-circuit the aggressive behavior early in its development.
- Communication skill training and problem-solving strategies.
- Methods for aiding the parent or caregiver in not only reducing his or her own anger level but also for teaching him or her how to do likewise for the child.

The following interventions promote change in families when other factors are identified as contributing to child physical abuse.

- Some families may be so impoverished or stressed that food, shelter, clothing, or utilities may need to be provided at the same time as counseling or parent education to reduce the anxiety or stress that may lead to future maltreatment.
- *Substance abuse* and/or *domestic violence* may be an underlying factor in physical abuse. If an assessment identifies the presence of these issues, they should be addressed as an intervention strategy to lower the risk of future abuse. Additional information regarding the link between child maltreatment and substance abuse and/or domestic violence is provided later in this chapter.

The following interventions are for children who are victims of physical abuse. Components of effective treatment for physically abused children include:

- A specific discussion of the child's perception of the circumstances surrounding the abuse as well as the details of the abuse itself. Depending on the level of emotional and cognitive development, children often blame themselves. Children need help identifying their shame and guilt and need to be informed that they did not cause the abuse.

- Child training in self-expression, self-control, and effective problem-solving. Interventions should teach children alternative ways to express their feelings and thoughts, especially anger and anxiety. In cases of child maltreatment, although the parent or caregiver is the abuser, children often adapt the behavior of the "out-of-control" parent or caregiver, which exacerbates the problem and perpetuates the cycle of abuse. Generally, to learn new behaviors in response to parents' behavior, mutual therapy involving both the parent or caregiver and the child is indicated.

☐ Interventions in Families Where There Has Been Sexual Abuse

The two main objectives in sexual abuse intervention and treatment are to deal with the effects of past abuse and decrease the risk of future abuse. Symptoms of posttraumatic stress improve when children are involved in therapy, even if their parents or caregivers do not receive treatment. However, parallel treatment for parents or caregivers improves the outcome for children. The following four types of treatment modalities are used in cases involving child sexual abuse (Faller, 1993):

Group therapy is appropriate for victims, siblings of victims, nonoffending parents or caregivers, and offenders. However, in cases involving sexual abuse, groups should be homogeneous. Combining family members who have different roles in the abuse, such as offenders and victims, is not appropriate.

Through group therapy children learn their situation is not unique and may relate with peers, thereby reducing their feelings of isolation. Group therapy can prevent future abuse by teaching children to say no and offering them an opportunity to role-play resisting sexual advances. Groups are effective in educating children regarding the nature of sexual abuse, the characteristics of offenders, and the process of victimization. Group and individual therapy can help children to dispel their misconceptions about abuse and allow them to view their role in the proper perspective.

Group therapy is particularly helpful to a nonoffending parent or caregiver as he or she explores insights into the relationship with the alleged offender. Even though the nonoffending parent or caregiver is not to blame for the abuse, he or she may have contributed to the risk of abuse by, for example, leaving the child for long periods of time with the offender or discounting the child's early disclosures.

Group therapy assists offenders in accepting responsibility for their actions. The group can assist in pointing out thinking errors that the offender might use to rationalize his or her sexually abusive behavior.

Individual treatment for victims, siblings of victims, nonoffending parents or caregivers, and offenders. Such treatment is helpful in building trust, modeled by the relationship that can be established between the individual and the treatment provider.

Child sexual abuse victims often exhibit behavioral reactions to sexual abuse that are manifested by sleep disturbances, enuresis, risk-taking behaviors, self-destructive behaviors, or sexualized activities. Individualized treatment can help the victim understand the relationship between the behaviors and sexual abuse, develop insight into his or her behaviors, and assist him or her in finding more appropriate expressions of emotions.

Individualized treatment is helpful for nonoffending parents or caregivers who have been sexually victimized themselves. Often the parent or caregiver is so overwhelmed by his or her own abuse that he or she cannot deal with the child's victimization.

Dyadic treatment is used to enhance or repair damage to the nonoffender/child victim relationship and the husband/wife relationship and eventually to create a different kind of relationship between the offender and the victim.

Family treatment is considered at the end of the treatment process and is usually not undertaken until there has been a determination that reunification is in the best interest of the child.

There are other intervention considerations in dealing with child sexual abuse. Sexual abuse treatment is a highly specialized field. Care should be taken to select clinicians who are skilled in the treatment of victims, nonoffending parents or caregivers, and offenders. Rarely is one individual qualified to handle all the issues involved in the complicated spectrum of sexual abuse. Multiple therapists can provide a check and balance for making important treatment decisions. In treating intrafamilial sexual abuse it is important for each family member to consent to share information with therapists treating other family members.

In cases of sexual abuse, family members experience much stress and pain. Therefore, you must be aware of any professional and personal biases that may affect your ability to work with victims and their families.

In screening individuals for group entry, cultural taboos should be explored regarding the discussion of sexual behavior in public or group settings.

☐ Interventions in Families Where There Has Been Neglect

Neglect is the most frequently identified type of child maltreatment occurring in the United States and the most difficult to define or treat. As with physical abuse, an understanding of the factors contributing to neglect influences the selection of prevention and treatment strategies.

Causes of Child Neglect

Neglectful parents or caregivers are often considered *psychologically immature,* usually as a result of their own lack of nurturing as children. Consequently, many neglectful parents or caregivers are unable to consider the needs of others and invest themselves emotionally in another person. This is often demonstrated by infrequent and negative patterns of communication or interaction between a neglectful parent or caregiver and his or her child. Parents or caregivers who neglect their children often have negative perceptions of themselves as parents or caregivers and little confidence that they can improve their skills. These personality traits, combined with poverty, a lack of resources, minimal supports, and high stress levels, can cause the parent or caregiver to feel hopeless (Pecora et al., 2000). An intervention strategy must include building feelings of hope, self-esteem, and self-sufficiency. Small successes, with neglectful parents or caregivers, should be applauded. For example, make a positive statement about him or her keeping an appointment, preparing a hot meal, vacuuming the living room rug, or interacting with his or her child.

Parental clinical depression is often associated with neglect. Further research is needed to firmly establish the relationship between depression and neglect; however, it should be considered as a factor in assessment and service provision.

Studies have found that parents or caregivers who neglect their children often have *poor social skills* and *difficulty with problem solving*. However, each family is unique. Caution should be used regarding generalizations about families who neglect their children that can lead to inappropriate case decisions.

Excessive use of alcohol or drugs is often present in cases of child neglect. Research results do not yet conclude that substance abuse causes neglect, but it is certainly a significant contributing factor.

Unemployment, high levels of poverty, and *lack of support* from family and/or the community are major sources of stress in neglectful families.

Multiple Services

Since families who neglect their children are likely to have multiple issues to resolve, the intervention plan must include multiple services. The following interventions have proven successful in reducing the risk of neglect (Gaudin, 1993):

- *Family-focused interventions.* A review of demonstration projects shows that traditional, in-office, one-to-one counseling by professionals is ineffective with neglect. Successful demonstration projects involve the entire family system, including both parents and children. To remedy chronic neglect, it appears that all family members must learn new ways of interacting.

- *Family preservation services,* supplemented with tangible resources to promote environmental change, help families alter previously acquired patterns.

- In situations involving neglect, *group approaches* that provide very basic child care information and skills, and problem-solving, home management, and social interaction skills have proven more successful with parents or caregivers than groups offering more general content on child development and the needs of children. Successful groups are designed to provide encouragement and support for families and to assist them in developing strengths and becoming involved in decision-making about their lives.

- *Casework techniques.* Intensive, weekly, in-home casework counseling focusing on concrete problem solving is effective in dealing with issues of neglect. Clearly defined structured intervention activities are more success-ful than loosely defined "casework" or "counseling" interventions. Struc-tured interventions incorporate well-developed service plans that include sequential tasks/activities.

Interventions designed to change family communication patterns and parenting techniques should consider cultural norms and not assume that universal ap-proaches are appropriate for all families. Issues such as displays of affection, dis-cussion of feelings, and confrontation about inappropriate behaviors may be handled differently within various cultures.

Interventions to strengthen informal support networks include:

- The worker's use of his or her skills to reframe or mediate negative perceptions the community or family may have regarding the parent or caregiver, or that the parent or caregiver may have regarding his or her support network.

- Use of volunteers or parent aides to expand resources.

- Social skills training to teach parents or caregivers how to make and maintain friendships. This can best be accomplished in groups through modeling, practicing, and rehearsing.

- Identification and linking with "natural helpers" such as a neighbor, a friend, a spiritual leader, or a church member.

- Linking parents or caregivers with existing supportive resources in the community such as churches, schools, cultural activities, or neighborhood groups.

The Importance of Treating and Offering Services to Neglected Children

Most neglect-related interventions focus services on parents or caregivers and do little to remedy the effects of neglect on children. Longitudinal studies indicate that child victims of neglect suffer serious developmental deficits. Remediation of these developmental deficits require supplemental nurturing with preschool children, school-aged children, and teenagers (Gaudin, 1993).

Therapeutic childcare for young children. Effective therapeutic childcare programs are staffed by individuals who understand the negative developmental effects of neglect and provide therapeutic interactions. Parents or caregivers should be in-volved in the therapeutic childcare and receive instructions on how to interact and provide a stimulating and nurturing environment for their children.

Interventions for older children and adolescents. School-age children who are victims of neglect often experience deficits in cognitive and academic functioning. There-fore, they may require intervention through special education programs to prevent school failure and dropout. Group counseling and personal skill development classes are also helpful to raise the level of social functioning of older children and adoles-cents. Volunteer and mentoring programs offer neglected children emotional nur-turing, cultural and recreational activities, and vocational and career counseling.

☐ Interventions in Families Where There Has Been Psychological Abuse

Although cases of physical and sexual abuse gain the most publicity and professional attention, neglect and psychological maltreatment often cause more long-term damage to children. Currently, some states do not include "psychological abuse" in their statutes because it is difficult to define, it often lacks an evidentiary basis for court action, and there is less consensus in the CPS arena as to when and how to intervene. However, psychological abuse is recognized by some as being one of the "core components" of child maltreatment because it is often inherent in other forms of child abuse and neglect.

Causal factors of psychological maltreatment (Pecora et al., 2000). Many parents or caregivers who psychologically maltreat their children were emotionally mistreated themselves as children. The way they are parenting their children is based on the way they were raised. Parents or caregivers who are emotionally mistreated as children often grow up to be emotionally needy and become dependent on their children to satisfy their own needs. When a child is unable to satisfy the parent's or caregiver's need for nurturance, the parent or caregiver feels rejected, insecure, and betrayed by his or her own child, thereby forming the grounds for psychological maltreatment of the child.

Parents or caregivers who psychologically abuse their children often experience social isolation because they withdraw themselves or the community rejects them. Although these parents or caregivers may have some type of relationship with other families in the community, most of the families they associate with suffer from the same situation and may not provide positive support for each other.

Parents or caregivers often have a sense of frustration and powerlessness created by high poverty levels, high percentage of unemployment, high crime rate, inadequate housing, and poor access to services.

Lack of parenting skills is an important risk factor in cases of psychological abuse. Parents or caregivers who psychologically abuse their children often lack knowledge of the developmental stages of children and have unrealistic expectations regarding their child's functioning.

Parents or caregivers who abuse drugs or alcohol are often "out of control" and tend to lash out at their children during times of frustration.

Implementing interventions in psychological abuse. Stressors including lack of financial resources, unemployment, inadequate housing, lack of appropriate medical care, unavailability of services, and community isolation drain parents or caregivers of time and energy, making it difficult to provide a positive environment for their children. When families are stressed by lack of resources, you may need to provide them with referrals to remedy their immediate needs.

Interventions may need to resolve problems in interpersonal relationships and improve overall family functioning. Interventions that may be helpful in modifying family functioning include (Pecora et al., 2000):

- *Family therapy.* May be useful in reducing psychologically destructive family patterns of interaction and inappropriate coping behaviors. The goal would be to provide emotional support and nurturance to all members and to help the family function in a healthy manner.
- *Parent-child counseling.* Parent-child interventions improve the parent-child relationship and attempt to eliminate dysfunctional patterns.
- *Infant-mother interaction.* Interventions with infants and parents focus specifically on the infant-mother interaction. Skills are taught to the mother to help her become more nurturing and to meet the needs of her infant.
- *Parent skills training.* Parenting interventions teach practical skills to parents so they can gain competence in their parenting role.
- *Increased social connectedness* to reduce isolation.

☐   Intervention in Families Where There Has Been Domestic Violence

The importance of building collaborative services and partnerships between CPS agencies and domestic violence programs should be understood (Foley, Berns, Test, Bragg, & Schecter, 2001). Due to the high rate of cooccurrence of domestic violence and child maltreatment, CPS, domestic violence programs, batterer intervention programs, child advocates, the court system, schools, law enforcement, and health providers need to work together to ensure child safety, stability, and permanence. Cross-training for domestic violence advocates, CPS workers, and other agencies is essential to conducting thorough safety/risk assessments and planning effective interventions on behalf of children.

A differential response can be used for children and families experiencing domestic violence. Many communities are designing services that assist the adult victim in securing safety and protection for his or her children without opening a child protection case. Cases that have identified risk factors associated with potentially severe and lethal domestic violence are served by CPS. In cases involving domestic violence it is important to assess protective factors and other resources available to families in order to determine the most appropriate intervention and service plan. Cases with lower levels of risk can be served through community-based programs.

Community-based interventions and partnerships can supplement the array of services for families experiencing domestic violence. Community-based domestic violence services may include temporary shelters, legal advocacy, support groups, hotlines, counseling and education groups, housing assistance, trauma services for children, case management, and education groups for perpetrators. In addition, an adult victim may need substance abuse counseling, money management skills, parenting classes, financial assistance, respite care, and job training.

CPS interventions in cases with domestic violence. In *Domestic Violence: A National Curriculum for Children's Protective Services* (1996), Anne Ganley and Susan Schechter propose the following intervention plan in child protection cases involving domestic violence:

- *Use of legal remedies and community resources.* The courts can be instrumental in protecting children by mandating participation in programs to reduce violence, issuing civil and criminal protection orders, evicting the batterer from the home or prohibiting access to the adult victim and children, and monitoring the batterer's compliance with court orders.
- *Supporting adult and child victims.* Support for adults concurrently protects children. You can support adult victims by validating their experiences, building on their strengths, assisting them in regaining control over their lives, and exploring their own options. A family-centered approach can promote child safety while engaging the adults and encouraging change.
- *Safety planning.* In domestic violence, safety planning must be included at every juncture of the case. Safety plans should be developed with the adult victims and children (if age appropriate). A few examples of information that may be included in an adult safety plan are (1) determining who to call and what to do when the batterer becomes threatening or violent; (2) making a list of persons or agencies that can provide safety and shelter; (3) saving money and making copies of important documents in the event the adult victim needs to flee to shelter with the children.

Special considerations in service planning in cases involving domestic violence include the following:

- You should *develop separate individualized service plans,* one for the adult victim and child, and one for the domestic violence perpetrator. Maintain confidentiality by not sharing the adult and child's plan with the perpetrator, particularly if it contains details around safety planning.
- *Develop safe procedures* for visitation and exchanges of children.
- *Remember the inappropriateness of counseling with the batterer and the victim.* Many of the professionals involved in a CPS case may not be aware of the dynamics of domestic violence. Sometimes it is assumed that domestic violence is a "marital issue" that requires marriage counseling. Advocate with the court as needed for safety first, and educate providers about the traumatic effects for the victims.
- In service planning, *include services to children.* Studies show that children who witness domestic violence typically receive treatment long after the traumatic incidents and only after serious behavior problems surface. Although some children do not show any significant effects as a result of their exposure to domestic violence, others exhibit increased levels of anxiety, depression, anger, and fear; aggressive and violent behaviors; lack of conflict resolution skills; lack of empathy for others and unhealthy peer relationships; poor school performance and cognitive functioning; higher rates of suicide, delinquent behavior, pregnancy, and alcohol and illegal drug use; self-blame, hopelessness, shame, and apathy; and posttraumatic stress disorder symptoms such as hypervigilance, nightmares, intrusive thoughts, and images of violence.

Managing and monitoring cases (Ganley & Schecter, 1996).

Case management with the adult victim. Each adult victim has a different timetable for implementing change. Research by Giles-Sims (as cited in Ganley & Schechter, 1996) reports that the greater a woman's support system, the quicker she can recover from domestic violence and assist her children. Therefore, once a woman leaves the support of a shelter, additional resources should be explored to prevent isolation, loneliness, and vulnerability.

Adult victims who are seriously affected by substance abuse, depression, or anxiety will take longer to recover from the effects of domestic violence and will need more intensive supports in the form of home-based services. Case management for these families may also require more frequent visits to monitor and ensure child safety.

Case management with the perpetrator. A perpetrator's progress should be monitored for whether he or she stops the abuse rather than for his or her promises or participation in a program. Progress can be monitored through contacts with the treatment program and the adult and child victim.

☐ Intervention in Families Experiencing Addictions to Drugs and/or Alcohol

Studies show that children who are raised by parents or caregivers who abuse alcohol and other drugs are almost three times more likely to be abused and four times more likely to be neglected than other children. This was confirmed in 1999, when 85% of states named substance abuse and poverty as the top two issues contributing to abuse and neglect referrals in their agencies. Drug and alcohol misuse are also contributing factors for increased placement of children in the foster care system, as well as for longer foster care stays. Finally, if parents or caregivers do not get appropriate treatment for alcohol or drug abuse, their children are more likely to reenter foster care once they have returned home (Child Welfare League of America, 2001).

Given the substantial impact of substance abuse on families and child protective services, it is important to use multiple intervention efforts to help families stop abusing alcohol and drugs, to provide services that are most effective in helping families stay together, and to implement approaches that promote family reunification.

Understanding families who abuse drugs or alcohol is essential. Most parents or caregivers do not intend to harm their children or ignore their children's needs. In fact, parents or caregivers who use drugs or alcohol frequently feel guilt and shame about how their drug or alcohol use may affect their children. Once addicted, however, the parent or caregiver loses control over his or her life and is preoccupied with the goal of obtaining and using drugs. The effects of alcohol or other drug usage are so powerful that they supersede previous parenting values. Parents or caregivers become so absorbed with their own needs for alcohol and/or drugs that the basic needs of their children for food, shelter, care, interaction, and supervision are often not met.

Although parents or caregivers who abuse alcohol or other drugs initially use compensatory strategies, such as leaving the child with a babysitter prior to using drugs, or waiting until the children are sound asleep, or paying all their bills as soon as they receive money, eventually the strategies break down, and the parent or caregiver cannot keep the child safe or meet his or her basic needs.

It is helpful to understand some of the factors that may contribute to alcohol or drug dependency. Individuals may use drugs to alleviate problems and emotional pain or to meet emotional needs. Alcohol or drug abuse may coexist with mental health issues, poverty, discrimination, low self-esteem, or a history of maltreatment during the adult's childhood.

Working with families who use alcohol or other drugs is extremely difficult due to the effect of the drugs on the family member's personality and the defense mechanisms he or she may use. A family member may use anger or denial to reduce anxiety or to avoid being confronted with reality. The use of these defenses is automatic but often results in the parent or caregiver being labeled "resistant."

A person abusing substances may also utilize silence or excessive talking (but not talking in specifics) and creating a "scene" as methods of keeping you at a distance. These avoidant behaviors are often used in an attempt to continue the addictive behaviors.

It is helpful to understand that "resistive and avoidant" behaviors are a way of preventing you and others from recognizing the person's sense of fragility and powerlessness. A family member may also use these challenging behaviors as a way to attempt to take control of his or her situation.

Due to the multiple issues that substance-abusing families present and the nature of the disease of addiction, as a worker you may naturally feel overwhelmed and hopeless. But don't give up. The family and you can experience positive results.

> Studies by the Substance Abuse and Mental Health Services Administration show that nearly one-third of persons in recovery achieve abstinence from their first attempt at recovery and one-third have brief periods of relapse but eventually achieve long-term abstinence. These statistics are consistent with the lifelong recovery rates of any chronic lifestyle-related illness, such as diabetes, asthma, and hypertension. (CWLA, 2001, pp. 2–3)

Recent alcohol and other drug treatment research finds that persons who are mandated to participate in alcohol or drug treatment have outcomes similar to those of people who voluntarily participate in treatment (Young, Gardner, & Dennis, 1998).

The following considerations are important in choosing alcohol or other drug abuse interventions. Continual assessment in the case is necessary to ensure the child's safety. Zuckerman (1994) writes: "If the mother is addicted, the child's safety can be assured only if an adult who does not use drugs is in the household and is willing to take care of the child or if the mother is actively involved in treatment that regularly monitors the child" (as cited in Rycus & Hughes, 1998, p. 292).

Due to the wide variety of substances that can be used, it is not usually possible for you to accurately diagnose which drug is used and to what degree. Therefore, anyone suspected of substance abuse should be evaluated by a professional in the drug or alcohol field, and substance abuse treatment professionals should be included on the service planning team.

The most effective programs in dealing with alcohol or other drug abuse are *family focused, nonpunitive, and supportive rather than confrontational.*

Due to Adoption and Safe Families Act timelines, *services need to be readily available.* Families lose valuable time if they have to wait for treatment services to begin.

Although there are *differing standards of confidentiality* between child protective services and substance abuse treatment providers, it is important to find ways to overcome those barriers by developing joint formal protocols, allowing you to communicate assessment, treatment, case management, and visitation information. (See Chapter 4 for more information.)

Culturally based treatment or programs with a reputation of being culturally aware and responsive may be more effective for individuals from various backgrounds. The availability of and desire for such treatment should be assessed.

There is a greater chance of success when you use an interdisciplinary approach that partners and collaborates with other professionals and agencies (CWLA, 2001). Some CPS agencies team with a substance abuse provider, located in the CPS agency, to assess and assist families with appropriate treatment plans. This teaming is proving effective in breaking down some of the defenses of denial and more quickly linking families to services. The team approach allows for frequent communication and case coordination to reduce service fragmentation.

Many agencies are forming interagency teams that include a CPS worker, a substance abuse treatment provider, and a public health nurse. These teams make joint home visits for the purpose of assessing and treating families. The interagency teams meet on a regular basis for formal staffings to share information and evaluate the family's progress. In order to gain a common knowledge base and framework for working with families, interagency teams participate in joint trainings. This process also helps familiarize professionals with each other's agencies, policies, and services.

As alcohol and drug abuse increases, many grandparents are caring for their grandchildren because the children's parents are unable to provide for their needs. Programs are being developed to provide a wide range of services designed to assist grandparents in caring for their grandchildren. Such programs may include stress management and education about addiction, including the concept of enabling addictive behaviors. Grandparents also need information about community resources, financial assistance, legal custody, food stamps, and medical care for their grandchildren.

Alcohol or other drug treatment programs are most effective when they use multifaceted approaches that include the following service components:

Detoxification units should be provided if they are needed.

Intensive family preservation services include family counseling, referrals for housing, legal services, and food. The frequent contact of family preservation models also monitors child safety and engages the family in the treatment process.

Alcohol or other drug abuse treatment should also address *parent education and training*, including the impact that alcohol or drug abuse has on parenting.

Alcohol or other drug abuse treatment should include *multiple weekly contacts with peers* (such as 12-step programs); *treatment related to maintaining abstinence; urine monitoring; education* regarding the effects of alcohol and drugs; and *individual counseling*. *Mentors or sponsors* also promote recovery.

Supportive services, including health care, spiritual counseling if desired, vocational counseling, transportation to and from treatment, and developmental and protective day care services assist parents or caregivers in attending treatment programs.

Special attention must be given to the needs of children. Often the medical and developmental issues of substance-exposed infants and children require health care services. Programs are needed that give parents or caregivers an opportunity to practice parenting skills within an environment that also ensures a child's safety, stability, and consistency. Classroom activities assist parents or caregivers in establishing predictable routines and structure.

Public school–funded preschool activities can be helpful to young children. After-school activities and mentoring programs benefit older children.

Children should be included in the alcohol or drug treatment process whenever possible. In growing up with a parent or caregiver who is chemically dependent they have experienced the effects of their parent's or caregiver's addiction. Therefore, children often need individual and family counseling to address the impact that parental alcohol or drug abuse has had on their lives.

If children cannot be safe at home, best practice would allow the mother and her children to be placed in a *residential treatment group home* to provide intensive family treatment without separating the children from their mother. Residential treatment stays are typically between 6 and 12 months in length.

Case management enhances aftercare and reduces recidivism.

Child protective services drug courts are proving to have a positive impact on motivation, participation, and success rates. Most CPS drug courts monitor cases closely by holding court frequently (in some cases weekly) to review the family member's treatment progress. This accountability offers rewards to individuals who are compliant with their service plan and immediate consequences to those who are out of compliance.

Relapse and safety planning should be included in the treatment process. Strategies that are based on knowledge of the stages of change might include helping the parent or caregiver predict situations in which relapse is high, rehearsing avoidance strategies, and developing a drug-free network of social contacts and a realistic perspective of the negative consequences of drug or alcohol abuse.

You should develop a safety plan for the children in the event the parent or caregiver relapses. Who can care for and supervise the children if the parent or caregiver chooses to use alcohol or other drugs? Who will meet the children's needs until the parent or caregiver can again care for them and participate in the recovery process?

If and when relapse occurs, encourage the parent or caregiver to make contact with support systems that have been helpful prior to the relapse period. Remind the parent or caregiver that he or she was successful in the recovery process for a period of time and can be successful again.

If the parent or caregiver cannot participate successfully in the recovery process, you need to pursue other permanency options for the child. Continually communicate to the family the reality of the Adoption and Safe Families Act and the time limits for reunification. Early in the case consider the poor prognosis indicators regarding the use of alcohol and other drugs as well as the mitigating factors and strengths. Without predicting failure, when appropriate, apply the principles of concurrent planning.

Develop and work a concurrent plan for the child's permanency. Engage maternal and paternal relatives in the process of developing a plan for permanency through adoption or transfer of guardianship to a relative.

Help the family to place the needs of the child first while supporting the family member with his or her chemical dependency issues. Family involvement models have been utilized for these purposes.

☐ **Interventions for Parents or Caregivers
with Severe Physical or Mental Disabilities**

Parents or caregivers who lack the ability and/or judgment needed to provide safe homes for their children often come to the attention of CPS. At times this occurs with mothers and fathers who have developmental disabilities, cognitive impairments, and/or severe mental health issues. Studies have found that over half the parents in the United States with cognitive limitations will at some time experience permanent or temporary removal of their children from the family home. Given the frequency of involvement with parents or caregivers who have special needs, consideration should be given to the use of adaptive equipment and supports (Muenzer-Day & Anderson, 1998).

In planning intervention strategies involving parents or caregivers with severe physical or mental disabilities, consult with individuals who have expertise in the field of disabilities. Supportive devices or adaptive equipment may be available to assist a parent or caregiver who has a physical disability in safely meeting the needs of his or her child. Programs that have proven most effective with parents or caregivers who have cognitive limitations are a combination of home visiting programs, parenting groups, center-based programs, and shared parenting models (Anderson & Lakin, 1998).

Home visiting programs are often effective because they provide an opportunity for the parent or caregiver to learn in the setting where they will use the skills, making generalizations and transfer of knowledge easier. In-home services can identify the unique and constantly changing circumstances and needs of each family. Examples include accessing transportation, developing strategies to decrease missed appointments, and addressing areas of concern such as housing conditions or nutrition.

Parenting groups have been used to teach discipline techniques, health and safety issues, and decision-making skills. The use of groups has been shown to be most effective when combined with home visitation programs, because home visitation allows parents or caregivers to transfer the ideas and skills learned in the group session to the home setting. Groups allow parents with cognitive limitations to establish needed connections. Often parents or caregivers are isolated because they tend to have small friendship networks, and family members may become "worn out" by the ongoing emotional and physical needs.

Center-based programs often provide services to parents or caregivers and children at a program site but, like group interventions, are most effective when combined with in-home services. Center-based programs have the benefit of providing services to parents or caregivers and children jointly and separately at the same site. Center-based programs can often serve larger numbers.

Shared parenting models provide an effective way for children to remain in contact with their parents or caregivers when the parents or caregivers cannot fully meet the child's needs. In situations where these severe cognitive limitations exist, the parent or caregiver and child live together and a provider serves as a "coparent."

Even with intensive supports, some parents or caregivers are unable to learn to adequately care for their children and keep them safe. In such cases, open adoptions have been used to help parents and children maintain a relationship after termination of parental rights.

Often families with disabilities have multiple service providers. It is helpful for service providers to collaborate and develop an integrated service plan. This provides for greater consistency and minimizes confusion. It also allows for better service coordination and eliminates duplication of services.

Teaching parenting skills to parents or caregivers with cognitive limitations involves knowledge of instructional strategies that promote successful learning. Some of these strategies include (Maneville & Snodgrass, 1998):

- Focus each parenting session on only one learning objective at a time and use a variety of learning modalities. Sessions should include encouragement and compliments so they are not an additional stressor to the parents or caregivers.
- Teaching should include concrete methods, combining "showing" with "telling." The person providing the training should demonstrate the desired behavior and then repeat it. Tasks should be broken down into parts.
- It is useful to provide pictures, charts, or other kinds of visual cues that will help in recalling the teaching.
- Skills are best taught in the setting in which they will be used, and learning should be experiential. Allow the parent or caregiver to practice and celebrate successes.

Keep in mind that a parent or caregiver with a disability can be successful, and that his or her right to parent is often protected by specific state statutes and by constitutional law. In many cities there are disability law centers that can assist in determining the legal requirements for parents involved in dependency and neglect cases as well as making referrals to services. As in any child protection case, the focus should be on child safety, and appropriate supports should be made available to parents or caregivers with disabilities.

Children of parents or caregivers who have developmental delays or severe mental health issues need extra support. In addition to family support, children benefit from early intervention services, homework assistance, and recreational and after-school enrichment activities. Maternal-child interaction is found to be the main parenting deficit for mothers with limited cognitive abilities. Therefore, daycare or preschool settings may be used to allow children to receive more stimulation and experience appropriate child/adult behaviors.

School-age children often need assistance with homework and encouragement in reading. A family member, friend, or an older neighborhood child may be able to assist in providing learning opportunities to children, given parental consent. Child involvement in after-school activities, camps, and neighborhood, cultural, or faith-based programs are helpful in supplementing the home environment.

■ Termination of the CPS Casework Process

Termination of the CPS casework process is the final phase of your work with the family. *Termination* is synonymous with *case closure* and refers to the point at which the service provision process ends. Keep in mind that you should begin to prepare for the termination of the casework process during the actual formulation of your service plan, since it is at that time that you and the family consider what must occur for goal achievement. Thus you are setting the criteria for termination and negotiating this process as you develop a service plan with the family.

☐ Evaluation Prior to Case Closure

The decision to close a case emerges from a case evaluation. As you evaluate the service plan, you will observe indicators for termination and levels of achievement that will help you to decide whether to terminate the casework process. The primary indicators are observable changes in behavior and family functioning. There should not be a recent occurrence of abusive or maltreating behavior, and the circumstances that previously led to maltreatment either are no longer present or are handled differently by the parent or caregiver.

Reassessing the case prior to reunification or closure focuses critical decisions on whether sufficient progress has been made by the family to ensure the child's safety. The factors and levels of risk at the time the case was opened for services should be compared to the factors and level of risk prior to reunification or closure. The question to ask is "How much progress has been made toward reducing the risk factors that required CPS intervention?" This comparison allows you to verify changes that have occurred. The evaluation should indicate that previous safety and risk factors are now significantly reduced and managed.

Prior to reunification or case closure you should review the family's progress in accomplishing the tasks, objectives, and goals as outlined in their service plan. You know it is safe to reunify or close a case when the family's behaviors are matching the behaviors that were defined as required in the original and any modified service plan objectives. The achievement of the goals and objectives indicate to you, the family, and service providers that the children are no longer in need of protection.

Not only should you reassess risk levels and review the accomplishments of the service plan objectives, but you should also evaluate the family's current level of functioning. There are some *basic levels of parent or caregiver achievement* that will assist you in determining whether it is safe to "step down," or close agency interventions with the family. Many family functioning scales are available; some basic principles to consider are the following: (1) The family should demonstrate that they have improved their level of functioning since first contact with your agency. (2) The parent or caregiver must understand why he or she was not previously successful in keeping his or her child safe. (3) The parent or caregiver should demonstrate that he or she has the motivation and capacity to learn new and more positive methods of assuming responsibility for his or her child. He or she should be able to generalize these new methods to other challenges that the family might face in the future. (4) The parent or caregiver should put the needs of the child above his or her own needs. Likewise, the parent or caregiver meets the child's needs. For example:

- The parent or caregiver engages the child in positive interactive communication or play. With an infant or young child, this is demonstrated when the parent or caregiver makes frequent eye contact with the baby and interactive mirroring of expressions occurs.
- The parent or caregiver uses positive strategies to manage the child's behaviors—for example, listens, redirects, sets boundaries, and provides praise and feedback. Remember to consider cultural differences in these areas, including seeking the advice of a cultural expert or trusted extended family member such as a grandparent or elder.
- The parent or caregiver anticipates the child's needs—for example, packs a diaper bag before leaving the house with the baby.
- The parent or caregiver recognizes the importance of routines in feeding, hygiene, and sleep and integrates routines of care in daily living schedules.
- The parent or caregiver knows when to seek medical care.
- The parent or caregiver says and reinforces "no" if he or she sees the child's request is not in his or her best interest.
- The parent or caregiver shows empathy for the child, if culturally appropriate. For example, during a supervised visit, a 3-year-old child ran into a coffee table and started whimpering. The Indian mother did not comfort

the child but simply said, "Sweetie, you need to watch where you are going and be careful so you don't hurt yourself." Indian children are taught to be careful and personally responsible for their actions. They may not be given "empathy" if the goal is to develop self-control and reduce the number of incidents of self-harm.

- The parent or caregiver deliberately strives to make sure the child is safe from harm.

(5) The family has shown the ability to access and use resources to assist them in problem solving.

If a child has been in alternate care, most agencies do not close a case immediately after reunification. Instead the agency facilitates and supervises family reunification to ensure the child's safety.

In some cases, terminating a relationship with a parent or caregiver may not mean reunification or case closure. It may mean that the parent or caregiver has not made the necessary changes to reduce the risks of future maltreatment and an alternate living arrangement is being made for their child. A child may have been placed with a relative for permanent guardianship. Under ASFA, this is a reason to not terminate parental rights. When you need to terminate a relationship with the parent or caregiver, it may not always be a positive outcome for the parent or caregiver but may reflect the best possible outcome for the child.

In such a situation, if a child cannot return to the home of the parent or caregiver, you should assist the parents or caregivers as they begin to process their grief and loss. You should refer them to available services and encourage them to continue to seek solutions to their problems and deal with grief and loss. Develop a life book for the child so he or she has a record of his or her history.

If a child has a permanent placement with a relative, be clear about the conditions under which the child may visit with the parent or caregiver, and anticipate the power issues that may occur with the relative caregiver. Determine a plan for the caregiver to seek assistance, if needed, to keep the children safe.

The judgments you make with regard to terminating a service plan and closing a case should be made in conjunction with the family, with your supervisor, and with the court (if there is court involvement).

☐ Reasons for Terminating the CPS Process

There are a number of reasons to terminate the CPS casework process. After having assessed the previous criteria, you should recognize that there are both valid and invalid reasons for discontinuing work with families.

Acceptable reasons for terminating the CPS process are as follows:

- *The children are no longer at risk of maltreatment.* The issues that brought the family to the attention of the agency have been addressed by successful achievement of the service plan goals, and no new safety factors have been identified.

- *Situations in the case may have significantly changed.* For example: (1) The child may no longer need protection because he or she is permanently living with another family member where there is no risk of maltreatment. (2) The child may have become emancipated. In some cases the child may, however, still be served through an independent living plan. (3) The abuser may have died or left the home permanently. (4) The parents or caregivers may have relinquished the children for guardianship or adoption. (5) The jurisdiction for the case may have been transferred to the American Indian child's tribal court.
- *The family's situation may be stabilized* and the family has been linked to community services for ongoing support, or the family may still have service needs but the needs may not be protective in nature.
- *The family has refused services* and there is no legal ground for intervention.
- *The family has moved* to another state or community and another worker or agency is taking responsibility for the family.
- *The family cannot be located* even after a thorough search.
- *The courts have ordered case closure.*

Unacceptable reasons for termination/case closure are as follows:

- Cases may be closed due to a minimal level of activity over a period of time. A worker may justify case closure by thinking, "The family must be doing okay because I haven't had any new referrals for a while." Case closure is inappropriate without evaluating the current status of risk.
- *Some workers are intimidated by a family and want to terminate the case so as to no longer have to deal with them.* In situations where you fear for your own safety, talk with your supervisor so he or she can put supports in place. Worker safety should not be compromised. In some instances, a case may need to be reassigned to a different worker or law enforcement assistance may be required in monitoring the family's progress.
- *A worker may want to close a case because he or she is angry or frustrated with the family about their lack of progress.*
- *"Hopelessness" can be contagious.* A worker can become as overwhelmed as the families he or she serves. Multiple problems and a scarcity of resources may cause a worker to lose a positive perspective and think, "What's the use?"
- Cases should not be closed because a caseload is too high or the worker is too busy. Case closure should be prioritized by evaluating the risk of future maltreatment, not as a means of controlling the capacity of the CPS system.

Cases may remain open that should be closed.

Workers may keep inactive cases open when, in fact, they should be closed. In the following situations it is inappropriate to keep the case open:

- *Cases may remain open because workers do not have or do not take the time to complete documentation that is required to close the case.* This practice can increase liability if, for example, a child is harmed when the case is "statistically" open but the worker has little or no contact.

- *Workers may keep a case open even though they are no longer working with the family* because they think, "If another problem develops we won't have to start over again; we'll already be involved" or "Having the case open may prevent abuse from recurring."

- *Workers may want to keep a case open because they like a family* and feel good working with them.

- At times workers may not want to close cases because *it will reduce their caseload size* and may result in the assignment of new, more difficult cases.

- *There is always the potential for a worker to have a bias toward certain types of families.* This may involve unresolved issues from the worker's own history, such as sexual, physical, or emotional abuse or neglect, domestic violence, or substance abuse. Workers who have not done intentional personal work regarding cultural or racial biases may keep cases open beyond the time when families have met their goals and court-ordered criteria have been met for having children returned. Supervisors should be aware of cases that are being held open past this point and work with workers to discover and appropriately address any personal issues that interfere with professional judgment.

All of these justifications for keeping a case open increase liability and take time and resources that could be applied to more critical cases. In addition, children in out-of-home placements are unnecessarily delayed in reunifying with their parents or caregivers and may experience more preventable loss due to disrupted attachments to temporary caregivers.

☐   The Termination/Case Closure Process

The decision to close a case is made during the evaluation phase to ensure that the goals and objectives in the service plan have been achieved or there is another acceptable reason for termination. If possible, termination/case closure should be based on a mutual agreement among you, your supervisor, the family, and the court (if involved). The actual termination phase becomes a casework activity of documentation, communication, and disengagement.

The following procedures can facilitate a positive case closure and prevent recidivism.

Early in the case, clarify your role with the family. Explain that you are there to assist them in accomplishing the objectives and goals outlined in their service plan, and when that purpose is achieved the case will be closed. Addressing case closure at the beginning of the case not only gives the family hope of success but also may prevent them from feeling that you are abandoning them later in the case.

After evaluating the family's progress, you should set potential time frames for case closure. During this time, your direct involvement with the family should be gradually decreasing. When families have made significant progress, acknowledge their daily successes.

Prior to termination/case closure, you should schedule an appointment with the family to discuss your work together. This appointment should give you the opportunity to put "the finishing touches" on the helping process. During the appointment you should review the entire CPS process with the family, paying particular attention to the difference between the family's earlier and current behavior and circumstances. Acknowledge the family's personal achievements in making improvements. Celebrate termination while realistically acknowledging ongoing challenges that may or will exist. You should help the family prepare to use existing problem-solving skills in future problem-solving efforts.

Transfer attachments from you to other supportive relationships in the community by linking families to community resources. Let them know that you are not the only person who can help them. It may be appropriate to reconvene a meeting with the extended family and community support persons to assess the family's progress and plan for their needs in reunification.

Help the family to recognize and deal with feelings associated with termination. If the family's relationship with you has been rewarding and mutually respectful, and if the relationship itself has been a key factor in helping the family to accomplish goals, members of the family may go through a number of reactions in the termination stage. They may evidence *denial,* in which they seemingly forget that termination is to occur or consciously avoid the subject and refuse to face the reality of impending termination.

The family may seem to regress or backslide in their ability to cope with problems. They may seek to become more dependent on you and express a fear of the loss of your support. They may express feelings of anger, rejection, self-pity, grief, desertion, or betrayal. These feelings may relate directly to you or to people in general and are indicative of the feelings of loss.

The family may express a need for continued help. They may feel that you will continue your supportive relationship and continue providing services if they demonstrate that there is still a need for services. For example, they may revert to old behaviors or create or verbalize new problems. They may feel or express doubts about their ability to maintain gains without your involvement.

Respond to and acknowledge the family's expressions of feelings. Reinforce, wherever possible, the progress and achievements the family has made, assisting them in seeing their role in making changes. Emphasize your faith in their ability to utilize their skills in the future without involvement or support from you.

Let the family know that closing the case does not mean you no longer care what happens to them. Reassure the family that if they have future needs, they can call and you will help them identify potential resources.

Notify other involved agencies of the decision to terminate your services. In some situations the termination of your relationship with the family does not mean that all activity with a case stops. For example, there may be continuing court action, or another worker may be involved in another social service activity such as adoption.

Remember that termination with the family is not complete until you have documented the closure according to your agency's policies. Documentation should include the relevant decisions and the rationale for closing the case. The case closure summary should also include any referrals or instructions that were given to the family.

■ Summary of Competencies

You, as a child protection worker, are in a central position to intervene in families when allegations of child abuse have been made. Your intervention comes at a time when families are often in crises. Your "knock on the door," when carried out in a thoughtful and planned manner, may be very effective in strengthening families to become more competent at solving their problems. Essential CPS worker competencies include the following:

Knowledge:

1. Knowledge of the casework principles necessary for the development and maintenance of the helping relationship.

2. Knowledge of responsibilities, procedures, and the process of negotiating, monitoring, and evaluating the service providers' work with families.

3. Knowledge of communication techniques that reflect respect, positive regard, and genuineness.

4. Familiarity with service resources available in the community and associated eligibility criteria.

5. Knowledge of components of a service plan or contract.

6. Knowledge of the dynamics of negotiating a service contract.

7. Knowledge of interventions and strategies that are effective in addressing all types of child maltreatment.

8. Knowledge of the attitudes, traditions, and rules of each social group your agency serves.

9. Understanding and following the criteria for and process of case termination.

Skills:

1. Ability to work effectively with children, parents or caregivers, and families.

2. Ability to prioritize (based on family strengths, problems, weaknesses) service needs on the basis of available information.

3. Ability to establish goals and objectives that build on identified strengths.

4. Ability to design a service plan that is clear and concise and addresses outcomes that are measurable and have meaning to the family, agency, and court (if involved).

5. Proficiency in determining which services are appropriate for each family member's needs.

6. Ability to identify and provide or refer families to culturally responsive services.

7. Expertise in using service providers to assist the family in reaching their goals.

8. Ability to coordinate services and negotiate timely outcomes for services.

9. Ability to keep accurate and up-to-date case records.

10. Ability to monitor and evaluate the family's progress.

11. Ability to effectively terminate services and the relationship with the family.

12. Ability to know when you are "in over your head," or when your personal issues have been triggered by the family in some way, and to seek advice from your supervisor or personal therapy, if warranted.

References

American Academy of Pediatrics. (2000). Developmental issues for young children in foster care. *Pediatrics, 106*(5), 1145–1150.

Anderson, L., & Lakin, K. C. (1998). Parents with cognitive limitations: What do we know about providing support? *Impact, 11*(1), 6–7.

Berliner, L., & Kolko, D. (2000). What works in treatment services for abused children. In M. P. Kluger, G. Alexander, & P. A. Curtis (Eds.), *What works in child welfare* (pp. 97–104). Washington, DC: CWLA Press.

Biestek, F. P. (1957). *The casework relationship.* Chicago: Loyola University Press.

Child Welfare League of America. (2001). *Alcohol, other drugs, and child welfare.* Washington, DC: CWLA Press.

Christensen, D. N., Todahl, J., & Barrett, W.C. (1999). *Solution-based casework.* New York: De Gruyter.

Dawson, K., & Berry, M. (2002). Engaging families in child welfare services: An evidence-based approach to best practice. *Child Welfare, 81*(2), 3.

DePanfilis, D., & Salus, M. K. (1992). *Child protective services: A guide for caseworkers.* Washington, DC: U.S. Deptartment of Health and Human Services, Administration for Children and Families, Administration on Children, Youth and Families, National Center on Child Abuse and Neglect.

Faller, K. (1993). *Child sexual abuse: Intervention and treatment issues.* U.S. Department of Health and Human Services, Administration for Children and Families. McLean, VA: The Circle, Inc.

Foley, R., Berns, D., Test, G., Bragg, H. L., & Schechter, S. (2001). *Guidelines for public child welfare agencies serving children and families experiencing domestic violence.* Washington, DC: American Public Human Services Association.

Ganley, A. L., & Schechter, S. (1996). *Domestic violence: A national curriculum for children's protective services.* San Francisco: Family Violence Prevention Fund.

Gaudin, J. M. (1993). *Child neglect: A guide for intervention.* Washington, DC: U.S. Department of Health and Human Services, Administration for Children and Families, Administration on Children, Youth and Families, National Center on Child Abuse and Neglect.

Gelles, R. J. (1996). *The book of David.* New York: Basic Books.

Holder, W. (2000). *Change-based CPS intervention: An overview.* Charlotte, NC: Action for Child Protection.

Katz, L. (1999). Concurrent planning: benefits and pitfalls. *Child Welfare, 78*(1), 6.

Macleod, J., & Nelson, G. (2000). Programs for the promotion of family wellness and the prevention of child maltreatment: A meta-analytic review. *Child Abuse and Neglect, 24,* 1127–1149.

Maneville, H., & Snodgrass, P. (1998). Helping parents be parents. *Impact, 11*(1), 2–3.

McCart Hess, P., & Ohman Proch, K. (1988). *Family visiting in out-of-home care: A guide to practice.* Washington, DC: CWLA Press.

McCurdy, K. (2000). What works in nonmedical home visiting: Healthy families America. In M. P. Kluger, G. Alexander, & P.A. Curtis (Eds.), *What works in child welfare* (pp. 45–55). Washington, DC: CWLA Press.

Muenzer-Day, D., & Anderson, L. (1998). Supporting parents and children during termination of parental rights. *Impact, 11*(1).

National Resource Center for Foster Care and Permanency Planning. (2001). *Concurrent planning handout.* New York: Hunter College School of Social Work.

Nelson, K. (2000). What works in family preservation services. In M. P. Kluger, G. Alexander, & P. A. Curtis (Eds.), *What works in child welfare* (pp. 11–21). Washington, DC: CWLA Press.

Pecora, P. J., Whittaker, J. K., Maluccia, A. N., & Barth, R., with Plotnick, R. D. (2000). *The child welfare challenge: Policy, practice, and research.* (2nd ed.). New York: De Gruyter.

Prochaska, J. M., & Prochaska, J. O. (2002). Transtheoretical model guidelines for families with child abuse and neglect. In A. R. Roberts & G. J. Greene (Eds.), *Social workers' desk reference* (pp. 379–384). New York: Oxford University Press.

Rycus, J. S., & Hughes, R. C. (1998). *Field guide to child welfare: Case planning and family-centered casework* (Vol. 2). Washington, DC: CWLA Press.

Skiba, R. J., & Nichols, S. (2000). What works in wraparound programming. In M. P. Kluger, G. Alexander, & P. A. Curtis (Eds.), *What works in child welfare* (pp. 23–32). Washington, DC: CWLA Press.

Tierney, J., & Grossman, J. B. (2000). What works in promoting positive youth development: Mentoring. In M. P. Kluger, G. Alexander, & P. A. Curtis (Eds.), *What works in child welfare* (pp. 323–328). Washington, DC: CWLA Press.

Tracy, E. M. (2000). What works in family support services. In M. P. Kluger, G. Alexander, & P. A. Curtis (Eds.), *What works in child welfare* (pp. 3–9). Washington, DC: CWLA Press.

Wright, L. (2001). *Tool box no. 1: Using visitation to support permanency.* Washington, DC: CWLA Press.

Young, N. K., Gardner, S. L., & Dennis, K. (1998). *Responding to alcohol and other drug problems in child welfare: Weaving together practice and policy.* Washington, DC: CWLA Press.

11

Amy Winterfeld
with contributions by
Deborah Esquibel Hunt

The Legal Framework for Child Protective Services

- History of the Judicial System and Child Abuse and Neglect

- The Current Law of Child Abuse and Neglect

- Similarities and Differences in the Juvenile, Domestic Relations, Civil, and Criminal Courts

- The CPS Worker and the Courts

- Legal Accountability

- Summary of Competencies

Courts and CPS agencies share the goal of ensuring that children have safe, permanent homes. To reach this goal, there must be an effective working partnership between agency workers and legal and judicial personnel. Forging this partnership requires a commitment to cooperate in the interest of children, knowledge of the legal framework for child protective services, and ongoing efforts to improve collaborative practice.

Court intervention, in cases of child abuse and neglect, may consist of a simple *ex parte* (one side only) order, a full trial by judge or jury involving all parties, or a myriad of other processes in between, in the various courts that deal with some aspect(s) of the problem. While the juvenile courts (or, in lieu thereof, family courts) remain the major forum for both *venue* (place of hearing or trial) and *jurisdiction* (authority over the parties and subject matter), other courts—domestic relations, civil, and criminal—also respond to issues that may arise in child protection matters (e.g., domestic violence). The complexity of child welfare cases may therefore result in CPS becoming involved in these additional forums, or in other specialized forums, such as family treatment courts that respond to families with substance abuse issues. Many cases of child neglect and abuse do not require court intervention. However, for those that do require it to secure legal permanency for the child or to provide for child safety in an emergency, your effectiveness in court will necessitate knowledge of and respect for court jurisdiction, rules, procedures, your role in each of these courts, and problems that may arise with respect to your role.

If the legal system is to be used to enhance the well-being of children and families, you as a CPS worker must be knowledgeable about the courts, skillful in cooperating with legal personnel, and able to use the court forum properly. This chapter is designed to provide you with basic information that, when used in concert with local and state statutes, will enable you to invoke the judicial process effectively. The chapter also contains material that will assist you in performing in this arena in a more informed and professional manner.

■ History of the Judicial System and Child Abuse and Neglect

Criminal cases involving child abuse in the United States date back to the mid-1600s. During this time period, after criminal action was taken against the parent, the child would often be committed to a public almshouse (a large institution for the poor of all ages) until bound out in a form of involuntary servitude or apprenticed. Early criminal actions often resulted in further harm to the child. There was no legal notion of a separate system or services for children. The early legal system not only failed to respond to the needs of neglected and abused children but often perpetuated the cycle of abuse.

The Mary Ellen Wilson case in 1874 is well known as the first civil cause of action to remove an abused child from the custody of an abusive caregiver that subsequently resulted in community response to the plight of maltreated children. The petitioner in the case was Henry Bergh, president of the ASPCA, who acted as a concerned private citizen but was represented by the attorney for the ASPCA, Elbridge T. Gerry, who prepared a petition for the legal removal of Mary Ellen from the home where she had been mistreated. Fortuitously for the child protection movement, because of Bergh's role as president of the NYSPCA, he also had connections to the legal system and the press. His action ultimately resulted in Mary Ellen's rescue and became the impetus for a formalized child protection system. This case marked the beginning of what we now know as "child protective services." In 1875 the New York Society for the Prevention of Cruelty to Children was established.

Landmark events in the development of legal protections for children were as follows:

- *1877.* The American Humane Association (Animal Division and, in 1878, Children's Division) was established as the first national organization to develop research, formulate policies, and advocate for best practices with respect to the role of both the legal system and child protective services in responding to maltreated children in communities throughout the United States.

- *1899.* The first juvenile court was established in Chicago as a completely separate judicial system for neglected and abused children, as well as delinquent children.

- *Early 1900s.* All states began to develop versions of the juvenile courts, with juvenile codes and specific juvenile laws regarding child abuse and neglect.

- *1962.* The term *battered child syndrome* was coined; it gradually came to be widely accepted by courts of law as admissible evidence in child abuse cases.

- *1967. In re Gault,* 387 U.S. 1, 87 S. Ct. 1428 (1967), held that juvenile courts had to comply with basic constitutional requirements for due process but recognized that there might be a difference between adult and juvenile proceedings in the area of due process.

- *1970s.* States began to enact child abuse reporting laws and "rape shield" statutes, and courts began to take notice of *battered wife syndrome.*

- *Early 1980s.* Further innovations in law facilitated proving child abuse, particularly child sexual abuse, in the juvenile and criminal courts. Child abuse reporting statutes had been enacted in all states and were becoming more sophisticated, complex, and detailed.

- *Mid-1980s.* Increasingly, courts of domestic relations became involved in the area of child abuse, especially in allegations of child sexual abuse in custody hearings related to separation or divorce.

- *Mid-1980s.* There was increasing involvement of civil courts in civil domestic suits brought by adults against their former caregiver(s), particularly those alleging sexual abuse of petitioners as children.

- *Mid-1980s.* Courts considered new problems of jurisdiction and venue relative to criminal, domestic relations, civil, and juvenile courts, particularly regarding allegations of sexual abuse of children. Jurisdiction or venue issues might arise when custody and/or visitation by the father was at issue in a domestic relations case, while charges were also pending against him in juvenile and/or criminal court. Courts had to resolve the issue of whether there was concurrent or conflicting jurisdiction.

- *Late 1980s–1990s.* Specialized *family treatment courts* began in some locations to address the needs of substance-abusing parents and provide the alternative of a treatment-based process that merges rehabilitation with the judicial system. By the late 1990s such courts numbered over 450 throughout the United States, including juvenile and family drug courts (Beck, 2002).

- *Late 1980s–1990s.* Specialized courts were also developed in many jurisdictions to concurrently handle issues of dependency and neglect, termination of parental rights and adoption, custody and visitation, child support, juvenile delinquency, and status offenses. These courts may be known as *unified family courts, family courts,* or *juvenile and domestic relations courts.* (Terminology varies by location.)

- *1990s.* State court improvement projects began in many states in an effort to make courts more effective and efficient in meeting the needs of abused and neglected children and their families. Speedier timelines for permanency planning under the Adoption and Safe Families Act of 1997 required courts to be more responsive and to cooperate with agencies to meet legal mandates, often without additional resources.

- *Late 1990s.* There was increasing emphasis on court involvement when necessary to ensure child safety—for example, court hearings for emergency removals or temporary custody. If the child could not safely remain at home, child protection began to be addressed through concurrent planning for legal termination of parental rights and adoption rather than agency placement in long-term foster care.

- *Late 1990s.* Courts and agencies have become more cognizant of the cooccurrence of child abuse and domestic violence and the need to assess for domestic violence issues and to protect children by addressing the needs of battered women when this is an issue in family dynamics (Petrucci & Mills, 2002).

■ The Current Law of Child Abuse and Neglect

☐ Legal Definitions (Case Law and Statutory) of Child Abuse and Neglect

Each state has its own statutory definitions of child abuse and neglect, and you should familiarize yourself with the definitions in effect in your state. The federal Child Abuse Prevention and Treatment Act (CAPTA) (42 U.S.C. § 5106g) also provides a threshold definition of child abuse and neglect, as follows.

- *Child abuse and neglect* means "at a minimum, any recent act or failure to act on the part of a parent or caregiver, which results in death, serious physical or emotional harm, sexual abuse or exploitation, or an act or failure to act which presents an imminent risk of serious harm" (42 U.S.C. § 5106g).

- *Physical abuse* generally includes the infliction of physical injuries such as burns; scalding in hot water; human bites; fractures; central nervous system injuries; any injury causing permanent damage to, loss of use of, or disfigurement to body parts; any life-threatening injury; bodily injuries requiring hospitalization, or a chronic or cumulative pattern of minor injuries; and exploitation by overwork.

- *Neglect* is generally defined as a situation in which the parent or caregiver is not providing the child with basic necessities (i.e., adequate food, clothing, shelter), and the parents' failure or refusal to provide these necessities either endangers the child's physical health and well-being or psychological growth and development, or poses a substantial risk of harm to the child. Most states also include educational neglect (failure to provide a school-age child with education), medical neglect (failure to provide necessary medical care to prevent death, disability, or disfigurement), and inadequate supervision (endangering the child, putting the child at imminent risk of harm or serious injury, or action/inaction resulting in the child not receiving basic necessities, due to lack of supervision) to their definitions of neglect. If the parents do not have the financial means to provide necessities, poverty alone does not constitute neglect, but parents should be offered community supports and services to meet their children's needs (Feild & Winterfeld, 2003). Some states also include excessive corporal punishment, parental mental illness or misuse of drugs or alcohol when either results in failure to protect the child, as well as exposure to domestic violence, in their definitions of neglect.

There are some exceptions here for religious treatment in lieu of traditional medical care, but generally not if a child would suffer death, disability, or disfigurement as a result of lack of medical care. Each state has its own statute, and you should familiarize yourself with the law in your state, noting when you may need to obtain a court determination about whether medical treatment for a child will be required. CAPTA provides that:

> A State shall, at a minimum, have in place authority under State law to permit the child protective service system of the State to pursue any legal remedies, including the authority to initiate legal proceedings in a court of competent jurisdiction, to provide medical care or treatment for a child when such care or treatment is necessary to prevent or remedy serious harm to the child, or to prevent the withholding of medically indicated treatment from children with life-threatening conditions. (42 U.S.C. § 5106i [b])

> *Emotional abuse* includes acts or omissions by parents or caregivers that have caused, or may cause, serious behavioral, cognitive, emotional, or mental disorders. Extreme or bizarre forms of punishment, such as torture or confinement of a child in a dark closet, are sufficient to warrant intervention.

> Abuse can also include educational deprivation, abandonment, or expulsion of the child or youth from the home by the parent or caregiver.

> *Sexual abuse* is also defined by the federal CAPTA law to include:

A. the employment, use, persuasion, inducement, enticement, or coercion of any child to engage in, or assist any person to engage in, any sexually explicit conduct or simulation of such conduct for the purpose of producing a visual depiction of such conduct; or B. the rape, and in cases of interfamilial relationships, statutory rape, molestation, prostitution, or other forms of sexual exploitation of children, or incest with children. (42 U.S.C. § 5106g)

State laws may further define these terms to include:

- *Exploitation or prostitution.*

- *Incest.* Marriage to or sexual intercourse with any ascendant or descendant, brother or sister, uncle or niece, aunt or nephew (also, often nonrelated caregivers living in the home with access to a child), with knowledge of their relationship.

- *Rape.* An act of anal, vaginal, or oral sexual intercourse with a child. Although a crime requires that the act be committed without consent, a child cannot give lawful consent to intercourse.

- *Sexual battery.* Touching of the anus or genitals of the victim by the offender using any instrumentality or any part of the body.

- *Child molestation.* Any sexually oriented act or practice by a parent, caregiver, or any other person that threatens or harms the child's physical, emotional, or social development.

In general, regarding government intervention with family, there is a *minimum acceptable standard of parenting* that is required. There is no clear definition of this standard. Factors considered are as follows:

- *Mental competency.* Low intelligence and/or mental retardation are usually insufficient to warrant formal intervention by child protective services, but parents with developmental delays may need community support services to adequately care for their children. Mental illness may warrant intervention to ensure child safety, protecting the child from physical abuse, neglect, or emotional maltreatment resulting from the parent's illness.

- *Religious beliefs.* Faith healing and obscure cults, if injurious to a child, can warrant intervention. For example, the state intervened where parents belonged to the cult of Melchizadek, they believed in no emotional attachments between parent and child, and only children's physical needs were met.

- *Emotional nurturing.* Where failure-to-thrive syndrome in a child has occurred because of lack of nurturing contact and appropriate external stimulation, the state has intervened. Small children born of an emotionally neglectful relationship, who have been shown no affection and appear withdrawn and passive, avoiding eye contact, and are nonverbal and unaware of how to play with toys would appear to be emotionally neglected and warrant state intervention. The distinct risk of "psychological decomposition" where a child is rejected by his or her parents can warrant state intervention.

- *Protection of child's physical well-being.* Courts in all states will intervene to protect children who have been physically abused. Intervention has also been found to be warranted where there has been:

> Drug abuse by pregnant mothers that has resulted in the child being born suffering adverse effects of drugs or drug addicted.

> Use of drugs or alcohol by parent that results in the parent losing control of his or her actions or putting the child at risk of physical harm.

> Failure of the parent to provide adequate healthcare.

> Excessive corporal punishment. Welts caused by belts or other instruments used for discipline, scalding in hot water, or cigarette burns inflicted as a punishment are examples of conditions that have been found by the courts to constitute abuse.

> Sexual misconduct with a child. Obviously rape, molestation, incest, child pornography, and prostitution have been deemed to be abuse by the courts. In addition, failure of one parent to protect the child from sexual abuse by the other parent has been found to be abuse. Having sexual intercourse in the presence of a child can be found to be abuse.

☐   The Legal Framework for CPS Practice

Your intervention is guided by your state statues and policies, as well as federal legislation. This federal legislation helps to set standards for CPS practice across the country by defining uniform goals for all CPS cases and specific requirements for practice, and by requiring accountability for states. Three key pieces of legislation that you should be familiar with are the Adoption and Safe Families Act (ASFA), the Adoption Assistance and Child Welfare Act, and the Indian Child Welfare Act (ICWA).

The Adoption and Safe Families Act of 1997 (Public Law 105–89). ASFA became federal law in November 1997 and guides many aspects of current child welfare practice. The law prioritizes child safety, permanency, and well-being as goals for the delivery of child welfare services and guiding principles for the child welfare system (Winterfeld, 1998).

In the provisions of this law, child safety is paramount. ASFA clarifies that "the child's health and safety shall be the paramount concern" (42 U.S.C. § 671[a][15]) in determining what reasonable efforts should be made to "to prevent or eliminate the need for removing the child from the child's home" or to make it possible for the child to safely return home.

Achieving *permanency* for the child also takes precedence over continuing with reasonable efforts to prevent or eliminate the need for placement. Instead,

> if continuation of reasonable efforts (to prevent placement) is determined to be inconsistent with the permanency plan for the child, reasonable efforts shall be made to place the child in a timely manner in accordance with the permanency

plan, and to complete whatever steps are necessary to finalize the permanent placement of the child. (42 U.S.C. § 671[a][15][c])

Concurrent planning is also allowed for the first time under ASFA, that is, efforts can be made to achieve timely permanency for the child by working toward reunification while simultaneously developing a contingency for an alternate permanent home if it appears that reunification with the parent is an unlikely outcome for the child (Biddle & Silverstein, 2001).

Reasonable efforts to preserve or reunify families are not required at all if there is a court determination that the parent has subjected the child to "aggravated circumstances" as defined in your state's law. Aggravated circumstances may include, but are not limited to, abandonment, torture, chronic abuse, sexual abuse, or other circumstances that constitute severe and repeated abuse. ASFA also specifies that reasonable efforts are excused under other specific circumstances, including (1) where the parent has committed murder or voluntary manslaughter of another child of the parent, (2) where the parent has committed a felony assault that resulted in serious bodily injury to the child or another child of the parent, or (3) where parental rights to another child were terminated involuntarily.

This law also requires that a *permanency plan* be developed for each child. If it is determined that no reasonable efforts to reunify a family are required, a permanency hearing for the child must be held within 30 days after that determination. Otherwise, a permanency planning hearing is required within 12 months of the date that the child is considered to have entered foster care. The hearing can be held sooner than 12 months after a child enters foster care, but it must be held not later than 12 months after the child enters care. The purpose of this time frame is to unequivocally establish that the state (child protective agencies) must set and act on permanency plans for children in foster care without delay.

Each child must have a *written service plan*. The service plan should contain a plan for assuring that the child receives proper care and that services are provided to the child, parents, and foster parents, as appropriate. The *purpose of the service plan* is to place children in the most family-like setting available, one that is located in the area of the parents' home and that promotes visitation and encourages reunification of the parents and child if possible and is consistent with child safety.

Other significant practice aspects of the Adoption and Safe Families Act of 1997 include:

- The state must initiate court proceedings to terminate parental rights when a child has been in foster care for 15 of the most recent 22 months.
- A criminal records check of foster and prospective adoptive parents is required, including fingerprinting.
- Foster parents, relative caregivers, and preadoptive parents must be notified and given an opportunity to be heard in court hearings and administrative reviews concerning children in their care (Grimm, 2001).
- Support is provided to develop programs that provide postadoptive services to families (Biddle & Silverstein, 2001).

- Permanency hearings are applicable to juvenile delinquents and status offenders.

The Adoption Assistance and Child Welfare Act of 1980 (*P.L. 96–272*). This act established, and ASFA continues to require states to establish, a *case review system* with respect to foster children. Each child's service plan is reviewed *every 6 months* (at least) to:

> determine the safety of the child, the continuing necessity for and appropriateness of the placement, the extent of compliance with the case plan, and the extent of progress which has been made toward alleviating or mitigating the causes necessitating placement in foster care, and to project a likely date by which the child may be returned to and safely maintained in the home or placed for adoption or legal guardianship. (42 U.S.C. § 675 [5][B])

ASFA now requires that *within 12 months of the child's placement* in foster care, a court must hold a "permanency hearing" to determine what is best for the child to provide him or her with the most long-term and secure permanent home.

Concurrent planning is also permitted under ASFA; that is, it allows for efforts to place a child for adoption or legal guardianship to be made at the same time as efforts to prevent or eliminate the need for placement or to return a child home (42 U.S.C. § 671 [a][15][F]).

Permanency planning options available under ASFA are specified in a child's written permanency plan at the permanency hearing. The goal in selecting a permanency plan for the child is to chose the option that will be the most stable and long-term, the least restrictive (most home-like), and free from state oversight (Fiermonte, 2001). A stable placement that provides a sense of belonging and well-being for the child may contribute to the child's healthy development and mitigate early losses caused by abuse or neglect. Permanency options include the following:

- *Reunification.* Return of the child to the parent, under circumstances where the child's safety and well-being will be secure. When the child will be safe in so doing, return to the parent is the preferred option.

- *Adoption.* The state will file a court petition to terminate parental rights and will place the child in an adoptive home.

- *Legal guardianship.* A judicially created relationship between child and caregiver that is intended to be permanent and self-sustaining, and in which the legal guardian takes on the following parental rights with respect to the child: protection, education, care and control of the person, custody of the person, and decision-making.

- *Relative custody.* Permanent legal custody of the child with family or extended family.

- *Another planned permanent living arrangement.* If there is a documented compelling reason that it is not in the best interests of the child to be placed for adoption, with relatives, or in legal guardianship, another planned permanent living arrangement for the child may be determined (42 U.S.C. § 675 [5][C]). For children over age 16, working toward independent living may be the permanency goal, while the child remains in the legal custody of the state.

Under the Adoption Assistance and Child Welfare Act of 1980 (P.L. 96-272), in cases where the child is placed voluntarily in foster care by parents, special requirements apply. The parents must enter into a foster care agreement with the agency that meets the following criteria:

- The parents are permitted to revoke the agreement and have the child returned, unless the agency obtains a court order determining that to return the child would be contrary to the child's best interest.

- The rights and responsibilities of both the parents and the agency are spelled out—for example, visitation rights, decision-making powers, financial support obligations, the parents' role in obtaining services for themselves and the child, the agency's right to bring further legal action with respect to the child, and the agency's responsibility to provide parents with information about their child.

- Within *180 days* of the child's placement, a judge must determine whether that placement is in the child's best interests.

The Indian Child Welfare Act (P.L. 96-608) of 1978 (ICWA). The child welfare system must take a specific approach when working with American Indian families that are eligible for membership in federally recognized tribes. Good practice with Indian children is founded on the understanding of the reasons that Congress enacted a separate law. As was noted in chapter 2, the Indian Child Welfare Act of 1978 demonstrated good faith by the U.S. Congress to prevent unnecessary removal of Indian children from their families. Testimony presented at congressional hearings indicated that up to 35% of all American Indian children had been removed from their families. In some communities, 90% of children had been removed. Most had never returned home; the majority of children adopted were permanently lost to their culture. Congress recognized that children had been removed without real cause. The extreme loss of children was leading to extermination of tribes. The well-being of Indian children was also a heavy consideration. Congress heard testimony that in adolescence the same Indian children experienced extremely high rates of mental health concerns, suicide, substance abuse, involvement with the law, and problems in school. While some children adjusted well, many others were to become permanently marginal, fitting in neither the mainstream nor the Indian worlds. Congress affirmed the Indian child's right to remain culturally connected and tribes' sovereignty in matters of child welfare. The following discussion addresses the legal issues that should be considered when intervening with American Indian families.

Because of American Indian children's unique political status as dual citizens, child welfare proceedings involving Indian children are treated differently from other such proceedings. (Note: An Indian child is defined under ICWA as "any unmarried person who is under age 18 and is either (a) a member of an Indian tribe, or (b) is eligible for membership in an Indian tribe and is the biological child of a member of an Indian tribe" (25 U.S.C. §1903 [4]). Always assess whether a child may have American Indian heritage and seek the assistance of local American Indian resource agencies, if needed, to determine if the child is eligible for tribal membership.

Jurisdiction. Indian tribal courts (rather than state courts) must hear cases involving Indian children who are *domiciled on reservations* or who are wards of the tribal court. When a child lives away from the reservation, the ICWA specifically allows jurisdiction to state courts for *temporary emergency placement.* Even if the child does not live on a reservation, the case may still be transferred to the tribal courts. (See *Mississippi Band of Choctaw Indians vs. Holyfield et al.,* 109 5. Ct. 1597 [1989].) Some states have specific state-tribal agreements regarding jurisdiction in Indian child welfare cases. Check with your supervisor and/or your legal department.

Notification requirements. In any state court case involving foster care, change of placement, preadoptive or adoptive placement, or termination of parental rights, the child, the child's parent or Indian custodian, and the tribe have the *right to intervene* (become parties to the court action). The tribe, parents, or Indian custodians must be notified of the proceedings by registered mail, return receipt requested. Designated tribal contacts are listed in the *Code of Federal Regulations.* Among other things, this enables the tribe to request a *transfer of jurisdiction* of the case to the Indian tribal court. At the tribe's request, a state court shall transfer, absent good cause. Good cause may include objection by either parent (court may overrule), declination by tribal court to take jurisdiction, or expert witness testimony.

> Practice Tip: ICWA standards still apply even if good cause is found not to transfer, and whether or not the tribe responds to notification.

Or the tribe may formally intervene in order to be a party to court proceedings. No placement may occur until 10 days after notification. Tribes may request an additional 20 days to prepare for court. Tribes have the right to intervene at any point in the proceeding.

> Practice Tip: Often the tribe prefers to allow children to remain in the jurisdiction of the state court and to work the treatment program with their parents. Some tribes want to intervene in the proceedings in order to have input regarding the issues of placement and to be apprised of the progress of parents toward reunification.

If the tribe is not known, notice is sent to the Bureau of Indian Affairs, in Washington, D.C., or to the regional office where the case originates.

This notice requirement is very strict; if the child's parent or custodian and his or her tribe are not notified of the proceeding and given time to respond, the whole case can be overturned.

> Practice Tip: Early tribal notification and involvement in planning for permanency assure best outcomes and fewer potential disruptions for the child.

Right to counsel. Indigent parents are entitled to a *court-appointed lawyer* in child removal, placement, or termination of parental rights proceedings. The judge may also appoint a lawyer for the child if it would be in the child's best interests.

Active efforts. Before an Indian child is placed in foster care, active efforts must be made and culturally appropriate services provided to keep the family intact. If active preventive efforts are unsuccessful, the judge must determine by *clear and convincing evidence* that continued custody by the parent would cause serious harm to the child in order for the child to be removed and placed outside of the home. Active efforts must be made to reunify the family.

Placement standards. When placing an Indian child, certain *preferences* must be followed. *Foster placement preferences,* in order, are as follows: members of the child's extended family; a foster home approved by the tribe; an Indian foster home; a tribally approved institution. *Adoptive placement preferences,* in order, are members of the child's extended family; other tribal family; other Indian family. A separate record must be kept indicating the efforts to follow the placement preferences.

The *cultural and social norms of the child's tribe* must be considered in any placement. Expert witness testimony may be presented to show the cultural norms of the tribe.

The setting must be the least restrictive, approximate a family, meet special needs, and be within reasonable proximity to the child's home.

According to guidelines issued by the Bureau of Indian Affairs, the wishes of the parent and an older child may also be considered. The tribe may also override the preferences and approve an alternative placement.

Termination of parental rights. A judge may not terminate parental rights over an Indian child unless the evidence shows *beyond a reasonable doubt* that continued custody is "likely to result in serious emotional or physical damage to the child." Under ASFA, placement with a relative is good cause not to terminate parental rights.

Voluntary placement or termination of parental rights. Where the child's parent or Indian custodian voluntarily consents to foster care placement or termination of parental rights, strict procedures must be followed, or the consent will be invalid. Under no circumstances may consent be given prior to the child's birth or within 10 days afterward. The consent must be (1) executed in writing; (2) recorded before a judge; (3) accompanied by the presiding judge's certificate that the "terms and consequences of the consent" were fully explained to and understood by the parent or Indian custodian; and (4) accompanied by the judge's certification that the consenting party fully understood the explanation in English or that it was interpreted into a language he or she understood.

An illustration of a CPS scenario involving ICWA: the Yarrow Family.

Ms. Yarrow has recently moved from the reservation to an urban area. She is 29 years old and has four children. Her oldest, a son age 14, is being raised by her mother on the reservation. Her three other children include a daughter, age 12, and two young children ages 4 years and 4 months. The oldest two children's father is in prison for vehicular manslaughter while intoxicated. As teenage parents, both Ms. Yarrow and the father had been heavy drinkers until the incident, which happened 6 years ago. Ms. Yarrow was able to get into a tribal treatment program and became sober. While in treatment she met the father of her 4-year-old daughter. The relationship lasted for a year, but he relapsed with his alcohol abuse and left the reservation. Ms. Yarrow has not heard from him since. Last year, she became involved with a migrant farm worker, who was in the country illegally. She became pregnant again. Language barriers made it difficult to communicate. He began drinking and became physically violent with Ms. Yarrow when he would drink. Ms. Yarrow moved in with her brother and his family until her baby was born. The boyfriend stopped coming around because he was afraid of Ms. Yarrow's brother. Because her daughter had to change schools, she became angry and withdrawn. The daughter began to stay away from home at nights and began drinking with friends. Ms. Yarrow's mother told Ms. Yarrow she needed to get away from the reservation and not come back for a long time, as she was afraid for her grandchildren. Ms. Yarrow did not want to leave her extended family, which had always been available to help her in times of crisis. Although she did not want to leave her older son, he was doing well in school and staying out of trouble.

Ms. Yarrow came to the city and was able to locate a cousin, with whom she stayed for the first several weeks while she tried to "get on her feet." Several decades earlier, her father's older brother and his family had come to the same city as a part of the federal "relocation" program. The relocation program was intended to provide employment opportunities and training to Indian people to compensate for the lack of jobs on the reservation. Unfortunately, like many program enrollees, Ms. Yarrow's family had found the cultural differences and isolation to be very difficult. The program had not anticipated the need for services and supports for families coming to a strange environment. Many were unable to get back to their home reservation and remained in cities living a marginal existence.

Ms. Yarrow moved in with the cousin, who lived in subsidized housing and eventually was threatened with eviction if Ms. Yarrow and her three children did not vacate the premises within a week. Ms. Yarrow had been looking for a job in the local newspapers, but she could not find anything that was close to the area where she was staying. Her daughter had begun to miss class and to stay out late again with new friends who were "gang identified." A truancy officer from the daughter's middle school came to the cousin's home and informed Ms. Yarrow that there would be a hearing the following week to determine if her daughter could stay in school. Ms. Yarrow had nowhere to turn. The other family members who lived in the city were abusing alcohol and frequently unemployed. One day she felt she could not cope any longer. She accepted the invitation of a relative to go to the bar and "relax." The cousin agreed to watch the children. Ms. Yarrow became highly intoxicated and blacked out. She was gone for 2 days. When she became sober, she called her cousin, who said that she had been forced to call social services because she could not take care of the children, as she had to go to work, and her landlord had increased his threats of eviction. Ms. Yarrow's daughter had run away. Despite being very fearful of the social services system, Ms. Yarrow called the number of the intake worker, who had left her card with the cousin.

Ms. Yarrow went to the crisis center where her infant daughter and 4-year-old were staying. The children were safe, and the worker, Jennifer, let her know that they would remain there until a temporary shelter hearing was held to place them in foster care. Jennifer asked Ms. Yarrow about how her children came to need state protection. Ms. Yarrow related the story of her coming to the city, her failed attempts to find employment and housing, her difficulty with her teenage daughter, and her relapse with alcohol. Jennifer was able to listen sympathetically to Ms. Yarrow's struggles and pointed out to her that she also has many strengths. She commended her for wanting to seek a better life, for having the courage to leave the violent relationship, and for staying sober for so many years.

As part of the standard assessment, Jennifer asked Ms. Yarrow if she was a tribe member and if her children were enrolled or were eligible for enrollment. At first, Ms. Yarrow hesitated, and asked why she wanted to know. In Ms. Yarrow's family history, many children had been removed and never returned. Jennifer explained that there is a specific law that helps Indian families to get back with their children and makes sure everything is done to respect the tribe's way of raising children. Because she sensed that Jennifer was sincere in her desire to help her, Ms. Yarrow said that she was a tribal member but she had never thought it important to enroll her children, even though they were eligible. She said that her oldest son was enrolled, because it was a requirement for getting into the Bureau of Indian Affairs day school that he attended at home.

Jennifer assured Ms. Yarrow that she wanted to help her get her children back. She told her that before she left the building, she would help her begin her paperwork for the Temporary Aid for Needy Families (TANF) program so that she could begin searching for a job. Jennifer suggested that Ms. Yarrow go to her local police department and file a missing person report on her daughter and that she contact the school to see if they had any information about friends or activities. Jennifer arranged for a visit with the children right after the interview. Ms. Yarrow was able to hold the baby and give her a bottle, while answering questions and comforting the 4-year-old.

Jennifer had had one previous Indian child welfare case and remembered that she needed to apply procedures different from those in other cases. She explained that she would need to consult with her supervisor regarding how to notify the tribe and what would have to be done to comply with ICWA in order to improve Ms. Yarrow's chances of success. She explained the timelines and court processes that Ms. Yarrow should expect in the next few weeks. Ms. Yarrow expressed her desire that the tribe not know about her situation, as she felt so ashamed. Jennifer gently let her know that it was her obligation under the law to notify the tribe, and in the long run the tribe might be able to help her with what she needed for her children. Ms. Yarrow was not comfortable with it, but she understood that if the court ruled that the children needed to be placed in foster care, she would not have a choice.

Jennifer learned that Ms. Yarrow was unable to go back to her cousin's home and arranged for a motel voucher for a few days. She asked if she would be able to stay sober. Ms. Yarrow expressed true regret for her relapse. Ms. Yarrow assured Jennifer that she wanted to get her children back and would do "whatever it takes." Jennifer checked for support resources within the Indian community and found a sobriety "talking circle" at a local treatment program. Ms. Yarrow said she would give them a call because she had felt very alone as an Indian person so far away from home.

Jennifer met with her supervisor the next morning. They reviewed ICWA law to see what needed to be done. First, they noted that if active prevention efforts are applied, and there is no immediate danger to the children, the children may be returned and not placed in foster care. They determined that the mother should have an alcohol assessment. After researching the Indian family resources in the area, Jennifer learned of an outpatient facility that provided culture-specific assessments and treatment for American Indian people.

The next day, Ms. Yarrow came to her scheduled appointment and visited with the children. Jennifer proposed that Ms. Yarrow schedule an alcohol assessment to determine if she would need help with alcohol issues before it could be considered safe to return the children. Ms. Yarrow agreed. From the assessment, it appeared that the alcohol abuse was an isolated incident and that the mother would benefit from alcohol education and support groups. A shelter that had an alcohol counselor on staff was located. If the mother could stay there with her two young children, she would also be able to attend alcohol education classes and complete random urinary analysis. At the hearing, the court determined that with placement in the shelter, random UAs, and parenting support, there was not clear and convincing evidence of immediate risk to the children. Since the children were not being placed in foster care, the tribe did not have to be notified. Ms. Yarrow was referred to the Indian center's parenting class, where she began to get to know other Indian mothers in similar situations. The teacher helped the class rediscover the cultural ways that had kept them strong through many difficult times. Ms. Yarrow continued with her TANF program and was able to finish her GED and get a job. The worker at the shelter helped her enroll in subsidized housing for single parents, where there was a childcare center for her children. Her job was located along a bus line that was convenient to her residence. Ms. Yarrow continued to do random UAs for 6 months, and continued to attend the parent support group. She finished her alcohol education classes and continued in her commitment to have a better life for her children. The case was closed within 6 months.

The police located Ms. Yarrow's daughter, who was placed in a temporary detention center. She was charged with misdemeanor status offenses, including running away and possession of alcohol by a minor. She had been assessed for substance abuse and mental health disorders. It was determined that she needed to be placed in a treatment facility where she would get help with her depression and her marijuana and alcohol abuse. The CPS agency was contacted and determined that she was beyond the control of her parent. A dependency and neglect petition was filed. Ms. Yarrow was glad that her daughter was no longer on the street and temporarily safe, and was receiving help. Because the CPS agency needed to place her in a residential treatment facility, the tribe was notified. The tribe filed a motion to intervene after the grandmother attended a tribal council meeting and asked for help for her granddaughter. She explained that she was not a bad girl but had been troubled by her father's incarceration and her mother's poor choices in relationships. The tribe requested a transfer of jurisdiction so that they might place the granddaughter with the grandmother and enroll her in the same school as her brother. Through the Indian Health Services hospital outpatient program, they were able to provide the mental health and substance abuse treatment she needed.

While Ms. Yarrow was sad to have her daughter leave, she believed that it would give them both the best chance to stabilize their lives. The court agreed, and jurisdiction was transferred and the placement accomplished.

Key Practice Points with American Indian Children

In order to carry out the principles of the ICWA, you should act in the following ways.

Understand the reasons for the law.

Exercise self-awareness to determine possible biases and stereotypes regarding American Indian people.

Assess every child and family for American Indian ancestry. Ask at each step of the process. Due to mixed ancestry, many Indian children have Hispanic last names or features of other races. American Indian children today may have white, black, or brown skin tone and have hair and eyes of all colors. Many American Indian children do not fit the prototype of features. Ask: "Does this child have American Indian tribal heritage?" Explain the rights and remedies that can be an advantage to Indian families in reunifying with their children.

ICWA applies to children who are *eligible* for membership and whose parent is a member of a tribe, and to children who are members. Remember that as sovereign nations, *tribes determine their own criteria for membership* and do not rely solely on a presumed "blood quantum." Certain tribes have no blood quantum requirement. Children may also be customarily or legally adopted by tribes and be considered members. *Always notify the tribe to determine eligibility.*

Learn who within your system is responsible for notifying a tribe. In some cases the worker is responsible, and in other systems the legal department may handle notification. If you determine that a child may be eligible for the application of ICWA, check with your supervisor or administrator on the specific protocols within your agency for tribal notification.

Ask the family and extended family to share specific cultural needs of American Indian children placed outside the home. Many tribes have specific taboos, such as against the cutting of hair, that should be respected in order to maximize cooperation with the family and tribe and to minimize unintended trauma to the child. Family group conferences are a good time to help educate foster parents regarding cultural needs and issues.

Keep in mind that the best interest standard for American Indian children is encoded in the Indian Child Welfare Act. Long-term safety and well-being for American Indian children means having a plan to stay as connected as possible to tribal culture and identity. Actively and creatively plan with the tribe and family for meeting these needs.

Consider the tribe a partner in the process. Document tribal contact for evidence of "active efforts." Even if the tribe does not formally respond to notice, attempt to build trust and respect with the tribe by calling, writing letters, or requesting to visit personally with a tribal representative. Remember the history with child welfare representatives, and have patience and compassion with responses that may seem indifferent, hostile, or rejecting.

Learn the sources for tribal contact information. The regional Bureau of Indian Affairs office and the Department of the Interior are sources. The World Wide Web can be searched for specific tribal names. Local Indian organizations, including your state governor's commission on Indian affairs, may help. Because of removal from tribal lands under federal programs, many American Indian families that would qualify for membership have lost contact with their tribes. The law may still apply. Therefore, it is a good investment in the long run to seek information early about possible tribal membership.

Seek out culturally responsive resources in your local community. Remember that giving people choices about comfortable services may increase compliance and benefits of treatment.

Help educate non-Indian foster parents about the unique history and culture of the child in their care. Encourage participation in American Indian cultural activities that affirm the child in his or her tribal identity. Help foster parents that may be considering adopting an Indian child to understand the legal risk and the right of the tribe to intervene at any point in the process.

Learn how ASFA, ICWA, and the Multi-Ethnic Placement Act (MEPA) interact, restrict, and complement each other.

The Interaction of ICWA with ASFA and MEPA

Since the enactment of the Adoption and Safe Families Act, there has been some tension regarding the effect ASFA may have on the practices required by the Indian Child Welfare Act.

Timelines. Primarily, the shortened timelines for permanency under ASFA can be interpreted to mean that ICWA requirements may be disregarded. In fact, ASFA timelines do apply to most American Indian children, who reside in urban areas and are under concurrent jurisdiction of tribal and local court systems. Many tribal social services systems receive Title IV-B federal funds, and the tribal children who receive such services are also subject to ASFA timelines for permanency. However, there is nothing in ASFA that would indicate that ICWA standards are modified. And since ICWA allows the tribe to intervene at any point in the dependency and neglect process, ICWA and ASFA should be simultaneously applied, from the beginning, to eligible American Indian children and families.

Legal and cultural differences. Applying both laws simultaneously requires an open heart and mind—in other words, good social work practice. Both laws have the intent of providing for the safety, well-being, and permanency of children. However, there are legal and cultural differences in how these are accomplished. For example, there are direct contradictions regarding permanency alternatives. ASFA promotes reunification with the parents. If parents do not complete the requirement within a short time, adoption is seen as the next option, and not necessarily by extended family. ICWA emphasizes the tribe's right to determine child welfare outcomes, and sets forth placement preferences that assure the child's right to remain connected to the extended family and tribe rather than to parents. Most tribal cultures do not conceive of "parental rights," and adoption does not have the same meaning. In most tribal communities, the parents are expected to make every effort to care for their children but are rarely expected to do this without significant support from other relatives. Multiple attachments are the cultural norm for American Indian children. Rather than focusing on the "disruption of attachment," the tribal perspective is that multiple attachments enhance the feeling of connection and security. If parents are found to be temporarily or permanently incapable of assuming responsibility for their children's welfare, other individuals with significant connection to the child step into the role. This often does not occur in a formal, legal way but rather occurs informally. ASFA does harmonize with ICWA by acknowledging that when children are placed with relatives, there is a compelling reason not to terminate parental rights. In addition, ASFA's requirement for "child-specific" recruitment of permanent homes provides an opportunity for child welfare systems to utilize extended family and other tribal families. And while most children may not be denied adoption because of cultural and racial matching, the Multi-Ethnic Placement Act specifically excludes children covered under ICWA. For successful outcomes, the child welfare system needs to be knowledgeable about these three federal laws. Workers need to be both flexible and prepared to learn a different cultural way of providing for care of children.

Legal questions are emerging regarding the interaction of the two laws. Since ASFA does not specifically exempt ICWA, nor does it contain guidelines regarding the integration of ICWA standards, case law is developing that has influenced court interpretation. For example, since active efforts are required by ICWA to prevent the breakup of the Indian family, there has been some question about whether situations defined by ASFA as meriting no reasonable efforts can be extended to cases involving Indian children. Case law has been contradictory.

Working together. In addition to learning to think differently about how permanency looks for American Indian children, child welfare systems need to make every effort to develop a respectful, collaborative approach to working with tribes. The conditions of federal treaties with tribes stipulated a trust responsibility of the federal government for certain aspects of social welfare of tribes. This did not imply a direct relationship between states and tribes. Until recently, tribes negotiated directly with the federal government for services. This lack of experience and historical mistrust between states and tribes has left child welfare and court systems unprepared to deal directly with each other. Early involvement of the tribe is critical to meeting the timelines of ASFA and for locating placements that will assure tribal connections for the child regardless of parental success in reunification. With early application of ICWA, respect for cultural and legal differences, and building relationships between tribes and state child welfare and court systems, ASFA and ICWA can be successfully applied for the best outcomes for children.

The Multi-Ethnic Placement Act of 1994 (P.L. 103-382) and the Inter-Ethnic Adoptions Provisions Act of 1996

The Multi-Ethnic Placement Act (MEPA) and clarifying amendments to that law found in the Interethnic Adoptions Provisions Act are aimed at preventing discrimination or delays in foster care or adoptive placement on the basis of race, culture, or ethnicity. The law (which specifically excludes children covered under ICWA) prohibits federally funded child welfare agencies from either (1) delaying or denying an adoptive or foster placement to a child on the basis of race, color, or national origin, or (2) denying any person the opportunity to become an adoptive or foster parent on the basis of race, color, or national origin. Instead, in each individual case, a child welfare worker should consider the needs of the particular child and the capacity of the prospective adoptive or foster parents to meet those needs. The child's needs with respect to racial, cultural, or ethnic identity may be considered, but so must the capacity of prospective foster or adoptive parents of any race, culture, or ethnicity to meet those needs.

MEPA also calls on agencies to make special efforts to recruit people of color as adoptive and foster parents in order to meet the need for additional adoptive and foster homes for children of color who are waiting for a family. However, a general rule favoring interracial placement is no longer applicable, as it is the intent of MEPA to remove barriers to interethnic adoption (National Council of Juvenile and Family Court Judges, 2000; Pecora, Whittaker, Maluccio, Barth, & Plotnik, 2000).

■ Similarities and Differences in the Juvenile, Domestic Relations, Civil, and Criminal Courts

"Child abuse" and child "neglect" are *legal* designations that can only be pronounced by a court of competent jurisdiction after full compliance with due process and equal protection of law to all parties brought before any court. The following types of courts may consider legal issues related to child abuse or neglect.

Juvenile court. Hereinafter the term *juvenile court* includes family courts that have juvenile jurisdiction. In juvenile courts, state (and, less frequently, federal) statutes specifically relating to juveniles generally establish court procedures and may define abuse and neglect. Case law of various state/federal courts of appeal, state supreme courts, and the United States Supreme Court may also contain defini tions. Courts have interpreted these statutes broadly.

Domestic relations and civil courts; unified family courts. Generally these courts also follow specific state statutes relating to child abuse or neglect definitions. Since these courts are civil, they will generally look to criminal and juvenile court statutes for definitions of abusive conduct that may also constitute a crime, and to case law for standards interpreting these statutes. Some states or localities have unified family courts where all court matters related to the same family can be heard in the same courtroom. Court jurisdiction follows the family, rather than having separate cases heard in separate courtrooms.

Criminal court. State (and, less frequently, federal) criminal codes *only apply* here. Statutes defining specific crimes can refer to general crimes against any person (e.g., assault, battery, etc.) or specific crimes against juveniles (e.g., carnal knowledge, indecent behavior with a juvenile, molestation of a juvenile, etc.). Statutes are narrowly defined and strictly construed.

If a perpetrator is not a caregiver and the conduct alleged meets the statutory threshold definition for a crime, the case will be tried in criminal court. If the perpetrator is a caregiver, the matter can be tried in criminal court and also heard in juvenile/domestic relations courts.

☐ Jurisdiction

Jurisdiction is the authority of a court to hear a specific type of case involving specific persons and make a legally binding decision in that case. Different types of courts may have jurisdiction over issues of abuse and neglect that involve the family and child with whom you are working.

Juvenile court. For the juvenile court to have jurisdiction, state laws, almost universally, mandate that the person accused of perpetrating or contributing to, or failing to protect the juvenile from, the abuse/neglect be a parent or caregiver. Juvenile court has *exclusive jurisdiction, except in the cases of Indian children residing on their reservation or who are wards of tribal courts,* to make a legal finding of abuse/neglect by the caregiver, although the case is generally designated as being "in the interest of the juvenile."

Civil courts. These courts can hear lawsuits for money damages by a minor (usually upon becoming an adult) against a caregiver (usually a parent).

Domestic relations courts. These courts have jurisdiction to hear suits between parents for separation and divorce, including cases in which child custody or visitation is at issue and one parent is accused of neglect or abuse of a child as part of that dispute.

Criminal courts. These courts conduct trials by judge or jury against any adult charged with violation of a criminal statute. The state (through the state's attorney or district attorney) brings the charge seeking criminal penalties such as a fine or imprisonment.

☐ The Rules of Evidence and Standards of Proof Required

Juvenile court. In neglect/abuse cases in the juvenile court, usually the standard of proof for the allegations in the case is by a *preponderance of the evidence* (generally accepted as 51%). If the agency is seeking a termination of parental rights, usually the standard is *clear and convincing evidence* (generally accepted as 66%). (Individual states generally have their own juvenile codes, so the standard of proof required may vary from state to state.) These standards vary in Indian child welfare cases (see the preceding section).

Many states have a specific code of juvenile procedure that follows civil rules, with certain provisions specific to juvenile proceedings. These codes may establish special rules in juvenile court hearings with respect to the following:

- Relaxation of evidence rules related to hearsay exceptions may occur.
- Videotape evidence may be used to prevent retraumatizing the child victim.
- There may be exceptions to rights of confrontation and cross-examination of juvenile victims.
- Usually there are no jury trials in juvenile court; decisions are made by a judge.
- Testimony by juveniles may be given *in camera* (privately, excluding spectators).
- Privileges against providing testimony about communications that may be considered confidential (e.g., statements made to a physician for diagnosis or treatment) usually fail, except the attorney-client privilege.
- Juveniles are usually entitled to their own attorneys, independent of the parents' or agency's attorney.

Usually hearings in juvenile court are confidential hearings and are not open to the public, except those with particular interest in the court or case—for example, court-appointed special advocates (CASAs)—as allowed by the judge. Testimony in all other courts generally is admissible in juvenile courts.

All pretrial motions are generally permitted in juvenile court, usually following civil procedure rules, in order to facilitate discovery of information through, for example, (1) interrogatories, (2) depositions, or (3) motions for discovery.

Domestic relations/civil courts. In these courts, the standard of proof is generally by a preponderance of evidence. Hearings in these courts are generally open to the public, and all evidence and testimony received is generally later admissible in criminal and juvenile courts, except in very rare cases when a judge orders closed hearings and sealed records, for example, contempt hearings for parents who disobey court-ordered visitation. Usually, cases heard in domestic relations or family court are decided by a judge without a jury. There is concern for balance between protecting the child by closed hearings and the need for public awareness of the child abuse problem. Courts in general, however, are becoming more sensitive to the needs of abuse victims.

Criminal courts. In these courts, the standard of proof is *beyond a reasonable doubt* (generally accepted as 99%). Felony trials conducted in criminal courts often have juries. Serious felonies almost always have jury trials. Court proceedings are open to the public.

State codes of criminal procedure are followed for pretrial discovery, allowing less latitude than in civil proceedings. (Each state has its own criminal code, so provisions for pretrial discovery may vary as to specifics.)

State codes of criminal procedure that govern procedures for criminal trials also allow much less latitude on the part of the judge. Generally, no "proffers" of evidence are permitted, as in other courts. Generally there is no waiving of the right to confrontation and cross-examination, but the U.S. Supreme Court recognizes the need for special rules where children are witnesses. (See *Maryland vs. Craig*, 110 S. Ct. 3157 [1990]; *Idaho vs. Wright*, 110 S. Ct. 3139 [1990].) Generally, there are fewer exceptions to the hearsay rule and other rules of evidence.

Problems arise because the victim is a child. To testify in court, witnesses must be "competent" in the legal sense (that is, they must be able to tell fact from fiction). Competency of child witnesses may be challenged for this reason, and their capacity to provide factual testimony may be called into question because of their youth. In addition, there may be controversy about the Constitutional rights of the accused to confront persons testifying against him or her through cross-examination, versus the protection of the child from further trauma by use of videotaped testimony.

Many jurisdictions now have child advocacy centers where the child victim can be interviewed in one location and at one time by a forensic interviewer who is skilled in working with child victims. Staff from the CPS agency, police, medical or mental health personnel, and prosecutors can be present outside the interview room (e.g., behind a two-way mirror) to view the interview and make sure that important questions are answered. In this way, additional trauma to the victim from multiple interviews by separate agencies is reduced, as the child need only be interviewed once, and the interview is videotaped for later use, either in court or to encourage an admission and plea bargain by the alleged perpetrator.

Procedures for alternative means of taking testimony from child witnesses, such as closed-circuit television testimony and videotaped depositions, are in use in many states but have been implemented differently in different jurisdictions. Recently, the Uniform Child Witness Testimony by Alternative Methods Act was approved by the National Conference of Commissioners on Uniform State Laws (American Bar Association Center on Children and the Law, 2002). States may approve this model act to provide procedures for child witness testimony in both criminal and noncriminal cases. For criminal proceedings, the suggested procedure is for the court to find by "clear and convincing evidence" that a child would suffer serious emotional trauma impairing the child's ability to communicate if required to testify inside the hearing room in front of the defendant. If the proceeding is not a criminal matter, the court must find by a "preponderance of the evidence" that an alternative testimony method is needed to protect the best interests of the child. The court should also specify what testimony method will be used and who may be present during the child's testimony. Cross-examination of the child witness is permitted to allow for a full and fair opportunity for examination and cross-examination.

☐ Rights to Due Process of Law

The due process clause is found in the United States Constitution in the Fifth Amendment, pertaining to the federal government, and in the Fourteenth Amendment, which protects persons from state actions. In all courts, due process demands that all parties receive adequate notice of any hearing or trial, with sufficient time to respond and prepare a defense, with ability to secure witnesses and to subpoena reluctant witnesses, to discover relevant information prior to hearing or trial, to confront and cross-examine adverse witnesses, and to appeal adverse rulings. Technically, CPS workers are not police and, therefore, not required to give "Miranda warnings" to caregivers. Such a warning is used only in situations where someone is being arrested; someone is being accused of a crime; and/or an interrogation of someone in police custody is being conducted.

However, if the CPS worker is the major state's witness, particularly in a criminal trial, a judge may rule otherwise.

In addition to these due process *procedural* safeguards, there are also *equal protection of law* safeguards of the Fourteenth Amendment, so that the substantive law is applied fairly to all those coming before any court.

Civil court. In a typical civil lawsuit pertaining to child abuse, the major participant (the "plaintiff" or "petitioner") is an adult who was abused as a child and files suit against a former caregiver (usually a parent or the "defendant"). The plaintiff is almost always now an adult, so that the issue is usually not the current abuse or neglect but that already suffered. Such a suit seeks monetary damages from the abuser or those responsible for supervision of the abuser (e.g., for emotional distress or negligent supervision of a third-party abuser).

Domestic relations courts. The "plaintiff" or "petitioner" is a spouse or former spouse, suing the other spouse or former spouse (the "defendant" or "respondent") for legal separation, divorce, or dissolution of marriage, and the suit will also determine related matters, such as child custody and when the noncustodial parent will be able to visit with the child. The custody/visitation issue is incidental to the separation or divorce. The suit seeks custody of the child and restrictions on visitation by the abusive spouse.

Criminal court. The purpose of the criminal trial is to penalize the offender and, therefore, the juvenile victim or witness is incidental to the trial. The defendant has a right to post bond prior to trial. Because the criminal trial can result in loss of property or liberty, the defendant's rights are considered paramount over those of the victim or accuser. Therefore, the child victim is much more likely to be subject to confrontation and cross-examination than in any other court proceeding. Recently delineated procedures of the Uniform Child Witness Testimony by Alternative Methods Act may provide guidance in this area.

Juvenile court. Of most importance in effective teamwork on behalf of children are your perspectives and philosophy about the juvenile court's important and distinctive role in child protection. This begins with a recognition that, while the juvenile court and the social service department are established by law and committed to its legal framework and both are primarily concerned with the protection of children, the juvenile court must base its decisions on procedures that observe due process of law. The theoretical concept on which the juvenile court is based, however, is different from the concept of the civil or criminal court.

Civil and criminal courts are focused on resolving disputes between adults and preserving Constitutional rights and equality under the law. In criminal courts, the focus is on rights of the accused. In domestic courts, child custody matters are incidental to the main proceedings, even though the standard is the best interest of the child.

In juvenile court, *children are not incidental* to any other proceeding, but are the focus of the proceeding. There are no criminal charges against the parent(s) or caregiver(s), and no fines or imprisonment that result. Instead, the state is bringing an action "in the interest of a minor." The juvenile should have his or her own attorney to represent her interests, which may differ from those of the parent(s) or agency. Many jurisdictions appoint a *guardian ad litem* (GAL) for the juvenile, who is generally an attorney (but in some jurisdictions is a nonattorney volunteer) who represents the best interests of the child and advocates for the child's interest by presenting information about the child and his or her needs and circumstances to the court. The GAL may also present information about the child's own wishes and viewpoint, or a separate attorney may represent the child for that purpose. Whether a separate attorney is appointed is a matter of each state's law. A child may have both a *guardian ad litem* and an attorney of his or her own, as well as a CASA (who is generally not an attorney, but a volunteer who has received special training and has met with the child) to represent the child's best interests and the child's own preferences in court.

The parents are served with a petition that notifies them of the case. At the hearing, the parents also have a number of rights: (1) to counsel (most states provide an attorney for parents who cannot afford to hire their own attorney); (2) to confrontation; (3) to cross-examination; (4) to present a defense; and (5) in some states, the right to a jury trial.

Under ASFA, foster parents also have the right to be notified of court hearings involving children in their care and to appear at such hearings and present information to the court.

There are strict limitations on the manner and length of detention for a child. Detention cannot be prolonged unless a court petition is filed and the reasons for the detention or agency custody of the child are approved by the court.

☐ Court Structure

All court proceedings have three distinct stages: preliminary to trial; the trial; and the disposition, decision, sentencing, or judgment phase. When the trial and dispositional phases are heard independently of each other, they are called bifurcated hearings. The following are illustrative of the highlights of each proceeding in each court; there are many more. There will also be variations among state laws and procedures, and among courts and judges within a state.

Criminal court

Preliminary phase.   In criminal court, the preliminary phase of the proceedings may include motions to discover evidence (i.e., bill of particulars), motions to dismiss the charges against the accused (i.e., motions to quash), motions to set bond or release the defendant from jail on his or her own recognizance, motions for preliminary hearings, or motions for probable cause hearings (to determine whether there is enough evidence to establish probable cause that a crime was committed).

The trial phase.   In a criminal proceeding, the charges against the accused must be proved beyond a reasonable doubt. The defendant also has the right to confront and cross-examine all witnesses against him or her and to subpoena witnesses on his or her own behalf. The defendant has the right to remain silent and may not be compelled to testify against himself or herself. He or she also has the right to be represented by an attorney, and one must be provided at state expense if the defendant cannot afford to hire one. Almost without exception, a criminal trial is aimed at proving that very specific criminal act(s) were committed at a specific place(s) at a specific time(s). The case is decided by the verdict of a jury or—if there is no jury, by the judgment of the court—which can be either "not guilty" (case is dismissed), or "guilty," which leads to sentencing. If the verdict is "guilty," the defendant has a right to appeal.

Sentencing phase.   This phase of a criminal case generally includes receipt of a presentence report, with information about mitigating versus aggravating circumstances of the crime, character references for the defendant, and recommendations of a probation officer as to an appropriate penalty and sentencing or community service alternatives. The penalty is generally decided by a judge and may include community service, some form of restitution to the victim (this may be in the form of payment for therapy), probation, a fine, imprisonment, or some other penalty.

Civil and domestic relations courts

Preliminary phase.   In a civil or domestic relations case, this phase also includes discovery of evidence through motions to discover (for example, a motion to subpoena documents), interrogatories (written questions submitted to the other party), and/or depositions (sworn testimony before a court reporter, taken outside of the courtroom). Preliminary activities in a civil or domestic relations case may also include requests for specific court actions or orders appropriate to a particular case, such as injunctions, limitations on visitation, restraining orders, medical or psychological evaluations, and so on. The court may or may not have the ability to provide resources such as social workers, psychologists, and so on, in support of evaluation requests.

The trial.   In a civil case, this phase is sometimes called the "hearing" or, in some states, the "trial on the merits." The proof required to prevail in a civil matter is by a preponderance of evidence. Parties in a civil lawsuit have the right to confront and cross-examine all witnesses against them and the right to subpoena witnesses in their own behalf. An individual also has the right to remain silent and not testify against himself or herself. An attorney is usually not guaranteed to a party in a civil case, but legal aid is sometimes available.

Judgment.   Entry of judgment is the final phase of a civil trial. It usually occurs immediately following trial, unless the evidence in the case is "taken under advisement" by the judge for a later decision. Judgments in civil cases may be subject to appeal. After a judgment is entered in a case, a civil matter is usually concluded, unless it is remanded back to the trial court for further proceedings upon completion of an appeal. While the matter is technically "concluded," it sometimes never ends, especially in the domestic relations courts, because child custody, visitation, or child support orders may be modified.

At the conclusion of a civil matter, either the plaintiff or defendant prevails, unless the entire matter is dismissed. In a trial to the court (that is, when the case is decided by a judge without a jury), written reasons for the judgment will generally be furnished by the court when requested by either party.

Juvenile court

When there are allegations of neglect or abuse by a parent or caregiver, juvenile court is almost always the forum in which court proceedings about these allegations will be heard. Since the vast majority of time and effort spent in the courts by the CPS worker is therefore in the juvenile courts, this particular court system is discussed in greater detail here.

The juvenile court was perhaps the first legal tribunal where an attempt was made to have law and science work side by side. Its philosophy was that the law must be aided by psychology, social work, and medicine in order to decide what constituted adequate treatment of delinquency, child abuse, and juvenile crime. It undertook to define and readjust social situations. Its approach was supposed to be scientific, objective, and dispassionate. The roots of this approach were in social work, equity, administrative law, and, of least importance, criminal law. Its method was supposed to be individualization and treatment of each child.

The juvenile court's early disassociation from the adversary system of criminal law resulted in a different approach and different procedures from other courts in the United States. Nontechnical rules of evidence were applied. For example, hearsay evidence was admissible. Law and the social sciences were combined, with an emphasis on understanding and treatment of the offender rather than more formal legal procedures (and safeguards). Other differences in the juvenile court included use of a different terminology and more informal procedures. The court was not adversarial in nature, and attorneys were not encouraged to participate.

Reassociation of juvenile courts with the legal system occurred because of criticism and dissatisfaction. Legal circles began criticizing the court. Humanistic groups also made certain negative judgments about the court. They asserted that the system was not working. They felt that the court did not help children, and they believed that judges, staff, and facilities were inadequate. It was recognized that the originators of the system had unrealistic expectations.

The juvenile and family court today is a court unit of its own particular class or kind (the Latin term is *sui generis*, meaning "of one's own kind."). While retaining some of its unique differences from the other courts, the juvenile court today operates under the adversary system and is, as are all other courts, a court of law rather than a "quasi-social" agency. As in other courts, the truth of the matter being considered is sought out through the use of questioning (examination) and counter-questioning (cross-examination). Attorneys try to bring out the most favorable interests of those whom they represent.

Juvenile court judges must consider all aspects of the cases that they see. They must look carefully at family interactions. They must assess the extent of the problem. Parental responsibilities and the best interests of the child must be considered. Family strengths and weaknesses must be examined. Decisions must be family centered but child focused.

Preliminary phase. In the juvenile courts, the preliminary phase of court proceedings often includes a hearing on temporary custody, usually called a detention hearing, if the child has been removed from the custody of the parent. It may also include psychological and other medical tests and hearings on other pretrial matters.

Hearing on custody removal usually occurs within 48 to 72 hours of the removal. An attorney for the child should be present. The worker must be prepared to demonstrate that there is probable cause. In other words, did abuse probably occur? In addition, for removal, what is the likelihood of further abuse? Unless there are emergency or exigent circumstances or the "aggravated circumstance," or other exceptions of ASFA apply, it must also be shown that reasonable efforts have been made to keep the child in the home.

There is wide latitude with regard to admissible evidence, including hearsay evidence, in the preliminary hearing. Some juvenile courts conduct pretrial conferences, which prepare the court and enhance communication. These conferences may prevent surprises, ensure that all facts are presented to the court, and shorten proceedings. State and federal rules for motions and orders in civil cases generally apply to pretrial conferences in juvenile court; some of these processes include advance disclosure of anticipated legal tactics or strategies for the case, and disclosure of witnesses, issues, and the pleadings (court documents) for the case. Stipulations, that is, agreements between the parties about facts or issues in the case, are discussed.

You should be aware which state law rules apply in pretrial discovery. These may include civil rules, criminal rules, juvenile court law, the juvenile code, the general welfare (TANF) law, and the child abuse reporting statute.

A proceeding in juvenile court is initiated by filing a petition alleging abuse and neglect. (The petition is generally called a dependency and neglect petition, but other terminology may apply in your state.) If you are responsible for initiating the filing of a petition, work with your agency attorney to ensure that it is completed in a format acceptable to the court. A petition usually contains certain facts, including identifying information about the parents and child, a statement of facts regarding the problem or issues of abuse or neglect, and a statement certifying that the facts presented in the petition are true.

The petitioner is the person responsible for presenting the case to the court. Usually the petitioner is the worker on behalf of the state or agency. The state or agency may be considered to be the petitioner. The parents are called respondents.

Adjudicatory phase (hearing or trial). The purpose of the adjudicatory phase of a juvenile dependency case is to make a *legal determination* as to whether the child is abused or neglected, through *legally admissible* evidence. The allegations in the petition must be proven by the standard of preponderance of the evidence, or clear and convincing evidence, whichever applies in the particular court. The trial proceeds as follows:

1. *The petitioner*, generally through the county or state's attorney, questions the first witness (often the CPS worker) with regard to his or her knowledge about the case. Questioning is usually confined to areas referred to in the petition. Other witnesses may follow.

2. *Cross-examination.* At the end of direct examination, the credibility and content of the testimony of each witness is tested by the parents' attorney through cross-examination. This questioning is sometimes limited to areas covered in the direct examination.

3. *Redirect and recross-examination.* This questioning occurs if the attorneys judge it to be necessary, giving an opportunity for further questioning.

4. *Voir dire examination* (preliminary questioning of a specific witness or juror) may be conducted to determine the qualifications and credibility of witnesses, and, in some states, the jury.

5. *Rebuttal* allows other information and provides an opportunity to raise other issues brought up by the defense.

6. Upon conclusion of all testimony and argument, the judge (or jury) reach a decision as to whether the state has failed to prove its case (and the case is dismissed), or whether the state has proven its case (and the child is deemed to be, *and so adjudicated*, a neglected, dependent, or abused child).

After the child has been adjudicated neglected, dependent, or abused, the permanency hearing follows. Its focus is on establishing a deadline to determine where the child will find a permanent home. The permanency hearing must be held within 12 months of the date that the child is "considered to have entered foster care." The date of the child's entry into foster care has been interpreted to mean the earlier of (1) the date of the first judicial (adjudicatory) finding that the child has been subjected to child abuse or neglect; or (2) the date that is 60 days after the date on which the child is first removed from the home (Hardin, 1999). Many states require an adjudication of abuse or neglect within 30 days if the child is removed from the home, so a permanency hearing must generally be held no later than 12 months after removal.

It is important to note that the 12-month time frame for the permanency hearing is a maximum time frame. The emphasis is on safe, timely permanency for children, and the permanency hearing may be held sooner than 12 months after removal. If it is clear that there are aggravated circumstances such that efforts to reunify are not reasonable, the adjudication of child abuse or neglect and the permanency hearing can take place concurrently, and must take place within 30 days.

At the permanency hearing the court hears any evidence of substantive value to decide on the proper permanency option for the child. The following permanency options should be considered:

- *Return home.* If it is safe for the child to do so, return home is an appropriate option. A date for return and a plan for managing logistics of the transition home should be specified.

- *Initiation of termination of parental rights and adoption.* When it is clear that a child will not be able to return home safely within a reasonable period of time, it is appropriate to consider termination of parental rights.

- *Permanent guardianship or transfer of custody.* If the child cannot safely return home, but adoption is not practical or appropriate, legal guardianship with a relative or other responsible adult should be considered. (For example, this option may be appropriate for a teenager living permanently with relatives who do not want to formally interfere with the parents' rights or in Indian child welfare cases, in order to fulfill legal requirements for maintaining tribal and cultural connections for the child.)

- *Other planned permanent living arrangements.* Low-priority options include group or institutional care (when severe emotional disabilities prevent the child from functioning in a family setting).

In order to determine the most appropriate permanent plan for the child, the court should hear information about the following areas (as recommended by the National Council of Juvenile and Family Court Judges, 2000):

- *What are the child's special needs?* Information should be provided to the court about the child's health and educational status, current placement and behavior, any special services the child receives (including progress and needs), cultural needs, and the child's siblings and plans for maintaining sibling contact.

- *Is reunification recommended?* If so, what corrections have been made to the circumstances or conditions leading to removal so that reunification is now in the best interests of the child? The date and detailed plan for return home should be resolved, including any follow-up supervision by the agency and services for the child and family that will continue.

- *Is termination of parental rights and adoption recommended?* Facts and circumstances showing that reasonable efforts were made and supporting grounds for termination and why it is in the child's best interest should be specified. Adoption by relatives should be considered, as should adoption by adults with whom the child has already formed a positive relationship. If these are not alternatives, a plan should be specified to recruit an appropriate adoptive home. ICWA requirements should be met for American Indian children.

- *Is permanent guardianship or permanent custody recommended?* If so, it should be explained what reasonable efforts were made and why this option is preferable to permanency through adoption and is in the child's best interests. Facts should be presented showing that the individual(s) selected to serve as guardians are appropriate as a permanent family for the child. Plans should be specified, as appropriate, for continued contact with parents, siblings, and other family members, for financial support from parents if appropriate, and for continuation of any special services and supports needed by the child.

- *Is another planned permanent living arrangement recommended* to provide the child with permanency and stability? If so, what reasonable efforts were made and what compelling reasons are there not to proceed with reunification, adoption, or permanent guardianship? How will services and supports to the child be continued, if needed, and what is the plan to prepare a teen for independent living, if appropriate?

At the conclusion of the permanency hearing, the court should determine the permanent plan for the child and why that plan is in the child's best interests. A written court order should state the permanent plan and any steps to be taken to reach the permanent goal for the child and the timeline for accomplishing them.

If the child is removed from the parental home, the court must make findings that reasonable efforts have been made by the agency to keep the child in the home (unless there are "aggravated circumstances" or other emergency exceptions under ASFA that apply—e.g., the parent has murdered another child or the parent's rights to another child have been terminated—such that reasonable efforts are not required). It is critical for the court to make written findings as to whether reasonable efforts provisions were properly complied with or were excused, because without such findings the agency cannot receive reimbursement funds for the child's care. If the child is covered by ICWA, these efforts must meet the higher "active efforts" standard. The placement of the child must be pursuant to a permanency plan filed by the agency. Some state statutes require the court to warn parents about grounds for termination of parental rights. If termination of parental rights is the permanency plan for the child and a petition for termination has not yet been filed with the court, the court's order at the end of the permanency hearing should state an expected time frame for filing a petition for termination of parental rights that is within 30 days.

For any permanency plan, if there will be further agency involvement with this family, a next court hearing date should be scheduled and its purpose stated.

■ The CPS Worker and the Courts

☐ Domestic Relations, Civil, and Criminal Courts

When a worker is originally involved in a case through the juvenile courts, and then subpoenaed to any of the these courts, the following are *some* of the issues that must be anticipated by the agency staff and their attorneys:

- Can the worker be subpoenaed to testify as a fact witness in these courts against his or her will, when originally involved only in the juvenile court case?
- Do "Miranda warnings," or other admonitions to clients, apply?
- Can the worker be made an "investigator" for these courts, in the role of, or in lieu of, police or private investigators?
- Does a privilege exist as to what was said to the worker by parent(s), child(ren), or other witnesses?
- Are these courts permitted to subpoena and read all agency records regarding this matter? The agency must anticipate these and similar issues, and have a written policy, approved by their attorneys, regarding the confidentiality of agency records that is understood by agency staff and workers. Failure to do so has resulted in lawsuits seeking damages against agencies and their staffs. These suits have been filed by parent(s), third parties whose names have been in agency records, the children (for making public what was supposed to be confidential in the juvenile court), and others.

More often, however, a worker is named as an independent *expert witness* by judges of the other courts rather than appearing as an *ordinary* (lay) *witness*. The CPS worker may also be appointed by the domestic relations courts to perform custody evaluations where the juvenile court is not involved. When testifying as an expert witness, the worker can render an opinion, but if acting as a lay witness, the worker can testify only about facts. The expert can testify to render an opinion about issues in the case, on the basis of information gleaned from an interview, review of records, and so on, but *not* from any *personal* work he or she has done in the case, unless the aforementioned problems and issues have been satisfactorily reconciled.

Expert witnesses participate in differing ways to enhance understanding of evidence presented in court. If scientific, technical, or other specialized knowledge will assist the trier of fact (the judge or jury) to understand the evidence or to determine the facts, a witness qualified as an expert by knowledge, skill, experience, training, or education may testify thereto in the form of an opinion or otherwise (Rule 702, Federal Rules of Evidence). Attorneys establish the expert qualifications of the witnesses during preliminary (*voir dire*) presentation of credentials and questioning. Once the credentials of the expert witness are established, the expert may testify only in his or her area of expertise—here, for example, child abuse and neglect.

Necessary Skills

There are professional skills that CPS workers must possess in the performance of their jobs, as summarized at the end of each chapter of this book. Here we refer to the *additional* skills necessary to work within the legal system and present testimony in court. These skills include:

- The ability to project credibility, "that quality in a witness which renders testimony worthy of belief."

- Impartiality, bringing no biases or preconceptions to one's testimony.
- Knowledge of the particular case.
- Knowledge of the general subject matter of child abuse and neglect.
- Being recognized as being skilled in subject matter.
- Following proper courtroom dress and decorum.
- Speaking clearly, to the point, and avoiding technical jargon when testifying in court.
- Being a poised witness on the stand, especially during cross-examination.
- Being familiar with basic rules of testimony and evidence.

Agency responsibilities. The issues raised earlier regarding your testimony and responsibilities in other courts (criminal or domestic relations) must first be answered and resolved to the satisfaction of the agency and its attorney. If doubt remains, an appeal to a higher court, or an emergency writ of review to the appellate court for immediate clarification, may be necessary to establish guidelines for your testimony. Within these guidelines, it is the responsibility of the expert to be:

- Impartial and unbiased toward all parties.
- Well acquainted with the literature and scientific works and studies relating to abuse and neglect, parenting, and current issues as they emerge.
- Cognizant of the limits of one's own expertise and prepared to offer the testimony of other experts—psychologists, psychiatrists, and medical providers—if needed.

All help to ensure that the judge or jury has the most complete, impartial, and accurate information possible in order to arrive at a fair and just conclusion.

☐ **Juvenile courts**

Child protection workers *bring important information to the court* in abuse and neglect cases, just as probation officers do in delinquency cases. (However, CPS workers are not considered to be "an arm of the court" as are probation officers.) Most juvenile judges do consider CPS workers to be the professionals with the most knowledge about assessing and responding to families, and because of this association, they are generally the exclusive agency to assess the case for the juvenile court. Child protection workers, therefore, have a special role in the juvenile court. The court must depend on workers to initiate actions and provide information on which far-reaching decisions will be made.

The major difference between the juvenile court and other courts is that in the juvenile court CPS workers are always fact witnesses and often, depending on their experience, training, and education, expert witnesses as well. State law generally mandates CPS workers to assess whether abuse or neglect occurred, the probability of future abuse or neglect, and the child's current safety. The CPS worker is there to protect the child and assess family strengths and weaknesses and subsequently respond to and affect the family through service provision. Law enforcement is there to *investigate* for possible criminal violation, gather evidence, and possibly arrest and confine those who pose serious danger to children, and to ultimately decide, in conjunction with the state's attorney, if there will be a criminal charge.

Various disciplines participate in juvenile court proceedings and have different roles and professional skills to bring to these proceedings. The *CPS worker's* role is to gather and assess information about the child and family and to invoke the judicial process when needed to provide safety and permanency for the child. The worker also provides required information to the court and contacts and consults with potential collateral witnesses. In court, the worker is usually called as a witness by the attorney for the CPS agency to testify about the information that he or she has gathered. The worker may also have the responsibility to prepare the family for court.

The *attorney's role* is to decide the legal merits of the case and, after consultation with the worker, to determine whether to take the case to court. The attorney prepares cases for court with respect to the clients (agency or state) they represent and presents (tries) these cases in court. Attorneys may disagree as to who initiates court action and who represents the child's interest. An attorney is appointed separately for the child. (In many states this attorney is referred to as the *guardian ad litem*, but in some states the *guardian ad litem* is not an attorney.) The child's attorney may agree with both the state's and the agency's attorney, or neither, and may also initiate court action on behalf of the child. Parents are also entitled to an attorney, or to have an attorney appointed by the court if they cannot afford one.

Often a *guardian ad litem* (*GAL*) or *court-appointed special advocate* (*CASA*) representative is appointed and has certain responsibilities. This advocate represents the interests of the child. This advocate possesses all the rights, powers, and obligations normally accorded to a legal advocate in a trial setting, except for acting as attorney. (In many states, however, the GAL is an attorney and does have the powers of an attorney.) This advocate personally investigates, consults with social services agencies, subpoenas witnesses, and prepares for trial. The advocate evaluates the needs of the child and the parents in order to determine what, if any, treatment is required in the best interests of the child. The GAL or CASA may continue to be associated with the case throughout its history in the juvenile court.

Other experts such as *psychiatrists, certified social workers, psychologists, pediatricians, and other therapists* may be consulted for evaluation, testimony in court, or for treatment of the child and/or family throughout the case.

Many communities have *multidisciplinary teams and agencies* to coordinate the involvement of the family with the court in an effort to avoid multiple traumatic interviews of the child and repetitive preliminary court hearings. These teams may also facilitate communication regarding actions taken by different courts that impact on a family and provide multidisciplinary perspectives to determine if court action is necessary or desirable. Involvement of the team may shorten court proceedings.

Invoking the judicial process. The CPS worker is the person responsible for invoking the judicial process, where a multidisciplinary team does not have that responsibility. The decision to go to court should always include consultation with, and the concurrence of, the worker's supervisor. Consider the criteria listed in chapter 6 when deciding to invoke the judicial process. An important philosophical premise is that the need to go to court does not represent defeat or failure. It can be a positive action to protect the child and help the family.

The legal implications of case assessment.　As a CPS worker, you determine the need to invoke the authority of the court. You assess the presence of, or potential for, abuse or neglect. You may obtain emergency orders to take temporary custody of the child when proof of danger exists. You may call for a quick hearing, requesting the cooperation of the parents.

You must be concerned with the full documentation of your efforts. Keep in mind that you may be required to testify. Good documentation also ensures compliance with child abuse reporting statutes and may help to protect you against allegations of malpractice.

While gathering information for court purposes, keep in mind that it is important to note the facts. Do not draw conclusions. Consider the facts from a judicial perspective. Factual information should be noted during the initial contact with the child and family and all subsequent contacts.

Remember that in order to bring any action to court you must be able to demonstrate that a law has been violated or that the legal threshold for child abuse or neglect has been met. It is critical that you be thoroughly versed in all state statutes that govern matters pertaining to child abuse and neglect and child protection, as well as agency rules, regulations, and policies and procedures for carrying out your job assignments.

The decision to file a neglect or abuse petition.　To support such a filing, you must gather information or evidence that is legally sufficient, that is, enough evidence to meet the burden of proof required. Witnesses must be credible and persuasive. To be admitted in court, evidence must meet the standards established in your state's rules of evidence and applicable constitutional exclusionary rules. Complainants, witnesses, and victims must be available for trials. There should be documentary and physical evidence if at all available.

In consultation with an attorney, you should estimate the influence of several factors on the case, before deciding whether to proceed to court. The length, uncertainty, and probable complications of the trial should be considered. The validity of statutory interpretations and other legal assertions that will have an impact in the court proceeding should be considered. The predicted or likely outcome of a trial should be estimated.

CPS worker contact with the court.　Some contact between the court and you, the CPS worker, is permitted. For example, you may contact the court for emergency intervention when needed to protect a child. Personal opinions about court decisions are best kept to yourself. Any pretrial discussion with the court or decisions by the court should involve all attorneys.

There is also impermissible contact with the court. You should not share more than essential information with the court and avoid sharing hearsay evidence. You should avoid ongoing discussions with the court before trials.

Reports, records, and record keeping. Reports to the court must be prepared with care and deliberation and comply with ASFA requirements. Attorneys and workers should discuss report content prior to sending it to the court. This sharing of information includes the parents' and the child's attorneys. Therefore, assume that the parents will be aware of the report's contents. The court report should not be admitted into evidence unless so stipulated by all parties. Be prepared for vigorous questioning about the report. The judge should not read reports in advance or at the pretrial without the consent of all parties.

When you consider the content of the report, you should:

- Omit potentially explosive information that may result in physical harm.
- Include psychiatric and psychological evaluations with caution. If a reference to these evaluations is necessary, it should be as brief as possible. The evaluations speak for themselves.
- Ensure that the report is brief, pertinent, and simple and does not contain jargon.

The content and format of a court report will depend to a large extent on your local court's preference and on agency policy.

The report should highlight those crucial aspects that the court and the attorneys need to know about the case to get the "big picture." Therefore, although kept brief, the report should include the following information.

Identifying information about the children and the caregivers, including birth dates, should be presented. (Special care should be taken *not* to identify the whereabouts of domestic violence victims, as this information may endanger the safety of the victim and her children.) Identification of the worker should appear in the report. The origination and reason for the abuse or neglect referral should be clear in the report, and the reason that the court report is being made now should be clear. A log of contacts with the family and others by type, purpose, and date should be included, and a summary of your activities and findings should be presented.

A brief statement of the family's condition (previous and current) should appear in the report. A statement of the problems should be included, and the problems should be categorized, consistent with the statute, for example, "physical abuse." Identification of others who know the family—for example, relatives, friends and professionals, and of any family strengths—should be included. As per the child abuse reporting laws, you are not allowed to name complaining witnesses who wish to remain anonymous. Supporting information, such as affidavits, reports, and memos, should be included.

The conclusions of the report should be clear. Your case plan and recommendations must be presented. Any special needs of the child and plans for responding to these needs should be included. Before you submit your report to the court, it should undergo supervisory review.

Agency records. The CPS agency's record should contain all activities and be up to date. Specific dates, times, persons interviewed, places, interview content, and other pertinent observations should be noted in the record. Copies of confidential information releases and date-stamped correspondence and reports should be present. Worker opinions and facts must be clearly distinguishable.

Information about witnesses should be contained in the record. However, the identity of any witnesses who want to remain anonymous and all other confidential information, evaluations, and reports should be kept in a separate section. In the event the records are brought to court, the judge must first examine this section to determine what he or she alone may consider, what may not be considered (i.e., obvious hearsay), and what is proper to consider in open court.

Agency records may be brought to court for reference material to refresh recollection (Myers, 1992–1995). To use the records in this manner, however, allows the opposing attorney the right to question you as to the *entire record*, except for the separate confidential section. Only a worker thoroughly familiar with the record can refer to it in court. If you are a new worker, then a supervisor who is familiar with the contents can testify. If there is no one with sufficient information regarding the record, the judge will *not* allow you to read from it.

The record must comply in form and substance with agency guidelines, pertinent state/federal statutes, and, most especially, any state or federal regulations or statutes with respect to individuals' privacy. It is important to note that federal law prohibits any disclosure of an individual's HIV status. Public Law 93-579, the Federal Privacy Act, specifies certain protections for individuals when federal agencies maintain records about them. The major provisions of this act are as follows:

- Individuals on whom records are maintained have rights of access to records, to copies thereof, and to correct and amend their records, and so on.
- The agency must obtain the individual's written consent before it can release information (a major exception is reports to the court).
- When an agency makes a disclosure of information, it must keep certain records.
- The agency must follow certain guidelines in gathering material for their records.

There are other rights, and there are also situations where the agency is allowed to maintain records and *not* disclose them to an individual (e.g., confidential information, court-ordered evaluations). Before information is released to a client, there should be a *legal opinion* authorizing the release.

The foregoing considered, what is not in the record is just as important as what is in the record. Material that should not be in case records (or in court reports) includes process (narrative) recordings; information about a client's political, religious, or other personal views; intimate, personal details with little or no relevance to the case or to the helping process; intimate, personal, and/or extreme details of physical illness; gossip; and problems and frustrations with other workers, agencies, the courts, and so on.

The CPS worker as an expert witness. As an expert you may utilize some of the expanding innovations in proving abuse/neglect in the juvenile courts, as well as to protect the child in the courtroom setting. Recent innovations include closed-circuit testimony or videotaped testimony (these may be challenged in criminal courts) and videotaped first statements and appearances of the child in preliminary hearings. Other innovations that may help children feel more comfortable in court include prior orientation of the child to the courtroom, the presence of a support person for the child in court, blocking the child's view of the perpetrator during the hearing, and restricted preliminary hearings and continuances.

It may be useful to present the work of joint assessment teams to support expert testimony conclusions and for members of the team to testify. Note also that for the purpose of testifying in juvenile court there are more exceptions to the hearsay rule than in criminal courts and, frequently, more than in domestic relations and civil courts.

The CPS worker as a fact (lay) witness. The only qualification for a lay (nonexpert, factual) witness is that the witness has seen, heard, smelled, or felt something, and the testimony will consist of these direct, firsthand observations and/or sensations. The lay witness must be restrained from opinion, characterization, and conclusion. In the juvenile courts, the most frequent CPS worker involvement as a witness is in this capacity.

To be prepared to be an effective lay (factual) witness, you should keep your records accurate, unbiased, and well documented; review and organize your record before you appear in court; and meet with the attorney representing your position prior to your testimony in court. (Keep in mind that the agency's attorney represents the agency, not you personally, and if you are concerned that your position may be at odds with the agency, or if the case is highly controversial or your conduct is in question, you may wish to seek legal counsel of your own.)

As you meet with the attorney in order to prepare for your testimony, you can help with case preparation by explaining to him or her in detail the case circumstances, findings, and opinions and your recommendations. On the basis of information that you provide, the attorney may review the legal strategy for the case with you, and specifically go over issues and questions to be covered in court. If necessary, to make you feel more comfortable with the courtroom process, you may wish to rehearse the anticipated courtroom scene.

You should also be certain that the family understands your role in the proceedings, including the fact that you will testify in court. After discussion with the attorney, you should advise other witnesses if they are to be subpoenaed and arrange for them to meet with the state's attorney.

The juvenile court follows rules of evidence under which you must work. The rules of evidence are all the laws that establish the order and structure about what is admissible evidence in a juvenile court proceeding. Many rules of evidence are similar from state to state, but be aware that each state has its own rules of evidence. You should ask the agency attorney to familiarize you with any issues with respect to evidentiary rules that may arise in a particular case, and how any evidentiary objections will be answered. Only *legally admissible* evidence can be used in court to *prove and establish facts.* In order to be admissible, evidence must be:

- *Competent.* Evidence is "competent" if no objection exists as to its being introduced in court to be considered by the trier of fact (such as an objection to hearsay).
- *Material.* The evidence is germane to some issues(s) involved in the case.
- *Relevant.* The evidence is not only material but also will further tend to prove or disprove, in logic, a certain fact or proposition.

There are many kinds of evidence that are considered to be competent. For the CPS worker in the juvenile court (and all other courts), the more common ones are as follows:

- *Direct evidence* refers to factual information that requires no proof of any other facts. This evidence is provided by someone who has firsthand knowledge of a situation (e.g., who saw it, heard it, touched it).
- *Indirect evidence* is called *circumstantial* evidence—for example, you heard screaming (direct) and then saw a child bleeding, but you did not see the abuse committed. Circumstantial evidence is competent, but to base a judgment or guilty finding on it only, it must exclude any other reasonable hypothesis.
- *Real evidence* refers to actual proof, because it can be viewed in court. Bruises, for example, represent real evidence.
- *Demonstrative evidence* refers to *things,* such as whiskey bottles or belts, compared to assertions of witnesses.
- *Documentary evidence* is other types of indirect and demonstrative evidence, such as writings, pictures, models, and so on.

There are also *exceptions to the rules of evidence* that facilitate proving neglect/abuse. Some of the exceptions that may be of major importance in typical juvenile court proceedings are the following:

- *Business records exception to hearsay rule.* This exception provides for the admission of evidence that may appear in the form of an entry in the records regularly kept by an organization in the normal course of its business.
- *Admissions.* Essentially confessions on the part of one of the parties, these are exceptions to the hearsay rule.
- *Fresh complaint rule.* Evidence rules in some states provide that a witness can testify about the first complaint of a sexual assault victim that occurred shortly after the attack. Check with the agency attorney to determine if this rule applies in your jurisdiction, and keep in mind that there is typically a delay of weeks or even years between the onset of sexual abuse and a child's disclosure about the incident or incidents (Myers, 1992–1995).
- *Res gestae events.* This exception covers events that "speak for themselves" under the immediate pressure of the occurrence (impulsive and spontaneous words or actions, "excited utterances" of participants).

You will testify, therefore, in accordance with the rules of evidence, so that your testimony will be admissible in court. In order to make your testimony more effective, you should speak clearly and demonstratively and use appropriate and understandable language, avoiding jargon. Always address only the questions that you are asked, without digressing to other topics. By having total familiarity with the case, you can ensure that your answers are accurate and sound spontaneous rather than memorized.

You should be aware that while your attorney has responsibility for developing testimony in court (through the questions that he or she will ask), there should be major input from you in prior preparation for the case. When you do testify in court, you are responsible for (1) presenting the truth, as you understand it; (2) presenting the information of which you are personally aware; (3) stating what you remember; and (4) being aware that consistency in your statements is very important.

Avoid being intimidated by attorneys. You should listen carefully to questions and answer only what is understood. Two-part questions should be answered in two parts, or ask for the question to be rephrased into two separate questions. You should answer all questions assertively and confidently. It is appropriate for you to advise the judge if you feel you are being harassed during questioning by the opposing attorney. (Hopefully, the state's attorney will object to any harassment). As you testify, you should be deliberate and calm. Listen carefully to the questions. Take your time to answer. Ask for questions to be repeated if you do not understand them.

It is also appropriate and acceptable for you to refer to the record or your notes for specific details that support your opinions and ensure the accuracy of information. If you are making estimates, be certain to make this clear. For example:

> "As nearly as I can estimate, it was 4:30 p.m." If you do not know the answer to a question, say: "I don't know." Avoid speculation.

Keep in mind that you are, in a sense, a follower in the courtroom. Others will direct and lead the proceedings. You are a resource person. When an objection is made, stop speaking and wait for the matter to be resolved before answering. You may be directed not to answer and simply wait for the next question. Do not try to force information to be included. Do not elaborate in your answers or volunteer further information. Give positive, direct answers only to the questions asked.

Opposing attorneys will try to discredit you. They may ask you what qualifies you to make such serious judgments in matters of such importance to children and their families. Be prepared to answer this type of questioning by considering your qualifications in advance. For example, how old are you? What is your educational background? Have you had special training? What personal qualities do you possess? (Are you a parent?) Personal questions, such as your age, marital status, and whether you have children do *not* reflect professional qualifications and should be strenuously objected to and even appealed by your attorney.

If you feel your qualifications are not as strong as they could be, do not try to defend them; just state the facts about yourself, but do so in a nondefensive manner. Even if you are a beginning worker, with preparation and anticipation of what you will be asked, you can be an effective witness. An actual example of such a situation, follows:

> Attorney: "How old are you?"
>
> Worker: "24 years old."
>
> Attorney: "Do you have a college degree?"
>
> Worker: "Yes."
>
> Attorney: "In what?"
>
> Worker: "Political science."
>
> Attorney: "Have you had any agency training?"
>
> Worker: "One week of orientation."
>
> Attorney: "You have not had any training in child abuse or neglect?"
>
> Worker: "No."
>
> Attorney: "How many child abuse referrals have you received?"
>
> Worker: "This is my first."
>
> Attorney: "Given that you are young, inexperienced, inappropriately educated, and untrained, how can you possibly think you are qualified to handle this case?"
>
> Worker: "I have met repeatedly with the family. I have observed their behavior. I have interviewed them and documented their responses. I have gathered and will testify on factual information. I do have opinions that I believe are valid. I have consulted with my supervisor. The decisions on this matter represent the agency's position, not mine alone."

It is inevitable that challenges will continue. Remain calm, be prepared, and remember that you represent the agency.

Keep in mind that as a lay (factual) witness, you are presenting important information about the case and are acting as a professional on behalf of the agency. Every action you take, including legal involvement, needs to be designed to help the child and the family. Therefore, their involvement in what you are doing is necessary.

Responsibilities. In the juvenile court, the responsibilities of the CPS worker include many of the same skills necessary in the other courts, and when appearing as an expert witness. In addition, because of the worker's more intimate involvement with the juvenile court system, judge, staff, attorneys, and other professionals who are involved in child protection, the worker should strive to maintain a collaborative working relationship with these specialized legal and judicial personnel. In this way, they will all be able to better serve the children and families whose lives may be so dramatically impacted by court proceedings.

■ Legal Accountability

Child protective services exists because children must be protected from abuse/ neglect and families must be helped to prevent further abuse/neglect. The *rights* of clients continue to increase through the reported decisions of cases filed in the state and federal courts, and through state and federal legislation. As these rights expand, so do the *duties* of the CPS worker, as well as the obligation to fulfill the duties and deliver the mandated services in a responsible professional manner. Failure to do so may result in legal and professional sanctions.

☐ CPS Vulnerability to Legal Actions

CPS workers are most vulnerable to such actions in the following situations:

Responding to child abuse or neglect reports. In responding to child abuse reports, the following issues may subject the worker and/or the agency to legal liability: no response, delay in response time, denial of service, cultural unresponsivensss, insufficient data collection for decision-making, or inadequate assessment of child safety or risk to the child.

Conducting home investigations. Workers are required to make investigative home visits in response to a child abuse or child neglect report. The child and family may experience the worker's presence as intrusive. Families have charged violation of privacy and violation of civil rights and liberties in situations when the agency has contacted neighbors, teachers, and other collaterals.

Ensuring protection of child. There have been efforts to hold child protective services legally liable for removal and subsequent placement of a child—for example, in an abusive institution or foster home, or in other inappropriate placements. Other liability issues have arisen for nonremoval of a child when the child is harmed further at home.

Failure to adhere to professional standards. Liability may result from noncompliance with state licensing standards. Agencies and workers should also make an effort to adhere to Child Welfare League of America, National Association of Social Workers, and other professional and ethical standards where appropriate.

Failure to protect civil and legal rights of child and/or parent(s). Concerns about violation of rights to privacy (for example, protections in Public Law 93-579 or other state or federal laws concerning the protection of individual's privacy and the privacy of records maintained about them) may exist where there are violations of confidentiality or improper material in the record. Reasonable effort requirements are still applicable, except for aggravated circumstances as defined under ASFA and state laws, for which reasonable efforts are not required under ASFA. So workers and agencies must remain mindful of reunification as a permanency alternative as established originally in Public Law 96-272. Failure to provide the least detrimental or least restrictive alternative that will protect child safety, or failure to provide specific services mandated by law, may subject the agency to liability. For example, under ICWA, the case may be dismissed on the grounds that procedures were not followed that are outlined in 25 U.S.C. sections 1911, 1912, or 1913 regarding notification to tribes, jurisdiction of tribal courts, and preservation of tribal connections for the child, as was discussed in more detail previously in this chapter.

Planning for follow-up. Inadequate planning to address issues presented in a particular case may also be a basis for liability, particularly when a child is unsafe as a result. Negligence or deliberate indifference in implementing a plan also may result in legal action.

Disregarding agency standards. Failure to adhere to agency policy, by neglect, indifference, or unwarranted use of discretion regarding the agency manual, agency procedures, agency directives, or instructions of the worker's supervisor, can also result in liability.

☐   Protection against Court Actions

Maintaining the highest possible professional standards is the ultimate defense against court actions and helps to ensure that all legal requirements will be adhered to and that families will be properly served. (When there are questions about the liability of a particular worker or agency, courts will look for guidance as to applicable professional standards to professionals who are recognized as having superior practice skills, agencies known for good practice, nationally promulgated professional practice standards, and the state's and agency's own rules and procedures.)

Agency requirements. To help protect against lawsuits, workers, supervisors, and administrators should, in consultation with the agency's attorney, develop manuals, procedures, and directives that comply with all laws previously mentioned; spell out, as clearly as possible, duties of workers, *leaving as little discretion as possible to individual workers*; and seek to establish and maintain quality services. In addition, administrators and supervisors should seek to adequately control caseload size and adequately train supervisors and line staff in the specialized field of child protection.

Agency staff who are responsible for hiring and training agency personnel should adequately screen and select qualified personnel and ensure that those staff remain qualified. Evaluations of both supervisors and line staff should include issues such as:

- Does this worker follow law applicable to child abuse and neglect regarding investigation, case decisions, and court reports?

- Does this worker consistently show awareness of procedures and policies that are part of the agency's stipulations for employee action?

- Is this worker capable of decision-making regarding the following areas: placement of children, diagnosis of various types of child abuse and neglect, termination of parental rights, effects of attachment and separation?

- Does this worker show a consistently positive and helpful relationship with community professionals who are also involved with child abuse and neglect cases?

- Does this worker consistently complete sufficient activities at the expected proportion of duties and in an organized manner?

- Do the worker's records on families correctly document the worker's ability to help families identify problems, set priorities, and work with them to negotiate and carry out service plans?

- Does this worker demonstrate skill in conducting purposeful interviews with families?
- Can this worker clearly identify instances where placement is needed, find appropriate placement, and move children out of placement or into a permanent setting quickly?
- Can this worker identify situations that need no further department intervention, and close cases or make referrals as appropriate?

Worker requirements. At the line worker level, minimizing exposure to liability derives from efforts to adhere to professional codes of ethics and good practice. (There is no protection against unethical or incompetent behavior in practice.) Workers should also maintain accurate, factual documented records that include clear statements about objective observations on which any interpretations are made. Adherence to written administrative policies and procedures when actions involving a child or family are taken is also essential. Assert your role as an agency representative at all times; for example, sign every document and chart notation in your capacity as an agency employee. You should also be thoroughly familiar with the policy and procedures manual governing your position and with the relevant laws covering your responsibilities. Have a clear understanding of your responsibility and the scope of authority delegated to you. For example, know which actions require prior supervisory or administrative approval and document that you have obtained it. Follow the requirements of the law when you respond to children and families.

Ask if your agency has a defined policy of providing legal backup for your actions if you have followed agency procedure. If a policy does not exist, decide in conjunction with your colleagues and supervisor if there is a need to establish one. Know if your agency maintains malpractice and liability insurance for all staff. If not, encourage the agency to secure this coverage. Secure and maintain adequate personal malpractice and liability insurance coverage if agency insurance is inadequate or nonexistent.

Maintaining membership and close ties with your professional association for support and consultation can also help to protect you against liability. Assist the agency in developing and maintaining a qualified professional staff capable of providing high-quality services and of making decisions based on sound professional knowledge and principles. Insist on orientation, training, and supervision in keeping with your level of assigned responsibility. Work with your colleagues to insist on realistic caseload standards as defined by national standard-setting bodies.

Developing professional collaborative relationships is also a means to promote good practice and protect against liability.

Utilize second opinions, consultations, and a multidisciplinary team review for diagnosis, treatment, service planning, and placement decisions in difficult cases, as well as for identification and clarification of legal issues.

Develop and maintain close contact with your agency's legal staff and/or other relevant attorneys. Work with others to develop and implement legislation or regulations that protect workers against personal liability and loss for actions taken in connection with their work.

☐ **In the Event of a Lawsuit**

Despite the best efforts of the CPS agency and its staff, it is not always possible to avoid lawsuits. Thus it is useful to have some knowledge about what to do when sued or threatened with a suit. The first steps to take are the following:

1. Explore verbally and in writing the possibility of your agency assuming full responsibility for defending you against legal actions. Request that a written response be used if you must seek consultation.

2. File a formal claim with your professional liability insurance company.

3. Notify and seek the assistance of your professional association. Provide information on the situation in writing and in detail.

4. Get additional advice and/or a second opinion from an attorney knowledgeable in the field. The legal steps to be taken can be complicated and extensive, depending on which type of lawsuit is involved. It should be of comfort for the worker and the agency to know that any type of suit against him or her will generally fail as long as there is no ill will, malice, or gross negligence on the part of the worker or the agency.

■ Summary of Competencies

The following knowledge and skill areas are important as you develop your professional competence and will help you to use the legal system effectively to enhance the well-being of children and families.

Knowledge:

1. Knowledge of agency policies and procedures, and of state and federal law regarding child protective service intervention and permanency planning for children.

2. Knowledge of legally mandated time frames in child protection cases.

3. Knowledge of different kinds/levels of jurisdiction a court may exert on behalf of the child (e.g., orders for supervision, emergency removal, or medical treatment; termination of parental rights) and of the procedure for initiating different levels of court action.

4. Knowledge of information contained in the particular case record, as well as delineation of which information is appropriate for a court petition.

5. Knowledge of the procedures for filing and processing a child abuse and neglect court petition, and of the key persons and witnesses who should be involved in the hearing.

6. Knowledge of proper dress and decorum for the courtroom.

7. Knowledge of basic rules of evidence, testimony procedures, and standards of proof, and due process considerations required in the legal process.

Skills:

1. Ability to gather information, organize information, and make recommendations to the court without biases or preconceptions.

2. Ability to project that quality in a witness that renders testimony worthy of belief.

3. Ability to be a poised witness on the stand, speaking clearly and to the point, and avoiding technical jargon, especially during cross-examination.

4. Ability to form cooperative working relationships with agency and court personnel, and to collaborate with other professionals and nonprofessionals involved in services to families.

5. Ability to remain supportive, helpful, persuasive, and persistent, even under difficult conditions and in anxiety-producing situations.

6. Ability to work toward preserving a positive casework relationship, and to implement court orders, even under difficult conditions.

7. Ability to organize and prepare a court petition.

References

American Bar Association Center on Children and the Law. (2002, November). Uniform act on child witness testimony. *Child CourtWorks, 5* (6), 1–2.

Beck, J. (2002). Family treatment court: Significant results in recovery and reunification. *Child Protection Leader,* 1–2.

Biddle, C., & Silverstein, D. (2001). Post-adoption services: Making ASFA-initiated adoptions work. *Protecting Children 17*(1), 2–10.

Feild, T., & Winterfeld, A. (2003). Guidelines on physical abuse—major injury, and neglect-inadequate supervision. *Tough problems, tough choices: Guidelines for needs-based service planning in child welfare.* Englewood, CO: American Humane Association, Annie E. Casey Foundation, and Casey Family Programs.

Fiermonte, C. (2001). Reasonable efforts under ASFA: The judge's role in determining the permanency plan. *Child Law Practice 20*(2), 21–27.

Grimm, W. (2001). Caregivers and courts: Realizing ASFA's promise of participation. *Protecting Children 17*(1), 12–19.

Hardin, M. (1999). *Improving permanency hearings: Sample court reports and orders.* Washington, DC: American Bar Association Center on Children and the Law.

Myers, J. E. B. (1992–95). *Evidence in child abuse and neglect cases* (2nd ed., vols. 1 & 2). New York: Wiley.

National Council of Juvenile and Family Court Judges. (2000, Fall). *Adoption and permanency guidelines: Improving court practice in child abuse and neglect cases.* Reno, NV: Author.

Pecora, P., Whittaker, J., Maluccio, A., & Barth, R., with Plotnick, R. (2000). *The child welfare challenge: Policy, practice, and research* (2nd ed.). New York: De Gruyter.

Petrucci, C., & Mills, L. (2002). Domestic violence assessment: Current practices and new models for improved child welfare interventions. *Brief Treatment and Crisis Intervention, 2*(2), 153–172.

Winterfeld, A. (1998). An overview of the major provisions of the Adoption and Safe Families Act of 1997. *Protecting Children, 14*(3), 4–8.

12

Susan Klein-Rothschild
Charmaine Brittain

Accountability in Child Protective Services

- ■ Accountability and CPS Goals

- ■ Accountability and Decision-Making

- ■ Accountability and Professionalism

- ■ Accountability and Outcomes

- ■ Accountability and Statewide Automated Child Welfare Information Systems

- ■ Using Data to Improve Outcomes

- ■ Accountability and Performance-Based Contracting

- ■ Summary of Competencies

Since the passage of child abuse and neglect reporting laws in the early 1970s, the scope, size, and complexity of child protective services has increased tremendously. The rapid growth in the field and the significant effects of interventions have created an environment in which fellow practitioners, funding sources (government and private), and the general public are demanding accountability for decisions made and actions taken.

Being accountable means accepting responsibility for performance, such as being able to show measurable ways in which CPS interventions make a difference, what works to assure safety for children, how permanency is achieved, or how we improve the well-being of children and families. Increasingly, we must pay attention to the consistency of decisions, to service availability, to cost justification, and to achieving results. Our ability to help children and families depends on our effectiveness as CPS professionals who recognize that part of doing a good job is being accountable.

This chapter gives you some basic information about professional accountability and decision-making. It also provides information on service and client measurement, performance-based contracting, outcomes, and using data to improve outcomes. Today, you and your agency must be able to demonstrate that you are following laws and mandated procedures, that you are making decisions on the basis of adequate information, that the services you provide are effective, and, ultimately, that you achieve positive outcomes for children and families. As a profession, we have shifted from process-based management (e.g., measuring quantity of service, number of clients served) to outcomes-based management (e.g., children are safe, permanency is achieved).

Workers may be under the misguided notion that outcomes-based management is used as a worker performance measure. Agencies who use outcome measures effectively also know that worker performance cannot be wholly inferred through outcome measures indicators. Instead, outcome measures focus on the CPS agency's response to ensure that children are safe, permanency is achieved, and child and family well-being is improved.

■ Accountability and CPS Goals

The Adoption and Safe Families Act of 1997 (ASFA) required the Department of Health and Human Services (DHHS) to develop a set of outcome measures to assess the performance of states in operating child protection and child welfare programs and to report the results annually to Congress. ASFA established safety, permanency, and well-being as national goals for children in the child welfare system and set key outcome indicators to measure states' performance.

While these federal goals guide practice, they are not enough to assure an effective and efficient system to protect children. Child protective services systems also have specific goals for different groups, and you and your agency are responsible for meeting them.

Federal Child Welfare Outcomes and Measures

1. Reduce recurrence of child abuse and/or neglect.
2. Reduce the incidence of child abuse and/or neglect in foster care.
3. Increase permanency for children in foster care.
4. Reduce time in foster care to reunification without increasing reentry.
5. Reduce time in foster care to adoption.
6. Increase placement stability.
7. Reduce placements of young children in group homes or institutions.

(Source: U.S. Department of Health and Human Services, Administration on Children and Families, Administration on Children, Youth, and Families, Children's Bureau, 1999.)

Goals for children and families

- Children are protected and, if safe, maintained in their own homes.
- Children receive services/interventions as a result of timely, appropriate decisions based on sufficient information.
- Families are involved in the assessment process and service planning.
- Children and families receive effective services.
- Children and families achieve realistic goals and intended outcomes.

Goals for CPS workers

- Workers are able to complete their work, keep scheduled appointments, and meet case timelines as outlined by state and federal law or agency policy.
- Workers are knowledgeable about and have access to resources.
- Workers are able to provide quality services effectively.
- Workers are able to evaluate the quality of their decisions.
- Workers document their decisions, their rationale for decisions, and their case activities on a timely basis.
- Workers use administrative data for decision-making.
- Workers communicate effectively with colleagues/peers, supervisors, court staff, community partners, and other professionals.

Goals for supervisors

- Supervisors ensure that unit workloads are equitable and reasonable.
- Supervisors identify and meet workers' training needs.
- Supervisors ensure that children/families are served as planned or required.
- Supervisors focus on client outcomes during case supervision.

Goals for the CPS agency
- The agency is in compliance with law and policy.
- Workers have a reasonable and equitable workload.
- The agency defines and monitors program goals and objectives.
- The agency ensures that services are effective and efficient.
- The agency budgets resources effectively.
- The agency ensures that staff are prepared for their jobs through classroom and on-the-job training.
- The agency is providing quality services.

Goals for the community
- Community members understand the role of CPS and know what to expect.
- Community members receive services that meet their particular needs.
- Community members' financial resources are used efficiently and effectively.
- Community members partner with CPS in an effort to keep children safe and promote the well-being of children and families.

■ Accountability and Decision-Making

Making decisions may well be the most challenging part of your job, yet it is essential in every aspect of CPS work. Decision-making is a process for helping to ensure accountability. Through adequate documentation of your decisions and the steps of making them, you prove your efforts toward being accountable. It is crucial to have adequate and accurate information to support your decisions.

The six basic steps for making all types of decisions are:

1. Describe the problem on the basis of current information.
2. Gather more information to inform the decision.
3. To make an initial assessment of the problem, process the information to generate alternative solutions.
4. Evaluate alternative solutions. Having a range of possible solutions gives you the opportunity to weigh the pros and cons of each and to make more effective decisions.
5. Make a decision and implement the plan. The more reasonable, feasible, and capable of addressing the problem a strategy is, the more likely it is that the various players will commit to it and make it work.
6. Reevaluate decisions. While it is important to commit to a decision and to take action on that decision, it is also important to reevaluate the decision to ensure that it continually achieves the intended outcomes. It also provides important information for making decisions in similar situations.

Many CPS agencies rely on decision-making tools to improve practice and accountability through structured assessment and decision-making. Most CPS agencies use a variety of instruments to help you make decisions and document case activity in areas such as assessment (safety, risk, and family functioning), case planning, family progress in achieving desired outcomes, and decisions (made by the family, the CPS agency, and interdisciplinary teams).

To make good decisions, you must have reliable information. This entails the following actions:

- Identify the needs and strengths of families and involve them in the process.
- Identify the decisions to be made.
- Classify and synthesize existing observations with a view toward assessing safety and risk.
- Determine the need for additional information.
- Identify the expected and measurable outcomes of the decisions.
- Evaluate the outcomes of past decisions. For example, if you were working with a child who had been removed from a parent's home at a prior time, it would be important to know the details of the previous episode—including what precipitated the removal, how the risks were minimized in the past, and the results of any interventions. Past behavior is typically the best predictor of future behavior. If a particular intervention was or was not helpful, that information could be invaluable in making decisions related to the current situation.
- Monitor the family to assess progress toward service goals.

The information you gather and organize is used to:

- Reach the decision.
- Communicate your reasoning about the decision to families, your supervisor, agency administrators, the courts, and other professionals. You also should document it for yourself for future reference.
- Describe the expected outcome so that the next steps, including subsequent decisions, can be identified. For instance, if you decide to remove a child from the parent's home to ensure immediate safety, you should be able to articulate your response to some key questions, such as: What specific factors made you decide that the child was not safe? What factors, if any, supported the child remaining in the home safely? What alternatives to removing the child did you consider?

Researchers have looked at how CPS workers think about the decisions they make. The National Center on Child Abuse and Neglect funded a 3-year study to examine the characteristics of decision-making in child welfare. Although this study found that there were certain case-specific factors that influenced decision-making, they also found that there were other influential factors not specific to the cases (Texas State Department of Protective and Regulatory Services, 1994). Factors that influenced decision-making included:

- Caregiver cooperation.
- Caregiver recognition of the problem.
- Family history.
- Collateral contacts.

Factors that influenced decision-making but were extraneous to the specific cases included:

- The time available to work on a case.
- The worker's perception of available resources.
- Role ambiguity (investigation versus assessment).
- Personal history.
- Agency culture.

It is important to understand how well you make decisions, what types of decisions you make best, and with which ones you may need help. Once again, having good information concerning how you reach decisions makes the task of evaluating your decisions much easier and more systematic. You should always:

- Assess the quality of your decision. Was the information on which you based your decision accurate and complete? Did the predicted outcomes of the decision occur?
- Seek feedback. As you evaluate your decisions, it will help to review them with your supervisor. Coworkers—and even families—are another good source of feedback. Obtain feedback in various ways by presenting a case to a group of peers, observing exchanges with family members, or asking a family about your performance and their expectations.
- Develop a feedback system. It is important to build a system for feedback. If it is not planned, it is often forgotten. Some suggestions for developing feedback systems include scheduling periodic reviews of a sample of your case decisions, creating a survey and distributing it to those who have knowledge of your work, and becoming involved in professional organizations that encourage discussions and feedback about casework.

Your supervisor plays an important role in the decision-making process. As a worker you make most of the decisions in a case. However, many key decisions are made by your supervisor or in cooperation with your supervisor, such as decisions to investigate a referral and substantiate an allegation. When this happens, the information available to make the decision is filtered through you to your supervisor, making it absolutely critical that the information you provide is as accurate and as complete as possible. Your presentation of the case to your supervisor can make a significant difference in the decision outcomes. You may discuss a case with your supervisor in which there are allegations of physical abuse. You raise concerns about the parent's lack of cooperation and limited communication. While these are real facts in the case, they do not describe the situation. Your presentation should also include information about mitigating strengths, such as a strong support network, or an ongoing relationship with a schoolteacher. Otherwise, decisions may be based on insufficient information.

■ Accountability and Professionalism

Organizing and planning work is an aspect of accountability that is related to your ability to make good decisions. Without some method of planning and keeping track of tasks, information, and decisions, your work may become disorganized.

You can use different planning methods to keep track of and organize your work.

- *Develop work plans* on a daily, weekly, monthly, and annual basis. Within these plans are reminders of key events or decisions such as deadlines for disposition decisions, court dates, and community presentations.
- *Plan resources.* This may include availability of specialized staff, training opportunities, availability of key community professionals, monitoring waiting lists for services, availability of team meeting participants, and availability of services. (See chapter 10 for more information on service planning.)
- *Assessing accomplishments* is another important aspect of accountability. You can do this by (1) reviewing case progress; (2) evaluating changes in families; (3) ensuring that services have been provided; (4) staying organized; and (5) asking for feedback from your supervisor, coworkers, and families.

Use your professional judgment when you share information with others both inside and outside the agency. Rules and policies on confidentiality are in place to protect families within the CPS system. You and your agency should take them seriously and abide by them. It is clearly not appropriate to provide your friends, family members, media representatives, and so forth with case records or other documentation about families served by CPS. However, in some instances, the appropriateness of sharing confidential records is unclear. For example, when seeking advice, should you share confidential records or information with a co-worker who is not assigned to the case? If your agency does not provide you with specific confidentiality guidelines, you must keep in mind how the best interest of families can be served while protecting confidentiality. Ask yourself:

- What rights to confidentiality does the family have by law and by policy?
- Who has access to confidential records in your agency?
- What procedures are used to share confidential information (e.g., staffings, multidisciplinary team meetings)?
- Is it necessary to provide the family's name or other identifiers?
- What are the potential consequences to the family of sharing certain information?

Confidentiality can become a communication barrier. If you cite confidentiality and refuse to share information, be sure that you do so in the interest of the family. As a representative of your agency, developing and maintaining good communications with reporting sources, other agencies, and the public is a part of the system of accountability. Ask yourself:

- Will sharing information be helpful to the family?
- Is there a way to respond without providing confidential information?
- Can the information be made anonymous or generalized?
- What is the procedure used to gain approval for sharing certain information?

For example, if a child was left alone in a car and died, the incident would probably result in significant media attention. It might seem like the best course of action would be to limit information-sharing by citing the family's right to privacy. It is important to determine if a limited response would simply protect the agency and/or worker from examination or if other children and families might actually benefit if you share some key facts. Children and families may be served better by focusing on broad examples rather than on the specifics of a particular case. Sharing some information could help prevent similar tragedies in the future. Know and abide by your agency's policies on who should respond to inquiries regarding high-profile cases. In all cases, use supervision to determine when and how much information you should share. (For more information on confidentiality, see chapter 4).

■ Accountability and Outcomes

Accountability is taking responsibility for the way you perform your job and the decisions you make. In your work with families, you are required to describe desired outcomes as part of a jointly developed service plan. Examples of problems caused by lack of clarity about outcomes can be seen at almost every level of intervention. It is essential that you and your agency focus on the outcomes of your interventions for a number of reasons. If you are not clear about the intended results of your work:

- You may not intervene in a planned, thoughtful manner.
- You are likely not to get buy-in from parents or caregivers.
- You may not know when you have veered off track.
- You may support unintended consequences that are contrary to the desired end.
- You may not know when you have achieved the desired results.
- You may be less successful and less accountable with families, your community, and yourself.
- You may have difficulty explaining your service plans in court.

Almost all CPS agencies set requirements for the frequency with which workers must see children and parents, but they rarely specify the intended purposes or outcomes of this contact. Worker visits with children in out-of-home placement vary in effectiveness. Some workers use monthly visits simply to confirm a child's existence. Alternatively, some use them as opportunities to gather information on and assess a child's level of safety and well-being or to promote growth and development through planned services or interventions. As you make the monthly visit, you should be clear about the purpose of the visit and the desired outcomes for that visit.

You must be able to measure outcomes. Outcome measures provide quantifiable, qualitative, or observable indicators of change in the status of a family, program, or system. If the family achieves the desired outcomes, risk will be reduced or eliminated, and safety, permanency, and child and family well-being will increase. Administrative data—or any data collected for compliance monitoring or fiscal purposes—can provide information on outcome measures.

It is essential to identify the outcomes and explain how they will be measured. Up until the late 1990s, many agencies only measured the quantity or frequency of tasks (e.g., number of contacts, number of service visits, correct documentation), and some still evaluate results in this manner. Today, however, the field recognizes the importance of focusing on and measuring results. For example, a parent could attend multiple parenting classes, but that does not necessarily translate into improved parenting skills. The focus needs to be on the desired outcome, such as assurance that the child is safe from harm.

Key Definitions

Outcomes are the overall results or changes for individuals or populations during or after participation in program activities (interventions). Outcomes may relate to behavior, skills, knowledge, attitudes, values, condition, status, or other attributes. They are what participants know, think, or can do; or how they behave; or what their condition is that is different following the program, service, or activity. Outcome measures go beyond simple observation, or clinical jargon, and describe family status in terms of quantities or measurable qualities. Some agencies use the term *goals* interchangeably with *outcomes*.

Outcome indicators are events or benchmarks used to track a program's success on outcomes. An indicator is a measure for which you have data and helps quantify the achievement of a desired outcome. Indicators help answer the question "How would we know an outcome if we achieved it?"

Outcome measures are the instruments (or items on an instrument) or methods used to collect and assess changes in observable and measurable knowledge, skills, attitudes, or behaviors. The term may be used interchangeably with *outcome indicators*.

Always distinguish the desired outcomes/results from the outcome indicators or measures. For example, an outcome would be that children are safe from harm while in foster care. An outcome indicator would be the substantiation rate for abuse/neglect for children in foster care.

Choose outcome indicators carefully, as other factors may influence the indicator and distort the intended outcome measurement. You could measure an outcome but miss a key factor in how the outcome was achieved. For instance, the rate of reunification with parents is an indicator of success in achieving permanency. If, however, you fail to measure family well-being at the time of reunification, then the rate of reabuse after children are reunified may be high, as well as the return-to-care rate; you may achieve permanency but jeopardize safety.

Outcome measures may not reflect the intended outcome accurately. For example, a community could measure the number of abuse and neglect reports and find a dramatic decrease in spite of population increases. This community could come to the conclusion that the rate of abuse and neglect is decreasing. However, if the same community were to learn that a large local constituent has set a new policy and stops reporting allegations of abuse, the indicator may be more reflective of reporting than of substantiation.

You could measure outcomes accurately and have multiple reasons for changes in the outcomes that are not always evident from the numbers. For instance, children may be safer in foster care as evidenced by the outcome indicator of abuse/neglect reports while in foster care, but the decline may be due to numerous factors such as training, privatization, or improved monitoring. Always interview key parties who are involved in providing services and pay particular attention to the process of how things are done to have adequate insight into the situation. Two different workers or units could have similar outcomes as a result of remarkably different practices and interventions. For example, a decrease in the number of out-of-home placements could be the result of fewer children coming into care, more children exiting care, or a combination of these.

The federal outcomes are a good beginning, but they are not all that is needed to guide practice and adapt it as necessary. Additional work by the agency, the unit, and the worker is needed to define outcomes that guide the work at every level and interpret the data that is gathered. These efforts feed into the final outcomes of safety, permanency, and well-being. For example, after reviewing the results of a number of cases, your agency may be concerned about the reabuse of children who are in a specific type of care or home. The concern could be about relative care, institutional care, or any other type of out-of-home setting. The agency may want to focus on the types of abuse reported in different settings to understand if there is a particular relationship between children's safety and the type of care in the community.

Following are key steps for establishing outcomes and indicators and identifying methods to measure and monitor them:

1. *Identify the key elements of the organization's mission and purpose.* Avoid identifying every objective. Focus on such things as safety, family preservation/continuity, community safety, permanence, well-being. For example:

> A recent federal audit found that the safety outcome was not achieved in your agency. Your agency and unit have determined that this is a key component of the CPS mission and the very purpose of your agency.

2. *Establish broad goals that facilitate achievement of one or more of the elements of the mission* (e.g., provide child safety from point of agency intervention). Limit

goals and make sure they are realistic. Make sure they are sufficiently broad but not too narrow or specific so that they do not consider the full purpose of an organization.

> Your agency sets two goals related to child safety. First, the rate of rereports of abuse or neglect will be reduced. Second, the rate of reports of abuse and neglect for children in foster care will be reduced.

3. Delineate key activities related to accomplishing goals. Be careful to specify all key activities related to the goals.

> Your agency identifies key activities related to these goals, including completion of child safety assessments on a timely basis, ongoing reassessment of caregivers on a formal basis, removal of children from dangerous settings, increasing community partnerships to support needs of caregivers, and increasing respite options for foster care providers amongst many others. Your unit assesses their own performance regarding these activities and identifies goals related to each of these activities.

4. Identify the types of data that measure each key activity. In the example:

> Financial data may be dollar expenditures for respite care for foster care providers, process data may be the completion of child safety assessments, utilization data may be the number and frequency of assessment contacts, and outcomes data may be the number of substantiated reports of abuse and neglect from point of contact with the agency. Identify all data sources for each activity.

5. Define where related data are now collected, insufficient areas, and possible sources. Be sure to consider all potential future sources of data. In the example:

> Data can be collected from several sources, including the automated data system, foster care reviews, and case notes. Your unit determines that no data source exists for determining whether respite care is needed and used. Your supervisor arranges to have the foster care coordinator conduct phone surveys with foster care providers on a regular basis to provide data for this activity.

6. Choose data sets that best serve as outcome indicators toward achieving goals. Select outcome indicators for their ability to adequately represent the outcome and offer a wide perspective on achievement of the outcome. In the example:

> Once a case is opened the rate of incidents of confirmed abuse/neglect will decrease and the rate of abuse in foster care will decrease.

7. Determine benchmarks for the selected performance measures. In the example:

> The current rate of incidents of confirmed abuse/neglect reports in foster care is determined to be 4%; your agency sets the goal of reducing the rate to 2%.

8. Establish reporting requirements, such as who will report what and when or when the data will be reviewed jointly. Be sure to specify a process for joint review of data. Encourage frontline staff to access reports and data.

> Your agency determines that reports will be generated and reviewed on a monthly basis between administrators and supervisors. Supervisors will be responsible for reviewing these data with their units.

9. *Make these things explicit in a contract, agreement, or alternative method.* The agreement is between the two parties involved. It could be between you and a family, between an agency and a consultant, or between agencies. The service plan between the agency and family is the most common contract used in CPS. Contracts should be sufficiently detailed and clear about outcome measures to be reviewed.

The aforementioned steps involve a good deal of analysis. It is most effective if individuals with different perspectives participate in completing these steps together. For instance, you might want to work with your supervisor and others to establish outcomes, measurements, and methods to measure and monitor them. This same process is helpful for intervention at all levels. A worker could follow this model when developing desired outcomes with a family, or an agency supervisor or administrator could follow this model when defining unit or agency key outcomes.

■ Accountability and Statewide Automated Child Welfare Information Systems

In CPS work, the results or outcomes related to a safe and nurtured child are not necessarily tangible or visible. With good documentation, however, you can trace the status of the child when referred, the decisions you made, the goals and objectives that were set, and the outcomes that were achieved. This supports accountability. The information needed to determine broad outcomes is dependent on data entered by the CPS worker.

☐ NCANDS and AFCARS

In the last several years the federal Department of Health and Human Services has implemented two major data reporting systems: the National Child Abuse and Neglect Data System (NCANDS), which captures data on children and families reported to CPS agencies, and the Adoption and Foster Care Analysis and Reporting System (AFCARS), which collects information on children placed in foster care or adopted from the foster care system.

NCANDS, authorized by the Child Abuse Prevention and Treatment Act (CAPTA), is a *voluntary system of reporting on the acceptance and investigation of child maltreatment allegations.* CAPTA requires states that receive a State Child Abuse Grant to provide information on the extent and nature of child abuse and neglect to the extent practicable. This information includes prevention services, the number of reports and investigations, child fatalities, types of maltreatment, characteristics of perpetrators, and services provided, as well as workforce information. The annual results of NCANDS reporting have been presented in the *Child Maltreatment* series published by the Children's Bureau.

AFCARS is a *mandatory data collection system* that collects automated case-level information on all *children in foster care* of whom the state CPS agency has responsibility for placement, care, or supervision. Information is also collected on children whose adoptions from the foster care system have been finalized. The AFCARS data allows for analyses regarding the numbers and characteristics of children in foster care and children who are adopted, the circumstances associated with children's removal from home, the length of time children spend in foster care, and many other factors.

Both the NCANDS and AFCARS data collection systems are designed to improve understanding about the number and characteristics of children served by CPS agencies throughout the United States. In addition, both systems track differences and similarities in the patterns of child maltreatment activity of various states. The systems also provide a mechanism for providing technical assistance to states in order to promote improved data quality and data collection and data utilization at the state level. The NCANDS and AFCARS data are the sources for measuring outcomes relating to the safety of children, including children not removed from their homes, and to the permanency issues of those children who are (see the preceding list of federal outcomes).

☐   SACWIS

Federally funded Statewide Automated Child Welfare Information Systems (SACWIS) provide the source data for the states' AFCARS and NCANDS submissions and other pertinent case-based data. Information collected in these databases includes demographic information, service plan components, provider information, case notes, fiscal records, and permanency goal history. The following considerations should be kept in mind:

- Many states have SACWIS systems or other computer systems that have the capacity to record and produce volumes of reports. Unfortunately, production of voluminous reports does not assure that results are interpreted or that there is an adequate focus on outcomes.

- You could easily become overwhelmed with data without clarity about what to use or how to use it. Similarly, without adequate direction, you may not see any direct value in the data system and the importance of entering in thorough and accurate data. Supervisors and administrators should help you interpret data to make the process more meaningful.

- All information is not equally valuable. There are many data elements that may be required for a multitude of reasons that are not a priority for all staff.

- Not all key information is included in computer systems. Since our work is directly with people, there are integral interactions that will never be collected fully in an information system. Other methods of data gathering are essential, including observing staff with families and interviewing key stakeholders. Some additional forms of documentation include activity reports, case assignment logs, travel reimbursement, calendars, leave requests, training plans for professional development, and skill assessments.

- The usefulness of a SACWIS system depends on the accuracy of the data it contains. It is essential that the frontline CPS worker enters accurate data so that management staff will have accurate information to use in deciding where to assign limited resources or to defend the actions of the agency in terms of achievement of required outcomes. If management is unable to present the work of the agency accurately, then it is less likely to obtain necessary funding resources to relieve workload pressures for the frontline worker. If the data in the automated system are unreliable, or if the data are reliable but no one values or uses the information, it is unlikely that the system will have long-term viability (English, Brandford, & Coghlan, 2000). The caseworker's role in the input of case data is a key aspect of agency accountability.

Accountability extends to maintaining professional standards for the accuracy and timeliness of documentation, in SACWIS systems as well as other formats for documentation. Your credibility as a professional hinges on the care you take to document your work as accurately, objectively, and completely as possible. At times, workers may feel overwhelmed and frustrated by the volume and complexity of the documentation. The bottom line is that the worker who has direct contact with the family is the only person who can provide this information.

Data collection should focus only on those areas deemed important by the agency and not on extraneous information. Thus, key outcomes related to safety, permanency, and well-being are of paramount importance. Activities associated with the key outcome areas are equally important to capture in the database.

To effectively use SACWIS systems to improve outcomes, consider the following:

- Identify what activities and data are really most useful related to outcomes measures, outcome indictors, and an analysis of goal achievement. As a worker, what is most helpful for you to know to better serve families?

- Ask other workers what is most valuable to them in the SACWIS system and why. They may give you clues as to how the system can be directly relevant to your work.

Garbage In = Garbage Out

- Discuss with others within the agency and/or state how they use the SACWIS system data and reports. Sometimes different individuals within the same organization will locate valuable sources not apparent to others.
- Know what reports are available, review existing reports, and identify those that provide needed data. Often reports that are provided to individuals at one level of the organization may be helpful to individuals at other levels of the organization.
- Consider eliminating or modifying reports that are not currently used to make them relate more directly to practice.
- Identify data that is best gathered through means outside of SACWIS. There are many insights that can be best understood and obtained through interviews with workers who are directly involved in working with families and providing the services.
- Consider requesting ad hoc reports specifying certain data parameters to customize the reports that will be useful to manage your workload.
- Consider how often to look at these data.
- Recognize the benefits and value of the SACWIS data and share examples for staff.
- Bring beneficial reports, data, or analysis to staff and unit meetings as a discussion item related to how you can use this information to improve outcomes with families.
- Seek out and review current child welfare research to connect information from your own system.
- Identify trends in practice and seek SACWIS data to confirm or support those trends for planning and program development.
- Request additional permitted values or pick list options to collect data on new trends (e.g., if there is a drug that appears to be gaining popularity and has a major impact on families—for example, crack or methamphetamines—make sure it is listed separately in the SACWIS system).
- Use administrative data regularly in supervision and communication with workers about what is provided, how it is provided, and the results achieved.
- Use administrative data properly and involve everyone in your unit in discussions on how to improve outcomes. For instance, one unit may be particularly concerned about initial out-of-home placements for children who are removed for safety reasons. The unit may want to examine the factors of reabuse, the length of time in placement, or the number of placements and see if any of these factors are influenced by the particular selection of the initial placement.
- Access reports and search the SACWIS system for relevant information. There is a possibility that by examining the data, the unit may learn that

children placed in certain placements do better or worse in key areas than children who are placed in alternative settings upon initial placement. When you know what is most effective, you can change practice in ways that improve outcomes for families.

■ Using Data to Improve Outcomes

In many fields, there is often a gap between research and practice, and the CPS field is no exception. Researchers and practitioners may differ in their short-term goals, although the long-term goal is the same. In addition, they use different terminology and language. Practitioners and researchers also work in different ways. Families will be better served when the field addresses the gaps and sees the benefit of each perspective. For example, research has empirically demonstrated that visitation between children and their parents is associated with reunification (Wright, 2001). While you may find this interesting, you need to understand its relevancy before you can think about developing visitation schedules that increase the quality and quantity of visitation between children and their parents. Attention to research data might inspire you to approach practice differently. Thus, outcomes may improve, making you a more accountable worker.

To use data effectively to improve outcomes for families, *researchers and practitioners must partner and use what really works*. It is actually a similar process to service delivery with families. For instance, workers who truly value families, and partner with families in completing assessments and case plans, are most effective. Practitioners who value researchers and partner with them by knowing current research and engaging in the process of planning for program evaluations could be more effective in using what works with families.

Researchers and CPS practitioners face some of the following *challenges*:

- Automated systems may collect a great deal of information, but not necessarily in the manner that is needed.
- The automated system may provide inaccurate data. This could be due to a number of factors such as missing data, different definitions, and recording errors.
- Practitioners' assumptions regarding significant factors may not be validated; these factors may not be found to be statistically significant.
- Data from the automated systems provide a foundation for areas needing change, but other data are needed to gain a full understanding of the meaning behind outcomes.

Some *strategies to meet these challenges* are:

- Findings should be provided in multiple ways and venues. Practitioners need time to discuss what the data really said, what it means, and how they could use the information.
- A process should be developed to help practitioners apply the data and outcomes in their work. Seminars and workshops can be held for different

groups within an agency or within a community. For instance, a particular study in one agency could provide information on a number of factors in achieving permanency for children. Each unit of the agency may need time and assistance reviewing the research results and discussing what the results mean for the particular unit. Some of the results may not apply directly, and other findings may have particular importance to different parts of the agency. There are differences across units, including work hours, environmental factors, and personnel factors. Findings do not automatically transfer to all programs areas and units in the same manner.

Partnership between practitioners and researchers can promote improved outcomes for families when they begin and end with discussions about what to examine, how to examine it, what it really means, and other factors to consider. This is likely to result in factors that neither would independently have identified, a process that is more complex than first presumed, and results that would not have been expected by either side. It is also likely to be of greater value.

■ Accountability and Performance-Based Contracting

Performance-based contracting is defined as explicit agreement on what participating parties expect of each other (Block, 1981). Performance is defined as achievement and completion, and performance-based contracting is an explicit agreement focused on the achievement of specified goals and outcomes, namely, the results.

Individuals or organizations—that is, a supervisor and a worker in an agency, a public agency and a private agency, or a worker and a family—can use performance-based contracting. Performance-based contracting is beneficial because it:

- Identifies outcomes and increases achievement of those outcomes, or success.
- Makes the process more objective.
- Provides clear direction for both sides.
- Decreases conflict and confusion because there is less room for ambiguity.
- Clarifies expectations.
- Makes results easier to measure.

Different types of performance-based contracting have been around for years in CPS practice. You have contracts with foster parents, private providers, and others (e.g., placement contracts, worker evaluations, treatment plans). Performance-based contracting is different from what has been done in the past because historically in CPS there have been agreements between parties about what you do and how you do it. Traditionally, there has been more of a focus on the process of what CPS does and not on how CPS helps achieve goals and actual outcomes.

Performance-based contracting takes the same focus on activities leading to outcomes within a CPS agency and extends it to contracts with other providers. As an example, let's look at a contract between the agency and a private consultant. "Jackson County" contracts with a psychologist to act as a consultant to a CPS unit. Traditionally, a contract would define how often the psychologist would meet with staff (e.g., twice a month), the purpose of the consultation (e.g., to provide support to CPS workers in making key casework decisions in difficult cases), and the types of issues and topics that would be covered (e.g., separation and attachment, prognosis, intervention strategies). A consultant could meet all of the conditions of the contract without meeting the needs of the staff in the child protection unit. How do we know if the consultant is helpful to staff in making key decisions? How do we know if there are any impacts in the cases addressed in the consultation? How do we assess the effectiveness of the consultant? Individual workers in the unit may view the consultant and the value added to their casework very differently. A performance-based contract with the same consultant would be focused more clearly on the results of the consultation (meeting the needs of the staff and desired goals of the consultation). Clear goals from the consultation would be outlined (e.g., specific decision points with CPS cases) and measurements defined (e.g., timeliness of achieving permanency or initiating alternative permanency actions). The clarity of the contract provides direction for all parties and helps all assess the effectiveness of the consultation based on agreed upon information and methods.

Performance-based contracting is becoming a more popular way of doing business for the following reasons:

- *A greater emphasis on accountability.* Those asking for accountability want to know about ultimate outcomes and achievements, not simply attempts or efforts. For example, funders want to be able to tout accomplishments for their investment. You also want to emphasize accountability in meaningful terms for families who receive your services to include issues beyond funding and cost savings.

- *A recognition that quantity does not equal quality.* The number of contacts workers have with children does not in and of itself tell you anything about the qualitative aspects of those children's lives.

- *The movement toward privatization.* Part of the discussion related to privatization includes a discussion about the quality of services received by families and the benefits of different service providers. This requires that we define quality and use measurements that can be applied to different providers.

- *The managed care movement.* An essential component of managed care is identifying what is the desired end goal with families so that "flexibility" and "creativity" in the process does not lose sight of the goal.

- *A greater flexibility and autonomy for workers.* Decision-making should be promoted at the lowest possible level. This philosophy can only be implemented when the individual with decision-making power has clarity about guiding principles, desired goals, and process parameters.

Establishing a performance-based contract is the first step toward achieving one's outcomes, but it does not end there. To assure success, the contract must be monitored and reviewed on a regular basis. The federal government has been implementing child and family service reviews that look at safety, well-being, and permanency. Each of these goals is viewed from a number of perspectives, including reading case files and interviewing families and community representatives, as well as focus groups with workers. The federal government is monitoring for outcomes, and in return for achieving outcomes, states and tribes will continue to receive federal dollars. States or tribes that do not achieve outcomes or do not make efforts to achieve outcomes risk losing their federal funds for child welfare services.

At every level—beginning with a worker and a family and extending to a contract with any service provider—intended results or outcomes are defined, and there needs to be a clear mechanism for monitoring or reviewing progress toward those outcomes. The key steps for establishing outcomes, measurements, and methods to measure and monitor them are pertinent for performance-based contracting. The final step becomes the performance-based contract itself. The elements of a written contract include (Block, 1981):

- *Boundaries.* Determine what is included as well as what is out of scope.
- *Objectives.* Define the broad goals, indicators, and measures.
- *Information.* Identify what will be shared between the parties to achieve the goals and objectives. Delineate the types of information, access to information, and who will provide what.
- *Roles and responsibilities.* Relate both parties' roles and responsibilities to goals, what is expected of both parties, and the level of support or involvement for everyone involved.
- *Deliverables.* Identify any products that will be delivered; for instance, if there is a report, what are the parameters related to reports.
- *Time schedule.* Establish the schedule for completion of all tasks and goals.
- *Confidentiality.* Designate privacy/confidentiality parameters.
- *Feedback.* When the contract is met and services are provided, is there any follow-up about what happened with and for families?

In other words, a contract for services that you and your agency develop with a family should include the scope of what is expected (e.g., services only to the child or to include services to other family members); the specific services to be provided (e.g., counseling and specific treatment strategies); the goals and measures (e.g., increased social skills measured by increased peer interactions, and number of friends); who will do what (e.g., define the level of involvement or support between the provider and the worker); what is reported (e.g., the content and frequency of written reports); when the outcome is expected (e.g., 6-month goal); confidentiality expectations (e.g., a signed agreement with the family for the agency and provider to share information to better serve the child); and a method for feedback and follow-up (e.g., staffing scheduled every 3 months to monitor progress and provide feedback).

■ Summary of Competencies

Accountability is a core value of CPS practice. CPS workers, supervisors, and agencies must be accountable on many fronts to serve children and families effectively. Accountability starts with the first contact with the family and drives CPS practice through case closure. Ultimately, what matters is that children are safe, permanency is achieved, and the well-being of children and families improves. You should be competent in the following areas.

Knowledge:

1. Knowledge of the importance of accountability.
2. Knowledge of the definition of accountability.
3. Knowledge of how to identify examples of accountability in CPS.
4. Description of professional accountability.
5. Understanding the relationship between information and accountable decision-making.
6. Knowledge of how to organize and communicate information to promote accountable decision-making.
7. Knowledge of the importance and value of outcomes in child protection services.
8. Knowledge of how to identify the strategies to use SACWIS systems data to improve outcomes for families.
9. Knowledge of the value and importance of the relationship between CPS practice and research.
10. Knowledge of how to identify the strategies for practitioners to use research to improve outcomes for families.
11. Knowledge to define performance-based contracting.
12. Knowledge of the benefits of performance-based contracting.

Skills:

1. Ability to distinguish the difference between outcome goals and outcome measures.
2. Ability to identify key child welfare outcome areas identified by the federal government.
3. Ability to describe the key steps for establishing outcomes, measurements, and methods to use to measure and monitor them.
4. Ability to describe the relationship between SACWIS systems and outcomes in CPS.
5. Ability to develop a performance-based contract.

References

American Humane Association, Children's Division; American Bar Association, Center on Children and the Law; Annie E. Casey Foundation; Casey Family Program; Casey

Family Services; & Institute for Human Services Management. (1998). *Assessing outcomes in child welfare services: Principles, concepts, and a framework of core outcome indicators.* Englewood, CO: American Humane Association, Casey Outcomes and Decision-Making Project.

Block, P. (1981). *Flawless consulting: A guide to getting your expertise used.* Austin, TX: Learning Concepts.

English, D. J., Brandford, C. C., & Coghlan, L. (2000). Data-based organizational change: The use of administrative data to improve child welfare programs and policy. *Child Welfare, 79*(5), 499-515.

Texas State Department of Protective and Regulatory Services. (1994). *First preliminary report of the Child Welfare Decision Enhancement Project on critical incidents affecting caseworker decision making.* Austin, TX: Author.

U.S. Department of Health and Human Services, Administration on Children and Families, Administration on Children, Youth, and Families, Children's Bureau. (1999). *Child welfare outcomes 1999: Annual report.* Arlington, VA: James Bell.

Wright, L. (2001). *Tool box no. 1: Using visitation to support permanency.* Washington, DC: CWLA Press.

Glossary

The terms appearing in this glossary were obtained and adapted from numerous sources, including previous publications of the American Association for Protecting Children (AAPC), a division of the American Humane Association. Another primary source for definitions was the U.S. Department of Health, Education, and Welfare, Office of Human Development Services, Administration for Children, Youth and Families, Children's Bureau, National Center on Child Abuse and Neglect, *Interdisciplinary Glossary on Child Abuse and Neglect: Legal, Medical, Social Work Terms* (Washington, DC: U.S. Government Printing Office, 1978). Other sources included Robert L. Barker, *The Social Work Dictionary* (Silver Spring, MD: National Association of Social Workers, 1987); U.S. Department of Health, Education, and Welfare, Office of Human Development Services, Administration for Children, Youth and Families, Children's Bureau, *National Child Abuse and Neglect Data System (NCANDS) Glossary (SDC and DCDC combined)*, available online at http://www.acf.d s.gov/programs/cb/dis/ncands98/glossary/glossary, 2000; Colorado Department of Human Services, *Colorado Child Welfare Practice Handbook* (Englewood, CO: American Humane Association, 1998); and *Random House Webster's College Dictionary* (New York: Random House, 1992).

Medical terms listed are adapted in part from *Dorland's Illustrated Medical Dictionary, 29th Edition* (Philadelphia: Saunders, 2000), and from Merriam Webster's Medical Dictionary Online, available at http://www.intelihealth.com/IH/ihtIH/WSIHW000/9276/9276.html, 2003. The discussion of ego defense mechanisms is adapted from *DSM-III-R, Diagnostic and Statistical Manual of Mental Disorders*, 3rd ed-rev. (Washington, DC: American Psychiatric Association, 1987). Legal terms are defined by Sol Gothard, M.S.W., J.D., Judge, Fifth Court of Appeal, State of Louisiana, and the *Court Referral Project Final Report* (Bismark, ND: Social Service Board of North Dakota, 1977). This glossary was compiled by Jesse Rainey, Research Assistant, Children's Services, American Humane, Englewood, CO.

acting out   A mechanism in which the person acts without reflection or apparent regard for negative consequences.

Adoption and Foster Care Analysis and Reporting System (AFCARS)   A mandatory data collection system that collects automated case-level information on all children in foster care for whom the state child welfare agency has responsibility for placement, care, or supervision. Information is also collected on children whose adoptions from the foster care system have been finalized. The AFCARS data allow for analyses regarding the number and characteristics of children who are in foster care and who are adopted, the circumstances associated with children's removal from home, the length of time children spend in foster care, and many other factors.

Adoption and Safe Families Act (ASFA) (Public Law 105-89)   Passed in 1997, ASFA provides both changes and clarification of policies of its antecedent legislation, the Adoption Assistance and Child Welfare Act. The legislation is intended to improve the safety of children, promote adoptions and permanent homes for children, and support families. Of significance, the legislation stipulates that child safety is of paramount importance during reunification efforts and provides exceptions to reasonable efforts requirements. The law also requires concurrent permanency planning; provides financial incentives and technical assistance to states to promote adoption activities; includes system accountability and reform provisions; and outlines state requirements for performance measures for state child welfare programs. It also promotes the study of kinship placement feasibility.

Adoption Assistance and Child Welfare Act (Public Law 96-272)   A law passed in 1980 that ties federal foster care funding to, and provides fiscal incentives to, the implementation of policies related to family preservation and permanency planning. Workers and courts are now obligated to demonstrate and certify that reasonable efforts were made to preserve families before children can be placed in foster care or made eligible for adoption. Further, the legislation provides fiscal incentives to support the adoption of children determined to have special needs.

adjudication   The giving of a judgment or decree.

adult-to-child language (ACL)   Communication between adults and children in which adults modify their language to make it easier for children to understand. It involves speaking slowly, with exaggerated enunciation, in short and simple sentences, minimizing the use of pronouns and modifiers, and focusing on objects currently visible and events that are currently happening or recently happened.

aggravated circumstances (As defined under the federal Adoption and Safe Families Act)   These may include, but are not limited to, abandonment, torture, chronic abuse, sexual abuse, or circumstances where the parent has committed murder or voluntary manslaughter of another child of the parent, or has committed a felony assault that resulted in serious bodily injury to the child or another child of the parent, or where parental rights to another child were terminated involuntarily. Additional aggravated circumstances may be defined by state law.

allegation   A charge, statement, claim, or declaration (often of a child maltreatment occurrence).

alternate care   When children cannot remain safely in their home, an alternate form of care is sought. Generally referred to as foster care, alternate care provides a substitute family experience where the individual needs of the child can be addressed. Attempting to meet the placement needs of children and youth is an important mandate of alternate care services. Several care options exist, such as placement with relatives or with recruited foster families, group homes, specialized living arrangements, or shared apartments. The latter two options are reserved for older children under special circumstances only.

anxiety disorders   Psychological conditions that cause children and youth to feel excessively frightened, distressed, and uneasy during situations in which most others would not experience such symptoms. Anxiety disorders can lead to poor school attendance, low self-esteem, deficient interpersonal skills, alcohol abuse, and adjustment difficulty.

apnea   Cessation of breathing.

appeal   A complaint to a higher tribunal of an error or injustice committed by a lower tribunal, in which an attempt is made to have the error or injustice corrected or reversed.

assessment   A professional, systematic, and informed approach to gathering and evaluating specific information about a child and/or family for the purpose of making decisions regarding allegations of maltreatment, protection of the child, services to the family, and family progress.

assessment track   An approach by the CPS agency to a report that includes situations in which there are needs that, if addressed, could stabilize the family and enable the parents to better care for their children. Typically, there are no serious safety issues immediately present.

attachment   An active, affectionate, reciprocal, enduring relationship between infant and caregiver that is thought to be essential to the development of the psychological foundation of the child. The establishment of attachment is based on how responsive the caregiver is to the infant's needs for physical care, nurturance, and social interactions. When the caregiver responds to the infant's needs, the infant comes to realize that he or she can count on the caregiver to meet any needs. This learned relationship is thought to be critical to the formation of trust and the development of future relationships.

attending   A nondirective listening technique that refers primarily to eye contact and body language but also includes following a client verbally.

Attention deficit disorder (ADD) and attention deficit hyperactivity disorder (ADHD)   Neurochemical disorders that interfere with attention. ADD is a condition characterized by inattention and impulsivity. If children show these symptoms along with hyperactivity, they are considered to have ADHD. Most children identified as having ADD are also hyperactive and restless (ADHD), have poor impulse control, and are prone to outbursts of anger and aggression. Often they are emotionally labile and immature, and are resistant to discipline.

axonal injury   A condition in which the axon (single nerve-cell process) is stretched and cut by a sudden acceleration, deceleration, or rotation force to the head.

battered child syndrome   A medical condition, primarily of infants and young children, in which there is evidence of repeated inflicted injury to the nervous, skin, or skeletal system. Frequently the history, as given by the caregiver, does not adequately explain the nature of occurrence of the injuries.

bipolar disorder   A mental illness in which mood and affect are maladaptive. Can be subcategorized as manic, depressed, and mixed (alternating between mania and depression).

bone scan   A process in which a small amount of radioactive phosphorus is injected into the bloodstream. The radiation, or "heat," from this injection is then photographed. Those areas of bone that are growing will demonstrate radioactivity. This method can detect fractures within 48 hours after they occur. It does not allow for dating of injuries.

burden of proof   The burden of producing evidence or persuading the fact finder within the legal system.

caregiver   A person responsible for a child's health or welfare, including the child's parent, guardian, or other person within the child's own home, or a person responsible for a child's health or welfare in a relative's home, foster home, or residential institution. A caregiver is responsible for meeting a child's basic physical and psychological needs and for providing protection and supervision.

case closure   The final phase of CPS work with the family. It is synonymous with *termination* and is the point at which the CPS provision process ends.

case management   A systematic approach to social work in which an emphasis is placed on systems in which a client must function rather than on inner thought processes to help facilitate client change. Case management involves coordination of the multiple services required by a child abuse and neglect client. Some of these services may be purchased from an agency other than the mandated CPS agency. In general, the role of the case manager is to monitor services by making sure they are relevant to the client, delivered in a useful way, and appropriately used.

casework   A method of social work intervention that helps an individual or family improve their functioning by changing internal attitudes and feelings, behaviors, and external circumstances directly affecting the individual or family. This contrasts with community organization and other methods of social work intervention that focus on changing institutions or society. Casework relies on a relationship between the worker and client as the primary tool for affecting change.

cephalhematoma   A usually benign swelling formed from a hemorrhage beneath the periosteum of the skull and occurring especially over one or both of the parietal bones in newborn infants as a result of trauma sustained during delivery.

cerebral edema   Excessive accumulation of fluid in the brain substance; causes include trauma, tumor, and increased permeability of capillaries as a result of anoxia (lack of oxygen) or exposure to toxic substances. Also called brain edema and wet brain. This type of trauma can occur either laterally (on one side) or bilaterally (on both sides of the brain).

Child Abuse Prevention and Treatment Act (CAPTA) (Public Law 93-247)   Passed in 1974, CAPTA ties federal funding for states to systems of identification, reporting, and response to child abuse and neglect. CAPTA has been revised and updated regularly since its enactment.

child development   Changes in physical characteristics, neurological makeup, behaviors, and personality traits that are observed in children and occur over time.

circumstantial evidence   Proof of circumstances that may imply another fact. For example, proof that a parent kept a broken appliance cord may connect the parent to infliction of unique marks on a child's body.

clear and convincing evidence   This evidence should produce in the mind of the judge a firm belief or conviction as to the truth of allegations.

closed fracture   A fracture of the bone with no skin wound.

closed question   A question that prompts a person to give a one-word answer (e.g., yes or no). This question restricts a person's response.

coining/*cao gio*   Described in Asian cultures as a healing method. Warmed oil is applied to the child's skin, which is then rubbed with the edge of a coin or a spoon in a linear fashion, usually on the chest or back. Repetitive rubbing leads to linear bruises and welts.

collaterals   Individuals (often professionals) who have contact with the child and/ or the child's family, such as medical personnel, teachers, neighbors, and clergy, and can provide information about the child's history and/or ongoing condition or situation.

complaint   (1) An oral statement, made usually to police, charging criminal, abusive, or neglectful conduct. (2) A state attorney's document that starts a criminal prosecution (also known as an "information" in some states). (3) A petitioner's document that starts a civil proceeding. (In juvenile court a "complaint" is called a "petition.")

compound fracture   Open fracture; a fracture in which the bone is broken and protruding through the skin.

concurrent planning   The simultaneous preparation of plans to (1) assist the child's parents or caregivers in completing a treatment plan that, when developed and adopted by the court and completed by the parents or caregivers, will allow the child to return to the parents' home; and (2) place the child in a setting that will become the child's permanent home if the parents or caregivers are unable to complete their treatment plan successfully.

conditional safety   The concept that the child is safe as long as the "condition" or parts of the service plan are followed by all participants.

confidential communication   A statement made under circumstances showing that a speaker intended the statement only for the person addressed. Thus, if communication is made in the presence of a third party whose presence is not reasonably necessary for the communication, it is not considered confidential.

confrontation   When engaged in an interview, the act of pointing out contradictions between what a person says and what a person does.

congenital syndrome   A syndrome related to a physiological or structural abnormality that develops before birth but is not related to heredity.

corporal punishment   Physical punishment inflicted directly on the body. Some abusing parents mistakenly believe that corporal punishment is the only way to discipline children, and some child development specialists believe that almost all parents must occasionally resort to corporal punishment to discipline or train children. Other professionals believe that corporal punishment is never advisable.

court-appointed special advocates (CASAs)   Screened and trained community volunteers appointed by the court to speak up for the best interest of abused and neglected children. They review records, collect information from everyone involved in the child's case, and sometimes help monitor the progress of the child. Responsibilities also include making recommendations to the court as to what is best for the child and monitoring the case until it is resolved.

credibility   That quality in a witness that renders testimony worthy of belief; for example, credible evidence provided is worthy of belief.

crisis intervention   The purposeful activities and involvement of child welfare and other professionals in a helping capacity at the point the family is in crisis. The basis for intervention involves moving the family from emotional disorganization to rational problem solving through counseling and other resource acquisition.

cross-examination   Generally, an adversary's examination of a witness after the witness has been examined by direct examination.

cultural responsiveness   Efforts made by CPS workers to understand the unique experience of the individual person, family, and community. Culturally responsive practitioners recognize and value multiple and diverse worldviews and histories. People's culture and history is the strongest influence in their relationships with their environments. A critical component of culturally responsive practice is relationship. Culturally responsive practitioners understand the history of the other, allow time for trust to develop, and are trustworthy in their capacity to keep commitments. Skills of the culturally responsive practitioner include humility, respect, being willing to learn, a capacity to listen deeply while tolerating silence, and awareness of personal biases and levels of power and privilege.

culture   The stable pattern of beliefs, attitudes, values, and standards of behavior that is transmitted from generation to generation. Culture facilitates successful adaptation to the group and to the environment. It is dynamic, includes within itself group differences, and changes over time. In the "strengths perspective," culture transmits hope and resilience, and is the source of meaning, belonging, and identity. Culture also mediates response to trauma and healing.

culturegrams   A series of concise, accurate, timely cultural information designed for educational reference. Includes information on history, customs, lifestyle, government, and so on.

cupping   A healing method described in Asian and Mexican cultures. A cup is warmed and placed on the skin. A vacuum is created between the cup and the child's skin as the cup cools, which leads to a bruise.

demonstrative evidence   Things, such as whiskey bottles or belts, as opposed to assertions of witnesses.

denial   Refusing to accept or reducing the importance of a real circumstance because of its emotional implications; for example, responding to a worker's intervention by not cooperating, being preoccupied with other things, or saying an incident "just did not happen." Also referred to as "minimization."

deposition   The testimony of a witness, taken in writing, under oath or affirmation, before some judicial officer, in answer to questions or interrogatories.

depression   A serious medical illness that can affect a person's mood, concentration, sleep, activity, appetite, social behavior, and feelings that lasts for a sustained period of time (e.g., more than 2 weeks). It can include persistent feelings of helplessness, hopelessness, inadequacy, and sadness.

dermatitis herpetiformis   Chronic, recurrent papular skin condition that is usually symmetric. Lesions are usually small, clustered in groups, very itchy, and usually seen on the extremities, buttocks, back, and abdomen. It may be mistaken for cigarette burns.

detention   State of being held in some form of legal custody.

devaluation   A mechanism in which a person attributes exaggerated negative qualities to self or others.

developmental assessment   Assessment of a child's developmental progress that typically consists of a combination of observations of the child and questions to the caregiver on the child's behaviors. The observations and questions often target how the child's behaviors and skills compare to the developmental milestones typical for the age of the child being assessed.

diaphysis   The shaft of a long bone.

direct evidence   The basic distinction between direct and circumstantial evidence is that in direct evidence a witness testifies to his or her own knowledge as to the ultimate facts to be proved, while circumstantial evidence relates to instances where proof is given of facts and circumstances from which the finder may infer other connected facts that reasonably follow according to common experience.

direct examination   In practice, the first interrogation or examination of a witness on the merits of a case by the party on whose behalf he or she is called.

displacement   Transferring the feelings from one relationship or situation into another; for example, the battered wife who batters her children may be displacing her own hostility toward her husband onto someone less dangerous.

disposition   This term has two definitions. (1) In court, the outcome of a *dispositional hearing*, which determines whether a minor, already found to be a dependent or delinquent child, should continue in or return to the parental home. The hearing also determines the conditions under which the minor should remain or return home, and the actions that are necessary to assure that outcome (e.g., service provision, parent progress). Disposition in a civil case parallels sentencing in a criminal case. (2) In the investigation process, the outcome of the *investigation* (e.g., substantiated or confirmed, indicated, founded, alternative response, and unsubstantiated, or unfounded).

disseminated intravascular coagulation (DIC)   A bleeding disorder characterized by abnormal reduction in the elements involved in blood clotting due to their use in widespread intravascular clotting. It may be caused by any of numerous disorders; in the late stages, it is marked by profuse hemorrhaging.

dissociation   The separation of a thought or feeling from consciousness; for example, when a sex abuse victim "pulls away" from the cognitive and emotional experience of the abuse. A most severe and rare outcome of dissociation is the clinical diagnosis of multiple personality disorder.

distal   Far from the point of reference, for example, the distal femur, and so on. The opposite of *proximal*.

documentary evidence   Indirect and demonstrative evidence, in the form of writings, pictures, models, and so on.

dual track response   Designed to allow more flexibility in the agency's response to child protection. This two-pronged approach recognizes both the variation in the nature of reports and the reality that one approach does not meet the needs of every case. Responses can vary from state to state in implementing this approach, but usually at least two categories exist. The first category includes reports that are immediately recognized as presenting serious safety issues for children, may require court intervention, and may also involve potential criminal charges. This is sometimes known as the "investigation track." The second category focuses on service provision and includes situations in which there are needs that, if addressed, could stabilize the family and enable the parents to better care for their children. Typically, there are no serious safety issues immediately present. This is often known as the "assessment track." Instead of *dual track* the terms *alternative response* or *differential response* may be used.

due process   The rights of person involved in legal proceedings to be treated with fairness. These rights include the right to adequate notice in advance of hearing, the right to notice of allegations of misconduct, the right to assistance of a lawyer, the right to confront and cross-examine witnesses, and the right to refuse to give self-incriminating testimony.

duodenum   The first portion of the small intestine.

early intervention services   Services to address a problem or delay in development as early as possible; available for infants and toddlers up to age 3.

ecomap   A diagram that depicts reciprocal influences between the client and his or her relations, relevant community entities, and environmental influences.

eczema   Allergic skin condition that causes reddened, dry areas on skin; may be mistaken for abuse.

Ehlers-Danlos (ED) syndrome   Rare inherited disorder of collagen, which is characterized by skin laxity, hyper extensible joints, and skin fragility. The skin of these children is extremely fragile. The diagnosis of this syndrome is made with the help of genetics.

emergency services   Services whose focus is protection of a child and prevention of further maltreatment through availability of a reporting mechanism on a 24-hour basis and immediate intervention. This intervention could include hospitalization of the child, assistance in the home, including homemakers, or removal of the child from the home to a shelter or foster home.

empathy   Ability to perceive accurately and sensitively the inner feelings of the client and communicate understanding of these feelings in language aligned to the client's experience of the moment.

encephalomalacia   Softening of the brain, especially that caused by an infarct.

encopresis   A condition in which older children (typically older than 4 years) regularly have stool or bowel movement accidents.

enuresis   The involuntary passage of urine; a common condition of children that may or may not be of psychological origin.

epidermolysis bullosa   A group of blistering skin disorders that may mimic burns. Blisters may develop in response to mechanical trauma.

epiphysis   The ends of the bone: the part of the long bone (on both ends) that is developed from the center of ossification. In a growing child, the epiphysis is separated from the shaft by a layer of cartilage, called the epiphyseal plate, or "growth plate." Often not seen on the x-ray of infants and young children because it is not yet ossified.

erythema multiforme   Skin condition that produces red, target-like lesions.

evidence   Any sort of proof submitted to the court for the purpose of influencing the court's decision.

expert witness   One who, by reason of knowledge, skill, experience, training, or education regarding a subject may testify in the form of opinion or otherwise, in order to assist in the understanding of evidence or to determine a fact.

external locus of control   A personality dimension in which people assume that the outcomes they experience in life depend on forces outside themselves; a feeling that they have little or no control over what happens (as opposed to people who assume that they are personally responsible for their life outcomes).

failure to thrive (FTT)   A nonspecific term applied to infants and young children who are failing to grow according to commonly described normal parameters. Failure to thrive may be organic, meaning that the growth failure is caused by an underlying disease, or nonorganic, meaning that the cause is psychosocial or environmental in origin. If the condition progresses, the undernourished child may become apathetic and irritable, and may not reach milestones like sitting up, walking, and talking at the usual age. Inadequate nutrition may have permanent negative effects on a child's mental development in some cases. May be referred to as "pediatric growth failure."

family assessment   A systematic, informed professional approach to gathering and evaluating specific information about a family. Uses information gathered from initial screening, safety assessment, risk assessment, and various other sources of information that shed light on family connections and capacities. This assessment includes family interactions and relationships, strengths and supports, developmental issues, physical and mental health, educational history, social adjustment, substance use or abuse, domestic violence, the environment, culture and the community, and any other factors that affect the family's ability to resolve concerns that led to involvement with CPS.

family-centered practice   Practice grounded in a conceptual approach that is based on the belief that the best way to protect children in the long run is to strengthen and support their families, whether it be nuclear, extended, foster care, or adoptive. It requires specialized knowledge and skills to build family capital—resources for strength and resilience—by providing services to the family, extended family, and kinship group, as well as by mobilizing informal resources in the community.

family dynamics   Interrelationships between and among individual family members. The evaluation of family dynamics is an important factor in the identification, diagnosis, and treatment of child abuse and neglect.

family group conferencing (FGC)   A decision-making process that encourages and broadens family inclusion and responsibility for the safety, permanency, and well-being of children. Families are engaged and empowered to make decisions and develop plans that protect and nurture their children from further maltreatment. Carried out in four stages (referral, preparation, actual FGC meeting, and follow-up), the conference involves bringing family members and friends together so that they can hear information on safety concerns and create a plan to assure child safety. It simultaneously fosters a partnership with the family and child welfare and other community agencies involved in supporting the family.

family group decision-making (FGDM)   A process that is based on the belief that extended family systems (broadly defined to include all persons designated by that family as family) should be engaged and empowered by CPS agencies to make decisions and develop plans that protect and nurture their children from further abuse and neglect. Such engagement and empowerment is more likely to motivate families to address the issues that are putting their children at risk of maltreatment. It is primarily being used by child welfare agencies when maltreatment of a child has been confirmed. However, its use is expanding to resolve concerns of juvenile delinquency, truancy, and economic self-sufficiency, as well as promoting and supporting adoption and transitions for teens to young adulthood.

family timelines   A historical timeline marking significant events in a family's history.

felony   Generally, any criminal offense for which a defendant may be executed or imprisoned in a state prison.

fetal alcohol effects   Effects that represent a partial expression of fetal alcohol syndrome.

fetal alcohol syndrome (FAS)   A condition in infants resulting from heavy and continual prenatal exposure to alcohol. This syndrome consists of growth retardation before and/or after birth, central nervous system dysfunction, and at least two of the following: (1) small head; (2) short or small eyelids; (3) thin upper lip; and/or (4) underdeveloped jaw area. Following birth, the infant may suffer from alcohol withdrawal.

fomites   Objects, such as clothing, toilet seats, or door handles, that are able to harbor microorganisms and can potentially transmit infections.

fontanelles   Soft spots (areas not covered by bone) in a newborn's skull.

forensic interview   An interview conducted by law enforcement for the purpose of collecting information on possible child abuse and neglect.

foster care review   Review, often occurring at least every 6 months, that monitors the safety of the children in foster care, the progress of the children and families toward permanency, the reasonable efforts toward permanency being made, and the decision-making process and time frames.

funneling   A line of questioning where the interviewer starts with broader, open-ended, and less threatening questions and moves to focused and more sensitive questions.

genogram   A family tree that depicts the histories, personalities, and relationships of family members.

greenstick fracture   Incomplete fracture; fracture in which the compressed side of the bone is partially bent/bowed and the other side is partially broken, as when a green stick breaks, but not completely fractured. Caused by compression and angulation.

guardian ad litem (GAL)   Adult appointed by the court to assure that the best interests of the child are being served. The guardian ad litem may be, but is not necessarily, an attorney.

hearing   Generally, a judicial examination of the issues of law and fact between parties.

hearsay   Secondhand evidence, generally consisting of the type: "I heard him say . . ." Except in certain cases, such evidence is usually excluded because it is considered unreliable and because the person making the original statement cannot be cross-examined.

hematoma   Accumulation of blood in an organ or tissue due to a break in a wall of a blood vessel.

hemophilia   A hereditary disorder in which blood fails to clot adequately and abnormal bleeding can occur.

Henoch-Schönlein purpura (HSP)   vascular inflammation that causes areas of distinctive rash, particularly on the lower extremities and buttocks, abdominal pain, and joint symptoms. The rash may resemble bruising. This illness is most commonly found in children between 3 and 10 years of age.

herniation   The abnormal protrusion of an organ or other body structure through a defect or natural opening in a covering, membrane, muscle, or bone.

hotline screening tool   Tool used by staff who take reports of possible child maltreatment; often consists of a form to collect key pieces of information and a checklist of criteria for the conditions or actions that constitute child abuse or neglect. On the basis of types and number of conditions/actions checked, the staff determine whether the report matches the state's criteria for child abuse or neglect, the severity of the potential maltreatment, and the required amount of time CPS investigators have to respond to the call. It may be called different names in different locations.

hydrocephalus   An abnormal increase in the amount of cerebrospinal fluid within the cranial cavity that is accompanied by expansion of the cerebral ventricles, enlargement of the skull and especially the forehead, and atrophy of the brain. In children it may occur prior to closure of the skull sutures and is typically characterized by enlargement of the head, prominence of the forehead, brain atrophy, mental deterioration, and convulsions.

idealization   A psychological mechanism in which a person attributes exaggeratedly positive qualities to self or others—for example, the child who idealizes the absent and abusive parent.

identification   The psychological process of feeling affinity with and like someone else and then behaving like the person. For instance, an abusive person may identify with her mother, who abused her as a child.

idiopathic thrombocytopenic purpura (ITP)   Bleeding disorder characterized by a marked decrease in the number of platelets in the system, resulting in multiple bruises.

indirect evidence   See *circumstantial evidence.*

impetigo   Superficial bacterial infection of the skin typically caused by *Staphylococcus aureus*. This condition produces lesions that appear as pustules and then later form crusts. These lesions are of different sizes and may produce blisters similar in appearance to cigarette burns. These usually do not leave scars, whereas cigarette burns may.

Indian Child Welfare Act (ICWA) (Public Law 95-608)   A law passed in 1978 that protects the role of Indian tribes in the decision-making around the protective needs and placement of American Indian children. The law includes mandates on state courts and procedural safeguards, such as tribal notification and active efforts to preserve the unity of families and the integrity of children's tribal and cultural affiliation.

infantile cortical hyperostosis (Caffey's disease)   Rare disorder present in infants up to 2 to 3 months of age as red, painful, swollen extremities.

infarctions   An area of necrosis (death) in a tissue or organ resulting from obstruction of the local circulation by a thrombus (clot of blood formed within a blood vessel and remaining attached to its place of origin) or embolus (an abnormal particle such as an air bubble) circulating in the blood.

initial assessment   Activities undertaken in order to evaluate the safety of the child, determine whether the report of neglect or abuse can be substantiated, and initiate services for the child and family. Used interchangeably with the term *investigation.*

intake   refers to all of the activities that must be performed in order to receive referrals alleging child maltreatment, assess whether a referral will be accepted as a report of child abuse or neglect, and determine the agency response and the urgency of that response. Intake provides a means by which the community can report its concern for children whose safety is in question, and it is the initial point of contact between the CPS agency and the community.

intellectualization   Thinking and talking about behavior from a perspective so as to avoid the emotional implications; for example, attributing a child's withdrawal to his developmental age rather than to the fact that he has been abused.

internal locus of control   A personality dimension in which people assume that they are personally responsible for the outcomes they experience in life (as opposed to people who assume that their life outcomes depend on forces outside themselves).

investigation   The activities that follow the process of intake in order to assess the safety of the child, initiate the appropriate intervention with the family, make a decision on the substantiation of the report if an investigation is conducted, and identify and initiate services for the child and family. Some locales use the term *initial assessment* for this stage in the casework process.

investigation track   An approach by the CPS agency that is used when a report is immediately recognized as presenting serious safety issues for children and/or potential criminal charges.

jurisdiction   Authority over the subject matter, the person, and the rendering of a particular order or judgment that was given.

juvenile court   A statutory (not criminal) court having special jurisdiction of a paternal nature over delinquent and neglected children; its practice and procedure are governed by rules applicable in civil cases. May include "family courts" that have judicial jurisdiction.

learning disability   A condition in which there is a significant discrepancy between a child's achievement (in reading, spelling, written language, mathematics, and/or language skills) and ability. The discrepancy between actual and expected achievement is not the result of lack of educational opportunity, emotional disturbance, physical disability, or health impairment.

leukemia   In this form of cancer there is a tremendous increase in the number of immature white blood cells that are unable to fight infection and an associated marked decrease in the production of platelets and red blood cells, often causing a child to "bruise easily."

liability   *Responsibility* is virtually synonymous with *liability*.

low ego control   Poor control of unconscious impulses geared toward gaining pleasure.

maltreatment   An act (or failure to act) by a parent, caregiver, or other person as defined under state law that results in physical abuse, neglect, medical neglect, sexual abuse, or emotional abuse. Or an act (or failure to act) that presents an imminent risk of serious harm to a child.

mandated reporter   A person designated by state statutes who is legally responsible for reporting suspected cases of child neglect and abuse to the mandated agency. Such persons, held liable for failure to report, vary by state but often include professionals such as pediatricians, nurses, school personnel, childcare providers, police, and workers who have frequent contact with children and families.

mediation   An intervention technique used in disputes between parties to help them reconcile differences, find compromises, or reach mutually satisfactory agreements.

metaphysis   The wider part of the long bone between the end and the shaft. It borders the growth plate. On the x-ray, it is identified as the flaring portion of the long bone.

microcephaly   Abnormal smallness of the head, usually associated with mental retardation.

Miranda warning   A statement given by law enforcement to a person taken into custody that he or she has the right to remain silent and is entitled to legal counsel.

Mongolian spots   Grayish-blue, clearly defined areas of increased skin pigmentation that are most commonly found on the buttocks or the back. They are present at birth and usually fade after the first few years of life. These are most commonly found in darker pigmented children.

motivational interviewing   Interviewing that focuses on strategies such as reflective listening, summarizations, open-ended questions, and affirmation-eliciting self-motivation statements; has been used at the early stages of engagement and reduces barriers for individual family members in their change process.

multidisciplinary team   A group of professionals, and possibly paraprofessionals, representing a variety of disciplines (e.g., law enforcement personnel, social workers, psychologists, and the community). These members interact and coordinate their efforts to diagnose and treat specific cases of child abuse and neglect and may also address the general problem of child abuse and neglect in a community. Their goal is to pool their respective skills in order to comprehensively and effectively address the child maltreatment problem.

Multi-Ethnic Placement Act (MEPA) (Public Law 103-82) and Inter-Ethnic Adoptions Provisions Act (IAP)   In 1994, the MEPA legislation eliminated policies that favored same-race placements. Amendments to MEPA, found in the Inter-Ethnic Adoption Provisions Act (IAP) legislation, established Congress's intent to prevent discrimination or delays in foster care or adoptive placement and specifically prohibited delays in or denial of foster care or adoptive placement on the basis of race, culture, or ethnicity. MEPA makes an exception for Indian children, ensuring them placement with extended, tribal, or other Indian families.

National Child Abuse and Neglect Data System (NCANDS)   Authorized by the Child Abuse Prevention and Treatment Act (CAPTA); a voluntary system of reporting on the acceptance and investigation of child maltreatment allegations. CAPTA requires states that receive a State Child Abuse Grant to provide information on the extent and nature of child abuse and neglect to the extent practicable. This information includes prevention services, the number of reports and investigations, child fatalities, types of maltreatment, characteristics of perpetrators, and services provided, as well as workforce information.

neglect   A type of maltreatment that involves a caregiver's failure to provide needed, age-appropriate care, despite being financially able to do so or being offered financial or other means to do so.

nonorganic   Arising from effects outside of the body; cause is psychosocial or environmental in origin.

open-ended question   A question that requires the person to give more than a yes or no answer. This question is used as a way to prompt a person to open up.

opinion   Although witnesses are ordinarily not permitted to testify to their beliefs or opinions, being restricted instead to reporting what they actually saw or heard, when a witness can be qualified as an expert on a given subject, he can report his conclusions. For example: "On the basis of these marks, it is my opinion as a doctor that the child must have been struck with a flexible instrument very much like this appliance cord." Lawyers are sometimes allowed to ask qualified experts *hypothetical questions*, in which the witness is asked to assume the truth of certain facts and to express an opinion based on those "facts."

organic   Arising from an organ or organs, or caused by an underlying disease.

osteogenesis imperfecta (OI)   Group of rare, inherited connective tissue disorders that are characterized by bony fragility and skeletal deformity. The incidence of this disorder is 1 in 25,000 to 30,000 live births; it is diagnosed with the help of a geneticist.

outcome indicators   Events or benchmarks used to track a program's success on outcomes. An indicator is a measure for which there is data and helps quantify the achievement of a desired outcome. Indicators help answer the question "How would we know an outcome if we achieved it?"

outcome measures   Instruments (or items on an instrument) or methods used to collect and assess changes in observable and measurable knowledge, skills, attitudes, or behaviors. The term may be used interchangeably with *outcome indicators.*

outcomes   The overall results or changes for individuals or populations during or after participation in program activities (interventions). Outcomes may relate to behavior, skills, knowledge, attitudes, values, condition, status, or other attributes. They are what participants know, think, or can do; how they behave; or how their condition is different following the program, service, or activity. Some agencies use the term *goals* interchangeably with *outcomes.*

ossification   Inflammation of bone caused by a bacterial organism.

osteomyelitis   A bacterial bone infection that may produce bone weakness and subsequent fractures.

pancreatitis   Acute or chronic inflammation of the pancreas, which may be asymptomatic or symptomatic, and which is due to autodigestion of a pancreatic tissue by its own enzymes. It is caused most often by alcoholism or biliary tract disease; less commonly, it may be associated with abdominal trauma.

paranoia   A mental disorder characterized by suspiciousness and systematized delusions.

party   Refers to those by whom (plaintiff) or against whom (defendant) a legal suit is brought, whether in law or in equity. The plaintiff or defendant can be one or more individuals and can be natural or legal persons (i.e., an artificial entity, such as a corporation). All others who may be affected by the suit, indirectly or consequently, are persons interested but are not parties.

passive   Not reacting visibly to something that might be expected to produce manifestations of an emotion or feeling.

passive aggression   A psychological mechanism in which a person indirectly expresses aggression toward others.

pathology   Any deviation from a healthy, normal, or efficient condition.

pathophysiology   The physiology of abnormal states; specifically, the functional changes that accompany a particular syndrome or disease.

performance-based contracting   Explicit written agreement on what participating parties expect of each other. Focuses on the achievement of specified goals and outcomes—namely, the results.

perinatal   Existing or occurring just before and after birth; generally between the twenty-eighth week of gestation and 28 days after birth.

perineum   The space between the anus and the scrotum or vagina.

periosteal reaction   The creation of new bone by the periosteum, a membrane several cell layers thick that covers bone, when a bone is fractured.

periosteum   A specialized connective tissue covering all bones of the body and possessing bone-forming potentialities.

permanency hearing   At the permanency hearing the court hears any evidence of substantive value to decide on the proper permanency option for the child. The following permanency options should be considered: reunification, adoption, legal guardianship, relative placement, or another planned permanent living arrangement. The permanency hearing must be held within 12 months of the date that the child is "considered to have entered foster care."

permanency planning   A decision-making process that involves identifying a permanent home and preparing the child and family, both the biological and foster or adoptive family, for the placement. The plan could include for reunification, adoption, independent living, or another living arrangement.

petition   A document filed in a juvenile or family court at the beginning of a neglect, abuse, and/or delinquency case. The petition states the allegations that, if true, form the basis for court intervention.

petitioner   The words *petitioner* and *plaintiff* are practically synonymous in legal nomenclature and refer to the party bringing the case to court for a decision. The petitioner in a child protection action is often the worker for the child protective services agency.

physical abuse   A type of maltreatment that refers to physical acts that cause or could cause physical injury to a child.

physical evidence   Any tangible piece of proof such as a document, x-ray, photograph, or weapon used to inflict an injury. Physical evidence must usually be authenticated by a witness who testifies to the connection of the evidence (called an exhibit) with other facts in the case.

phytophotodermatitis   Skin reaction to psoralens (chemical compounds found in citrus fruits). Skin in contact with psoralens manifests red marks that may look like bruises or burns if exposed to sunlight.

poor prognosis indicator   A piece of information or measure about the family (caregiver, child, or family) that reflects the family's likelihood for a poor outcome (or likelihood of future maltreatment is unacceptably high). These indicators could be in the areas of substance abuse, domestic violence, mental health, and other areas of family functioning. When multiple poor prognosis indicators are present, the likelihood of successful resolution of the situation is small, and efforts should be directed toward other permanency options.

postnatal   Occurring after birth, with reference to the newborn.

post-traumatic stress disorder   An anxiety disorder in which a traumatic event is repeatedly experienced in the person's mind to the point that it can interfere with daily functioning. These experiences can take the form of flashbacks to the event, nightmares, daydreams, and so on.

prenatal   Existing or occurring before birth, with reference to the fetus.

preponderance of evidence   Evidence that is of greater weight or more convincing and that on the whole shows that the fact sought to be proved is more probable than not.

probable cause   A suspicion of guilt that is well grounded; a reasonable basis for belief that a crime has been or is being committed.

probing question   A question that explores a problem by continual examination at progressively deeper levels.

proffers of evidence   An offer of proof, that is, an advance statement made to the court about what will be offered in evidence in a case.

projection   Blaming others for one's problems or the actions (such as the abuse)—for example, the noisy, meddling teacher, the bad child, the uncooperative spouse or worker.

proximal   Nearest; closer to any point of reference; as opposed to distal (e.g., the end of a bone closest to the body trunk).

psychological maltreatment   A type of maltreatment that refers to acts or omissions—other than physical abuse or sexual abuse—that cause or could cause conduct, cognitive, affective, or other mental disorders. This includes emotional neglect, psychological abuse, and mental injury and frequently occurs as verbal abuse or excessive demands on a child's performance and may result in a negative self-image and disturbed behavior. Also referred to as *emotional maltreatment.*

psychosomatic symptoms   Physical symptoms that have psychological causes.

purpura fulminans   Purpura of an often severe progressive form, especially of children, that is characterized by widespread necrosis of the skin and is associated with a severe illness, results from an inherited or acquired defect of a certain biochemical pathway, or is of unknown cause.

rationalization   Justifying behavior to get oneself socially and psychologically "off the hook"; for example, "My son's behavior warranted the beating."

reaction formation   A mechanism in which a person substitutes behavior, thoughts, or feelings that are diametrically opposed to her own unacceptable ones; for example, the parent who feels guilty about her lack of bonding with her child and overindulges him.

real evidence   Evidence that is addressed directly to the senses without intervention of testimony.

recapitulation   The process of reviewing and summarizing discussed topics.

recidivism   The recurrence of a situation, for example, repeated child abuse and neglect.

redirection   An interviewing strategy used to help an interviewee organize his or her thinking, maintain focus, or move a conversation in a less confrontational direction. It is also used to refocus an interview.

referral   A process in which a report of possible child maltreatment is provided to a CPS professional in order to initiate an investigation of abuse/neglect if it meets statutory and agency guidelines. Referrals typically come from staff who screen incoming child maltreatment reports.

reflection   Paraphrasing what a person has said (content) or identifying and verbalizing a person's feelings.

repetition   A technique used whereby a worker goes over key points or steps to make sure that he or she has grasped the main points a client has tried to make.

report   An allegation of child maltreatment that is typically provided by someone in the community who suspects a child of being abused and/or neglected. A report is also known as a "referral."

repression   A mechanism in which the person is unable to remember or to be cognitively aware of disturbing wishes, feelings, thoughts, or experiences.

respondent   Anyone who answers or responds may properly be called a *respondent*. *Respondent* is not a technical word but is often used to mean the defendant in a lawsuit.

rickets   Bone disease resulting from vitamin D deficiency, renal and hepatic disease, and/or certain medications that may cause bone irregularities similar to those caused by trauma. The radiographic findings in this disease are specific to the disease and usually not confused with abuse. The diagnosis is confirmed by laboratory studies.

risk assessment   A structured process used to assist in determining the future risk of harm to a child and in key decision-making processes in child abuse and neglect situations. Effective risk assessment models focus on both the strengths and needs of the family environment.

safety assessment   A formal assessment that assists in determining whether a child is currently safe, and if not, what needs to happen to ensure safety. It focuses on the potential harm to the child that could be immediate or in the near future; also focuses on the strengths and needs of the family environment.

safety plan   A plan that is developed by the worker and the family to assure that the child will be conditionally safe. It is based on the strengths of the individual family members and their ability to monitor their own behavior. It is put in place during the investigation process and must be revisited at each contact. Such plans often are developed after the safety assessment has been completed.

salmon patches   Pink marks that are commonly seen on the nape of the neck, the eyelids, above the nose, and on the midforehead of newborns. These may also be referred to as *stork bites*.

scapegoat   A person bearing the blame for others and/or receiving the brunt of punishment.

schizophrenia   A group of psychotic reactions characterized by fundamental disturbances in reality relations and concept formations, and behavioral, affective, and intellectual disturbances in varying degrees. There is often progressive deterioration and regressive behavior.

screening   The process of determining whether a referral will be accepted as a report of child abuse or neglect, based on whether the referral falls within the guidelines established by state law and agency policies, and whether the agency has an appropriate role with the child and family.

scurvy   Rare condition resulting from vitamin C deficiency that may cause irregularities and fractures of the bones.

service plan   An organizational approach to documenting case issues, goals, objectives, and tasks for a family involved with the CPS system. Typically the service plan is developed with the family.

sexual abuse   A type of maltreatment that refers to the involvement of a child in sexual activity to provide sexual gratification or financial benefit to the perpetrator, including contacts for sexual purposes, molestation, statutory rape, prostitution, pornography, exposure, incest, or other sexually exploitative activities.

shaken baby syndrome   A type of head injury in abused children. This type of abuse involves infants who are held by the arms or trunk and violently shaken. There may or may not be impact with an either hard or soft surface in addition to the shaking. Commonly, infants with this identified form of injury are less than 2 years of age and are usually less than 6 months of age. Presenting symptoms are often irritability, poor feeding, and lethargy. The child may present for medical care with a history of apnea (not breathing spells), seizures, or visual impairment, or as an unexplained infant death. The history given at the time of presentation is often vague or not present at all. The term is used interchangeably with the term *shaken impact syndrome.*

shared parenting   An intervention in which the parent and child live in foster care together and the foster parent acts as a "coparent" to model appropriate parenting, as well as provide a safe place for the family to live.

skeletal survey   A series of x-rays taken of the child's entire skeleton to look for indications of new or old injury. Includes the skull, chest, spine, and extremities. Should be done in cases of suspected physical abuse for all infants and children under 2 years of age; rarely used in children over 5 years of age.

skull sutures   Immobile joints that separate the bones of the skull.

social isolation   The limited interaction and contact of many abusing and/or neglecting parents with relatives, neighbors, friends, or community resources. Social isolation can perpetuate a basic lack of trust, which hinders both the identification and treatment of child abuse and neglect.

somatization   A mechanism in which the person becomes preoccupied with physical symptoms disproportionate to any actual physical disturbance (common among sex abuse victims).

splitting   A mechanism in which the person views himself or others as all good or bad, failing to integrate the positive and the negative qualities into cohesive images. Often the person alternately idealizes and devalues the same person; for example, the parent or caregiver who is either defiant or compliant with the worker with little apparent provocation.

State Automated Child Welfare System (SACWIS)   A statewide automated computer system in which child welfare agencies track their activities in a system-wide database. It must meet the requirements established by the U.S. Department of Health and Human Services, Administration for the Children and Families, to support the state's federal reporting for Adoption and Foster Care Analysis and Reporting (AFCARS) and the National Child Abuse and Neglect Data Systems (NCANDS).

strawberry marks (hemangiomas)   Red marks that are usually not present at birth but appear during the first 4 to 6 weeks of life. These marks represent blood vessel growth just below the surface of the skin.

strength cards   Cards that combine simple, positive, affirming concepts with lighthearted graphics to create a versatile tool that reinforces the important principle that everyone has strengths.

subpoena   A command to appear at a certain time and place, on a certain date, to give testimony on a certain matter.

summarizing   A technique used to pull together thoughts, feelings, and plans expressed and developed during an interview.

suppression   A mechanism in which a person intentionally avoids thinking about disturbing problems, desires, feelings, or experiences.

target event   The specific event of abuse and/or neglect that is the current focus of an interview.

tattooing   Discoloration of skin from fabric dye, giving the appearance of a bruise.

Temporary Assistance for Needy Families (TANF)   Provides assistance and work opportunities to needy families by granting states the federal funds and wide flexibility to develop and implement their own welfare programs.

temporary custody hearing   Typically occurring within 48 to 72 hours of a case being assigned for investigation; a hearing held for the purpose of determining whether a child needs to be temporarily placed in the custody of the state (or county, if a county-administered system) to assure his or her safety.

termination   The final phase of CPS work with the family. It is synonymous with *case closure* and is the point at which the service provision process ends.

termination of parental rights   When reasonable efforts have been made (or are excused by the court due to aggravated circumstances) and facts support grounds for termination, and when it is in the child's best interest, a court order of termination of parental rights may be sought.

testimony   Evidence given by a competent witness under oath or affirmation, as distinguished from evidence derived from written and other sources.

torsion   Twisting or rotating about an axis.

traction   Pulling along an axis.

undoing   A mechanism in which a person engages in behavior designed to symbolically make amends for, or negate, previous thoughts, feelings, or actions; for example, a child who feels responsible for his abuse, attributing the abuse to his angry feelings, becomes a very good or model child.

universalizing   Creating understanding that a person's problems are shared by others.

vasculitis   Inflammation of a blood or lymph vessel.

venue   Related to the locality of the court or courts that possess jurisdiction.

verbal cue   A nondirective listening technique that encourages a person to continue speaking (e.g., "right," "sure," "yes").

voir dire examination   Preliminary questioning that determines the qualifications and credibility of witnesses.

witness   A person whose declaration under oath is received as evidence for any purpose.

Women, Infants, and Children (WIC)   A program operated by the Department of Health for low-income mothers and their children 0 to 3 years of age. It provides financial assistance for baby supplies and food, as well as medical care.

wraparound services   A philosophy that requires services to be community and strength based, individualized, culturally competent, and requiring parent involvement. Wraparound services also require interagency collaboration and the ability of agencies to access flexible funding. The term developed from the goal of integrating services into a "system of care" to support family members and keep children in the least restrictive placement in their home communities.

Index